SUPERIOR PERSON

Kenneth Rose, a renowned historian and biographer, is a Fellow of the Royal Society of Literature and a contributor to *The Dictionary of National Biography*. He was awarded the CBE in 1997.

Also by Kenneth Rose

George V (Phoenix Press)

The Later Cecils

SUPERIOR PERSON

A Portrait of Curzon and his Circle in Late Victorian England

Kenneth Rose

5 UPPER SAINT MARTIN'S LANE
LONDON
WC2H 9EA

A PHOENIX PRESS PAPERBACK

First published in Great Britain
by Weidenfeld & Nicolson in 1969
This paperback edition published in 2001
by Phoenix Press,
a division of The Orion Publishing Group Ltd,
Orion House, 5 Upper St Martin's Lane,
London WC2H 9EA

A CIP catalogue record for this book
is available from the British Library.

Printed and bound in Great Britain by
Clays Ltd, St Ives plc

ISBN 1 84212 233 9

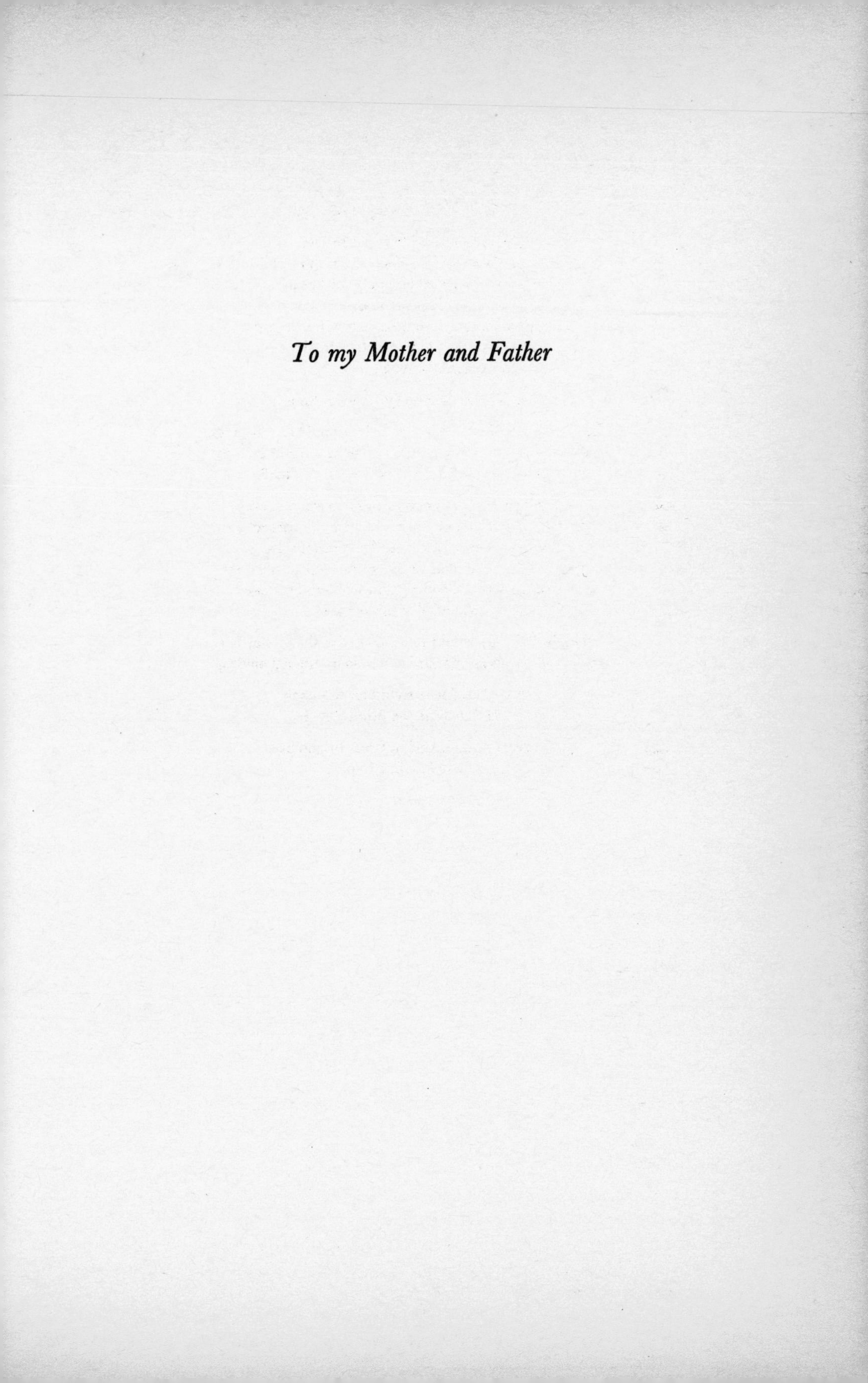

To my Mother and Father

My name is George Nathaniel Curzon,
I am a most superior person,
My cheek is pink, my hair is sleek,
I dine at Blenheim once a week.

– *The Masque of Balliol, 1881*

CONTENTS

LIST OF ILLUSTRATIONS

Grateful acknowledgement is made for permission to reproduce the following pictures: 1, 2, 3, 5, 7, 12, 13, 14, 15, 16, 17, 18, 19, 21, 24 – by courtesy of Lord Scarsdale and the Kedleston Trustees; 4, from *Eton in the Seventies* by Gilbert Coleridge (John Murray); 6, Ernest Benn Ltd; 8, from *Mary Gladstone: Her Diaries and Letters*, ed. Lucy Masterman (Methuen); 9, 26, from *King Edward and His Times* by André Maurois (Cassell); 10, by permission of the Master and Fellows of Balliol College, Oxford; 11, 22, 23, Radio Times Hulton Picture Library; 20, from Lord Ronaldshay's *Life of Curzon* (Ernest Benn Ltd), by permission of Lord Zetland; 25, from *Recollections and Reflections* by J. E. C. Welldon (Cassell).

Maps showing Curzon's journeys

Drawn by Design Practitioners Limited

INTRODUCTION

The character and creed of George Nathaniel Curzon, first and last Marquess Curzon of Kedleston, crystallized early in life. In his devouring industry, his relentless ambition, his commanding intellect, his fervent imperialism, his zest for enjoyment, his genius for friendship, there was little difference between the schoolboy who persuaded Mr Gladstone to address the Literary Society at Eton and the self-assured Parliamentary Under-Secretary who was appointed Viceroy of India before he was forty. That is the first theme of this book: a study in precocity. It covers the years 1859 to 1898.

India wrought a change in him. The intolerable burden of work which he insisted on assuming and was temperamentally incapable of delegating to others proved too heavy for a constitution which he had wantonly over-strained since his days as an Oxford undergraduate. That is the second theme: the corroding effect on Curzon's friendships of ill-health, authority and frustration during the years of his Viceroyalty, 1898 to 1905, and sometimes beyond.

There is a third theme: the compactness and self-sufficiency of a patrician class whose right to rule was never questioned by themselves and only rarely disputed by others. The wheels of history, H.A.L. Fisher once observed, are seldom moved by the poor. As late as the turn of the century, government remained largely in the hands of a few hundred aristocratic and land-owning families. Others penetrated their circle in increasing numbers by marriage and money and merit. But the shared intimacies of Eton and Balliol, of country house and London club, continued to influence policy at home and abroad. It was still the age of gunroom diplomacy.

SHORT BIOGRAPHY

1859	Born
1872–8	Eton
1878–82	Balliol College, Oxford
1882–3	Journey to Mediterranean
1883	Fellow of All Souls College, Oxford
1885–6	Assistant Private Secretary to Lord Salisbury
1886–98	Conservative MP for Southport
1887–8	First journey round the world
1888	Journey to Central Asia
1889	Publication of *Russia in Central Asia*
1889–90	Journey to Persia
1891–2	Parliamentary Under-Secretary of State for India
1892	Publication of *Persia and the Persian Question*
1892–3	Second journey round the world
1894	Publication of *Problems of the Far East*
1894–5	Journey to the Pamirs and Afghanistan
1895	Married Mary Leiter (who died in 1906)
1895–8	Parliamentary Under-Secretary of State for Foreign Affairs and Privy Councillor
1898	Created Baron Curzon of Kedleston in Peerage of Ireland
1898–1904 1904–5	Viceroy and Governor-General of India
1904–5	Lord Warden of the Cinque Ports
1907	Chancellor of Oxford University
1908	Elected Representative Irish Peer, with seat in House of Lords
1911	President of the Royal Geographical Society
1911	Created Earl Curzon of Kedleston
1915–16	Lord Privy Seal in Coalition Government of Asquith
1916–19	Lord President of the Council and Member of War Cabinet in Coalition Government of Lloyd George
1916–24	Leader of the House of Lords
1916	Knight of the Garter
1916	Inherited Kedleston from his father
1917	Married Mrs Grace Duggan
1919–24	Foreign Secretary in Governments of Lloyd George, Bonar Law and Baldwin
1921	Created Marquess Curzon of Kedleston
1924–5	Lord President of the Council and Leader of the House of Lords
1925	Death

ANCESTRY OF GEORGE NATHANIEL CURZON AND DESCENT OF THE BARONY OF SCARSDALE

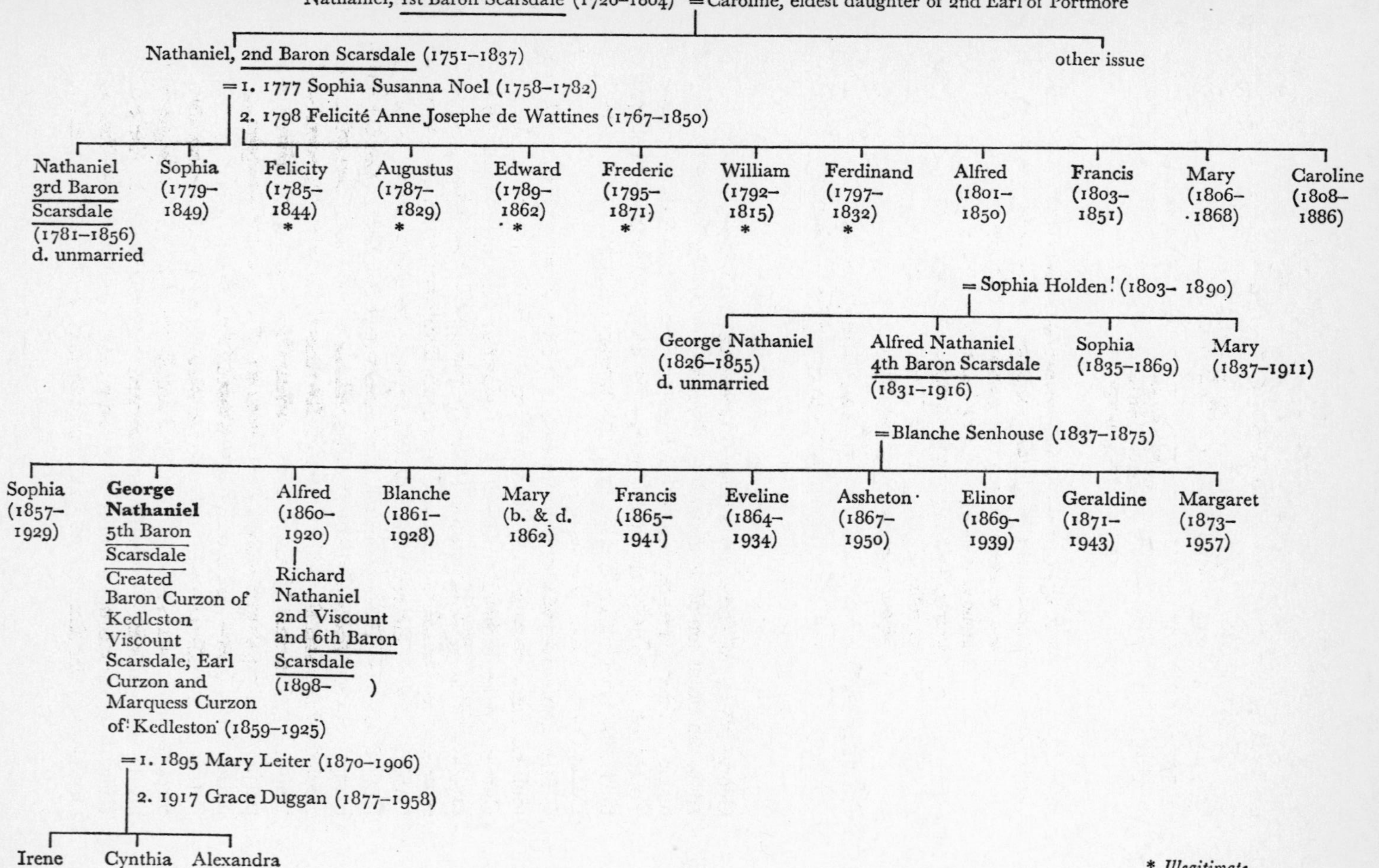

Chapter One
KEDLESTON

It is a pity that save in rare cases families have been so careless of their own memorials, except, and sometimes even when, these are of brick or stone or marble, so destructive of papers and correspondence, so contemptuous of the furniture or relics of older times, so Philistine in their ideas or modes of reconstruction.

– *Introduction by Lord Curzon to his monograph on Kedleston Church*

George Nathaniel Curzon was born at Kedleston, near Derby, on 11 January 1859, the eldest son of the fourth Lord Scarsdale. 'In most churches,' one of his sisters liked to assure visitors to Kedleston, 'you will find the tombs of any Tom, Dick or Harry. Here there are only Curzons.' For nearly nine centuries the family have lived in Derbyshire, embodying the spirit of their motto, 'Let Curzon holde what Curzon helde'.

They came over with the Conqueror, a branch of the original stock that took its name from one of the two towns in Normandy called Courson. Curzon's pride in his Norman ancestry sometimes aroused the envy, not to say the malice, of his enemies. It appealed particularly to Lloyd George's sense of mischief when he and Curzon sat uneasily together in successive Cabinets. Lloyd George would describe to a little circle of cronies how in Guizot's life of William of Normandy he had read of the chance meeting on a bridge between William's father and an unknown pretty girl whom the Duke carried off to his castle. 'What a remarkable thing,' Lloyd George concluded, 'had it not been that William's father and mother crossed the bridge at that particular time, there would have been no William the Conqueror, no Norman Conquest – and no George Nathaniel Curzon.'

It was natural enough that Curzon should enjoy tracing his descent through twenty-one generations from King Edward III or recording during his travels through Persia the amazement expressed by the Ilkhani of Kuchan at an unbroken tenure of the same estates for more than 800 years. Occasionally the family tree was illuminated by a kinsman as splendid as

Robert, Cardinal Courson, spiritual director of the Fifth Crusade, who was mortally wounded at the siege of Damietta in 1218. But most of his forbears, Curzon confessed, 'were just ordinary country gentlemen'. One was made a baron by Henry VIII and another a baronet by Charles I. In 1761, Nathaniel Curzon was created Baron Scarsdale by George III, a generous mark of Royal favour for one who as a schoolboy had carved his name on the Coronation chair in Westminster Abbey. A few members of the family distinguished themselves as High Sheriffs and Members of Parliament. Some took Holy Orders, others went to sea. One died in the hunting field, another on the field of Waterloo. Nearly all are commemorated in brass and marble and alabaster within the walls of the tiny medieval church of Kedleston.

Curzon was proud enough of his lineage to write to the Home Secretary, Sir John Simon, on hearing in 1915 that a supposed enemy alien had been allowed to change his name to Curzon. Simon's reply was correct but unsympathetic:

Dear Curzon,

I have now ascertained the facts about the shopkeeper who calls himself Curzon. The business is carried on by two brothers, who are both natural-born British subjects. Their name was originally Jonas but was changed to Siegenberg many years ago. It was further changed to Curzon by Deed Poll in August last. You will see, therefore, that your correspondent is mistaken in supposing that these people are Germans ...

I find in the Home Office file an earlier communication about these people, but I am afraid we cannot interfere with British subjects changing their name by Deed Poll, though I am sorry it has taken this form. If Jonas had called himself Jones, it would have been less noticeable.

Yours very truly,
John Simon.

Conscious of his ancestry though unimpressed by his ancestors, Curzon did, however, retain throughout his life an almost mystic sense of reverence for Kedleston itself. The present house was built in the third quarter of the eighteenth century. It replaced a more modest dwelling of red brick put up hardly more than sixty years before but rejected by the first Lord Scarsdale as too cramped a setting for the works of art he had collected during the Grand Tour. With patrician abandon he not only ordered a comparatively new mansion to be demolished but also moved the entire village to the respectful distance of nearly a mile from the site of his intended palace, and was granted permission by Act of Parliament to divert the public highway.* The little church of All Saints was alone allowed to remain, sheltering apologetically behind a wing of the new house.

* George III. 33. Cap. 33.

Three architects were responsible for Kedleston. Matthew Brettingham, who helped to prepare the plans for Lord Leicester's Palladian house at Holkham, drew the preliminary design. It envisaged a central block from each front of which would extend a pair of curved galleries ending in smaller but hardly less imposing wings. James Paine, a fashionable architect of the day, carried out only part of Brettingham's plan. He built the main mass, strengthened it with a heavy, almost intimidating, six-columned portico approached by a double staircase and flanked it with a pair of embracing arms and their pavilions. In defiance of the harsh Derbyshire climate, his sweeping anthem in stone faces resolutely north. Yet there is an austere loveliness about Kedleston on a winter's morning as pale sunlight gilds the classical statues that crown the portico and flights of geese sweep across the park and the mist dissolves to reveal the graceful arches with which Robert Adam spanned Cutler Brook.

In the summer, however, the house should be viewed from the gentle hill to the south. On that side of the building, perhaps out of deference to his patron's pocket, Paine omitted the proposed curved galleries and supporting wings that complete the north front. It thus stands unsupported, but also unencumbered, seeming to float upon an ocean of green like a huge but finely proportioned silver ship towing two lesser vessels in her wake. Adam, to whose inspiration the house owes most, reinforced the illusion by adorning the south front with a portico of singular cunning. 'The double arcs of the staircase,' a later architect, A. S. G. Butler, has written,' plunge forwards and downwards and the lines of their balustrades toss themselves back in the beautiful twists of natural perspective like high waves from the bow of a great liner cutting the sea.'

Adam completed the exterior of Kedleston and brought his genius to its decoration. Some of his ceremonial rooms are designed as if to offer cool relief from a burning Italian sun. There is the cold perfection of the marble hall, its ceiling resting upon twenty soaring Corinthian columns of solid alabaster hewn from Lord Scarsdale's own quarries; and the high chill dome and shining empty floor of the saloon mock the heating system which Adam ingeniously installed in cast-iron altars. Other rooms, however, are alive with colour and warmth, with cavernous fireplaces and inlaid chimney-pieces, with elaborate cornices and delicate plasterwork, with bedposts carved like palm trees and chandeliers of Waterford crystal. Silk walls and tinted ceilings, portraits and landscapes, books and bibelots soften the stately magnificence of an eighteenth-century nobleman's house. And from the tall windows stretch vistas of parkland and lake that have captured all the felicity of a Capability Brown or a Repton.

Horace Walpole wrote one of the earliest accounts of Lord Scarsdale's majestic enterprise. He described it in September 1768 as:

a fine park with old timber, beautiful gateway with lovely iron gate by Adam. A vast house with four wings, of which two only yet built and magnificently finished and furnished; all designed by Adam in the best taste but too expensive for his estate... There are many and large pictures, but most copies or sadly repaired bought for the house in Italy. Music room, pretty organ by Adam. The ceilings by him are light, but have too great a sameness ... settees supported by gilt fishes and Sea Gods, absurdly like the King's Coach... Vast kitchen with a gallery like a chapel, over the chimney these words, 'Spare not and waste not'.

Three years later, *The Farmer's Tour through the East of England*, by Arthur Young, paid respectful tribute to Lord Scarsdale's sense of husbandry:

Lands that were so wet, as almost to be boggy, are by draining converted into excellent pasture; and various other tracts of a barren or inferior quality are now improved to the utmost, so that you no where see any land that is not cloathed with a fine verdure. This is one great national advantage of the nobility and gentry improving the environs of their houses – they are excellent farmers, whether they design or not.

Another contemporary visitor, Dr Johnson, was less impressed. The first time he visited Kedleston he embarked on a flight of fancy that has not worn well. 'It would do excellently,' he said, 'for a town hall. The large room with the pillars would do for the Judges to sit in at the assizes; the circular room for a jury chamber; and the rooms above for prisoners.' On 19 September 1777, he accompanied Boswell on a second visit. The diarist, who had armed himself by reading *The Farmer's Tour through the East of England*, described it in these words:

The day was fine, and we resolved to go by Keddlestone, the seat of Lord Scarsdale, that I might see his Lordship's fine house. I was struck with the magnificence of the building; and the extensive park, with the finest verdure, covered with deer, and cattle, and sheep, delighted me. The number of old oaks, of an immense size, filled me with a sort of respectful admiration: for one of them sixty pounds was offered. The excellent smooth gravel roads; the large piece of water formed by his Lordship from some small brooks, with a handsome barge upon it; the venerable Gothick church, now the family chapel, just by the house; in short, the grand group of objects agitated and distended my mind in a most agreeable manner. 'One should think (said I), that the proprietor of all this must be happy.' 'Nay, Sir (said Johnson), all this excludes but one evil – poverty.'

Boswell later repeated the conversation to his wife. 'It is true,' she replied, 'all this excludes only one evil; but how much good does it let in?' Perhaps Johnson had been merely simulating a distaste for Kedleston in order to deflate the enthusiasm of his travelling companion. In the end good humour broke through as he caught sight of a copy of his *Dictionary* in Lord Scarsdale's dressing-room. Boswell records the eagerness of his 'Look 'ye!' when his eye lighted on it, followed by the rotund Virgilian sentiment: '*Quae terra nostri non plena laboris?*' – 'What land is not filled with our labours?'

That intimidating parliamentary orator, John Bright, with whom Curzon sat in the House of Commons for a year or two, used to say that old abbeys suggested to him only superstition, old castles only violence. Curzon took a less misanthropic view of architecture. 'A house,' he wrote in his literary testament, 'has to my mind a history as enthralling as that of an individual. If an old house it has a much longer existence, and it may be both beautiful and romantic which an individual seldom is.' He was sensitive to his surroundings and he revered the past: the two themes fused in his love for Kedleston, which ran through his life as an unbroken thread. Although in retrospect his childhood seemed to him to have been of almost unrelieved unhappiness, he never associated those hateful memories with the house itself. The self-appointed guardian of its classic lines, he used to rebuke his sisters for cluttering up the Adam chimney-piece of their schoolroom with unworthy little ornaments. Half a century later he would denounce with the same fervour 'the middle class suburban fittings' which a consultant architect thought proper to instal during a prolonged period of restoration.

The rigidity of Curzon's aesthetic standards dominated even his friendships. He warmed towards Lady Salisbury* when she told him that her husband was making alterations at Hatfield without employing professional advice. He cooled towards Lady D'Abernon when she declined to admire a piece of landscape gardening of his own design. Lord Newton, too, incurred his displeasure. 'Curzon,' he wrote in his diary, 'who when last here found fault with a very substantial but necessary tower on top of the house containing bedrooms, which had been built about 100 years ago, was quite surprised to find that I had not removed it.' Like his Eton contemporary, Sir George Sitwell, who believed that no garden could fail to be improved by a sheet of water and a line of statues, he would wonder at the faint-heartedness of those on whom he pressed advice. To be an amateur in the highest sense was an indispensable qualification in his eyes, and those insensitive to problems of perspective and arrangement he thought hardly worthy of his attention. Finding himself one night next to a young peer at dinner, he said, not unkindly or with any intentional arrogance, 'I suppose you live in a flat'.

Arnold Bennett used to regard a pineapple on his sideboard as the symbol of ultimate worldly success. For Curzon it was a splendid house – or better still, a succession of such residences. 'I will not disguise from you, my dear Lang,' he wrote to a newly appointed Archbishop of York who had just moved into the Palace of Bishopthorpe, 'what pleasure it gives me, as the years advance, to see my friends inhabiting spacious places.' Although the doors of Kedleston were always open to him during his father's long lifetime, he had no house of his own, either in London or in the country, until his marriage in 1895. Then, with financial help from his rich American father-in-law, he and his wife took No. 4, Carlton Gardens, overlooking St James's

* Alice, wife of the fourth marquess.

Park, and The Priory, Reigate, a plain but elegant Georgian house, for use at the week-end.

The peerage he received on his appointment as Viceroy in 1898 enabled him to couple his name with that of the house he loved: it was as Curzon of Kedleston that he governed India for seven years. And by a smiling whim of fate, Government House, Calcutta, had been built by Lord Wellesley a century before on the model of Kedleston.* The Court of Directors of the East India Company had then deplored 'the style of Asiatic pomp and display', believing that 'nothing of this kind is requisite for the support of the British authority in the East, which was acquired and has been preserved by other means'. That was not an argument to appeal to Curzon. He delighted in expounding to Viceregal guests a comparison between the two houses. Kedleston had only two projecting wings, Calcutta had all four; Kedleston's corridors had two storeys, Calcutta had three; Kedleston had a grand staircase, Calcutta had four small and pokey flights. He was also at pains to explain, in a much-imitated pronunciation owing something both to the eighteenth-century and to his native Derbyshire, that whereas the Indian pillars of the great hall were mere lăth and plăster, those of his own home were constructed of the purest alabăster.

The silent education in sensibility which Curzon had received from Kedleston in his childhood also enabled him to apply the fruits of his travels to the restoration of Indian monuments. Outraged by the condition into which they had been allowed to fall, he wrote despairingly of 'a utilitarianism which makes one shudder and feats of desecration from which even a Goth would have shrunk'. Few important remains escaped his alert eye and capacity for exhaustive research. One day he would be found scrambling up bamboo scaffolding at Chitor or measuring stone elephants at Mandu. On another he would order the removal of whitewash from the Red Fort at Agra or rebuke the officials in Delhi who wantonly used the Pearl Mosque as a treasury. From 1899 to 1903 he was his own director of antiquities; then he summoned Sir John Marshall as his archaeological adviser. To an increase in the official grant from £7,000 to £37,000 a year he added substantial personal gifts – a lamp for the Taj Mahal, copied at much expense from one known to have hung in the Mosque of Sultan Beybars II in Cairo; the wages of a Florentine craftsman needed to replace the mosaic panels of the Audience Hall in Delhi; a Koran stand for the Mosque of Wazir Khan, Lahore.

Calcutta's Victoria Memorial Hall, for which he raised nearly half a million pounds, gave Curzon a splendid opportunity to build what he called 'by far the finest structure that has been reared in India since the days of the Moghuls'. Another Viceroy, Lord Hardinge, was not impressed. 'A no less striking memorial to himself,' he observed sourly. Curzon had his revenge in this skirmish of aesthetic wits. Visiting the British Embassy in Paris twenty

* The capital was not moved to Delhi until 1912.

years later, soon after Lord Hardinge had been replaced as Ambassador by Lord Crewe, he wrote: 'It was such a pleasure to see that beautiful house without tiger skins, the silver caskets, the elephant tusks and common photographs of Charlie Hardinge. Instead there were some quite good oil paintings, all portraits from Crewe House, not those of the first order, but quite good, including some Romneys, Reynolds, Gainsborough, etc.' No Viceroy could fail to acquire a collection of Indian trophies. But the place for them in a classical house, Curzon insisted, was 'in some rather out of the way corner'. At Kedleston they are insulated in their own museum.

Kedleston never ceased to haunt Curzon's heart and mind during his seven years in India. When Mahdo Singh, Maharaja of Jaipur, came to England in 1902 for the Coronation of Edward VII, Curzon arranged that he should visit Kedleston. 'I watched the rabbits playing on the green turf,' the Maharaja afterwards told his friends, 'and I thought I could sit watching these little creatures in the sun, and could rest there for ever, playing a flute, and I wondered how English sahibs could ever go to India.'

Returning to England on leave in the summer of 1904, Curzon spent several weeks at Walmer Castle, in Kent, the residence of the Lord Warden of the Cinque Ports. His appointment to that honorific office touched his sense of history. He was able to add his name to a roll that included Wellington and Dalhousie, Palmerston and Salisbury; among his successors have been Sir Winston Churchill and Sir Robert Menzies. But the pride he took in acquiring so celebrated and picturesque a house overlooking the English Channel soon turned to bitterness. Beneath its ancient structure lay even more ancient drains from which Lady Curzon caught an infection that brought her almost to death's door. Before departing again for India in the autumn, Curzon resigned the office, glad, as he put it, to be rid of 'that charnel house ... unfit for human habitation'.

A year later he was back in England. But it was a dismal homecoming, clouded by the political dispute that had forced his resignation and cut short his second term as Viceroy. Nor was he allowed for long to find solace in either the woman or the house he loved most in the world. After little more than ten years of an enchantingly happy marriage, his wife's frail health at last gave way and she died in July 1906. In an agony of grief, Curzon turned to Kedleston, but only to raise to her memory as beautiful a shrine as human craftsmanship could contrive. 'It was,' Sir Shane Leslie has written, 'as though a Gothic chantry had been made to enclose an Arabian Night.' The monument itself, in Kedleston church, consists of Bertram Mackennal's recumbent effigies of George and Mary Curzon, at peace beneath a veiled celestial crown that is held aloft by two angels. In white marble, it expresses the timeless passion of the Latin inscription:

M. V. C.
QUI JAMPRIDEM AMABAT
HODIE AMAT
CRAS AMABIT
IN AETERNUM AMANDAM
G. N. C.*

To show the tomb to advantage he laid a floor of rare translucent green quartz from the Ural Mountains, then scoured the world for objects that would enhance the setting. From Italy came bronze candelabra and crimson velvet, panels of embroidery and silver lamps. Portugal yielded a crucifix, Mexico a lectern, Spain two carved and painted wooden representations of the Descent from the Cross and the Adoration. Years went by before he was satisfied with the perfection of his private Taj Mahal that glows like a jewel in the damp Derbyshire dales. Thereafter his thoughts seldom strayed far from Kedleston.

Meanwhile his father lived on, and the son who had ruled 300 million Indians was not prepared to linger at Kedleston as his guest. Curzon therefore took a furnished lease of Hackwood, the eighteenth-century house near Basingstoke that had been the home of the Dukes of Bolton. Like Chatham in retirement at Burton Pynsent, he busied himself in renovation and landscape gardening. 'Hundreds of men are removing a neighbouring hill, to improve the view,' a visitor wrote in 1907. It cost his host several thousand pounds to demolish that mound of solid chalk, in places fourteen feet high, which partly obscured the vista from the ground-floor window. Nor, while still living as a tenant in Hackwood, could he resist taking the lease of Montacute, in Somerset. Built in the late sixteenth century, it was cherished by Curzon as the most beautiful house of middle size in England.

His love of architecture was not, however, the selfish plaything of a rich man. He wrote in his will:

> Convinced that beautiful and ancient buildings which recall the life and customs of the past are not only a historical document of supreme value, but are a part of the spiritual and aesthetic heritage of a nation, imbuing it with reverence and educating its taste, I bequeath for the benefit of the Nation certain properties which I have acquired for the express purpose of preserving the historic buildings upon them.

His official biographer, Lord Ronaldshay, ingeniously wonders whether Curzon might not have been inspired by another great proconsul, and quotes from Shakespeare the threnody of Mark Antony on Julius Caesar in the Forum – the same lines that Curzon had first heard as a boy at Wixenford:

* G.N.C., who long loved M.V.C., loves her today and will love her tomorrow, so worthy is she of eternal love.

Moreover he hath left you all his walks,
His private arbours, and new-planted orchards,
On this side Tiber: he hath left them you,
And to your heirs for ever – common pleasure,
To walk abroad, and recreate yourselves.

Curzon's benefaction was twofold. In Lincolnshire he bought the medieval castle of Tattershall, restored the ruin to its former grandeur, retrieved the historic fireplaces which Pugin had taken as his model in the Houses of Parliament, and left it to be enjoyed by his fellow-countrymen in perpetuity. Bodiam Castle, in Sussex, he also bought, repaired and bequeathed to the National Trust. Such gestures prompted Sir Mark Sykes, Member of Parliament and Orientalist, to draw a cartoon of a ragged Lord Curzon against a background of the noble buildings he had restored. On the pavement is his upturned cap and by his side a notice that reads: 'KIND FRENS PITY MEE I WOS WONS A VISEROY BUT LOST MI ALL BILDIN CASSELS AND ADDIN TO THE BEWTIS OF INGLAND.'

It was not enough that Curzon should save ancient monuments from decay: he must also write their histories. Government House, Calcutta; Walmer Castle; Hackwood; Montacute; Tattershall; Bodiam; Kedleston – each was a labour of love undertaken in the scant period of leisure that a busy public life allowed him. Some were published during his lifetime, others posthumously, and one or two remained only in the form of a manuscript or pencilled notes. He has left his own account of what such scholarship involves:

> A search must be made in Patent Rolls, Close Rolls, Pipe Rolls, Charter Rolls, Parliamentary Rolls, Inquisitions, visitations, in the published State Papers, and in any documentary source that tells of the grant or inheritance of lands, the proceedings of Law Courts or of Parliament, or the gifts and awards of Kings ... The recognised but often recondite sources of parochial and county history require to be explored – Charters, Court Rolls, Indentures, Deeds of Sale, Mortgages, the genealogies of families, the wills of persons, the County Histories... private muniment rooms, personal correspondence, biographies or memoirs, sometimes family tradition ... general works on the Castles of England, or in papers written by antiquarians in the Proceedings of learned Societies, or in separate publications.

Even that did not conclude his meticulous research. He would pore over drawings and engravings, plans and photographs, then stump over the ground with a measuring rod and sometimes a spade.

It was not until 1916, when Lord Scarsdale died at the age of eighty-five, that Curzon was able to realize a boyhood ideal – the renovation of Kedleston and the recording of its history. The preliminary task he described in a letter written in September to Grace Duggan,* who was to become his second wife in the following year:

You can conceive the labour of cleaning out a house the contents of which have barely been touched for a hundred years – the accumulations of my father's 60-year reign! He kept every bill – even for 1/6 or 2/10! There is every detail about the whole of this great estate and thousands of other things. There are all the school books of every member of the Curzon family for a century. There are scores of portfolios filled with drawings, deeply buried in dust, some white with mildew. There are the trinkets and personal belongings of many generations and all the worthless literature of the early Victorian period. All these I have to go through personally, examining every paper, burning 19 out of 20 but now and then finding a record of local interest or value. I want to get all this done before you and I take in hand the renovation. There is much about the history of the house and the place that is buried in mystery and which my father never knew – as he had no understanding of such things and dared not grapple with the memorials of his predecessors. Somebody must do it and I seem fated to be the man.

In one way it was a disappointing quest. He could find no trace or record of the various mansions or manor houses that were known to have stood on the same site for six centuries before the building of the red-brick house in 1700, and only a single picture and a single plan of that house. Nor, except for title deeds and wills, was there any manuscript earlier than 1650. From 1760, however, the muniments were full and continuous.

There was another difficulty. In bleakly practical terms, Lord Scarsdale lived too long. Had he died or handed over Kedleston to his eldest son soon after Curzon's return from India in 1905, the labour of renovation and recording could have begun during the decade that Curzon spent in the political wilderness with comparative leisure at his disposal. From 1915 until his death ten years later, Curzon was almost continuously in high office, able to snatch only an occasional week-end in Derbyshire. Even then there were interruptions. Called to the telephone one day by his butler in order to hear from his private secretary† at the Foreign Office of the death of a European statesman, he delivered this majestic rebuke: 'Do you realize that to convey to me this trivial information, you have brought me the length of a mansion not far removed from the dimensions of Windsor Castle?'

Curzon was denied, too, the interest and encouragement he had hoped to inspire in the second Lady Curzon. 'All ask for Gracie and want to see the beautiful lady,' he wrote to her from Kedleston in 1921. 'One day you will take up your duties as chatelaine of this place as you used to do at Windsor.‡ The old tradition still survives in this untarnished spot, and the people are

* She was the widow of Alfred Duggan, of Buenos Aires, and a daughter of J. Monroe Hinds, United States Minister to Brazil. She died in 1958. One of her sons was Alfred Duggan, the historical novelist.

† Robert (later Lord) Vansittart, 1881–1957.

‡ Before her second marriage, Mrs Duggan had a house at Windsor.

single-minded and respectful.' Lady Curzon, however, younger and more cosmopolitan in her tastes, had no relish for the subdued tenor of a country life so remote from the social whirl of London. 'Kedleston,' she wrote unkindly to her husband from Hackwood, 'I would so much rather not go at all – there is nothing for me to do there – after all one's home is where one's heart is.' So he resigned himself to a lonely mission that he estimated could hardly be achieved in less than four years. He was not quite alone during those eagerly sought interludes at Kedleston. Scorning what he called a man 'of established eminence', he engaged the late A. S. G. Butler, a young and promising architect, as his assistant. It was a partnership that flourished in spite of occasional exasperation on both sides. Butler's own account of his engagement epitomizes their relationship:

It appeared that he wanted to restore the eighteenth-century mansion to its original purity and elegance; and it was his aim to make the home of his ancestors a possible place for himself to live in at the end of his life. That meant all modern comforts and appliances being worked in without detracting in the least from the artistic quality of the building. And it is not easy to fit into a palace, designed chiefly for the enjoyment of high entertainment and lofty conversation, every kind of convenience noble guests expect today and all the apparatus and inter-related rooms their staffs demand. The work had to be perfectly done – even the visiting valets' bathrooms – but of course done without sumptuousness or any note of modern vulgarity. So, after one suddenly arranged and quite short interview in Carlton House Terrace, we made a twelve-point treaty – on Foreign Office notepaper – and I went to Derbyshire with Lord Curzon for a week-end, on trial.

I can still recall most clearly that curious first evening at Kedleston, though it is now nearly twenty years ago. We seemed to drive interminably from Derby station in a small horse-drawn brougham, much of the time passed in a mauve darkness because the blinds had to be partly down. That was to prevent our being seen in the streets. I did not ask why we should not be seen, but accepted the fact as part of a sort of Oppenheim novel I had jumped into. We reached the broad park at Kedleston in the dusk of an October evening, and, driving over the high stone bridge spanning an artificial river – we saw the house looming in dark and slightly sinister silhouette.

There was nobody there except the agent for a few moments: so I spent the first of about fifty week-ends practically alone with Lord Curzon. We dined about nine-o'clock, and at half past ten he started showing me the whole house. I knew about it from books, but had not expected quite such a wealth of exquisite detail and such really grand planning. Lord Curzon clearly had a passion for the place; and as I became infected with his zeal and increasingly excited by his schemes for making it more splendid still, he became most friendly and I felt, towards three o'clock in the morning, that I was probably established there. For I suppose even an unknown architect and an eminent statesman can hardly spend so much time as we did – confined together as it were in a remote country monastery – without either having an early and disastrous row or establishing a basis at least of trust and, I might add, of affection: and Lord Curzon, when he was not in one of his well-known irritable and sometimes uproariously abusive states – brought on, I gathered, to a great extent by physical suffering and bodily discomforts – was a delightful companion and could be, at times, that difficult thing, a real partner in the work to be done. I mean he made himself into an architect – which he was as much as Lord Burlington at least – and we toiled at the designs and details in the closest union, except that I held the pencil which drew our joint conceptions. Sometimes he joined in almost too much, especially when, after hours of trial by models made of sheets and standing about discussing at perhaps unnecessary length, I settled down to envisage on paper what we really wanted made. Then he would sit beside me in an armchair with his leg on its wooden rest, and watch with a glittering but quite kindly eye every line I drew and each movement of my compasses. This occurred in a small boudoir he had prepared for me near his study, and such were my exertions in the heat of the room from the roaring fire, I would remove both collar and tie and even let my shoes fall off under the table without provoking any comment from the Foreign Minister.

No problem was either so trivial or so burdensome that it failed to engage Curzon's entire attention. He would recline in a new bath, lined with clean copies of *The Times*, to test whether its proportions were suitable;* he would reject an estimate of over £7,000 for laying out a garden and determine to do it himself. There were many other such dramas – plagues of flies and gardeners who planted herbaceous borders of monstrous asters more suited to a municipal park than to a nobleman's seat; ungrateful tenants too idle to collect a gift of Christmas beef in person and an obstreperous lavatory in the State dressing-room that could be heard all over the house. There were compensations, too. He plunged about 'in deep mud, amid rain and cold and mist and snow', until with the spring the pleasure ground emerged in sunlit splendour and the church tower caught the eye again and again in felicitously arranged vistas. He identified pictures and statues and corrected careless attributions. He wrote the history of Kedleston church – alas, the only one of a series of monographs on Kedleston that he completed. And although he did not live to achieve the ambition of entertaining his Sovereign at Kedleston in all its restored glory, he enjoyed dispensing a milder hospitality. 'I eventually packed him off with a pheasant, two partridges and two colossal pears', Curzon wrote of a departing guest.

A few days before his final illness in March, 1925, Curzon saw Kedleston for the last time. This is how Butler recalls him:

> He was lying in the State bed, that superb design by Robert Adam with tall carved and gilded columns upholding a canopy, tufted with smoke-blue feathers at each corner. The high bed-head was heavily embroidered with heraldry – an effect of acid blues and gold – and the counterpane matched it. He was lying there wearing grey gloves in the cold silk-lined room and reading a magazine of adventure stories.

Less than a month later, after a funeral service in Westminster Abbey, he made the last journey of all to Kedleston. His coffin, hewn from one of his

* The first permanently fixed bath at Kedleston had been installed in 1885, a dozen years before Windsor Castle acquired the same amenity.

beloved oak trees two centuries old, lay all night in the great marble hall. Next day it was carried simply to join those of his kinsmen in the church.

With an attention to detail that characterized his life, Curzon composed his own epitaph. Ironically, it was found on a sheet of writing paper bearing the superscription of No. 10 Downing Street, the one house he had so long and vainly hoped to occupy. It reads:

In divers offices and in many lands
As Explorer, Writer, Administrator and Ruler of men,
He sought to serve his country
And add honour to an ancient name.

In lapidary inscriptions, Dr Johnson observed, a man is not upon oath. When the author of an apostrophe happens also to be its subject, cynicism is almost irresistible. But there can be no true understanding of Curzon's complex character unless the intellectual curiosity and proud patriotism implied in his epitaph are accepted at their face value. His ancient lineage was both an inspiration and a challenge: a call to public service and a spur to surpass the limited achievements of his ancestors. Although some of his ambitions turned to dust, Winston Churchill's epitome of his life endures: 'The morning had been golden; the noontide was bronze; and the evening lead. But all were solid, and each was polished till it shone after its fashion.' Each, too, was permeated by an abiding love of Kedleston, a rock-like support in a world of shifting fortunes.

Not long after Curzon's death, his widow went down into the vault of the church to gaze at his coffin. On one of the shelves her eye caught a postcard bearing in her husband's writing the words: 'Reserved for the second Lady Curzon.' It was the highest compliment he could have paid her.

Chapter Two

CHILDHOOD

> It is said that famous men are usually the product of unhappy childhood. The stern compression of circumstances, the twinges of adversity, the spur of slights and taunts in early years, are needed to evoke that ruthless fixity of purpose and tenacious mother-wit without which great actions are seldom accomplished.
>
> – *Sir Winston Churchill's Life of Marlborough*

For all the architectural splendour of his surroundings, Curzon spent his childhood in what was essentially a mid-Victorian parsonage. His father, the Rev. Alfred Nathaniel Curzon, became Rector of Kedleston in 1855, when he was twenty-three, and held the living until he died sixty-one years later. Following the tradition of the age, he was the fourth successive member of the family to be presented to the benefice, the advowson of which had belonged to the Curzons for 600 years.

The Rector from 1795 to 1832 was the Rev. David Curzon, fourth son of the first Lord Scarsdale. He carried almost into the reign of Queen Victoria the habit of preaching with top boots under his gown and of dining convivially at the Bell Inn, Derby, after a day's coursing.

Decorum was restored by his successor, Alfred Curzon, seventh son of the second Lord Scarsdale, and Rector from 1832 to 1850. Alfred's grandson, George Nathaniel, describes in his history of Kedleston church the air of demure rusticity that characterized the services of those days. Until an organ was installed in 1870, a violoncello, a violin and a trombone provided a precarious accompaniment to the venerable chants of Tate and Brady. 'Each person,' Curzon continues, 'sat in his appointed place according to his position and rank; every man who owned a silk hat wore it on the Sabbath; the music and singing were equally primitive; the extreme of simplicity justified by the rubric prevailed; and when the park keeper, garbed in his best Sunday apparel of green plush coat and vest, and the village constable advanced to their seats under the tower they bowed low to the parson as they passed the pulpit.'

On Alfred's death in 1850 the incumbency was kept warm for five years by his brother Frederic, who held it jointly with the living of Mickleover. In 1855 Frederic vacated it in favour of his nephew Alfred Nathaniel, Alfred's second son. The new Rector, secure in the belief that an elder brother would inherit both the peerage and its responsibilities, could expect to pass a lifetime of placid ministration in a country parish. But within a few months his elder brother, George Nathaniel, was dead, thrown from his horse in Rotten Row;* and in 1856, on the death of his bachelor uncle, the third Lord Scarsdale, the unambitious heir succeeded to both Kedleston and the Barony.

There seems, however, to have been a moment of doubt whether the right of succession of Alfred Nathaniel was so beyond challenge as to satisfy the rigid demands of English peerage law. The new Lord Scarsdale's grandfather, the second Baron, was the cause of the uncertainty. He married twice. By his first wife he had a son, Nathaniel, who as the undisputed heir to his father succeeded him as third Baron Scarsdale in 1804 and died unmarried in 1856. After the death of his first wife in 1782, the second Baron was obliged to live abroad to escape a heavy burden of debt caused by gambling and the exactions of moneylenders. There he formed an alliance with a Flemish girl, Felicité Anne Josephe de Wattines, who bore him ten children. But as their only traceable form of marriage did not take place until 1798, the six children born before that date were illegitimate. It was not until 1926 that children born out of wedlock were legitimized by the belated marriage of their parents; and even had such retrospective legislation operated in the previous century, the legitimized children would still have been debarred by peerage law from succession to the Barony of Scarsdale, or to any other inherited dignity. None of the children born to Lord and Lady Scarsdale after their marriage in 1798 suffered, of course, from such a disqualification. Thus the heir to the childless third Baron was his half-brother, the Rev. Alfred Curzon: born in 1801, he was the seventh son of the second Baron, but the next eldest

* Lord Curzon wrote: 'He had been engaged to a young lady of high rank whose parents however broke off the match, because they had a wealthier suitor (whom she ultimately married) in view. Just as he was leaving the Row, he passed the young lady & her mother in their carriage. As he took off his hat his horse reared and threw him with his head against the curb. He was taken into St George's Hospital where he lingered for some hours and then died.

'The same story may be referred to as illustrating the extraordinary smallness & concentration of London Society in the middle of the 19th. century. The lady who had been engaged to my uncle and whom I afterwards knew herself told me the tale. When her mother broke off the match with my uncle in favour of the rich banker the act was looked upon by the narrow circle that then constituted Society as such bad form, that when the mother and daughter appeared at the opera at Covent Garden a few nights later, they were publicly hissed by the occupants of the boxes and stalls. ... '

legitimate son after the third Baron. Alfred died in 1850 and his elder son in 1855. On the death of the third Baron in 1856, the peerage therefore passed to Alfred's only remaining son, Alfred Nathaniel.*

The new Lord Scarsdale, however, was haunted by a doubt. Was the marriage contracted abroad by his grandparents in 1798 as valid in English law as they had hoped? If it was, then the children born after that year were legitimate and he himself was indisputably secure in his claim to the title. But if it was not a valid marriage, then his father had been born out of wedlock and he himself left without right of succession to the peerage, which in the absence of any lawful male issue of the first, second or third Barons, would now become extinct. That was not all. Should his late father's legitimacy be challenged at any time, he might lose not only the title but also the Kedleston estates. By a family settlement made in 1816, the estates, in default of lawful male issue of the second Baron and of his eldest son, would pass to the second Baron's illegitimate issue in order of seniority. Two illegitimate sons were in fact still living in 1856. They were Edward Curzon, a retired admiral, and Frederic, Rector of Mickleover. Until their nephew, Alfred Nathaniel, had established the validity of his grandparents' marriage in 1798, he could never be certain that either of his uncles would not institute proceedings to deprive him both of peerage and of estates.

In 1856 the new Lord Scarsdale – if such he was – invited the English courts to examine the circumstances of his grandparents' marriage and to decide whether or not it was valid in English law. The ceremony had taken place in the house of a Roman Catholic priest in Altona, near Hamburg: the ebb and flow of the French revolutionary wars had not made it easy for the second Baron and Mlle de Wattines to find a domestic haven. A trunkful of legal precedents and opinions in the muniment room at Kedleston today testifies to the thoroughness of the investigations carried out on behalf of the claimant. His cause succeeded and in 1857 the fourth Baron Scarsdale was able to enter on his heritage.

There still remained a remote danger that the two illegitimate uncles might appeal against the declaration in an attempt to lay hands on the valuable Kedleston estates. To do so, however, they would be obliged to prove that their mother and father had never been married. Charity prevailed in every sense. The uncles stated that out of regard for their parents' memory they would not pursue the case. And their grateful nephew responded by continuing to pay them a handsome annuity out of the revenues of the estates.

Curzon, too, comes well out of the story. When he came to write the history of Kedleston church, a meticulous work of scholarship, privately printed in 1922, he gave all his illegitimate great-uncles and great-aunts the prefix of 'Honourable', a triumph of ancestral pride over historical pedantry.

* See family tree, opposite page 1.

Burdened by an estate of 10,000 acres and the multitude of local duties demanded of a land-owner, Lord Scarsdale soon ceased to officiate in Kedleston church. But he never divested himself of Holy Orders or resigned his living. A succession of curates took the services under his scrutiny, while he himself retained responsibility for both the moral and material welfare of his flock. It cannot always have been easy for him to remember at any single moment whether he was pastor or peer. Visiting a sick parishioner one day, the Rector knocked at the front door of a cottage. There was no answer. Eventually the invalid's wife appeared from behind the house. 'The front door is locked, My Lord,' she told him, 'would you mind coming round the back?' 'I do not come to back doors,' the squire of Kedleston replied.

Scarsdale was the archetype of the old-fashioned country nobleman, whose ambition hardly extended beyond the horizons of his estate. His days were punctuated by events as little exciting as committees of the water authority in Derby or meetings of the governing body of Repton School, to which he belonged for forty years. He was just and punctilious in the administration of business, but could display fierceness if his rights were infringed. A neighbouring rector who advertised his willingness to take paying guests, with trout-fishing thrown in as an inducement, was swiftly reminded that the riparian rights belonged to his Brother in Christ, and there was an unseemly exchange of courtesies as their gigs passed each other on the Derby road.

Nor did Scarsdale allow his cloth to inhibit him from the traditional pursuits and sympathies of a countryman, such as shooting and the tolerance evoked by the hard realities and loneliness of cottage life in the nineteenth century. Both facets of his character are shown in one of his favourite stories which has been handed down and perhaps even a little burnished by his family. For several years he leased from Lord Derby a grouse moor at Crag, on the borders of Derbyshire and Cheshire. Arriving there one 11 August, he sought out the head keeper, and after hearing the prospects for the shoot next day enquired what other news there was since he had last been there.

'None, My Lord.'

'None? What a dull dog you are! Surely something must have happened in the last twelve months?'

'Oh, yes, now I recall. You know Joe —, him that farms down in th' holla, where we sometimes kill t'partridge?'

'Yes, what about him?'

'He just begat a son cum his 73rd barthday by his own thard darter.'

'Perfectly disgraceful! How dare you tell me such a thing?'

'Beg pardon, your Lordship, no offence. But such is life in these here wild parts.'

The Rev. Lord Scarsdale also took a man-of-the-world interest in the peccadilloes of his grandfather, the informality of whose marital arrangements might have cost his grandson the peerage and all that went with it. Discovering from family papers that the second Baron had belonged to the Society of Beggars Benison, he undertook much correspondence in an ultimately successful attempt to penetrate its history. The result was not edifying. The club had been founded in 1732, inspired by the legend of a reward bestowed on a young beggar girl by King James VI of Scotland who, when travelling incognito, had been carried across a burn on her back. It was not, however, a charitable association in the accepted sense, but a Scottish counterpart of the Hellfire Club. There were phallic punchbowls and wine-glasses, obscene initiation ceremonies and two mottoes with but a single theme – 'Be Faithful and Multiply' and 'Lose No Opportunity'.

Although Lord Scarsdale was himself an abstemious man and tolerated no luxury in his family, he enjoyed dispensing the hospitality expected of him. To the end of his life he refused to delegate the duty of carving to less skilled hands: a perfectionist in such matters, he kept the gravy spoon warm in a silver bowl of hot water at his elbow. A frequent guest was Sir Henry Wilmot, a schoolboy friend at Rugby who later won the Victoria Cross during the Indian Mutiny and was Member of Parliament for South Derbyshire – the seat that Curzon unsuccessfully contested on Wilmot's retirement in 1885. Scarsdale's port was as good as his beef, and the family still speak of the night the old veteran raised his glass to Angelica Kauffman's painted ceiling in the dining-room, a representation of 'Love embracing Fortune', with the poignant invocation, 'Come down, old girl, come down'.

In July 1856, three months before succeeding to the peerage, Scarsdale married Blanche, a daughter of Joseph Pocklington Senhouse, of Netherhall, Cumberland. She bore him eleven children, of whom one died in infancy. Her husband recorded the birth of his eldest son laconically: 'Tuesday, January 11, 1859. Dear Blanche safely confined of a boy at 10.30 A.M., no doctor or nurse being present.' Lady Scarsdale, too, kept a diary during succeeding years. It contains details of family comings and goings, the weather, texts of sermons, the clothes she wore each day and successive winners of the Derby. But there is nothing of her intimate thoughts, not a word to suggest that her children ever caused her anxiety or brought her pride. She remains an elusive figure.

Lord Scarsdale, too, immersed in local affairs, was an undemonstrative man who did not find it easy to achieve an intimate relationship with his children. Even when George surprised and delighted him by winning an Eton prize, that most Victorian of papas could not resist tempering a rare letter of congratulation with a chilling warning:

> Your success has given us all the greatest pleasure, and you may feel very sure your Mama and I fully appreciate all the application and study necessary for the

desired result. You deserve credit and I am sure you will receive it, but do not, dear Boy, be unduly puffed up! ... Do not celebrate your success by wearing your hair long and wrapped around your ears!! You know what I mean, and I do detest long hair.

The ambitions of a boy who early in life determined to dedicate himself to Parliament and to foreign travel meant little to a father who never again left England after going on the Grand Tour at the age of twenty and whose only two recorded excursions into politics were to support Gladstone's repeal of the duty on paper in 1860, and to vote in 1883 against the opening of museums on Sunday. The place of a land-owner, Lord Scarsdale believed, was on his land and in the midst of his tenants: not, as he put it, 'roaming about all over the world'.

There is, however, touching evidence that he cared desperately about his son, however much he felt constrained to conceal his concern. When he died in 1916, St John Brodrick wrote to commiserate with Curzon. It cannot have been an easy letter to write. Curzon believed that Brodrick, Secretary of State for India during the latter years of his Viceroyalty, had betrayed him both as a Cabinet Minister and as one of his oldest friends. Except on formal business the two men rarely corresponded again and when they met by chance confined their conversation to polite nothingness. Now, more than a decade after Curzon's resignation, Brodrick sought an occasion for reconciliation:

Your father's death brings back to me so much of our early life that you will, I hope, forgive me for writing you a line of sympathy on a loss which comes to you at a specially trying time. For many years, after my visit to Kedleston in 1879, he treated me with a kindly confidence, and more than once came to consult me on points in your outlook on which he was anxious. For, with all his reserve to outsiders, he was prodigiously proud of you and alive to everything which might affect your career.

It seems difficult to realise that your possession of Kedleston, which did not seem unusually remote in those days and which was naturally interwoven with your thoughts of the future, comes to you when you have other great houses and have long passed all ordinary standards of achievement.

And in 1887, when Curzon wrote to his father from Singapore to describe the strength of the British influence in the Far East, Lord Scarsdale shyly, but with unconcealed pride, sent on his son's letter to the Prime Minister, Lord Salisbury.

To the end of his days, Curzon believed that he had passed a miserable childhood. 'I suppose no children well-born and well-placed,' he wrote, 'ever cried so much or so justly.' Of this unhappiness, intensified rather than relieved by the splendour of his surroundings, his parents were apparently unaware. After the fashion of the time they placed the early education of their children in the hands of a governess. Miss Paraman, Curzon admitted, 'taught us good habits – economy, neatness, method and a dislike of anything vulgar or fast'. But she reinforced her lessons with a fierce and crushing discipline. Curzon has left his own account of her sadistic regime:

> In her savage moments she was a brutal and vindictive tyrant; and I have often thought since that she must have been insane. She persecuted and beat us in the most cruel way and established over us a system of terrorism so complete that not one of us ever mustered up the courage to walk upstairs and tell our father or mother. She spanked us with the sole of her slipper on the bare back, beat us with her brushes, tied us for long hours to chairs in uncomfortable positions with our hands holding a pole or a blackboard behind our backs, shut us up in darkness, practised on us every kind of petty persecution, wounded our pride by dressing us (me in particular) in red shining calico petticoats (I was obliged to make my own) with an immense conical cap on our heads round which, as well as on our breasts and backs, were sewn strips of paper bearing in enormous characters, written by ourselves, the words Liar, Sneak, Coward, Lubber and the like. In this guise she compelled us to go out in the pleasure ground and show ourselves to the gardeners. She forced us to walk through the park at even distances, never communicating with each other, to the village and to show ourselves to the villagers. It never occurred to us that these good folk sympathised intensely with us and regarded her as a fiend. Our pride was much too deeply hurt.
>
> She made me write a letter to the butler asking him to make a birch for me with which I was to be punished for lying and requesting him to read it out in the Servants' Hall. When he came round one day with a letter and saw me standing in my red petticoat with my face to the wall on a chair outside the schoolroom and said 'Why, you look like a Cardinal!' I could have died of shame.
>
> She made us trundle our hoops as young children, all alone, up and down a place in the grounds near the hermitage where were tall black fir trees and a general air of gloom and of which we were intensely afraid. She forced us to confess to lies which we had never told, to sins which we had never committed, and then punished us savagely, as being self-condemned. For weeks we were not allowed to speak to each other or to a human soul.

Yet Curzon never doubted that Miss Paraman was devoted to her charges. After the fashion of nannies throughout the ages, she afterwards spoke of the Curzon children as models of every virtue and to the eldest, Sophy, she bequeathed what little money she had in the world.

> She represented [Curzon later wrote], a class of governess and a method of tuition (in entire independence of the parents) which have both disappeared. With children who are constantly with their parents such a system would be incapable of concealment ... Not one of us ever reproached her with the past; and I believe that had it been recalled to her memory she would have dismissed it as a baseless and wicked fabrication.

George's parents treated her almost as a member of the family and within a fortnight of Lady Scarsdale's death, Lord Scarsdale handed her a gold necklace which his wife had wanted that devoted governess to have.

Curzon was never a man to waste good agony, and his sombre memories were possibly clouded by the mood of self-pity into which he would sometimes be driven by the ill-health, pain and exhaustion of his middle age. In other autobiographical notes he sheds a warmer glow over early years at Kedleston:

We used to go as children every year to the seaside either to Brighton, or St. Leonards or Broadstairs or Llandudno or Maryport; and among the most cherished recollections of my childhood were the Chain Pier with the little shops where things made of shell were sold at Brighton; Warrior Square in Hastings; the covered wooden steps leading down to the sands at Broadstairs; the big white lighthouse on the cliff; the house where Sir Moses Montefiore lived between Broadstairs and Ramsgate; a harp being played on the pier at Margate on an excursion Saturday; a Confirmation Service being held in St. Peter's Church by the Archbishop of Canterbury, Longley, in 1863; (it was the first time I had ever seen an Archbishop and the first time I had ever heard bells peal a tune – they rang 'Abide with me' I remember) ... the wall-flowers on the parapet of the banqueting hall at Conway Castle; the target in the sea at which the Artillery volunteers used to practise at Maryport; the Roman Camp above the town, and an expedition with my grandfather to see salmon caught in the coops and nets on the Derwent River above Workington.

The contemporary schoolboy diary of his younger brother Alfred also helps to dispel some of the shadows that clung to George's early memories. There were few luxuries at Kedleston, but a succession of shopping excursions and pantomimes, Christmas trees bearing nearly 500 objects and birthdays punctiliously marked (even by Miss Paraman) with a rich harvest of presents. At school the boys were sent hampers from Fortnum & Mason, and in the holidays few children could have enjoyed a happier time roaming the estate or visiting the country houses of other members of the family. There was riding and hunting and shooting and fishing and football and 'cricket with the flunkeys'.

But even as a mere child George could not escape the call to public service. He was only eight when required to deliver the first of those exhortatory addresses which punctuated his career. Written by his father and learned by heart, it was to mark the building of a new school at Kedleston:

I am very much pleased at being desired by my Father to lay the first stone of this school, which I hope will be an ornament to the village and a blessing to the parish; and I trust that many children here may learn those truths which may fit them to fulfil their duty towards their God, their parents and their neighbours as long as they live.

For a small boy whose self-confidence had taken many a knock from Miss Paraman it must have been an ordeal. He was sensitive, too, about his appearance, particularly the abnormal breadth of his head that throughout life required him to have his hats specially made. The tiny Demosthenes, however, acquitted himself well at his first engagement and as a reward was allowed to ride home on his father's grey cob.

In May 1869, when he was ten, Curzon was sent to the private school at Wixenford, in Hampshire, run by the Rev. R. Cowley Powles.

> I remember to this hour [he later wrote] the horrible moment when I saw the fly and white horse drive away carrying my mother, who was dearer to me than anyone in the world, and also the long wait two to three hours alone in the bare Wixenford dining room before I was taken over to the schoolroom and introduced to the second master and other boys. Fortunately Powles gave me a fascinating book to read describing the adventures of a Prince rather after the Arabian nights fashion and though I have long ago forgotten both the title and the story, I shall never forget the enthralled absorption with which, half in homesickness and half in terror of what might be to come, I clung to that volume.
>
> Powles himself [Curzon's unpublished memoir continues] we all liked and respected. He was rather weak and sometimes querulous but was a perfect gentleman, an amiable character and a graceful scholar ... I shall never forget his features – his thick hair beautifully brushed and coiled in a heavy twist over each ear whence it projected on to his cheeks; his thin flexible overhanging upper lip which wobbled up and down as he talked, and his amiable academic laugh. Well, too, do I remember the gold-rimmed glasses which hung by a chain round his neck and which he was always fingering in an uneasy way and rubbing clear with his yellow silk handkerchief.

Curzon's library at Kedleston contains a more tangible record of his first headmaster: a printed sermon entitled 'Means of Avoiding Sin'. Powles had moved his school from Blackheath to Hampshire in order to bring it within the spiritual influence of his old friend the Rev. Charles Kingsley, who had the neighbouring parish of Eversley. 'We have just come back from church,' George wrote to his mother a few days after his arrival, 'where Mr. Kingsley preached; he preaches so simply, so that all may understand; such a great many labourers, farmers and working men come to this church.' Mrs Kingsley added the material bounty of plum cake to her husband's eloquence, and that the boys also found attractive. Frederick Denison Maurice, the Christian Socialist, was another preacher of whom Curzon approved.

In material terms, too, Wixenford was an agreeable change from the frugality imposed by Miss Paraman on her charges. 'At meal times,' he wrote of his childhood at Kedleston, 'she took all the dainties for herself and gave us nothing but tapioca and rice pudding which we detested and which we used to drop into our caps when she was not looking and carry away and hide in chinks in the wall where she was not likely to discover them.' Wixenford offered a more sybaritic diet. During his first week at school, Curzon wrote daringly to his mother: 'Will you tell Miss P. we do not have bread and scrape here but bread with more butter on than we have at home.' And as confidence grew, he became more imperious in his demands:

> Now for my requests. First, as it is the half term, a hamper is undoubtedly requisite under the present circumstances, as we hadn't one last term. This hamper must contain: one fine fat brawn, as usual, several pots of superior jam, including, mark me, apricot, etc., whilst pots of potted meat are indispensable. Oh! but above all things, one of those very jolly cakes which are so nice and big and which Mrs. Halliday fully knows how to fabricate.

Every letter from Wixenford to Kedleston was preserved. They were written on paper prettily adorned with flowers and sometimes with colourful designs called transferables. Cricket and rounders, warm clothes and cod liver oil, requests for garden plants, postage stamps and invisible ink – Curzon was not a precocious correspondent in those days. But already there were intellectual stirrings. 'Will you ask Mama,' he wrote to a younger brother, 'if she will mind Mr. Powles putting down on the bill a book of music of pieces by the *very best authors*, Beethoven, Mozart, Haydn, Clementi.' The curriculum also included literature:

> Last Thursday a gentleman Mr. Beaumont came here and read us part of Julius Caesar in Shakespeare imitating the voices of all the characters very well. He goes about reading at Eton and other places. He read to us about an hour and a half and the part about the assassination of Caesar and Mark Antony's speech in the Forum were very nice: we got rather tired at the end: he was rather old I should think... *

In his very first letter home, George mentioned Mr Dunbar, the headmaster's assistant – 'a short, stout gentleman with a moustache, whiskers and a little beard; he scolds more than Mr. Dyne'. Unlike the mild mannered Mr Powles, Archibald Dunbar was a man of passionate temperament and sadistic impulses, always on the look-out for imagined slights – and a dextrous beater when he thought he had detected them. In the supposed interests of education he imposed upon his pupils a rule as stern as that of Miss Paraman; and if he, too, drew inspiration from the works of Kingsley, it was from the diatribe against Cardinal Newman rather than from the sentimentality of *The Water Babies*. George saw Wixenford no less than Kedleston through a mist of schoolroom tears.

> As a master [he later wrote of Dunbar] he was for the most part detested by the boys to whom he was savage and cruel. On the other hand he made great favourites – of whom I was one – and though he never spared us one jot or tittle of his displeasure or punishment if we had provoked either, he could be extremely nice to us when he

* But Mr Beaumont still had life in him. Sixteen years later the young Winston Churchill heard him read *Julius Caesar* at Brighton.

was in a gracious mood and was as genuinely fond of us as we were – at a distance – attached to him.

His vigour and resourcefulness were overpowering. He practically shunted poor old Powles and 'ran' the school by himself. He executed all or nearly all the punishments whether by spanking on the bare buttocks or by caning on the palm of the hand or by swishing on the posterior. I remember well all three experiences. He was a master of spanking, though he used to say that it hurt him nearly as much as it did us. I remember that it was at about the 15th blow that it really began to hurt and from thence the pain increased in geometrical progression. At about the 28th blow one began to howl. The largest number of smacks I ever received was I think 42. But comic to relate I still remember the delicious feeling of warmth that ensued about 5 to 10 minutes later when the circulation was thoroughly restored and the surface pain had subsided. He was very cruel with the cane to some boys whose hands were covered with weals. With the birch I think he never gave beyond 10 or 12 strokes – and that for some peculiarly grave offence in his bedroom at night.

Curzon probably fared little worse than most children of his age and class. Lord Salisbury, for instance, his first political master, hated his schooldays so bitterly that only after an interval of thirty years could he bear to revisit Eton. So heavy was the depression produced by his memories that he never repeated the visit, although a frequent guest at Windsor, on the other bank of the river. He also admitted that his intimate acquaintance with the obscure byways of London sprang from a youthful dread of meeting fellow Etonians in the more fashionable streets during the holidays.

The little victim of Miss Paraman and Mr Dunbar was made of tougher fibre. As in the schoolroom at Kedleston, so at Wixenford the storm clouds would give way to fitful sunshine. Curzon became head boy of the school and in his last term won an unprecedented five prizes, including one for the best collection of moths and butterflies.

I also [he recorded] under Dunbar's supervision kept the school accounts, i.e. I was the private banker of every boy in the school. I still have the tin cashbox in which I kept the money and the account books. We had cheque books specially printed for us and money could only be drawn by a cheque properly signed. I believe I was never out by even a penny at the end of the term, and undoubtedly the plan was a wise one as inculcating both business habits and economy.

The Wixenford Herald of 2 February 1870, the magazine in which the boys advertised their treasures for sale, lends support to the commercial ability of the school banker: 'Curzon has stamps of Brazil, Canada, Danubian Principalities, Portugal, Pony Express, also large stock of monograms, seals and postmarks.' How opulent sounds his stock-in-trade compared with the pathetic offer of Thorneycroft: 'Six feet of strong string in exchange for three used postage stamps.'

Curzon never forgot his early mentors: but he forgave them. As a junior Minister in Lord Salisbury's Government he attended Miss Paraman's funeral in 1892. For years, too, he maintained a warm correspondence with the Wixenford tyrant. In his very first week as an Eton boy he wrote to his mother that he was expecting a visit from Mr Dunbar, and two days later described the pleasant hours they had spent together: 'He was so kind. He took me out to dinner which was a very good one indeed. He brought me 5 very nice pictures and while here bought me 3 more so that I have a good many pictures in my room already but I have no chair.' His old schoolmaster called again in May and each week sent him the *Graphic* magazine. That is not the customary relationship between a heartless instructor and an embittered pupil.

The story, however, has a less happy ending. By his morbid touchiness, Dunbar successively exasperated and alienated all those for whose regard he so desperately yearned. 'That we remained firm friends, even affectionate friends for over 20 years,' Curzon later wrote, 'is a phenomenon which I am even now at a loss to explain.' The final breach was probably caused by Dunbar's taking offence at an intended act of kindness on Curzon's part. Hearing that Dunbar was in financial difficulty, Curzon made an offer through a third party to buy back his own letters over the years. Dunbar received the proposition with indignation and seems to have destroyed every one of his old pupil's letters before his death in 1923.

By a conscious effort of charity and understanding, Curzon was thus able in later years to recall his early tribulations without bitterness. Yet he did not emerge altogether unscathed from the needless curbing of high spirits, the severe correction of childish misdemeanours, the humiliating malevolence designed to break his will. Miss Paraman's treatment provoked in him a spirit of rebellion and an intolerance of opposition which in the years ahead sometimes warped his critical faculties. At times he could appear as unreasonably sensitive as Mr Dunbar himself, and one theme of the present volume is his alienation in middle and later life of many of the intimate friends of his youth. Even his Sovereign exposed himself to a snub during Curzon's years as Foreign Secretary. One morning in December 1923, Curzon was expected in audience at Buckingham Palace; but finding himself too ill to move from his bed in Carlton House Terrace, he sent a message asking to be excused. George v thereupon determined to dispense with protocol and to hold the audience at Curzon's bedside. 'It was all I could do to stop him,' Curzon wrote to his wife. 'To tell the truth I knew the King well enough to be sure that even though he came in his great good nature, he would make a fine story of it afterwards. So eventually I prevailed and went to the Palace at 6 p.m.'

The slights and taunts of Miss Paraman may also have implanted the seeds of a relentless ambition to succeed, as much to discomfit his enemies as to achieve fame. It was an attitude of mind that a Balfour – although perhaps not a Churchill – would have scorned as a little vulgar, a shade lacking in the philosophical detachment expected of governing men. Of another Prime Minister, Rosebery, it was said that he wanted the palm without the dust. Curzon had no such reservations and even found merit in its very dustiness. An ancient lineage and a splendid house encouraged him to take an aristocratic view of life: but again and again he would obscure it with a parsimony, an attention to detail and a narrowness of vision generally supposed to be characteristic of the middle classes.

Nowhere was it more marked than in his attitude to personal expenditure. Compared with the drab and hungry existence endured by so many of his less fortunate contemporaries in mid-Victorian England, Curzon's childhood was enviably secure. The memory of the privations imposed by Miss Paraman nevertheless overshadowed his recollections of schoolboy treats and bred in him a strain of austerity from which only his aesthetic pursuits and the claims of hospitality were immune. Here the influence of his father may also be discerned. After Lord Scarsdale's death in 1916, Curzon composed an epitaph containing these lines:

Just and unblemished in his commerce with the world
Whose vanities he held of no account.

Scarsdale's will, it is true, was proved at a gross figure of £454,694; but throughout his stewardship of sixty years the estate was heavily mortgaged and the household run on simple lines.

Curzon would sometimes boast of being a self-made man, in the sense that his ambitions had been realized by his own efforts, not through the case of inherited wealth. There was, however, an unattractive side to his success story. 'When I got to Paddington,' he once wrote to his father, 'I gave the cabman 1/–. He grumbled and said he ought to have 1/6 as it was over 2 miles but I said that I had given only 1/– in the morning and that I wouldn't give him any more and while he was grumbling I walked away.' Curzon was then thirteen: but the encounter could have taken place at any moment during the next fifty years.

Poverty itself vanished with his marriage to an American heiress in 1895. Yet a dual set of values continued to affect the balance of both his private and his public life. He would, his second wife has recalled, pay £10,000 for a picture but grudge the expense of a new dressing-gown. One moment he was writing a State paper calculated to change the course of history, and the next fussily disputing a tradesman's account of a few shillings or complaining to his publisher that the margins of his latest book were one-quarter of an inch narrower than those permitted to another statesman-author.

Having been impressed from childhood with the need to be methodical and self-sufficient, he never learned to use a secretary. As Viceroy of India he once wrote to a friend:

> It is supposed to be a mark of efficiency and even greatness to get your work done for you by other people. I frankly disagree. I say that if you want a thing done in a certain way, the only manner in which to be sure that it is done, is to do it yourself. It is supposed that big men ought to have a soul above detail. I assert that every really great man from Caesar to Napoleon has been a master of detail.

In similar vein he criticized an earlier Viceroy, Lord Dufferin: 'He was careless about detail, interfered very little in departmental business, and left the conduct of minor matters to his Private Secretary and officials.' Incapable of appreciating that in great offices of State such habits of administration were virtues rather than faults, Curzon perpetually immersed himself in needless trivia to the detriment both of his health and of his judgement. Throughout life he wrote in his own hand not only a voluminous private correspondence but also the vast bulk of official documents. He hardly ever dictated, light-heartedly explaining that he had ceased to employ an amanuensis since the occasion on which his 'sanguine hope' had emerged in the printed text of a despatch as 'sanguinary hope'. Night after night through the long years of his public career, he chained himself to his desk until the early hours of the morning. If copies of letters had to be kept, they would be taken down by a clerk from the interminable sheets of his flowing script. And because he could trust nobody to meet his own standards of perfection, he would even draft acknowledgements and other purely formal papers for his secretaries to sign and send out under their own names.

These lifelong flaws in an Olympian façade may well have sprung from the iron discipline and nervous tension of Curzon's early years. In retrospect, however, he came to realize that he also owed to his early mentors a moral and mental training without which he might have been known to posterity as no more than a Derbyshire country gentleman. A determination to succeed in the face of formidable obstacles and sustained opposition; a sense of order and method, of accuracy and industry; a respect for knowledge and a lively curiosity – these were the foundations on which, in the milder climate of Eton and Oxford, he built one of the most impressive intellects of his time.

Chapter Three
ETON

> You know what I think of your Eton career, and there are many like myself who at its close would scarcely have known what limit the future would assign to you.
>
> – *Letter of St John Brodrick to Curzon, 10 January 1880*

'I am all right here,' George wrote to his mother in the very first letter he sent her from Eton, in the spring of 1872. 'We got up at 7 this morning and began exam at 7.30 in a huge room: all the walls were carved with names and I saw *Curzon* carved twice: I suppose Uncle George did it, and the date of one was 1813 or 1818.' He boarded at the house of the Rev. Charles Wolley Dod, 'a grim and monstrous barrack', as he called it, on the site of which School Hall now stands. Nor did he find his housemaster any more cheerful an institution. As a boy himself at Eton, Wolley Dod had been an able scholar and promising athlete, and in later life achieved some renown as a field naturalist. He loved fishing, and to catch a fine Thames trout would put him in a good humour for days. His pupils also remembered a dramatic little anecdote he once told them, with a sensible conclusion: 'Once when I was out shooting, a trigger of my gun caught on a button and the gun went off, so I took out my knife and cut off all my buttons.' Shyness, however, prevented him from winning the confidence of the boys in his house. He was tall and thin, with narrow reddish whiskers, had a sarcastic manner and in imitation of his speech was known as Wollah Doddah. His usual manner of addressing a small boy was: 'Small boy'. He was learned and conscientious and unsympathetic.

Curzon was utterly unsuited to the tight rein on which Wolley Dod drove his pupils. In his unpublished 'Notes for a Biography', he described the clash of temperament that darkened his first two or three years at Eton.

> I recall distinctly how little I was in harmony with many of the masters and how completely they misunderstood me, or was it that I misunderstood them? I think that the misunderstanding was partly due to three features or faults in my own character which years afterwards seem to me to stand out quite clear.

The first was the tendency, common with boyhood, and particularly public-school boyhood, to conceal my virtues, such as they were, and to represent myself as worse than I was. The second was a sort of innate rebelliousness which has been with me all my life. The third was a passionate desire to win, to be the first in whatever I undertook, and to defeat competition.

These three qualities were perpetually combining together to produce curious results. Thus as a small boy I was one of the most undisciplined boys in old Wolley Dod's house. I was one of the most studious because I burned to excel, but one of the rowdiest because I had high animal spirits and liked to depict myself as not wholly a 'sap'. Moreover I rather despised the dear old gentleman's capacity either to impart instruction or to maintain order.

For the same reasons I was always at war with mathematical masters. I had perhaps a natural distaste for mathematics, and I certainly had an extreme contempt for mathematical masters who seemed to me, and were popularly regarded in the school, as representing a lower order of character and intelligence. ...

Contact with this type of master sharpened all the rebellious elements in my nature. At the same time I never neglected my studies, and a sudden challenge from the indignant master invariably found my answer ready and right, my work well done, my sum or problem beautifully worked out. Thus I was always among the first in the class, though one of its apparently least satisfactory members.

Awed by the skill with which Curzon defied authority, his contemporaries soon abandoned the use of his first and increasingly inappropriate nickname, Moonface. His tutor, reporting to Lord Scarsdale on the progress George had made by the end of his second Half at Eton, was less easily dazzled:

Your son continues to show great aptitude for first class scholarship and is very quick at learning. He is very amiable in manner and is upon the whole very well conducted. There are however one or two points to which I should like to pay particular attention ... a tendency to say silly things and to make silly answers about the lesson. This cannot fail to have a demoralising tendency in the formation of his character and I have spoken very seriously about it to him. ... Being young for his place in the school, and a popular and well-mannered boy, he is in some danger of being spoilt by associating too much with boys older than himself. I believe him to be very well principled, but the notice of older boys is too apt to make young ones conceited and forward. Your son served a very short apprenticeship as a lower boy. I am anxious therefore not to bring him too forward for his age. The moral position a boy of that sort can be placed in is as 'steerer' of a long boat. I say this from 20 years' experience and hope if he should have any inclination to seek such a position that you will not encourage it.

It was a ponderous indictment of a boy who was not yet fourteen. In the following month George was reassuringly writing to his mother with that ageless schoolboy plea: 'I am very low in cash.'

Chafing under Wolley Dod's unsympathetic scrutiny, he looked longingly towards the circle which gathered round another Eton master. 'Why should a man,' Oscar Browning asked, 'directly he becomes a schoolmaster be thought as unfit for civilized society as if he had taken Orders?' His boys enjoyed appetizing food and comfortable rooms; an unusually large staff of servants and concerts of chamber music; the conversation of Ruskin, Pater and George Eliot during the Half and foreign travel during the holidays. His house, he determined, should be a nursery for statesmen.

Browning had taught Curzon in school and, like Wolley Dod, was aware of the dangers to which a handsome and precocious boy was exposed. Rashly he felt it was his duty to protect Curzon from unwholesome influences, a responsibility that more properly belonged to the boy's housemaster. He invited him to use his magnificent private library, on which he spent £300 a year, and to receive unofficial tuition in working for the Prince Consort's French Prize. Having been struck in the eye by a cricket ball during the Summer Half of 1874, George had more leisure than most boys and eagerly accepted Browning's invitation to climb Parnassus. Their friendship grew. Returning borrowed volumes of Dante and Tennyson, George was soon signing his letters, 'Yours affectionately'. Wolley Dod, his mind aching with not unreasonable suspicion, complained to the Head Master of the interest taken by a colleague in a boy who was not his pupil.

Dr James John Hornby had been appointed Head Master in 1867 to guide Eton through a period of enforced reform, the result of a Royal Commission on the Public Schools which revealed deplorable deficiencies in both curriculum and management.

> Nothing can be worse than this state of things [declared Lord Clarendon its chairman] when we find modern languages, geography, history, chronology and everything else which a well-educated English gentleman ought to know, given up in order that the full time should be devoted to the classics, and at the same time we are told that the boys go up to Oxford not only not proficient, but in a lamentable state of deficiency with respect to the classics.

For many reformers Hornby moved too slowly. Attempts to goad him into further activity, wrote a later Head Master, Edward Lyttelton, were resisted with a courteous immobility to which educational history affords no parallel. As a young assistant master he once complained to Hornby that he had no house to live in, no pupil-room or class-room in which to teach. Hornby merely said: 'Dear, dear', and changed the conversation to Alpine climbing. His judgements were delivered with a striking and economical turn of phrase, 'I rather wish Shelley had been at Harrow', he was once heard to murmur. But behind his apparent indolence lay a precise knowledge of the rate at which Eton could absorb unfamiliar subjects; and it was under his Head Mastership that modern languages, geography and history began partly to displace the classics and so equip Etonians with an education more suited to an age of accelerated change.

Headstrong and tactless, Browning made no effort to disarm the mistrust that his radical views aroused not only in Hornby but in many of his colleagues. He wrote a memorandum of 200 pages warning the Royal Commission on Public Schools against the growing cult of athleticism; he made frequent expeditions to London; he placed Liberal Party election posters in his windows; he was even so revolutionary as to teach history up to the threshold of the nineteenth century. The Head Master also suspected him of neglecting routine duties. One day he suddenly collected the exercises of Browning's pupils. 'Apparently none of them had been corrected,' he remarked on returning them. 'True,' replied Browning, 'but they would have been if you had not taken them away.'

Now came Wolley Dod's accusations, which cannot have been unwelcome to Hornby. He sent for Browning, and began: 'So I hear Mr. Wolley Dod has a good-looking pupil.' Browning was indignant: 'Do you mean to say that you have allowed any master to tell you I took notice of a boy because he was good-looking?' The Head Master replied with evasive rudeness: 'I don't know, I'm sure.'

There followed one of those protracted rumpuses which haunted the Victorian public school. In a small and closed community there were often occasions for misunderstanding; and when nerves were strained, tempers roused and motives doubted, those silk-gowned titans sought relaxation as well as vindication in a battle of the pen. They exchanged page upon page of closely reasoned and wounding abuse, once, twice, three times in a day. They made innumerable copies of their correspondence for general circulation. They appealed to long-suffering members of the governing body. They hinted that in the absence of satisfaction they would raise the matter in the newspapers, even in Parliament. They were eloquent and self-righteous and obsessed.

Browning denied with contempt the charge of Wolley Dod that he had imposed his 'irrepressible attentions' on Curzon, but had at last to submit to the Head Master's insulting decree: he and Curzon were not to meet except on specifically authorized occasions. Warre Cornish, later Vice Provost of Eton, tried to intercede on behalf of his colleague. He pointed out to Hornby that if Browning was unfit to meet Curzon, he was unfit to be a master. 'So he is,' was the Head Master's bland reply. While recognizing that Hornby's authority in matters of discipline could not be challenged, Lord Scarsdale declined to share the Head Master's interpretation of his subordinate's motives and wrote an understanding letter to Browning:

I exceedingly regret this very unpleasant complaint of Mr. Wolley Dod's, with reference to your conduct towards my son George. I am fully aware of your warm feelings and keen desire that he should grow up a manly, true, pure-minded lad and though it is possible that your notice of him may have tended to annoy his tutor – I give you full credit for acting from the purest motives and I do not wish the kindly relations between you and my boy to fall through. I quite believe that you were instrumental in rescuing George from companions of more than doubtful repute, and that your sole desire and object has been to elevate and improve his character ... and I can only hope no further unpleasantness may ever occur on this head.

George, too, wrote a letter of affectionate farewell to Browning, prefaced by the hope that Hornby's ruling would soon be relaxed:

I can't say how distressed I am to think that I am prevented from seeing you, and all through the unkind, ungentlemanly and obstinate conduct of my tutor, whom I detest the more I see him. But I must thank you with my whole heart for all the inestimable good you have done me, for you have always been open to me as the best of counsellors, and have opened my eyes to the company by which I am surrounded and have warned me against evil companions.

It is impossible in retrospect to accept the sinister implications of the Head Master's action. That most upright of men, Lord Scarsdale, rejected them out of hand and allowed his son to spend much time in Browning's company during the holidays, even to travel abroad with him. Nor is it certain that Hornby believed Browning to be an evil influence: rather did he find him a troublesome and negligent colleague whom he hoped to taunt into resignation. But with uncharacteristic docility Browning swallowed the insult. To leave Eton amid a spate of rumours would have deprived him simultaneously of his reputation and of his livelihood.

Little more than a year later the watchful Hornby pounced again and in September 1875 dismissed Browning on the technical but valid point that he had wilfully exceeded the permissible number of boys in his house.* At the age of thirty-eight he found his income reduced from £3,000 to £300 a year and the vocation to which he had devoted his life snatched from him. But O.B., as he became universally known, was of too robust a spirit to vanish into the shadows. Resuming the Fellowship at King's College, Cambridge, to which he had been elected as a young man, he stimulated generations of undergraduates, outraged his colleagues, embraced Christian Science, studied Esperanto and paid court to a dwindling band of Emperors wherever he could find them.

There is a peculiarly sad aspect of any schoolmaster's life, epitomized in a letter written by H.E.Luxmoore, an Eton colleague of Browning and one of the few to rally to his defence against Hornby. He wrote of his former pupils:

Generation after generation pass away from one, with just now and then a single lasting friend among them all – but most of them with never a goodbye or a visit from their college – one sees them across chapel perhaps, or meets a middle-aged man who says 'I'm sure you don't know me' and it's too true, but it's his fault because he passed out of one's life and kept no touch nor cared to. Why should he, with life

* The domestic life of Eton is based on houses, each containing about forty boys. House-masters, although possessing considerable autonomous powers, are obliged to conform to the general directions of the Head Master.

opening before him, choice of innumerable new friends and the sense of stuffy confinement that goes with the word 'school'?

Curzon was more considerate towards the Eton master who had first extended his horizon. 'Whatever I am,' he told his wife when together they met O.B. at a garden party at Marlborough House, 'I owe it all to Mr. Browning.' Far from neglecting to pay his debt of gratitude, he corresponded regularly with him over the years, invited him to India as an honoured Viceregal guest in 1902 and later lent him £100 so that he could write a history of the world in eight enormous volumes.

It was not quite O.B.'s last demand. In 1919, when he was eighty-two and living in busy retirement in Rome, he wrote to Curzon: 'Could you possibly get me made a KBE? I should ask for it on the ground of propaganda, for which many have been decorated. I doubt if any one, except perhaps George Trevelyan, has done more than I have to make English and Italians understand each other.'

As the Cabinet Minister who had planned the recently instituted Order of the British Empire, Curzon was well placed to secure an honour for Browning. But a KBE, or knighthood in the Order, was pitching his services too high. Instead, a few weeks before his death in 1923, O.B. received the lesser distinction of an OBE. He showed no disappointment. The initials were irresistible.

When a young daughter of Warre Cornish spoke disapprovingly of some schoolboy scandal that had recently come to light, her mother told her not to be a prig. 'It's the traditional, ancient, aristocratic vice of Eton,' she explained. 'What do they know of it in those modern, sanitary, linoleum schools?'

The Head Master and his staff, however, took a less romantic view of that perennial problem, and throughout the entire episode that began with Wolley Dod's complaint to Hornby and ended with Browning's dismissal, one theme inspired all three – a determination to save George Curzon from the corrupting flattery of older boys. The monastic life which public schools continue to impose on their pupils was accentuated in the nineteenth century by the long years during which boys remained under such restriction. They stare insolently out of group photographs, huge young men, brawny and bewhiskered, lounging indolently by the Thames until well into their twentieth year. Most of their contemporaries, by contrast, were released from a perfunctory schooling at the age of twelve to seek work in the factories and shops of an expanding industrial England.

It was fortunate for Curzon that among the boys who took an interest in him were Edward and Alfred Lyttelton. The two youngest of Lord Lyttelton's eight sons, they fused a high standard of scholarship with outstanding athletic talent, a cheerful zest for life with a reverent yet unpriggish attachment to

Christian principles. Edward Lyttelton began his correspondence with Curzon on an unlikely note. The younger boy had placed a bet on George Frederick, the Derby winner of 1874, with a friend called Johnstone. But unexpectedly it was from Lyttelton, captain of the cricket XI, that he received his winnings of 12*s.* 6*d.*, together with a friendly warning: 'I am glad to hear you did not scorch your fingers over the Derby. I didn't myself either, but I shall take good care how I embark on such matters again, and I can't help advising you to do the same. It isn't very satisfactory to win and highly unpleasant to lose.' A few weeks later, shortly before Lyttelton left Eton for Cambridge, he asked Curzon for a photograph. The distribution of such souvenirs among contemporaries is a sentimental Eton custom which still survives. But for a nineteen-year-old hero of the cricket field to make such a request to an undistinguished athlete four years his junior – an eternity in the hierarchical structure of a public school – was an attention that could be misconstrued. Lyttelton hastened to explain his motives to Curzon:

Perhaps it may have seemed odd to you that I who have had so very slight a claim to be considered as one of your acquaintance, should have asked so coolly for your likeness, and I should like to give you an explanation of this and other things.

I have heard a good deal about you at one time and another from Oscar Browning whom I have already known for a long time now, and always liked and in many ways respected.

What he told me and what I have been told by other people could scarcely fail to awaken in me a considerable interest in a boy of your position, surrounded by so many dangers, and needing at times a helping hand.

I have always been very observant of the various phases of life presented at Eton, and the more I observed, the more it struck me that in a case like this there were difficulties in my path which should warn me to be careful. I well know the sort of view which the world takes of any big fellow hemmed in by the social chains of being what is called a swell, taking any notice of one younger. I know the tone so prevalent which either in jest or earnest ascribes any motives but the right ones to a fellow in my position supposing I had, as I often wished, made some effort at becoming acquainted with you.

These considerations induced me against my will, but out of regard for you and the harm it might do to others if I was incautious, to keep aloof and behave as you may have thought rather oddly in this matter. I could not help, then, making an effort to carry away with me something to remind me of one who has occupied a considerable share of my thoughts giving me cause now and then, but seldom, for anxiety and always for feeling much interest.

It is only a few short hours that I have to spend at Eton now, and grievous to me the thought is, for with all the wickedness I love the old place ... I can only add that should we ever meet as I hope we shall in days when I shall be free from these considerations, I shall hope to know you well enough to warrant my asking for a photograph, without it needing an apology. I send you in parting my best wishes for the remainder of your Eton life which if spent well will prove a good starting point for what is to come after.

'It is needless to say I should prefer this being kept private', he wrote at the top of his letter. But the correspondence continued and their friendship flourished.

A few months later, a chance encounter enabled Curzon once more to surmount the barriers of custom and to embark on friendships with two boys both considerably his senior and at the pinnacle of their Eton careers. Of Alfred Lyttelton, Edward's younger brother, Curzon wrote many years later: 'No athlete was ever quite such an athlete, no boyish hero ever quite such a boyish hero.' Accompanying Lyttelton from Slough to London to begin Long Leave, a short break in the middle of the Half, was St John Brodrick, son of the eighth Viscount Midleton and a member of Sixth Form hardly less loaded with Eton honours. Brodrick recorded the meeting:

Just as the train was moving a tall, breathless, pink-cheeked and well-groomed boy with black hair was shoved into our carriage. He was covered with shame at intruding on so great a personage as Alfred, but recovered a little when we congratulated him on having been pronounced winner of the Prince Consort's French Prize that day, which, as it happened, I had won the year before. So, reassured, he gaily entertained us until our arrival at Paddington. It was the first introduction of either of us to George Curzon, and from that day in 1874 began a friendship which lasted without shadow for nearly thirty years.

Winning the Prince Consort's French Prize was a characteristic *coup*, one of many inspired by the sense of grievance which Curzon hugged throughout his schooldays and resurrected in his vivid autobiographical notes of later years:

The masters with one or two rare exceptions (the principal was Oscar Browning, who always gave me encouragement and inspiration, hence my lifelong attachment to him), would not regard me as a serious personage, or at least not as thoroughly serious as I was. I accordingly experienced a sweet revenge in 'scoring off' them with their own weapons. I was a fierce worker and used to sit up half the night over my books. I have frequently at Wolley Dod's heard the morning birds begin to sing and I remember that it used to be invariably at about 4.15 a.m. in the summer.

The two French masters (Frank and Harry Tarver) regarded me as an impossible pupil, so I determined to win the Prince Consort's French Prize in independence of them. I did so, winning by a larger percentage of marks and at an earlier age than had ever been done before.

Then I resolved to win the Italian prize. The Italian master was a long-bearded and ridiculous old personage named Volpe. I soon came to loggerheads with him over some irreverent pun on his name. I accordingly left his class and did all my work by myself with the aid of an excellent edition of Dante containing a prose translation by one Carlyle. I became a master of the first 12 cantos of the 'Inferno', and a very passable writer and translator of Italian. Anyhow, to Volpe's surprise and indignation I won the prize, beating his favourite pupil, a boy named Maquay, who was half of Italian extraction and had been brought up at Florence.

I can recall a similar adventure as regards the History prize. The lecturer for this was Cornish – a charming man and afterwards one of my greatest friends, but with a querulous despairing manner that was vexatious. He was dissatisfied with my work and said I would come to nothing. From that moment I resolved to win the prize in spite of him. I left his class the next term, did all my reading by myself in out-of-school hours, entered for the prize, much to his and the general astonishment and won it with consummate ease.

Looking back, I think I must have had an extraordinary gift for assimilating the contents of books, committing to memory precisely what was wanted, and writing just what an examiner required. I won the Holiday Task prize every term that I tried for it, never looking at the book or books during the vacation, but spending the week before the examination in a savage effort of concentration which fixed everything in my mind and left me no time to forget.

In this way, Curzon won more prizes during his five years at Eton than any other boy in the history of the school.

I particularly excelled in writing Latin verses, not I think because I had the least sense of poetry or the smallest imagination, but because I had great facility and command of words; and I was extremely proud of having been 'sent up for good' more times (I think it was 23) than any other boy had ever been. I forget if Welldon equalled me – he certainly was not ahead.

At the same time, I was never in the front rank as a 'scholar' mainly I think because of the extreme incompetence as a classical teacher of my tutor Wolley Dod. This was realised in my last year or two both by the latter and by the Head Master, and I was transferred to the tutorial care of E. D. Stone. Here again Stone was quite incapable of understanding my temperament: he looked upon me as a nimble-witted farceur, and I well remember the dismay depicted on his face when at the close of one 'half', in which he had frequently upbraided me for lack of seriousness and purpose, the papers announcing the result of the First Hundred Examination came out – and I was the first of the whole school, having beaten all the swell Collegers whom he was constantly holding up to me as a pattern.

This vein of devilry on my part and of blunt obfuscation on that of the masters continued throughout my Eton career. They never could realise that I was bent on being first in what I undertook, but that I meant to do it in my way and not theirs.

The Head Master was well aware of the boy's precocious talents, and on one occasion played a witty little trick on him. When announcing the result of a Latin declamation prize, he said: 'The best has been written by Foley, the second best by Mr. Curzon.'* Curzon heard the announcement with dismay. But Dr Hornby had not finished. 'Unfortunately,' he added, 'in the greater part of what he has written, Foley has been anticipated by Cicero. The prize therefore goes to Mr. Curzon.'

* To this day Eton dignifies the sons of peers by the prefix 'Mr'.

Curzon's academic triumphs, much less his covetable friendships, did not persuade Wolley Dod to relax his heavy-handed supervision. On 16 March 1875, George sent his mother eleven pages of complaint about his tutor: 'He especially *spites* me ... He pitches upon me on every possible occasion, and makes my life as much of a burden as he can ... I have been so loaded with his punishments during the last week that I haven't had a moment to myself.'

A week later, as the boys came up to London for the Easter holidays, Lady Scarsdale took to her bed in the family house in Lower Berkeley Street with a sore throat and headache. At first she was not thought to be seriously ill and George took advantage of being allowed to resume his friendship with Browning by accompanying him to the Albert Hall to hear Bach's Passion on Good Friday and to the British Museum on the following day. His mother's condition deteriorated on the Monday. 'Dearest Mama gets much worse, a very critical case,' George's younger brother Alfred wrote in his diary on Wednesday. 'Mama very bad, calls out dreadfully. ... Dr. Jenner came again in evening, and gave up all hope of Mama's recovery.'

On the Friday other members of the family were summoned, but Lady Scarsdale did not recognize them. The younger children were packed off to Brighton and it was there that Alfred received a telegram from George on Sunday: 'The Spirit fled at half past three this morning.' A letter of manly consolation followed:

> It is a very hard trial for us all and especially for poor Papa but we must try to bear it and comfort him – I have just written to Denman's and ordered black trousers for each of us ... I slept at 1 Grosvenor Crescent last night but was awoke this morning at twenty minutes to four and we drove here in a cab as fast as possible but we were too late – for dear Mama died at half past three quite peaceably, with no pain. We went in and saw her today, her face was like it used to be, with a happy smile on, but of course very grey and calm, like marble. Aunt Mary put white flowers all over the bed. We shall not see the dear face again.

For fifty years Curzon preserved among his papers a withered camellia, melancholy souvenir of that last farewell. And in November, having been sent home from Eton in the middle of the Half after breaking a collar-bone at football, he was moved by the autumnal mists of Kedleston to set down the misery of his loss in verse:

Monarch of the grassy parkland,
Sheltered by ancestral trees,
For a century thy pillars
Have grown hoary in the breeze.

For a century around thee
Bud hath blossomed, flower hath blown,
Many a wooded glade thou ownest,
Many an acre is thine own.

Still as ever, proud thou standest,
Green thy meadows as of yore,
But a chill of desolation
Mid the sunbeams clouds thee o'er.

Merry voices that but lately
Laughing echoed through thy halls
Sound no longer there, and silence
Reigns instead within thy walls.

Heedless of thy frowning presence
Lichen creep along the stone
And the weeds grow long and dreary
Where thou standest all alone.

Blanche Scarsdale, whose constitution had been weakened by the bearing of eleven children in sixteen years, was only thirty-seven when she died. 'Her ladyship,' the local newspaper recorded, 'had been attacked ten days previous to her decease with symptoms of blood-poisoning attended with great exhaustion. The case becoming serious, and typhoid symptoms supervening, Sir W. Jenner was called in, in addition to the family surgeon.' A few years later an undergraduate friend of Curzon happened to tell him how an illness from which he was suffering had been aggravated by a corroded pipe discharging sewer gas into his bedroom. 'My own mother,' Curzon replied, 'died of blood poisoning from a similar cause, so I have some reason to appreciate its terrors.'*

Among Curzon's acquaintances at Eton was George Sitwell, later to be immortalized in the stately volumes of his son Osbert's autobiography. When Osbert in his turn was about to go to Eton, Sir George presented him with a

* Infectious fevers struck rich and poor alike during the middle years of the nineteenth century and began to abate only after the Public Health Act of 1866 had led to widespread improvement in sanitation. Sir William Jenner, who failed to save Lady Scarsdale, had presided over the death of the Prince Consort from typhoid in 1861. The Prince of Wales, later Edward VII, came within a hair's breadth of suffering his father's fate in 1871 when staying at Londesborough Lodge, near Scarborough: a fellow guest, Lord Chesterfield, was less fortunate. Ten years earlier, the insanitary conditions of the War Office were believed to have been responsible for the deaths within a few months of the Secretary of State (Lord Herbert of Lea), the Under-Secretary (Sir Benjamin Hawes) and the Assistant Under-Secretary (J. R. Godley). Another contemporary and friend of Curzon, George Leveson Gower, attributed his frequent fevers as one of Mr Gladstone's private secretaries from 1880 to 1885 to the foul drains of No. 10 Downing Street. He, however, lived to be ninety-three.

small, thin volume of Horace's *Odes*. A crib, he told his son, only showed a determination to get on. And of his own school friends, the one who had displayed the most skill and persistence in cribbing had since achieved by far the most distinguished career – George Nathaniel Curzon.

Sir George's memories were sometimes touched by fantasy. There exist, however, circumstantial accounts by Curzon himself of other misdemeanours which he committed in his war against authority:

> Out of school I carried my indiscipline or independence to a pitch that was never suspected of so hardworking and orthodox a student, and which I can still recall with a smile.
>
> I made it a point of honour to attend Ascot races every year, not because I cared in the least for racing, but because it was forbidden and therefore dangerous. It was not forbidden to go, but it was forbidden to be seen in a carriage, which was the only means of getting to Ascot and back – a distance of 7 miles each way – in the interval between the two callings of absence, i.e. about 3.15 p.m. to 6.20 p.m. As a small boy I succeeded in going every year, being usually picked up by some friendly stranger in a carriage or coach.
>
> One year I did better. I was staying out, i.e. was excused from attending school and expected to remain indoors, for some malady or other. I knew that my tutor, Wolley Dod, had gone away on a day's fishing. So I slipped up to Windsor in the morning, introduced myself to an unknown American couple at the White Hart Hotel, and went to Ascot and back in their carriage, spending an entire day most comfortably and undetected at the races.

The most sublime of his escapades, he thought, was to arrange a game of tennis with three friends in the panelled dignity of Upper School one rainy afternoon, the balls bouncing disrespectfully off the busts of Chatham and Canning. He also had a zinc lining made for the bottom drawer of his oak bureau in which he would keep an illicit cellar. 'It was not,' he wrote, 'that I cared for drinking, but I enjoyed the supreme cheek as an Eton boy of giving wine parties in my room. I used to make excellent champagne and claret cup, procuring the ice, soda and herbs in the Eton shops: and many a time on a Sunday afternoon or after a long cricket or football match have I entertained a party of my friends and even of Old Etonians.' Less enterprisingly, he carved his name on a sixth form desk under the nose of Dr Hornby himself. That wise Head Master was not to be drawn: he said nothing to the culprit but quietly gave orders for all the desks to be planed smooth. And when a deputation of senior boys that included Curzon cheekily asked whether they could wear tall white hats in summer, Hornby replied: 'No. You might be mistaken for bookmakers.'

In 1877, Curzon succeeded Alfred Lyttelton as president of the Eton Literary and Scientific Society. It had been founded by Oscar Browning six years before and survives to this day as a monument to his imaginative concept of education. With that daunting thoroughness which Curzon brought to all his offices, even as a schoolboy, he bequeathed much useful advice to his successors in thirty-five pages of flowing script. Members of the teaching staff, he wrote, should not be encouraged to attend: 'as a support they increase its stability, as a ruling power they would probably ensure its retrogression.' Bleakly, he warns against 'a goodly phalanx of masters in the background, from each of whom, in spite of previous protestations of ignorance and inability to speak, a full 10 minutes may in most cases be expected'. The society, he continues, may find it difficult to produce suitable speakers, but 'a few courteous words are always effective with any member who seems inclined to play either truant or the obstructive, and conciliation is in almost every case the best system of action'. Neither then nor in later years was Curzon a slave to such persuasive methods.

His responsibility for finding speakers to address the Literary Society gave him an eagerly grasped opportunity to establish friendly relations with Mr Gladstone. Curzon wrote to him in April 1878 asking whether he would lecture:

> I have heard it observed that an Eton audience beats any other in the expression of its pleasure and gratitude. Should you do us the honour to come, might I suggest some such subject as the Homeric question as one in which Eton is specially interested and which no one is so fitted as yourself to expound.

The theme was one to touch Gladstone's heart. In his library at Hawarden, known as 'the Temple of Peace', he had a separate desk for his classical studies. After the tumult and bustle of politics, he used to say, he felt himself 'in heaven' when breathing the pure atmosphere of Homer. Greek scholars, however, sometimes spoke disrespectfully of his learning. 'He has six theories about Homer,' Dr Jowett of Balliol observed, 'they are impossible singly and mutually destructive of each other, but he holds them all.'

Gladstone was not popular in so strongly fortified a Tory community as Eton. Oscar Browning, a defiant Liberal, had years before suggested to Dr Hornby that Gladstone ought to be invited to address the school: he was laughed to scorn. More recently, Gladstone had been tactless enough when lecturing at Marlborough to comment on Eton's reluctance to move with the times. Reports of the speech had been ill-received by his old school, and Curzon himself admitted to having 'rushed into a rather spluttering and feeble reply to the editorial columns of *The Etonian*', a rival journal to the official *Eton College Chronicle*.

It was therefore with caution that Gladstone replied to Curzon's invitation:

> If it is in my power to serve in any degree, however slight, the welfare of Eton and anyway its studies, you may rely upon it the disposition will not be wanting.
>
> But I must not obtrude myself or run counter to discipline. The first question

therefore I have to ask is whether I am to understand you as conferring the distinct wish of your fellows as well as your own: and the second is whether my coming to treat informally of Homer would be agreeable to the wishes of Dr. Hornby.

It took more correspondence and two visits to Gladstone's house in London – he was then out of office – before the compact could be sealed. Curzon's first interview with him took place on 30 May:

> Sent in my card. He was at breakfast with a large party of ladies and gentlemen, but came out at once, shook hands most kindly, and took me into small side room where he said he looked upon the visit as a bargain which was certainly to be kept. Said he considered himself bound to do anything for Eton.

On 20 June, Curzon called again. 'Introduced me to Mrs G. and young G. (like a sleepy assistant behind a silk-mercer's counter),' he recorded.

The lecture on Homer proved a success and Eton boys more charitable than Jowett. One of them described the scene:

> His prestige, his pale face, his blazing eyes, his sweeping gestures and the *timbre* of that marvellous voice, which had an almost physical effect upon the nerves, kept the audience spell-bound. But I remember wondering how it was possible that one should not be able, afterwards, to recall a single point of a discourse which at the time seemed the most important communication ever vouchsafed to the world.

Curzon was often to hear Gladstone in later years, both as an undergraduate visitor to the galleries of the House of Commons and subsequently as a fellow Member of Parliament. Politically and intellectually a gulf often divided the two men: but the hypnotic absorption of the Liberal leader in whatever he chose as his theme never ceased to fascinate, however extravagant and even oppressive it became. 'He will talk about a piece of old china as if he was standing before the judgement-seat of God,' one of his contemporaries recalled. Curzon was neither intimidated nor deterred by the torrent of eloquence. From the time of his first meeting with Gladstone as an Eton boy he remained almost mesmerized by the great man's personality; and their friendly relationship, occasionally punctuated by expressions of mild censure, lasted until 1897, the year before Gladstone's death, when Curzon sacrificed the whole of a precious day in Scotland to drive from the place where he was staying in order to pay his respects.

Descending from Olympus on the morning after his Eton lecture, Gladstone showed his young host where, as a boy, he had carved his name on the wall opposite College Chapel, a signature almost obliterated by time and the seats of countless Etonians. They called at Curzon's room in Mr Wolley Dod's where Gladstone professed to be aghast at the luxury of pictures and china, armchairs and flowers, compared with the plain living of his own day. But he did not fail to notice a volume of translations from the classics by himself and his brother-in-law, Lord Lyttelton, lying tactfully on a table. In the rooms of the Eton Society, better known as Pop, Gladstone examined the minute books of past debates, including his 'Tory opinions fossilised in faded ink'. He was delighted, too, to come on a painted photograph of himself. Had he entered a moment or two before, he would have been less enchanted. His recent unpopularity had provoked the members of Pop to turn his likeness to the wall, and as Curzon and C.M. Smith, the President of Pop, were escorting him up the stairs, Smith suddenly remembered their angry gesture. With an agility which won him renown on the cricket field, he leapt ahead in time to replace the portrait in a position of honour before Gladstone reached the door. 'I don't think he noticed it was still swinging,' Smith wrote hopefully.

That was not Gladstone's last encounter with the pictures of Pop room at Eton: for a busy man he allowed them to occupy a disproportionate amount of his time. On making way for Lord Rosebery as Prime Minister in 1894, he sent his successor a letter. It asked him, as yet another distinguished Old Etonian Prime Minister, to address the authorities on the current depravity of the school. Gladstone, it seems, on his last visit there, had noticed a picture of a Derby winner adorning the walls of Pop. The owner of Ladas was undismayed by this revelation. 'It was,' he mildly observed, 'a circumstance which, for personal reasons, did not cause me so much disquiet.'

A third Liberal Prime Minister, Henry Asquith, although not himself an Etonian, saw something of Curzon at Eton. Speaking in the House of Lords on Curzon's death in 1925, he recalled how he had visited the school nearly half a century before as an examiner for Oxford and Cambridge certificates, a role by which he supplemented his slender income as a young barrister. Even while Curzon was a schoolboy, Asquith recalled, 'he showed the readiness of resource and the unrivalled self-command which never failed him during all the vicissitudes of public life'. Curzon recorded the encounter in less complimentary terms. At the *viva voce*, he wrote, 'many of my friends came out from the interview with him, chafing under what they thought was his superciliousness of manner. It was universally agreed that I was the proper person to "take him down".' The carefully planned impertinence, an ironic lecture on the tendency of classical commentators to confuse the younger Cato with the elder, was ill-received, and Asquith dismissed him from the room with a frigid, 'Thank you, Mr. Curzon.'

Curzon's six years at Eton progressed towards their close in a glow of triumph. He made his peace with Mr Wolley Dod, was invited to play tennis with him, and presented him with a silver cup. He became Captain of the Oppidans and his fine amplifying style resounded endlessly throughout the debates of Pop, that self-perpetuating oligarchy which is the apotheosis of an Eton career. He edited *The Etonian* and published a selection of verse and prose from it entitled *Out of School at Eton*. The little volume was favourably reviewed and brought him the slender financial reward of £3 11*s*. 11*d*., although the loss on *The Etonian* itself amounted to £2 7*s.* 7*d.* In only one ambition did he fail; he could not persuade the editors of influential national periodicals such as the *Nineteenth Century* to publish his articles on current topics, among them an essay on 'The Value of a Classical Education'.

Undemonstrative man that he was, Lord Scarsdale found both pride and consolation after his wife's death in the achievements of his eldest son. At 10.30 P.M. on 4 June 1877, having returned from the celebrations at Eton,* he sat down in London to send George a cheque for £5 as a token of the pleasure he had found that day. But one wound was never to heal. 'Thoughts of your darling Mother', he wrote, 'were uppermost in my heart, oh that she could have been at my side.'

'This is decidedly egotistical', Curzon labelled the record he made of his last Fourth of June in the following year. So it is, but an endearing document:

> June 4, 1878. The proudest day, I *expect* of my life. Speeches in the morning. Remarks overheard ...
>
> 'Where is C? I heard him last year and liked him so much.'
>
> 'Isn't he splendid?'
>
> 'What wouldn't I give to be his sister?'
>
> As soon as they were over, gents, whom I had never previously seen, seized me by the hand: 'Well done, you were the best of them all!' An elderly French lady tremendously voluble with her, '*Je vous félicite, Monsieur.*'
>
> In the evening, Tent Dinner at Surley. Toasts. Queen and Royal Family, Eight, Eleven, Ladies, Floreat Etona. Ponsonby my great friend got up and proposed health of Captain of Oppidans. Drunk with musical honours in tent and all down boat tables. Had never been done before. Later on my health proposed by *Dod.* Such fun!
>
> All the above is pure unadulterated conceit, but as the truthful memento of a successful day may suffice in after years to recall the pleasurable emotions which it at the time excited.

A more sobering note was struck by Reginald Brett, son of the Master of the Rolls who was later created Lord Esher. Brett had left Eton two years before Curzon's arrival, but was inspired to join those bent upon taking a protective interest in one so talented. He wrote to Curzon during the boy's last year at Eton: 'Guard against flattery, unconscious flattery – if you will – of people who desire to please you. Of all human influences it is the most subtle in undermining independence of mind.' And in letters to Curzon the following summer he described an encounter with Cardinal Manning, while both were staying at Studley Hall, the house in Yorkshire of Lord Ripon, a Roman Catholic: 'He is not an adroit priest. He uses flattery, but not wisely'; and again, 'He is a wily old serpent and of course elaborately pleasant'. Brett's strictures on flattery would have come better from a pen other than

* The Fourth of June, the birthday of King George III, is still the principal festival in the Eton calendar.

his own. It was he who, some years later, described to one of his sons the intimate relationship he had established with King Edward VII:

> The King said to me, 'Although you are not exactly a public servant, yet I always think that you are the most valuable public servant I have', and then I kissed his hand as I sometimes do.

Curzon's reply to Brett's homily was deferential yet not without dignity.

> I know what you say about flattery is quite true [he wrote]. I do not know myself that I have been spoilt by flattery or even that I have received it ... I can safely say one thing, that if I am being flattered, in nine cases out of ten I feel what humbug it is and how undeserved. ... I particularly like being told about character; faults in my own, good points in other people's. There is nothing I like better than the former; it is the province of a friend to criticise one, at least I think so; and I owe to good friends of mine many little improvements or rather endeavoured abandonments of faults which I should not have noticed myself.

With his breadth of interests, ambitious eye and habit of immersing himself utterly in whatever task happened to engage his attention, Curzon gave fewer backward glances at Eton than most of his generation. It remained for him a distant prospect. To the end of his days he preserved his cheap little Eton desk and bookcase at Kedleston with the same care he gave to the magnificent gilded furniture designed by William Kent: but only because he valued all possessions. He kept his Eton notebooks, too: but then he hardly ever threw away a scrap of paper in his life. As Viceroy of India he gave dinners to fellow Etonians within travelling distance of Government House: so did other proconsuls. In one unexpected way, however, he revered his old school. Cavalier in his treatment of so many men who later crossed his path, he retained for the Head Mastership of Eton a high and sincere regard, whoever happened to occupy the office. He liked to recall the celebration of the Fourth of June in 1904 when Hornby toasted him in College Hall as an honour and a model to the school. On becoming Chancellor of Oxford University in 1907 he personally included Edmond Warre, Hornby's successor, among those national figures on whom he bestowed honorary degrees after his installation. The next Head Master, Edward Lyttelton, received reverent attention as well as the affection of forty years when in 1915 he wrote to Curzon, by then Lord Privy Seal, on the social problems of the day. And Cyril Alington, who succeeded Lyttelton, wrote with amused irony that probably the most glorious moment of his life was when he found himself being addressed with real respect by that master of disrespect, Lord Curzon.

For Curzon believed that institutions were the plinths of civilization, and Eton was the first of them to touch his heart as well as his mind.

Chapter Four
BALLIOL

To meet members of the two Houses of Parliament, and other members of the College.

– *Invitation issued by Dr Jowett for 24 June 1893*

Only half in jest, St John Brodrick spoke of the brief interval which Curzon must endure between Eton and the Cabinet. For a schoolboy whose ambitions already reached out towards the highest offices of state, an apprenticeship at Balliol College, Oxford, in the dawn of its golden age under Benjamin Jowett, seemed inevitable. Curzon had tried for a scholarship at the college during his last year at Eton but had failed. Brodrick, already an undergraduate, wrote to give him the private report of the examiners:

> They thought you a little wanting in accuracy – and your brilliance (which they admitted) off the point. Having got this into their heads, they, I suppose, assumed that you had gone out of your way to put in touches. I hope this dreadfully prosaic and literal report will not discourage you. There are two examinations in the world entirely adapted to the exclusion of men of wide culture from honour – one is the Balliol Scholarship, the other 'honour mods' – and although I would have gladly seen you 'score' in both, I should not myself regret, if I were you, the loss of them when you consider your brilliant reputation in other lines.

Curzon was nevertheless entered for Balliol as a commoner and after a summer holiday learning a little French in Paris he prepared to go up to Oxford in October 1878. Then he was struck by a misfortune that clouded the remainder of his life: he developed an incurable curvature of the spine. As a high-spirited boy, he had endured more than a fair share of accidents. 'He fell backwards down an 8 ft. wall this morning,' Lady Scarsdale wrote from Kedleston a few days after George's twelfth birthday, 'and fortunately his thick strong black cap saved his head – he has a great crack through it. We fomented his arm well and have since bandaged it with a lotion, excellent for a sprain.' Three years later he hurt his back in a fall from a pony during the holidays. And in October 1875 he broke his right collar bone playing football at Eton. 'Very slim, not too strong on his pins, and very easily knocked over,' was how his brother Frank recalled him. The bone was not set properly and a fortnight later George dictated a letter to another brother, Alfred, scrawling his initials at the bottom with his left hand:

> We went to see Sir James Paget, a great doctor, this morning: he did not do any thing to my arm but I am to go to bed at 6 o'clock and a man is coming to fix a thing made of pasteboard and leather on my shoulder which will gradually make it all right.

Whether or not the curvature of the spine which developed in the autumn of 1878 had its roots in those schoolboy tumbles is impossible to prove. But it is significant that while he was still at Eton his friends knew of his weakness and begged him not to sit up late at night. Now, on the threshold of his Oxford career, came a frightening and dramatic development. In a letter written in pencil – a sign that for the rest of his life gave intermittent warning to his correspondents that he had had to take to his bed – he told Reggy Brett:

> Since I came back from France, I have felt shooting pains in my side – in the region of the hip, and noticed the unusual prominence of that member. I went up to London about it and saw the best man. They said it was weakness and over-work – and that I must give up Oxford for the present and lie down on my back. Paget, to whom it was settled I should go – as a final opinion – saw no harm in going to Oxford if I obey strict injunctions – wear an appliance – lie down a good deal and take no violent or indeed very active exercise. ... I feel – myself – that I must be very careful and indeed Paget said if there is not improvement at Christmas I shall have to resort to the lying down.

Brodrick wrote with affectionate concern to say that almost everyone he knew had collapsed in one way or another between eighteen and twenty-one, but had afterwards seemed to get a second wind.

Determined that it should be a whirlwind, Curzon soon tired of the restrictions imposed on him by the doctors. 'Short of profligacy or alcoholism,' Brodrick had sadly to admit, 'I do not think any man could have done more than he did to shatter his health.' After days crammed with the excitements and discoveries and companionship of Oxford life, he would put a fearful strain on his constitution by sitting up working or talking until the early hours. In thus neglecting to conserve his strength as a youth, he was to pay a compound penalty of suffering for the next half century. 'Now George,' Alfred Lyttelton addressed him on Christmas Day 1880, 'I want to harangue you about going to bed in rather better time.' The familiar admonition went unheeded and Curzon continued to live as if his spine were made of steel. In a sense it was. Never again could he be free of the steel waistcoat into which he had to be strapped each day. Years later, embittered by the taunts of his enemies, he dashed down on paper some angry words repudiating the insatiable appetite for public life he was believed to cherish:

I am supposed to seek the footlights. Little do they know what a business it is to get me on to the stage. How many of them I wonder have any idea of the long hours spent in bed, of the aching back, of the ulcers and nerve pain in the leg, of the fearful steel cage in which I have to be encased when I undergo any strain in which standing up is involved. They think me strong and arrogant and self-sufficient. Little do they reck that it is an invalid addressing them, who has only been driven to the duty because it is a duty, who has to be mechanically supported in order to stand upright for an hour and who presently goes back to his bed to writhe in agony as an expiation for his foolishness.

Throughout Curzon's career, caricaturists continued by word and pen to profess that he both sought and found pleasure in imperial pageantry and the intimacy of royal personages. Ironically enough, those were precisely the activities for which he had least relish. 'I am very tired,' he wrote as Viceroy, 'after a 15 mile ride on an elephant this morning: one of the most horrible forms of locomotion, and to anyone like myself, with a weak back, of actual pain, that you can well imagine.' As Foreign Secretary, too, he wrote to tell his wife that he had been invited to dine by a friend to meet his Sovereign. 'I have declined for myself,' he said, 'since these dinners in breeches etc. where I have to stand up for hours afterwards and talk both to the King and Queen are penance and almost an agony to me and I am happiest here alone.' As long as he ruled India he could not escape imprisonment in the gilded rack of a howdah; but to relieve the aching tedium of court ceremonial he turned the sword of his Privy Councillor's uniform into a sort of shooting-stick, a blunt ferrule at its point and a hilt that divided into two to form a seat.

Under Benjamin Jowett, elected Master of Balliol in 1870, the college exerted a profound influence in almost every field of national life. Among the undergraduates during his first dozen years who distinguished themselves in politics were Asquith, Milner, Lansdowne, Grey, Brodrick and Curzon himself. Rennel Rodd, Arthur Hardinge, Cecil Spring Rice, Louis Mallet and Charles Eliot in diplomacy; Samuel Alexander in philosophy; T. F. Tout, Richard Lodge, Charles Firth, J. H. Round and R. L. Poole in historical scholarship; J. W. Mackail, W. P. Ker, H. W. Fowler, Anthony Hope and Sidney Lee in literature; St Loe Strachey, A. B. Walkley, J. A. Spender and Sidney Low in journalism; Cosmo Gordon Lang, Archbishop successively of York and Canterbury. As the turn of the century approached, more than forty Balliol men sat in the same House of Commons. For seventeen successive years, 1888 to 1905, Balliol monopolized the Viceroyalty of India. Between 1878 and 1914, more than 200 Balliol men passed into the Indian Civil Service. Here indeed was a fitting monument to the dominating figure of Victorian Oxford, a legend even in his own lifetime:

Superior Person

First come I. My name is J–W–TT.
There's no knowledge but I know it.
I am Master of this College,
What I don't know isn't knowledge.

This celebrated jingle, one of forty written by Balliol undergraduates about contemporary Fellows, Scholars and Commoners, was published in 1881 in a broadsheet entitled 'The Masque of B–ll—l', soon withdrawn when sensitive victims hinted at libel. 'Very unfair,' was the comment of Tennyson on the rhyme about his friend, 'Jowett never set up to be omniscient.' Perhaps the poet had forgotten the occasion when, staying at Balliol, he had read Jowett a new poem. 'I think I wouldn't publish that, if I were you, Tennyson,' was his response. Tennyson had been stung to reply: 'If it comes to that, Master, the sherry you gave us at luncheon was beastly.'

Within the University, however humble at heart, Jowett was a formidable figure. Young dons earned his particular contempt: 'They want to marry and they have no money. They want to write and have no originality. They want to be fine gentlemen and are deficient in manners.' Not even Heads of House were immune from his censorious economy of phrase. Thomas Fowler, President of Corpus, once stopped him in the street. 'Master,' he said, 'I must congratulate you on the appearance of your new volume of Plato. May I send you a few suggestions?' 'Please don't,' Jowett replied.

No undergraduate ever forgot the Master's white tie and swallow-tail coat, his cherubic face and high-pitched voice, his devastating retorts and appalling silences. Walter Lawrence, a contemporary of Curzon and later his private secretary in India, asked Jowett one day whether Jane Austen had been much read at the beginning of the century. 'I don't know,' he replied peevishly, 'I did not live at the beginning of the century.'

He was sometimes suspected of reserving his particular attention for undergraduates of aristocratic family, and the charge was not without foundation. His explanation, however, was convincing: 'Anyone who tries to get hold of young men of rank or wealth must expect to be accused of snobbishness, but one must remember how important it is to influence towards good those who are going to have an influence over hundreds or thousands of other lives.' He gave hardly less unsparingly of his time and advice to those who had struggled to reach the privileged shelter of Balliol, helped them with extra tuition, invited them on reading parties in the vacation, sometimes made discreet gifts of money. All shared his hospitality at breakfast parties where table-talk was a solecism, or enjoyed more convivial occasions in a drawing-room illuminated by the conversation of Matthew Arnold and Robert Browning, George Eliot and Algernon Swinburne. Snubbing and encouraging by turn, drawing young men of every social class into the social neutrality of the college, Jowett moulded both intellect and character to meet the growing responsibilities of those who aspired to rule.

Like the august head of his college, Curzon was paid the compliment of inclusion in 'The Masque of B–ll—l'. Of the several versions which circulated far beyond Oxford for a generation or more, the best known ran like this:

My name is George Nathaniel Curzon,
I am a most superior person,
My cheek is pink, my hair is sleek,
I dine at Blenheim once a week.

The first two lines are generally attributed to J. W. Mackail, later appointed to the Order of Merit for his contribution to scholarship; the last two to Cecil Spring Rice. Both have much to answer for. To those who had not penetrated what Margot Asquith later called Curzon's enamelled self-assurance, the verse seemed exact. He was undeniably superior to most contemporaries in the quality of his mind and the maturity of his character, in the sustained industry of his working hours and the generous warmth he brought to his friendships. He was tall and handsome, with the complexion of a milkmaid and the elegance of one of Ouida's guardsmen. He was a welcome guest at the Duke of Marlborough's house. On one visit the dinner party went on so long that he was asked to stay the night and, having brought no luggage, was accommodated with a nightdress of Lady Randolph Churchill. Line by line, the quatrain can be explained away: in its entirety it is lethal.

The label of superior person was to stick to him through life like a burr. Partly it came from the steel waistcoat which supported his spine and imposed on him a rigid bearing which both amused and irritated his acquaintances: only the most intimate of his circle were aware that his aura of aloofness masked discomfort and sometimes pain. Partly it was a personal failing. Before going up to Oxford, Curzon received some solemn counsel from Alfred Lyttelton: 'One thing I want you to do ... is to take stock carefully of your present opinions and aims, and after a year's life there compare the realization of your aims with your intention.' F. E. Smith, Lord Birkenhead, who was fascinated by Curzon and would like to have written his biography, maintained that Curzon took this advice – but that the constant and favourable comparison he drew engendered in him an awareness of his own superiority. Another interpreter of Curzon's character, Lord D'Abernon, suggested that his epitaph should be: '*Immense orgueil: justifié.*'

There was certainly an inability on his part, even as a schoolboy, to resist the crushing retort, the wounding jibe, the cold dismissal of ignorance or of social inferiority, the unrelenting exposure of error. Reggy Brett warned him that he had been accused 'of a general superficiality of heart and mind ... plenty of intellect and not enough heart'. Another candid friend, Alfred Lyttelton, repeated the lesson:

> If, because a man is wanting in manner or in social gifts, one treats him with contempt undisguised, such a man goes about seeking for every ill-rumour which he can attach to one and ... will not cease till he has paid out his grievance to the utmost farthing. ... Permit the people you may dislike to go their way without showing them your dislike, unless by pressing their acquaintance they render it necessary. ... Believe me, for every one, but more particularly for any one going in for political life, to make enemies unnecessarily – even sincere ones, which seems so congenial to you – is a great error.

Such kindly warnings from those who cared for him were politely acknowledged, occasionally refuted and invariably ignored.

Curzon was a precocious politician. While still at Eton he had taken a Conservative line in debate, withering his few Liberal opponents with devastating sarcasm. At Oxford he exchanged those early prejudices for a more reasoned doctrine based upon the Disraelian creed of Tory paternalism, or social reform without class warfare. He spoke tirelessly at the Oxford Union and in May 1880 was elected President, an office which both Asquith and Milner had held a few years before. Curzon's intellectual dexterity, his elaborate diction, his sedate self-confidence inspired wonder and envy among his fellow members, but rarely affection; that homage he received only from a circle of intimates who sensed the genuine warmth which lay behind his too-conscious affability.

He found another platform for his Conservatism in the Oxford Canning Club. Before his arrival it had fallen into easy habits. Meetings would resolve themselves into games of whist or sweepstakes on the Derby. It was difficult to assemble a quorum and even rarer to find speakers. Sometimes the same paper would be read twice, and one night Cochrane-Baillie doctored the traditional mulled claret with castor oil. Curzon, who became secretary in 1880, changed all that. The historian of the club calls him its second founder. With all the restless energy that he afterwards brought to the administration of a continent, he breathed new life into its indolent constitution. Its Toryism was no longer expressed in halting periods and games of chance. Instead there were informative addresses followed by discussions which seldom ended before 11.30. The voice of reaction gave way to fluent democratic sentiments on universal military training and the Imperial aspects of free trade, rural depopulation and a cheap Press. At the beginning of one term he read out a list of twenty-five possible subjects which he hoped might inspire members to read papers. He drew up a series of elaborate and exhaustive memoranda on the rules of the club. So polished were his minutes that members subscribed to have them printed for general circulation when he laid down his office in 1882. Engulfed by this relentless spirit of change, there must surely have been an occasional member who sighed for the bad old days. Curzon did, it is true, start the custom of an annual dinner: but the bill for broken glass came to a paltry £1 19*s.* 3*d.*

'He was master even in those early days,' a fellow-member of the Canning has recorded, 'of a style always vigorous and effective, and at times rising to a stately eloquence.' There lay his weakness as well as his strength. John Morley used to compare verbose orators to a train of fifteen carriages conveying but a single passenger. Sometimes Curzon's majestic language would be matched by his theme; more often it awed his audience without convincing them. Jowett was aware of this shortcoming. Writing to acknowledge a gift of game from Lord Scarsdale, he told Curzon with well-meant brutality:

> I think you have many advantages and one disadvantage. 'Too much to say' in a speech or in conversation. It is a good fault *if corrected*, but a most serious one if left uncorrected because it destroys the impression of weight and of thought and gives the impression, probably very undeserved, of conceit and self-sufficiency.

Curzon's platform oratory nevertheless impressed the leaders of his party. Within a few weeks of ceasing to be an undergraduate, he was recommended by Lord Salisbury to the Conservative Association in Preston as a prospective parliamentary candidate. But as he complained to Brodrick: 'They won't have anything to do with unknown fledglings.'

Like most Oxford men of his generation and upbringing, caring more for breadth of education than for the means of earning a living, Curzon read the classical course peculiar to his university. It was, and remains to this day, in two parts. For six terms he worked for Classical Moderations, known as Mods, an examination based upon a precise knowledge of Greek and Latin texts. It was followed by a further six terms during which he studied for the school of *Literae Humaniores*, or Humane Letters, known as Greats, a gruelling syllabus that includes ancient history and philosophy, both ancient and modern. Greats, to quote one of Oxford's most distinguished scholars of the twentieth century, exercises the mind in three quite different directions. In ancient literature, it introduces the student to a world unlike his own; in ancient history, it trains him in the use of evidence and the assessment of historical fact; in abstract thinking, it requires him both to interpret the philosophy of others and to form some kind of philosophy for himself. For mental discipline, for sustained application, for exactness of meaning, for the expression of opinion in graduated terms, it would not be easy to devise a more searching test.

Curzon was fortunate in his tutors. J. L. Strachan-Davidson, for more than thirty years Senior Tutor and from 1907 Master of Balliol, taught Roman history and political economy. The son of a Scottish merchant in Madras, he was largely responsible for the close connection of the college with the Indian Civil Service. He collected coins, spent part of each winter on the Nile for the sake of his health and achieved immortality more in the hearts of his pupils than in the contorted rhyme on him in 'The Masque of B–ll—l':

STR–CH–N D–V–DS–N am I, the lean
Unbuttoned, cigaretted Dean,
Brother numismatists, you see a
Historian in a Dahabeeah.

Strachan-Davidson's smoking habits were a source of endless delight and fantasy in the college. In his early days he cherished an Egyptian pipe with a three-foot stem of cherrywood and a bowl of red clay. Then he took to cigarettes, still an uncommon practice in the late 1870s. He would roll them himself, not very neatly, and had an indulgent contempt for the manufactured article. His gigantic pouch of fine-cut Turkish tobacco always lay on his table; and one evening a shy undergraduate picked it up and would have taken it away under the belief that it was his own cap had not its owner noticed the mistake.

R. L. Nettleship, Classical Tutor and Junior Dean, taught Curzon philosophy. He, too, was pilloried:

Roughly, so to say, you know,
I am N–TTL–SH–P or so;
You are gated after Hall,
That's all. I mean that's nearly all.

He was, however, more than a stage don in pursuit of elusive shadows, a shy disciplinarian whose meaning vanished into a whirlpool of qualification. Like other academics of his own and successive generations, Nettleship sought elation and danger in the Alps, and died of exposure in a snowstorm while attempting an ascent on Mont Blanc in 1892. 'He was wonderfully beloved by the undergraduates,' Jowett wrote, 'because they knew that he cared for them more than anything else in the world.'

The author of the Balliol rhymes about both Jowett and Nettleship was the undergraduate H. C. Beeching, later Dean of Norwich, who also appears in that acidulous anthology:

I am the apostle B—CH–NG,
Ruskin Swin–Burne-Jones my teaching;
I write poems; but one saith
My poems are a form of death.

'I wrote it myself,' he said, 'I thought it safer.'

It was not only from his college tutors that Curzon received instruction and advice. Richard Farrer, too, like those other self-appointed mentors, the Lyttelton brothers and Reggy Brett, felt obliged to assume some responsibility for Curzon's character and conduct. Farrer's father was a Yorkshire landowner, barrister and Fellow of Merton College, his mother a sister of Lady Midleton, St John Brodrick's mother. He was a year or two older than Curzon and had preceded him from Eton to Balliol in 1875. His Oxford career, however, had been clouded by disappointment, a First in Mods being followed by an unexpected Second in Greats. That setback helps to explain the laborious but affectionate little homily with which he greeted Curzon's twenty-first birthday:

It suddenly occurred to me that this is your natal day; so, although the post has long since departed, I assume the calamus in order to wish you many happy returns of the day and all prosperity during your future life. There is no fellow among my friends or acquaintances who starts on his majority with greater gifts, or who shows more likelihood of turning them to good account. Only beware of the besetting danger of any young man possessed of talent, position and good looks – I mean that of trying to do too many things at once. You are still young in Oxford life; and *do* devote the best of your faculties during the remainder of it to securing University honours: they are worth a deal more hereafter than one has any idea of at the time. I speak with feeling, as having once underrated them and now regretting the mistake: they are not to be knocked off promiscuously like Eton prizes.

Curzon responded with becoming modesty to Farrer's admonition:

My dear Ricardo [he wrote], I know how true what you say is, and that Oxford life and work is not to be treated in a chance and casual manner. I hope that this coming term, several former distractions being absent, I shall be able to buckle down in greater earnestness. Anyhow, I recognise that there is something more to be done than indulge in delightful but not perhaps very profitable intercourse with charming friends. ... One of my chief desires shall be not to fall so far short of the opinions of my friends as to lose their esteem. ...

In the summer of 1880 Curzon disproved Farrer's fears by taking a First Class in Mods. Replying to the congratulations of Spring Rice, he wrote that he had been leniently treated, being awarded thirteen 'firsts' and three 'seconds' on his sixteen papers. 'Chitty's class,' he added, with a touch of condescension, 'is a fine performance: a lasting testimony to what sheer labour can do.'

As the more severe ordeal of Greats drew near, Alfred Lyttelton sent words of encouragement:

I see you are keeping a brave heart my dear boy not withstanding the weariness of the long stiff task – it would do you good to hear Gladstone speak of the great service which the mere grind of the Oxford exams have yielded him. Every serious call which exceptional labour has made on him has reminded him of the Oxford schools and made him rejoice at the sheer grit which they provided. His first holyday was taken to hear the debates in the Lords on the Reform bill in 1831 and I should not wonder if another student isn't stretching eagerly out over the world of politics into the midst of which he will soon plunge. What a future there is before a Conservative, young, patient and gifted.

But the grind of eight and sometimes ten hours work a day for months on end was proving unpalatable to Curzon. 'I am thoroughly sick of work,' he wrote to Farrer, 'and have long realised that I did not begin putting my back into Greats till a year too late, and shall be quite content still further to dignify class two by the insertion of my name.' Nor did he take a more optimistic view of his chances in a letter written between the end of the examination and the announcement of the results. Although satisfied with the quality of his history papers, backed by some good translations, he had found philosophy 'a terribly hard paper, the questions very wide and involved —the source of much bitter complaint'. In logic, too, he had again misunderstood one important question and written bosh. As Dr Jowett said, when asked whether logic was an art or a science, 'It is neither. It is a dodge.' Curzon continued in his letter to Farrer:

Now you see my extremely critical position. My history is pulling me up, greatly backed by my translations. My Logic and Philos[y] are remorselessly pulling me down. Which will win?

Honestly I think either – I tell you the truth. I do not think I am absolutely out of the chance of a First, but upon my word I am far from in it. And putting all together, bearing in mind the superior importance attached to philosophy and also remembering the evil luck that has hung about all our friends here and at Cambridge and which has probably fixed upon me for its last victim, I am inclined to believe that the betting is on a Second.

You will perhaps think of encouraging me. I really don't need it. I know with tolerable exactness my position and that only one thing can better it, viz. my viva, for which therefore I shall not be wholly idle. But a bad viva will condemn me to the Valley of the Shadow of Death.

It was therefore without surprise that he heard early in July of his being placed in the Second Class. Years later he jotted down for his friend Ian Malcolm an account of how nearly he had achieved a First:

Two names were in doubt, another man's name and mine. My Balliol tutor happened to be one of the examiners and could not, owing to a very proper rule, adjudicate on my merits. The papers of the other candidate were therefore submitted to him. If he passed then we were both to get our 'First'. If he did not, we were both to lose. The verdict was negative, and by his unconscious axe my head fell.

His note is unconvincing. It seems hardly credible that the fate of one candidate should have depended on the papers of another. In any case, the only one of his Balliol tutors to be an examiner in Greats that year was Strachan-Davidson, the historian, whose inability to adjudicate on his pupil's merits could have affected the marking only of history papers. Yet it was in philosophy and logic, as Curzon realized immediately after the examination, that his weakness lay. This is confirmed by a more plausible explanation which he sent Farrer a few weeks later, having received an unofficial report from W. L. Courtney, Fellow of New College and another of the examiners:

It was long disputed and only given against me on the last day, just before the publication of the list. ... I and a man named Furneaux of Corpus were first out, each of us receiving votes, but not sufficient for a First. ... My history was, as I expected, up to a First throughout. So were my translations: but the philosophy was only marked 2; and this, I think unfairly, was held to spoil my chances. I say unfairly, for I think that if two out of the three branches of subjects are up to a First, and the third is moderate, the former ought to influence the final decision and not the latter.

Later generations of university graduates may not find it easy to appreciate the consternation and concern caused by Curzon's failure to achieve a First Class in Greats. The change in mood over the years can be illustrated by a passage from the autobiography of Bishop Welldon, one of Curzon's friends and contemporaries:

I was taught as a boy to look upon anybody who had won a first-class in the Schools at Oxford or in the Mathematical or Classical Tripos at Cambridge as a superior being. In those old days he seemed to me to command the same homage as a judge or a cabinet minister commands now. The Cambridge University Calendar was a sort of second Bible in my home.

For most of Curzon's circle their class of degree was a matter of pride rather than of utility. Few were in pursuit of an academic career, where such qualifications matter; and in other professions a second-class degree carried little if any stigma. Those bound for politics might nevertheless reflect that seven of the fifteen members of Mr Gladstone's first Cabinet had taken Firsts in Classics at either Oxford or Cambridge.

On learning that Curzon had failed to achieve a First, Lord Scarsdale wrote to his son in terms of cheerless condolence:

I have had a presentiment all along that you would not get what we wished for; although with very many a second would be highly thought of, I am quite aware that it has little value in your eyes: for there is, no doubt, in the estimation of the public, an enormous difference between the two distinctions.

Nor was Mr Cowley Powles any more encouraging. The Headmaster of Wixenford reminded his former pupil that he did not have to make his way in life, and sent good wishes for his future – 'and you will enjoy it if you use it for the good of others rather than for personal ambition'.

Curzon's friends showed more warmth in their letters of sympathy. Edward Lyttelton, who had himself taken an unexpected Second Class in the Cambridge Tripos, wrote soothingly: 'Well old boy, this is of course a mouldy bore but few people if any have shown themselves better able to bear what little failure you have had to bear than yourself. ... The outside world is beginning to look upon the Oxford classes as affairs of luck more and more.' Alfred Lyttelton, too, another victim of the examiners, added his measure of balm: 'An unkind fate has robbed you of the most glittering spoils of labour. ... Of course you could have got the 1st class for certain had you denied yourself the Union, the Canning and those other literary, political and social enterprises which have earned you the name of the most famous Oxonian that in my knowledge of Oxford I can remember.'

And from Olympus, Dr Jowett himself declared that the result should be regarded only as an accident, and that Curzon should not for a moment consider abandoning the political career which was his natural sphere.

It was Curzon's first major check in his effortless ascent of Parnassus, and his disappointment, although stoically borne, was profound. 'In the public eye,' he wrote bitterly, 'I am stamped with the brand of respectable mediocrity.' In spite of the academic serenity he later achieved, he could never afterwards recall having been placed in the Second Class without a twinge of dismay. St John Brodrick, who like Farrer and the Lyttelton brothers achieved the same respectable award, was more sanguine. He called it the Oxford cachet of most men of first-class ability who have varied interests. That is an exact description of Curzon's career as an undergraduate.

Chapter Five
BAND OF BROTHERS

In spite of the story of Aristides, I have not got tired yet of hearing Rennell Rodd call you perfect.

– *Oscar Wilde to Curzon, November 1883*

'I had thought beforehand that life would be quite insupportable, and that I should have to retire somewhere and hide my face from the world,' Curzon wrote soon after his failure to obtain a First Class in Greats had darkened his last days as an undergraduate. Like Dr Jowett, however, Curzon's friends refused to accept the verdict of the examiners as a conclusive test of his ability. Their healing words restored his self-confidence, stiffened his determination and sent him advancing once more in pursuit of life's glittering prizes. This, then, is the moment to pause and dwell on the circle of intimates whose consolation tided him over what otherwise would have been an episode of prolonged unhappiness and dejection.

They were a generation of tireless correspondents. On thick glazed paper that has stood the test of time they wrote punctiliously to enquire about health and to warn against fatigue; to congratulate on a First and to commiserate on a Second; to exchange gossip and to renew the ties of friendship. By later standards their vocabulary was extravagant, even embarrassing. 'Most charming George', 'My shapely boy', 'My glorious George' – such are the endearments that punctuate their letters, and in an age that did not readily use Christian names outside the family. Sometimes their budgets of news were cast in a tortuous argot, leaden with facetiousness. Gladstone was the Gladder; Brodrick, the Brodder; Jowett, the Jowler; Spring Rice, Sprunks; Leveson Gower, Loose'un or the Laxer; the Archbishop, the Archboss; and George himself, Cussboss. People became peep-hole; tenants, tentools; and the crisis between Turkey and Greece, the Tugger-Grugger. Then solemnity would break in, and in flatterous tones that do not seem to have been unwelcome they unanimously prophesied for each other a swift ascent to the highest places in Church and State.

Most of them afterwards achieved eminence. Edward Lyttelton was Head Master successively of Haileybury and of Eton. His brother Alfred, a barrister, entered Parliament and became Colonial Secretary. St John Brodrick, later created Earl of Midleton, was successively Secretary of State for War and for India. J. E. C. Welldon was Master of Dulwich, then Headmaster of Harrow before going out to India as Metropolitan and Bishop of Calcutta in the same year that Curzon embarked on his Viceroyalty. Cecil Spring Rice ended his diplomatic career as Ambassador in Washington, Arthur Hardinge as Ambassador in Madrid, Rennell Rodd as Ambassador in Rome. George Leveson Gower, after an apprenticeship as one of Mr Gladstone's private secretaries, sat in the House of Commons and held minor Government office. Reginald Brett, later Viscount Esher, was Secretary to the Office of Works and Deputy-Governor of Windsor Castle; in worldly terms his rise to power may better be measured by the appointments he declined – Governor of Cape Colony, Secretary of State for War and Viceroy of India. Richard Farrer, a young Fellow of All Souls might have gone as far as any had he survived beyond the age of twenty-seven.

Except for Rodd, a Haileyburian, all were Etonians. Their later fame was less a tribute to the quality of the education they had received than to the fidelity with which so many families that still constituted a ruling class continued to send their sons to Eton. As Cecil Spring Rice said, one might as well talk of the P. & O. boats breeding Viceroys as of Eton breeding Governor-Generals: it was the only line for them to go by.

They were speeded on their way by two Eton masters who dedicated themselves to equipping boys with the habits of statesmanship. One was Oscar Browning, whose Socratic influence on Curzon and Spring Rice was profound and enduring. The other was William Johnson, tutor to two Prime Ministers, Rosebery and Balfour, as well as to Brett and all the Lyttelton brothers. Among the most inspiring of Victorian teachers, he had been dismissed from Eton by Hornby three years before another pupil of his, Oscar Browning, suffered the same fate. The precise cause of his going is still unknown, but is believed to have been a complaint by a parent to the Head Master that Johnson had written letters to his son in terms excessively affectionate even by the sentimental standards of the age. Sad at heart, he departed to Devon, where schoolboy disciples continued to visit him and to hold his friendship dear. He changed his name to Cory and is remembered by 'Heraclitus', an exquisite translation from the Greek Anthology, some poems of lesser merit and a posthumous volume of letters and journals described by a contemporary as 'the most singular compound of genius and silliness, insight and simplicity, knowledge of books, ignorance of the world, amiability, prejudice and craze'. Johnson also wrote the words of the Eton Boating Song, with its haunting couplet:

Band of Brothers

And nothing in life shall sever
The chain that is round us now.

Curzon's generation loved their pale blue chains. Having lingered at school long past the age at which most of their contemporaries were already immersed in the problems of adult life, they nevertheless seemed reluctant to cast themselves loose from the microcosm of their youth. 'Only forty-eight hours now between me and insignificance,' Alfred Lyttelton said to Brodrick after a farewell dinner given in his honour by Oscar Browning to masters and boys. And even after another three years had passed, when he was on the point of leaving Cambridge, he wrote nostalgically to Curzon, then in his last year at Eton:

I think I shall regain cheerfulness if I can fancy myself talking with you, old boy, over a too sumptuous tea in the most comfortable of Eton rooms, the curtains drawn, and much enduring fags dismissed ... Perhaps you will write back and tell me the sort of things which I liked hearing so much when I came to Eton.

Brett, too, continued to take an obsessive interest in the school. 'He is,' Edward Lyttelton wrote from Cambridge, 'the most learned, not only in the state of the feeling of the masters, but all the gossip, transitory, prejudiced and inane, among all the boys. There is scarcely anyone better worth talking to on the subject, albeit his principles are somewhat obscure.' As early as 1872, when he was nearly twenty, Brett had begun to correspond with the precocious fifteen-year-old Alfred Lyttelton. He once more took the initiative five years later in establishing a friendship with Curzon. 'Dear George,' he wrote to Eton in February 1878, 'there is no particular reason why I should not break the ice and write first.' Curzon responded to the attention of the older man, already making his mark as private secretary to Lord Hartington, heir to the Duke of Devonshire and one of the leaders of the Liberal Party. A few weeks later Brett wrote again with undisguised enthusiasm:

Now that you have written to me it is possible that we may get to know each other and may become fast friends. It is a new start in life, and has all the excitement of a fresh start about it for me.

By the summer, their correspondence had flourished into intimacy and Brett's thoughts returned again and again to his schooldays. 'All my life long,' he wrote, 'I have looked backward rather than forward, and consequently feel your departure from Eton, and from associations which I have in common with you, nearly as much as you feel it yourself.'

Edward Lyttelton, a future Head Master of Eton, varied his diet of gossip, while not abandoning its staple element. 'There's no place for comfort like the University,' he wrote to Curzon from Cambridge, and added:

I wish you could see us this term grinding just within the borders of health, then football or tennis, grind again, then a noisy dinner with the comrades in the hall, and then best of all, a short academical discussion in each other's rooms after. The range of subjects covered is extensive: the state of Europe: of Eton: morality among boys: bigotry among masters: the difference between Christianity professed and real: the relative merits of Eton and Association football: the chances of a freshman on first arriving here: the possibility of a criterion in art criticism: the way to realize the Deity. I have discussed all these merrily within the last four days.

Another of Curzon's early friends who had gone up to Cambridge, Jock Wallop, later Lord Portsmouth, was aware of the spell which Eton continued to cast, but sturdily chose to please himself: 'O.B. is always abjuring me not to become a slave to "The Set", as he terms it, but though I don't keep exclusively to it, I am bound to say that I am Tory enough to prefer Etonianism, with all its supposed disadvantages.'

Gazing back philosophically upon the tribulations he had endured before his election as Master, Dr Jowett once observed that a man must make a compact with himself not to remember everything. Those of Curzon's friends who preceded him to Balliol, the only Oxford college to find favour in their eyes, imposed no such inhibitions on themselves. They made a second home of the Etonian Club where, Spring Rice wrote to Curzon, the *Eton College Chronicle* was more popular than the *Daily Telegraph.* But he at least consciously widened his circle of friends and in the same letter delighted in the company of Samuel Alexander, the philosopher from Australia, and J.A. Hamilton, who as a Lord of Appeal in Ordinary was later created Lord Sumner.

From the moment of his chance encounter with Curzon in the train between Slough and Paddington, St John Brodrick grasped every opportunity of strengthening their friendship. As an undergraduate he used his influence behind the scenes – unsuccessfully the first time – to have the younger boy elected to Pop. Like Edward Lyttelton, he also coveted a photograph and wrote from Oxford in supplication. 'My dear Curzon,' he began humbly, 'this mode of commencement has rather a formal appearance, but our hitherto short correspondence would hardly warrant my assuming the Christian name in use among so many of your friends.' Later he thawed. 'I know you agree with me,' he wrote, 'that it is something beyond a mere community of interests which has enabled us to talk so unreservedly on so short a friendship about subjects which most people, if they enter on them at all, touch upon only when they have proved their confidence in each other.' Eton remained an unbroken thread between them. Brodrick could not resist boasting to him that he was the first member of Pop for at least ten years to become President of the Oxford Union. And shortly before Curzon came into residence at Balliol he sent useful advice on how much wine he should bring – a dozen of port at 42*s*, a dozen of decent claret at 48*s*. and some pale sherry. 'You are not expected to entertain at all your first term. In the case of most fellows it would be considered rather curious if you did, but in an Eton fellow it is quite optional.'

Nearly all their families were land-owners, some substantial. In 1883, Lord Scarsdale owned 9,929 acres, with an annual rent-roll of £17,859. Lord Lyttelton owned 6,939 acres, worth £10,263 a year. Lord Midleton, Brodrick's father, owned 9,580 acres, bringing in £10,752 a year. Lord Portsmouth, Wallop's father, owned no fewer than 46,984 acres, producing an annual income of £36,271.

J.E.C. Welldon, however, known to his intimates as Doon, came from a more middle-class background. His father was second master at Tonbridge School, his mother the daughter of the head of a printing firm in Ipswich. As a King's Scholar at Eton his career was of effortless distinction. He won the Newcastle Scholarship, blue riband of the studious, alone equalled Curzon's feat of being 'sent up for good' on twenty-three occasions, and was President of the Literary Society. An impregnable fortress when playing at the wall, he was no less effective at the field game, Eton's peculiar brand of football: and in later years Curzon spoke of how that 'mighty leg could kick a ball higher and farther than any other of our recollection'. At Cambridge he won the Bell and Craven Scholarships, was senior Classic and senior Chancellor's Medallist, and in 1878 was elected a Fellow of King's. Curzon, who was five years his junior, arrived at Eton not long before Welldon left for Cambridge, so never knew him when both were in the school. Just after Welldon had taken his degree, however, he was asked temporarily to replace a master who had broken down in health. By that time Curzon was Captain of the Oppidans, and a lifelong friendship sprang up between them.

Having to make his way in life by his own efforts, Welldon displayed an earnestness that was not always appreciated by more romantically-minded members of the circle. A reproachful letter from Curzon to Brett on the subject brought this answer:

> When you say that I 'don't like' the excellent Welldon I suppose you mean exactly what you say. It is true I 'don't like' him, but I don't dislike him. I am perfectly neutral. Not armed neutrality, but perfectly friendly. I should not care to see much of him. He is too academical: a word which sums up a whole heap of attributes which are to me not disagreeable but simply tiresome. I adore young people casting about and eager for knowledge, but am bored with people who profess to have it all cut and dried.

It was, however, the pastime of Curzon and his circle to have everything cut and dried for many years ahead. 'When you are Secretary of State for Foreign Affairs,' wrote Spring Rice a good thirty-five years before Curzon assumed that office, 'I hope you will restore the vanished glory of England, lead the European concert, decide the fate of nations, and give me three months leave instead of two.' Welldon thought Curzon more likely to go to the Treasury. Repeating to him a conversation with Oscar Browning, he ends his letter: 'I need not say how kindly and affectionately he spoke of you;

yet forgive me if I say it will be a proud and strange boast for him to make in future years, that he has trained a *Conservative* Chancellor of the Exchequer.'

Welldon's own career showed much early promise. Before he was thirty he had taken Holy Orders and been appointed Master of Dulwich College. Although a Cambridge man, he had also attracted the notice of Bob Raper, as he was known to generations of Oxford undergraduates. Raper belonged to that not uncommon type of university don who, to quote Curzon's own words, 'would sooner be the unknown king-maker than occupy the precarious elevation of a throne'. For more than forty years a Fellow of Trinity, he determined the election of four successive Presidents: on three of those occasions he might have had the office himself, but declined. The role he chose was that of a one-man appointments board. He had many friends both inside and outside the Ancient Universities and received almost daily budgets of intelligence from high table and senior common room, from episcopal palace and ministerial private office. In the intervals of classical tutoring and college business he would himself send out innumerable letters in a hand so minute that he could boast of never having had to continue on to a second page. The documents that flowed from his pen resembled medieval palimpsests: they strained the eye but repaid study. Few vacancies in public or academic life escaped his knowledge, and he would rarely fail to produce a suitable candidate on demand. Curzon received several letters from him over the years, either offering advice about his own career or commenting with shrewdness on the prospects of his contemporaries. Welldon's appointment to Dulwich in 1883 evoked the following assessment from Raper:

> I hear his friends are disappointed as they thought he would get something better – but £2,000 a year and no necessity of doing anything seems not so bad for aet. 26 or 27 to rest on; even tho' an Archbishopric be his ultimate destiny, it is not vacant.

Edward Lyttelton, writing to tell Curzon that Welldon's testimonials included eulogies from Mr Gladstone and the Archbishop of Canterbury, also had doubts about Dulwich:

> In one way it is a nuisance. He will get no training there in managing boys out of school which is three-quarters of the work. The place is day board of young stockbrokers, and as so often happens, when such a place gets a young University swell, it will be raised gradually into an upper class school for which it was not by nature intended, with many resisting grumbles on the part of the local governors.

Welldon did not have long to wait for a wider field of action. In the summer of 1884 he was mentioned as a possible successor to Dr Hornby, about to retire as Head Master of Eton; the appointment went in fact to the vastly more experienced Dr Warre. But less than a year later Brodrick was writing to Curzon:

> Have you heard of Welldon's probable elevation to H. Mastership of Harrow? He was not going to stand, but 17 masters signed a memorial asking him to do so,

and 7 added their signatures conditionally on a layman not being acceptable to Governing Body. ...

There seems no doubt of his promotion, which is a grand thing and will I suppose clear Eton for Edward after Warre. By that time you will be a Cabinet Minister and Alfred Solicitor-General. Goodbye dear old Boy.

Brodrick's prophecy was only a little wide of the mark. Welldon secured the appointment to Harrow, where the young Winston Churchill boarded in the house he held as Headmaster. Edward Lyttelton duly succeeded Dr Warre as Head Master of Eton, although he had to wait until 1905 for his predecessor to relinquish the office, meanwhile spending fifteen years as Master of Haileybury. In 1905 Alfred Lyttelton was indeed in the Government, not as Solicitor-General but as Colonial Secretary. Curzon, too, would have been a Cabinet Minister, except that he was in his last year as Viceroy of India, driven to resignation by what he considered the perfidious conduct of the Secretary of State for India – who happened to be the Right Honourable St John Brodrick. Well might Alfred Lyttelton write to Curzon: 'I have so often to contend with the rooted middle-class idea that a youthful member of the aristocracy does not mean business that I am fully in sympathy with a determined effort to give no basis whatsoever to it.'

George Brodrick, Warden of Merton College and uncle of St John, attributed the succession of Second Class degrees taken by Curzon's generation of Etonians at Oxford and Cambridge to 'too much society at an early age'. Within the charmed circle of a few hundred families there was perpetual entertainment and sport to be enjoyed by presentable young men – and at no cost other than travelling, tips and washing bills. Few of Curzon's contemporaries were rich, and even the expenses of a journey from one haven of hospitality to another had to be calculated with care. As tramps mark the gateposts of houses according to the degree of charity dispensed there, so Dick Farrer, returning to his home in the North, passed on a useful report from Hams Hall, Lord Norton's house near Birmingham: 'I am here for the Sunday only, thinking to do it cheap on the way to Yorkshire. The place is just what you might expect – substantihole but dull as ditcher, which fact is worth making a menthole note of.'

Better fare awaited visitors to Hatfield, where more than sixty guests stayed in the house for the coming-of-age of Lord Cranborne, Lord Salisbury's eldest son and heir. Curzon described it all in a letter to Farrer:

We bachelors, some 15 in number, were established in a commodious house, till lately the Salisbury Arms, just outside the gates. Thence we had complete command of the entire proceedings, sauntering up in a phalanx some ½ hour late for dinner. Everything was done in princely style; hundreds of tenants, kids and paupers were fed from day to day. Jim was receiving incessant deputations and presents and making innumerable modest and appropriate speeches. Every night there was a sphere; 150 swells coming down in a special from London for the principal one. There were athlete sports (Pammer and I desired to enter for 3-legger but were not allowed), fireworks and every variety of entertainment. Beer flowed like water. We played tennis, lawn tennis, rode, tricycled, and having casually strolled out without any preparations for a couple of hours in the park one afternoon, 5 of us did to death 226 conies. The pen of a Disraeli might fittingly have been employed to immortalise the week.

Curzon's own coming-of-age at Kedleston was on a more modest scale. 'I had a very jolly celebration at home of my birthday,' he told Farrer. 'The tentools presented me with a magnificent candelabrum, in accepting which I had to make something of a speech. The house servants and labourers also gave me handsome presents. My tongue was on the wag the greater part of the day: at night we had a servants' dance.'

In spite of his spinal weakness, there is hardly a letter which does not record his attending a ball. He danced at Grosvenor house, not yet an hotel but still the residence of the Duke of Westminster. He danced in Switzerland 'with young English ladies to whom a London ballroom was as Abraham's bosom to Dives, a far distant and unattainable region of felicity'. He would have danced at a party given by the Duchess of Bedford in honour of the Empress Augusta of Germany; but when he asked Dr Jowett for leave to be away from Oxford, the Master replied: 'I don't think much of Empresses. Good morning.'

'I have had just over four weeks of season, which I have enjoyed enormously,' Curzon wrote to Farrer in the summer of 1882. 'During that time I have only dined at home once, and have been to a dance every night (excluding Saturdays and Sundays) but one. So much for actual festivities. But it is not so much to them that I would point as the principal sources of enjoyment, as to the opportunities which seem to multiply year after year of strengthening old friendships and acquiring new.'

The most illustrious was that of Mr Gladstone. 'Much pleasant conversation on Homer,' he wrote on meeting Curzon again at Eton in 1882. Both were the guests of Edward Lyttelton, the Prime Minister's nephew, who had just become an assistant master and was soon to take Holy Orders. Curzon's own account of his reunion with Gladstone was less cordial:

Nearly all Sunday we talked incessantly, mainly about Church subjects and old times. One thing we all noticed, his deficient sense of mutual perspective as applied to the criticisms of character. Two or three persons in the course of a single conversation were 'Among the most remarkable persons of intellect that he had ever known.' Two of them, I recollect, were unknown clergymen, and not one had ever established the smallest claim to fame.

Curzon's newer acquaintances included Augustus Hare, who devoted his life to writing guide books, painting in water colours, telling ghost stories and recording his placid adventures in high society. 'Dining at Louisa, Lady Ashburton's,' the diarist wrote, 'I sat near George N. Curzon, eldest son of Lord Scarsdale, the sort of fellow I take to at once, and we made great friends in one evening, unfolding ourselves in a way which makes me sure we shall meet again.' Hare's barometer of talent rarely gave a false reading, and the compliment was returned. 'A delightful man,' Curzon told Spring Rice, 'he said nothing would persuade him to go and stay with Jowett, though he knows him well. It would be "ideal boredom".' Later in the year they met again at Oxford, and Hare's name passed into the fanciful currency of the Curzon coterie. Farrer, describing the sport he had enjoyed in Hungary as the guest of Baron de Hirsch, boasted of all the Augustuses he had shot.

Through Rennell Rodd, Curzon penetrated more Bohemian circles. A childhood spent travelling abroad with his parents had liberated Rodd from many of the conventions and prejudices of the later Victorian era and extended his horizons beyond those of his contemporaries. Sensitive to beauty in all its forms, he was while still at Balliol on terms of easy familiarity with Morris and Whistler and Burne-Jones. It was Rodd who introduced Curzon to the novelist Ouida at her villa near Florence, a meeting spiced with social daring. Some years before, during their correspondence in the holidays from Eton, Jock Wallop had told Curzon of the disapproval with which even the unconventional Oscar Browning frowned on Ouida's romantic novels of passion among the well-born:

> I greatly shocked him by confessing – to his inquiry – that I read Ouida, the merits of whose books I endeavoured to prove by lending him *Pascarel*, which I I have read these holidays. In my attempt to prove that the moral tone of the book was not really bad, I let him open it at any place he pleased. Unfortunately, he came upon just the *wrong passage*, a defence of which at the moment was utterly impossible, much to our amusement.

Curzon's reputation and morals survived his introduction to Ouida and in later years his heart was touched by her dedication to improving the lot of animals in a callous world. He sent her money when she was destitute and after her death composed the inscription for a memorial fountain in her birthplace, Bury St Edmunds: 'Here may God's creatures whom she loved assuage her tender soul as they drink.'

Curzon and his friends were as much at home in the butts as in the ballroom. One of the few bonds of intimacy that brought him close to his father and his brothers was their shared love of shooting. Lord Scarsdale carried a gun until he was over eighty, killing a brace of partridges on the last occasion he went out. He encouraged his children in the sport, and from the age of ten they were able occasionally to escape the surveillance of Miss Paraman to spend a day walking with the guns. In the autumn of 1875 Lord Scarsdale bought his eldest son a 16-bore gun from Purdey. Public life never allowed Curzon the regular practice without which even the born shot cannot develop his skill: for in the late nineteenth century, shooting was too serious a matter to be confined to the week-end and most parties would assemble on Tuesday and disperse on Friday. But he enjoyed rough shooting as much as banging away at what he facetiously called 'the paternal grice'. In pursuit of rabbits while staying with Lord Wharncliffe in 1882, 'I developed unexpected and unwonted accuracy in my attempts upon that animal's existence this autumn, a deadliness not extended in similar proportion to the fowls of the air. However, a little at a time.' By 1884 he had obviously improved his aim and the Kedleston game book records that in a single day he shot seven elusive woodcock to his own gun.

Unlike many of his generation, Curzon attached more importance to the sport than to the bag. His friend George Wyndham, writing to his own father at the turn of the century, described how conviviality was giving way to relentless slaughter among a certain type of land-owner:

> They live for shooting and 'record' bags on their several estates. And, in order to secure these bags, they have abandoned most of the old precepts, shooting at everything near and far, taking the best places at their own shooting, being rude to their guests who shoot badly and generally destroying the amenities of what was a pretty sport by turning it into a vulgar and arduous competition.

The worst offender was Lord de Grey, later second Marquess of Ripon, who between 1867 and 1900 personally killed no fewer than 370,728 head of game, including 142,343 pheasants, 97,759 partridges, 56,460 grouse, 29,858 rabbits and 27,686 hares.

Large numbers of game meant little to Curzon. 'As regards wild-fowl shooting,' he wrote of a visit to Korea, 'the great nuisance is that there is no means of disposing of the slain, and after a time mere slaughter palls.' But as Viceroy of India he found relaxation in the wonderful sport provided for him as a matter of course whenever he was on tour. 'I went out a day or two ago with the great snipe shooter here,' he told his brother Frank. 'A man named Dodd, who got the record bag of 131 couple to his own gun in a single day. The birds were fearfully wild, as there was no sun, but we managed to get 50 couple. Luckily I shot just as well as he did.' And in Sind he established what he believed to be a record bag for a single day of 153 duck. He was an accomplished shot with a rifle, too. Shooting in Assam with the Maharaja of Kuch Behar, he killed stone dead, one after the other, three tigers moving at a gallop.

But what he enjoyed most of all when shooting was the fresh air and the exercise and the chaff. He also liked the cheerful anecdotes with which his friends would pepper their letters, such as Farrer's story of the Belgian cook at a house in Scotland who came out with the guns one day:

A sheep was found dying from natural causes close by the spot where he had made a laudable but futile attempt to peep a hare, so he was persuaded he had caused its death and went home boasting of having slaughtered '*un mouton sauvage*'.

George Leveson Gower, too, had a fund of improbable episodes to relate, as when Lord Calthorpe, shooting with Lord Cowper at Panshanger, complained to his host's younger brother Henry about the way in which the coverts were driven. 'Am I my brother's keeper?' Henry replied.

Although Curzon's delight in shooting was later curbed by bouts of spinal pain, by the burden of office, by long journeys abroad and by the austerities of war, he was meticulous throughout his life in keeping a game book. Statistically unremarkable, it nevertheless contains some revealing autobiographical notes. Here is one from the year 1910, when he followed his father's custom of leasing Crag Hall, an estate belonging to Lord Derby:

The shoot of September 13 was variegated by the novel incident of a 'strike' of the majority of the drivers during lunch. They receive 4/6d and drink, and they suddenly struck (by premeditation) for 6/-. I refused to give way: and we went on with 7 men. I declined either to yield or to take on any of the strikers: but we managed with the aid of the Estate and Home Farm to collect sufficient drivers for the 15th.

In his last years he again discovered the pleasures of shooting at Kedleston. 'Yesterday after lunch,' he wrote to his wife on Whit Sunday, 1918, 'I went out with Frank to shoot rooks and jackdaws. The first time that I have fired a gun at Kedleston for over 21 years and the first I time have shot a rook here for 30!' In the following year he took his step-sons out for their first partridge shoot. 'It was also the first time I have shot partridges here for 25 years! They did not hit much but blazed away merrily. ... We came back to a late lunch at 2.30 P.M., and I have been resting since, since I walked for 3½ hours without intermission over rough ground – a great effort for me.' A snipe and a wild duck one day, four of the fat Canadian geese in the park the next: it was in recapturing the joys of his youth that Curzon found solace from the political humiliation and anguish that clouded the sunset of his life.

Unexpectedly in a boy who showed no outstanding ability on the playing fields of Eton, Curzon loved watching cricket. During the school holidays he would accompany his brothers to the Derby cricket ground, particularly if W.G. Grace were playing; and to see his first Varsity match at Lord's he took an illicit day off from Eton, brazenly travelling back in the same railway carriage as the Provost, Dr Goodford. His initial interest in the game was strengthened by his friendship with the Lytteltons. Alfred put up his name for the M.C.C. during the Varsity match of 1878, and he found himself a member exactly a year later. Among recreations, he wrote, he knew of no pleasure to compare with sitting on the roof of the pavilion at Lord's on a sunny day, and he could recall all the memorable games he had witnessed over the years.

'My dear old Alf,' he wrote from Simla in the summer of 1901, 'a letter from you is like a fresh wind from the ocean and it fans and cheers me right away in the heart of the Himalayas. ... My chief regrets at being in India are that I can't see Jessop* slog or shoot a grouse myself.' He could have had no better mentor than the man whose play W. G. Grace himself described as the champagne of cricket. At Hagley, the Lyttelton seat in Worcestershire, the children were taught the elements of the game indoors as soon as they could stand, and Chippendale tables and chairs bore the scars of their early enthusiam. The family could themselves field an eleven – eight sons, a father and two uncles. At both Eton and Cambridge, Alfred succeeded Edward as captain of the eleven; in the years they successively captained Cambridge, 1878 and 1879, the eleven remained unbeaten. As an assistant master at Eton, Edward celebrated Queen Victoria's Golden Jubilee by erecting a notice on his house: '50 not out'. And as Head Master and a fashionable preacher, he confessed that he never walked up the nave of a church or a cathedral without bowling an imaginary ball and wondering whether it would take spin.

There were, however, puzzling contradictions and paradoxes in the Lyttelton character. 'I think Edward is much the better fellow of the two,' Curzon told Browning as a schoolboy, 'though Alfred is so jolly.' Both brothers combined Christian idealism and earnest self-examination with a boisterous euphoria sometimes indistinguishable from brutality. Their father, learned, upright and universally respected, would nevertheless encourage napkin fights at dinner that sent guests clambering for safety on to the sideboard; and he could never resist lightly flicking with his whip anyone he met or passed when bowling along a road in his gig. These disturbing outbreaks of high spirits alternated with fits of melancholia, during one of which he committed suicide in his sixtieth year. Mr Gladstone, it is said, used to lament that he had not persuaded his brother-in-law, a brilliant scholar and translator of Milton into Greek, to undertake an English verse rendering of his own beloved Homer: a daily portion of routine but intellectually congenial labour, he thought, might have kept Lyttelton's mind from brooding and so averted the disaster.

The gales of laughter and wild jokes of the Lytteltons contrasted oddly with their tenderness as lovers and their absorbed devotion to music. Laura Tennant, who was married to Alfred in 1885, once asked her sister Margot: 'Wouldn't you have thought that, laughing as loud as the Lytteltons do, they

* G.L. Jessop (1874–1955), one of the hardest-hitting players in the history of cricket.

would have loved [Edward] Lear? Alfred says that none of them think him a bit funny and was quite testy when I said his was the only family in the world that didn't.' Dazed by the heady triumphs of Eton and dubbed by his sisters, only half in jest, 'King Alfred', he cannot always have found it easy to preserve a sense of proportion.

In the eyes of the twentieth century, Curzon and his friends sometimes seem cruel and insensitive. Domestic animals, social inferiors, foreigners – these were the favourite butts of their savagery. 'In Parnassus,' Farrer writes of his tour of Greece in 1880, 'canine assaults become an exciting sport, as constituting about the only circumstance under which a human being is justified in indulging in the unspeakable delight of heaving stones with all his might at a living mark.' No irony was intended. George Leveson Gower describes how he was once walking back to Balliol with Curzon after a game of tennis. Curzon was carrying the balls, which belonged to Leveson Gower, in a net bag. When a stray dog appeared, he began to bombard it with a stream of balls, using his racket with much force. The dog, resenting the attack, bit all the balls he could reach instead of more logically biting Curzon. When the bag was empty, Leveson Gower told Curzon that he would have to pay for the balls. Curzon replied that the dog, not he, had bitten them, and that the dog would have to pay.

'Don't be absurd!' said Leveson Gower.

'Well, then, his owner.'

'But I don't know to whom he belongs.'

'That's not my fault.'

Leveson Gower mourned his tennis balls but managed to conceal any sympathy he felt for the dog. Edward Lyttelton, too, described in his memoirs how as an Eton boy he relished hurling fives balls at dogs; stones he reserved for throwing at cart drivers. But the animal kingdom took its revenge on him a year or two later when he was working for the Classical Tripos at Cambridge. Ploughing through the speeches of Thucydides one evening, he was distracted by an unmelodious cat under his window. 'I seized a cudgel,' he wrote, 'and spent ten minutes in an unavailing chase. That incident caused me to omit one speech which, I need hardly say, was set in the examination.' He missed his First.

Horses alone were exempt from ill-treatment. Walking down Northumberland Avenue, Leveson Gower and Rennell Rodd once came on a cabby beating his horse. Before they could intervene a clergyman had called a policeman and had had the man arrested. The whole party marched off to Bow Street, where the two Balliol men gave evidence. The episode ended satisfactorily with a sentence on the cabby of a month's hard labour. 'A fortnight would have been enough,' Rodd conceded magnanimously.

It would be tempting to assume that the reputation for arrogance which clung to Curzon from his Oxford days was no more than a manifestation of exuberant youth. But the evidence of that candid observer Leveson Gower does not read prettily. One evening, he relates, having supper at a ball with Rennell Rodd and other friends, Curzon missed Leveson Gower and told a waiter to go and fetch him from the ballroom. The waiter pleaded that he did not know Leveson Gower. 'Oh, you can't mistake him,' Curzon said, 'he's tall and fair and rather stout and probably very hot.' So the waiter went off and approached a guest who seemed to fit the description and delivered his message. The man was puzzled and said he did not know Curzon, but when the waiter persisted he went down to the supper room. As he approached the table Curzon, instead of apologizing, called out: 'Who are you? You are not the Laxer. We don't want you. Go away!' The stranger was naturally furious at such churlishness, but took no further action.

Curzon was not always so fortunate in escaping the fury of those whom he had offended. In Lord Charles Beresford, that most peppery of admirals, he seems to have met his match, although the encounter was followed by this *amende*:

My dear George,

I am afraid that I was very rude last night, but the fact was you happened to pinch me on my broken leg and it made me wince, and I suppose being an Irishman and consequently pugnacious, I got furious, but you know me quite well enough to know that I should be very sorry if I was rude.

Yours very truly,
Charlie Beresford.

One of the friends whom Rodd brought into Curzon's life was Oscar Wilde. He had come from Trinity College, Dublin, to Magdalen College, Oxford, taken a First Class in both Mods and Greats and won the Newdigate Prize for 1878 with his poem, *Ravenna*. Rodd, too, was a poet who two years later won the Newdigate on the theme of Sir Walter Raleigh, a success that prompted Wilde to call on him. He was touched by the attention of the older man and even after they had quarrelled wrote of Wilde's 'really genial and kindly nature which seemed at times in strident contrast with his egotism, self-assertion and incorrigible love of notoriety'. The breach in fact took place as a result of a generous impulse on the part of Wilde. Rodd had in 1881 published a little volume of verse entitled *Songs in the South* which he dedicated 'To My Father'. As a gesture of friendship, Wilde offered to have the book published in the United States. To Rodd's embarrassment, however, it appeared under the more esoteric title, *Rose Leaf and Apple Leaf*, and was dedicated 'To Oscar Wilde, "Heart's Brother", These few songs and many songs to come' – the strictly personal inscription which Rodd had written for his new friend in a presentation copy of the original edition. Even more misleading, Rodd thought, was Wilde's effusive foreword to the American edition:

Amongst the many young men in England who are seeking along with me to continue and to perfect the English Renaissance – *jeunes guerriers du drapeau romantique*, as Gautier would have called us – there is none whose love of art is more flawless and fervent, whose artistic sense of beauty is more subtle and more delicate – none, indeed, who is dearer to myself – than the young poet, whose verses I have brought with me to America.

There was much more in the same vein, an unwelcome commendation in the eyes of a young man destined for the Diplomatic Service. Rodd admitted that 'where a thing has been kindly meant, one cannot find fault'. But his friendship with Wilde did not endure. It is doubtful whether the author of *Dorian Gray* would ten years later have felt able to commend in the same fulsome terms the increasingly sturdy sentiments of the poetry which Rodd continued to publish. Thus in 1891, as a Second Secretary at the British Embassy in Rome, he produced a volume entitled *Songs of England* and dedicated it to Curzon in these lines:

Since you believe in that great work her sons have still to do,
Persuaded that her service means the world's best service too,
These first-fruits of my English Songs I dedicate to you.

Rodd continued to have his admirers, and in 1893 Mr Gladstone declared that his poem on the defeat of the Armada was 'finer than Macaulay'.

The coolness between the two young poets did not deter Wilde from friendship with other members of Curzon's circle, although his sybaritic philosophy accorded oddly with their manly idealism and unsophisticated humour. In February 1882 he sent 'My dear George Curzon' a rhapsodic account of his first lecture tour in the United States:

The excitement of a sane strong people over the colour of my necktie, the fear of the eagle that I have come to cut his barbaric claws with the scissors of culture, the impotent rage of the ink-stained, the noble and glorious homage of the respectable – you shall know it all ...

Well, it's really wonderful, my audiences are enormous. In Chicago I lectured last Monday to 2500 people! This is of course nothing to anyone who has spoken at the Union – but to me it was delightful – a great sympathetic electric people who cheered and applauded and gave me a sense of serene power than even being abused by the Saturday Review never gave me; I lecture four times a week – and the people are delightful and lionize one to a curious extent – but they follow me and start schools of design when I visit their town – at Philadelphia the school is called after me and they really are beginning to love and know beautiful art.

As for myself, I feel like Tancred or Lothair – I travel in such state – for in a *free* country one cannot live without slaves – and I have slaves – black, yellow and white. But you must write again – your letter had a flavour of Attic salt.

Yours (from Boeotia),
Oscar Wilde.

'When are you at home?' he wrote in the following year on Curzon's return from the Levant. 'I will come round one morning and smoke a cigarette with you. You must tell me about the East. I hope you have brought back strange carpets and stranger gods.' A few weeks later, on his second crossing of the Atlantic, Wilde was captivating the staid Brodrick, who found himself a fellow-passenger in the R.M.S. *Britannic*:

> On the whole [he wrote to Curzon] we have been wondrous lucky as to companions – Oscar Wilde has been the life and soul of the voyage. He has showered good stories and bons mots, paradoxes and epigrams upon me all the way, while he certainly has a never failing bonhomie, which makes him roar with laughter over his own absurd theories and strange conceits. Of course you know all this – but I don't know that I have ever laughed so much as with and at him all through the voyage.

That autumn Curzon defended Wilde against an attack in the Oxford Union and received a spirited letter of thanks:

> You are a brick! and I thank you very much for your chivalrous defence of me in the Union – so much of what is best in England passes through Oxford that I should have been sorry to think that discourtesy so gross and narrow-mindedness so evil could have been suffered to exist without some voice of scorn being raised against them.
>
> Our sweet city with its dreaming towers must not be given entirely over to the Philistine. They have Gath and Ekron and Ashdod and many other cities of dirt and dread and despair and we must not give them the quiet cloisters of Magdalen to brawl in or the windows of Merton to peer from.

A year or two later, when Curzon stood on the threshold of a political career, Wilde sought his help in becoming an Inspector of Schools. 'I know how the party think of you,' he wrote, 'you brilliant young Coningsby.' Curzon seems to have done his best, but it was not as an Inspector of Schools that Wilde eventually won renown.

No whisper of scandal had yet touched Wilde: had it been otherwise, Curzon and his friends would not have admitted him to their circle even in the role of buffoon. In spite of the extravagant language of endearment in which Victorian undergraduates wrote to each other, they were shocked by any suggestion of homosexual practice and the tolerance with which later generations viewed such aberration was unacceptable. Shortly before Curzon set out for Greece in 1882, Farrer gave him much practical advice about hotels and guides. 'I send a letter,' he wrote, 'to ——, the only Greek friend I have. He comes from Salonica but ought to be now arriving in Athens for the season.' Six weeks later Curzon added a warning to the report on his progress which he sent Farrer from Cairo: 'Don't give anyone else recommendations to ——. He turns out to be a b–gg–r! Thank heaven I don't say so from personal experience, though he did once look in to my bedroom.'

For the less esoteric lusts of the flesh, Curzon and his circle showed a healthy enthusiasm. 'At Pesth,' he wrote to Farrer during his Grand Tour, 'the women have figures that make one stare and itch.' He told another friend: 'Never was such a travelling companion as you. Energetic, unselfish, amusing, equally provided with philosophic reflection and bawdy anecdote, agile with every natural endowment from the brain to the c—k.' They took particular pride in the exploits of George Leveson Gower. A youth of imposing stature and invincible good nature, he was well-read and well-travelled and much in demand as a raconteur from Marlborough House to Chatsworth. He also had a prodigious appetite for eating and drinking and dancing and womanizing. In a letter to Farrer, Curzon recorded one vignette of Leveson Gower's favourite pastime: 'G. L. G., having had a woman twice before dinner yesterday evening, presumably in the same shirt in which he subsequently dined, presented a limp and crumpled appearance.' And from the British Embassy in Berlin, his first diplomatic post abroad, Rennell Rodd sent Curzon these lines of verse:

I have said every day, and I repeat it again
That the sex we call fair is most damnably plain,
So plain, my dear Cussboss, that even the Laxer,
If he came to Berlin, would soon have to go back, Sir:
I have hardly met even a passable whore
All the way from the Schloss to the Brandenburg Tor.

Curzon's private correspondence is peppered with sly allusions to romantic conquests and sexual prowess. Girls, however, could be accepted on equal terms only if they confined themselves to flirtations in London ballrooms and charades in country houses. Except as occasional and heavily chaperoned visitors, they were not encouraged to intrude on what had hitherto been the wholly masculine preserves of a university. Curzon suffered one of his rare defeats in debate at the Oxford Union when he spoke against a proposal to allow women students to use its library: the motion was carried by 254 votes to 238.

Throughout the early years of his life he showed a similar obtuseness to the demands of women for equality in public affairs and opposed their admission as Fellows of the Royal Geographical Society in a vein of jaunty vulgarity:

> We contest *in toto* the general capability of women to contribute to scientific geographical knowledge. Their sex and training render them equally unfitted for exploration, and the genus of professional female globe-trotters with which America has lately familiarised us is one of the horrors of the latter end of the 19th century.

Twenty years later, as President of the Royal Geographical Society, he relented, and as forcefully commended their admission.

Women [he wrote] have read some of the ablest papers before our society; they have conducted explorations not inferior in adventurous courage or in scientific results to those achieved by men; they have made valuable additions to the literature of travel, and have been invited to lecture in our great universities; above all, as research students and as teachers, they enjoy opportunities for which they are at least as well equipped as men.

But he never thought them fit to vote, contemptuously dismissing the case for women's suffrage as 'the fashionable tomfoolery of the day'.

Dr Inge, the Dean of St Paul's whose acidic aphorisms failed to conceal a kindly heart, declared his dislike of women at universities on more limited grounds: 'They ruin the men's chances in Mods by getting engaged to them, and in Greats by jilting them.' Curzon, for all his high-minded anti-feminism, barely escaped the double danger. Early in 1881 he became briefly engaged to be married, but the betrothal did not survive parental disapproval of so young a match. The transient fiancée seems to have been one of the three daughters of Mr Thomas and Lady Harriet Wentworth-Vernon, with whom Curzon stayed at Wentworth Castle, in Yorkshire, during the Christmas vacation of 1880. The visit had a sad ending. Dick Farrer, who was a fellow guest, sent his friend a report after Curzon's withdrawal from the battlefield of the heart. Like Gibbon, he leaves so delicate a topic in the decent obscurity of a learned language, employing a form of dog-Greek intelligible only to students of the classics. Translated, it reads:

The unlucky young lady appears to have been kept up all night talking by her mother, which accounted for a very wearied and unhappy appearance. But by dinner-time her great natural good sense reasserted itself and she was as cheerful as ever, laughing heartily and naturally and cutting little jokes and dancing away with zest up to 1.0 a.m. ... You have acted the best possible part in a most horribly trying situation.

The only other light to fall on the episode is shed by an unsigned letter to Curzon from No. 11, Connaught Place, the London house of the Wentworth-Vernon family, commiserating on his failure to achieve a First in Greats:

I see the announcement. Pray don't give the matter a moment's thought! No one who knows you *can* think less highly of you, of your powers, or of your magnificent, generous, tolerant nature – instinctively, but I quite believe unconsciously, raising and educating morally and intellectually every one you associate with ... It is not to be told how great is the loss to me of the liberal education I derived from intercourse with you! or how immense and torturing is my sacrifice!

Such was the love and devotion that Curzon could inspire when hardly more than a boy. Not all his friends shared his boldness: for most of them, an early marriage was a daunting and remote prospect. While still at Cambridge, Alfred Lyttelton attended the wedding of a brother. Next day he suddenly halted in the middle of a walk with a friend and exclaimed: 'Good heavens! What can Charles and Mary be finding to talk about after being shut up together for 24 hours?' Cecil Spring Rice, learning Italian in Florence, wrote to Curzon: 'I want next not to see the news of your marriage but of your being in Parliament: so many of our friends seem bent on making their families not so much great as numerous.' And Curzon himself told Farrer: 'None of our friends seem bent on marrying just yet, and I think they are wise in waiting a bit, for to my mind nearly all the nicest people are already married.'

Brodrick, however, married Lady Hilda Charteris, a daughter of Lord Wemyss, when he was twenty-three. And Brett, the oldest of the circle, married Eleanor van der Weyer, daughter of the Belgian Minister in London, when he was twenty-seven. Of Curzon's other friends, Alfred Lyttelton in 1885 married Laura Tennant, sister of the girl who was to become Margot Asquith; enchanting and sweet-natured, she died in childbirth less than a year later. In 1892 he ended six years of loneliness by marrying the accomplished Edith Balfour, known to her family and friends as D.D. Edward Lyttelton married in 1888. Rennell Rodd, Leveson Gower, Hardinge and Curzon himself postponed matrimony until the 1890s and Spring Rice until 1904. Welldon and Farrer died unmarried, one at eighty-three, the other at twenty-seven.

High spirits and generosity of affection did not always protect Curzon and his friends from an occasional primness of mind: the moral failings or weaknesses of those outside their circle evoked pitiless disdain. During a visit to Paris just before he went up to Oxford, Curzon encountered 'that young blackguard Savernake [afterwards Ailesbury] who had been sacked from Eton for twice refusing to take a swishing – in addition to other enormities – but who had been taken in hand by an amiable Cambridge man named Bull (afterwards a master at Wellington College) who found the only possible method of discipline was to knock the young ruffian down about once a week'.

Another unsatisfactory contemporary, they thought, was Lord Garmoyle, heir to Lord Cairns, a recent Lord Chancellor. He, however, was spared the hit-or-miss treatment of the amiable Mr Bull. Instead, Farrer wrote to Curzon, 'a perfect stranger of great wealth, admiring Lord Cairns as a fellow North Irishman, bequeathed £50,000 to his eldest son: consequently the only result of the object of his good wishes is the absolute emancipation from his control of a very loose youth'.

Drunkenness, too, was abhorred. From Scotland Farrer once sent Curzon a description of the arrival of an heir to a dukedom at a shooting party. 'He drove up with me from the station last night. He sucked a flask all the way and arrived quite drippy, so as to have to be taken at once to his bedder.

Today after lunch he fell down in a bog and was unable to rise. He is about 35 but cannot walk two miles without being killed by fatigue.'

Although priggish, Curzon and his friends were perceptive. Lord Savernake, having in 1886 succeeded his grandfather as fourth Marquess of Ailesbury, was within a very few years expelled from the Jockey Club for fraud and declared bankrupt with liabilities of £345,462. His death in 1894 aged thirty was said to be mourned only by the Radical Party, who grieved to lose so deplorable an example of an hereditary legislator. He was subsequently presented to posterity in the pages of the *Complete Peerage* as 'a young man of low tastes, bad character and brutal manners'.

Lord Garmoyle died from pneumonia in 1890 at the age of twenty-eight, but not before he too had made history. As defendant in a breach-of-promise case, he was obliged to pay unprecedented damages of £10,000.

But the heir to the dukedom survived, surprisingly, for nearly twenty years, having in the meantime succeeded to the family honours and presided with decorum over the fortunes of the Mendicity Society.

Chapter Six
CLASSICAL LANDSCAPES

Upon my word, these Gruggers are a queer lot.

– *Curzon to Richard Farrer,*
29 January 1883

Between 1877 and 1895 there was hardly a year which Curzon did not spend partly in foreign travel. He owed his initial enthusiasm to Oscar Browning, who liked the company of lively-minded young men on his rambles round Europe. In the Christmas holidays of 1877 Curzon was permitted by his father to accept O.B.'s invitation to a tour of the French Riviera and the cities of northern Italy. Lord Scarsdale's faith in Browning's integrity had remained utterly unshaken by the distressing episode that ended in Browning's dismissal from Eton two years before. If the Head Master still had doubts, he kept them to himself, for O.B. was by now beyond his reach and Curzon on the eve of his nineteenth birthday. Browning, however, never ceased to smart from a sense of injustice; and to the end of his life nearly fifty years later he would return again and again to his well-known grievance.

'You will soon be going abroad with the protuberating O.B.,' Edward Lyttelton wrote to Curzon on Christmas Eve, 'don't let him talk about Hornby, and only sparsely about Eton at all.' Alfred found positive virtue in Browning's failing. 'It is always a relief,' he told Curzon, 'if no obligation is imposed on one to talk.'

It was an uneventful trip, marked by a single mild adventure: for the first time Curzon exercised that art of harmless deception which later enabled him to penetrate into the most closely guarded places of the world. The two travellers reached Milan in January, soon after the death of King Victor Emmanuel, and determined to attend the requiem mass in the Duomo. There seemed little hope that two obscure foreigners would obtain places for so memorable a national occasion. They nevertheless put on black evening clothes, white ties and tall hats, and made their way to the Prefecture in search of official tickets. There was none to be had. What they did find, however, was a procession of minor judges, all dressed in the same sombre garb as themselves, about to set off for the service. In a moment they had insinuated themselves in the judicial ranks, and so walked through the streets and into the Duomo. Browning, as loquacious in Italian as in English, passed off their presence with ease. Curzon, a less experienced actor, was only briefly embarrassed by the remark of his neighbour in the cortège, that he appeared to be an exceptionally youthful judge. 'I acknowledged the precocity,' he wrote, 'but refrained from otherwise adding to the information.'

One lesson of this successful foray remained with him throughout his travels. He passed on the advice in the book he later wrote on Persia:

> Of all the necessaries of outfit, commend me, after a long experience, to a suit of dress clothes. Were I setting out to-morrow either for Lhasa or for Timbuctoo, they should accompany me; for I am convinced that I should find them equally useful were I to meet in audience either the King of the Negroes or the Dalai Llama of Tibet.

He added: 'I remember having heard that Gordon started in a dress suit from Cairo for Khartoum.' But that seems a less convincing recommendation.

During all his years of exploration, Curzon was never deterred from achieving his ends by dubious means: of such stuff are great travellers made. In 1885 he was able to watch a horrifying performance of the Aissaouia, or religious self-mutilation, in the holy city of Kairouan, by pretending to be the son of General Boulanger, at that time the French Commander-in-Chief in Africa. In 1889, when about to be received in Teheran by the Shah Nasr-ed-Din, he was suddenly reminded by the British Minister, Sir Henry Drummond Wolff, that a black silk hat was obligatory. Having failed to find one in the town, he promptly stole that of an eminent French archaeologist whom he met at the house of a Persian Minister, and retained it until after his audience at the palace. Nor did he scruple to adorn himself with a colourful constellation of foreign orders and decorations – bought from Nathan's, the theatrical costumiers – before going to Kabul in 1894 as the guest of the Amir Abdur Rahman.

Among the pleasures that Browning drew from his peregrinations was his reception as a distinguished scholar at the courts of Europe. This harmless ambition exposed him at Cambridge to a ridicule not untinged by jealousy. Blue-stocking princesses came to tea at King's. The Kaiser William II earned from him the encomium, 'He is the nicest Emperor I have ever met'. In middle age, he was alleged to have taken up hockey so that he could be struck across the shins by Princes of the Blood Royal. And Arthur Benson contributed to the legend with the story of the undergraduate who called on O.B. one day and found him supervising his valet in packing for a visit to Italy.

'Yes, I am going abroad, I am going to Lucca. I believe there is a Grand Duke there.'

'I am afraid I don't know.'

'Yes, I am sure there is. Hopkins! Pack my second-best dress-coat.'

Curzon, too, did not readily miss an opportunity of meeting the rulers of those countries through which he passed. His pursuit of potentates, however, was no mere caprice of snobbery. The more remote the land, the more help he demanded from those in authority. He would as coolly cross-examine an emperor as a shepherd, and as meticulously record the information he extracted from each.

He was wise to do so. Within a decade or two, nearly all the rulers who had received him during his journeys to the East suffered violent death or untimely dethronement. The King of Korea, whom he visited at Seoul in 1892, saw his Queen murdered in the palace and later was forced to abdicate. The Emperor of Annam, who presented Curzon with a golden decoration at Hue, was deposed and subsequently banished. The Mehtar of Chitral was assassinated in 1894, only two months after Curzon had stayed with him, and by the half-brother who had dined at the same table. The Shah Nasr-ed-Din of Persia met a like fate two years later. The King of Cambodia was dethroned; the Amir of Bokhara was expelled; the Khedive Abbas Hilmi was exiled; Habibulla, elder son of the Amir of Afghanistan, was murdered in his tent.

Among the marginally more stable dynasties of Europe, his experience of crowned heads was also touched by the macabre. In 1880, again in Browning's company, he visited the picturesque castle of Herrenhausen: sitting in a room surrounded by furniture fashioned in the shape of swans, he heard the steady tramp overhead of the mad King Ludwig of Bavaria, who later was found drowned in the lake. And with Rennell Rodd he dined with King George I of Greece, afterwards assassinated in the streets of Salonika. Monarchs might well turn pale on hearing that Curzon, an unwitting harbinger of doom, had crossed the frontier and was making haste for the capital.

In the summer of 1878, between leaving Eton and going up to Oxford, Curzon went to Paris with Welldon. They spent ten days practising the language in the house of a homoeopathic chemist who knew no English. The end of the holiday was clouded by Curzon's discovery for the first time that he had developed a curvature of the spine, an affliction that sent him back to England in despair and cast an intermittent shadow of pain over the half century that remained to him. It was not long, however, before resilience of spirit and the bodily support of a steel waistcoat enabled him to resume a life that was abnormal only in the relentless energy with which he drove himself.

Two years later he again went abroad with Browning. 'For a month,' he told Farrer, 'I continued to find O.B. what I had always previously found him to be and what few persons will dispute his being – viz., the pleasantest of companions, admirably informed on all subjects, with a great, perhaps an exaggerated capacity and inclination for imparting it to other people.' They saw the Passion Play at Oberammergau, about which Curzon produced a huge bale of manuscript that never found a publisher. They drove in a two-horse carriage through sixty miles of Bavarian highland. They steamed placidly round the Swiss lakes and 'walked up mountains of respectable but not remarkable height'.

The first journey that entitled Curzon to call himself a traveller rather than a tourist took place between December 1882 and June 1883. It embraced Rome, Naples, Athens, Corfu, Cairo and the Nile, Palestine, Constantinople, Pesth, Vienna, Dresden, Prague and Berlin. As far as Corfu he had the company of Welldon and Edward Lyttelton. Alfred was to have joined them in Athens, but his practice at the Bar confined him to London. His place, therefore, was taken by Warre Cornish, the Eton master.

Throughout these months of travel Curzon pursued his lifelong habit of recording his impressions in copious diaries and letters, and of keeping accounts with the same meticulous attention he had given to the petty-cash box at Wixenford. His style was always luminous and elegant, although sometimes touched by pretentiousness, as when he observed that 'the plain of Marathon was alive with flitting magpies guiltless of the timidity of their English cousins'. As befitted a man who had read Greats, his imagination was fired by the recognition of ancient and hallowed places. In Rome he gazed upon 'the unmistakable paving stones in their original beds which echoed to the chariot wheels of Scipio, Sulla, Caesar Germanicus, Titus and Trajan'. He reconstructed the heyday of the Colosseum – 'those endless tiers crowded with a sea of faces, a vast awning stretched over that gigantic and open roof, the floor even turned into a miniature lake on which rode galleys and ships of war, or given up to the combats of men and beasts'. But his awe was pleasantly spiced by humour, as when he asked himself a conundrum – what in St Peter's would be the remark of the British sportsman who, after slowly pacing down the nave of York Minster, was heard to observe: 'A long shot for a partridge.'

'A villainous passage from Naples,' Curzon recorded, 'Edward was reduced to a corpse during 5/6 of the voyage. Welldon was not much better.' Curzon himself was less affected by sea-sickness and managed to continue working on an essay on Justinian that later won him the Lothian Prize at Oxford. The firmest of friendships do not always survive the cumulative irritations and frayed nerves of foreign travel: but in the excitement of making new discoveries and of recognizing old acquaintances from classical texts and textbooks, the harmony between Curzon and his companions remained intact. Their journey turned into a triumphal progress when it became known that Lyttelton was a nephew of that dedicated Philhellene, Mr Gladstone. On the way to Delphi, there turned up an old man of eighty-five who had been his guide during the ascent of Parnassus in 1856: he insisted on lending Edward his horse, while the rest of the party were more humbly accommodated with mules. Curzon was already too set in Conservative ways to relish the cause of such tributes, and wrote a waspish account of Lyttelton, 'in knickerbockers and fives shoes, rising from our humble and half-finished dinner to address the delegation in mediocre and metallic French'.

Athens fulfilled every expectation, Curzon's highest praise naturally being reserved for the Acropolis. As he passed through the pillars of the Propylaea, he wondered where the world would have been without 'the philosophy of Socrates, Plato and Aristotle; the history of Thucydides; the poetry of Aeschylus and Sophocles; the eloquence of Demosthenes; the sculpture of Phidias; the example of Aristides and Pericles'. Architecturally, too, his emotions were aroused by the exquisite proportions of the Parthenon. Prolonged study convinced him that it would be impracticable to restore the marbles rescued by Lord Elgin from destruction to their original places in the frieze, and that for the British Museum to return them to Athens for any other purpose would merely ensure their passing 'from a magnificent to an inferior museum'.

Over the years, however, he became convinced that the British Museum should allow its lonely Caryatide to rejoin her five sisters that support the portico of the Erectheium; and that four panels from the Temple of the Wingless Victory should likewise be returned by the British Government to their original site. In 1890 he wrote to enlist Mr Gladstone's help in removing 'an anomaly amounting to an eyesore', pleading that the gesture would be 'both a graceful act and a service to art'.

Gladstone replied cordially but in a characteristic vein of circumlocution:

> Your proposal is of the utmost interest. You are in every way entitled to open the question. It is of course, however, one of some delicacy. Joe Hume said in Parliament that wherever there is delicacy there is something wrong! In this case there has been something wrong, the matter appears to rest with the Trustees and the Government (I am no longer a Trustee). I think I can say at this early stage that in the special work of restitution which you devise you have nothing like objection or opposition to expect from me.

But Sir Frederic Leighton, President of the Royal Academy and a trustee of the British Museum, declared that 'from the point of view of Art', the service rendered by the Caryatide in London was greater than it could be in Athens. And although he, like Mr Gladstone, promised not to speak out publicly against the restoration, his coolness seems to have been decisive. The Caryatide to this day reposes in the British Museum, while a terra-cotta substitute usurps and defaces her rightful place in the Erectheium.

Curzon's first visit to Athens in 1883 also enabled him to meet Heinrich Schliemann, the prosperous German merchant whose excavations at Mycenae and Troy changed the course of classical archaeology. Curzon described him as 'reputed to be worth £10,000 a year ... a short, uneasy-eyed ugly little man, his hair shaven close to a bullety head, a grizzling moustache on his upper lip, and a collapsible figure. ... He told me that, though a German by birth, he had yet written his books on Troy and Mycenae in English and afterwards had them translated back into the German tongue.' It is possible that Curzon had first met Schliemann at Eton, where he stayed as the guest of Oscar Browning. But it was a short visit. 'There is nothing to dig, nothing prehistoric,' the archaeologist complained. His host's suggestion that there were some respectable old fossils in the shape of the Provost and Fellows was ill-received, and Eton saw him no more. Curzon belonged to the breed of traveller that does not hesitate to make use of the most fleeting acquaintanceship; before leaving Athens he had picked Schliemann's brains about the further stages of his journey and later wrote to him for advice on inspecting the excavations at Troy.

Curzon's reverence for the ancient glories of Greece did not extend to her nineteenth-century inhabitants. He observed that the central street of Athens 'is filled with a clamouring crowd from morn to night. At no moment of the day is there any respite in the clatter of aimless conversation.' The people 'argue and declaim and gesticulate ... and those who have been shaking their hands in one another's faces at one moment are exchanging cigarettes the next'. The Greeks, he felt, were not yet fitted for a system of parliamentary government. 'A people just awakening from the night of four hundred years of Turkish oppression is hardly fit to receive the mead of full enlightenment.' He was magnanimous, however, in conceding that although he had lost rugs and umbrellas in Greece, 'this may have been owing as much to our carelessness as to the instincts of the people'.

However patronizing such sentiments may sound in twentieth-century ears, they were mild and courteous compared with the fierce and irrational disdain for foreigners held by many of the governing class of Victorian England. Initially reflecting the arrogance of a Palmerstonian foreign policy, it was a brand of xenophobia that survived Great Britain's subsequent decline both of power and of prestige. Lady Salisbury, with whom Curzon had stayed at Hatfield for the twenty-first birthday celebrations of her son Cranborne, used to tell her friends how Lady Palmerston had once said to her: 'My dear, you will some day be in my position, and when you are, I advise you to pay no visits at all.' 'So I never pay any,' Lady Salisbury continued, 'except to the Foreign Ambassadresses. Of course, I don't include those of the South American Republics or any others of the people who live up trees.'

Lord Ronald Gower, sculptor of the Shakespeare memorial fountain at Stratford, experienced traveller and cousin of George Leveson Gower, struck a more violent note in his diary:

If possible, this visit to Naples has increased my disgust of the place and its population. A more deformed, bestial-looking lot of men and women than are the Neapolitans it would be hard to match, and De Brosse's account of them holds good to this day — *'C'est la plus abominable canaille, la plus dégoutante vermine qui ait jamais rampé sur la terre'*.

Curzon's immediate circle of friends shared such contempt for those who had the misfortune not to be British. During a visit to Italy, Alfred Lyttelton noticed on the station at Venice 'a small, grubby Italian, leaning on his walking stick, smoking a cheroot'. The challenge was irresistible. As his train drew away, he flung a half-sucked orange 'full at the unsuspecting foreigner's cheek'. After which, Edward records, his brother 'collapsed into noble convulsions of laughter'.

The concomitance of foreigners, cigars and railway stations was apparently enough to outrage the feelings of any decent Englishman. Lord Ribblesdale, who married one of Curzon's most intimate women friends, Charty Tennant, writes thus of his father:

I remember a particularly tempestuous episode, when he was seeing off my eldest brother to India, at Victoria Station. In the confusion of changing his railway carriage at the last moment, a great-coat of my brother's was left in the first compartment he had entered. My father claimed the coat, loudly and truculently, from the occupants of the carriage, two dark-complexioned gentlemen smoking black cigars; they complied with his request with enthusiasm, throwing the coat out of the window with such a will that it knocked my father's top hat sideways. With a leap forward he was on the step of the train, and just about to blacken further the traveller's dusky eye, when the whistle blew, and he was pulled back on to the platform by the onlookers.

Nor can Curzon himself be acquitted of brutal insensitivity. In the authoritative two-volume work on Persia he wrote after an exhaustive tour of the country, he confessed without shame to

having once or twice, with intentional malice, spurred my horse to a gallop, as I was overtaking some party of wayfarers thus accompanied: for to see the sober asses kick up their heels and bolt from the track as they heard the clatter of horsehoofs behind, to observe the amorphous bundles upon their backs shake and totter in their seats, till shrieks were raised, veils fell, and there was imminent danger of a total collapse, was to crack one's sides with sorely-needed and well-earned laughter.

Denizens of the Colonies were generally spared violence, but evoked a full measure of social contempt. 'There is no society out here,' Charty Ribblesdale wrote to Curzon from Natal in 1884, 'the people of the place are all desperately uninteresting, other women all weary or vulgar. There are a few nice men passing thro' in their regiments but there are only 2 men in the whole place I care to speak to, one is General Sir Leicester Smyth, he changed his name from Curzon and is a brother of the Duchess of Beaufort, and the other is the Governor, Sir Henry Bulwer.'

Jock Wallop, the eloquence and maturity of whose conversation with Curzon in the library at Eton had stupefied their contemporaries, became private secretary to the Governor of Tasmania on leaving Cambridge, and wrote to tell his old friend what he was enduring in the Antipodes: 'The people are very kindly and hospitable, but one cannot help feeling that going out is more like attending a series of servants' balls or tenants' entertainments.'

The most implacable xenophobe of Curzon's circle was Richard Farrer, who in 1882 published *A Tour in Greece*. It is a handsomely bound quarto volume of over 200 well-printed pages, with elegant engravings by the author's friend and travelling companion Lord Windsor. It is also perhaps the most peevish and pejorative work written by a highly educated, intellectually able and personally attractive upper-class Englishman of the late nineteenth century.

From the moment he set foot on Greek soil his existence was joyless. There were the fleeting pleasures of landscape and architecture, but the inhabitants simply did not know their place. On arrival at Piraeus he was 'packed into a fly with one of these not too fragrant gentry'. When he visited the Tower of the Winds, there were 'many loafers who assisted at our inspection'. The galleries of the Greek Parliament 'were crammed with an unsavoury rabble'. In the interior of the country, roads would be blocked 'by a mob of aborigines crowding about the vehicle'. And when he stopped for the night, 'one old lady makes a determined attempt to assist at our ablutions, from which no persuasion short of the forcible and accurate projection of shooting-boots will induce her to desist'.

The moral tone of Greece was not at all what a Balliol man had a right to expect. 'In point of universal sympathy with crime, the Hellenic population is not far behind the Irish ... they appeared to have nothing to do but talk and pilfer.' They even had difficulty in mastering their own language. 'Much harmless amusement may be obtained by getting some gentleman or lady to read a little classical poetry which, being by them pronounced solely according to accent, loses all approximation to metre, and becomes a mass of false quantities sufficiently monstrous to bring any offending schoolboy into prompt and sharp contact with the birch. No amount of explanation will make them see the absurdity of this performance.'

In a crescendo of churlishness Farrer describes how, during a visit to a monastery, he insouciantly spurns the feast specially prepared in his honour: 'We find that the largest, and therefore most elderly rooster, has been sacrificed in our absence and is even now browning on the spit; while bread, cheese, wine and aromatic mountain-honey are spread out in the guest chamber. But the prospect of dining in Athens is more agreeable, and we have to make ready for departure.'

Curzon could sometimes be unfeeling, but he would never have written a book as insubstantial and bigoted in its judgements as *A Tour in Greece*. The letter of qualified congratulation he wrote to the author hardly glows with approval:

I have just finished reading your book on Greece which I bought as soon as it came out. I was far from grudging the skiv,* for apart from its being an offering on the shrine of affection, I knew I should be repaid by the amount of information I was certain to derive. It has given me many useful hints about our journey. The writing is always easy, unaffected, stylish and amusing.

If I might make a criticism it would be that except in one or two notable cases (e.g. the chapter on Olympia) it scarcely rises in dignity to the level either of the subject matter or of the magnificent guise in which the book is presented to the public.

You will answer and with perfect truth that your share of the work was merely intended as a running accompaniment to the pictures and that you did not mean it to be anything else than slender either in bulk or style. The same was the intention of the publisher who got Dickens to write the running comment on the pictures already supplied, which soon won immortality as the Pickwick Papers.

And I think you might have given a little more scope to your undoubted power of description and your intimate acquaintance with the Classics. I know it wasn't your subject: but then your object – simple and unambitious – scarcely harmonises with that gorgeous paper, printing and exterior.

You mustn't be offended at this criticism, we always speak out to each other or ought to.

Arthur Hardinge also read the work. 'His book,' he wrote to Curzon, 'pretty and clever as it is (and good I should say on classical Greece), is marred by violent party feeling and a John Bullish spirit of indignation at every little discomfort.'

* Slang for a sovereign.

Chapter Seven
UNTO CAESAR

To those who believe that the British Empire is, under Providence, the greatest instrument for good that the world has seen.

– Dedication of Curzon's *Problems of the Far East*, 1894

By the early weeks of 1883, Curzon's Grand Tour had carried him through Greece to the island of Corfu. There he said farewell to his fellow Hellenic travellers – Welldon, Lyttelton and Warre Cornish – who had to return to tutorial duties in England, and embarked in an Austrian steamer for Alexandria. He was put out at finding himself 'the only Englishman among a lot of frowsty Germans'. It was a disagreeable voyage in other ways, taking nine days instead of the scheduled three. Trying to escape the full severity of a storm, the captain ran the vessel aground on the mainland, and the smaller boat to which passengers were transferred was no match for a second storm off the west coast of Peloponnesus. Eventually the ship sought shelter in Navarino, unexpectedly giving Curzon the opportunity he had long wanted of seeing the ancient site of Pylos. 'The entrances to the bay do not tally with Thucydides, being much wider,' he noted, 'in other respects the correspondence is exact.'

In Alexandria he examined the damage caused by bombardment from the British fleet the previous summer. 'The practice of our artillery must have been first rate: immense holes torn in every direction through massive masonry. All the Egyptian guns (Armstrongs from Newcastle) still stand in their places with heaps of unused shells hard by.' Then to Tel-el-Kebir, where four months earlier Sir Garnet Wolseley had defeated the army of the rebellious Arabi Pasha. Twice he rode over the battlefield, 'still strewn with cartridges, water bottles, broken guns, bits of uniform, shells and the graves of the slain'. He examined the ground with the same thoroughness he had brought to his survey of the battle of Marathon, fought 2,300 years before; for in matters of military tactics and strategy he was not the headstrong amateur that critics of his frontier policy in India later supposed.

Disappointment awaited him in Cairo. There he had hoped to be joined by Richard Farrer and to complete the tour in his company. But since the beginning of 1881 Farrer had been struggling against the ravages of tuberculosis and was now too ill to endure a prolonged journey. 'It is not the solitude I mind,' Curzon told him, 'for I rather like it, and can at any moment relieve it by association with the scores of English here; it is the thought of what I have lost in losing your society. For we should both have gone with scholar's interest in the places: and now I may be sandwiched among a lot of people who don't know the capital of a pillar from the backside of an idol.'

Reserving the sights of Cairo for his return, he took a Cook's steamer up the Nile. 'How you would – with me – have enjoyed this trip,' he wrote to Farrer from Luxor. 'The temples, colossi, tombs are splendid, of proportions so stupendous that the ordinary senses find themselves bewildered, and rich with the blazoned history, every letter of which is now intelligible, of 4,000 years ago.' He could not share the popular verdict that the great hall at Karnak was the noblest architectural work ever designed and executed by human hands. But the two enthroned Colossi of Thebes, the vocal Memnon and his mute companion, touched his enquiring mind.

A year or two later he fulfilled his determination to solve the problem of the sound reputed centuries before to have emerged from the depths of one of the figures: Juvenal described it as the snapping of a harp string. Helped by his old Oxford tutor, Strachan-Davidson, Curzon wrote a closely reasoned paper of thirty-five large octavo printed pages, attributing the phenomenon to the expansion of fissured stone caused by the sudden heat of the rising sun. The investigation illustrated the intellectual effort and cogency which he would invariably bring to historical or archaeological problems: and no less the richness of prose with which he could clothe the fruits of his research:

> There they sit, the two giant brethren, scorched by the suns of more than three thousand summers, ringed by unnumbered yearly embraces of the wanton stream. By their side Stonehenge is a plaything, the work of pigmies. They are first even among the prodigies of Egypt; more solemn than the Pyramids, more sad than the Sphinx, more amazing than the pillared avenues of Karnak, more tremendous than the rock-idols of Aboo Simbel. There they sit, patient and pathetic, their grim obliterated faces staring out into vacancy, their ponderous limbs sunk in a perpetual repose, indifferent alike to man and to Nature, careless of the sacrilege that has been perpetrated upon the mortal remains of the royal house whose glories they portrayed, steadfast while empires have crumbled and dynasties declined, serene amid all the tides of war and rapine and conquest that have ebbed and flowed from Alexandria to Assouan. There they sit and doubtless will sit till the end of all things – *sedent aeternumque sedebunt* – a wonder and a witness to men.

Such a style did not commend itself to all his contemporaries. On hearing Curzon deliver a public lecture on another historical theme, H. A. L. Fisher remarked to G. M. Young: 'If he had given me all the nouns, I could have put in all the adjectives.'

The architecture of Cairo left a lasting imprint on his mind. The arches and domes, the mosques and minarets, the open courts and coloured mosaics, laid the foundations of that profound knowledge which as Viceroy of India he brought to the preservation of ancient monuments. Like any lesser tourist he also went out to inspect the Pyramids and the Sphinx but was cool in his appreciation. Although awed by the sheer bulk of the Pyramid of Cheops,

> a lot of fuss is made about ascending it and about supposed giddiness. As a matter of fact it is ridiculously easy and could be undertaken with an effort by any lady. A strong Bedouin holds each hand and simply pulls you from stone to stone. Many of these are more than three feet deep, but legs of my abnormal length found nothing alarming in these dimensions, and I was at the top in ten minutes from the bottom. The investigations of the interior is more laborious. Crouched down in a tunnel about three and a half feet high, suffocated with dust, streaming with perspiration, slipping to and fro on the polished and sloping stone floor, you are alternately pushed and pulled along by Bedouins who at intervals raise a shout of 'Hurrah' intended to impress you with the magnitude, but only doing so with the meanness of the undertaking.

He found the Sphinx no less overrated, 'half buried in the sand, standing in a hollow, shamefully mutilated, of comparatively small proportions'.

It was with a jaundiced eye, too, that he gazed upon the Egyptian people. 'Civilisation,' he wrote, 'is foiled by a country which refuses to be civilised, which cannot be civilised, which will remain uncivilised to the end.' For all his intellectual equipment, Curzon could not always resist the tempting half-truth of an epigram. His summary judgement of the Egyptian character persisted throughout his life and ultimately defeated his efforts as Foreign Secretary to negotiate a settlement of the Middle East problem.

His dissatisfaction with Egypt was partly the mood of the moment. 'I confess to having got slack by a continued stay in Cairo,' he told Farrer:

> One gradually dropped after the London fashion into a social set, made great friends, formed decided affections, found every moment occupied and sight-seeing (the raison d'être of my presence abroad) at times an effort. My correspondence went rather to the wall and altogether I experienced a sense of disorganisation, almost of disintegration, which after a while began to be painful. ... Our friends of all degrees from Lady Wharncliffe to a pretty actress living with an Egyptian officer came to tea daily ... The most charming person I met there was the Baroness de Malortie (English herself but married to a foreigner) whose face, an extremely beautiful one, is familiar from photographs in Bond Street windows. I got to know her most intimately (this for your *private* ear only) and I count her one of my dearest friends. All this made life at Cairo seductive, but it also made it rather unprofitable. For here one was living the London life over again without the London justification.

An uneasy conscience was not the only spur that sent Curzon on his travels again. Just as he was later to infuriate Calcutta University by imputing to Indians a concept of truth inferior to that cherished in Europe, so in Egypt he disdainfully matched those romantic legends peddled by the guides against the sober learning and reasoned conclusions of an English scholar and gentleman. It pained him to be shown historic shams, such as the tree under which the Virgin is said to have reposed with the Infant Christ; and although he tried to be just by recalling that even Herodotus had not only been told a good many lies by the Egyptians but had himself told a few more, the Balliol man would not be comforted. 'Tradition is very active everywhere in the East,' he wrote from the steamer between Port Said and Jaffa, 'but I look for a real plethora at Jerusalem.' His melancholy predictions were to be fulfilled: and in their unfolding it may well be that he lost the Christian faith of his upbringing.

'Palestine is a country to see once, not to revisit,' Curzon informed Farrer. 'The scenery is not often picturesque or even pretty. There is much greater need of cultivation than in Greece and much less chance of making it pay. For the surface in many places is all rocks and stones. No Jew with his eyes open (and you never saw one with them shut) would think of going back: and if the Millennium is only to arrive when they have returned, our descendants will still be expecting it in 3000 A.D.'

Only the most fervent of visionaries could in 1883 have foreseen the establishment of the State of Israel little more than sixty years later, and Curzon was not of their number. He was, it is true, a senior member of the Lloyd George Government which in 1917 approved the Balfour Declaration But his personal hostility was implacable, particularly after he had replaced Arthur Balfour himself as acting Foreign Secretary at the beginning of 1919. Writing to Balfour in March about reports of a new Zionist programme, he said:

> I confess that I shudder at the prospect of our country having to adjust ambitions of this description with the interests of the native population or the legitimate duties of a Mandatory Power; and I look back with a sort of gloomy satisfaction upon the warnings that I ventured to utter a year and a half ago in the Cabinet as to the consequences of inviting the Hebrews to return to Palestine.

Such an attitude may appear understandable in a statesman beset by the unsettled Arab world of the immediate post-war period. It is more difficult to excuse the tone of schoolboy facetiousness to which he reverted in the following August when writing to the author of the Balfour Declaration about its most grateful recipient:*

* Chaim Weizmann. 1874–1952. First President of Israel, 1948.

This is merely a line to say how much startled I am at a letter from Dr. Weizmann to you, dated July 23, in which that astute but aspiring person claims to advise us as to the principal politico-military appointments to be made in Palestine; to criticise sharply the conduct of any such officers who do not fall on the neck of the Zionists (a most unattractive resting place); and to acquaint us with the 'type of man' whom we ought or ought not to send.

It seems to me that Dr. Weizmann will be a scourge on the back of the unlucky Mandatory, and I often wish you would drop a few globules of cold water on his heated and extravagant pretensions.

Curzon's judgements not infrequently crystallized early in life. Having determined in 1883 that Palestine was an unsuitable national home for the Jews of the Diaspora, he seems to have resented every stage in their subsequent reunion as a personal affront. It would, however, be wrong to equate his dislike of Zionism, a political posture, with the evil creed of anti-Semitism. Brought up on the Bible, he filled notebook upon notebook during his tour of Palestine with eloquent recollections of the Old Testament. Thus Esdraelon, he recorded, had produced 'the two finest bursts of poetry in the Hebrew, perhaps in any tongue: the noble paean of conquest and the most pathetic dirge of despair'. Engraved on his memory, too, were the wailing prayers of the Jews at their wall of lamentation, 'the most impressive sight I have seen abroad'; and the Sunday he spent on Mount Carmel, reading as part of the morning service 'that glorious chapter I Kings xviii ... the most dramatic scene in Jewish history'.

The shrines of his own faith he found distressingly artificial. 'The Church of the Holy Sepulchre is a nest of fallacies, fiction and superstitions. So indeed are most of the Holy Places. Everything took place in a grotto. This shows the practical spirit of the local custodians, for grottoes are sempiternal while buildings crumble and need repair.' In later years he expanded these initial sentiments of bitterness and shocked disappointment into a Voltairian exercise of sustained irony:

I experienced no surprise, indeed, at learning that there is hardly a place or scene in the Old or New Testament which has not been identified with scrupulous accuracy. Thus, to see the House of Joseph, or the Tomb of the Virgin, or the Sarcophagus of David, or the burial-place of Nicodemus, or the home of the kindly man by whom Paul was let down in a basket and who is known as George the Porter, or even the spot where the cock crew to Peter, were sensations that might well have been foreseen. Nor, when I came to the Moslem Sacred Sites, was I greatly startled to be shown the round hole in the rock, inside the Mosque of Omar at Jerusalem, through which Mohammed rose to heaven on the back of his athletic steed, or even the fragments of the saddle which that animal bore, although this saddle was rather unexpectedly made of marble. Further, I had not known beforehand that the rock itself was only prevented from following the Prophet in his aerial flight by the special intervention of the Archangel Gabriel, whose finger-prints are still visible where he held it down.

But what I had altogether failed to anticipate was that the most famous men of the Scriptures, with an admirable regard for the convenience of posterity, should have concentrated their main activities on approximately the same site or sites. Thus, after I had exhausted the sights of the Holy Sepulchre, it was a great relief to know that without leaving the building I could see both the grave of Adam, who, I thought, had ended his days at some considerable distance, and the place where Abraham attempted to sacrifice Isaac; whilst in the dome of the rock Mohammed had struck his head against the ceiling so hard that he left an unmistakable impression side by side with the place – also unmistakable – where David and Solomon had prayed.

All these discoveries, however, paled before the realisation that in Palestine and Syria men could be buried several times over without exciting any surprise. It is true that I had read in England of two, if not three, well-attested skulls of Oliver Cromwell, and that I was familiar with the explanation given by the owner of one of these to the visitor who complained that he had already seen the skull of the Protector elsewhere, and that it was a good deal bigger. 'Oh, but our skull,' had been the reply, 'was the skull of Oliver Cromwell when he was a little boy.'

I was therefore prepared for some uncertainty about the relics of the dead. Moreover, I realised that there might be some reason for a double record in the case of Lazarus, whose tomb I encountered first at Bethany, and afterwards at Larnaka in Cyprus. Again, we know that John the Baptist was beheaded; which may explain how it came about that I saw the mausoleum of his body at Samaria, and of his head at Damascus. But it did not explain how, on another occasion, I came across the greater part of his remains at Genoa in Italy. The Virgin Mary had also two graves, one in the Garden of Gethsemane, and another at Ephesus (with the tomb of St. John thrown in). But the hero of the greatest achievement was undoubtedly Noah. It is true that history contains no record of the stages by which he trekked from Ararat to the Holy Land. But let that pass – for it was only a minor discovery in comparison with others. I had, I thought, already left him safely buried at Hebron, when later on, in the neighbourhood of Baalbeck, I came upon him again; and this time he was interred in a tomb forty yards long by two or three feet wide, thereby throwing an entirely new light upon the methods by which he may have escaped the Flood, without ever building or entering the Ark. Noah must, as I say, have been a person of exceptional stature, even in a part of the world where the Sons of Anak, 'which come of the giants', and compared with whom all other men 'were as grasshoppers', would appear to have abounded. But even in his day the standard of human height must have been rapidly deteriorating; for the grave of Eve, near Jeddah in the Hejaz, which corresponds accurately to the dimensions of her body, is not less than 173 yards long by 12 yards wide; so that compared with the ancestral Mother of Mankind, the builder of the Ark was only a pigmy. At Jeddah, however, the guardians of her tomb have a ready and indeed a plausible explanation of this decline, for they say that when Eve fell, with her fell the stature of the race which she originated.

If Curzon found it difficult to reconcile such widespread deception with an unquestioning acceptance of Christian belief, he did not disclose his doubts. 'To go into a fictitious Holy Sepulchre,' he wrote to a friend, 'to walk along a modern *via dolorosa*, to see an imaginary Holy House at Nazareth does not – cannot – make me sceptical as to the truth of the narrative which they only secondarily illustrate.' At the same time he confided to his notebook that Palestine had exerted no more influence on him. 'I feel a kind of interest I never did before in the circumstances of the gospel narrative. But they do not appeal to me with a different force. They breathe a thousand memories; but they teach no lesson. I do not find it any easier after visiting the country and dwelling place of Christ to live more like Christ.'

Departing from his habitual discretion, Lord Ronaldshay asserts both in his official biography of Curzon and in his own memoirs that Curzon found himself unable, while still a young man, to accept the essentials of the Christian creed. He claims, moreover, that Curzon's loss of belief began during his tour of Palestine. 'It is uncertain,' Ronaldshay writes, 'when exactly the full realisation of this intellectual revolt against the miraculous in the Christian doctrine flooded in upon him; but no one who reflects upon the self-examination to which he subjected himself as a result of his visit to the Holy Land ... can doubt, in spite of his vehement protestation at the time, that it was then that the corroding acid of scepticism first bit into his mind.'

The probability that Curzon had by his early thirties abandoned his belief in Christianity is obliquely supported by the testimony of two other friends. When in 1890 Edward Lyttelton was appointed Master of Haileybury, his reply to Curzon's congratulations included these pointed questions:

> They tell me your old church-going habits have broken down, and that you have put away religion? Is this so? If so why? Forgive brevity – 170 letters in 2 days.

The laconic style of Lyttelton's letter – reminiscent of those written as Prime Minister half a century later by one of his pupils at Haileybury, Clement Attlee – did not invite a generous response, and none has survived. The theme, however, recurs five years later in an obscurely phrased but patently troubled letter which Brodrick wrote as Curzon was about to cross the Atlantic to marry:

> My dear old boy,
>
> We may possibly meet before you start on Wednesday but if by chance we do not I send you a line to wish you God speed on your expedition – which after all is perhaps the most important of your travels since no event is really as great in any man's life as marriage.
>
> And now I am going to plead with you that in the brief leisure of the voyage you will look back 20 years and give a thought to what I am going to say.
>
> I think you know how high I rated the promise of your life as well as our friendship from the moment you set foot in Oxford.
>
> But probably your best well wisher hardly contemplated a more brilliant career than you have achieved. You have won the ear of the House of Commons and of the country on certain subjects on which your reputation is unique; you are universally marked out for high office; you command great audiences.
>
> Withal you have troops of friends and everything which brightens life, and henceforth you will have the command of great wealth.

Except in the matter of health I think Providence has done all – more for you than we could ever have asked or thought.

In the old days, the picture of your life had the halo round it that your successes and the Creator's glory ran together. Nothing seems more beautiful than a character which with every attraction of this world is still cast in the mould which makes for eternity.

I do not believe you could ever lose faith, but I believe you too honest to invoke the most High unless you can justify your works.

One thing only I will venture to tell you about marriage. If ever religion is required it is there.

Love, mutual ambition and interest go far, but not quite far enough.

Think of this a little and see if, in the new life, you cannot recreate the old standard.

Do not think I write as a saint: I would give a good deal myself to have as pure a life and purpose now as in the last year at Eton.

It is only the true friendship I bear you which makes me not afraid to write this – knowing also that with your daily increasing influence your account will be heavy.

Do not think of answering this in all the press before you go. There is no one else for whom I would write it.

Always your affť.
St John Brodrick

Lyttelton's reproach and Brodrick's sorrowful hints at ungodliness speak for themselves. What cannot be established is how far Curzon had, as a young man, accepted the doctrine of Christianity that he subsequently rejected. He shared the Anglican upbringing of his class and generation but seems to have had little taste for the niceties of doctrine. Nor is there evidence that his churchmanship was other than formal. As the son of the Rector of Kedleston he could hardly have avoided regular church attendance: Eton and Oxford, too, encouraged no latitude. He would certainly have heard the story of the Balliol undergraduate who hoped to shirk early services in college chapel by pleading that he had lost his faith in God. 'You will find God by tomorrow morning,' Jowett replied, 'or leave this college.' Faith was one thing, conformity to the established pattern of community life another.

Some of Jowett's early work on St Paul's Epistles had been condemned as heretical and there was determined opposition to his appointment as Regius Professor of Greek. But when his enemies thought they had trapped him into a refusal to subscribe to the Thirty-Nine Articles, he refuted them with Johnsonian brusqueness. 'Give me the pen,' he said. Throughout his years at Oxford he was painfully resolving in his mind the ultimate problems of belief; but the opaqueness of his conclusions never permitted him to dispel the shadow of unorthodoxy that lay across his reputation. He once asked Turgenev whether there was any value in a contemporary German religious revival. 'No,' replied the novelist, 'it is all schlim-schlam and vish-vash, what you call Broad Church.' Jowett refused in fact to accept that label, claiming that what was broad had limits. He would have preferred some expression conveying more the sense of a diffusive and expansive spirit that leavened humanity. 'Always the same, of course,' Cecil Spring Rice wrote of a sermon delivered by Jowett in the University Church, 'no religion good and no religious man bad.' It was unconventional, too, for the Master of Balliol to observe that 'there seems to be much more in the New Testament in praise of poverty than we like to acknowledge'.

Those who held that Christian morality was dependent upon Christian dogma found no merit in Jowett's beliefs. Lord Scarsdale, planning a university education for his schoolboy son, had at first been reluctant to send him to 'a free-thinking place' like Balliol. Even after the Master's death in 1893, resentment lingered. As honorary secretary of the Jowett memorial committee, Curzon wrote to Lord Salisbury, Chancellor of Oxford University, asking him to speak at the inaugural meeting. Salisbury's reply was ungracious:

> The letter summoning me to the Jowett meeting runs thus: 'A general wish has been expressed that measures should be immediately taken to perpetuate the memory, and (as far as may be) to maintain and carry forward *the work of* the late Professor Jowett.' The words I have underlined alarm me a little. . . . I hope the 'work' when it is defined more closely will not involve any reference to Jowett's special theological cranks?

Curzon's own allegiance to religious life was less emotional than that of the Master, less rigid than that of the Chancellor. He was reverent and interested, but betrayed neither the signs of a soul tormented by doubt nor the fervour of a man who has found the key to the Kingdom of Heaven. He could never have written to Rennell Rodd, as Rennell Rodd wrote to him: 'The last month in London has more than ever set me *à l'outrance* with the spirit of today, where no one seems to have any object and purpose in life beyond making money and social success.' It is true that Curzon liked listening to sermons and as a young man made a special journey to hear the ebullient Spurgeon preach at the City Tabernacle. He also added his signature to those of Alfred Lyttelton, Welldon and Brodrick in persuading Professor Henry Drummond to deliver a series of private lectures on Christian themes at the Duke of Westminster's house in Park Lane. To a crowded audience of young men drawn from society and the professions, the Scottish theologian spoke successively on 'The Programme of Christianity', 'Evolution and Christianity' and 'Natural Selection in reference to Christianity'.

Curzon's appreciation of such pursuits, however, was intellectual, not spiritual: he analysed content and performance with the same critical attention he gave to parliamentary oratory. Perhaps unconsciously, he was also treading the footsteps of Jowett, who at the age of twenty-nine had concluded: 'I never hear a sermon scarcely which does not seem equally divided between truth and falsehood.'

In later life, too, he shared Jowett's insistence on the value of corporate worship as an essential of community life. From the moment he inherited Kedleston in 1916, he devoted much time, labour and money to restoring the ancient beauty of the village church and to writing its history. Through the agency of his favourite sister, Blanche, who chose and coached the choir, he immersed himself in every detail of parochial life, even the selection of the hymns. Whenever he could escape from the cares of the Foreign Office in London, the decorum and regularity of his own attendance set a worthy example to his tenants. Modern churchmen may nevertheless have detected a lingering strain of the Victorian age in his attitude towards preferment. In his search for a suitable incumbent for Kedleston – a benefice long adorned by members of his own family – he visited No. 10 Downing Street one day to see whether the Prime Minister had a candidate on his list of ecclesiastical patronage. 'As he will periodically come into personal proximity with myself and my wife,' Curzon explained, 'it is, of course, essential that he should be a gentleman.'

The year before Jowett's death, when Margot Tennant visited him for the last time, he gave her his blessing. 'My dear child,' he said, 'you must believe in God in spite of what the clergy tell you.' To that extent Curzon, too, retained the same steadfast faith to the end of his days. He held the universe to be an expression of divine purpose that transcended all sectarian activity. To the conception of an omnipotent and omnipresent God, he wrote, 'all creeds, dogmas and formulae are subordinate; in its light, sacraments and ceremonies become mere forms; the so-called Holy Scriptures a highly idealised branch of human literature. Jesus Christ takes his place alongside Buddha as the preacher of a rare and sublimated ethics and as the type of perfect humanity.'

He nevertheless clung with deep and humble fervour to some of the tenets of Christianity. 'Though my views about religion are not very orthodox,' he told Lord Roberts, 'I am a firm believer both in the duty and efficacy of prayer, and I do not think I have ever missed a day in my life myself.' Nor did he abandon the certainty that death was but a temporary separation and that earthly ties of love and friendship would one day be renewed in eternity.

Curzon's belief in divine purpose did not only sustain him through the vicissitudes of pain and bereavement that punctuated his private life: it also inspired him in what he conceived to be the highest duty ever laid upon man – the civilizing mission of the British Empire in the East. Although the full force of the role did not come to him until in 1887 he set foot in India for the first time, his awareness of an imperial mission had been awakened in him even as a schoolboy. In a career dedicated to public service he would often justify the task by displaying an intellectual armoury of State papers and statistics; but its core was spiritual and it found its apotheosis in the years he spent as Viceroy of India. A few weeks before he sailed for Bombay in the winter of 1898, he and Welldon, the newly appointed Metropolitan of India, were entertained by a gathering of fellow Etonians. In his speech Curzon recalled the joys and adventures of boyhood and youth they had experienced together. He continued:

> Little did we think that the day would one day come when at the same time he and I should be going forth to the same great continent, to take our share in that noble work which I firmly believe has been placed by the inscrutable decrees of Providence upon the shoulders of the British race.

Seven years later, within hours of leaving India for the last time, he delivered before a British audience at Bombay an apologia of his rule. It was one of the bleakest moments of his life. The triumphs of his statecraft had turned to dust; those who had once been his friends had driven him to resignation; and the proconsul who had touched 300 million people with the benevolence of his authority was about to return, as it seemed, to political extinction. Yet his faith in Great Britain's imperial mission continued undimmed and the peroration of his speech still rings majestically and confidently down the years:

> A hundred times in India have I said to myself, Oh that to every Englishman in this country, as he ends his work, might be truthfully applied the phrase 'Thou hast loved righteousness and hated iniquity.' No man has, I believe, ever served India faithfully of whom that could not be said. All other triumphs are tinsel and sham. Perhaps there are few of us who make anything but a poor approximation to that ideal. But let it be our ideal all the same. To fight for the right, to abhor the imperfect, the unjust, or the mean, to swerve neither to the right hand nor to the left, to care nothing for flattery or applause or odium or abuse – it is so easy to have any of them in India – never to let your enthusiasm be soured or your courage grow dim, but to remember that the Almighty has placed your hand on the greatest of his ploughs, in whose furrow the nations of the future are germinating and taking shape, to drive the blade a little forward in your time, and to feel that somewhere among these millions you have left a little justice or happiness or prosperity, a sense of manliness or moral dignity, a spring of patriotism, a dawn of intellectual enlightenment, or a stirring of duty, where it did not before exist – that is enough, that is the Englishman's justification in India. It is good enough for his watchword while he is here, for his epitaph when he is gone. I have worked for no other aim. Let India be my judge.

The alert but perplexed young man who roamed Palestine in the spring of 1883 afterwards recalled the disappointment of the holy places with amused irony rather than a pang of loss. The needs of tourism and superstition had jolted him out of his adherence to an unquestioning Christian belief, but he found both consolation and forgetfulness in obedience to the call of Great Britain's imperial destiny.

He never ceased to reproach himself, however, for an act of negligence committed during his tour. A year or two before, walking down Pall Mall with a friend, he had been introduced to 'a figure rather shabbily dressed in a seedy black frock coat, trousers that did not come down to the boots and a very dilapidated black silk "topper" with particularly narrow brim and silk mostly brushed the wrong way'. Curzon did not then catch his name and was astounded to hear after they had passed on that he had met General Gordon. In 1883 he heard that his hero was living only a few miles from Jerusalem on the Jaffa road, and proposed to ride out to call on him. In particular he wanted to discuss the theory put forward by Gordon which identified the site of the Crucifixion and Holy Sepulchre with the bare hill, said to resemble a skull in its outline, that stood outside the Damascus Gate. But the friends with whom Curzon was staying thought it would be too much trouble. 'Like a fool,' Curzon wrote when recalling the episode, 'I was persuaded, but have ever since regretted my weakness.' He never had another chance to meet Gordon, who was killed at Khartoum less than two years later: and the student of Curzon's early career can only speculate on what chord of mystical imperialism their conversation might not have touched.

Chapter Eight
FELLOWS

> This delightful spot exists for the satisfaction of a small society of Fellows who, having no dreary instruction to administer, no noisy hobbledehoys to govern, no obligations but towards their own culture, no care save for learning as learning and truth as truth, are presumably the happiest and most charming people in the world.
>
> – *Henry James on All Souls College, 1877*

The course of Curzon's career, which has been allowed to range forward in pursuit of his early friendships and travels, must now return to Oxford. It is the autumn of 1882, and the bitterness of his failure to take a First in Greats, although mitigated by sympathy and encouragement, has not abated. The rest of his life, he is said to have declared, would be spent in showing the examiners how wrong they have been. One way would be to shine in another Final Honours School, just as Farrer had redeemed his Second in Greats by achieving a First in Law two years later. But it was a long grind, in itself offering no appreciable advantage to a young man who, like Curzon, did not intend either to practice at the Bar or to teach.

A swifter if somewhat inferior path to academic glory lay in winning a University prize. Already Curzon had just missed capturing the Chancellor's Latin Verse Prize in 1881, being placed *proxime accessit.* The same fate had awaited his 108 large quarto sheets on the set theme of the Lothian History Prize, 'John Sobieski, King of Poland'. R.W.Raper wrote to one of the examiners to enquire how his friend had done, and received this reply from G.W.Kitchin, later Dean successively of Winchester and of Durham:

> 'The Sword of the Lord and of Gideon' was placed second by both Stubbs* and myself independently. It was a decidedly good narrative essay, with a considerable amount of careful reading. .. The fault of it was a certain pretentiousness of style and character which gave it sometimes a look of dullness.

* William Stubbs. 1825–1901. Outstanding historical scholar. Bishop of Oxford, 1889.

In the following year, 1882, he had been too preoccupied with the approaching ordeal of Greats to compete again for the Lothian. The subject for 1883 was 'Justinian', the Emperor who codified the Roman Law. Although he feared fierce competition from both the Law and History Schools, Curzon determined to enter. He faced one particular difficulty. As he had already arranged to leave England for a Mediterranean tour within a fortnight of his decision to compete, he could depend neither on time enough in which to master the necessary sources nor a tranquil atmosphere in which to write. For two weeks he shut himself up in the reading room of the British Museum filling notebooks which, together with a Gibbon and a French edition of Procopius, he packed in his luggage before departing for Italy in December 1882. No composition, he said, was ever put together at such a jumble of times or in such a jumble of places. He wrote away laboriously in trains and at sea and in a Cook's steamer on the Nile; at intervals of sightseeing and of seasickness. Then he sent off his 140 neatly penned quarto pages to Oxford and continued his travels. It was while sitting in a Buda Pesth café in May that he opened an old copy of *The Times* and read of his success. Later he wrote from Dresden to tell Farrer of the circumstances in which he had brought off his triumph:

> The fact is I kept it universally dark. It would have distressed me to publish to the world another rebuff. ... No one knew anything about it except the Brodder, who detected my reading at the British Museum for it before starting abroad, and Edward and Welldon who often saw me writing while with them ... Justinian was the subject. Though not a hero and though 1,000 years anterior in date, he has for me at least avenged Sobieski.
>
> I only enter into these explanations to you because we feel a rare sympathy with each other on such matters, and because I know you will look for them from me just as I under similar circumstances should from you.

In their agreeable fashion, Curzon's friends hastened to congratulate him. The most disingenuous of messages came from Rennell Rodd. 'I may fairly say,' he wrote, 'I am more pleased than if I were to have got it myself, for I don't think one is ever envious of what one knows is out of one's reach.' Cranborne, too, wrote to tell Curzon, who was still abroad, that his success had been remembered by a special toast at the Canning Club.

The Lothian was not the limit of Curzon's ambition in the field of University prizes. There was also the Arnold, an endowed prize worth, like the Lothian, about £40, but requiring an essay of such length and depth as to stand the buffets of publication. Thus Bryce's *Holy Roman Empire*, had originated in his winning entry for the Arnold of 1863. Nobody had ever won both historical prizes, although Arthur Hardinge came within striking distance of doing so. Having captured the Lothian in 1880 with an essay on Queen Christina of Sweden, he prepared an assault on the Arnold for 1883, the subject being 'The Causes of the Greatness and Decay of Carthage'. In a letter he sent from the Foreign Office to Curzon, then in Cairo, Hardinge related the misfortune that overtook him:

> You are good enough to ask about Carthage! Alas! my child has miscarried! I had written a good part of it, when about the second week in November, I had the misfortune to lose the half-formed foetus in a hansom cab. I had all my paper, notes, etc. in a small black bag, which a stupid club servant forgot to take out with the rest of my luggage. I made repeated enquiries at Scotland Yard but in vain. The cabman probably kept the bag and burnt the essay; though even a sordid plebeian might have found something to interest him in my account (derived from authentic sources) of the orgies connected with the Phoenician and Carthaginian 'nature worship'. Since then I have had neither time nor inclination to begin again, but perhaps it is as well – some 'Greats' man would have been sure to get it.

It is not certain that Curzon would have undertaken the burden of competing for the Arnold but for a chance encounter in the Bodleian Library late in 1883. He happened to see Anthony Hope Hawkins, a Balliol contemporary who had been runner-up for the Lothian that year, absorbed in making notes. Curzon at once assumed that Hawkins was out for revenge by winning the Arnold, and determined to thwart the plan. That he knew nothing of Sir Thomas More, the subject of the prize that year, did not deter him. With a will to succeed which even Curzon's admirers find daunting, he spent fifteen weeks living alone in his father's house in London. By day he toiled away in the reading room of the British Museum. By night he worked at his desk until four or five in the morning. Then he slept for a few hours before making his way to Bloomsbury soon after eleven. Sustained by a diet of tea and brief moments of relaxation at a music hall, he steadily assembled not so much an essay as a volume consisting of 242 pages, carefully annotated and flawlessly written in his flowing hand. With Curzonian verve, he worked on his manuscript to the very last moment, taking the train to Oxford a few hours before the entries had to be handed in. Even then he was putting the finishing adornments on it until almost midnight. As the clocks began to strike twelve, he awoke the janitor of the Old Schools, handed over the labour of the past weeks and apologized for incommoding him. Disarmingly, he added that his was the prize-winning essay. It was. Curzon delighted in having once more seemed to disprove the verdict of his obtuse examiners in Greats; nor could he have been at all displeased that Hawkins was not even placed *proxime accessit*. That lesser distinction went to W.H.Hutton, a cousin of Curzon who later became Dean of Winchester. There was a simple explanation for the supposed rout of Hawkins. Curzon had been utterly mistaken that December day in the Bodleian when he assumed that Hawkins was out for revenge. Hawkins never entered for the Arnold.

Hutton later expanded his essay on More into a book which became a standard work. Curzon declined to publish his, claiming that whatever the examiners may have thought, it did not reach the high standards he set himself. And Hawkins, better known to later generations as Anthony Hope, went on to win more popular acclaim than either with *The Prisoner of Zenda* and *Rupert of Hentzau.*

These were comforting triumphs of their sort, more regarded in the Victorian Age than in our own, but not enduring enough to satisfy Curzon's desire for academic achievement. There was only one way in which he could finally erase the lingering memory of having missed his First in Greats. It was by winning a Prize Fellowship at All Souls. Founded in 1438 by Henry Chichele, Archbishop of Canterbury, to commemorate the souls of King Henry v and of those 'whom the havoc of warfare hath drenched with the bowl of bitter death', the college enjoined its Fellows to serve God in Church and State. Like other ancient institutions, it fell into slothful ways during the eighteenth century. Providing a man possessed the barest academic qualifications and could establish his descent from the brothers of Archbishop Chichele, he found little difficulty in being elected to a lifetime of well-endowed ease: for alone among Oxford colleges, All Souls admitted no undergraduates, except a handful of Bible Clerks. Between 1815 and 1856, seventy-eight of the 113 Fellows could claim to be Founder's Kin. Some would have achieved distinction even by competitive examination: Lord Robert Cecil, for example, elected in 1853, who as Marquess of Salisbury later became Prime Minister. Others were more at home in the hunting field or at the whist table than in the magnificent library which Colonel Christopher Codrington, an eighteenth-century Colonial Governor, bequeathed to All Souls and which Dr Johnson commended to George III during their celebrated encounter at Windsor in 1767. 'If a man has a mind to *prance*,' he said on another occasion, 'he must study at Christ Church and at All Souls.'

With the nineteenth century came a restless itch for reform. In 1858 the revised statutes eliminated the privileged preferment of Founder's Kin, and as a result of the Royal Commission of 1877, the examination for the election of Prize Fellows came to include three papers in either Law or History, an English essay, a general paper and translations both written and *viva voce*. In most years two able young men who had recently taken their Final Schools were elected to Fellowships which lasted for seven years and carried an annual stipend of £200. For many ambitious graduates, however, the attractions of All Souls lay less in the emoluments than in the dignified stepping stone it provided to the world of affairs. As a place of scholarship, not of teaching, it combined the amenities of a country house or of a London club with the intellectual stimulus of a learned society.

Within three weeks of hearing the depressing result of a Second in Greats,

Curzon once more turned his thoughts towards Oxford. 'Do you recommend me to stand for All Souls this year?' he wrote to Farrer, who had been successful in 1880. 'I am very doubtful. I don't know much history and am not inclined to read all August, September and October. What is your candid opinion? It seems to me only a 100 to 1 chance – particularly as I have only got a 2.' Farrer's reply was not encouraging:

Your idea does credit to your pluck, and don't forget that if you got in, the present failure would be wiped out in the public estimation. At the same time, I can't recommend you to stand this time. Since I went to Oxford, no Greats man (with the possible exception of Raleigh) has got in the election after his Schools.

Three months later, in November, Curzon must have regretted that he followed Farrer's advice. For he heard from the omniscient Raper that All Souls had considered none of the candidates of sufficient merit to warrant election to a Fellowship. Raper went on to give Curzon some further details:

Strachey best but formless, the rest void. Some doubt whether Spring Rice was really able – no doubt he lacked knowledge and wrote nonsense (this is confidential), the verdict was they thought the whole lot weak and lacking knowledge to an absurd extent. Surprise was expressed at your not being in and it is thought there would have been an election if you had.

Raper's private intelligence service was known to be well organized and accurate: in later years he used it to good effect in pulling strings and finding suitable jobs for deserving pupils. It nevertheless seems surprising that All Souls should so unhesitatingly have rejected both John St Loe Strachey, who took a First in Modern History and later became editor of the *Spectator*, and Cecil Spring Rice, who took Firsts in Mods and Greats and passed first into the Foreign Office.

Curzon could not repress a twinge of dismay on reading the last sentence of Raper's report, which he passed on to Farrer:

Your college, you see, elected no Fellows and everyone says I was a d—d fool not to go up as it seems they might have elected me had I given them any provocation. But I agree with you in thinking that this was unlikely: and I don't think I regret having abstained.

Struggling against ill-health in Sicily, Farrer replied in December with mingled apology and encouragement:

I have received no information from the spot as to whether social or intellectual unfitness was the cause of the non-election. I feel morally certain you'd have wired it if you had started. But how could I tell? Greats man after Greats man goes in after the long's reading and fails: and how could I advise you, overworked as you were, to add on four months work with every chance of a disappointment? ... I still think that with your powers of utilising odd moments you could do it without much trouble next time.

There was nearly a year to wait for the contest and Curzon left for a long tour of the Mediterranean and Central Europe. He was back in England in June 1883, having in the meantime heard that he had won the Lothian Prize. At Kedleston he set himself a stiff course of reading that included several volumes of Gibbon, and wrote to St John Brodrick about the spell of grandiloquence it had cast over his pen. Unexpectedly, Brodrick had read Gibbon four years before. 'It is a very interesting period,' he confided to Curzon, 'though I do not care for the style.'

In mid-October, Curzon wrote again to Brodrick, striking the note of pessimism with which he approached all examinations:

> Next week I may perhaps go up to Oxford; but it really seems hardly worth while. The effort to get even a superficial grasp of the entire range of history in less than three months, I have found to be excessive, if not absurd. And it seems preposterous to go and compete with men who have studied history for years and to challenge their profundity with one's own shallowness. ... Still I shall probably enter by way of satisfying myself that my scruples against entering are well founded.

They were happily not well founded. On 3 November 1883, Lord Scarsdale noted briefly in his diary: 'G. elected Fellow of All Souls. Stomach much deranged.'

Asquith was later to allude to certain Balliol men who had 'exchanged the plain living and high thinking of their college for the immoderate luxury and moderate learning of All Souls'. The Fellows of All Souls certainly lived well, as indeed they do today. The academic year was punctuated by gaudies and oyster suppers, but such occasions were not confined to All Souls. For most of the week, moreover, there were but four or five residents. Only on Saturdays and Sundays did the college fill with lawyers and politicians, civil servants and men of letters, prelates and professors. It was then that Curzon as junior Fellow, or 'Screw', was obliged to mix the mayonnaise, decant the port and, in his first year, deliver a Latin oration. There was no lack of conviviality, but nothing to merit Asquith's repetition of a traditional Latin jest, '*bene nati, mediocriter docti*'.

Nor could it be said with justice that All Souls was deficient in learning. Among those who flourished during Curzon's seven years as a Fellow were A.V.Dicey and W.P.Ker, Hensley Henson and Cosmo Gordon Lang, Charles Oman and John Andrew Doyle, who combined a mastery of domestic business with the writing of authoritative works on the English in America and the breeding of racehorses. A remarkable list can also be compiled of those who sat for the examination and failed. Between 1873 and 1912, unsuccessful candidates for Prize Fellowships included Frederick York Powell, later Regius Professor of Modern History; T.F.Tout, the medieval historian;

Hastings Rashdall, philosopher and historian of the universities of Europe; Frederick Kenyon, President of the British Academy and Director of the British Museum; Lord Robert Cecil, a son of the Prime Minister, Lord Salisbury, and architect of the League of Nations; his brother Hugh, later Lord Quickswood and Provost of Eton College; A.F. Pollard, the Tudor historian; W.S. Holdsworth, Vinerian Professor and historian of English Law; John Buchan, Lord Tweedsmuir; Hilaire Belloc; Philip Kerr, later Lord Lothian and Ambassador to the United States of America; Lewis Namier, the historian of the age of George III; and Philip Guedalla. Some may consider that All Souls lost occasional opportunities of adding lustre to itself; the college prefers to believe that the eminence of those it rejected intensifies the distinction of those few whom it chose. In any case, not all the candidates could have been elected: the maximum quota was two.

The other Prize Fellow of All Souls elected in the autumn of 1883 was Charles Oman. Born exactly a year and a day after Curzon, he was senior scholar successively of Winchester and of New College, Oxford. As part of the Wykehamist custom of the age, he had endured during his first fortnight at school a series of sadistic beatings by senior boys that were either concealed from or ignored by the dons, as Winchester calls her masters. The reign of terror might have lasted longer and become hallowed by tradition had not a peculiarly savage episode come to light: a boy received a thrashing of thirty strokes, five ground ashes being broken in the process. The victim wrote a restrained and manly account of the experience to his father, who ventilated the scandal in the national Press. A shocked Head Master thereupon ordained a gentler regime which Oman and his contemporaries were fortunate to inherit after only two weeks of suffering.

Oman never forgot the misery of that early bullying any more than Curzon effaced from his memory the disciplinary methods of Miss Paraman. Both, however, came to look back without anger on their schooldays, sometimes in unexpected ways. In later life neither took much interest in horse-racing. But each had cause to recall the victory of the colt George Frederick in the Derby of 1874. It enriched Curzon by 12*s*. 6*d*. and a homily from Edward Lyttelton: to Oman, winner of the school sweepstake at Winchester, it brought £7 10*s*., an enormous windfall for a boy of fourteen whose parents were far from rich. Already a discerning numismatist he spent £2 of it on Roman coins.

Bored by the nuances of classical exegesis, he took only a Second in Mods at Oxford. But he was in no danger of missing his First in Greats, buttressing his chances of success by becoming the first undergraduate to add an archaeological subject to the obligatory papers. He went on to take a First in History, followed by a Fellowship at All Souls. And in the same year that Curzon carried off the Arnold Prize, Oman won the Lothian with an essay on 'The

Art of War in the Middle Ages'. All Souls had no cause to regret the elections of 1883.

A later Fellow, Leo Amery, described Oman as 'massive in person, omniscient and categorical on every subject from numismatics and etymology to mediaeval and modern warfare'. He became a lifelong friend of Curzon, although never admitted to the intimate circle of those who exchanged Christian names. Their relationship sprang from shared intellectual pursuits rather than from impulses of the heart: but free from the abrasive touch of political controversy, it endured better than most.

From his travels to remote places, Curzon used to bring back imaginative little presents for Oman: a Sassanian ring picked up in the Khyber Pass, a bag of Bactrian coins bought in the bazaar at Kabul, gold coins of the Guptas and early Mohammedan rupees. Oman repaid these kindnesses by helping Curzon to write his Romanes lecture on 'Frontiers', and in 1907 performed a more lasting service by acting as his chief of staff during the election of a new Chancellor of the University in succession to Goschen. After a spirited campaign, Curzon beat Lord Rosebery by 1,101 votes to 440, and at once wrote with exuberant gratitude to 'the consummate tactician who has laid the plan of battle and the gory warrior who is still knee-deep in the piles of slain'. He continued:

> Again and again I thank you for your inimitable and unselfish exertions so gloriously crowned and only hope that some day I may have an opportunity of repaying some portion of my debt.

The opportunity did not come for thirteen years. Then Oman was created a KBE for his wartime services to the Foreign Office and Curzon sent him a letter of graceful, yet in a sense graceless, approbation:

> I have not so far congratulated you on your recent honour because having enjoyed the happy responsibility of placing you in the list, I felt it would be rather like congratulating myself on my own acumen. Still, lest you should misinterpret my silence, you must allow me to send a line merely to say that your literary and other labours connected with the war so disinterestedly undertaken seemed to me, as they did to others, to make this a very suitable moment for honouring a career that quite apart from this would have merited special recognition.

Curzon rarely missed an opportunity of renewing their ties of friendship at All Souls gaudies. He also maintained a copious correspondence with Oman about Bodiam Castle, which he bought in order to preserve for the nation. From the later humiliations of his political career, it refreshed Curzon to turn to the niceties of medieval warfare: and in letter after letter he consulted the Professor of History on moats and drawbridges, on poles and pikes, on whether the noxious material once hurled down from the perforated stone bosses of ancient fortifications was molten lead or boiling oil, quicklime or pitch.

The nineteenth century offered clever but needy young men wider avenues of advancement than our own age is prepared to admit: and it was at All Souls that Curzon made almost the only friend of his life who had not enjoyed the conventional education of his own class. Poverty and the lack of a formal schooling had prevented Herbert Hensley Henson from going up to Oxford other than as a 'tosher', or non-collegiate student, a status that smacked of both academic and social inferiority. Having, in spite of this handicap, taken a First in History, he was encouraged by W.H. Hutton to enter for the Fellowship examination at All Souls. He was elected a year after Curzon.

It was the turning point of his life. In a community utterly free from hierarchical barriers, Henson was readily admitted to the society of the learned and the eminent on equal terms.* He took Holy Orders and received the college living of Barking; then he attracted the notice of Lord Salisbury, who as Prime Minister nominated him to the Rectory of St Margaret's, Westminster, and to a Canonry of Westminster Abbey. From that moment his advancement to high ecclesiastical office was assured. But even after twenty years as Bishop of Durham he could not assuage a regret – perhaps even a grievance – that he had never been to a great public school. When the Etonian Welldon, recently appointed Headmaster of Harrow, preached at the University Church in 1886, Henson wrote in his journal: 'He is a young man, tall and stalwart, yet withal vigorous and manly. He interpolated into the Bidding Prayers petitions for Eton and Harrow, which was bad taste.'

From beneath a formidable pair of eyebrows that more than made up for his lack of inches, Henson scrutinized the world and found it wanting in both morality and manners. He was a trenchant talker, diarist and correspondent, whose command of the written and spoken word sometimes concealed his genuine humility. Not all his colleagues at All Souls cared to hear him speak of 'that state of resentful coma which is dignified by the Universities with the name of research'.

It would hardly have been surprising if the personalities of Henson and Oman had grated on each other. For all his confident and stylish pronouncements, Henson was disconcertingly prickly and watchful against being patronized; and Curzon could be brutally insensitive. Yet their relationship never fell below affection. On one of the saddest days of Curzon's life, while Welldon conducted the funeral of Mary Curzon at Kedleston, it was Henson who preached at the memorial service in London.

In later years they met at the House of Lords, and when separated they corresponded fitfully on the great issues of the day. 'A melancholy suspicion begins to grow and fix itself in my mind that the British Empire is breaking up,' Henson wrote to Curzon in 1922. 'May Heaven grant that my fears be as baseless as they are distressing!'

* A very junior Fellow once addressed the greatest of the college's honorary Fellows as Mr Gladstone. The old man smiled and said: 'Gladstone here, please.'

For all their affinity, Curzon and Henson differed sharply on the merits of a third contemporary at All Souls. Cosmo Gordon Lang had come up to Balliol from Glasgow University, enjoyed similar triumphs to those of Curzon at the Oxford Union and the Canning Club, taken a Second in Greats followed by a First in History, and been elected to his Fellowship in 1886. He took Holy Orders, became Dean of Divinity at Magdalen College, laboured in a densely populated parish, ascended effortlessly to the episcopate and was Archbishop successively of York and Canterbury.

With gracious condescension, Lang would refer in public to 'my old friend from All Souls days'. Henson neither appreciated nor reciprocated such blandishments, and in that exquisite calligraphy which he held to be the mark of a civilized man rarely touched on Lang's personality without sharpening his quill or adding acid to his inkpot. 'He had,' Henson wrote of him, 'like most Scots, an unerring instinct in the choice of friends, drawing towards the titled and socially or professionally influential with the sure procedure of iron moving to a magnet.'

The ease with which Lang drew ahead in the race for preferment contributed to Henson's antipathy. But what eroded the last traces of goodwill was Lang's reaction to the nomination of Henson as Bishop of Hereford. The appointment was controversial and there were some who doubted Henson's orthodoxy. In congratulating him, the new Bishop recorded, Lang was 'embarrassed and lukewarm, evidently scenting trouble ahead'. And when the Archbishop of York declined to attend his consecration, Henson never forgot or forgave what he regarded less as a personal slight than as an act of treason to the brotherhood of All Souls.

Lang had cause to regret his betrayal, and on hearing of Henson's translation from Hereford to the Northern Province, wrote mournfully: 'I expect a good deal of mischief and worry from Durham.' A characteristic encounter is said to have taken place at Bishopthorpe, the Archbishop's palace near York. Henson overheard Lang showing his new portrait by Orpen to a group of other guests with the complacent comment: 'They say that in that portrait I look proud, pompous and prelatical.' 'And to which of those epithets does your Grace take exception?' Henson enquired.

Less sensitive than Henson to social pretensions, Curzon found only pleasure in Lang's company, and their intimacy came to be blessed by Queen Victoria herself. 'The Queen saw the other day a great friend of the Viceroy,' she wrote to India in the last year of her life, 'the Revd. Canon Lang, who is a most able and excellent man.'

Lang also held the unofficial but honorific office in All Souls of 'Lord Mallard'. It is said that when workmen were laying the foundations of the college, they disturbed a mallard which over the centuries became the theme of much traditional mummery. There were torchlight processions with a stuffed bird dangling on a pole, and a song to its glory which for more than thirty years Lang would sing in a voice of memorable sweetness at the gaudies on All Souls Day and at the annual bursar's dinner. The refrain went, 'It was a swapping, swapping Mallard.' In 1901, Lang found time during the ceremony to send Curzon a single-word telegram to India: 'Swapping.' Back came the Viceroy's reply: 'It was.'

Some resented the influence which Curzon supposedly exerted over Lang. When both were in middle life, a secretary of the Archbishop once pointed to a portrait of Curzon and said: 'That's the man who has been his curse.' Lang never modelled himself deliberately on Curzon; but there were more than superficial resemblances. Each came increasingly to revere an ordered society in which forms mattered almost as much as creeds; each cherished a sense of occasion, even of drama, and cared for the elaborations of ceremony and the arts of oratory; each could relapse into bonhomie with a charm of manner that was not wholly unconscious. During rare moments of leisure, too, their pleasures were similar. Curzon read detective stories – he called them 'ephemeral literature' – and Lang filled his bookshelves with yellow-backed French novels.

It was Curzonian that, having become Primate of the Northern Province, Lang should determine never again to enter a shop in York. But it was no less Curzonian that he should divide his summer holiday between Balmoral and a tiny cottage as sparsely furnished as Curzon's plain little bedroom in Carlton House Terrace. Each, too, recognized a spiritual quality in the other that was sometimes hidden from the world. When Lang as a young cleric determined to desert the comfort of Oxford in order to minister to the busy parish of Portsea, Curzon was the only one of his friends to applaud the decision. Thirty years later, preaching at Curzon's funeral service, Lang absolved him of just those charges of egotism and arrogance with which he himself had sometimes been reproached: 'Faults and failings there may have been in that forceful, vital, masterful personality, but they were of the kind we can leave trustfully in the pardoning and perfecting hands of God.'

The All Souls Betting Book, in which for more than a century and a half the Fellows have made light-hearted wagers with and about each other, casts an agreeable glow over the intimacy of their society. Within three weeks of his election, Curzon was betting Rowland Prothero* half a crown on a minute point of University athletics: he lost. He recouped, however, three months later by betting Oman five shillings that E. A. Freeman would be the next Regius Professor of Modern History. He bet on general elections; on the

* 1851–1937. President of the Board of Agriculture 1916–19. Created Lord Ernle.

length of the Codrington Library; on whether England would be, or would have been, at war with Russia within a year of May 1885; on the weight of a tennis racket.

The results of such wagers were often, as the Great Duke of Wellington said of Waterloo, 'the nearest run thing you ever saw in your life'. In 1885 Curzon bet J.R. Maguire, the future MP for North Donegal, that Maguire would be married before him. Ten years later Maguire won the bet, having deliberately postponed his wedding for forty-eight hours after Curzon had announced the date of his. But it was Curzon's turn to scrape home by similar astuteness when he bet that the number of times the name of H. Hensley Henson appeared in the book was nearer twenty than thirty: his opponent paid under protest on discovering that H. Hensley Henson appeared twenty-three times and H.H. Henson four times.

Henson's wagers reveal a catholicity of interests. He bets in shillings on his weight being at least four stone less than Oman's, and in magnums of champagne that he will not be married by 1897 (he was married in 1902). More significant is that in the spring of 1886 a friend so doubted the seriousness of Henson's intention to take Holy Orders that he bet him half a crown he would not be an Anglican clergyman within two years. Helped in part by the persuasion of Arthur Hardinge, he was ordained on 5 June 1887. And a few weeks after making the original bet, he promised to give the same Fellow £5 if and when he became a bishop; by 1918, however, when he at last was appointed to Hereford, his opponent had been dead fourteen years.

All Souls also took an interest in how Curzon's career would develop. In June 1886 Oman bet seven shillings to six that within the next fifteen years Curzon would have been a member of a Cabinet. By June 1901, however, Curzon had done no better politically than become Parliamentary Under-Secretary for Foreign Affairs. Incidentally he had been Viceroy of India since 1898: but that did not count and Oman lost his bet.

Unburdened either by pupils or by academic research, a young Fellow of All Souls might have been tempted to idle away his first year or two in college. That, for all his high spirits, was not Curzon's habit. Within a few months of his election he won the Arnold Prize, and subsequent chapters will show how relentlessly he equipped himself for a public life that began with his election to Parliament in the summer of 1886. He travelled abroad for months each year. He mastered the problems and personalities of current politics. He had himself adopted as Conservative candidate for South Derbyshire. He wrote thoughtful articles for the quarterlies and execrable limericks for the *Oxford Review*. He enjoyed the society open to men of promise.

After dining out one evening in 1885, Gladstone observed:

Mr. George Curzon is evidently the possessor of quite extraordinary ability and he will, if I mistake not, be one day the Conservative Prime Minister; but I am bound to say that what struck me painfully in him was the absence of any sort of reverence for anything like age or tradition.

They nevertheless shared an almost passionate allegiance to All Souls. Mr Gladstone, elected an honorary Fellow in 1858, went into residence there for ten days at the beginning of 1890. Curzon, travelling in Persia, could not be present at the decorous revels, but by good fortune two young Fellows, Charles Oman and C.R.L. Fletcher, each wrote and subsequently published an illuminating account of the visit. Never was the Grand Old Man more absorbed in his surroundings, more earnest, more eloquent, more tireless, more exhausting – in a word, more Gladstonian. He gave an incomprehensible lecture at the Union on 'The Connection of Homeric with Modern Assyriological Studies'. He read the lesson in chapel. He so delighted in wearing cap and gown that he would hardly be parted from them. He recalled that in his day no undergraduate could have been dressed for less than £30, whereas nowadays £10 would do. And when the junior Fellow one night by mistake filled up a claret decanter with port, Gladstone topped up his half-empty glass of wine, took a sip and said: 'Really, Mr. Warden, this claret of yours is a *most* generous brand.'

Curzon shared a like regard for All Souls and even after his Prize Fellowship had run out in the autumn of 1890 he took advantage of every college occasion open to a quondam Fellow. In 1917, as a member of the War Cabinet, he wrote to Sir Charles Grant Robertson, college historian and his official correspondent as Chancellor of the University: 'At the Cabinet table there are almost always present two Fellows – Young (as secretary) and myself. Frequently two others, Prothero and Adams. Not bad.'*

He was thwarted, however, in an ambitious design that would simultaneously have commemorated his Chancellorship of the University and adorned the college. He proposed to have made a series of stained glass lights to replace the plain eighteenth-century ones in the great window of the Codrington Library. His own likeness would occupy the central position, and around him would hang other eminent men associated with All Souls and the University, such as King Henry VI, Chichele, Codrington, Sheldon and the Duke of Wellington. The Fellows hesitated, not wishing to hurt Curzon's feelings. Then W.P. Ker, the scholar of English and Scandinavian literature intervened, protesting against a plan that would turn the green and silver light of the library into the likeness of the smoking-room in a transatlantic liner. The college was thus persuaded to decline Curzon's magniloquent benefaction.†

* G.M. Young. 1882–1959. Civil servant and historian. W.G.S. Adams. 1874–1966. Editor of the War Cabinet reports and later Warden of All Souls College.

† On the other side of Radcliffe Square, Brasenose College has had no such inhibitions. The plaque erected in the ante-chapel to the memory of Walter Pater depicts the tree of

Curzon was wounded by the apparent ingratitude of All Souls, although he continued fitfully to enjoy the life of the college and to entertain there as Chancellor of the University. In 1921, however, when Queen Mary received an honorary degree, the drains of All Souls were being repaired and Curzon had to hold his luncheon at Balliol – '*also* my college', he explained to his Royal guest. Only the unremitting attention he gave to the smallest detail of any such occasion saved it from what in his eyes might have been a social disaster. While preparing for the entertainment, the Bursar of Balliol sent the Chancellor a specimen menu. Curzon returned it with a single sentence written across one corner: 'Gentlemen do not take soup at luncheon.'

knowledge. The heavily moustached face of Pater grows out of the top of the trunk, surrounded by branches which bear the heads of his four peers – Leonardo and Michelangelo, Plato and Dante.

Chapter Nine

PRELUDE TO PARLIAMENT

> I am glad to hear you have had Sir Stafford to Luncheon, you had better have young Curzon, whom you met here, instead of all those Radicals, more particularly Chamberlain, who is a blackguard and would like to be Prime Minister in order to turn everything topsy-turvy.
>
> – *Lady Chesterfield to Lady Dorothy Nevill, June 1884*

Writing to his father from Wixenford at the age of eleven, Curzon casually mentioned that he supposed Parliament would soon be opening. It was an interest that never deserted him. He followed the affairs of Westminster as a schoolboy, dedicated himself to the Conservative cause at the Oxford Union and the Canning Club, and during University vacations spent long hours in the galleries of the House of Commons or on the steps of the throne in the House of Lords, that undignified perch traditionally reserved for Privy Councillors, the Dean of Westminster and the eldest sons of peers.

Disraeli entirely captured his imagination. On one of his first visits to the Commons, Curzon saw him dressed in the bizarre fashion of a black velvet coat and check trousers; a year or two later he noticed how in the Upper House they had given place to the frock-coated sobriety of elder statesmanship. 'There was an air of expectancy whenever he spoke,' Curzon wrote. 'Men were on the lookout for the jewelled phrase, the exquisite epigram, the stinging sneer. He was like the conjuror on a platform, whose audience with open mouths awaited the next trick.' During the critical debate on Afghanistan in December 1878, Curzon sat through a long evening to hear him deliver his famous peroration against the doctrine of peace at any price and call upon the House to brand 'these dogmas, these deleterious dogmas, with the reprobation of the peers of England'. The division took place at 2.30 in the morning, after which Curzon left by train for a distant shoot.

Curzon was still an undergraduate when a sense of history persuaded him to attend Disraeli's funeral at Hughenden. 'I recall the profound and unfavourable impression created by the absence of Mr. Gladstone,' he wrote, 'but this omission was more than rectified by the magnanimous tribute paid to his memory a few days later by his great survivor in the House of Commons.'

More than twenty years after Disraeli's death, Curzon was invited to write his official biography, a task already declined by both Brett and Rosebery. He refused, claiming with an excess of modesty that he did not possess the perception or the analytical powers or the literary style. A few jottings about his early hero are all that remain of his long hours at Westminster.

With Mr Gladstone, Curzon achieved a respectful familiarity that bordered on friendship. During his first eight years as a Member of Parliament he sat opposite him in the House of Commons: but for as many years before, he rarely missed an important speech by the greatest orator in his recollection – 'indeed almost the only orator'. Curzon's description is worthy of his subject:

> His movements on the bench restless and eager, his demeanour when on his legs, whether engaged in answering a simple question, expounding an intricate Bill, or thundering in vehement declamation, his dramatic gestures, his deep and rolling voice with its wide compass and marked northern accent, his flashing eye, his almost incredible command of ideas and words, made a combination of irresistible fascination and power.

Every mannerism of the Grand Old Man, like those of Winston Churchill in a later age, was noted and dilated on and chuckled over. How he would point his finger in scorn at an opponent; how he would swing right round and appeal to his supporters; how he would scratch the top of his scalp with the extended thumb of his right hand; how he would sport a flower in his buttonhole on great occasions; how he would unwittingly warn the House of a long speech in prospect (Curzon once heard him speak for three and a half hours in introducing the first Home Rule Bill) by producing a little bottle of beaten egg and sherry. 'It stimulates, it lubricates,' he explained to John Morley.

From the galleries of the Commons the undergraduate, and later the young Fellow of All Souls, came to know every oratorical gesture by heart: but he could not give Gladstone his political allegiance. 'Why O why are you not a Liberal, George?' Edward Lyttelton asked him in 1881. In a sentence, it was because Liberalism seemed to offer neither contented government at home nor the high adventure of imperialism abroad. For those political aims Curzon turned to the Tory Democracy of Lord Randolph Churchill, younger son of the seventh Duke of Marlborough, who had been elected for the borough of Woodstock* in 1874. It was Disraeli's romantic conception of Young England brought up to date: aristocratic Conservative leadership combining with the working classes as a political force. Against so bold a

* It is on the doorstep of Blenheim Palace.

strategy, Liberalism could be made to appear both timid and condescending.

Churchill's opportunity came with the sweeping triumph of Mr Gladstone in the general election of 1880. On the Liberal front bench the Prime Minister was flanked by such formidable lieutenants as Chamberlain and Hartington, Harcourt and Dilke. The official Conservative Opposition by contrast was inadequate and discredited. Disraeli had gone to the Upper House – he described himself as 'dead, but in Elysian Fields' – and Sir Stafford Northcote, for all his experience of public life and sensible judgement of national issues, was too amiable, too diffident and too ailing to breathe life into the defeated party he led only in name. To the indignation of the Liberals and the embarrassment of his own front bench, Churchill determined to assume the burden himself.

He had only six years parliamentary experience; but he was not without allies. The Fourth Party, as it came to be called, was an insolent partnership consisting of Lord Randolph; Henry Drummond Wolff, a diplomatist; John Gorst, a lawyer; and, for a year or two, Arthur Balfour. Their purpose was twofold: to avenge the humiliating rout of 1880 and to ensure that the Conservative Party acquired effective and imaginative leadership. The first of these aims was to be secured by embracing the cause of working-class welfare: the second by the advent of Lord Salisbury.

Thirty years later, with a Viceregal frown of disapproval, Curzon recalled the scenes that Lord Randolph incited in the Commons: 'The tomahawk was always in his hand. It is impossible to describe the gleeful ferocity with which he swept off the scalps of friend and foe. Some of these speeches contained the grossest errors of taste, and nearly all were marked by a vein of almost burlesque exaggeration.' At the time, however, Curzon delighted in the cavalier tactics and intricacies of Parliamentary procedure by which Churchill usurped the power of decision from the leaders of the Conservative Party in the Commons. When his own front bench chose to remain silent on whether Charles Bradlaugh should be allowed to take his seat, it was Lord Randolph who, in the name of Christianity, challenged Gladstone's apparent indulgence of atheism. He played on the Prime Minister's subtleties of mind and infinite shades of meaning as on an organ, revelling in the ferocious prolixity he provoked and its obstructive effect on the Government's legislative programme. On the platform, too, he attracted immense audiences by the savagery of his philippics: who else would have dared to describe Gladstone as 'the Moloch of Midlothian'? In more satirical vein he mocked his addiction to felling harmless trees. 'The forest laments in order that Mr. Gladstone may perspire', deserves a place in any anthology of political invective.

Only occasionally did Gladstone descend to striking back at the Fourth Party with their own weapon of ridicule. It happened once when Churchill, Wolff and Gorst, in their haste to harry the Government, failed to coordinate their tactics: each in succession made a speech that was effective in itself but destructive of the arguments deployed by the other two. Mr Gladstone rose and quoted the first chapter of the Book of Joel: 'That which the palmerworm hath left hath the locust eaten; and that which the locust hath left hath the cankerworm eaten; and that which the cankerworm hath left hath the caterpiller eaten.'

For the hierarchy of his own party, Churchill reserved an insolence even more offensive than the jibes with which he mocked the Liberals. He dubbed the bearded Northcote, 'The Goat'. Two other solemn colleagues, Sir Richard Cross and Mr W.H. Smith, became 'Marshall and Snelgrove', and their attachment to the domestic virtues of the middle classes earned them the sneering appellation, 'Lords of suburban villas ... owners of vineries and pineries'. Towards Cross in particular he behaved with studied brutality. Speaking once to an amendment which did not appear on the printed order paper, Churchill groped for the precise words. Cross saw an opportunity of propitiating his tormentor, so passed him a manuscript note of the amendment which he had made. Lord Randolph merely said: 'A pretty pass we have come to in the House of Commons when we have to consider amendments passed about from hand to hand on dirty bits of paper.'

'In Parliament,' Curzon wrote to Farrer on 2 December 1882, 'the session is just over. Randolph Churchill has made most remarkable strides in estimation both inside and outside the House. He may not always have been judicious, but he has shown extreme capacity and is walking away from all his contemporaries.'

Curzon's much apostrophized visits to Blenheim as an undergraduate allowed him to pay personal allegiance to the leader of the Fourth Party at the outset of the venture. 'A smart fellow,' he wrote to Farrer in the autumn of 1880, 'possessing all the audacity which his performances give him credit for.' He began to speak at meetings in his support and sent a stream of articles to the periodical Press. Churchill was grateful and wrote with unusual cordiality: 'I must write you a line to thank you very much for your speech at Woodstock last week. I hear from two or three reliable sources that your audience was interested and delighted with the way in which you treated the topics of importance at the present moment.' By November 1882, Curzon's persistent efforts on behalf of the Conservative cause brought him gratifying recognition. The episode is best told in a letter to 'Dearest George' from St John Brodrick, who had been elected for West Surrey two years before:

This is only a line in case you don't hear of it from others to say that Sir H. James [Attorney-General] introduced you to the House early on Saturday morning in somewhat of the following flattering language:

'And here I must be allowed to refer to a remark made in a public speech by a gentleman who when he enters this House will rise to high distinction among the party opposite, I mean Mr. Curzon (query – Who's Curzon etc. etc. all round) who said at Derby a few days ago, "*Business, if it is to be business, must be brief*"' (Cheers).

The rest I didn't catch being engaged in assuring my neighbour (who was inquisitive) that you were not a Howe, or a Teynham, or a Zouche. ...*

In March 1884, within a few days of winning the Arnold Prize, Curzon was adopted as Conservative candidate for South Derbyshire, the sitting Member, Sir Henry Wilmot, having announced that he would retire at the end of the current Parliament. The prospect of a Liberal defeat loomed large as the session advanced. There were embarrassing entanglements and humiliating setbacks in Egypt, in Afghanistan, in the Transvaal and above all in the Sudan, where General Gordon was besieged and murdered at the beginning of 1885. Ireland was in a state of perpetual eruption tempered only by coercion and reaching its climax in the assassination in Phoenix Park of the new Chief Secretary for Ireland, Lord Frederick Cavendish, who had married a sister of Edward and Alfred Lyttelton. The Government eventually blundered to its doom in June on a proposal to increase income tax from 6*d.* to 8*d.* in the pound. In normal circumstances there would have been an immediate general election. An electoral Redistribution Bill, however, had just become law after agreement between the parties. Old constituencies had been abolished but new ones not yet defined. During the interim period it would obviously be unsatisfactory if the country continued to be ruled by an administration which had just lost the confidence of the House of Commons. Lord Salisbury, therefore, without enthusiasm but with that sense of public duty that marked his entire career, agreed to form a caretaker Government.

That the Queen should have sent for Salisbury rather than for Northcote – who was deeply mortified and did not long survive that and other disappointments – was in itself a triumph for Lord Randolph and his adherents. From the other side of the Commons that shrewd Radical, Joseph Chamberlain, whose relations with Churchill were turbulent but ultimately amicable, had observed in the previous year:

Tory democracy, of which we shall hear a great deal in the future, is represented in this House by the Member for Woodstock. I pay the greatest attention to anything he says, because I find that what he says today his leaders will say tomorrow. They follow him with halting steps, somewhat unwillingly; but they always follow him. They may not always like the prescription he makes up for them; but they always swallow it.

And now they had swallowed it to the extent of making him Secretary of State for India at the age of thirty-six, with responsibility for annexing Upper

* Peerages held by other branches of the Curzon family.

Burma. Nor were his henchmen forgotten. Gorst became Solicitor-General; Arthur Balfour, President of the Local Government Board; and Wolff was despatched on a special mission to Turkey. It was a splendid victory for a party which, as Winston Churchill wrote, could be contained by one single enormous sofa.

Curzon hoped that after the general election in November his own assiduous attention to Conservative fortunes would see him in the House of Commons as Member for South Derbyshire. Meanwhile he received a mark of high favour from the Prime Minister himself. Lord Salisbury invited him to become one of his assistant private secretaries.

'It is the shadow before the substance,' a friend assured him, 'and I feel that I am only getting my hand in to congratulate you some day, when your shoulders will be considered broad enough and your head old enough to bear great responsibilities.' To serve a Minister as a junior private secretary was a valuable apprenticeship to political power. Brett worked for Hartington, Farrer for Northcote, Leveson Gower for Gladstone; and in 1883, W. H. Smith had written to Curzon urging him to follow in their footsteps.

The kinsmen or family friends of Ministers, they were prepared, for little or no pay, to make themselves useful in return for the opportunity of learning how the State administered itself. Today their places would be occupied by promising young civil servants, already earmarked for promotion. In the nineteenth century, however, the structure of Whitehall was less rigid and the wheels of government more readily lubricated by patronage. The duties of a junior private secretary, moreover, were largely routine. Not until the close of the century was the typewriter considered a seemly instrument in the transaction of official business, and all correspondence had to be laboriously copied into letter books. Such was the drudgery of aspiring young men who had just spent years reading for Greats or for the Classical Tripos.

It is not surprising that Leveson Gower should have fallen asleep one hot day in Downing Street when making a précis of some tedious documents. He was awoken by the Prime Minister, the only occasion in his recollection on which his chief ever entered the private secretaries' office. Characteristically, Gladstone regarded himself as the guardian not only of Leveson Gower's official life but also of his spiritual welfare: and the private secretary used to relate how his mid-septuagenarian master deprived him of a late Sunday breakfast by sweeping him off to a distant church and back at a relentless four miles an hour.

Salisbury, too, drew his new assistant private secretary into the family circle. They had much in common to bridge the thirty years that separated them. Salisbury came of a line a little less ancient than Curzon's, but like him he achieved more eminence than any kinsman for centuries past. The Prime

Minister had been too miserable as an Eton boy to share Curzon's romantic reverence for the school. But both had experienced comparative poverty which drove them to earn money by journalism and both had been fired by ambition to become Fellows of All Souls. Their intellectual interests varied. Curzon absorbed history and the classics. Salisbury grudged the pressures of office that kept him from his laboratories. Everybody had their gin shops, he used to say, and his were book stalls and stores of scientific instruments. Lady Gwendolen Cecil, Salisbury's daughter and biographer, has told of the occasion when the household at Hatfield was roused by a loud explosion. Her father emerged from his laboratory, covered with blood and severely cut, to explain to his terrified family – with evident satisfaction at the accurate working out of chemical laws – that he had been experimenting with sodium in an insufficiently dried retort.

As Lord President of the Council in later years, Curzon had Ministerial responsibility for scientific research. His antipathy to the subject may well have been inspired by Salisbury's excursions into physics. Hatfield was one of the first houses to have electric light.* 'There were evenings,' Lady Gwendolen has recalled, 'when the household had to grope about in semi-darkness, illuminated only by a dim red glow such as comes from a half-extinct fire; there were others when a perilous brilliancy culminated in miniature storms of lightning, ending in complete collapse.' There was also an early telephone system, and from all over the house could be heard the voice of its owner testing it with the words: 'Hey diddle diddle, the cat and the fiddle; the cow jumped over the moon.'

Salisbury was as assiduous a worker as Curzon. But whereas the private secretary trained himself early in life to write at speed whether travelling, at his desk or in bed, his chief required absolute seclusion for his thoughts to flow. Downing Street he spurned, except for the most official business. He preferred to use his room at the Foreign Office – he was Foreign Secretary as well as Prime Minister – or his house in Arlington Street. Above all, he liked to escape by train to Hatfield. For this purpose the horse which drew his brougham had been trained to do the journey from the Foreign Office to King's Cross in seventeen minutes. So sensitive was Salisbury to interruption that each room at Hatfield where he worked was fitted with double doors widely spaced enough to prevent him from hearing any rattling on the locked outer one. His secretaries did not appreciate these defences and would attempt daring raids on the Prime Minister's papers – only to find that he had tricked them by transferring himself to some unexpected retreat. It was a symptom of a defect which he shared with Curzon: neither was willing or able to delegate responsibility to subordinates. When remonstrated with on the waste of energy it involved, Salisbury would always return the same

* Electric light was installed at Hatfield in 1881 and at Kedleston seven years later. All Souls waited until 1909 before committing themselves to it.

answer: 'I am too busy not to do the work myself.' But, unlike Curzon when he too came reluctantly to employ private secretaries, the Prime Minister never deviated from a high and sustained standard of courtesy:

His affability [wrote Curzon in his diary] is almost embarrassing, for he poses as the recipient rather than as the donor of the obligation. He pays as much attention to the words of a boy of 21 as to those of a statesman of 70. When I mentioned my willingness, now that I have no occupation, to do any work for him that he was good enough to give me, he expressed himself in terms of the warmest gratitude. He said he should be very glad of my assistance in the compilation of speeches and the like – a kind of work which his other secretaries could not so easily undertake.

Three weeks later, Curzon described one such mission:

I called on Lord Salisbury, having received a summons from him. He wanted me to look up all the facts connected with the suppression of the Catholic Association in '29 by Peel's and Wellington's Government before they repealed the Catholic Disabilities. It was with a view to the proposed proclamation of the National League. He did not want me to draw up a report, but to master the facts and be able to answer questions.

I spent the afternoon in the British Museum Reading Room over the Annual Register, Hansard, etc. I found an extraordinary coincidence between the circs. and events of the two times. But Peel was successful. Will Lord S. be the same?

On the following day Curzon took the result of his researches to Arlington Street:

Lord S. asked me questions and listened to my replies, taking no notes. He is a man of singularly powerful memory. At Newport (October 1885) he delivered his famous speech 1¾ hours long without a single note from beginning to end. I was within five feet of him at the time and could see. I fancy he ponders his speeches beforehand but commits little or nothing to memory. And yet there is a wonderful literary finish about the result. Rosebery told me at Mentmore last year that he thought Lord S. the ablest and most polished speaker in England – high praise from an opponent who is himself a master of the same style.

Curzon loved oratory for itself, studied the art as other men pondered the points of a racehorse or the pleasing proportions of a garden, and carried it into an impatient age that scarcely bothered to hide its scorn for such adornment. 'Whether in the House of Lords, or at a Lord Mayor's banquet, or at a public meeting,' Curzon wrote of Salisbury, 'he appeared to suggest embodied wisdom; he was the philosopher meditating aloud. It seemed a mere accident that the reflection was conducted audibly and in public rather than in the recesses of the library at Hatfield. His massive head, bowed upon his chest, his precise and measured tones, his total absence of gesture, his grave but subtle irony, sustained the illusion.' It was indeed a transformation from his turbulent early days in Parliament when, on being urged that his comparison of Gladstone to an attorney needed a public apology, he readily gave one – to all attorneys.

Curzon's first attempt to enter the House of Commons in 1885 coincided with a sharp improvement in the conduct of parliamentary elections. The Ballot Act of 1872 had ensured that voting should be secret, a measure which politicians of the old school regarded as an affront to the sturdy character of the race. Dr Jowett, however, approved of the reform; and a scholar of Balliol, having said in the Master's presence that he thought secret voting un-English, was cut short by the question, 'Do you think bribery and intimidation English?' The Corrupt Practices Act of 1883 made further changes in electoral law, ending the scandal by which each vote had sometimes cost the successful candidate as much as £1 and the unsuccessful candidate only a fraction less.

Although spared such distasteful bargaining, Curzon laboured under other handicaps. The new register introduced by the Redistribution Act added two million voters to the electorate. Curzon's constituency of South Derbyshire was drastically affected and its former balance upset by an influx of enfranchised miners and factory workers. Nor was his manner on the platform adapted – or even adaptable – to unsophisticated audiences. Sometimes, as at Repton, he was encouraged by an attentive row of schoolmasters: but their votes were no more valuable than those of the artisan. 'His eloquent and scholarly orations,' a reporter wrote in the *Derby Mercury*, 'which have inspired in the more educated portions of his audiences nothing but admiration and respect, have gone over the heads of his more ignorant hearers, and have left, probably, in many cases, nothing but a confused notion that he was "a very clever young gentleman".'

He found the grind of electioneering distasteful. Lord Cranborne, the Prime Minister's eldest son, who was standing for north-east Lancashire, wrote to him from Darwen in the middle of the campaign:

> I am sorry to hear your account of your own chances – I trust that the gloomy vein in which your thoughts run is due as much to the disgusting character of the work in which we are engaged as to your prospects.
>
> This kind of thing is indeed beastly. I remember telling you I was going to have only 12 meetings – I was young and sanguine – I have had about 25 reported meetings (not to speak of 3 or 4 unreported) and I have arranged a lot more. I gather that this is nothing to the number of meetings you have, and that being so, I am only surprised that your gloom has not driven you to suicide.

Curzon nevertheless continued to carry out a burdensome programme. A fortnight before the poll he wrote to Brodrick:

I have been for three days canvassing among the collieries and potteries of my worst district. You have no conception of the tyranny which prevails. No shop-keeper dare admit he is a Conservative, for fear of losing his custom. Even the publicans have to pretend that they are Radicals ... Some of the men won't so much as speak to me or look at me ... I had my forty-ninth meeting to-night and have fourteen more before the poll on November the 27th. It is my only chance, as the other man is not much of a speaker.

A particularly disagreeable occasion was when he went to talk to the railway men during their dinner break – he called it their luncheon hour – and was received with a volley of paper pellets filled with soot. It was in every sense the writing on the wall.

The result, announced on 28 November, showed that Curzon had been beaten by 2,092 votes in a poll of 10,280. 'Those miners are the very devil,' Cranborne wrote in commiseration, 'the great Ashmead told me he has calculated we have lost some 72 seats by the miners' vote.' The Prime Minister, too, sent a sympathetic letter to his assistant private secretary.

My dear Curzon,

A line to tell you how sincerely sorry we all were to hear of your mishap in Derbyshire. For some reason or other the opinion of the miners seems to have set very strongly against us everywhere and new voters show that inclination which it seems they have to get over like the distemper. I am very sorry indeed that the effect has been that for the time you will be shut out from the natural theatre where your powers could assert themselves. I hope sincerely it may be for a very short time.

Ever yours truly,
Salisbury.

Miners, railway workers and other newcomers to the electoral roll undoubtedly swayed the result. It is true that a few years later George Leveson Gower said of the same constituency: 'They were very pleasant audiences, chiefly railway men, the sort of fellows who sing songs and take up points quickly and are readily warmed into enthusiasm.' But he was a Liberal.

The general election of November 1885 produced a confused political pattern. The Liberals had a majority of more than eighty seats over the Conservatives and could count on the support of eighty-six Irish Members if they brought in Home Rule; such a course, however, would inevitably split the Liberal party and provoke the anti-Irish dissidents to support the Conservatives. Salisbury's situation was no happier than Gladstone's; he too was unable to reconcile the two bodies of opinion within his party, one demanding repressive measures against the Irish nationalists, the other willing to negotiate. 'I am feverishly eager to be out,' Salisbury wrote to a colleague, 'internally as well as externally our position as a Government is intolerable.'

He decided, however, to remain Prime Minister until the new Parliament met in January. And Curzon concluded that a young man still in search of a seat could do no better than continue to serve his leader as an assistant private secretary.

'At Hatfield,' he recorded in the diary that he kept, alas, for barely a month, 'a great deal of politics is talked, but it is in the shape of desultory criticism. One never gets any idea of what is likely to happen. I asked Lord S. his views about the possible duration of the Govt. He quite expected to be turned out before long – but thought the sword might not fall till Easter.' The Queen's business must meanwhile be carried on, and Curzon saw something of diplomacy as well as of politics.

Holding the offices both of Prime Minister and of Foreign Secretary, Salisbury used to receive foreign ambassadors to the Court of St James, a task he sometimes found so intolerably boring that he would stick a paperknife into his thigh to keep awake. Curzon, a guest at Hatfield, encountered the most persistent of them, Rustem Pasha, the new Turkish Ambassador. 'Neither a Turk nor a Mussulman,' he wrote, 'but an Italian and a Catholic: a supple man, it struck me, but of inflexible purpose. He spoke of his Governorship in the Lebanon. His methods were those of Cromwell with the Irish or Bismarck with the German Poles.' Salisbury rarely refused to see him. 'If I don't give him something to write home,' he explained, 'they will probably dock his next month's salary.'

Curzon found more than one old friend established in Lord Salisbury's inner circle. Wallace Cochrane-Baillie, who in 1879 doctored the mulled claret of the Canning Club with castor oil, had survived the disgrace to become another of the Prime Minister's assistant private secretaries. Arthur Hardinge, too, had recently been selected from the junior ranks of the Foreign Office to be Lord Salisbury's précis-writer – through the influence of Cranborne, he believed. It was a covetable job, requiring more from its holder than an ability to prepare digests of documents, and generally it marked him for early promotion. 'With you and Hardinge to attend to the public weal in a thoroughly Etonian spirit,' another friend wrote to Curzon, 'I hope the State will prosper.' When the Government changed early in 1886 and Lord Rosebery became Foreign Secretary, the post of précis-writer, inevitably it seemed, went to yet another member of the Balliol coterie, Cecil Spring Rice.

Curzon attended the obsequies of the Conservative administration. On the morning of 27 January 1886, he called at Arlington Street with the fruits of his researches for a speech. 'Lord Salisbury said he hardly expected to have the opportunity of using my information as the Government would probably be out that night.' So it proved. The crucial issue was an amendment to the Address that traditionally opens each session of Parliament. It demanded that agricultural labourers should have facilities for acquiring smallholdings –

a policy that has gone down to history under the catch phrase of 'three acres and a cow'. For the mover of the controversial amendment, Curzon had only contempt: 'Jesse Collings is a dull old twaddler, but has earned the right to speak on the subject by making himself and it a bore.' Since negotiations between the Conservatives and the Irish Members had proved abortive, most members of the Government welcomed an end to their precarious position at Westminster. 'The division was 329 to 250 – you might have heard the Parnellites shouting on St Stephen's Green. Government out, and seemingly very glad of it too. What will the other fellows do? I am sorry we are out, for there is an end to my work with Lord Salisbury for the present. He wants very little help when in Opposition, being particularly self-dependent and personally industrious.'

Yet Curzon had no cause for dismay. The new Prime Minister, Mr Gladstone, seemed determined to bring in a Bill establishing Home Rule for Ireland – a course that would surely split the Liberal Party, precipitate another general election and once more enable the defeated candidate for South Derbyshire to stand for Parliament. Nor had his months with Lord Salisbury been wasted. He had consolidated his reputation as an able and industrious acolyte of the Conservative cause; he had earned the friendly interest of the party leaders; he had deepened his knowledge of political practice and manœuvre. It was a mark, too, of his social talents that on the day the new Government took office, he dined with the Speaker of the House of Commons, Arthur Peel. He described the evening in his diary:

> I had a long talk with the Speaker. ... He mentioned, not I think without covert allusion to Mr. Gladstone, a phrase once used of Lord Derby. 'He is not a master of language because language has the mastery of him. When he rises to speak, he does not know what he is going to say. When he is speaking he does not know what he is saying, and when he sits down he does not know what he has said.'*

In the year 1886 there cannot have been many men of his age – he was just twenty-seven – able to chat on equal terms with the First Commoner in the kingdom and be entrusted with confidences that bordered on the indiscreet.

In spite of a local connection that weighed in his favour, Curzon decided to abandon South Derbyshire. A swing from Liberal to Conservative of at least one vote in ten would be needed to win the seat at the next election, and he looked about for an easier contest. After much correspondence he was adopted as Conservative candidate for Southport, in Lancashire, a constituency which in the previous year had returned a Liberal Member by a

* This shaft of invective is often attributed to Winston Churchill, who as First Lord of the Admiralty launched it at Lord Charles Beresford during a debate in 1911. But it has a longer history.

majority of no more than 160 in a poll of 7,322. Financial negotiations were protracted. The local association at first suggested that Curzon should pay the cost of the election, about £1,000, as well as an annual contribution towards the party organization of between £150 and £200. When he protested, with the utmost truthfulness, that he could not afford anything approaching such sums, the Southport Conservatives yielded. They reduced the figures to £600 for the election and £50 as an annual tribute: and eventually they agreed to bear the entire election expenses, including those personally incurred by the candidate.

Curzon's understandable anxiety to be adopted did not, apparently, deter him from a magnanimous gesture. In the middle of settling the terms of his candidature he heard that Sir Frederick Milner, a North Country baronet who had been defeated at York in 1885, was also in the field for Southport but had decided not to press his claim. Curzon thereupon wrote to Milner, asking him to reconsider his decision. 'I am a young man,' he said, 'with plenty of time before me, and can afford to wait a bit, but I would like to see you back in the House at once.' The tale does not entirely convince, although it rests on the authority of Milner himself in a letter to *The Times* forty-five years later. By then, however, he was nearly ninety and his memory may have played him false. Curzon was surely too ambitious to offer the Southport seat to a rival of no particular influence who had sat only two years for York before his defeat. One possible explanation, if the facts were as Milner gave them, is that Curzon was doubtful whether he himself could afford so expensive a seat. Another solution, based on no more than speculation, is romantic rather than political. Throughout 1886, Curzon wished to marry a young widow, Lady Grosvenor, who at the end of the year plunged him into depression by becoming engaged to his friend George Wyndham. Could he have been hoping to advance his affair of the heart by renouncing Southport in favour of Lady Grosvenor's first cousin, Sir Frederick Milner? Whatever the motive, his offer was courteously rejected.

In the Commons, meanwhile, not even Gladstone's powers of persuasion were able to convince his party of the merits of Home Rule for Ireland. In June the House rejected the Bill by thirty votes, ninety-three Liberal Unionists having crossed the floor to support the Conservatives. Gladstone immediately appealed to the country and the second general election within a year returned the Conservatives to power with a substantial majority of seats over all other parties. Among the victors was Curzon, who in a poll of almost 7,000 defeated the sitting Member for Southport by 461 votes. His successor as Conservative candidate in South Derbyshire could do no better than halve the Liberal majority of 1885.

Southport was a demanding constituency for a young man whose ambitions were centred on Westminster. Nor did its political complexion accord with that of so dedicated a Tory as its new Member of Parliament. In 1900 the seat was won by Edward Marshall Hall, the celebrated advocate, and from Viceroy's Camp, Curzon sent him a letter of helpful advice:

> Except in times of imperial crisis it unquestionably inclines to the Radical side. Therefore you cannot take too much trouble about it. ...
>
> Banks [one of the wards] is quite hopeless. For twelve years I laboured at that place. I visited every house in it over and over again. I tramped along those roads and along those muddy flats all to no purpose. I got fewer votes there in my last election than in my first. I should not waste much time there. ...
>
> The place in which to strike out and to build up your future majority is in the Radical suburbs of Southport. Get the women and the young men there on your side, and you can afford to disregard the soured Radicals of middle life. ...
>
> The constituency is exacting in petty demands, and placed a great strain upon my correspondence. In larger matters it was singularly lenient. It never cost me more than £250 a year during the twelve years that I represented it, except in election years.

Neither Southport nor its Member of Parliament from 1886 to 1898 ever regretted their compact.

Chapter Ten

MAIDEN SPEECH

After dinner a clever maiden speech was delivered by young G.N. Curzon in the perfect style of the Oxford Debating Society.

– Sir Richard Temple's *Letters and Character Sketches from the House of Commons*

It was an unwontedly silent George Curzon who took his seat in the short session of the new Parliament from August to September 1886. Young men, never much encouraged by party leaders to draw attention to themselves, are expected to conduct themselves with particular modesty when their party is in power. The Member for Southport was thus denied the advantage seized by the Member for Woodstock six years before. Nor was he temperamentally fitted for such impudent tactics: his months in Salisbury's private office had done nothing to diminish his natural *gravitas*. Indeed, he was regarded as a man who could influence the Prime Minister in matters of patronage. Bishop Ryle wrote from the Palace at Liverpool begging him to intercede with Salisbury so that a vacant Crown living might go to a local curate:

> If the Premier sends us some stranger from outside the diocese [the Bishop continued], I believe it will give very grave dissatisfaction. I hear incessant complaints that in the distribution of Church Patronage the present Government seems to forget that no part of England fought harder and did more for the present Premier than the diocese of Liverpool! But alas, my poor clergy seem left out in the cold.

Salisbury's distaste for the exercise of political and ecclesiastical patronage was profound. He declared that the first days of a new Government reminded him of the zoological gardens at feeding time, and came near to believing that bishops died merely to spite him. Curzon nevertheless seems to have had some success in the delicate matter raised by Ryle. The living was given to one of the hard-working Liverpool curates.

Soon after Parliament had been prorogued in September, Curzon went up to Bradford to speak at a meeting of the National Union of Conservative Associations. Into his theme of imperialism he wove a much-applauded tribute to 'the incisive eloquence and brilliant leadership' of Lord Randolph, who a few weeks before had been appointed Chancellor of the Exchequer and Leader of the House of Commons. They were the last words of commendation that fell on Churchill from Curzon's lips. For on 23 December it was announced that the most mercurial of all Salisbury's colleagues had resigned.

The ostensible cause was Lord Randolph's rejection of the Service Estimates in spite of the view taken by the Cabinet that international tensions warranted no reduction. That the Prime Minister himself shared the view of the Ministers who presided over the Admiralty and the War Office should have warned Churchill not to press the matter to the point of resignation: for Salisbury regarded any unnecessary expenditure on defence with the eye of a Scrooge. 'If you believe the doctors,' he once complained, 'nothing is wholesome; if you believe the theologians, nothing is innocent; if you believe the soldiers, nothing is safe.' As for the alarmist attitudes of the military Chiefs of Staff, 'if they were allowed full scope they would insist on the importance of garrisoning the moon in order to protect us from Mars'.

Both Churchill's impetuous offer of his resignation and the readiness with which Salisbury accepted it lay less in the dispute on Service Estimates than in a growing antipathy between the two men. Partly it was doctrinal. However much Churchill had contributed to establishing Salisbury as Leader of the Conservative Party, the Prime Minister came increasingly to appreciate the dangers that lurked in his Chancellor's restless creed of Tory Democracy. In November, the month before Lord Randolph's resignation, Salisbury warned him of the perpetual dilemma of Conservative rule:

> We have so to conduct our legislation that we shall give some satisfaction to both classes and masses. This is specially difficult with the classes – because all legislation is rather unwelcome to them, as tending to disturb a state of things with which they are satisfied. It is evident, therefore, that we must work at less speed and at a lower temperature than our opponents. Our Bills must be tentative and cautious, not sweeping and dramatic. But I believe that with patience, feeling our way as we go, we may get the one element to concede and the other to forbear. The other course is to produce drastic symmetrical measures, hitting the 'classes' hard, and consequently dispensing with their support, but trusting to public meetings and the democratic forces generally to carry you through. I think such a policy will fail.

On a personal plane, too, Salisbury found Churchill an exhausting colleague. During his first Ministry he was asked by a friend how he fared. 'I could do very well with two Departments,' he replied, 'in fact I have four – the Prime Ministership, the Foreign Office, the Queen and Randolph Churchill; and the burden increases in that order.'

The months which Curzon spent as an assistant private secretary to the Prime Minister did not extinguish the radicalism that he so admired in Churchill; but once his hero had resigned in circumstances that could not fail to embarrass the Salisbury administration, he felt free to re-examine his political philosophy. And it was undoubtedly a reverent regard for the Prime Minister's moral and intellectual qualities that enabled Curzon, without any apparent spiritual torment, to displace within his own breast the discredited creed of Tory Democracy by a staider, Cecilian brand of Conservative belief. In an article written a few days after Churchill's resignation, Curzon commended to readers of the magazine *England* 'the advantages of stable government, of a continuous policy with foreign Powers, of a regard for Colonial and Imperial interests, of respect for such institutions as reconcile a historic grandeur with an ability to meet the requirements of the age, and of a sensible endeavour to amend such old laws as have grown faulty, or to make such new laws as may be necessary without soaring into the empyrean of philosophic abstractions'. The voice of Young England was still.

The agility with which Curzon readjusted his political balance also owed something to an unlikeable strain of arrogance in Churchill's character: like many men who are indifferent to the feelings of others, Curzon was acutely sensitive to snubs and slights. While working for Lord Salisbury at Hatfield he recorded this sketch in his diary:

> Randolph was in rather a distant and haughty mood. Lady Salisbury and I agreed that he does not go the right way about it to attract the young men. The one thing he wants is a strong Parliamentary following – the popular following he has already got. I used to know him well and to be on familiar terms with him. So much so that when first he contemplated leaving Woodstock, he recommended the local committee to invite me to stand in his place. Which they did. But since he has become a great swell, he will scarcely look at his subordinates and the barest civility is all that one can expect. In London it is difficult to get people to meet him at lunch or dinner: as four out of five of those who may be asked to the party he describes as asses or bores. Lady Dorothy Nevill says there are only about a dozen men whom he will tolerate. One of them is Chamberlain.

Curzon thus had reason for sharing Salisbury's relief at being delivered from the restive presence of Churchill at the Treasury. 'I was at Hatfield that night,' he later wrote, 'and I remember the thanksgivings and hosannas that went up.' The Chancellor who thought himself indispensable was not only replaced – by the Liberal-Unionist Goschen – but also disgraced. For with characteristic want of caution he had written his letter of resignation from Windsor Castle, where he was the guest of the Queen, without giving her the merest hint of his proposed course. He oscillated, to borrow Curzon's phrase, between the adventurer and the statesman.

When Parliament reassembled in the last days of January 1887, there were fears that an embittered Churchill might revert to the habits of the Fourth Party and turn on his recent colleagues as savagely as Disraeli had rent Peel forty years before. Cranborne, presumably reflecting his father's mind, wrote gloomily to Curzon from Hatfield, warning him of Lord Randolph's oratorical powers and the corresponding weakness of the Conservative front bench. Churchill proved more tractable. In a good-tempered speech on 31 January, he confined his astringency to the overtures made by Salisbury towards the Liberal-Unionists, those former supporters of Mr Gladstone who could no longer stomach their leader's insistence on Home Rule for Ireland. 'I frankly admit,' he said, 'that I regarded the Liberal-Unionists as a useful kind of crutch, and I looked forward to the time, and no distant time, when the Tory party might walk alone, strong in its own strength and conscious of its own merits; and it is to the Tory party and solely to the Tory party, that I looked for the maintenance of the Union.'

Lord Randolph's quip was still the talk of the House when Curzon caught the Speaker's eye a few hours later. *Hansard*'s Parliamentary reports at that time relied only partly on verbatim transcripts: often they were in the form of elegantly written digests in oblique speech. So it was with Curzon's first recorded words at Westminster. They occupy eight and a half columns of print which, allowing for their abbreviated form, would probably have taken not less than twenty minutes to deliver.

Mr W. H. Smith, who had succeeded Churchill as Leader of the House of Commons, that night wrote his customary letter to the Queen on the day's proceedings:

> The ordinary Irish members succeeded each other in dreary succession. ... Mr. George Curzon then rose – speaking for the first time but with a coolness and self-possession which was most enviable. He referred lightly to Lord Randolph's speech and said he had no intention of 'wrestling' with Lord R. as he knew his fate would be that of Jacob when he wrestled with the Angel and one of my colleagues remarks that it is the first time in his life that Lord R. has been likened to an Angel!

Taking advantage of the debate on the Address, which offers some latitude in the choice of subject, Curzon did permit himself a gentle tilt against Churchill. He borrowed the aphorism of Charles Lamb, that 'literature is a very bad crutch but a very good walking stick', and applied it to Lord Randolph's description of the Liberal-Unionists. That party, he insisted, was not the crutch of the Conservatives but their staff. Then he turned to rebut the attack which Gladstone had made on Salisbury for simultaneously holding the offices of Prime Minister and Foreign Secretary. The Liberal leader, he riposted, had committed a worse violation of the Constitution – his attempted introduction of Home Rule for Ireland. For the rest, Curzon glided confidently over the major political topics of the day and sat down to sustained acclaim.

Neither the themes nor the language in which they were cast can alone explain the chorus of almost unrelieved praise that Curzon's speech evoked. It displayed no touch of that glittering wit, that epigrammatic insolence with which F. E. Smith sprang to sudden fame twenty years later; it lacked all trace of that becoming modesty, that hesitant sincerity which is an even surer passport to a sympathetic hearing. Curzon's manner, however, was of such polished ease as to command an enthusiasm far surpassing the generous applause which the Commons traditionally accords a maiden speaker.

'It was a nine days' wonder in Parliamentary circles,' wrote one who heard him, 'and men asked each other whether Curzon would keep up that reputation thus made at the first attempt. ... In respect of style, diction and elocution he is one of the most finished and accomplished speakers in the House of Commons.' Another observed that 'it was at once amazing and amusing to witness a very young man, with looks even younger than his years, calmly haranguing the House with a coolness, an assurance and a fluency which would have done credit to the most experienced and impassive Cabinet Minister of twenty years standing'. The writer added that in appearance Curzon was like a distinguished historical personage sitting for his portrait: he even used the phrase, 'an air of ineffable superiority'. *The Times*, in a leading article, called it 'a brilliant maiden speech'.

Fourteen years later, from Viceregal Lodge, Simla, Curzon wrote to a recently elected member of Parliament, Winston Churchill:

> Just a line to congratulate you upon the successful inauguration of your Parliamentary career. I did not write to congratulate you upon your maiden speech because I have never known a case in which a young member who was expected to make a good maiden speech, has not been described as having done so. I remember in my own case making a maiden speech (I think that I ran a tilt at your father in it) which *The Times* next morning described as brilliant and which was plastered with amiable but uncritical praise. All the while I knew well enough that it was execrable. I therefore never compliment maiden speeches.

With the exception of this disingenuous, belated self-assessment, Curzon's maiden speech seems to have evoked only one disparaging note. That bucolic parliamentarian Walter Long declared, in the language of the racecourse: 'He was overtrained.'

In an age that still appreciated the melodrama of debate, Curzon delighted in the oratory of others without either jealousy or enmity. Gladstone, approaching eighty, dwarfed them all.

> We who sat opposite him in his later years [Curzon wrote], saw in him the likeness, now of an old eagle, fearless in his gaze and still exultant in his strength, now of some winged creature of prey, swooping down upon a defenceless victim, now of a tiger, suddenly aroused from his lair and stalking abroad in his anger. Mr. Gladstone seemed to me to be master of every art of eloquence and rhetoric. He could be passionate or calm, solemn or volatile, lucid or involved, grave or humorous (with a heavy sort of banter), persuasive or denunciatory, pathetic or scornful at will.

Until 1885 Gladstone would remain in his place night after night, however protracted the business, to the end of the sitting. By 1890 he had begun to make grudging concessions to his years. He would still turn up in the afternoon for question time, lingering until 7.30 if the debate interested him: but he would hardly ever return after dinner as in the old days. That did not prevent him from dining out four nights a week when, from far down the table, he could be heard declaiming on the immense and gratifying strides taken by dentistry during his own lifetime or enumerating the names of all the inns between Liverpool and London where coaches used to stop before the days of the railway.

Curzon's friendship with Sir William Harcourt, the man popularly assumed to be Gladstone's political heir, went back to his days as an undergraduate. Spending part of a vacation in 1879 with his Cambridge friends, he had called on Harcourt, the then Professor of International Law. To illustrate the importance of the spoken word in nineteenth-century politics, Curzon would afterwards tell the story of how on that occasion Harcourt had handed him a paper, saying as he did so: 'That speech will make me Home Secretary in the next Administration.' It did: and both in bulk and in ability he was not the least considerable supporter of the Grand Old Man – a phrase which incidentally he coined. He was a robust, outspoken land-owner whose deep regard for the memory of Sir Robert Walpole caused Gladstone much pain. In fact of all the sixty-five Cabinet colleagues with whom the Liberal leader ever sat, he admitted to having found Harcourt the most troublesome. Yet it was Harcourt who, at Gladstone's last Cabinet in 1894, pulled from his pocket a handkerchief and a bale of manuscript yellow with age, from which he delivered a tearful valediction that included an elaborate metaphor borrowed from the solar system. Mr Gladstone was much disgusted.

Harcourt's speeches cast a glow: but they also smelt of the lamp. When staying once with Curzon at The Priory, Reigate, he defended himself by pleading that it would be insulting to deliver extemporaneous harangues to the House of Commons. 'I reminded him,' Curzon wrote, 'with truth, that his own impromptu efforts were among his best, but the civility incumbent on a host prevented me from adding, as I might have done, that his carefully prepared orations, written out and read aloud from the box, were almost uniformly his worst.' And he would ruefully recall Harcourt's Budget of 1894, which introduced Death Duties. Without any attempt at concealment, the Chancellor studiously intoned his entire speech from sheets of paper, a procedure that only in recent years has become common practice. Curzon counted sixty-seven pages, then stopped in sheer weariness.

That alert parliamentary journalist Sir Henry Lucy believed that whether Harcourt was in a swaggering, bullying mood, or whether he adopted his more ponderous tone of statesmanship, the result was the same: he offended his audience. 'Unconsciously,' Lucy wrote of him, 'he assumed the attitude of the principal accessory who usually stands at one of the corners of a monumental piece and drops a stony or metallic tear over departed Youth, or Valour, or Domestic Excellence. ... Sometimes, towards the end of a week, the House of Commons begins to think it has had a little too much of Sir William Harcourt as *L'Allegro*; but the punishment of his *Il Penseroso* is apt, after the first sixty minutes, to grow insupportable.' He had, however, his lighter moments, and when telephoned by a bore would pour ink into the receiver, secure in the belief – for he lacked Lord Salisbury's scientific knowledge – that it would trickle into either the ear or the mouth of his inquisitor.

On the Liberal benches behind Gladstone and Harcourt sat Henry Asquith, who had entered the Commons in the same year as Curzon and made a similarly striking impression. Gladstone admired his speeches but thought them 'forensic'. The qualification was deserved. During an election campaign a few years later, a heckler referred to riots at a Yorkshire coal mine while Asquith was Home Secretary, and asked him why he had murdered working men in 1892. 'It was not in 1892,' he retorted, 'it was in 1893.'

With that chill lucidity went a complete absence of the juridical humming which has always tested the patience of the House of Commons and destroyed the political reputations of so many able lawyers. 'Whenever I have heard him on a first-rate occasion,' Curzon wrote, 'there rises in my mind the image of some great military parade. The words, the arguments, the points, follow each other with the steady tramp of regiments across the field; each unit is in its place, the whole marching in rhythmical order; the sunshine glints on the bayonets, and ever and anon is heard the roll of the drums.'

Once he had recovered from his first disagreeable encounter with Asquith at Eton, Curzon established a relationship with him that was always cordial but never quite achieved intimacy – not even after Asquith's marriage to Margot Tennant, one of Curzon's earliest and closest women friends. But Balliol, where Asquith was a few years Curzon's senior, was one bond between them; and a reverence for the classical languages was another. Curzon liked to recall that the only two Greek quotations he ever heard in the House of Commons were both delivered by Balliol men, Henry Asquith and Lord Percy.

Years later, when the House of Lords was debating Home Rule for Ireland in February 1914, Curzon completed the trilogy. He applied to Asquith in the original Greek the warning words used by the priestess of Delphi to Croesus before he embarked upon the enterprise that ultimately destroyed his kingdom. And when they sat together in the Coalition Cabinet of 1915–16, they would sometimes relieve the rigour of business by tossing across the table to each other classical conundrums and epigrams.

Gladstone, Harcourt, Asquith – the Conservative benches on which Curzon sat in 1887 could boast of no such giants. The Leader of the House was W. H. Smith, a kind, conscientious, self-effacing servant of his party who was known to his contemporaries as 'Old Morality'. With a fortune based on the firm of newsagents and book-sellers founded by his father, he had entered the Commons in 1868 and only nine years later became First Lord of the Admiralty. It was considered quite daring of Disraeli to offer the appointment to a man whose early life had been spent in trade. Queen Victoria agreed to him only with reluctance, fearing 'it may *not please* the Navy in which so many of the *highest rank* serve, and who claim to be equal to the Army – if a man of the Middle Class is placed above them in that very high Post'. Far from resenting such reservations, Smith shared them. When in 1886 the Queen wished to give him the Grand Cross of the Bath, he persuaded Salisbury to decline on his behalf 'a decoration which, until recently at all events, has only been given to men of his social standing for very distinguished services'. With the same humility he bore the taunts both of W. S. Gilbert, who immortalized him as Sir Joseph Porter in *H.M.S. Pinafore*, and of Lord Randolph Churchill, who displaced him in fact if not in name as Leader of the Opposition during the Gladstone Government of 1880–5. Having succeeded to the Leadership of the House on Churchill's resignation from the Government in December 1886, he was obliged to suffer the further indignity of an intolerable obstruction to business from the Irish Members. In poor health, he worked himself literally to death, consoled by a belated appointment as Lord Warden of the Cinque Ports.

Smith never flinched: but he never inspired. It was to the uncertain figure of Arthur James Balfour that the Conservative ranks in the Commons increasingly looked for guidance and assertive action. At a time when Curzon's Eton reputation was at its height, that perceptive tutor William Cory had selected Balfour, who was ten years Curzon's senior, as more likely to occupy the office of Prime Minister. During his early days in the House the fulfilment of Cory's prophecy appeared remote. He was then known as Captain Balfour, by virtue of a commission in the East Lothian and Berwickshire Militia. Yet he seemed indifferent both to military glory and to the prizes of politics. He preferred to attend gargantuan Handel festivals at the Crystal Palace and afterwards to pick out the themes on a concertina, which he called 'the infernal'.

Balfour first caught the attention of the Commons as a languid but valued member of Randolph Churchill's Fourth Party, from which he unobtrusively dissociated himself in order not to embarrass his uncle, Lord Salisbury. His promotion to be President of the Local Government Board in the Conservative Government of 1885 evoked no surprise and his parliamentary performances little applause. 'Arthur Balfour,' wrote Curzon, describing the last hours of Salisbury's first Administration in January 1886, 'made quite a fiasco – a lame halting feeble speech. I was astonished.' Thus his appointment as Chief Secretary for Ireland in March 1887, at a time when Irish affairs excluded almost all other business at Westminster, was greeted with widespread derision. One newspaper declared that it was 'like breaking a butterfly to extend Mr. Balfour on the rack of Irish politics' or 'like throwing a lame dove among a congregation of angry cats'.

The jeers were short-lived. As the long limp figure uncoiled from the Treasury bench night after night, the Members crowded into the chamber to hear him enunciate a policy of Cromwellian strength. The delicate, almost epicene features, the pince-nez, the velvet smoothness of voice and bland courtesy of manner enraged rather than disarmed the Opposition. Until 1887, Gladstone had reserved for only two political opponents the rare distinction of being referred to as 'my honourable friend'. One was Stafford Northcote, once his private secretary, the other was Arthur Balfour. Now Northcote was dead, and Balfour became 'the right honourable gentleman', or, in tones of chilling contempt, 'the Chief Secretary'.

Having moved in the same world as Balfour since his undergraduate days, Curzon knew him well. His months as a private secretary to Lord Salisbury cemented their friendship and after a visit to Hatfield he noted in his diary: 'Arthur Balfour was as usual cynical and charming. He is one of the most attractive men in Society: and Society just at present is passing thro' a phase of worshipping intellect.' A few days before Curzon delivered his maiden speech in January 1887, Balfour told him of his impending election to the Carlton Club:

> My dear George [he wrote], 'tis done: – and you will be elected at the first committee meeting. The Carlton is a beastly club: – infested by the worst of the species viz: – the bore political. But you are quite right to belong to it. It must be suffered, like late hours and constituents, as a necessary, though disagreeable, accompaniment of a political career.

Curzon's gratitude did not extend to an appreciation of Balfour's new-found mastery over the Opposition during that troubled session. 'I recall his first speeches as Irish Secretary,' he later wrote. 'They were both ineffective and hesitating.' Those words, however, were written more than twenty-five years later, when intervening events in India had cooled his regard. It was an opinion that in 1887 found few adherents on either side of the house.

The passions of Curzon's first parliamentary session were exacerbated by the intervention of the Liberal Unionists, those former followers of Gladstone who rejected his determination to grant Home Rule for Ireland and could be relied upon to vote with the Conservatives on the Irish question. The most revered of them was Lord Hartington, later to succeed his father as eighth

Duke of Devonshire. His reputation for integrity at the time Curzon first sat with him in the Commons was buttressed by his having refused to become Prime Minister on three separate occasions. The first was in 1880, when the Queen sought an alternative to Gladstone. The second was in July 1886, when Salisbury offered to serve under him in a Government composed of Conservatives and Liberal Unionists. The third was when Salisbury repeated his plea after the resignation of Randolph Churchill.

'Harty-Tarty was dullish, sensible and gentleman-like,' Disraeli said in 1875 of his maiden speech as temporary leader of the Liberal Party in succession to Gladstone. Bearded and impassive, he mistrusted all showiness, all oratorical flourishes. 'How that man does talk,' was his verdict on Arthur Balfour. Brett, who for several years served as his private secretary, wrote of him: 'No one I have known ponders longer over State problems; the bent of his mind is slowly critical, and very slowly constructive.' Such cerebration was not allowed to intrude on the pursuits of leisure. Gladstone complained that he would not read anything, not even *Treasure Island.* Brett described how 'he would leave the card-room at the Turf Club only just in time to be late for dinner, however exalted the rank of his host.' And his passion for racing once led Salisbury to sigh that all arrangements for solving a Ministerial crisis had been necessarily hung up 'till some particular quadruped has run for something'. But Hartington's calm reflective mind and freedom from any taint of opportunism gave ballast to the cause of Liberal Unionism.

That could not be said of all his colleagues. George Goschen, Randolph Churchill's unexpected successor at the Treasury, occasionally amused the House by inadvertence, as when, during the peroration of a Budget speech increasing the tax on most forms of alcoholic drinks, he knocked over the glass of port which sustained his oratory. Mostly, however, he was listened to with dislike by the party he had deserted and without respect by the party he had joined. Balfour privately referred to him as 'a jobbed man'. And when, in the absence of W. H. Smith, Goschen acted as Leader of the House, his new-found Conservative colleagues observed that although he had manners, they were all bad.

Joseph Chamberlain's exchange of Home Rule for Unionist Liberalism earned him enmity but never contempt. While still at Oxford, Curzon took the measure of the Birmingham manufacturer whose republican sentiments had shocked the House of Commons. 'Really a most dangerous man,' he told Brodrick in January 1882, 'very confident, quite determined, immensely powerful St John, we shall hate that man before we have done with him.' Curzon and his friends never grew to like Chamberlain. But the hatred he inspired during the battle for Home Rule came from the Liberal and Irish benches he had deserted, not from the Tory ranks to which he had tied his fortunes. Long after the traditional Unionists had wearied of the chase, Chamberlain would continue to pursue Mr Gladstone with the relentless and unforgiving fervour of the convert. The Irish Members shouted, 'Judas!' at him. And even his former leader was moved to observe with unusual bitterness: 'He never spoke like this for us.'

With the tragic theme of Irish Nationalism was intertwined the personal destiny of its protagonist at Westminster, Charles Stewart Parnell. The publication in *The Times* of letters apparently proving that he had condoned murder; his vindication by a Commission of Judges which found that the letters were forgeries; his ovation in the Commons; his disgrace in the O'Shea divorce case; his struggle for the leadership of his party behind the doors of Committee Room No. 15; his short-lived victory and early death – such was the drama which overhung the parliamentary initiation of the new Member for Southport.

> I sat opposite the Nationalist Party in the House of Commons [Curzon later wrote], during the twelve years in which they were forcing the Home Rule question from the obscurity of a local fad to the rank of the first political issue of the day – the years of political and agrarian crimes in Ireland, and tumult in Parliament – the years in which Parnell flared into a sudden and sombre prominence and as suddenly disappeared. Parnell was not eloquent, much less an orator. ... But as he hissed out his sentences of concentrated passion and scorn, scattering his notes as he proceeded upon the seat behind him, he gave an impression of almost daemonic self-control and illimitable strength.

Even men of normally mild behaviour and utterance were infected by the political fervour of the times. St John Brodrick's Uncle George, the Warden of Merton College, on hearing that John Dillon, a leading Irish Nationalist, had been invited to address a Liberal meeting at Oxford, was moved to observe publicly: 'If the Whitechapel murderer could only have been discovered, he also would have been invited to address an Oxford association which I could name if I thought proper.' The Warden was thereupon summoned before the Judges' Commission and released, thanks to Alfred Lyttelton's forensic eloquence on his behalf, with no heavier penalty than a rebuke.

Within the chamber of the Commons there was such an unprecedented press of Members to hear Mr Gladstone on Home Rule that for the first time in memory rows of chairs were temporarily laid out below the gangway. Moved by the spirit of the times, too, the gentle Lord Cranborne was inspired to call Michael Davitt, another Irish member, a murderer. On being challenged, Cranborne replied that he had been talking to himself, but that the observation had been quite true. Later he apologized to the House and resumed his seat amid loud groans from the Irish benches.

Resting on the triumph of his maiden speech, Curzon was not tempted to match the oratory of either the Tritons or the minnows. In March 1887, however, the House heard him compare the Opposition to Janus. 'They had two faces,' *Hansard* reported him as saying, 'one of peace, the other of war. They wore the face of peace when they wanted to dupe and cajole the English House of Commons, but they wore the face of war in Ireland when they wanted to hound on and inflame the Irish peasantry.' Except to ask a question about unemployment among chain-makers in Staffordshire, he spoke no more during the session.

The tradition of British parliamentary life that preserves amity between members of opposing political parties was strained but rarely broken during Curzon's first years at Westminster. However limited their social range, his friendships embraced all shades of political belief. Brodrick was a Conservative, Leveson Gower a Liberal and Alfred Lyttelton felt impelled to reject Gladstone's obsessive belief in Irish Home Rule and to become a Liberal Unionist: a departure from family orthodoxy that first angered his Uncle William but later came to be accepted with magnanimous understanding. The closing chapters of this book will show how in middle life Curzon seemed almost wantonly to shatter those friendships which had sustained and enchanted his youth. Such misanthropy found no place in his early years. Sometimes, it is true, pain would darken his naturally cheerful temperament or he would brood with morbid sensitivity on some real or fancied wound to his vanity. Then the clouds would roll away and reveal a warmth of character that both radiated and inspired affection.

There was another reason why Curzon's friendships were insulated from the corrosion of political dispute. However intense the parliamentary drama, he seemed to gaze upon the scene from afar. He went dutifully through the motions of debate and division, but he did not love them as a Pitt or a Gladstone or a Churchill loved them. He appreciated the art of oratory, but otherwise regarded Westminster as little more than a legislative machine. He observed its foibles indulgently, but he could not share them. The cheers and counter-cheers, the scenes and stratagems, the gusts of laughter and sudden awed silences found no lasting place in his heart. He was not a House of Commons man.

He was in short an administrator, not a politician. He had chosen a political career because that seemed the swiftest path to power, the way in which he could ultimately achieve noble and imaginative designs, particularly the consolidation of British rule and influence in the East. But for the wiles and ruses of parliamentary tactics, for what Lytton Strachey has called the delicious bickerings of political intrigue, he had neither taste nor time. Even those who were genuinely fond of him resented that he should so often prefer the library to the lobby or the smoking room.

What saved Curzon from positively disliking the House of Commons was a sense of history. It was a quality that prompted him throughout life to keep every letter or other scrap of paper that might one day be of value to posterity; to record his own impressions of memorable occasions and conversations; to seek the acquaintance of eminent men. The last of these traits exposed Curzon to much ribaldry from his enemies, as obtuse as it was malicious. They assumed, or perhaps chose to assume, that his pursuit of the famous – and corresponding exclusion from his life of the dull and the humble – sprang from motives that were arrogant and self-seeking and vulgarly snobbish.

His critics were only occasionally correct. As a schoolboy he had brazenly badgered Mr Gladstone into addressing the Eton College Literary Society because he liked to shine at every task he undertook – and Mr Gladstone was a fine catch. That he afterwards lost no opportunity of renewing his acquaintance was only natural in a young man of his imagination. Today, nearly a century later, who would not give much to enjoy the talk and to savour the rich personality of the man who dominated later Victorian politics? And if, incidentally, those titans could hasten his own progress along the road of public service or exploration, he can hardly be rebuked for enlisting their help.

Curzon, when on his travels, used similarly to present himself to the rulers of those countries through which he passed, not out of self-importance, but because he knew that in a hierarchical world they were the men who could command safe conduct and local knowledge. For mere rank, however exalted, he showed a lifelong indifference. When he was Viceroy he once wrote to a friend about the burden of entertaining 'these dreadful princelings who persist in making India the scene of their visitations. I have got two Frenchmen, d'Orleans and d'Auvergne, a German is I believe knocking about – one Mecklenburg-Schwerin – and I fancy that a Russian Grand Duke is in the offing. I regard them all as an unmitigated nuisance.' As Foreign Secretary, too, he told his wife of an invitation to a private luncheon party to meet the Queen of Spain. His comment was decisive: 'Catch me going!'

Chapter Eleven
LORDS

> Gilbert and Sullivan have produced a new comic opera called *Iolanthe*. It is a satire upon the House of Lords, and as such elicits yells of delight from the mob.
>
> – *Curzon to Richard Farrer, 2 December, 1882*

In spite of an increasing preoccupation with travel and scholarship, Curzon was assiduous in attending to the demands of his Lancashire constituency. 'Oh! you can't imagine the weary, weary strain of daily letters,' he wrote after seven years in Parliament. 'I cannot afford a secretary sufficiently intelligent to be of real use, and every day I have to sit down to some three hours of weary plodding. ... Thus next week I have got to go away making long speeches in the country. And all this while I have four or five articles on hand for magazines, lecture for the Royal Geographical Society; business of boards, and the Lord knows what.'

His record as a backbencher at Westminster was unexpectedly meagre. He spoke infrequently even on imperial affairs, shunned social questions and, except to record the votes demanded by the party whips, took almost no interest in the controversies of Irish Home Rule that continued to burden the legislature for year after year. 'I don't care a damn about the Bill,' he told Spring Rice, 'but the whole House has discussed it with portentous seriousness from the start, just as if it was coming into operation tomorrow.'

There was, however, a single domestic theme on which he would both speak and write with regularity and eloquence: reform of the House of Lords. The sturdy Toryism of his early youth had found no fault with the Upper House. At the Oxford Canning Club in 1881 he complained that the strongest attacks on the Lords came from the least fitting quarter, 'from a House which was much inferior in dignity, wisdom and ability'. Once elected to the Commons, Curzon brought a more critical mind to the subject. He realized that unless the composition of the House of Lords ceased to be wholly hereditary, the institution would one day either be abolished or at least stripped of its right to veto the legislation passed by the Commons. That was a contingency which as a Conservative he naturally deplored. He also had a personal interest in trying to forestall such curbing of powers. As the heir to a peerage he would sooner or later have to abandon his career in the Commons, and dreaded the prospect. But to be obliged to exchange a seat in the Commons for the gilded impotence of an emasculated House of Lords would be an even more intolerable fate.

The protagonist of the movement to abolish the House of Lords was Henry Labouchere, the Radical MP for Northampton. Each spring, with the regularity of the cuckoo, he would rise from the Liberal benches to introduce his well-worn theme. And since he was renowned for the sustained, solemn-faced frivolity he brought to that age of sober broadcloth and lofty sentiments, he never lacked an audience.

There is an agreeable parliamentary tradition by which the Member who follows a maiden speaker offers his congratulations. Immediately Curzon had addressed the Commons for the first time in 1887, that task fell to Labouchere. 'We have seldom heard a more clever and certainly seldom a more lively maiden speech,' he said. To this polite prologue he added some pointed words on the Irish question: 'The Tories will never believe that people can govern themselves – they always think that it is necessary for some superior class to step in and govern them.' Although his stricture was directed at the Conservative benches in general, he could hardly have chosen a more vulnerable target than the young Member for Southport, already feeling his way towards an elevated philosophy of paternal imperialism. The antipathy between the two men was temperamental as well as political and, except for occasional gleams of cordiality, lasted throughout the twelve years they sat on opposite sides of the House of Commons. Labouchere described Curzon's manner as that of a divinity addressing black beetles and delighted to bait him in the pages of his whimsically named paper, *Truth.*

Curzon was never at his best in attempting to humble Labouchere. Too often he would admonish him in the prim tones of a governess, bidding him show 'a little more wisdom and a little less wit'. He scored more effectively when he borrowed his opponent's weapons of libel and lampoon, scornfully doubting whether so dedicated an enemy of the House of Lords would ever have succeeded in entering the House of Commons without the influence of a peer, his uncle Lord Taunton. Many assumed Labouchere's relationship with Lord Taunton to be even closer than nepotism. 'I have just heard your father make an admirable speech in the House of Lords,' a well-meaning acquaintance once remarked. 'The House of Lords?' Labouchere replied. 'Well, well, that is very satisfactory. Since his death the family have always been a little uneasy as to his whereabouts.'

In pleading annually for the abolition of the House of Lords, Labouchere preferred personalities to principles, and found a convenient example in the misfortunes of Lord Ailesbury. 'It is rather ridiculous,' he observed, 'that a man who has been warned off a racecourse and expelled from the Jockey Club should come down here to legislate for the people of England by hereditary descent.' He also turned his disrespectful gaze upon the patronage extended to peers, particularly the political appointments of Master of the Buckhounds and of Lord Chamberlain: 'One noble Lord gets a salary for galloping after Her Majesty's dogs, another receives £2,000 a year for walking about with a stick.'

Labouchere's selective survey of the least deserving members of the Upper House – he discerned a high proportion of 'unsuccessful politicians and successful money grubbers' – provoked Curzon to make his own analysis of its composition. From its membership of between 500 and 600 peers, he enumerated twenty-three Cabinet Ministers, four Viceroys of India, six Viceroys of Ireland, four Governors-General of Canada, eight Colonial Governors, six Ambassadors, two Speakers of the Commons, eight Judges, seventy-eight Government officials, 120 Privy Councillors and 194 former MPs. One hundred and fifty-three of them held, or had held, commissions in the Armed Forces. And although some of the categories overlapped, he concluded that 144 peers had been ennobled for public services to the nation.

Curzon nevertheless shared Labby's concern about the chance imperfections of any wholly hereditary assembly and the dilution of its effectiveness by 'the idler, the spendthrift, and the habitual absentee'. In a plea that came daringly from the Conservative benches, he urged that modification of the hereditary principle should be carried out by his own party, to forestall more drastic action by the Radicals: 'Why should we not, by means of life peerages, make the House of Lords representative of the middle classes of this country, and even of the labouring classes too, and of the dissenting denominations, and, more than that, of every branch of industry and business? ... There would be a House of working bees, not drones, and the House would be reduced to manageable dimensions.'

Curzon's campaign was not an assault on the power of the aristocracy to which he belonged. The right of that class to play a substantial part in the governing of England was undisputed by all except the Radicals until well past the turn of the century. Defining an aristocrat as the son of a man with an hereditary title, Harold Laski claimed that between 1884 and 1905, fifty-eight per cent of all Cabinet Ministers fell into that category. Liberals as well as Conservatives subscribed to a belief in the value of inherited talent, and Mary Gladstone wrote of her father's new administration in 1880: 'The Cabinet is highly respectable, rather aristocratic, with a democratic dash in the shape of Mr. Chamberlain.' There were seven peers and three younger sons of dukes in the Cabinet formed by Lord Salisbury in 1886. He, as it happened, was the last peer to lead a Ministry. But his determination simultaneously to hold the two most important offices of State – he called them the *only* two important offices of State – was no more than mildly challenged.

Labouchere's strongest argument for abolition of the Upper House was that it could at any moment wield a Conservative majority. 'The fact is,' he said, 'the House of Lords play with loaded dice against the Liberal Party. When the Liberal Party are in office, they practically have to share power with the committee of the Carlton Club.' That was not a prospect to daunt Curzon. He called it 'a necessary feature of a Second Chamber', and claimed that 'there never has been a second chamber in the history of the world which did not contain a Conservative as against a Radical majority.' Those who had suspected the Member for Southport of preaching revolutionary sentiments were reassured; and he enlisted the broad support of twenty-three other heirs to peerages who sat with him on either side of the House of Commons.

Curzon developed his theme of House of Lords reform in two successive numbers of the *National Review*. It is a plan that, while still unrealized eighty years later, does at least command a substantial measure of support in all parties. The Upper House, he proposed, should contain four elements – hereditary peers, qualified by some form of public service; life peers, nominated by the Government of the day; another non-hereditary category of peer, elected by the House of Commons for a stated number of years; spiritual peers, but representing only the Established Church.

The corollary of such a reconstruction of the House of Lords was that no hereditary peer, even if qualified, should be compelled to sit in the Upper House. Like the unqualified peer, he should be free to stand as a candidate for the Commons and to take his seat there if elected. It was at this point that Curzon's thesis once more touched his own future. He foresaw that the prospect of an agreed, all-party plan to reform the composition of the Lords was remote; and that not even the most ingeniously nominated Upper House would offer as much scope for an ambitious politician as a wholly elected House of Commons. He therefore turned his mind to other ways in which a Member of the Commons might avoid compulsory banishment to the Lords on succeeding to a peerage.

He had two dedicated allies. Both St John Brodrick and Lord Wolmer, Lord Selborne's son, were heirs to peerages who, like Curzon, could expect more fruitful careers in the Commons than in the Lords. In 1894 they brought in a Private Members' Bill by which a Member of the Commons could retain his seat on succeeding to a peerage. The measure, entitled the Peers' Disabilities Removal Bill, received a formal first reading, but languished when none of its sponsors was successful in the ballot for the necessary parliamentary time.

A few weeks later they seized another chance to ventilate their proposals when Mr Bernard Coleridge, Liberal MP for the Attercliffe Division of Sheffield, succeeded to a peerage on the death of his father, the Lord Chief Justice. It is the duty of the Government Chief Whip in such circumstances to initiate a by-election in the vacant constituency. He does so by moving for a new writ on the ground that the sitting member has been 'called up to the House of Lords'. That procedure, however, sometimes delays the by-election for a considerable time until the new peer's summons to the House of Lords has been prepared. To ensure that the vote of a Government supporter should not be lost for a moment longer than necessary, the Chief Whip on this occasion in June 1894, adopted another formula:

> That Mr. Speaker do issue his warrant to the Clerk of the Crown to make out a new Writ for the election of a Member to serve in the present Parliament in place of the Hon. B. Coleridge, who, since his election, has accepted the office of Steward of the Chiltern Hundreds.

It was a form of words used to enable a Member to resign from the Commons by technically disqualifying himself on appointment to an office of profit under the Crown; and incidentally it was a procedure that allowed a by-election to be held with the minimum of delay.

But as Joseph Chamberlain pointed out from the Opposition front bench, there were grave constitutional irregularities in the Chief Whip's departure from custom. By referring to the new Lord Coleridge as 'the Hon. B. Coleridge' twelve days after his father's death, the motion for a by-election implied that he had not succeeded to the peerage. It furthermore suggested that up to his appointment as Steward of the Chiltern Hundreds he had remained a Member of the Commons. Thus by accepting the Chief Whip's motion, the House had decided that a man might be a Member of the Commons and not a peer, even although he was the eldest son of a deceased peer; and seemed to have created a special class of person, neither peer nor commoner, who could claim to sit in either House at will. That was just such a category as Curzon and his friends yearned to join.

Intervening in the debate, Curzon admitted that they had pondered 'whether there was in existence, or capable of being called into existence, any machinery by which, even after the deaths of the peers whom they would succeed, they might continue to show their affection for the House of Commons by remaining in its ranks'. And now, it appeared, the Chief Whip had produced the example they sought: the heir who succeeded to a peerage did not need to leave the Commons. Coleridge, it was admitted, had vacated his seat in the Commons, but only by applying voluntarily for the Chiltern Hundreds. It was a course he had not been legally obliged to take.

The entire House, not least Curzon himself, knew that the argument rested on no more than a quibble. But at least it forced the Government to refer the matter to a select committee, however slender the chance that it would commend the action of the Chief Whip as a constitutional precedent.

Meanwhile, Curzon, Brodrick and Wolmer had sworn a compact. Whichever of their fathers should die first, the heir would evoke a clarification of the law by refusing to relinquish his seat in the Commons. Since Lord Selborne was nearly twenty years senior to both Lord Scarsdale and Lord Midleton, it was hardly surprising that the responsibility for making the gesture should fall on Wolmer, whose father died in May 1895. The new peer was nevertheless alarmed, not so much at challenging the accepted practice of Parliament as at incurring a fine of £500, which he believed to be the statutory penalty for continuing to sit as a Member of the Commons when disqualified. Curzon reassured him, not only by offering to guarantee £100 of any such fine but also by producing a long reasoned statement on peerage law which he had drafted during his recent travels. He had intended to submit it to the committee set up as a result of the Coleridge case: now it would serve a more practical purpose.

The triumvirate of reluctant heirs showed the authorities every consideration. On 13 May, Curzon and Brodrick had a letter published in *The Times* stating that Selborne, as he had now become, proposed to raise the question whether a peer could continue to sit in, or be elected to, the Commons. 'He will take this step deliberately and after due forethought, not with a view to his own position or to an individual case alone, but in order to raise in a constitutional manner a grave constitutional issue upon which a Committee of the House of Commons, after sitting for eleven months and after receiving the most conflicting evidence, has as yet arrived at no decision.'

That same afternoon, Selborne took his place as usual in the Commons, the first time he had done so since his father's death. Labouchere at once called the attention of the Speaker to the presence of a stranger in their midst, and Selborne was asked to withdraw while the House began a two-day debate on his right to sit.

Arthur Balfour offered Selborne scant support. 'It seems to me,' he said, 'that every subject of Her Majesty has a right to be either a representative in this House or in the other but that no subject can have a right to choose what his status shall be. We cannot, in addition to peers of Parliament and commoners, have a third class to whose own good will it shall be left to decide whether they shall have the status of Commoners or the status of peers.'

Curzon pointed out that an Irish peer had precisely such a choice: he could sit in the Commons or stand for election to the House of Lords as a Representative Irish peer. And he went on to plead for a distinction to be drawn between a peer of the realm and a Lord of Parliament. Selborne, he claimed, was certainly a peer of the realm, but did not become a Lord of Parliament until he had been called to the House of Lords by a writ of summons. There were, moreover, precedents by which a peer could refrain from applying for such a writ.

Such ingenuity was in vain. The House decided that Selborne was ineligible to continue sitting as a Member of the Commons and moved for a by-election to elect his successor. Curzon regretted that it had not been possible to put the question to a court of law, and prophesied that one day such a change as he wished would come to pass. But it was not in fact until 1963 that the second Viscount Stansgate, after a protracted campaign that would surely have won Curzon's admiration, succeeded in divesting himself of his peerage and of returning to the House of Commons as Mr Anthony Wedgwood Benn.

But the early pioneers of the struggle received little encouragement. Labouchere, with offensive geniality, dubbed them 'The Peerikins'. And Lord Salisbury, replying to the toast of the Her Majesty's Ministers at the Royal Academy banquet, quenched their little flame of hope under a torrent of ponderous irony. 'It has been the practice of ages,' he said, 'that fathers should reform the sons. But our sons, holding that the experience of the past has been somewhat onesided in that respect, have been kind enough to propose to reform us. We have nothing to complain of in the prescriptions which they have offered, though they are somewhat analogous to those which in classic times Medea attempted also for the purposes of of retribution. And we have borne with patience and with Stoicism the tender and the affectionate attentions of our highly accomplished and condescending offspring.'

Chapter Twelve
CLUBS

> I have been in countries whose practices would render the people admirable candidates for the Crabbet Club. At Chitral I fraternised with fratricides, parricides, murderers, adulterers and sodomites. I start tomorrow for Kabul, where a female donkey is the object of favourite solicitude.
>
> – *Letter of Curzon to Wilfrid Scawen Blunt, 1894*

However pressing the claims of politics, travel and journalism, Curzon was no less addicted to the intense and almost hieratic social life of his age. His long years as a bachelor – he did not marry until he was thirty-six – left him more than usually free to enjoy the staid conviviality of clubs during the years they reached their apotheosis. England was prosperous, servants were cheap, wives inured to the regular disappearance of their husbands behind impregnable stone façades and impenetrable plate-glass windows. And Alfred Lyttelton, without any undertone of irony, could expatiate on the simplicity of his needs: 'All I want for dinner is soup, fish and a bird.'

Curzon belonged to half a dozen clubs. In spite of Arthur Balfour's warning that he would find the Carlton infested with political bores, he thought that haven of Toryism 'the friendliest of Clubs'. He used it for the rest of his life and as Foreign Secretary would frequently dine there to escape the inadequacies of his own chef at Carlton House Terrace. When Balfour returned from the Paris Peace Conference in September 1919, Curzon met him at Victoria and took him straight off to the Carlton. 'There we had an excellent dinner and a bottle of champagne all alone, and talked *ad lib.*' A few days later he wrote to his second wife during one of her frequent and prolonged absences: 'I am all alone in London and I lunch and dine at the Carlton in the company of old Harry Chaplin who is 79: but eats an enormous dinner with all the gusto of an epicure.' That Chaplin should choose to dine at the Carlton was itself a form of benediction on the club. His friends would recall with awe how, after an ambrosial dinner given by Hartington, he had congratulated his host but pointed out reproachfully that the grapes which adorned the ortolans should have been stoned.

On leaving Eton in 1878, Curzon had been put up for the Athenaeum by Oscar Browning and found himself a member fifteen years later. His seconder was Lord Salisbury, who at one time lunched there regularly, but abandoned the habit because his umbrella was stolen so often. 'It's the bishops,' the Prime Minister would say, apologizing for the other members.

When at work on his books of travel, Curzon used the libraries of both the Athenaeum and the Constitutional Club. For relaxation, he would cross the road to dine at White's, approving of the unwritten rule that reserved the armchairs in the bow window for 'elderly peers and distinguished veterans'. He enjoyed the robustly Johnsonian flavour of conversation at the Beefsteak Club – 'with each man's tongue guarding his own head', as Kipling put it. Then, as now, it was a haunt of eminent actors, and Curzon liked to tell the story of how, dining there early one night, he fell into conversation with the only other occupant of the single long table. 'I explained that I was going to see a play called *Diplomacy* for the second time, and that I very seldom repeated a visit to the same piece. He told me that he too was going to see the same play and in reply to a further question said that it was for the 87th time. I expressed considerable astonishment at his partiality for a play which I thought hardly deserved such a compliment, when it transpired that he was the actor (named Coghlan) who took the principal part.'

It was at the Beefsteak that he renewed his acquaintance with Henry Irving, whom he had met as a fellow breakfast guest of Mr Gladstone's at No. 10 Downing Street. Although never a dedicated theatre-goer, Curzon missed few of the most memorable performances. He first heard Sarah Bernhardt in Paris in 1878. 'I always thought her by far the most gifted actress that I ever saw: and her death scenes were masterpieces of dramatic force and pathos. Her main forte lay in her exquisite voice upon which she used to play, as David did on his harp before Saul. It could range over the entire diapason of sound and feeling, from savage fury to unutterable tenderness and despair.'

Curzon also belonged to Grillion's, a dining club founded in 1812 to enable members of rival political factions to meet socially on neutral ground. Its healing power proved effective even on the night Lord George Hamilton and John Morley came into the club and found only two other members, standing silent and widely apart. They were Lord Salisbury and Lord Derby. Earlier in the day Salisbury had publicly compared Derby's conduct to that of Titus Oates: by the end of dinner they were talking to each other.

The Crabbet Club, which Curzon esteemed most, cut no less sharply across the political differences that otherwise separated old friends. Its president and founder was Wilfrid Scawen Blunt, the traveller, poet, politician, amorist and breeder of Arab horses, whose estate in Sussex gave its name to the club. Blunt belonged to that not uncommon type of Englishman which encourages every manifestation of rebellion abroad while maintaining a stern and unbending conservatism at home. 'I leave today for Egypt,' he once wrote in his diary, 'after having taken all my male servants down to Shipley to vote for Turnour, the Tory candidate.' And although he denounced the British occupation of Egypt as an intolerable tyranny, he was reported to have beaten trespassers on his estate near Cairo until the blood ran down their backs. The squire of Crabbet's comment on meeting John Sargent, the portrait-painter, is also revealing: 'A rather good-looking fellow in a pot hat, whom at first sight I took to be a superior mechanic.'

Yet Blunt had a warm and generous side to his nature. As a child he used to prick constellations of holes in the lids of the boxes containing his caterpillars, so that the captives might think they were still out of doors and could see the stars. In later life his obsessive efforts on behalf of supposedly enslaved peoples were no less romantic. For having incited Lord Clanricarde's tenants to resist arrest during the Irish troubles of 1887 he spent two months in Galway jail. 'I was delighted to see you had run Wilfrid Blunt in,' Salisbury wrote to Balfour. The Chief Secretary was less vindictive, and readily accepted an invitation from George Wyndham, his private secretary, to meet Blunt at dinner soon after the prisoner's release.

The same spirit of political tolerance governed the Crabbet Club, at least during its final and most fruitful years. The first founder was George, thirteenth Earl of Pembroke who, to mark his coming of age in 1871, invited the closest of his friends to Wilton for cricket, rowing and conviviality. The gathering became an annual summer event and five years later was transferred to Blunt's house in Sussex. Although the club professed no politics, nearly all its members were Tories, two or three of them Members of Parliament. As Blunt's anti-imperialist and Home Rule activities became more impassioned throughout the 1880s, so the membership melted away. Hardly any of the Wilton members even troubled to answer his invitations to Crabbet and Pembroke himself, a substantial Irish landlord, felt obliged to snap the threads of friendship.

In 1887, therefore, a few months before retiring temporarily to prison, he reconstructed the club to include several younger men, most of them recent Oxford undergraduates sympathetic to Irish Home Rule. Among them were Willy and George Peel, sons of the Speaker of the House of Commons, and Loulou Harcourt, devoted son of Gladstone's Chancellor of the Exchequer. Two years later George Wyndham was elected and brought in his own circle of friends: drawn from all political parties, it included George Curzon and George Leveson Gower.

The laboured humour of the Crabbet Club constitution set a tone of badinage in which political acrimony found no place. It included these clauses:

> The Club is a convivial association, which has for its object to discourage serious views of life by holding up a constant standard of its amusements.
>
> Though public life in its various branches is not forbidden to Members, they are expected to subordinate such interests to the higher interests of the Club. A Member accepting a seat in the Cabinet, the Viceroyalty of India, an Archbishopric, or an Embassy, must submit to re-election before he can resume the privileges of Membership.
>
> Similarly with regard to marriage, which though not discountenanced in Members is still held to be a grave danger, a period of retirement from the Club of at least 12 calendar months is appointed, after which, and then only on written application couched in a proper spirit, shall the Member be re-admitted.
>
> The Crabbet Club being based on strict bachelor principles, it is a fundamental law of the Club that ladies are ineligible for membership.
>
> No subscription is required of Members or other duty than of regular attendance at the annual meetings. Absence from England, sickness confirmed by medical certificate, or matrimonial entanglement publicly announced in the *Morning Post* shall be considered sufficient reason for non-appearance, but the ordinary excuse of 'Previous Engagement' shall not be accepted, and if repeated twice in consecutive years shall be held equivalent to a resignation of Membership.
>
> A Member becoming obnoxious to other Members may be expelled from the Club on the agreement of two thirds of the Members present at an annual Meeting, but this shall not be on political, religious or other serious grounds.

On the first Saturday of July, members of the club would arrive at Crabbet for what Curzon called an 'immortal wassail' lasting two days. Never more than twenty in number, they contributed to the material side of the entertainment according to their means: a ham or a tongue, a *pâté de foie gras* or a box of cigars, a case of champagne or a bottle of brandy. Blunt himself, however, was a teetotaller. The club colours of evergreen and white were flown from a mast before the front door, reflecting the motto borrowed from Shakespeare, 'In Youth and Crabbed Age'. Some members spent the day playing lawn tennis for a silver goblet: before breakfast one morning Cust and Curzon defeated Blunt and Wyndham, all four stark naked. Others swam in the lake, and the entire company turned out to salute their president as he rode by in flowing robes at the head of his Arab stud.

Not all the guests appreciated the boisterous masculinity of Crabbet. George Leveson Gower, for whom forty-eight hours without feminine company was an eternity, deplored the club's having been founded upon the Moslem principle that women have no souls and are therefore unfitted for higher and rational converse. It is true that Blunt allowed two women to attend the annual Sussex saturnalia. One was his wife, Anne, Byron's granddaughter; the other was his daughter, Judith, who as Lady Wentworth became a recognized authority on the breeding of Arab horses. 'They would be better away,' Leveson Gower complained. 'Two women to twenty men is a bad combination, as it neither gives the unrestricted freedom of purely male society, nor the interesting opportunities of a society where the two sexes are more evenly mixed.'

There was an oriental flavour, too, about the banquet on Sunday. They feasted off a kid roasted whole that reposed on a mountain of rice. Then each member competing for the office of Laureate would read aloud his poem and submit himself to ballot. There was no rule which debarred a once-successful poet from again carrying off the prize in subsequent years. But a sense of justice seems to have ensured that the laurels should grace a different brow at each successive meeting of the club. In 1891 Curzon submitted a piece entitled 'Charma Virumque Cano' that opened with an endearing flourish of self-mockery:

CHARMS and a man I sing, to wit – a most superior person,
Myself, who bears the fitting name of George Nathaniel Curzon.
From which 'tis clear that even when in swaddling bands I lay low,
*There floated round my head a sort of apostolic halo.**

It failed to win him a prize, but was judged worthy to be printed in the annals of Crabbet. Two years later he swept the board with a sprightly entry on the theme 'Sin'. It ended with the chorus.

And so when some historian
Of the period Victorian
Shall crown the greatest exploit of this wonder-working age,
His eye shall light on Crabbet
And, if truth shall be his habit,
The name of everyone of us will shine upon that page.

To us will be the glory,
That shall never fade in story,
Of reviving the old axiom that all the world's akin,
That the true link of union
Which holds men in communion
Is frank and systematic and premeditated Sin!†

Both poems vividly refute those who persisted to the end of Curzon's life in sneering at his supposed pomposity and self-importance. In a sense he was the victim of his own drollery. 'It is,' Desmond MacCarthy once wrote of Oscar Browning, 'always dangerous to make jokes about yourself, for the humourless are sure to repeat them as examples of your astonishing lack of self-awareness,

* See Appendix, page 386. † See Appendix, page 388.

while the malicious fling them back at you as stones.' Curzon throve on the anecdotes that clung to his reputation, particularly in later years. It pleased him to hear how, when watching troops bathing behind the lines of the Western Front, he had observed: 'Dear me, I never knew that the lower clăsses had such white skins.' Or how he had rejected his inkstand in the Foreign Office because it was made of plebeian brăss and glăss. Or how he would talk of a béāno, under the delusion that it was an Italian word for a festival. Stored up, repeated, sharpened, multiplied, even embroidered by himself, such stories masked the vast proportions of his intellect and distorted the impression he made upon colleagues and public alike. Perhaps, by weaving about him a legend of anachronism, they helped to deny him the highest of all political offices, ostensibly withheld on constitutional grounds.

Certainly his rampant high spirits could sometimes be wearisome. At one meeting of the Crabbet Club, a new member threw himself on the mercy of the company as 'a respectable mediocrity'. In a voice trembling with indignation, Curzon protested: 'We have had, hitherto, all sorts of people elected to the club, of whom the less said, perhaps, the better. But we have never yet had one who laid claim to the title of "respectable mediocrity". A mediocrity I might, perhaps, *à la rigueur* put up with, but a *respectable* one would be past endurance.' And when introducing Oscar Wilde he made a speech so tactless and embarrassing in its implications that Wilde turned crimson and could stutter only a few words in reply.

There fortunately exists a happier vignette of Oscar Wilde at the Crabbet Club before he disappeared into the shadows. A miniature reunion took place in the autumn of 1891, when Blunt, Curzon, Wilde and Willy Peel had breakfast together in Paris. Wilde told them he was writing a play in French that might make him an Academician, and they all promised to go to the first night – George Curzon as Prime Minister.

'We sat down over twenty to dinner,' Blunt wrote in his diary on 1 July 1893, 'and did not leave the table till half-past one. ... George Curzon was, as usual, the most brilliant, he never flags for an instant either in speech or repartee: after him George Wyndham, Mark Napier, and Webber.'

George Wyndham, a cousin of Blunt, began his career in the Coldstream Guards and fought in the Sudan. He left the Army in 1887 to marry the widowed Lady Grosvenor, much to the disappointment of her other suitor, George Curzon. Elected to the House of Commons in 1889, he eventually achieved Cabinet rank. At heart, however, he was more a man of letters than a politician. 'This young and debonair figure,' Curzon wrote of him, 'like a Greek hero in the range of his attainments and perfections, possessing the physical beauty of a statue and endowed with the chivalry of a knight errant, the fancy of the poet and the deep tenderness of a woman.' Sarah Bernhardt thought him the handsomest man she had ever met; and something of Wyndham's luminous mind may be seen in a description of Crabbet he sent to a friend:

> The woods grow up in virginal unconsciousness of the axe to the very door. On one side a wilderness sown with Desert plants and dotted with windsown English bushes; on the other a Sussex paddock with Arab brood-mares and their foals. Below in the hollow a pond full of trout, on which the swans sleep and swim lazily through the day. The house is overgrown with June roses and the lawns after dark are very silent and conducive to the complete and satisfactory solution of all problems, moral and aesthetic, by the active brains of young and uninstructed men pacing in the moonlight.

Mark Napier, one of the several lawyers who belonged to the Crabbet Club, had spent eight years of his youth sharing chambers in the Temple with another struggling barrister, Henry Asquith. During all that time, he later told Blunt, the future Prime Minister earned no more than £500 – a lean regime that drove Asquith to add to his income by becoming a school examiner and so to his first encounter with Curzon at Eton. Napier persevered with the law and sometimes acted as Blunt's legal adviser. He also visited India during Curzon's Viceroyalty to settle a claim by an Indian Prince. 'It had been hung up for thirteen years,' Blunt noted, 'but he got it pushed through by George Curzon in ten days. Such is the virtue of the Crabbet Club.'

The last of the quartet which won Blunt's commendation for brilliance at that Crabbet meeting of 1893 was Godfrey Webb. As a Clerk in the House of Lords he could depend on long weeks of relaxation and was much in demand as a guest throughout the summer and autumn. 'For hours together,' Margot Asquith wrote of him, 'he would poke about the country with a dog, a gun and a cigar, perfectly independent and self-sufficing, whether engaged in sport, repartee or literature.' He had a bachelor's love of children and an inspired gift of winning their confidence. Among older friends his conversation was enriched by desultory scholarship that sometimes flowed deeply, and he could hold his own with authority on topics as varied as bird life and the plays of Shakespeare. His wit, perhaps contrived by later standards, was at the time considered daring. Charty Ribblesdale, when heavy with child, once asked him whether he did not think her gallant. He replied: 'Well, you are very buoyant if you are not gallant – you must be one or the other.' There was always a welcome, too, for Webb's Basque valet, Saubaud, who used to load for his master at shooting parties. Whenever a bird sailed away unharmed, he would shout consolingly: '*Vous l'avez bien blessé, Monsieur.*'

Harry Cust, a year or two junior to Curzon at Eton, was in those early days thought at least his match in the race to be Prime Minister. As a young man, too, his brilliance illuminated the social life of the age. 'Gifted with an astonishing quickness of interest,' Curzon wrote of him, 'a genuine love of reading and scholarship, a rich vocabulary, a fastidious literary sense and a wonderful memory, he was the unchallenged leader of the dinner table. Quip, retort, repartee, quotation, allusion, epigram, jest – all flashed with lightning-like speed from that active workshop his brain.' Having been called to the Bar in England, he presented himself in Paris for the *Baccalauréat en Droit,* when the following interrogation took place:

'*Qu'est-ce que c'est une théorie?*'

'*Une théorie, Monsieur le Juge, c'est une généralisation centralisatrice.*'

In later years he could never resolve whether his improvisation had been sublime or bathetic: and Lord Haldane, appealed to as a philosopher of profundity and wisdom, after deep thought pronounced himself unable to decide.

'He was a fastidious critic and a faithful friend,' Margot Asquith wrote of him, 'fearless, reckless and unforgettable.' In the early days of their acquaintanceship, Curzon disliked Cust. Reserve later thawed into warmth, and it was as 'My dear old Harry' that he would begin his letters. There nevertheless persisted a strain of mistrust, even of disapproval. Cust's brilliance shone fitfully. At its best it inspired him to write the poem '*Non Nobis*', printed in the *Oxford Book of English Verse* during his own lifetime, at first anonymously, later under his own name. Yet he lacked staying power. One contemporary said of him that he had energy but not industry. Another thought that he lost his seat in the Commons because he neglected it. A third observed: 'Cust was throughout his life consistently run after by women, and such was his temperament that they seldom had to run very far or very fast.'

It was largely as a journalist that he achieved fame of a sort. Dining out one night in 1892, William Waldorf Astor listened to Cust's conversation, then crossed the room to offer him the editorship of his latest acquisition, *The Pall Mall Gazette.* To direct an influential evening newspaper was not, in the eyes of the Crabbet Club, as dishonourable a fate as to become a Cabinet Minister or a Viceroy, an Ambassador or an Archbishop. It nevertheless brought Cust a stern reminder of the irresponsibility that was expected of him:

My dear Cust,

I feel it incumbent upon me as President of the C.C. to write to you a few words of warning in regard to the dangerous form of public life on which you are about to embark. ... We have as examples before us Stead and Morley, who have made use of the *Pall Mall* as a stepping-stone to their positions of dull respectability. ... You have been put forward at this critical moment of England's social history to do battle against the Non-Conformist Conscience. ... The Club has its eye on you.

Yours ever presidentially,
Wilfrid Scawen Blunt.

Cust did not fail his mentor. Headlines became engagingly flippant. A leading article on the Eastern Question was entitled 'The Voice of the Turkey'. When the fate of the Chinese Statesman Li Hung Chang was in the news, the headline was 'Li Chang – Hung?' A school-board controversy concerning a Mr Diggle was presented to the public as, 'To Diggle I am not able; to Beggle I am ashamed'. Before long, Astor received a letter from John Morley, the former editor, who by now had become Chief Secretary for Ireland in Gladstone's last Government: 'The nature of the attacks on me in the *Pall Mall* make it impossible for me to hold personal communication with Mr Cust.' Astor had troubles of his own with his mercurial editor, who refused to print a single line of the manuscripts which the proprietor laboriously composed and optimistically submitted for publication. At the same time, and in spite of Astor's pained remonstrances, jokes in bad taste about his native and much loved United States of America continued regularly to appear. Astor endured such humiliation for four years: then he dismissed Cust at a week's notice. The editor had the final word. His last poster read, '*Qui Cust-odit Caveat*' – 'Who hates Cust, let him beware'.

Charles Gatty, who was introduced to the Crabbet Club by George Wyndham in 1890 and won the laureateship in the following year, had a more varied life than most of his fellow members. In his youth he visited Australia to inspect the newly opened up gold-fields and to gather specimens of seaweed for his mother, an authority on that branch of marine biology and incidentally a daughter of Nelson's chaplain in the *Victory*; Gatty himself later served on the narcissus committee of the Royal Horticultural Society. For twelve years he was curator of the Liverpool Museum, followed by two years as private secretary to his fellow convert to Roman Catholicism, Lord Bute. He edited a newspaper started by Lord Wolverton in Yeovil, helped the Duke of Norfolk to compile a hymnal and after Wyndham's death wrote a moving volume to his memory called *Recognita*. He loved the music of Palestrina, staying in grand houses and reading aloud. His regard for the Irish led him to open a shop near Victoria Station where, in shirt sleeves and apron, he sold such characteristic Hibernian products as rosaries, butter and tweed.

Gatty was also inspired to stand as a Home Rule candidate for West Dorset in 1892. He lost the election but won a subsequent victory of another kind. In the course of the campaign his Tory opponent, Mr H.R. Farquharson, hinted that Gatty had as a schoolboy been expelled from Charterhouse for immorality. Farquharson, the sitting Member for the constituency, had also repeated the allegation to St John Brodrick in the lobby of the House of Commons: and Brodrick in his turn had told Curzon. After consulting Wyndham, Gatty brought an action against Farquharson for libel and slander and engaged Alfred Lyttelton as one of his counsel. The case was heard before Lord Coleridge, the Lord Chief Justice, in June 1893. In evidence it emerged that Gatty had not been expelled from Charterhouse: but at the age of thirteen he had complained of the immorality of other boys, and the headmaster had thought it better for him if his father removed him from the school. The jury thereupon brought in a verdict in Gatty's favour and awarded him damages of £5,000 and costs. Less than two weeks later, on 1 July, the Crabbet Club held its annual meeting for 1893 and Curzon, in his poem 'Sin' that won the laureateship, included these lines:

> *And* Gatty *shall defend us*
> *And get damages tremendous*
> *If any jealous critic vents his stupid spleen*
> *in slander.*

The damages were not, as it happened, as tremendous as Curzon supposed. On 20 July the Court of Appeal upheld the verdict but reduced the damages to £2,500.

Even before Lord Elcho became a member of the Crabbet Club he had subscribed to its fundamental principles by making catastrophic losses on the Stock Exchange. To prevent him from exposing himself to further disaster, his father, the Earl of Wemyss, set up a trust fund of £100,000 for his benefit, with Arthur Balfour and Alfred Lyttelton among the trustees. Jogging along as best he could on its limited income, he was a Member of Parliament from 1883 to 1885, and again from 1886 to 1895. He spoke little on affairs of State, but his annual speech on the motion to adjourn the House for Derby Day was always received with cheerful appreciation.

Moving the adjournment of the Commons on 3 June 1890, he put political matters into a Crabbet-like perspective:

> The withdrawal of a great Government measure would cause less excitement than the withdrawal of the favourite; and greatly as the country respects the right hon. Gentlemen on the Government Bench, the news that the whole of them were laid low by a severe attack of influenza would be received with a feeling mild in comparison with that which would be displayed if the horse which has been principally backed were to suffer from a mild attack of the same complaint.

Two years later, he perversely opposed a similar adjournment motion, and again carried the day:

> I admit that perhaps in the early years of a Parliament, as in the early youth of an individual, eccentricities are pardonable which in their old age are absolutely inexcusable. I can understand a Parliament, worn out perhaps by the feverish energy of its own youth, taking a holiday at Epsom; but for a Parliament in our unfortunate stage, with at least one foot in the grave, with the marks of approaching Dissolution

written on every line of our faces, to go masquerading to Epsom in an official capacity is more or less an act of indecency.

Like other shy men he had a wit of agreeable dryness, not least when referring to his huge bald dome of a head, as familiar a landmark as his cigar. '*My* hair preferred death to dishonour', he would say, gazing at the sparsely trellised crown of a cousin.

Although meetings of the Crabbet Club took place only once a year, its spirit of irreverence persisted in the correspondence which Blunt maintained with his fellow members. In November 1891, soon after Curzon had received his first Ministerial Office as Parliamentary Under-Secretary of State for India, Blunt wrote to him from Rome:

I feel it to be my duty as President of the C.C. to write you a few words on the occasion of your elevation to the rather dangerous eminence of an Under-Secretaryship of State. According to Article V of our Rules, public life is not discouraged in any of its branches, and indeed we are gratified when Members of tried fidelity are placed in positions of useful authority. It is only then that the dull political world can be leavened. Nevertheless you will understand that it cannot but be an anxious thought to me, who stand to you in the position of a spiritual father, that after so short a noviciate in our society (barely six months) you should be then suddenly launched on the more perilous paths of our Apostolate.

You will find yourself in a world of temptation at the India Office, where I remember to my sorrow that even one so light headed as Randolph Churchill was very nearly transformed into a responsible politician. I have, however, a better trust in you and am much cheered by the character given of you by the Opposition prints and even, in a vein of high comedy, by *The Times*. In any case I shall have discharged my duty to you by these few words of caution, blessing and encouragement in the higher paths. Remember that outside the walls of the Club we are in the position of Lay Jesuits, instructing the world in folly by an elaborate show of seriousness. Personally I have the fullest confidence in your sound appreciation of the emptiness of things, and even were I to live to see you in the Cabinet my trust would not be shaken. Take care only of your physical health. Our motto I think should be 'Mens insana in corpore sano'. Also do not forget that the first Sunday of July is devoted to a higher than official business.

That supposedly grave Liberal Statesman Lord Houghton – he had not yet been created Lord Crewe – struck the same profane chord when in the following year he replied to Blunt's congratulations on his appointment as Lord Lieutenant of Ireland at the age of thirty-four. First he paid tribute to Curzon, who had recently lost his junior post at the India Office on the defeat of Lord Salisbury's Government:

. . . I apprehend that, during a brief term of power, he has done more from sheer gaiety of spirit to destroy our Empire in Asia than any average Viceroy could effect in ten years or the Emperor of Russia in a hundred. This is a record of which any man may be proud.

Houghton then turned with enthusiasm to his own good fortune:

My sphere of action will be less vast, but its opportunities are, in some respects, more striking. The control of a considerable patronage, wielded with a rigid determination to appoint no man who is not only absolutely unfit for the post which he is to fill, but for any post whatsoever. The occupancy of an exalted, though fictitious, social position, with a purpose of rendering everybody within reach (including the occupant) as grotesque as possible, the power of effecting miscarriages of justice in the most arbitrary manner to the grossest extent – all these things afford a prospect of usefulness, which I fully appreciate. I shall hope to fill my office in the spirit of burlesque, and to leave behind me a reputation compounded of those handed down by Caligula and Le Roi d'Yvetot.

Curzon's appointment as Viceroy of India in 1898 inspired another exchange of letters with the President. 'I write to condole with you,' Blunt wrote, 'on the appointment which I grieve to think severs your long and meritorious connection with the Crabbet Club. As in H's case I notice that you have no single qualification but that of Crabbet Club membership fitting you for the high post you are called on to fill, and the appointment is a new tribute, and the most conspicuous the club has yet obtained, of its inestimable merits as a nursery of irresponsible statesmen. I trust … that you may prove the best, the most frivolous (even remembering Lytton) and the *last* of our Viceroys.'

'I know well that I have merited expulsion from the Crabbet Club,' Curzon replied humbly, 'but I hope by a consistent course of disaster to be unanimously re-elected on my return. … Only you must not come out and compel me to lock you up, which would be subversive for Club discipline. For your good wishes, bless you, dear Wilfrid.'

And so their friendship continued over the years, bridging the vast gulf that separated them in political belief. Perhaps the most moving letter of all was written by Curzon in 1911 to thank Blunt for a donation to the rebuilding fund of the Royal Geographical Society. It had, he said, given him all the more pleasure 'because I know it to spring from personal affection which I most heartily and eternally reciprocate. In this respect we remain forever young.'

Chapter Thirteen

HEARTS

Your letter gratified me more than I can say ... such intellectual strawberries and cream.

– *Laura Tennant to Curzon,*
5 August, 1884

Curzon was no misogynist. However deeply he seemed to be absorbed in the masculine activities of a masculine world – Parliament and foreign travel, All Souls and the Crabbet Club – his nature craved the stimulus of feminine companionship and the warmth of feminine affection. He rarely lacked either. He could demonstrate every facet of manly attention, from brotherly chaff to consuming possession: he could excite every womanly emotion, from maternal sympathy to melting infatuation, from roguishness to passion.

The love of four sisters illuminated his long years as a bachelor. They were the daughters of Sir Charles Tennant, who after making a substantial fortune out of railway development and Australian land, bought the Glen estate of 4,000 acres in Peeblesshire. His vast baronial mansion, which preserved the intimacies of Victorian family life relieved of all its most irksome restraints, provided his daughters with a home of boundless hospitality at which to entertain their friends. In 1879 he outraged the feudal traditions of the Lowlands by successfully standing for his local parliamentary constituency against the Tory member who had held the seat for twenty-eight years without once making a speech in the Commons. Such excessive devotion to the Liberal cause did not, however, deter aspiring politicians of all parties from paying court to his daughters.

There were Charlotte, known as Charty, who married Lord Ribblesdale; Laura, who married Alfred Lyttelton; Lucy, who married Thomas Graham Smith; and Margaret, universally called Margot, who married Henry Asquith. The eldest sister, Pauline, known to her sisters as Posie, was never more than a figure of shadow in Curzon's life.

Mr Gladstone's daughter Mary, an indefatigable letter-writer and diarist, has left a vivid impression of her own introduction to the Tennant family:

It is the maddest, merriest whirl from morn till night – wonderful quickness, brightness wit, cleverness – the 4 sisters all so pretty and fascinating in their different ways. Lady Ribblesdale tall, distinguished, and a sort of sunny serenity about her aged 25. Mrs. Graham Smith, married straight from the schoolroom, small, pretty, clever. ... She draws with great spirit and dash, plays the violin capitally, sings and is full of ardour and interest over everything in the world, books, politics, art, great men. Then comes Laura, the sharpest little creature, like a needle, delicate and yet able to do everything beautifully, like riding, lawn tennis, playing, etc., full of life and fun and up to anything in the world, and yet some 'Weltschmerzen' in her eyes and full of aspiration in her graver moments. ... She is fair and quite different in looks to the others, but very piquante. Lastly comes Margot, aged 18, perhaps the most really pretty and clever of the lot, her hair curling darkly all over her head, eyes large and deep, skin very pearly without much colour, and the most bewitching mouth. She sings, draws, plays violin and pianoforte, all with originality and charm. ...

Such was the quartet of sirens who cast their romantic spell over George Curzon.

His attachment to Charty, the eldest of the four, was slow to prosper. She had married the handsome and sporting Lord Ribblesdale while Curzon was still at Eton, and for two or three years continued to rebuff the attentions of the younger man with teasing irony. The very first letter from her which Curzon preserved, written to him soon after he had ceased to be an Oxford undergraduate, sets the tone of their early correspondence:

I made sure you had forgotten my existence and put me on the shelf ... with a hundred other ladies whose poor little heads you tried to turn and with whose affections you tried to trifle. But I was wrong for once. Hurrah!

Hot-blooded flattery from Curzon's pen was met by a cool riposte from her own. 'I wish,' she wrote to him in the autumn of 1883, 'I could think I was worthy of all or indeed any of the attributes with which your youthful and fantastic brain has been good enough to surround me. I can't think why it is we never met at the end of the season. I repudiate your charge or supposition indignantly – is it meant as a covert insult to my figure?' From this pleasantry she passed in the same letter to a homily only lightly touched with humour:

You say you have two passions, and I notice that with your usual gallantry you put 'women' before 'work'. Take my advice, which is always good, and transpose the order of these two words and put 'work' first. Not because I do not think you as well fitted to be successful with one as with the other; for your career should be brilliant indeed if you are as successful with your second passion as report says you are with your first. But because you will be the more worthy of your passion for women, or rather your passion for women will be the more worthy if you allow nothing to interfere with your passion for work. Do not, however, altogether despise the attractions of maidens and of languid lawn tennis in order to become a listless litterateur.

Lady Ribblesdale next wrote to Curzon from Natal, where she was spending six months with one of her married sisters. Distance did not soften her insistence upon the proprieties of the age. 'As you say,' she wrote in August, 1884, 'a year has elapsed since our meeting ... but I have not changed my views on the subject of Christian names since then. I don't wish you to call me by mine, and I would much sooner not call you by yours. ... It would not help to cement our friendship which I hope will always be a firm and true one, indeed I think there are very few cases where Christian names are an advantage.'

Less than a year later Curzon had utterly pierced the defences of her heart, From 'Dear Mr Curzon', she passed to 'My very dear friend' and so to 'My very beloved George'.

I was overjoyed at getting your delicious letter this morning [she wrote on 6 June 1885], it gave me a thrill of delight. I half hoped it would meet my anxiously expectant eyes and the hope made me bestir my sleeping self the instant my maid put my morning's bundle of missives by my bed. ... You don't know how happy it makes me to think, or rather know, you care a little about me, and I am sure this discovery fills me with as much pride and delight as the discovery of endless proportions for which Christopher Columbus is so celebrated. Do you know, it is more surprising even to me than it was to him, and may it be as endless.

Charty Ribblesdale's abrupt surrender to Curzon's charm seems to have been the result of what her husband called a 'clumsy indiscretion'. She was, however, unrepentant at an episode which can be reconstructed only through the rapturous sentiments that she poured on to paper:

Though I was miserable at the time, I do not and cannot regret it now, for how should I ever have got to know you as I do now? I look upon them as three precious hours well spent in which I have gained blessing, for what greater blessing can there be on this weary earth than a friend who loves one? Mind, I recarnalize this word as much as you do a kiss! You love several, but I feel proud to be amongst them. It is more and more a wonderment to me why you should care about me, dear old George, you know so many much cleverer, beautifuller, more attractive people than me, why do you? Is it because I like you? I am very fond of you but I don't think this is the reason, for gratitude is very far from being akin to love! I put you in an air-tight corner of my heart all by yourself where nobody dare intrude. Like you, I have got two or three private compartments sacred to their owners who are life tenants and nothing and nobody can ever oust!

I always feel friendship is so one-sided, one gives and the other receives. I don't mean the time-honoured adage of '*un qui baise et l'autre qui tend la joue*', I am afraid I committed both of these hideous enormities, but what I do mean is ... you are a feast to me. I delight in your society, enjoy it exultantly! I feel my return to you is a very poor one, a lady of slow wit and halting periods as compared to you, dear old thing, but my consolation for this is that mercifully thanks to a curious and unjust law in nature, people don't like one for what one is worth or what one can give; if they did I should run a poor chance.

Only occasionally did subsequent letters from Charty Ribblesdale to Curzon glow with the same fervour. 'Do come and see me,' she wrote in April 1886, 'I long to see you again and felt so jealous of Tommy when he told me he had met you at luncheon. ... I hunger to look upon you and talk to you and hear you talk. Have I still got a little corner in your heart? I believe I have tho' I have behaved badly to you and never wrote to you from Gib., as I always meant to.' And exactly a year later: 'It was so good having you here last night, it always binges me up and puts me on my best legs, seeing you. You are such a tonic to my spirits. It is funny, because I don't consider your spirits extra superfine in quality. I suppose it is because I love you and feel you are a link with all I love best. That heavenly feeling of confidence is so delicious and inspiring. Did you like your dindin here, I enjoyed it hugely. I don't mean the food.'

A more placid tone now began to permeate their correspondence. 'What an old sweet you were, George, to send me that delicious pin. I love him, he is so fat, old-fashioned and respectable, so unlike his master – his complement, I suppose. I delight in him and wear him constantly and I like him all the more because I think he has a wise expression as if he had seen a good deal of life and knew a good deal.' From so gay an acknowledgement of Curzon's thoughtful little present she passed to a threnody of the London house she and her husband had been obliged to give up:

> It was with a heavy heart that I left dear little Brook Street. When I was emptying out the drawers, etc., I felt as if I were emptying out my heart and putting up tombstones everywhere.
>
> It is so unspeakably sad the way in which everything rushes by one into the shadow land of the past! This chapter of my life, the most precious, sacred 18 months of it, is closed for ever. I shall never sleep under that roof again, and all the living links that made that time a reality are broken. It is curious how one clings to a bit of paper, a table, a chair, anything that keeps events living realities. It is so tragic the way they hurry past into the twilight. I long to follow them into that mystic other side but there is no road for poor plodding feet, and we must wait till we can make 'the clouds our chariots and walk upon the wings of the wind'.
>
> I buried the poor little house deep down in my heart and watered its grave with some very bitter tears and prayed a wrung-out prayer of consecration over it, dedicating it to its new mistress, and now it is all over.

The closeness of Lady Ribblesdale's friendship with Curzon seems to have been accepted by her husband with tolerant understanding. Immortalized in Sargent's portrait of him booted and spurred, Lord Ribblesdale held a commission in the Rifle Brigade before entering politics as a Liberal. He became a Lord-in-Waiting to the Queen and Master of the Buckhounds, both political appointments. It was, however, as the target of what he called 'the impersonal rudeness of a super-man' that he won renown in debate. Speaking in the House of Lords on Home Rule, he stated his mistrust of coercion and his intuition verging on conviction that a way must be found of managing Ireland by consent. 'Confessions,' Lord Salisbury replied, 'are always interesting, from St Augustine to Rousseau, and from Rousseau to Lord Ribblesdale.' The victim minded such ridicule no more than a toss in the hunting field and learnt to bear both sorts of misfortune with equal good humour. Lying in bed one day with a broken leg, he received a visit of unusual commiseration from Mark Napier. 'Don't take any *half*-measures,' the lawyer urged him waggishly, 'have the damned thing *off*, that's what I say!'

Lord Ribblesdale also brought a distinctive stateliness to public life, a quality which Curzon caught exactly in the set of verses he wrote to greet his guests at a dinner he gave in 1890:

Tommy in style and garb betrays
A courtly elegance of ways,
Wherewith in Pope or Dryden's days
Less rarely was a man born.

Nor was Charty Ribblesdale ever lacking in devotion to her husband. There is much tenderness in her description of a long and tedious illness endured by Ribblesdale in the new year of 1889:

I have got so educated to invalidism [she told Curzon] that I can't think what wives do who have not got sick husbands. I live from day to day and try not to peep into the future more than I am obliged to. It is a dreary outlook and I dread 1889! The doctors say that Tommy must be very careful for a whole year, and then he will be as strong as ever, but not unless. This means to an active man like Tommy who has never been ill in his life a tremendous amount of self-denial and almost more than he possesses, I fear. He is much better, but his spirits are very bad, and we have not dared tell him what a stretch of discipline he has before him.

I suppose after so many relapses one is apt to lose heart. I have lost all courage and cannot realise now that he will ever be quite well! We are ordered a sea voyage, a long one! – hideous prospect. We both loathe the sea; however I would welcome even the black hole of Calcutta as a desirable residence if I knew it would make Tommy well.

By a whim of fate almost predictable in its perverseness, Ribblesdale recovered his health, surviving until the eve of his seventy-first birthday thirty-seven years later: it was his wife who had to endure exhausting years of ill-health leading to a premature death. Charty had always had a horror of the family weakness of tuberculosis. Nursing her elder sister Posie at Davos in 1886, she poured out her heart to Curzon:

This is a sad dreary little place, and I feel as if I were living in a graveyard. I long to go up to everybody and say, 'How long have you to be down here?' One of the saddest parts of it is the ceaseless gaieties in the way of dances, theatricals, concerts which go on at the 15 hotels! I always think of the Dance of Death! There is such fearful satire about it! The people are deadly dull as well as deadly ill. I feel a sort of sense of suffocation when they come to tea here.

Posie died in the winter of 1888. 'She was my particular sister,' Charty wrote to Curzon, 'and my good angel from my earliest recollection. All there is of good in me (little enough, God knows) is hers. I used to call her my little kingdom of heaven.' Then tuberculosis claimed Lady Ribblesdale, too. Years of nursing and isolation could effect no cure. She died in 1911.

'Promise me,' Charty Ribblesdale once wrote to Curzon at a time of dejection, 'you will always be as you were in the beginning to me, never grow old to me, for you will always be to me part of that happiest time of my life when there were no shadows anywhere, and darling Laura's dawn seemed almost too bright.'

The legend of Laura Tennant resists scepticism. It cannot be diminished or explained away by the pity of her early death or by the extravagant delight which her coterie took in each other's company. Loving and beloved, she seems to have inspired in all who knew her a devotion that was total, selfless and unassailable. She was small and pale and delicate, but with an extraordinary beauty of movement. She was gay and innocent and imaginative. She was open-hearted and affectionate and utterly untroubled by those social distinctions that so often disturbed the Victorians. 'She could not be happy,' a contemporary wrote of her, 'unless the crossing-sweeper liked her, and unless she knew all about his joys and griefs and home life.'

Her sweetness of character also showed itself in a tenderness towards those who vainly sought to marry her. She moved, it was said, encircled by a crowd of rejected lovers who remained her adoring friends. They included Rennell Rodd, who wooed her with verses of his own composition, and Gerald Balfour, a younger brother of Arthur Balfour. 'Do me this infinite service,' she wrote to Curzon when Gerald Balfour's hopes had finally been extinguished, 'and don't let him guess you know anything. I like him too well to give him one pang of pain, and God knows I have given him enough already.'

Laura Tennant would never intentionally wound any admirer. But there was a fastidiousness about her which repelled the self-satisfied, all-too-conscious cavalier. Sir Charles Dilke, the Liberal Member of Parliament whose promising ministerial career was ended by his involvement in a particularly unsavoury divorce case, found this on visiting Glen as the guest of the Tennants. On his second night in the house he met Laura in the passage on her way to bed, and said: 'If you will kiss me, I will give you a signed photograph.' She replied: 'It is awfully good of you, Sir Charles, but I would rather not, for what on earth should I do with the photograph?'

Her letters to Curzon, which begin in the summer of 1884 and end with her marriage to Alfred Lyttelton a year later, glow with affectionate warmth. Some passages are alive with schoolgirl banter: 'If you intend me to write, you'd better give me a shilling box of stationery with a picture of Ophelia or

Mrs Langtry outside – extra superfine cream.' This letter, the first in their correspondence, begins, 'You nice old boy,' and ends, 'Yr. pal in sincerity and all friendship, Laura Tennant'.

Later, telling him of the her life at Glen, she reveals the soul of a poet:

I get up at light. I read Gibbon before breakfast. I write, yes I write for hours and hours and seem never to have finished. I have such deep arrears of letters unanswered. And I walk or lie on my dear mother earth and read again. I eat, not very much – that's part of my plan – and I sleep and sometimes go out in the moonlight and dream, because at the bottom of my heart I have a hankering after my friends and after much that I have said goodbye to. I am really quite happy, simply because I could never be unhappy in the most beautiful place in the broad earth. Such proud purple, such glowing green and such shadows under the trees, such pink lights on the hay fields. Oh, it is very very beautiful and all dearly beloved. I know every light on the heather, I know every gleam on the Tweed, and you must know it too someday, George, and we will walk into the moor mists and faraway into the sky.

The Mediterranean in springtime evoked the same joyous lyricism:

Here it is delicious – so blue and warm. The orange trees exulting in their gold and the almond trees blushing at the kiss of the sun and the tender olives in their sad mysterious grey, looking like little nuns who once loved – and must love no more, only repent and be silent for ever. ... I sat all morning on the shore listening to the melancholy rhythm of waves and revelling in the despair of it all.*

Curzon stayed at the Glen for the first time in September 1884. It was a house full of talk and laughter and intense activity. There were none of those artificial barriers between the sexes which some Victorian parents took a morbid satisfaction in erecting and which prompted one genteel hostess to have the luggage of her men guests and her women guests stored in separate baggage-rooms. 'We miss you *so* much,' Laura assured him afterwards, 'you were so kind, so bright, so easily entertained, that you won a large place in the Hearts of the Everlasting Hills.'

She displayed a supreme self-confidence in guiding the course of her friendship with him. At one moment she would write teasingly of his supposed power to charm: 'I have been reading about Bernal Osborne and I think you are very like him, especially when he said his intentions to Miss Julia were *not* honourable.' Behind the banter, however, lay a quality of the spirit and a wisdom beyond her years:

Unless a man and a woman's friendship is built on more foundations than the appreciation of a good story in common or a kiss or a sitting out under the chaper-

*Like all assiduous correspondents, Laura sometimes repeated passages in her letters to other friends. A week or two after sending Curzon the vignette of Bordighera quoted above she included an almost identical paragraph in writing to Mary Gladstone, quoted in *Some Hawarden Letters*, page 179. Spontaneity, however, is not invariably an ingredient of a good letter, and Laura was writing not for posterity but to give pleasure.

onage of a half palm-hid Venus, or even the love of a poet or a novel, it will not stand, it will fall, and sink or cease to exist. So our friendship must be built on one Faith, one Hope, one Love. The Faith is the perfectability of Man, the Hope of that Perfectability and the Love of it. Unless we are baptized together into that church it is not much good imagining one's friendship will be a blessed one.

And she went on to administer a gentle rebuke that echoes the warning of her sister Charty:

You don't mind my speaking out, I know you are far too nice to mind it, but I don't want people to talk and I have heard people say things not true about you because they have heard you call women by their Christian names. You will be carefuller, dear George, and don't be unfair to yourself. You will *always* have *hot strong* friends but you ought to have *no* enemies.

It was in her company the same year that he visited the Tennyson family at their house near Haslemere, an experience memorable in itself but ever afterwards sharpened by his recollection that Laura, too, had been present. The climax of the day came at ten o'clock in the evening, when the poet read aloud from his works – 'a guttural, solemn chant in a rolling resonant monotone'. Then, Curzon continued in an autobiographical note, 'that brilliant child acted to us one thing after another of Sarah Bernhardt, with perfect imitation of style and gesture and, above all, voice'.

For all the warmth of their friendship, there is no evidence that Curzon ever hoped to marry Laura Tennant. During the year that their acquaintanceship ripened into affection, each was pursuing another affair of the heart. Curzon, as will be seen, was laying siege to the widowed Lady Grosvenor; and Laura was being wooed by Alfred Lyttelton. She was not in a wholly teasing mood when in August 1884 she commended to Curzon the homely virtues of Glen: 'I have been living an exemplary life of simplicity and industry, quite the sort of life that is calculated to fit me in days to come for a home of hideous domesticity and womanliness. Oh yes, George, I shall mark the jam beautifully and have ways of washing the tablecloths and no one will ever think I was once long ago fond of anything so frivolous as you – no one.'

Early in the new year Laura and Alfred Lyttelton announced their engagement to be married, and she hastened to assure Curzon of his own continuing place in her heart: 'You will promise not to take it for granted that I am going to change or do anything but be your affectionate old friend Laura as long as I have breath. I am nearly dead writing answers to the dullest and commonplacest letters you ever read, all saying I must be glad I have a rock or a harbour or a shield! Dear Dear!'

A few weeks before the wedding in May, she told Curzon: 'I hear every day from my old King Alf and he loved you for taking care of me as you did.' Had Curzon been the intimate friend of either Alfred or Laura alone, he might have felt inhibited from pursuing his friendship after their marriage.

But Alfred had been his hero since Eton days and Laura had bound him captive more swiftly but no less surely than her husband. He gave them his heartfelt blessing, and it was reciprocated. On the last day of their honeymoon in June they wrote him a joint letter, a tribute to his genius for friendship that has few parallels. It is headed, 'An hour before the death of one honeymoon – an hour before the birth of an eternal honeymoon', and served to reassure Curzon beyond any doubt that he retained an imperishable place in their affection:

My dear old George,

Your letter was so charming that I must send one responsive line tho you bade me make no answer. A number of people will assure you when you are about to embark on it that honeymooning is a fraud and that our ancestors who founded the institution did not understand the feelings of the moderns. Discredit these revolutionists and believe that barring just an hour or two of strangeness and perhaps of depression (begotten of fatigue and reaction from the unnatural riot of the few days preceding the wedding) the time is a noble one full of tranquil harmony, fruitful in blessed hopes for the future founded on the sure experiences which only solitude can give.

Don't change, my precious boy – we shall not.

Ever your affectionate
A. L.

My dear old George,

Your letter was like you, a real trump and I think you'll believe me it added a great mark of joy in what was already an Aurora.

I hope we may never be to each other anything else but dear good friends.

Come soon to see us – at 21 C[arlton] H[ouse] Terrace. Bless you.

Your affectionate and real friend
Laura Lyttelton

Curzon received only one more letter from her. Written on 5 February 1886, it consists of a few lines of gratitude for his 'darling little present' and a renewal of the love that she and her husband bore him: 'Alfred and I both want you to come to dine quite *à trois* tomorrow – so you will, won't you? Till then and affectionately and for always, your friend Laura.'

That same month, moved by some premonition that she had not long to live, she composed her will. 'I have not much to leave behind me should I die next month,' she began, 'having my treasure deep in my heart where no one can reach it, and where even Death cannot enter.' On 24 April, Curzon received a telegram from her brother-in-law, Lord Ribblesdale: 'All over between nine and ten this morning.' At the age of twenty-three and after less than a year of marriage, Laura had died in childbirth.

Her death evoked a degree of grief and dismay unusual even for the demonstrative age in which she lived. Mr Gladstone spoke for all who knew her in a noble letter of Christian consolation to his nephew Alfred. 'If life is measured by intensity,' he wrote, 'hers was a very long life – and yet with that rich development of mental gifts, purity and singleness made her one of the little children of whom and of whose like is the Kingdom of Heaven. Bold would it indeed be to say such a being died prematurely.'

Curzon, too, struck a sublime chord. He recalled the memory of 'one of those ethereal emanations that sometimes flash for a moment from the unseen and disappear again into it, leaving a wonder and enchantment that till the end of life creates a thrill in the heart of every one who beheld the spectacle'. Those words were written years after her death and embodied in the panegyric with which he mourned her husband Alfred. Shorter but no less poignant is the epitaph he inscribed on the last letter he ever received from Laura: 'The blessed child'.

Unlike her sisters, Lucy Tennant passed an unhappy childhood. She grew up into a shy and sweet-natured girl whose talent as a painter far surpassed the standard of competence demanded by every Victorian governess. Her modesty and delicacy of mind, perhaps also bouts of ill-health, deterred her from quite the same exuberance of friendship with which her sisters invested Curzon: but she loved him no less. 'When we talked of the people who are liked,' she told him after one of their infrequent meetings, 'I wanted to place you high on the list, but could not say it out while you were looking at me. Now, behind the screen of these *pattes de mouches* I could be very brazen and say what I think. ...' And sure enough, in spite of her marriage to Thomas Graham Smith, endearments begin to fall from her pen with the fervour of Charty Ribblesdale and the tenderness of Laura Lyttelton.

Whenever Curzon set off on his travels, the sisters would mourn and mope as if he were destined never to return to the hospitality of the Glen or of Grosvenor Square:

My dearest George,

I could not say last night a word of what my heart held of affection and good wishes for your journey – you are such a dear friend – the best of faithful friends and to me you have been something that no other friend has ever been – and so I don't like your going away for so long and shall long for your coming back.

This cushion has many loving thoughts of you stitched into it. Think sometimes affectionately of me George dear when you are at the end of the earth and send a word or message when you can.

Please give bearer or send me a few addresses and dates. God bless and keep you safe dear.

Your devoted
Lucy

All too rarely, the intensity of Lucy's endearments would be relieved by a touch of humour. Attempting to lure Curzon down to Wiltshire, she apologized for the presence of other guests – 'a vestal emerged from the sea mists of

Banffshire and a horse and his rider from the cheesemaking West Country with a face and intellect like its staple commodity'. More often, as she herself confessed, 'facts have a small space in my letters to you – feelings have a bad practice of taking up all the paper'.

For the rest, Lucy emerges from the shadows only as the uncomplaining victim of successive misfortunes. Her sisters seemed continually to be writing to Curzon about her slow convalescence after an internal haemorrhage; about her 'fatuous horse-breaking husband'; about her prolonged tortures from arthritis; about the bombardment of importunate letters, telegrams and messages she was obliged to endure from Harry Cust; about the difficulty of getting two nephews into a good house at Harrow. They did not appeal to Curzon in vain. There was nothing of the superior person about the rising young politician who was never too busy for sympathy, reassurance and advice.

Here a trio we meet,
Whom you never will beat,
Tho' wide you may wander and far go;
from what wonderful art
Of that Gallant Old Bart.,
Sprang CHARTY and LUCY and MARGOT?

To LUCY he gave
The wiles that enslave,
Heart and tongue of an angel to CHARTY;
To MARGOT the wit
And the wielding of it,
That make her the joy of a party.

It was appropriate that even in the doggerel with which Curzon saluted Laura's three surviving sisters, Margot should have had the last word. The youngest of the Tennants, she was generous and indiscreet, curious and courageous, high-spirited and spiritual. She became the friend of Dr Jowett and of John Addington Symonds, of Mr Gladstone and of General Booth. She was as happy in a library as in the hunting field, as at ease in the East End as in Marlborough House.

'I don't believe anyone, George, is as fond of so *many* things as I am, do you?' she once wrote to Curzon. 'Reading writing art music the poor etc. etc., what don't I like? I know – the sea. I hate the sea. I can look at it with admiration but have no feelings for it – no love – it's cruel & inexorable & goes on so *much* longer than any of the things one loves.'

Like her sisters, she was more than a little in love with him and proved the most devotedly copious of all his correspondents. Her sentiments were artless, her syntax uneasy, her punctuation negligible. Her thoughts flowed on to paper like a torrent of glittering bubbles: and all too often, as is the way with bubbles, they captivated for scarcely a moment before dissolving into nothingness. Elusive and emotional, her letters do not often survive the stiff formality of print.

Curzon's devotion to her was unfaltering, even when, early in their acquaintanceship, she irritated him profoundly by opening one of his letters to Laura. 'I was so dreadfully sorry you minded,' she wrote contritely, 'it was quite a blow to me to think anything I could do to you might not be right. You see Laura being away, she told me to open her letters but I quite forgot the other party might mind. I promise I'll *never* do it again. So now it's all right, isn't it?' Curzon forgave her: and it was to him that she poured out her heart in sorrow when Laura's marriage to Alfred Lyttelton seemed to threaten a sisterly intimacy of twenty years:

> Oh, George you were so nice to me, so sympathetic, so real bless you I didn't think you ever cd. be so nice, you understand things so quickly and don't *remind* one of the fact. I can't help it, it may be selfish but its true I *mind* Laura going, she's part of myself & I shall shriek at the empty bed now & work off what I've wanted to say by biting my pillow and burying my head.

In return for the consolation of his friendship, she offered him unstinted affection, and sometimes flattery:

> I have just finished *Curzon's Monasteries of the Levant* – the name endeared it to me – you might write *Curzon's Improvements on Other People's Experiences*. It would be vastly entertaining. You *are* an improvement of most people, so it would be accurate as well as candid, a rare combination.

Many of her letters were written to Curzon on his travels. 'You old darlin' calling me the Princess of girls,' she began in September 1887, 'it is very gratifying not to be forgotten even in Japan. Bring me home an idol of some sort or a bit of bright coloured silk scarlet or orange to put round my waist or throat & all I can get for you here is love, but so much George ... that the envelope wd. split if I sent it all so I must needs keep it. ... I hope when you are low yr. thoughts turn to a place buried in the restful hills where the echoes of the burn are never heard except by the peewit & the curlews & the moor mists wreath round the sun.'

Two years later, as he set out for his arduous journey across Persia, she again sped him on his way:

> Dearest dear George,
>
> This is a line of good-bye & Bon Voyage for you to put in yr. pocket & read with yr. other letters when you are rather sad as everyone must be at leaving England & dear old boy *do* be careful of yourself. Keep your chest warm, buy chest protectors. *Please* see to this & dont over tire yourself, put brandy in your flask & never sit in

wet boats – you must not smile I'm serious because I think you've not got the strongest lungs & are inclined to over do it.

Now dear George God bless you a post card with yr. address will bring you a letter from yr. only & first girl who always cares for you & always will wherever you are on the globe.

Yr. Marge

She turned to him for protection, too, when she became aware of what Dr Johnson once called the hiss of the world. 'Don't let people say nasty things of me,' she pleaded, 'cause there's no reason for it.' That was not entirely true. She delighted in defying the conventions of the day. Her wild escapades in the hunting field, her flirtations in country houses, her pursuit of men of letters, her disdain for the small talk of the drawing-room – such a way of life disturbed the tranquil notions of her elders and made enemies among her contemporaries. They mistook her impatience for arrogance; her intellectual excitement for affectation; her independence for naughtiness, if not worse.

Her sharpness of tongue also affronted those leisured and much-arranged ladies who took it upon themselves to set the tone of society. In a letter to Curzon she described one acquaintance as 'that rather vulgar woman who looks under her eyes at one and speaks broken English in an arch undertone'. Another had a 'vast foolish decorated face and good heart'. She spoke disrespectfully even of the President of the Crabbet Club:

Wilfrid Blunt, lazier than ever, has just read me a sonnet he has written to me. I begged him to bowdlerize one line where he talks of my lips being thrilling to his! No being cd. inspire me with less thrill and if he kissed me he wd. give me a headache.

Her critics had their revenge when in 1893 Mr E.F.Benson, son of the Archbishop of Canterbury, published his novel, *Dodo*. Margot felt its sting. 'The heroine, a pretentious donkey with the heart and brain of a linnet,' she afterwards wrote, 'was supposed to be myself.' But, she added, Dodo could not really be modelled on her, 'as I was not beautiful and did not hunt in summer'.

As the years of her girlhood slipped away, Margot's friends began to wonder whether so stormy a petrel would ever subside into matrimony. 'I hear you are going to marry Margot Tennant,' Arthur Balfour was asked. 'No, that is not so,' he replied, 'I rather think of having a career of my own.' It turned out to be another future Prime Minister who claimed her hand. In December, 1892, she reported to Curzon on her growing friendship with the widowed Henry Asquith, who had recently become Home Secretary in Mr Gladstone's last Government – a promotion which Curzon described as 'sudden, unsuspected, agreeable to his friends, but scarcely deserved'. Margot was more tolerant: 'He improves with success, I think: he is more flexible and can be delightful company.' Early in 1894 they were engaged to be married.

The Queen was astonished that so staid a statesman, the epitome of middle-class caution, should wish to wed the mercurial Miss Tennant. Unfamiliar with court etiquette, Asquith wrote to enquire from her private secretary, Sir Henry Ponsonby, whether he need seek Royal consent to the union. The Queen noted grimly on the back of his letter: 'How curious ... *that he* sh^{d} ask if my consent is required to his marriage. If this *was* required the Queen w^{d} not give it as she thinks she is most unfit for a C. Minister's wife. V.R.I.'

Curzon responded with affection and generosity to Margot's new-found happiness. She replied:

Dearest of dears

What a noble & lovely present you have sent us such a beautiful piece of embroidery it is a feast of fine colouring and delights me.

It was like you to give me a little personal pin to wear by myself & for myself & I *thank* you.

You have been, & are *inexpressibly* dear to me George & if by May 10th (wh. is our wedding date) I cease to be yr. first girl I can & will for as long as you let me remain

Your true & your most loyal loving
Margie

Four Prime Ministers signed the register after the marriage service in St George's, Hanover Square – Gladstone, Rosebery, Balfour and Asquith himself. Only four days later Margot interrupted the tranquillity of her honeymoon to thank Curzon yet again for the rock-like constancy of his friendship:

Dearest George,

Your letter was a great delight to me & I shall keep it for my life. If I cd. really think I had brought 'real good' to one who spreads everything dear that the world can give around him why I sd. feel deep down pride but oh! George I'm not good I'm only living & I *love you.* So you cried a little – well – I too cd. have *sobbed* but I felt it wd. have been like a wine glass in the sea so deep was my emotion & I never cried a tear till I said goodbye to Charty in the train & then I felt it was all over & my ring was pressed into my finger by an enthusiastic old servant on the platform & with a wave & a gasp I sank back in the train *knowing* I was married.

It is very beautiful down here I never saw such starred underground of spring spangles – violets buttercups & perriwinkles. There is nothing new in the idea! but there is something sad about the Spring – a sort of abundant self sufficiency wh. makes it less sympathetic than autumn I think. We read a great deal, always to ourselves for I hate reading out loud or listening & yesterday we had a heavenly day at Bath with R & Charty – laughed all the time – you will give me dinner when I get back wont you I want to be made much of! & air my trousseau

Yr own ever loving
Marge

In the autumn of 1882, only a month or two after ceasing to be an undergraduate, Curzon confided to Brodrick that he had recently enjoyed a 'tête à tête with my dear Lady Grosvenor', and that he hoped soon to be taking her to the play. The fourth and youngest daughter of the ninth Earl of Scarbrough, Lady Sibell Lumley was only nineteen when in 1874 she married Lord Grosvenor, son and heir of the first Duke of Westminster. Her husband, however, was plagued by ill-health and after only ten years of married life she found herself left a widow with three children. Sibell Grosvenor's beauty and sweetness of character, not to mention her inherited possessions, attracted a swarm of eager suitors. None was more persistent than George Curzon.

Even before Lord Grosvenor's death, he had established a warm friendship with her. 'I went to Eaton not long ago,' Alfred Lyttelton wrote to Curzon in April 1883, 'and made great friends with Lady Grosvenor, upon whose table I saw a photograph of you.' And later that year he was teased by Charty Ribblesdale. 'I expect the reason we did not come across each other was that you were better occupied with S–b—l or some other fair angel in gauze.' Everyone loved her. 'Nothing can be more delightful than hearing Sibell playing on the organ in the Library at Eaton,' Lord Ronald Gower recorded in his diary, 'it is like seeing and listening to another St. Cecilia.' Mary Gladstone also adored her: 'She is a little sweet soul and the keynote is unselfishness.' So, too, did Margot. 'Sibell's lovely little eager pathetic face has gone like a vision,' she wrote to Curzon from Whittinghame, Arthur Balfour's house in Scotland.

For three years, in the intervals of politics and travel and flirtation with the Tennant sisters, Curzon begged her in vain to marry him. Neither side of the correspondence has survived, but the sympathetic concern of Laura, Margot and Charty illuminate his anguish. Although he confided to none of them the reason for his leaden heart, family gossip handed down over the years points to Lady Grosvenor's reluctance as the cause. Laura wrote to him in February, 1885:

My dear old George

I of course having eyes to see behind the earthquakes saw you were in lower spirits than usual, and all the fantastic froth of your conversation may have misled the others but had no blinding effect upon me. Well dear old friend I don't quite know what puts you down in the Profounds, but I do know by much bitter experience what it is to be there and so I offer you my hand to hold yours and my most full hearted sympathy.

The subtleties that turn ones laughter into tears are more marvellous in my eyes than the molecules that turn apes into babes or dust into dodos, but I don't think tears of ours are spilt for nothing and I believe they are drawn up into the sky to fall in thirst quenching showers, flowers creating and earth wooing rain!

Let me be of practical use to you always. You and I are friends and you know the beauty of friendship is honesty and trust. Alfred is anxious none of my friends should feel I had become different and as long as he believes in me and trusts me as he does I cannot think you will ever have reason to find me anything else but

Your old and affectionate friend
Laura Tennant

Later that year Margot took up the consoling refrain:

You dear, dear,

I do so hate seeing you the least low, you who are born to be bright & gay & make others the same & always have up till now – not that you were dull, that you cdnt be, in fact seeing people as they are & feel is a mark of confidence & was rather nice, only you made me so sorry for you. I longed to be able to help you. I ask nothing & want to know nothing but nothing is worth making yrself miserable about – everyone who likes you likes you so much you are so sympathetic & dear, yr. friends will always feel the same for you, amongst the best & truest is yr

Margot always

In the following week Charty, too, wrote to Curzon:

Laura and Margot have of course tried to pump me, but they have discovered nothing from me. They were certain there was something up, and Laura appeared to me to have been told quite as much by you as I was! We are all entirely in the dark. ... Poor dear, I have been thinking of you so much and wondering what new phases of mental torture you have been passing through.

Curzon's rival in his quest for Sibell's heart was George Wyndham. A soldier by profession, he wooed her with the passion of a poet. 'She makes one despair of the world,' he wrote, 'because other women are so different from her, and hope for it because she has been born and reared amongst their littlenesses and meannesses.' His campaign was as arduous as that of Curzon. By 1886, when it became common knowledge that each was pressing his suit, their friends began to take sides. Poor Sibell, distracted by doubts and indecision, could not make up her mind until the end of the year. Legend has it that she then accepted both Georges on the same day. More credible is the undoubted fact that she was married to Wyndham on 7 February 1887.

From Davos, where she was nursing her sister Posie, Charty hastened to comfort the rejected suitor with a mild denigration of the betrothed pair that probably appealed to Curzon less than she thought:

You have been so persistently and continuously in my thoughts, never out of them in fact, that I must write and tell you ever since I heard the hard stern, no, I don't think I can dignify it by that name, tough is more the word, tough news I have thought of nothing but my dearest old George and his numbed heart and cruel blow.

I *am* disappointed in Sibell, she has descended, fathomless fathoms in my estimation.

In fact now it is almost too tough a bit of news for me to digest, but I feel the incapacity of my digestive powers are an insecure peg to hang any doubts upon!

It must be true as Margot says Mary Elcho says it's all settled. Was Alfred right in his ancient verdict that she would succumb to anybody who was persistent enough? My dear old boy you don't know how my heart aches for you. I know it is not in any mortal's power to comfort you, but everybody likes sympathy, and I know you will care to know that I have been very near you all this time and holding your hand all these past 3 days and now I feel as if I were touching it. I do feel you would have been wasted on her, at least all the finest and rarest parts of you. But I don't suppose this is any consolation to you. ...

You know I was tremendously keen you should cut out George Wyndham, in spite of this great impassable gulf of non-appreciation, but now it is not to be.

It seems to me from the mere naked yet unashamed fact, that she prefers that impressive masher to you, shows how unworthy she was of you.

Well I hope the poor lady is happy, it is always dreadfully sad when one's best friend arrests his identity as it were and becomes a part of somebody else, whoever she marry, be he the archangel Gabriel himself, but when it is not an angel, and not even a fallen angel, it is sadder still. He is more of the cherubin type, who continually do cry!*

Fortunately, Curzon was not without distractions during that winter of discontent. Exactly one week before Sibell's wedding, he delivered his much-praised maiden speech in the House of Commons.

Nor did he afterwards brood with bitterness over Sibell's defection: both she and George Wyndham remained his intimate friends. One aspect of the marriage may even have given him a little sardonic amusement. Sibell's devotion to her new husband, Curzon cannot have failed to notice, stopped short of assuming his name. To the end of her life in 1929 she continued to be known, by her own wish, as Lady Grosvenor.

In October 1920, when he was sixty-one, the Secretary of State for Foreign Affairs received an unexpected and disagreeable reminder of another episode in his amorous bachelor days. There arrived at Carlton House Terrace a letter from a solicitor's office in Lincoln's Inn Fields. The writer spoke of having acted for a certain noble family, and asked Curzon to call on him one morning to discuss 'a matter of some interest to you'. Curzon replied that he was too busy to do so, and remained unmoved by further requests for a meeting.

Early in the following month, the solicitor composed and sent to Curzon an enigmatic document in the form of a play, the entire action of which takes place in a solicitor's office. Scene I, which opens in 1892, reveals a wronged husband about to bring an action for divorce against his wife on the strength of some compromising letters written to her by her lover, Mr A. In Scene II, a few weeks later, the husband is advised to abandon proceedings, as he him-

* Percy Lyulph, the only son of George Wyndham and Sibell Grosvenor, married in 1913 Diana, the youngest daughter of Tommy and Charty Ribblesdale. He was killed in action in 1914.

self could not go into court with an impeccable character. Scene III takes place twenty-eight years later, i.e. in the present. The solicitor and his clerk are discovered talking about the case. They recall that the wronged husband, now dead, has never paid the firm outstanding fees of £100 for legal services rendered; but that they still have in their possession twenty-eight of the compromising letters. So they decide to put a proposal to their author, Mr A., who is still alive: if he will discharge the debt of the man he wronged in 1892, they will burn the letters in his presence. The play ends with an epilogue, in the form of a soliloquy by its author, the solicitor:

> As I consider that with a view to avoiding any possible scandal or annoyance in the future it would be best that the remaining documents should be destroyed, whatever may be Mr A.'s decision I shall probably destroy them, but as owing to that which I have already done and propose doing I have been and shall be the means of bringing about a state of circumstances which Mr A. may consider from his point of view desirable I regard the suggestion I have made a reasonable one.

Curzon replied stiffly to the dramatist, reminding him that Mr A. had already paid for the letters to be destroyed many years before. Somewhat lamely, the solicitor persisted in his assertion that he had a legal lien on the letters for moneys due to him: but that as he had just destroyed them, he trusted that Mr A. would now feel it a matter of honour to discharge the ancient debt of £100.

The solicitor, however, had met his match. Curzon scrawled across the copy of the play that, surprisingly, he preserved in his archives: 'Indignantly declined to pay £100 blackmail for the destruction of the surviving letters.'

Chapter Fourteen
SOULS

Around him that night –
Was there e'er such a sight? –
Souls sparkled and spirits expanded;
For of them critics sang,
That, tho' christened the Gang,
By a spiritual link they were banded.

– From verses written by Curzon to welcome his guests at a dinner held at the Bachelors' Club, 10 July 1889

Curzon's circle of friends had intellects as well as hearts. They were no less bent on pleasure than their contemporaries, but pursued it in ways that stimulated the mind as much as the emotions. Life was too exciting and leisure too precious to be frittered away on the fashionable pastimes of the rich: cards were ephemeral and racing frivolous, not to say vulgar. Instead they sought fulfilment in the arabesques of conversation and the adventures of ideas, in books and in music, in the beauty of nature and the ingenuity of landscape gardening. Even their romances were invested with an elegance of wit and an exuberance of sentiment that to hostile eyes seemed artificial. They cared much for intelligence but nothing for convention. They were self-sufficient but not supercilious. They were a coterie, perhaps a cult, but never a conspiracy.

In Paris they would have been taken for granted: in London they earned a mocking sobriquet. It was Lord Charles Beresford who coined it. 'You are always talking about your souls,' he exclaimed at a dinner party given by Lady Brownlow in 1887 or 1888, 'I shall call you the Souls.' A sailor by profession, Charlie Beresford was a stranger to the tradition of silence often attributed to the Royal Navy. Throughout life he spoke his mind with a candour from which not even his wife was exempt. Walking down the steps of the Royal Yacht Squadron at Cowes one day he saw her approaching in the artless style of make-up which she affected. 'Here comes my little frigate in a fresh coat of paint,' he said. His conduct at the bombardment of Alexandria brought him national fame when, in command of the gunboat *Condor*, he drew the fire of the Egyptian shore batteries in order to spare the British iron-clads. In the House of Commons, where serving officers were at that time permitted to sit, he employed the same audacious tactics: and again in the skirmishes he fought with his no less impulsive but shrewder rival, Admiral Lord Fisher.

Not all the Souls appreciated Beresford's banter. 'To me,' Arthur Balfour wrote, 'the name of Souls seemed always meaningless and slightly ludicrous. It seems to imply some kind of organization and purpose, where no organization or purpose was dreamed of. It seems to suggest a process of selection, possibly even of rejection, by a group which, in so far as it had any separate existence, was a spontaneous and natural growth, born of casual friendship and unpremeditated sympathy.' The Souls themselves rarely used the name except in irony. They preferred to call themselves the Gang, with an emphasis more on shared confidence than on a self-conscious exclusiveness.

An almost complete roll of the Souls may be culled from the verses which Curzon composed and declaimed at a dinner he gave at the Bachelors' Club on 10 July 1889. As a bachelor without a country house of his own he could not easily return the incessant hospitality he received from his married friends. It was an inspired thought not only to invite about fifty of them to a single dinner party, but to ensure that they should remember the evening in rhyme. The moment they had taken their seats, on each of which lay a printed set of verses, he began:

Ho! list to a lay
Of that company gay,
Compounded of Gallants and Graces,
Who gathered to dine,
In the year '89,
In a haunt that in Hamilton Place is.

Having then apostrophized each guest in turn, the laureate concluded his recitation with a self-congratulatory flourish:

Now this is the sum
Of those who had come,
Or who ought to have come to that banquet,
Then call for the bowl,
Flow spirit and soul,
Till midnight not one of you can quit!

And blest by the Gang
Be the rhymester who sang
Their praises in doggerel appalling.
More now were a sin –
Ho, waiters, begin!
Each Soul for consommé is calling!

Almost exactly a year later, on 9 July 1890, Curzon repeated the occasion. Although the second set of verses lack the verve and sparkle of his initial outrage, the opening stanzas bear repetition:

A second time these friends are met,
Again the festal board is set,
The envy of a world to whet,
  Again 'tis George N. Curzon,
The author of the original crime,
The minstrel of a former time,
Who mounts his Pegasus of rhyme
  And claps his rusty spurs on!

Lost of our last year's ranks are some,
But most, the Lord be praised, have come,
And others, to make malice dumb,
  Have joined our gallant order.
To those, to these, the grateful host
Here lifts his glass and gives the toast,
Here dips his pen and makes his boast
  To be his guests' recorder.

It was no accident that led Curzon to reserve the first of his salutes for Arthur Balfour.

  There was seen at that feast
  Of this band the high priest
The heart that to all hearts is nearest;
  Him may nobody steal
  From the true Commonweal
Tho' to each is dear Arthur the dearest.

The aura with which Balfour's friends surrounded him continues to glow across the years. They cherished his grace of mind and body, his absorption in speculative philosophy, his seeming detachment, as Beatrice Webb called it, from the greed and grime of common human nature. They basked, too, in the warmth of his gentle courtesy and ready laughter, his almost feminine intuition and instinctive sympathy. He was elevated but never remote.

Music was a perennial bond that bound him to the Souls. With Lytteltons, Gladstones and Tennants (but hardly ever with the tone-deaf Curzon) he would sit enraptured through concerts at the Crystal Palace, Exeter Hall or St James's Hall, then return to his house, No. 4 Carlton Gardens, to renew the enjoyment with his friends. Sometimes they would use the concertina to recapture themes: at others his pair of concert grand pianos with a mass of music – mostly Handel, Beethoven and Schumann – arranged for the two instruments. For him music was a solace and a stimulation, but always an intellectual exercise. Never could he entirely escape from the shackles of logic. He would stand at the top of the great double staircase in Carlton Gardens, torn with doubts about which way to turn. 'The worst of this staircase,' he would say, 'is that there is absolutely no reason why one should go down one side rather than the other. What am I to do?'

Golf, too, set the wheels of his mind spinning with the same urgency as if he were at work on *A Defence of Philosophic Doubt*, or *The Foundations of Belief*. 'Forgive my dictating what is only a personal letter,' he wrote to Curzon in 1896, 'but time presses, and I find it difficult to squeeze in the claims of both golf and politics into the 24 hours.' Another Soul, Harry Cust, was similarly addicted to the game. He called it 'the last – would to God it had been the first – infirmity of noble minds'. Curzon, precluded from playing golf by his spinal weakness, took a vicarious pleasure in following the game. On being invited to become Lord Warden of the Cinque Ports he regretted being unable to play on the excellent courses of Kent, although a year or two later he consulted Alfred Lyttelton about laying out a nine-hole course in the park at Hackwood.

Balfour was exposed to much adulation from his fellow Souls. Mary Gladstone said that an ideal dinner party should consist of the eight Lyttelton brothers, A.J.B. and herself. Charty Ribblesdale told Curzon, after Balfour had been staying at Glen, that 'it was very dear of him to give us four days of his precious and clamoured-for presence'. All would refer to him, without a trace of mockery, as King Arthur. Sometimes, it seemed to his adoring circle, he did not respond with the enthusiasm they deserved. Talking to him one day of Lady Desborough and of his own niece Blanche, Margot Asquith said: 'You're fond of me and of Ettie and of Baffy; but you don't really care – you wouldn't *mind* if we all died.' He replied: 'I should mind if you all died on the same day.'

Although he never married, there was one woman to whom Balfour remained constant. Godfrey Webb, the court jester both of the Crabbet Club and of the Souls, used to say: 'What shall it profit a man if he gain the whole world and lose his own particular Soul.' That place in Balfour's heart was occupied by Mary Elcho, the sister of George Wyndham and wife of Hugo Elcho, later Earl of Wemyss. Balfour's latest biographer has devoted much conscientious study to determining whether their love for each other found physical fulfilment, and his verdict has been disputed. It is not a theme that need be re-examined: sufficient to know that Lady Elcho possessed a beauty of countenance that persisted into old age, and a charm of character spiced rather than marred by vagueness. She would refer to the eleventeenth century, and once described how, when in Scotland, she had 'quite inadvertently dined at Balmoral'. Her husband, having sown his wild oats early in life, was not always a willing accomplice of her hospitable instincts. On the occasion when she was moved to give a fancy dress ball, Lord Elcho had to be cajoled into donning an eighteenth-century suit of apricot satin. He dressed reluctantly and prepared to make what he hoped would be an unobtrusive entrance. He found his ballroom full of men and women, every one of them clad in the soberly correct fashion of the later Victorian age. His wife had forgotten to write 'Fancy Dress' on the invitation cards.

No Souls were more Soulful than the Tennant sisters. 'I have embarked on Gibbon – are you horrified that I have never read him?' Laura once wrote to Curzon. 'I suppose it's shocking. I never read facts if I can read fables! I don't mean novels. I have read very few novels, but any speculative reading I love. My soul hankers after philosophy and poetry.'

Lucy, too, determined to put her leisure to some purpose. From Wiltshire she subscribed to a correspondence course of English Literature organized by Glasgow University and answered a set of written questions once a fortnight.

> One is calmly requested [she told Curzon] to outline the careers of Pope, Addison, Swift or Johnson, to compare their styles and criticise their works. While lower down the paper are questions on the play of Julius Caesar, the chief people to be characterised and compared and speeches to be paraphrased. I have never seen an exam paper, so I imagine it is something similar. ... It all affords me so much amusement and litters the floor with tomes of every description.

And when she had to spend weeks in bed through illness, Charty and Margot produced a characteristic panacea. Each read John Morley's book on Rousseau, then prepared an analysis of the philosopher's life and character. 'It was such fun,' Charty wrote to Curzon, 'reading them out to Lucy and seeing the effect each had on her.'

They appointed Curzon their guru, and the role was not unwelcome to him. 'I want to improve my mind and follow your good example seriously,' Charty told him. 'I want to read some history, can you tell me the name, a comprehensive one and not reaching from here to Australia?' Later she proposed to write an essay on the art of conversation: 'Will you do one too? It doesn't matter how rubbishy, the worse it is the better we shall like it. Do join us if you are not too busy. I have just finished an essay on fashion. ... I am afraid you will think it sad twaddle.'

Margot was even more demanding:

> Dearest George,
>
> I know you are always so busy, so am I. Wd. you be very kind & either call round tonight or tomorrow night between 6 & 7 or write to me one or 2 hints & criticisms on *Maud*. We belong to a class & Churton Collins lectures on Tennyson. He asks us to write a paper criticizing Maud giving the plot etc. he does not admire it himself

but I *do* immensely & know you do. I think it is to love what *In Memoriam* is to sorrow – every bit of dramatic power & passion that Tennyson has gone into it: but one word from you wd. help me: I sd. like to write a good paper *immensely* only doubt my powers. Jowett once said it was based on the feeling of Shakespeare's sonnets tell me how? & if you agree?

Do you mind being thus bothered.

Ever yr. loving
Marge

The reservations which Churton Collins expressed about *Maud* are likely to have been as much personal as poetic. A few years before Margot became his pupil he had offended Tennyson by the savagery of his attack on a book by Edmund Gosse, a rival man of letters. Feeling, he confessed, as if he had been flayed alive, Gosse was reluctant to show his face in literary society until the stinging words of Collins had been forgotten. But he could hardly refuse an invitation from Tennyson: and it was from that rough-tongued poet that he received unbelievably soothing balm. 'Well, Gosse,' the poet boomed down the table at him, 'would you like to know what I think of Churton Collins? I think he's a Louse on the Locks of Literature.'

In retrospect it may sometimes seem surprising that friendships could survive the cold intellectual scrutiny of those observant sisters. Evan Charteris, a younger brother of Lord Elcho and the biographer of Edmund Gosse, wrote to Curzon about his visit to the Tennants in the summer of 1888: 'The Glen family are in their usual vigour, and have been reviewing a varied succession of male and female creations, analysing and drafting them off into their several categories, and dismissing them with the inevitable sense of thraldom and absolute submission.'

Surrounded by a house party of Souls, Laura once wrote this to Curzon:

The menu talked to me.

Salt	Alfred
Pepper	Arthur
Mustard	Hugo
Bread	St John
Butter	Lord Vernon, who makes his livelihood by dairy produce.

As for the pepper, one never knows if it is going to make one sneeze or cry. I like Mr Balfour but he is a little impossible and I don't fancy he thinks much of your friend.*

Balfour, like all who knew Laura, came to adore her. But he was not an easy guest to entertain. Although he would never betray his feelings by a

* A few weeks earlier she wrote an almost identical letter to Mary Gladstone, in which Hugo Elcho was the pepper and Arthur Balfour the mustard. Published in *Some Hawarden Letters*, page 179.

harsh word, much less a grimace, he could go quite pale from boredom. Harry Cust invented his own protection against wearisome guests when he found himself in Soulless company. He would embark on long, flat, interminable reminiscences of his childhood, until his audience screamed for mercy. It was called Boring the Bore.

The games which the Souls played among themselves were far removed from the bridge and baccarat and billiards of the rest of the *beau monde.* One consisted of writing on a given subject in the style of Shakespeare or Browning, Carlyle or Meredith. Another, their favourite, was a sophisticated version of 'Twenty Questions'. Instead of commonplace objects, however, they had to guess such conceptions as a *tête-à-tête*, odd man out, the last straw, the eleventh hour, a lost cause, a contrast or an interval. In so rarefied an atmosphere, the question, 'Abstract or concrete?' would often lead to prolonged and profound dispute. It was therefore changed to, 'Is it tangible?'

Further perils lurked in another of their pastimes. 'We have got a new game (don't shiver and yawn!),' Margot told Curzon, 'moral and intellectual receipts for mutual friends! quite chilling.' Balfour's foundations of belief may well have been shaken when Margot was once staying with him and he picked up a sheet of paper in her writing which began: 'So Arthur Balfour is dead. ...' Her husband was also addicted to these lapidary exertions, which have been described by his Chief Secretary for Ireland, Augustine Birrell: 'All of us know that when the Prime Minister is bored – and he is frequently bored – at a Cabinet meeting, he distracts himself by composing tributes to his colleagues. He looks round the table, selects a victim, and we know upon what exercise his mind is engaged. It is highly uncomfortable when, after circling round the table, the Prime Minister's obituary eye rests meditatively upon oneself.'

Charty Ribblesdale one night made each of her guests in turn define 'prejudice' and 'tact'. Arthur Balfour did well with the first. 'Prejudice,' he said, 'is principle from your opponent's point of view.' Unexpectedly, however, the prize went to St John Brodrick, who defined prejudice as 'the point where sympathy and interest meet', and tact as 'the tribute which intelligence pays to humbug'. Charty was astonished by his performance. 'The most tactless man in the room,' she told Curzon, 'defined tact better than anybody, wasn't this remarkable?'

St John Brodrick was as much renowned among the Souls for his gaffes as he was loved for his golden good nature. The most celebrated example was when he and his wife Hilda, a sister of Lord Elcho, were staying with Lord Pembroke at Wilton. Another guest admired the colour of her hair and Brodrick observed what an extraordinary thing it was that since they had had a red-headed footman, Hilda's hair had got redder and redder. 'Poor Hilda looked very uncomfy,' Charty Ribblesdale reported to Curzon, 'and there was general embarrassment! This was his only faux-pas.'

Speaking as a guest of honour at a Balliol gaudy, he dwelt on 'the unfortunate effects of the intrusion of professors into politics'. A few feet away from him sat Sir William Anson, Warden of All Souls, Conservative MP for Oxford University and his colleague in Arthur Balfour's Government. Delighted by St John's blunder, George Leveson Gower and other Liberals at the dinner cheered him to the echo.

On another occasion he was talking to the Duke of Northumberland about his son and heir, Lord Percy, who sat as Member of Parliament for South Kensington. He told the Duke what a pity it was that Percy would soon have to take his father's place in the House of Lords, thus ending a brilliant career in the House of Commons. Lord Lansdowne, who was also present, noticed the pained look on the Duke's face and tried to laugh off the tactlessness of Brodrick's unwelcome prognostication. 'I suppose you think the same about my own son, who is also in the Commons?' Lansdowne joked. 'Oh, no,' Brodrick replied solemnly, 'I was talking only about *brilliant* elder sons.'

In his pre-prandial verses of July 1889, Curzon paid graceful tribute to Lord and Lady Pembroke:

From Wilton, whose streams
Murmur sweet in our dreams,
Come the Earl and his Countess together.
In her spirit's proud flights
We are whirled to the heights,
He sweetens our stay in the nether.

The host again struck his lute in their honour when they dined with him the following year:

Straight from the canvas of Vandyck
A stately pair steps forth, alike
By nature well equipped to strike
With love and admiration;
Humour and sentiment combined
In guise romantic but refined,
George Pembroke's these – his lady's mind
Courts daring speculation.

George, thirteenth Earl of Pembroke and original founder of the Crabbet Club, was the son of Sidney Herbert, Secretary for War during the Crimean campaign and the protector of Florence Nightingale. In 1874 Disraeli appointed Pembroke to be Under-Secretary for War, a characteristically imaginative gesture. But the work proved too arduous for his delicate health, and he resigned in the following year. He was a victim of tuberculosis, a disease that even as late as the last two decades of the nineteenth century took a heavy toll as much among the rich as the poor. In 1890 Curzon, too, was suspected of weakness of the lungs, and from Aix-les-Bains received a letter of sympathy and advice from his fellow invalid:

> I hear ill news about your health – of your being threatened with serious illness which gives me great concern. For I know well what the bitterness of it must be to you. Not so much on account of the loss of health or even of life, but of the threatened ruin of all your hopes and plans and the snatching away of the success that you have always so steadily earned and which is so easily within your reach. I can't tell you how sorry I am to think of you being haunted by such a dread, even though it should be a mere bogey after all, as I trust it may prove to be.
>
> I wish you were here breathing this pellucid air instead of the damp plumcake that serves for atmosphere at Oxford, where I hear you are. I expect you ought to be a great deal in the open air. The Blunts used to get on horses and ride into the desert whenever they were ill and never seemed to suffer from exposure or anything – till they returned to civilization and England, which always had a disastrous effect and you seem to have something of the same peculiarity.

Pembroke added the name and address of a French doctor who had cured Wilfrid Blunt by injecting creosote oil (he thought) under his skin and so fattening him up. It is doubtful whether Curzon tried such a bizarre treatment. He did, however, take with him to Switzerland in January 1891 a present of a rug from the Tennant sisters, together with their hopes 'that it will enfold you as warmly as do our hearts'. That and the crisp climate of St Moritz seemed to have worked wonders, and by the summer he was fit enough to accept junior ministerial office. Pembroke was less fortunate. He died five years later aged forty-five.

Pembroke's wife was Lady Gertrude Talbot, daughter of the eighteenth Earl of Shrewsbury. Known to friends and family as Gity or Gety or Guity, she had a commanding presence, an imperious voice, splendid chestnut hair, and a display of pearls wound three times round her neck, even over the rough seaman's jersey she wore when sailing with her husband. She also had mannerisms which evoked among her fellow Souls a mild irritation not untouched by affection. 'Lady Pembroke will not fit any household quite,' Margot once wrote to Curzon from the Glen, 'she has lurid proposals to make at all times and if fine reads out loud indoors and if wet enough tramped the hills till my heels ached.' Charty also thought her a difficult guest:

> I found Gity rather hard work, she is the most unadaptable being I have ever met, they bore down on us from their yacht at a most unfortunate time when there was nothing but family in the house, and the ancient mariner with the albatross round his neck had an ideally easy time of it in comparison to me, for I had the whole of her on my shoulders, and she is one of those restless creatures who don't let you call your soul your own.

One friend said that 'she sailed about and she sailed alone', another that she 'stumbled upwards into vacuity'. Her conversational excursions into the infinite did sometimes seem pretentious. But her vagaries of belief protected her friends from boredom. During one of the Pembrokes' yachting holidays the men were pleased with themselves at having caught a lobster. Then Gity appeared and insisted that they should put it back in the sea, as it was cruel to boil lobsters alive. They showed her that it was bright red, having already been cooked. She didn't believe them. She said lobsters were always red: so it went overboard.

The story of Lady Pembroke and the lobster comes from the pen of one of the most ethereal of the Souls. Frances Horner was the daughter of William Graham, Liberal Member of Parliament, early patron of the pre-Raphaelites and himself a painter of talent. Her marriage to Sir John Horner, the predecessor of George Leveson Gower as Commissioner of Woods and Forests, brought her not only a loving husband but also Mells Park, a house of magical beauty in Somerset. It was there that the Souls relaxed in their own scintillating way. Alfred Lyttelton, startled to hear peals of laughter coming from the morning-room, traced it to his hostess and Charty Ribblesdale. They were reading aloud from Schopenhauer's *World as Will and Idea*, in which the philosopher describes the efforts of the unborn children to enter the world through the medium of lovers' meetings. In London, too, she had her own salon even as a girl, with Burne-Jones at her feet and Ruskin at her elbow.

Another Soul who shed joy about her was Ettie Grenfell. Unlike most of her friends she was insensitive to music and painting: but that was her only want. Margot Asquith, who could be uncomfortably candid about her friends, had no reservations about her: 'Her genius lay in a penetrating understanding of the human heart and a determination to redress the balance of life's unhappiness ... she ought to have lived in the days of the great King's mistresses. I would have gone to her if I were sad, but never if I were guilty.' A descendant both of Lady Melbourne and of Lady Palmerston, Mrs Grenfell herself was the last of the great Whig hostesses. From her uncle, Lord Cowper, she inherited Panshanger, in Hertfordshire, with its collection of pictures. Both there and at Taplow, by the Thames, she and her husband delighted to welcome large parties of their friends.

Willie Grenfell, later created Lord Desborough, was as memorable a figure as his wife. In contrast to the sedentary habits of the Souls, who rarely exerted themselves beyond a little mild tennis or golf, he was one of the outstanding athletes of his generation. Playing cricket for Harrow against Eton in 1873 he took four wickets for twenty-seven runs, including those of Edward and Alfred Lyttelton. At Oxford he rowed in the dead-heat Boat Race of

1877 and again in the crew of 1878 which beat Cambridge by ten lengths. He represented England at fencing in the Olympic Games, swam twice across Niagara pool, climbed the Matterhorn three times by different routes, killed a hundred stags in a single season in Scotland and won the punting championship of the Thames in three successive years.

Edgar Vincent, later Lord D'Abernon, began life as an officer in the Coldstream Guards and acquired some knowledge of international affairs on being seconded as assistant to the British Commissioner for the evacuation of the territory ceded to Greece by Turkey. In 1882 he resigned his commission to assume the post in Constantinople of British, Belgian and Dutch representative on the Council of the Ottoman public debt. Within a few years he was governor of the Imperial Ottoman Bank with a growing reputation as an adventurous international financier. Curzon was always his friend, even when as Viceroy of India he disapproved of Vincent's speculative practices.

Lady Helen Vincent was worthy of her husband both in the liveliness of her mind and in her patrician distinction of looks. Amid so many reigning beauties, it is not easy to award a single palm: but the blue haze of her eyes set in a complexion of transparent loveliness could not easily have been eclipsed. She, too, was gifted with the art of hospitality and Stoke D'Abernon, the family house near Esher, saw much of the Souls.

Lord and Lady Wenlock were another well-balanced couple. He was a courteous and unassuming Yorkshire land-owner who had once sat for a few months in the House of Commons. His heart, however, was more in local affairs, in his acres and in his guns. From 1891 to 1896 he was Governor of Madras, an appointment that allowed his wife to show her considerable skill at painting in water colours. She also cared to keep herself abreast of all the latest important books published in England, and charged her faithful correspondent, George Leveson Gower, with the task of despatching monthly parcels.

A. G. C. Liddell, known to the Souls as 'Doll', has described Constance Wenlock's 'elfin grace and originality – a far-away look in her face as if she belonged to another world'. It was, however, not some remote spirit ground of her own seeking, but the silent prison of the deaf. She would therefore carry about with her a silver ear-trumpet, but in an unusual form resembling an entrée-dish. Her adventures with it enlivened many parties. At a luncheon in Florence she suddenly presented it to her neighbour, an Italian duke, who gallantly filled it with green peas. And at one of her own balls, where she happened to leave it on a piano, it was mistaken for an ashtray: later in the evening the Prince of Wales took her in to supper and, as he addressed an opening remark to her, was garnished with a shower of cigarette ends.

In an age that both recognized and deferred to distinctions of class, it was inevitable that the Prince of Wales, as the social arbiter of his day, should include some of the Souls among his personal friends. At the very least, their birth demanded that they should be presented at Court or attend a Levée. Many achieved a closer intimacy with their future Sovereign by holding public office or by excelling at field sports. Nearly all could afford to offer that sybaritic, bonhomous hospitality which was the surest road to an Edwardian heart. There were few country houses where the intoxicating dialectic of the Souls did not occasionally give way to cigar smoke and guttural laughter and practical jokes. One Sunday, staying at Stanway with Hugo and Mary Elcho, the Prince of Wales insisted on a rubber of bridge under the tulip tree. The game ended dismally with a sudden clap of thunder and a burst of rain, and the village said it was divine judgement on his having played cards on the Sabbath.

The Souls were outwardly respectful to the Prince but had private reservations about his character. Lady Frederick Cavendish, a sister of Edward and Alfred Lyttelton, echoed what was in the minds of all her family and friends when she wrote this entry in her diary:

> He does not get on with me, nor indeed much with any but chaffy, fast people, though always kind and delightful in manner like most of 'em: he is amiable and truthful, and has sense and good feeling; my conviction is that, when he succeeds to the Throne and has *duties* to do, he will do far better than now seems likely; but the melancholy thing is that neither he nor the darling Prss. ever care to open a book.

Thirty-six years later, Margot Asquith, staying at Windsor soon after her husband had become Prime Minister, recorded a similar verdict:

> Royal persons are necessarily divorced from the true opinions of people that count, and are almost always obliged to take safe and commonplace views. To them, clever men are 'prigs'; clever women 'too advanced'; Liberals are 'Socialists'; the uninteresting 'pleasant'; the interesting 'intriguers'; and the dreamer 'mad'. But when all this is said, our King devotes what time he does not spend upon sport and pleasure grudgingly to duty.

Neither in judgement nor in behaviour was Curzon quite so austere. It is significant that he invited so un-Soulful a character as Henry Chaplin to both his dinners at the Bachelors' Club. A fox-hunting Lincolnshire squire and intimate friend of the Prince of Wales, Chaplin won the Derby of 1867 with his colt Hermit. In spite of later ventures on the turf that brought him near to financial disaster he retained discerning tastes in horses and hospitality, and his friends suggested that all the Crowned Heads of Europe should each give him £100,000 a year so that he could teach them to spend their money. As a Conservative Member of Parliament he became successively first President of the Board of Agriculture and President of the Local Government Board. He was, however, more at his ease in the Shires than at Westminster, where he would fortify himself in debate with sips of what Sir Henry Lucy charitably called 'unfiltered water'. Winston Churchill once said of him: 'If you look through the door of the House of Commons when he is speaking, and cannot hear what he says, you would imagine him to be one of the greatest and most effective orators in the House.' Chaplin was created a peer in 1916 and survived into old age, a gourmet to the last. 'Yes, my gout is very bad,' he confessed to a kind enquirer, 'but thank heaven I have earned every twinge of it.'

Curzon was not alone among the Souls in his relish for more boisterous pleasures than parodies and paper games. 'We were rather pyrotechnic, I grant you,' Laura Tennant wrote to him of one evening's entertainment, 'at first we were almost shooting stars but towards the end the vulgar catherine-wheel and squib.' The Souls who talked so brilliantly of politics and religion, of books and pictures and people, were the same young men who not long before had thought that there was hardly any pursuit so exquisite as the baiting of foreigners and dogs. The strain of high spirits persisted in less brutal form. At Stanway one evening George Wyndham turned somersaults on the floor while spouting Virgil, then went and serenaded Arthur Balfour (who had retired at midnight) with, 'The lark now leaves his wat'ry nest'.

Richard Haldane, the Liberal statesman who floated balloon-like on the fringes of the Souls, was always a welcome butt. Curzon used to refer to him as 'Schopenhauer' – a misnomer, as it happened, for he was a dedicated Hegelian – and dubbed him the greatest master of copious irrelevance the House of Lords had ever known. 'He carried his words, as it were, on a silver salver,' H. G. Wells wrote of him, 'so that they seemed good even when they were not so.' For all his learning, his administrative ability, his physical and moral courage (particularly when persecuted during the First World War for his professed love of German philosophy) Haldane had an unfortunate manner that invited irreverence.

An all-night sitting in the House of Commons once gave Curzon the opportunity of playing a prank on him. By then Under-Secretary for Foreign Affairs, Curzon had his own room at Westminster to which he invited his friends one by one for whisky and sandwiches. Each in turn was guided to a chair with a weak seat, the guests all remaining to see the trick performed on the next victim. Last of all to be summoned was Haldane. The room was crowded to overflowing, but one chair remained vacant. Haldane sank his well-nourished bulk into it – and remained stuck in the frame.

'Those who have only known Lord Curzon in an official capacity,' Rennell Rodd wrote in later years, 'would hardly credit him with the Rabelaisian humour and the inventive spirit of mischief which he displayed.' One such episode which might have earned him the commendation of the Prince of Wales was the dinner he gave Rodd in 1893 on his departure for Zanzibar as Agent of the British Government. Suddenly there was a sound of shouting from an ante-room, the door burst open, and a Frenchman rushed in, clamouring to see 'Monsieur Rodd', who had just left a post at the Paris Embassy. He loudly declared that Rodd had seduced his daughter, and demanded reparation. Curzon, although pretending to be scandalized by the intrusion, had arranged the whole affair. Rodd remained unmoved: he recognized the man as Saubaud, Godfrey Webb's valet. It was a happy occasion that Rodd can hardly have failed to recall in the grim months ahead when, broken down by fever, he wrote to thank 'my glorious George' for his friendship and encouragement.

Another agreeable scene took place in Paris, where Curzon entertained a party of friends at a restaurant. But in the middle of dinner George Leveson Gower had to leave to catch a train. 'The poor Laxer must not start hungry on his journey,' Curzon announced. So he seized a large napkin, wrapped up six quails in it, placed the bundle in a wicker wine basket, presented it to the departing traveller and escorted him ceremoniously and with many bows to his carriage. Leveson Gower was gratified to hear a bewildered Frenchman say to the lady who was dining with him, '*C'est évidemment un personnage d'importance*'.

There was an element of caprice in Curzon's character that sometimes baffled his contemporaries and misled later students of his career. Fundamentally, he was a serious young man. He had a relentless ambition to achieve high office and the self-discipline and concentration required to equip himself for it. But when he relaxed, he could uncage high spirits hardly distinguishable from boorishness. It was a fault which he readily discerned in others. Staying with Prince and Princess Wagram at Cannes in April 1890 he was delighted to hear that H. M. Stanley, the explorer, had accepted an invitation to lunch. His pleasure, however, was marred by the behaviour of another guest. 'In addition to the Wagrams, Stanley and myself,' he wrote, 'there was only Lord Brougham, who, though a clever man, surprised and disappointed us by his malapropos frivolity, taking no interest in discussions of politics, travel or Stanley's adventures, but always when he could leading the conversation into the stupid channels of social gossip or risqué suggestion.'

Curzon's irritation was understandable. Yet that same spring, at a dinner party given by the British Minister to Greece in honour of the King of the Hellenes, he too could not resist an unkind piece of clowning. Among the guests was Sir George Bowen, a retired Colonial administrator with an aggravated tendency to repeat his anecdotes over and over again. On that particular evening he had just told the same story twice – the second time after a very brief interval. Curzon, with a serious face, at once told him his own story back. Bowen listened without any trace of surprise, and said he could guarantee the accuracy of the facts.

Rennell Rodd, who also attended the dinner, recorded that the King was hardly able to keep a straight face. But there were others who found Curzon an impossibly bumptious fellow. The German governess employed by some friends with whom he was staying once asked him innocently: 'Please tell me, Mr Curzon, what is the meaning of your English word "bounder" that I sometimes hear you called?' 'It is,' he replied, 'one who succeeds in life by leaps and bounds.'

The Souls were unappreciated outside their charmed circle. Queen Victoria thought that they really ought to be told *not* to be so silly. The *Birmingham Gazette* sneered that they had failed to live up to their name, and that in place of intellect there remained only fad and fancy. Lord Bowen, the judge, declared that he would become the high priest of a rival group, the Parasols, and sit under a large umbrella listening to its members confessing their sins to each other.

Half a century later, Lady Violet Bonham Carter, Asquith's eldest daughter by his first wife, sprang to the defence of the Souls, many of whom she had known in the evening if not the high noon of their glory. They were, she said, 'tolerant of everything except stupidity – and silence ... thanks to them, it was no longer smart to be exclusive or fashionable to be dull ... they were lighthearted but not frivolous; unconventional, but neither fast nor loose.'

Lady Violet's apologia was eloquent and just. The Souls themselves, however, would surely have thought it unnecessary. It was not so much their supposed intellectual pretensions as their impregnable self-assurance that annoyed their contemporaries. They had every reason to be self-assured. In spite of the agricultural depression of the last quarter of the nineteenth century, income tax was little more than 6*d.* in the pound and death duties did not begin to cast a shadow over landed estates until Harcourt's Budget of 1894. On such firm financial foundations rested their independence of action, and hence of mind.

John Morley, a radical who burdened himself with many social inhibitions, was once persuaded by St John Brodrick to attend a week-end party otherwise composed entirely of Souls. 'These two days have been delightful,' he afterwards wrote to his host, 'but most blighting to one's democracy.'

Chapter Fifteen
EASTERN WINDOWS

> You are, Alfred says, the best traveller in the world, and that when we go to Rome and to the dazzling East, it would be like leaving our purses or dressing cases behind to go without you.
>
> – *Lucy Graham Smith to Curzon, 3 January 1887*

Curzon belonged to the last generation of parliamentarians whose duties at Westminster occupied little more than half the year. Occasionally, as in 1888, there was a short autumn session which he greeted with annoyance. In most years, however, the Houses of Parliament rose in August or September and did not meet again until late January or early February. Before his election to the Commons as Member for Southport, Curzon had visited almost every country in Europe. Now he determined to plan more ambitiously. The prestige of a legislator would command him hospitality and assistance denied by officials to other travellers, not to mention a readier market for the newspaper articles and books which, he hoped, would help finance his travels.

By the standards of his class and of most of his friends, he was a poor man. Not until 1911 did Members of Parliament receive a salary, and earlier attempts to secure their payment found no favour with Curzon. In March 1889 he opposed such a proposal, lest the House of Commons should begin to attract 'the idle, the necessitous and the unscrupulous'. He was content to continue living on an allowance from his father of less than £1,000 a year. The modesty of Lord Scarsdale's contribution did not spring from meanness. The Kedleston estate was burdened by many charges and its income of just under £18,000 a year barely adequate to maintain the huge house, to pay wages and pensions and to raise and educate a large family. Lord Scarsdale spent little on himself except for the shooting and an occasional few weeks at Bath, and only after long years of frugality was he able to leave on his death in 1916 a gross estate of over £450,000.

Curzon supplemented his parental allowance from three sources. During the seven years of his Fellowship at All Souls he received a stipend of £200 a year. As a contributor to periodicals such as the *National Review* he made another £200 or £300 a year. And he had one or two part-time business appointments. In 1887 he became a director of the Clerical, Medical and General Life Assurance Society. Since his qualifications for a seat on the board were not obvious, it may well be that he owed the appointment to Lord Midleton, St John Brodrick's father and a fellow director. His other colleagues included Dean Farrar, author of *Eric, or Little by Little*, Sir William Jenner, who had attended Lady Scarsdale in her last illness, and Sir James Paget, who had set Curzon's shoulder after a football accident at Eton. As the total remuneration of the sixteen directors was limited to £3,000 in any one year, Curzon can hardly have drawn more than £200 as his annual fee. He received the invitation to join the board while passing through Hong Kong and was required, he recorded with annoyance, to send a telegram of acceptance at two dollars a word.

In the following year he became a director of the old established but newly registered Hadfield's Steel Foundry Co. Ltd. Mr (later Sir Robert) Hadfield had just succeeded his father as chairman, and was embarking on a programme of expansion and research. A fellow Derbyshire man and one of the leading metallurgists of his time, he was an enlightened employer, too; as early as 1891 the men in his Sheffield factories were working an eight-hour day. Hadfield was particularly assiduous in developing the armaments side of his business. For a fee of £250 a year Curzon not only immersed himself in the technicalities of shells and fuses, but showed himself a master of surreptitious salesmanship. Before he himself became a Minister, he was quite shameless in importuning St John Brodrick, who since 1886 had been Financial Secretary to the War Office, to renew and increase Government orders for munitions. And he apologized very humbly when Brodrick resented his implication that military methods could be in the least dilatory.

'I must seek some unambitious quarter near Piccadilly', he told Brodrick soon after his election to Parliament. 'As you rightly indicate, I am a veritable pauper.' Although the Conservative Association at Southport had agreed to pay almost all his election and other political expenses as a tribute to their energetic young Member, he still found it difficult to raise his promised contribution of £50. Including subscriptions and railway fares, the constituency cost him nearly £200 during his first six months in Parliament and prevented his going abroad in the autumn of 1886.

By next summer he had saved several hundred pounds and on 4 August 1887, six weeks before Parliament was prorogued for the summer recess, he set out on his first tour round the world. He had two travelling companions. One was the Rev. J.E.C. Welldon, by now Headmaster of Harrow. The other was the Rev. Stuart Donaldson, son of the first Premier of New South Wales and an Eton housemaster. He had an attractive character. Twenty-five years later, on being appointed Vice-Chancellor of Cambridge University, Donaldson preached an impressive sermon on the multiplicity and complexity of his new cares. Arthur Benson, his successor as Master of Magdalene College, caught the eye of a colleague and both recalled that the Vice-Chancellor's duties in his first week of office had included two days' shooting.

Curzon's preparations for the trip were meticulous. He made long lists of all the articles to be included in his substantial baggage: corkscrew, sealing-wax, insect powder, opera glasses, sun umbrella, dust coat and Eno's salts. Alfred Lyttelton contributed an air cushion and a portable bath. Shortly before the S.S. *Oregon* sailed for Quebec, however, Curzon found that in spite of careful packing he had omitted an important item: he could not find the key to his portmanteau. He rushed to the nearest locksmith in Liverpool and by miraculous good fortune the very first key fitted. 'What are the odds against this?' he wrote triumphantly in his diary.

Life aboard the ship was slow, comfortless, dirty and smelly. Although the vessel was only four years old, she had the ingrained, inveterate grime of a collier, and the steward was positively mephitic. The passengers, too, were a disappointment. 'There are few ladies or gentlemen among them. The social status of the remainder is indicated by the aristocratic names they bear – Tulk, Tottle and Thistle!' Presumably in deference to his superior social status, Curzon was invited to organize a committee for the entertainment of the ship's company, but inspiration failed: he could think only of showing them Welldon, prostrate in his bunk from sea-sickness. As he abandoned the beetles in his cabin and gazed moodily out on an Atlantic vista of icebergs, porpoises and whales, he recalled with a spasm of envy that it was the first day of the grouse-shooting season.

Neither Montreal nor Toronto served to raise his spirits. He found the towns slovenly and undeveloped. 'It is hard to believe,' he added, 'that we are on British soil and amid our fellow subjects. All the same, they are very angry if you mistake them for Yanks.' But the beauty of the Niagara Falls was memorable, and he filled page after page with respectful tributes to the powers of nature.

Curzon's longstanding and necessary sense of thrift was outraged by a charge of four dollars for a berth in the sleeping-car between Toronto and Chicago. 'Our first impulse on the occurrence of these abominable extortions was one of uncontrollable resentment and savage remonstrance. But gradually as they recurred with pitiless reiteration our senses and our powers of protest alike became blunted and we ended by stumping up our dollars with as much equanimity as we hand 1/- to a hansom cab driver in England. The first lesson to learn in a strange country is good-humoured conformity to its vile idiosyncrasies.'

Throughout his long journey across the American continent Curzon never quite learnt that lesson, and a perpetual counterpoint of discontent runs through his narrative journal. But the pampered motel-user of the twentieth century will surely spare him a moment of sympathy as, in a shed lacking even a table, he squats on his bed and writes up the day's notes, a pen in one hand, a candle in the other. He describes the slaughter-houses in Chicago and the hot springs in Yellowstone Park, the tabernacle to seat 10,000 in Salt Lake City and the waterfalls of the Yosemite Valley. He was also much moved to meet a private soldier in the United States Army who turned out to be the son of an English clergyman, 'driven by poverty and bad ways to this low station of life, but retaining the manners and appearance of an English gentleman'.

Foreign soil has been the graveyard of many a friendship. Yet when, on the Pacific coast, the time came for Welldon and Donaldson to return to schoolmastering and for Curzon to board a boat for Japan, they parted with every manifestation of sadness and affection. The separation with Welldon, Curzon wrote, was a source of infinite sorrow, 'as he is the most interesting and unselfish fellow traveller in the world. The pleasure and advantage of his society in this first quarter of my journey round the world I shall never forget.' The Headmaster of Harrow returned the compliment in a poem which Curzon found awaiting him after Welldon's departure:

Farewell, dear George, and though you go
To scenes which I may never know,
Yet by the portals of the day,
In Hindostan or fair Cathay,
Forget not one whose dearest end
Is but to prove his friend's best friend;
Nor deem it little that which we
Have lately crossed from sea to sea
There has not passed in all these days
Between us any thought or phrase
That you or I were loth to tell
Save this one thankless word, 'Farewell'.

Curzon's ill-humour again descended on board the S.S. *Belgic*, bound from San Francisco to Yokohama. 'The misery of this day is a horror! But for the most scrupulous honesty I would obliterate it from my diary altogether. For I, who profess to be an excellent and seasoned sailor, and who have only once before been sea-sick in my life, was sick no less than 7 times.'

Nor did he find consolation in the society of his fellow passengers, most of them American missionaries:

I cannot confess to the slightest interest in their company. They are not self-sacrificing martyrs going out to danger and perhaps death in a distant country. But very commonplace middleclass folk who have taken up mission work as a profession – no doubt from the highest motives, but all of them comfortably salaried and sustained in the dull mediocrity which appears to be their common possession. As a lot they are about as interesting as would be a corresponding number of young English shop assistants of the upper middle class. They have no life about them, no talk, no spark of interest, and contribute about as much excitement to the voyage as would a company of tortoises.

He therefore abandoned himself to books, consuming two at a time, a light work and a more sober work together. In this way he sampled Milton, Macaulay, Stevenson, Goethe, Voltaire, Thackeray, Carlyle, George Eliot, Cervantes, Froude and Disraeli. 'I have read more books in the past four months,' he wrote that autumn, 'than I have in the preceding four years.' Among the fifty or sixty volumes, Horace earned the warmest praise: 'Delicious reprobate! Unblushing advocate of the two things my father warned me against when I went to Oxford, viz. "Wine and women." What a mistake to read him as we did at Eton, as a solemn business. It is the veriest relaxation.' And Curzon cheered up enough to perform at the ship's concert: he imitated Tennyson's declaiming of 'Tears, idle tears', which he had heard as a guest at the poet's country house three years before.

The Japanese Government was cautious in its admission of foreign tourists. Soon after landing at Yokohama, Curzon was therefore obliged to seek a special passport in addition to the handsome document measuring eleven inches by fifteen and bearing the arms both of the Queen and of Lord Salisbury which in those unrestrictive days were carried by British subjects on only the longest and most arduous journeys. The Japanese passport was a menacing instrument, expressly warning its possessor that 'he is to conduct himself in an orderly and conciliatory manner towards the Japanese authorities and people'. It also included a list of specific prohibitions. The bearer was forbidden to travel at night in a carriage without a lantern; to attend a fire on horseback; to disregard notices of 'No Thoroughfare'; to drive quickly on a narrow road; to neglect or refuse to pay ferry or bridge tolls; to destroy or deface notice-boards, house signs or mile posts; to scribble on temples, shrines or walls; to injure crops or trees or other property on the high road or in public gardens; to trespass on fields, plantations or game preserves; to light fires in woods, or on hills or moors. Japan cannot have been fortunate in her earlier visitors from abroad.

The country nevertheless enthralled Curzon. Not until he returned in 1892 did he deliberate on her internal politics and her role in international affairs. In 1887 he was content to see her through the eyes of an enthusiastic globe-trotter. He was enchanted by the beauty of tombs and temples set in a landscape whose name, the Plains of Heaven, he recognized to be hardly an exaggeration. He was gratified by the universal politeness of the inhabitants: 'Your shopkeeper as you enter prostrates himself and touches the floor with his forehead. This is no veneer of manners, but the inbred gentlemanliness and gentleness of the people.' As an inveterate bargain-hunter, he was surprised by their comparative honesty: 'They are neither such robbers nor quite such artful deceivers as their brethren in Cairo or Constantinople: for instead of asking three times the expected sum, they are content with a demand of a little less than twice the value.' He approved, too, of a nation apparently emancipated from false modesty: 'A people who are even now semi-nude and a few years ago were almost wholly so, and of whom both sexes bathe together naked in the public baths, do not know what indecency is.'

Only in attempting to ape European habits did the Japanese evoke that note of scorn which sprang so readily to Curzon's lips as he travelled among races unfortunate enough not to be English. It pained him that 'officials in ill-fitting swallow tail coats, atrocious trousers and gold-laced hats should make believe that their costume had come from London and that they knew how to wear them'. But for the cheerful, humble rickshaw boys he felt only compassion – 'fourpence an hour for labour which an Englishman would not undertake for 2*s.* 6*d.*, and which ultimately, poor little fellows, costs them their lives'.

It was with contemptuous humour, however, that he watched a bout of traditional wrestling at Kioto, the ancient capital of Japan, and embodied the experience in the only magazine article to emerge from his month in the country. A paragraph or two will serve to illustrate Curzon's deftness as a journalist:

> Either wrestler first advances with great solemnity to the edge of the platform, and faces the crowd. Lifting his right leg high in the air, and extending it as far as possible from the body, he brings it down on the ground with a vigorous stamp, at the same time that he also brings down his right hand with a resounding smack upon his right thigh. Then up goes the left leg, and along with it the left hand, and down come both with a thud at a similar angle on the left side; which done, and having strained and tested his sinews by this remarkable manœuvre, the wrestler straightens himself and gazes proudly around at the gaping audience.
>
> Then he lounges to a corner of the platform, sips a mouthful of water from a small wooden pail, and squirts it through his lips over his arm and chest and legs. Next, a paper napkin is handed to him by an attendant, with which he carefully wipes his face and body. Finally, from a little wooden box affixed to the corner-pole, he takes a pinch of salt between his fingers, and tosses it into the air for luck. ...
>
> Some seven or eight minutes must have been consumed in these formalities, and patience is well-nigh exhausted, when at length they proceed into the middle of the ring, and again squat down like two monstrous baboons, exactly opposite each other, and with their foreheads all but touching. ... They are seen to rise slightly from the crouching attitude, and to face each other with alert eyes and outstretched arms, ready to grip or to rush in. But not yet is the visitor sure of his money's worth; for even at this advanced juncture one or other of the antagonists will casually loaf out of the ring, stroll back to his corner, and resume the water and salt masquerade. ...

At length, however – after all these struttings and stridings, these rinsings and rubbings, and feints and fiascoes – our Daniel Lamberts are once more in the ring.

From such unwholesome mummery he turned with relief to greet 'a young fellow who was at Repton School when I stood for South Derbyshire in 1885, and who remembered coming out into the market place to hear me speak. I must have left a great impression upon him, for he persisted in calling me "Sir".'

Home thoughts from abroad were seldom absent from Curzon's mind as he journeyed the world. 'No Englishman', he wrote, 'can land in Hong Kong without feeling a thrill of pride for his nationality. Here is the furthermost link in that chain of fortresses which from Spain to China girdles half the globe. ... The sound of the bugle reminded us that a British garrison was securely stationed below, and that we were beneath the folds of the Union Jack.' He departed for a brief visit to China, during which he congratulated himself on suffering no insult from the xenophobic inhabitants of Canton: 'Strangers are too often themselves responsible for any difficulty in which they find themselves placed by the swaggering and abusive tone they adopt towards the coolies in the streets.' Then back to Hong Kong for the celebration of Queen Victoria's golden jubilee. The salute of guns, he recorded, killed three men, and the firework display two more.

Singapore quickened the pride he took in British administration overseas, a theme of which he never grew weary. 'To me,' he once told an audience in Derbyshire, 'the Empire is so sacred and so noble a thing that I cannot understand people quarrelling about it, or even holding opposite opinions about it.' What at home was an article of faith became the most vivid reality of his life as he set foot in each of our possessions abroad:

> Out here in the East one cannot fail to be very much struck by the stamp of men who represent the British Government. The popularity and prestige of a big Colonial Empire must very largely depend upon its Consuls and Proconsuls. It was so with Rome. It is so with Great Britain. I record it to our credit and praise that – so far as my experience goes – our home Government is served by as able and enlightened a body of men as ever carried or sustained a conquering flag in foreign lands. The industry, the capacity and the service of these men are beyond praise. Would we had some better means of rewarding them than by a K.C.M.G. and some more efficient method of profiting by their advice than the neglected despatches addressed to the Secretary of State and pigeon-holed in the Colonial Office at home.

These were not the sentiments of a demagogue designed to flatter an audience of Colonial Servants or consular officials: they were inscribed in a private notebook that their author had no reason to think would one day be published. His narrative of Singapore continues:

Fine buildings, good streets, roads and wharves, excellent police and local administration, neatness, order and decorum – these are what I should expect. What might excusably be found wanting but what I everywhere find present is a satisfied and grateful acquiescence in our domination. ... The French do not share this particular kind of prestige. As far as I can gather they are not popular in the East. Their diplomacy is tortuous, their commercial policy is ungenerous, and their rule irksome. ... Our real commercial rivals are the Germans, who are irrepressible, thrifty, industrious, without conceit or false pride, ready to stoop to anything that means money, contented with the slenderest profit, they are steadily pushing their way, in many cases undermining and superseding the British pioneers who have gone before.

Curzon's class-consciousness could be unattractive. It not only assumed the existence of well-defined social classes, a supposition generally accepted throughout Victorian England. To certain classes it also attached moral and intellectual standards that did not bear close scrutiny. Abroad, however, he gazed indulgently, even with admiration, upon fellow countrymen whom at home he would have ignored and sometimes despised:

Nothing, indeed [he wrote], is more striking in travel than the character and personality of the men who are sustaining in positions of varied trust the interests of Great Britain in far lands. The larger atmosphere of life and the sense of responsibility seem to free them from the pettinesses of a home existence that is too apt to be consumed in party conflict, and to suggest broader views of men and things. The same high tone exists through the various strata of society and employment, and the clerk behind the counter of the English bank will be no less a gentleman both in birth and education than the Governor in his palace or the Minister in his Legation. I do not think that the same can be said of the Germans, or of the French, or of the Dutch.

Occasionally his patriotism led him into bathos. It was not enough for him to claim that his compatriots' passion for games kept them the healthiest of all foreign settlers in the East. He had to add that 'while the German grows fat and the Frenchman withers, the Englishman plays lawn-tennis under a tropical sun'.

Curzon had less regard for the military forces who guarded the British Empire. An evening in Singapore, he noted, consisted of 'billiards and a ferocious argument with the General, who drank too much champagne and bellowed out the most outrageous nonsense'.

In December 1887 Curzon set foot in India for the first time. He came by way of Ceylon, where he was entertained by the Governor, Sir Arthur Gordon. 'Though reserved and even rude at times,' Curzon wrote, 'he is an able and accomplished man.' But it was a relief to exchange the excessive etiquette of Government House for a tour of 'the jungle-buried cities which were mighty capitals when Rome was only a village on a hill'. His appreciation of Buddhist antiquities was marred by a generous measure of affliction. 'The monks,' he grumbled, 'a seedy and stingy lot, refused to supply me with a match, so that I could not see their great statue properly.' The food was monotonous: 'Our dinner just now. 1st. course, stewed fowl. 2nd. course, fried fowl cutlets. 3rd. course, roast capon. 4th course, chicken curry. I feel like a walking poultry yard.' By day, 'an infernal mosquito is blowing his miserable but merciless trumpet right in my ear, confound the rascal.' By night there were harrowing treks in bullock carts: 'I had to curl up like a caterpillar with stomach ache. Not a wink of sleep: jolt, jolt, jingle, jingle, mixed with the most diabolical noises from the driver.'

He was, however, an adaptable traveller. During a tedious journey to the mainland and so up through Madras he worked away at a treatise on the similarities between Sinhalese and Hellenic architecture, then turned his mind to the long disquisition on reform of the House of Lords which later appeared in the *National Review*. And in the interval he wrote his own Baedeker. For all its wealth of archaeological detail, it did not lack humour. As he sailed into Calcutta harbour he came to the end of the last page in his notebook: 'At 5.45 I entered the Capital of the East. A sentence so pompous as the above will fitly close Vol. II and allow me to open in a more modest style Vol. III.'

Calcutta was hardly the city to imbue him with modesty. 'Other countries have but one capital – Paris, Berlin, Madrid. Great Britain has a series of capitals all over the world, from Ottawa to Shanghai.' He was moved, too, by his first sight of Government House, built nearly a century before on the model of Kedleston. In 1898, when thanking the townspeople of Derby for a congratulatory address on his appointment as Viceroy, he recalled the moment of recognition:

> It is strange by what small events and by what petty coincidences the current of life is shaped and turned. For it is certainly true that it was the fact of that resemblance that first turned my thoughts to the question of the Government of India; and when I left the doors of Government House in Calcutta on the first and only occasion on which I have visited it, in 1887, it made me feel that some day, if fate were propitious and I were held deserving of the task, I should like to exchange Kedleston in England for Kedleston in India

To a different audience he told a different story. Addressing a dinner given in his honour by fellow Etonians a month before the ceremony in Derby, he offered this version of his precocious interest in India:

> Sir James Stephen came down to Eton and told the boys that listened to him, of whom I was one, that there was in the Asian continent an empire more populous, more amazing, and more beneficent than that of Rome; that the rulers of that great dominion were drawn from the men of our own people; that some of them might perhaps in the future be taken from the ranks of the boys who were listening to his words. Ever since that day, and still more since my first visit to India in 1887, the fascination and, if I may say so, the sacredness of India have grown upon me,

until I have come to think that it is the highest honour that can be placed upon any subject of the Queen that in any capacity, high or low, he should devote such energies as he may possess to its service.

The precise moment at which he began to see himself a future Viceroy is unimportant: Kedleston and Eton may each stake her claim to history. Both versions, however, have a truth in common – that what above all crystallized Curzon's ambitions and continued to haunt him until they were realized was his first sight of Calcutta in the winter of 1887.

A Christmas reunion with two Balliol friends added to the pleasure of his stay. One was Lord Herbrand Russell, an aide-de-camp to the Viceroy. As an ensign in the Grenadier Guards at the battle of Tel-el-Kebir he had been the last officer to carry the colours of his regiment into battle. Having in later years succeeded his brother as eleventh Duke of Bedford, he dedicated much of his life to zoology and established collections of animals both at Whipsnade and on his own estates at Woburn. The other Oxford contemporary was Walter Lawrence, who in 1877 had been placed first in the open competition for the Indian Civil Service and later served Curzon with sustained devotion as the Viceroy's private secretary.

Even without such useful friends to gild his path, Curzon would have been assured of a courteous welcome from the Viceroy of the day, Lord Dufferin, whom he had met briefly in Egypt five years before:

> With that inimitable flattery which he bestows on all alike, he assured me that there was no one whose career he had watched more closely ever since. Prince and paragon of diplomatists! Everything is grist that comes to his mill, and he slaves to make everybody his slave. With that suave insinuating manner, that languid glance of the glassy eye, and that alluring smile – which are his alone – he chattered on, called me 'My dear fellow', talked about his work which he said was the hardest he had ever had to undertake.

Few travellers have excelled Curzon in the deftness with which he could pin his impressions to paper. Browsing late in life in the museum of his recollections, he declared these to be his most prized:

> The music of many nightingales floating across the water from the coasts of Athos; the incredible glory of Kangchenjunga as he pierces the veils of the morning at Darjiling; the crossing of a Himalayan rope-bridge, sagging in the middle, and swaying dizzily from side to side, when only a strand of twisted twigs is stretched between your feet and the ravening torrent below; the first sight of the towered walls, *minae murorum ingentes*, of Peking; the head and shoulders of an Indian tiger emerging without a suspicion of sound from the thick jungle immediately in front of the posted sportsmen; the stupendous and terraced grandeur of Angkor Wat; the snowy spire of Tenerife glimmering at sunrise across a hundred miles of ocean; the aethereal and ineffable beauty of the Taj.

In the weeks that followed his cheerful encounter with Lord Dufferin, he added two of the most enduring to his store of memories. First there were the

Himalayas. 'So far were they uplifted from earth,' he wrote, 'and so high did they encroach upon heaven that one could scarcely believe them connected with the commonplace globe upon which we were crawling 28,000 feet below. ... Long did we stand and stare and wonder, gloating over our extraordinary privilege.' Then to the Taj Mahal, at Agra. 'Designed like a palace and finished like a jewel,' he wrote to Brodrick, 'a snow-white emanation starting from a bed of cypresses and backed by a turquoise sky, pure, perfect and unutterably lovely. One feels the same sensation as in gazing at a beautiful woman, one who has that mixture of loveliness and sadness which is essential to the highest beauty.'

A day or two later and he was in Delhi, where he decided to make an unscheduled excursion to the north-west frontier. The poet in him relished the contrast. 'Melancholy and barren to a degree,' he described the Khyber Pass, 'dark ugly stony hills, showing patches of sandy soil but only the most meagre vegetation. For sheer repulsiveness I would compare it to the valley of the tombs of the Kings at Egyptian Thebes.' Sped on his way by Viceregal letters, he moved to Quetta and, in a special train ordered by the Chief Commissioner for Baluchistan, was conducted to Chaman, on the Afghan Frontier. He gazed down over the Kadanai plain towards Kandahar and 'felt a thrill of satisfaction at being for the moment on the very uttermost verge, the Ultima Thule, of the Indian Empire'.

For all its brevity, Curzon's survey of the outposts that guarded the approaches to India exercised a profound effect on his thought. He was never a soldier, but he had the mind of a strategist: and fifteen years later, obsessed by the dangers to an Indian Empire that had been placed personally in his charge, he pursued what came to be called a 'forward' frontier policy. His doctrine is embodied in a letter which in 1903 he addressed to Lord George Hamilton, Secretary of State for India:

> You there lay down the proposition as likely to govern the whole of our future policy in Central Asia that H.M.G. is never likely to incur the risk of international complication unless some gross or irreverent insult is offered to our honour or to our Flag. Those are not the conditions under which our Empire was built up; and I also say, without the least hesitation, that they are not those under which our Empire can possibly be maintained. If we are not to defend our own frontiers, to ward off gratuitous menace, to maintain our influence in regions where no hostile influence has ever yet appeared, until the national honour has been grossly affronted, the practical result will be that you will not be able to take a step upon your frontiers until they have actually been crossed by the forces of the enemy.

Lord Salisbury's comment on earlier requests by Curzon for a more belligerent frontier policy had been succinct and conclusive: 'He always wants me to negotiate with Russia as if I had 200,000 men at my back, and I have not.' When Salisbury's nephew, Arthur Balfour, succeeded him as Prime Minister, there was no less reluctance on the part of the Government to challenge Russian intentions on the frontiers of India. Curzon, however, persisted in throwing forward a protective screen, notably by means of the expedition he sent to Tibet. It was yet another source of the friction between Calcutta and Downing Street that ultimately led to Curzon's resignation as Viceroy in the summer of 1905.

Sailing back to Europe from Bombay in time for the reassembly of Parliament in February 1888, Curzon carried with him more than a trunkful of curios, a bundle of notebooks and an imagination aflame with the kaleidoscopic impressions of his six-month odyssey.

The artist in him responded to the stimulus of oriental landscape and architecture, the scholar to the synthesis of anthropology and chance. As Viceroy, he liked to tell the story of the English sportsman in India who examined the arrows in the quiver of a native hunter belonging to one of the aboriginal tribes. He found the first arrow tipped with stone – a relic of the neolithic age; the next was tipped with electric telegraph wire – a theft from the twentieth century.

But it was on the politician and the administrator that his first visit to the East left its most indelible stamp. 'The strength and omnipotence of England everywhere in the East is amazing,' he wrote to his father from Singapore. 'No other country or people is to be compared with her. We control everything, and are liked as well as respected and feared.' As for British rule in India, he never ceased to believe that it was a sacred trust in which the balance of advantage lay decisively with the governed rather than with the governors. His appeal to history was eloquent and convincing:

> For where else in the world has a race gone forth and subdued, not a country or a kingdom, but a continent, and that continent peopled, not by savage tribes, but by races with traditions and a civilization older than our own, with a history not inferior to ours in dignity or romance; subduing them not to the law of the sword, but to the rule of justice, bringing peace and order and good government to nearly one-fifth of the entire human race, and holding them with so mild a restraint that the rulers are the merest handful amongst the ruled, a tiny speck of white foam upon a dark and thunderous ocean?

He believed not only that British government in India was benign, but that it was also essential to the survival of civilized intercourse. 'We must remain in India,' he said, 'because, if we were to withdraw, the whole system of Indian life and politics would fall to pieces like a pack of cards.' Curzon was not alone in taking so paternal a view of imperial responsibility. However much it came to be derided in the next half century, it was a doctrine that in his youth found almost universal acceptance among governing men. Where Curzon differed from more visionary administrators was in holding that the incapacity of the Indian for self-government was impervious to education and thus permanent.

Chapter Sixteen
CENTRAL ASIA

> I wonder if it may be permitted to a politician to remember the days when he was only secondarily a politician, and when he found the chief zest of life in travel, not indeed in aimless and desultory travel, but in travel with that most generally unpopular of all attributes, a purpose.
>
> – Curzon's introduction to *Tales of Travel*, 1923

'Wherever I go,' Curzon wrote in 1887 during his journey round the world. 'the first question, accompanied with a look of suspicion, that I receive is this – "Are you going to write a book?" On my giving satisfactory assurances to the contrary, the brow relaxes, the manner expands and I am treated without the slightest reserve. Were I that most dreaded, and I must add despised, of all creatures, viz. the globetrotter who is also a bookmaker, I should not have nearly so good a time or be made so much at home.'

It was nevertheless in just such a compromising role that he set off for Russia less than a year later, trusting that what hospitality or information might be denied him as a writer of articles for the *Manchester Courier* and other provincial newspapers would be conceded to an influential Member of Parliament and serious commentator on international affairs. Ostensibly his task was to describe a journey along the 900 miles of the recently opened Transcaspian railway in Central Asia. His ultimate purpose, however, was more ambitious.

Inspired almost since childhood by the civilizing mission of the British abroad, he determined to develop his theme through a series of volumes embracing the entire continent of Asia in all its aspects – geographical, historical, ethnological and political. Each was to survey a region where British interests might be threatened, particularly by a Russian Empire which, the explorer Nansen calculated in 1914, had been expanding for the last four centuries at the rate of fifty-five square miles a day. They were Central Asia; Persia; China, Japan and Korea; Indo-China; the Indian Frontier; and Afghanistan. Only the first three were ever published. He found no leisure to complete the works on Indo-China and Afghanistan, although fragments of each were later included in collections of essays on his travels. The volume on the Indian Frontier was in type – and the author had even corrected the final proofs – when he was appointed to India in 1898. In deference to the belief of the Prime Minister, Lord Salisbury, that its publication would jeopardize the Viceroy's freedom of action, the work was suppressed.

Curzon was fortunate in the spacious months of relaxation which Victorian legislators allowed themselves. But even when Parliament was sitting he did not waste his time. In the libraries of the House of Commons and of the British Museum he would devour every available work on the countries he next intended to visit until, he boasted, he knew the places so well that it was hardly worth going there.

On 6 September 1888, he left London for St Petersburg, confessing to St John Brodrick how much he would miss his round of country-house parties, 'a large slice out of the happiness of the year'. Margot Tennant was sad to see him go and enquired whether she would be able to write to him on his travels – 'or will your middle-class method break down there?'

In St Petersburg, where he stayed with his Balliol friend, Arthur Hardinge, *chargé d'affaires* at the British Embassy, he delighted in 'the grandiose splendour and civilised smartness of the capital – with its architecture borrowed from Italy, its amusements from Paris and its pretentiousness from Berlin'. It was not in fact only from Italy that the builders of St Petersburg had borrowed their architectural notions. Charles Cameron, the eighteenth-century Scottish architect, copied his *Salle Grecque* in the Palais de Pavlovsk from the great marble hall at Kedleston – a circumstance that surely pleased Curzon as much as it gratified Dr Johnson to hear that his works were to be translated into Russian and read 'on the banks of the Wolga'.

Frustration also awaited Curzon in St Petersburg. Before leaving London he had been assured by the Wagons-Lits Company that they would secure a special permit, or *autorisation speciale*, without which he could not enter Transcaspia. But they had failed him, the application having disappeared without trace into the quicksands of Russian bureaucracy. He therefore had to initiate the process all over again by seeking permission for his journey from five separate authorities – the Governor-General of Turkestan, whose headquarters were at Tashkent; the Governor-General of Transcaspia, who resided at Askabad; the head of the Asiatic department of the Ministry of Foreign Affairs; the Minister of Foreign Affairs; and the Minister of War. Eventually he was successful, largely because of the jealousy that existed between the Ministries of War and of Foreign Affairs, each of which was only too anxious to disoblige the other by acting independently. It was not, however, until he had left St Petersburg, lingered in Moscow and arrived at Vladikavkas, on the Caucasus, that permission arrived from the capital by telegraph. He thus became only the third Englishman to make his way to the East by the Transcaspian railway since its opening in May 1888, the two previous passengers being the correspondent of *The Times* and a sportsman called Mr St George Littledale who was travelling to the Pamir mountains in pursuit of the *Ovis poli*, or wild sheep.

With a sense of deliverance, Curzon continued his journey down to Baku, on the shores of the Caspian Sea, where he boarded the steamboat *Prince Bariatinski*. Next afternoon he landed at Uzun Ada, or Long Island, the Western terminus of the Transcaspian Railway. It was an unattractive place, without a blade of grass or a drop of fresh water, and only the presence of a solitary toy shop convinced him that children could be born and live there. But once he had made his way to the station, ankle-deep in sand, he found that even the second-class railway carriages were comfortable and well adapted to receive passengers who brought their own bedding. It was just as well. 'There are so-called hotels at Askabad, Merv and Samarkand,' he wrote, 'but they would be called hotels nowhere else.' The arrangements for meals he thought decidedly good. Although there was no restaurant car, the train stopped for a mid-day and an evening meal, supplemented by 'constant and almost irritating pauses of from five to twenty minutes, which can be sustained by the consumption of first-rate tea at 1*d*. a glass, or superb melons at less than 1*d*. each, and of grapes at a fraction of a farthing a bunch'. Second-class travel, moreover, cost no more than 1*d*. a mile. It was therefore with a feeling of relief only faintly tinged with regret that Curzon confessed his inability to enter into competition with earlier visitors to Transcaspia, who 'pursued their explorations slowly and laboriously, either in disguise or armed to the teeth, amid suspicious and fanatical peoples, over burning deserts and through intolerable sands'.

The Russian occupation of Turkestan in 1865 had made the construction of a railway essential if the newly acquired territory was to be sustained and protected. In 1873, Ferdinand de Lesseps, the engineer responsible for the Suez Canal, suggested that an international line should be driven the 7,500 miles from Calais to Calcutta, passing through Transcaspia. The idea languished. Instead, the Russian General Annenkoff was entrusted with building what was essentially a military railway 900 miles in length from the eastern shore of the Caspian to Samarkand, in the heart of Central Asia. It was an audacious enterprise, achieved in the face of an acute scarcity of water and a perpetual shifting of sand-dunes. The army was responsible not only for the construction of the line, but also for its daily administration. 'The bulk of the staff,' Curzon wrote, 'is composed of soldiers of the line. The engines are in many cases driven by soldiers; the station-masters are officers, or veterans who have been wounded in battle; and the guards, conductors, ticket-collectors and pointsmen, as well as the telegraph and post-office clerks attached to the stations, are soldiers also.' Thus did Russia ensure the consolidation of her conquests in Central Asia and prompt the globetrotting Member of Parliament for Southport to observe with pardonable portentousness: 'The sands of an expiring epoch are fast running out; the hour glass of destiny is once again being turned on its base.'

Installed in a broad-gauge railway carriage, Curzon settled down to enjoy the three days of effortless travel that were to transport him from Uzun Ada to Samarkand. Around him were stowed his bedding and his portable rubber bath, his tinned meat and chocolate, his notebooks and his flea powder. His journalistic conscience was disturbed by the difficulty of gathering facts and figures about the rolling stock – 'it is, indeed, as hard to extract accurate statistics or calculations from a Russian as to squeeze juice from a peach-stone'. Nor was there much else to engage his attention as for more than twenty-four hours the train rolled slowly through Kara Kum, the desert of black sand.

On the afternoon of the second day, the train halted at Geok Tepe, where, seven years before, General Skobeleff's army had stormed the fortress in one of the most bloody encounters of the Russian drive into Central Asia. As at Tel-el-Kebir in 1883, Curzon paced the battlefield, reconstructed the action, gloomily noted the debris of war and a carpet of bleached bones. Then on through fertile country to Askabad, the capital of Transcaspia and seat of the Russian Governor-General. Here Curzon's suspicions were aroused by the construction of a broad road leading to the Persian frontier. 'Already,' he wrote, 'the north of Persia and Khorasan are pretty well at Russian mercy from a military point of view.'

Merv, once called Queen of the World and believed to be the cradle of civilization, resolved itself into 'a nascent and as yet very embryonic Russian town, with some station buildings, two or three streets of irregular wooden houses. ... No ancient city, no ruins, no signs of former greatness or reviving prosperity.' What he did see, however, was enough to remind him how impotent Great Britain had been in attempting to check the Russian annexation of Merv in 1884. 'The flame of diplomatic protest blazed fiercely forth in England,' he recalled with bitterness, 'but, after a momentary combustion, was as usual extinguished by a flood of excuses from the inexhaustible reservoirs of the Neva.' It would have been a very different matter, he implied, had George Nathaniel Curzon sat penning despatches at the desk of the Foreign Secretary.

Once more the train drew away to the East across a land wiped almost clean of history and Curzon composed its epitaph:

> In these solitudes, the traveller may realise in all its sweep the mingled gloom and grandeur of Central Asian scenery. Throughout the still night the fire-horse,

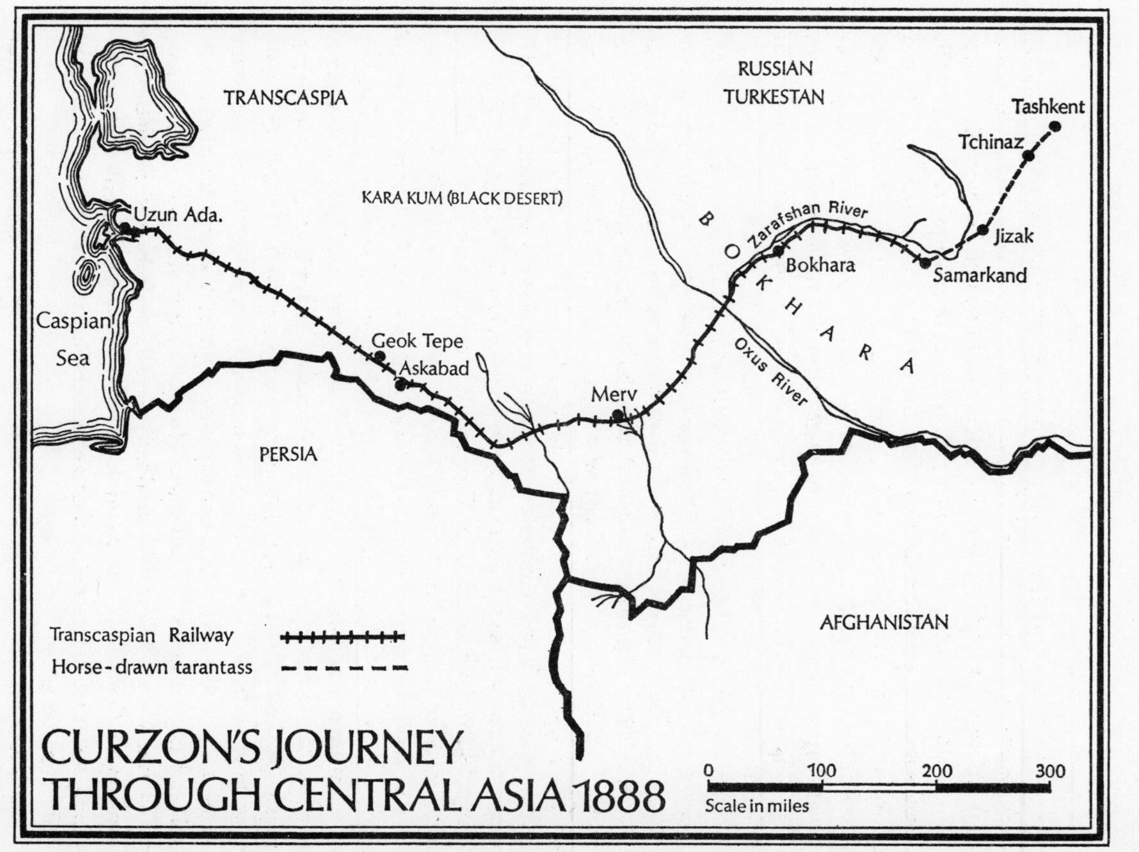
TRANSCASPIA
RUSSIAN TURKESTAN
KARA KUM (BLACK DESERT)
Tashkent
Tchinaz
Jizak
Samarkand
Zarafshan River
Bokhara
BOKHARA
Uzun Ada.
Caspian Sea
Geok Tepe
Askabad
Merv
Oxus River
PERSIA
AFGHANISTAN
Transcaspian Railway
Horse-drawn tarantass
CURZON'S JOURNEY THROUGH CENTRAL ASIA 1888
0
100
200
300
Scale in miles

as the natives have sometimes christened it, races onward, panting audibly, gutturally, and shaking a mane of sparks and smoke. Itself and its riders are all alone. No token or sound of life greets eye or ear; no outline redeems the level sameness of the dim horizon; no shadows fall upon the staring plain. The moon shines with dreary coldness from the hollow dome, and a profound and tearful solitude seems to brood over the desert. The returning sunlight scarcely dissipates the impression of sadness, of desolate and hopeless decay, of a continent and life sunk in a mortal swoon. The traveller feels like a wanderer at night in some desecrated graveyard, amid crumbling tombstones and half-obliterated mounds. A cemetery, not of hundreds of years but of thousands, not of families or tribes but of nations and empires, lies outspread around him: and ever and anon, in falling tower or shattered arch, he stumbles upon some poor unearthed skeleton of the past.

Oasis gave way to desert and in its turn to the orchards and gardens that fringe the banks of the Oxus. Again and again Curzon murmured to himself some lines of Matthew Arnold:

... the majestic river floated on
Out of the mist and hum of that low land
Into the frosty twilight, and there moved
Rejoicing through the hushed Chorasmian waste
Under the solitary moon.

He was moved not only by the euphony and aptness of this passage from *Sohrab and Rustum*, but also by fond recollections of the poet. That very Easter they had been fellow-guests of the Pembrokes at Wilton, where Arnold was much chaffed for his disposition to flirt with Lady Charles Beresford. 'Well,' he had replied, 'my doctors have always told me that I have a weak heart, and it is evident that it is true.' A day or two later he died suddenly of heart failure, having in the meantime sent a friendly and encouraging message to Curzon. 'I only received the note after his death,' Curzon recalled, 'and was much touched by this voice from the grave.' Five months later, as his train grumbled across successive sections of a temporary wooden bridge more than a mile long, Curzon looked down into the coffee-coloured waters of the Oxus and once again spoke the soft cadences of the poet.

'The Gihon of Eden,' he mused, 'that "encompasseth the whole land of Ethiopia", the Vak-shu of Sanskrit literature, the Oxus of the Greeks, the Amu Daria, or River-Sea, of the Tartars – no river, not even the Nile, can claim a nobler tradition or a more illustrious history. Descending from the hidden "Roof of the World", its waters tell of forgotten peoples and whisper secrets of unknown lands.' The exact site of its source, a problem which had teased generations of travellers, was just such an enigma to engage Curzon's mind. Six years later, in the course of an arduous expedition that brought him the gold medal of the Royal Geographical Society, he solved it.

Meanwhile the line ran through green, well-timbered country that paved the approach to Bokhara, capital of a quasi-independent State already succumbing to Russian influence. At first Curzon could see no more than a distant outline of minaret and dome: for the train, having skirted the city walls, perversely drew away into the shelter of a modern Russian-built station nearly ten miles from Bokhara itself. Although some of the local merchants had wished the station to be sited nearer the city, the general attitude of the Bokhariots towards the railway was one of suspicion. It was regarded as foreign, subversive, anti-national and even Satanic: they called it Shaitan's Arba, or the Devil's Wagon. Even in Russia such an attitude was not uncommon. Readers of Dostoyevsky's *The Idiot*, published in 1866, will recall how Lebedyev was taunted with believing that 'railways are a curse, that they are the ruin of mankind, that they are a plague that has fallen upon the earth to pollute the "springs of life" '. To which he replied: 'The railways alone won't pollute the "springs of life", but the whole thing is accursed; the whole tendency of the last few centuries in its general, scientific and materialistic entirety is perhaps really accursed.'

The Russian railway authorities readily adopted the suggestion of the Bokhariots that the line should not approach the city. It gave them an excuse for building a rival town and a cantonment of troops for its protection: an unobtrusive yet effective safeguard against possible unruliness on the part of a recently occupied and still semi-independent state. But already the merchants of Bokhara were regretting their early hostility to the line, much as English land-owners had come to lament the wealth lost by their having opposed the advance of the railway across their estates. Everywhere, Curzon noted, apprehension had given way to ecstasy: 'I found the third-class carriages reserved for Mussulman passengers crammed to suffocation, just as they are in India; the infantile mind of the Oriental deriving an endless delight from an excitement which he makes not the slightest effort to analyse or to solve.' Sometimes, it must be confessed, he did live up to the reputation of a Superior Person.

As a distinguished visitor, he was met at the station by a three-horse carriage from the Russian Embassy, where he lodged during this break in his railway journey. He drove past orchards of mulberries and peaches, figs and vines, through one of the eleven tall gates that pierced the walls and so to his guest chamber. It was an agreeably unpretentious apartment containing a carpet, a bedstead and a table. Washing was not encouraged, as the only jug known in Bokhara was a brass ewer holding as much as a teapot and the only basin a receptacle with a small bowl in the middle of a large brim – barely enough to pour over the hands. 'I created a great sensation,' Curzon wrote, 'with an indiarubber bath.' Every day attendants brought him supplies of mutton, chickens and fruit, and the Amir sent traditional offerings of sugar-plums, dried raisins, sweetmeats, little cakes and huge slabs of brown bread.

With insatiable curiosity, Curzon roamed at length round this city of 100,000 inhabitants in which even the pauper 'walks abroad with the dignity of a patriarch and in the garb of a prince'. He found them a friendly people: 'An acquaintance of the previous day would salute you as you passed by placing his hand on his breast and stroking his beard. I never quite knew what to do on these occasions. For not having a beard to stroke, I feared it might be thought undignified or contrary to etiquette to finger the empty air.' Recalling the boast of a devout Sunnite of Bokhara, that he could worship Allah in a different mosque on each day of the year, Curzon decided that the number must probably be halved. He visited many of them, but was repulsed from ascending the Minari Kalian, or Great Minaret, which he had seen from the train. Instead he climbed to the highest point of one of the numerous cemeteries and was able to look down on a panorama of flat clay roofs and occasional turquoise domes.

Then he descended for what was always a refreshing interlude in his travels, a haggle in the bazaar:

> The shopkeeper is very amenable to personal attention. He likes to be patted on the back and whispered to in the ear; And if, after a prolonged struggle repeated perhaps for two or three days, you can at length get hold of his hand and give it a hearty shake, the bargain is clinched and the purchase is yours. The people struck me as very stupid in their computations, requiring calculating-frames with rows of beads in order to make the simplest reckoning, and being very slow in exchange. But I thought them a far less extortionate and rascally lot than their fellows in the marts of Cairo or Stamboul.

It depressed him to see ugly Russian calicoes and cottons displacing the far lovelier native materials, and hideous brocades from Moscow debauching the instinctive good taste of the East. He was disturbed, too, by the display of Russian spirits and champagne at every railway station along the line. Although their sale was forbidden in Bokhara, Curzon feared that the interdict would not last. 'Western civilisation in its Eastward march,' he sighed, 'suggests no sadder reflection than that it cannot convey its virtues alone, but must come with Harpies in its train, and smirch with their foul contact the immemorial simplicity of Oriental life.'

In other ways the customs of the country had remained unchanged for centuries. In the bazaar one morning, Curzon saw a crowd collecting round a mounted horseman and heard howls of pain coming from the centre of the throng. It turned out to be an inspection by the Reis-i-shariat, a censor of morals whose duties included the checking of weights and measures. Convicted of fraud, a shopkeeper had just been stripped bare in the street, forced to kneel down and flogged with a leather whip. 'The features of the crowd,' Curzon noted, 'expressed a faint curiosity, but not a trace of another emotion.'

Curzon himself was rather a connoisseur of crime and punishment. In

Canton the previous year he had watched a salt smuggler being beaten 'with unnecessary gentleness', a mitigation which the prisoner's family had achieved by bribing the jailer. Curzon found no such leniency in Bokhara. In the past three years, he discovered, a false coiner, a matricide and a robber had paid for their crimes by being hurled from the top of the Great Minaret and dashed to pieces on the hard ground beneath. Shortly before Curzon's visit even fiercer retribution had been inflicted on the assassin of the Divan Begi, or second Minister of the Crown. The culprit having been handed over by the Amir to the family of the murdered man, he was beaten with sticks and stabbed with knives; his eyelids were cut off and his eyes gouged out; he was tied to the tail of an ass and dragged through the streets to the market place, where his body was quartered and thrown to the dogs.

One of Curzon's companions who penetrated the prison also reported a hundred inmates huddled together in a low room, chained to each other by iron collars round their necks, wooden manacles on their hands and fetters on their feet, so that they could neither stand nor turn nor scarcely move. Whatever influence the Russians chose to exert over the Amir of Bokhara, it did not extend into the field of penal reform.

The personal habits of the Amir were no less inviolate. 'Batchas, or dancing boys,' Curzon recorded with distaste, 'are among the inseparable accessories of the Palace, and represent a Bokharan taste as effeminate as it is depraved.' He would nevertheless have welcomed a personal audience with the Amir, whom he had seen only at a distance. As was his custom, he had come prepared for such an occasion by packing a suit of evening clothes in his baggage. He waited in vain, however, for a summons, then magnanimously lent them to a fellow traveller who had managed to secure a coveted invitation but lacked the formal garb which protocol demanded. Curzon consoled himself by noting that 'a more comic spectacle than an English gentleman in a dress-suit riding in broad daylight in the middle of a gaudily dressed cavalcade through an Oriental town cannot be conceived'.

Failing to be received at court was his only disappointment. 'For my own part,' he wrote, 'on leaving the city I could not help rejoicing at having seen it in what may be described as the twilight epoch of its glory. Were I to go in later years it might be to find electric light in the highways. ... It is something, in the short interval between the old order and the new, to have seen Bokhara while it may still be called the Noble, and before it has ceased to be the most interesting city in the world.'

Through the well-irrigated valley of the Zerafshan river, the Transcaspian railway carried Curzon on to Samarkand, its eastern terminus. Here once more he found himself on Russian territory, the seat of the mighty Tamerlane having been annexed by the armies of the Tsar in 1868. Russia, it is true, had since made vague declarations that she would restore Samarkand to the Amir of Bokhara. 'It is unnecessary to say,' Curzon wrote, 'that there never was the slightest intention of carrying out such an engagement, which if a Russian diplomat alone could have given, an English diplomat would alone have believed.'

He was enchanted, however, by the spaciously laid out modern town, so generously planted with trees that from a distance it might be mistaken for a thickly wooded park. 'A certain primness and monotony of appearance,' he continued, 'may perhaps be charged against the Russian Samarkand. But compared with other places I had seen it was almost a paradise.' It pleased him, too, to recall that the sylvan retreats of Tartar nobles were little different from the neat residences of Russian generals and colonels.

From such domestic contemplation he turned to examine the ancient town on the other side of the gentle valley. The Righistan of Samarkand, he declared, was even in its ruin the noblest public square in the world. 'I know of nothing in the East approaching it in massive simplicity and grandeur, and nothing in Europe, save perhaps on a humbler scale the Piazza di San Marco at Venice, which can even aspire to enter the competition. No European spectacle indeed can adequately be compared with it, in our inability to point to an open space in any Western city that is commanded on three of its four sides by Gothic cathedrals of the finest order.'

The aesthetic pleasure he drew from contemplating the triple glory of the *medresses*, or religious colleges, that framed the square was marred by the melancholy state of decay into which they had been allowed to fall. Even the Tomb of Tamerlane was in a sadly dilapidated condition. For such neglect Curzon blamed the Russians. 'What with the depredations of vandals, the shock of earthquakes and the lapse of time, the visitor in the twentieth century may find cause to enquire with resentful surprise what has become of the fabled grandeurs of the old Samarkand.'

The future Viceroy, whose protection and restoration of the architectural treasures of India are to this day recalled there with gratitude, offered an imaginative solution. 'A Society for the Preservation of Ancient Monuments should at once be formed in Russian Central Asia,' he wrote, 'and a custodian should be appointed to each of the more important ruins.' But already he had seen enough of Russian administration to realize how unacceptable his suggestion would be. 'This is a step,' he added, 'which can hardly be expected from a Government which has never, outside of Russia, shown the faintest interest in antiquarian preservation or research, and which would sit still till the crack of doom upon a site that was known to contain the great bronze Athene of Pheidias, or the lost works of Livy.'

The railway went no farther than Samarkand. But rather than embark immediately on the return journey to the Caspian, Curzon accepted an invitation to spend a few days in Tashkent as the guest of General Rosenbach, the Russian Governor-General of Turkestan. The journey of 190 miles could be undertaken only in a horse-drawn tarantass, 'a kind of ramshackle wooden boat, resting on long wooden poles, which themselves repose on the wooden axles of wooden wheels ... a sorrowful and springless vehicle'. An air cushion offered scant protection to Curzon's weak back, and he later confessed to hankering after the second-class carriages of the Transcaspian railway as eagerly as the Israelites, in similar surroundings, lusted after the flesh-pots of Egypt. His ordeal, he implied, entitled him to a more lavish measure of comfort than General Rosenbach cared to provide:

> Madame de Ujalvy-Bourdon in her book spoke of Government House as 'a veritable palace, with a truly splendid interior which could not be surpassed in any capital in Europe'; but I fancy that her faculty of perspective must have been temporarily disorganised by the prior experiences of a tarantass and the Kirghiz Steppes. As a matter of fact, its furniture and appointments are almost jejune in their modesty. The only two large rooms, the ball-room and the dining-room, are practically unfurnished. There is no throne-room or dais; and the only emblems of royalty are the oil-paintings of the late Czar and his wife, and of the present Emperor and Empress, which hang upon the walls.

What a contrast, he sighed, to the state observed by the Indian Viceroy, 'who in a country famed for its lavish ostentation, its princely wealth, and its titled classes, is obliged to support the style of a sovereign, who resides in a palace the corridors of which are crowded with gorgeous figures in scarlet and gold liveries, who drives out accompanied by a brilliant escort, and whose levées are as rigid in their etiquette as those of Buckingham Palace or St James'.'

Oppressed by so desirable and yet seemingly so distant a prospect, he wandered along the leafy avenues of the town. But it could offer only the limited attractions of military garrisons the world over: a church and a club, billiards and cards, vodka and valses. A particular seediness infected Tashkent. The traditional refuge of damaged reputations and shattered fortunes, it remained even in Curzon's day a place of compulsory banishment for those out of favour at St Petersburg. In one of the principal houses lived a Grand Duke, a first cousin of the Tsar who had married the daughter of a police officer and was reputed to drink and to beat his wife. 'The exile of this degenerate scion of royalty,' Curzon noted, 'is understood to be lifelong.'

The local museum was a disappointment, lacking both scientific arrangement and funds. Having gazed dutifully upon a poor specimen of the *ovis poli* and a preserved *reshta*, the light yellow worm nearly a yard long which is absorbed into the human system from impure water, Curzon went on to examine the library. And there, to his joy, he discovered the best collection of works on Central Asia published since 1867 that could be found in the world.

'Not only books and pamphlets,' he wrote, 'but even magazine and newspaper articles are admitted to this collection, in which I am driven to think that these humble pages may some day repose.' His stroll round the town had not been in vain.

Years later he had cause to remember that unexpected bounty of Tashkent. For on taking up residence in Government House, Calcutta, he found that the resources of the Indian Empire did not extend to providing the Viceroy with a library. 'Would you believe it?' he wrote incredulously to the Permanent Under-Secretary of the India Office in London, 'he has to bring with him or to purchase every book himself.'

'Well, my dear Sir, and how did you leave those damned fellows, the Russians?' the British Ambassador in Constantinople asked Curzon, who was making his way home by the Black Sea route in time for the reassembly of Parliament. Curzon, so often a martyr to the congenital shortcomings of foreigners, was exceptionally benign towards his recent hosts:

> If it is an exaggeration to say that every Englishman enters Russia a Russophobe, and leaves it a Russophile, at least it is true that even a short residence in that country tempers the earlier estimate which he may have been led to form of the character of the population and its rulers. This is mainly attributable to the frank and amiable manners and to the extreme civility of the people, from the highest official to the humblest *moujik*. The Russian gentleman has all the polish of the Frenchman, without the vague suggestion of Gallic veneer; the Russian lower class may be stupid, but they are not, like the Teuton, brusque. The stranger's path is smoothed for him by everyone to whom he appeals for help, and though manners do not preclude national enmities, at least they go a long way towards conciliating personal friendships.

Curzon was no less ready to applaud the technical triumph of the Russian military engineers in having subdued the desert and laid a railway across hundreds of miles of the most unpromising terrain. But when he turned to analyse the political design that lay behind its construction, appreciation gave way to apprehension. The mere existence of the line, he thought, served to consolidate Russia's most recent conquests. 'A railway in the deserts of Central Asia is a far more wonderful thing to the Eastern mind that one through the teeming territories of Hindostan: the passage of the sands more remarkable than the piercing of mountain ranges. Fatalism, moreover, if it starts by provoking a sanguinary resistance, ends in producing a stupefied submission. A sense of utter powerlessness against the Russians has been diffused abroad among the Central Asian peoples.'

Great Britain, therefore, should not for a moment countenance the deceptively pacific proposal put forward by General Annenkoff for the extension of the Transcaspian line into the heart of Afghanistan and for its junction at Kandahar with the Indian railway system. It would, Curzon urged, undermine British commercial supremacy in her traditional markets by flooding them with Russian goods. It would be regarded throughout the East as a crowning blow to British prestige, already imperilled by a succession of pocketed affronts and diplomatic reverses. It would imply the consolidation of Russian dominion to the very gates of Kandahar and bring a potential enemy a month nearer to the frontiers of India.

In a detailed examination of the strategic factors governing the defence of India, Curzon concluded that Russia, after long preparation and at a suitable time of the year, could use the Transcaspian railway to poise a force of 100,000 men on the northwest and Northern frontiers of Afghanistan. Yet to meet such a menacing concentration, there were in India only 70,000 British and 148,000 native troops, of whom barely one half could be spared for frontier defence, kept in the field for any length of time or adequately reinforced.

Fortunately, he believed, Russia was not bent upon the invasion of India. 'So far from regarding the foreign policy of Russia as consistent, or remorseless, or profound, I believe it to be a hand-to-mouth policy, a policy of waiting upon events, of profiting by the blunders of others, and as often of committing the like herself.'

Consoling in its way, such an interpretation of Russian intentions nevertheless allowed no relaxation on the part of Great Britain. In its very capriciousness, Russian foreign policy could be as oppressive to her neighbours as a direct threat of aggression. The more Russia flaunted her strength and powers of assimilation in Central Asia, the more nervous she would hope to make the Government of India; and the more insecure Great Britain felt in India, the more conciliatory was likely to be her attitude to Russia in Europe. The object of Russian policy, Curzon discerned, was not Calcutta, but Constantinople.

'Whatever be Russia's designs upon India,' he wrote, 'whether they be serious and inimical or imaginary and fantastic, I hold that the first duty of English statesmen is to render any hostile intentions futile, to see that our own position is secure and our frontier impregnable, and so to guard what is without doubt the noblest trophy of British genius, and the most splendid appanage of the Imperial Crown.'

To reach such a conclusion, Curzon need hardly have crossed the Caspian, rolled through Merv and Bokhara, bumped his way from Samarkand to Tashkent. In evaluating the Russian threat to India, as in much else, he had crystallized his views early in life. On 7 May 1877, he presided over a meeting of Mr Wolley Dod's house debating society at Eton to consider the question: 'Are we justified in regarding with equanimity the advance of Russia towards our Indian frontier?' He himself wrote the minutes:

The President expressed the opinion that the policy of Russia was a most ambitious and aggressive one. It dated its origin from the time of Peter the Great, by whom the schemes of conquest had first been made. He did not imagine for a moment that the Russians would actually invade India, and were they to do so we need have no fear of the result; but ... a great question of diplomacy might arise in Europe in which the interests of England were opposed to those of Russia. It might then suit Russia to send out an army to watch our Indian frontier. In such a case as this England's right hand would obviously be tied back.

The succinctness of the schoolboy did not satisfy the Member of Parliament and Fellow of All Souls. Twelve years later, on his return from Transcaspia, he wrote a 400-page work entitled *Russia in Central Asia*:

To the great army of
Russophobes who mislead others, and
Russophiles whom others mislead
I dedicate this book
which will be found equally disrespectful
to the ignoble terrors of the one
and the perverse complacency of the others.

Another decade, and the author was Viceroy of India. 'In 1888,' ran one of his earliest letters to the Secretary of State for India, 'I wrote a chapter in my book on Russia in Central Asia, upon Anglo-Russian relations and the future that lay before them in Asia, and although that chapter is eleven years old, I do not think that there is a statement of opinion in it that I would now withdraw or a prediction that has so far been falsified.'

But the almost obsessive strength and consistency of his beliefs blinded him to his true constitutional role in India. The Viceroy was not, as Curzon would have wished him to be, an Oriental potentate whose majestic judgements none dare challenge. Rather was he the servant and instrument of a British Government which, prepared to allow him latitude on internal questions, would not permit him to pursue a foreign policy that was wholly independent of Whitehall and of Westminster. Curzon himself recognized that the stresses between Russia and India could not be resolved in isolation from European affairs. He nevertheless determined that the Viceroy should remain unfettered by Cabinet and Parliamentary restraint; and in this miscalculation he ultimately tried the patience of the Home Government to breaking point.

One perceptive reader of *Russia in Central Asia* who saw the danger was Sir William Harcourt. Writing to congratulate Curzon on being appointed Viceroy of India in 1898, he added, not entirely in jest: 'Let me beg as a personal favour that you will not make war on Russia in my lifetime.'

Chapter Seventeen

PERSIA

> I am grieved, but not surprised, at your preference of Persia to Scotland. ... But I know that there is no use in preaching to you. Travelling is worse than drink.
>
> – *Arthur Balfour to Curzon, 9 September 1889*

In September, 1889, fortified by a week of Wagner operas at Bayreuth, Curzon departed once more for the East. For nearly six months he travelled alone through Persia, a journey that in retrospect made his earlier expeditions seem little more arduous than the saunters of a dilettante. No longer at the end of each day's exertions could he depend on the welcoming comfort of an hotel bedroom or ship's cabin or railway sleeping car. Such amenities simply did not exist in Persia. Sometimes he might look forward to the shelter of a British Legation or Consulate or telegraph station, occasionally to the traditional hospitality of a local ruler. But British officials abroad, in spite of their generous instincts and thirst for home news, often flinched from the visitor with literary ambitions; and native potentates found it unsettling to entertain so dedicated an enemy of their Russian neighbours in Transcaspia.

'Come back without another book in embryo,' Balfour had urged him, 'authorship is killing work.' Curzon could neither afford to follow such advice nor wished to do so. To meet the initial expenses of travel he undertook to write a dozen articles – later stretched to seventeen – for *The Times*: he received £12 10*s*. for each. The ultimate purpose of his tour, however, was to produce what he called a full-length and life-size portrait of Persia, a task that no English author had attempted for two centuries. Including the journey itself, it took him three years of scarcely uninterrupted labour.

He first read almost every one of the works on Persia written in European languages since the fourteenth century: there were between 200 and 300 of them. When he came to write his own *Persia and the Persian Question* – two stout volumes containing nearly 1,300 closely printed pages – he could boast that each of his references was the result of independent reading and that none of them had been copied second-hand.

Curzon was no less meticulous in preparing his baggage for a journey of nearly 2,000 miles on horseback across some of the bleakest landscapes in Asia. For riding, he wore a Norfolk jacket with a single button at the neck and lots of pockets; stout breeches cut not too tightly at the knee; Russian top boots of soft leather, at least two sizes too large; and an ingenious hat, the outer shell of which stripped off, enabling the wearer to present himself as if he had 'just stepped out of Bond Street'. For protection against a sudden drop in temperature he carried a Cardigan waistcoat; to shield his eyes against the glare of the sun, blue spectacles; to propitiate local grandees who did not care to see muddy or dusty footprints on their carpets, a pair of galoshes; to revive himself when exhausted, a flask holding a quart of spirits. Since Persians of rank looked upon a short coat as grossly undignified, he carried in his Gladstone bags a full-skirted frock coat; he also, of course, packed that suit of dress clothes without which he would never venture beyond the shores of England.

Saddle, sleeping-bag, blankets, rubber bath, air cushion, folding candlestick, telescope, frying pan – he left nothing to chance. As a small boy he had spent part of his first winter at Eton making his own brand of ice-cream out of milk, sugar and jam placed in the snow to freeze. Sixteen years later he cooked his own dinner almost every night under the Persian stars and took pride in his mastery of household hints. 'Crosse and Blackwell's tinned soups are quite excellent, and, besides being easily prepared, are almost a meal in themselves ... sardines, potted meats, chocolate or cocoa, Liebig's beef tea, and good tea or coffee, are useful adjuncts which should be procured in Europe. Lump sugar can be bought in the humblest Persian village.'

At the very outset of the journey, however, the care with which Curzon had packed his equipment and provisions was frustrated by the Turkish customs officials at Constantinople. On his arrival there from Paris by the Orient express, not even the possession of a diplomatic courier's red passport saved him from the indignity of having every piece of his baggage opened and searched. What particularly aroused Turkish suspicions were boxes full of watches and other trinkets intended as presents for the local potentates Curzon would meet on his travels. His protests that he was a Member of Parliament were brushed aside with scorn. As a commercial traveller in cheap jewellery, he was told, he would have to pay the usual duty in full – an imposition from which he was saved only by the arrival of the Embassy *Kavass*. He described the episode to Margot Tennant.

> They tore out all my things packed for Persian travel; they swore the saddle was a new one; they crashed into my Liebig soups; they ravished my chocolate; they made me pay special duty on my Waterbury watches, taken out to conciliate respectable Persian Khans. They made me swear, anathematise, curse, blaspheme, condemn them to a thousand hells of eternal fire; and after over an hour of this they let me go

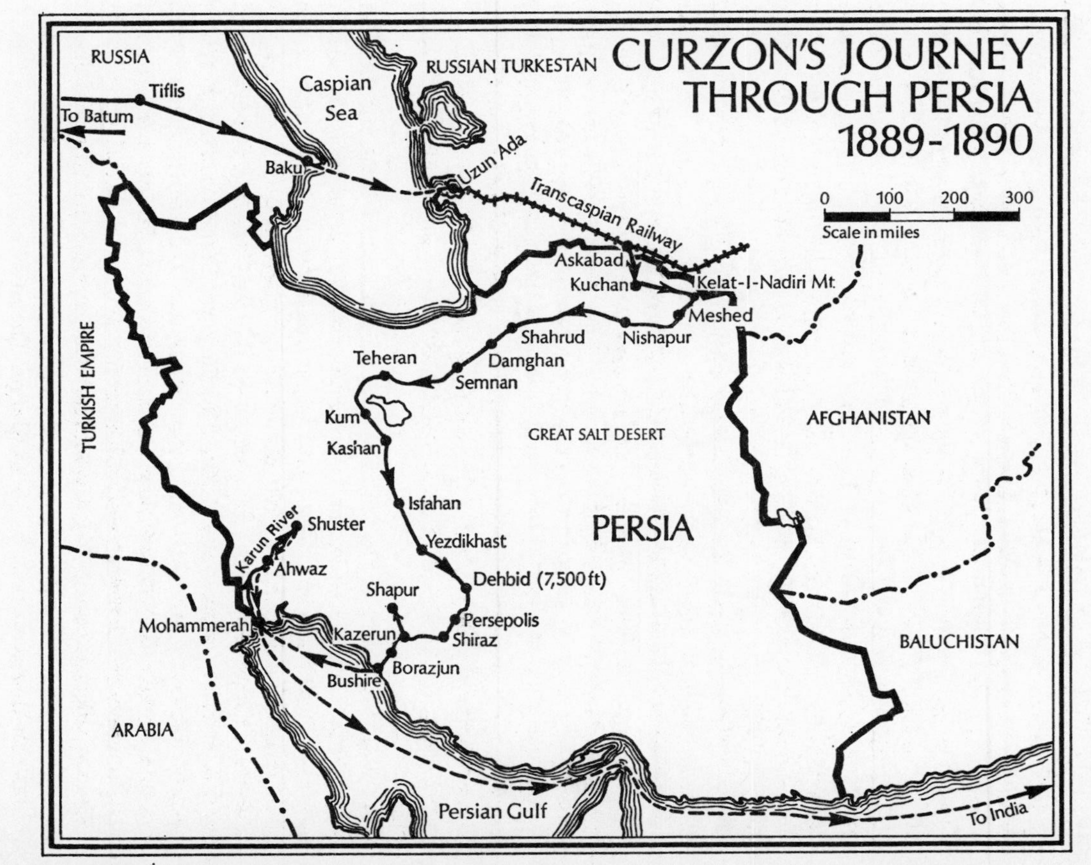
CURZON'S JOURNEY THROUGH PERSIA 1889-1890
0 100 200 300
Scale in miles
RUSSIA
Tiflis
To Batum
Caspian Sea
Baku
RUSSIAN TURKESTAN
Uzun Ada
Transcaspian Railway
Askabad
Kuchan
Kelat-I-Nadiri Mt.
Meshed
Nishapur
Shahrud
Damghan
Semnan
Teheran
Kum
Kashan
Isfahan
Yezdikhast
Dehbid (7,500 ft)
Persepolis
Shiraz
Shapur
Kazerun
Borazjun
Bushire
Shuster
Karun River
Ahwaz
Mohammerah
TURKISH EMPIRE
ARABIA
GREAT SALT DESERT
PERSIA
AFGHANISTAN
BALUCHISTAN
Persian Gulf
To India

panting, lacerated, foaming, unsubdued. As I think of it now I still consign them in my choicest vocabulary to the concentrated flames of a thousand Gehennas.

Retrieving his tumbled possessions, Curzon boarded a British oil tanker that carried him through the Black Sea to Batum. There he caught a train for Tiflis, and so on to Baku, 'more pungent and less inviting than ever'. Having now rejoined his route of the previous year into Central Asia, he once more crossed the Caspian Sea in the steamer *Prince Bariatinski* and landed at Uzun Ada. Although he found that the western terminus of the Transcaspian Railway had grown in the past twelve months, military control of the port had not yet imposed any trace of iron discipline on the travelling public. 'It appeared to be difficult to persuade these inveterate Orientals,' Curzon wrote, 'either to regard the price of a ticket as a fixed quantity or to comprehend the French system of the *queue*. They fought and jostled each other at the tiny opening; and when the ticket distributor named the price, in true Asiatic fashion they offered about half the sum in the expectation of a leisurely haggle and a possible bargain.'

Curzon took his seat in the train and gazed upon the familiar desert scene of his first journey along the line. This time, however, he descended after only 300 miles, at Askabad, the capital of Transcaspia: it was from here that in 1888 he had noticed a broad road running south towards the frontier with Persia. That way, too, lay his own route. 'I watched the noisy departure of the locomotive,' he confessed, 'with the feelings of one who is saying goodbye to an old and faithful friend.'

From Meshed, nearly 170 miles away, the British Consul had thoughtfully sent a horse, baggage mules and a guide. Curzon set off towards the south and in a few hours crossed into the Persian frontier province of Khorasan. Yet the menace of Russia's expansionist policy continued to haunt his thoughts. Her Transcaspian conquests, as he had seen with his own eyes, had brought her little more than a barren wilderness, punctuated by a series of detached oases at the base of a mountain range: on the other side of that mountain range lay a country whose valleys and plains concealed an abundance of wealth: minerals, fruit, grain.

Curzon's own advance on Kuchan was not without drama. He was gratified to be met on the road by an emissary of the Ilkhani, or Chief, whose capital he was to visit on the following day. The messenger wished to know at what hour Curzon proposed to reach the town, so that his master might prepare a suitable welcome. Curzon replied that he would be there at noon. When, however, he arrived at the agreed rendezvous, neither carriage nor escort awaited him. 'I was sufficiently versed in Oriental etiquette,' he wrote, 'to know that in matters of ceremony a foreigner is taken at his own estimation, and that any failure to vindicate his titular importance is ascribed not to modesty but to weakness.' So he halted outside the walls, sending a horseman to protest at the discourtesy to which he had been exposed. In a few minutes there was a clatter of hoofs and a somewhat dilapidated brougham accompanied by a cavalcade rumbled up to where he was waiting. The leader conveyed the Ilkhani's apologies, explaining that the messenger had mistaken the hour and begging Curzon to occupy a house that had been prepared for him. 'My wounded dignity having received this balsam, I mounted the vehicle; my horse was led before; my escort came behind; and the Khan's cavaliers galloped in front, clearing a way through the streets and bazaars with astonishing rapidity.'

Lodged in an apartment hung with coloured prints of the Crowned Heads of Europe, Curzon regained his equanimity, although he could not fail to notice that Queen Victoria was only half the size of the Emperors of Austria and Germany and a mere third that of the Tsar. Donning his frock coat, he enjoyed some pleasant exchanges with the Ilkhani, a formidable-looking fellow – 'the reverse of handsome', his guest called him – with a reputation for relapsing into bouts of intemperance.

'I had great difficulty,' Curzon wrote, 'in explaining to him my own profession and the position of my family. Parliament he had never heard of; and when I told him that I was a member of the great *mejilis* (council), he replied, "Are you a soldier?" The status or rank of an English nobleman conveyed nothing to him; but he put the pertinent questions, "Has your father many soldiers?" and "Who made him governor of his property?" ' They feasted off chicken and mutton, omelettes and rice, Kuchan wine ('extremely nasty'), sour milk and sherbet. Curzon sealed their friendship with the gift of a silver watch and was despatched upon the next stage of his journey in a brand new victoria, built in Moscow. Nowhere could he escape the shadow of Russian designs upon Persia.

After twenty-two miles of dust and bumps, Curzon excused himself from continuing farther in his frail carriage, which returned to Kuchan. He was anxious not only to avoid discomfort but also to inspect at his leisure the famous frontier stronghold of Kelat-i-Nadiri. It is a rampart of rock, sixty miles in circumference, springing from the bottom of a valley to a height of almost 800 feet, as level along the summit as though pared by a plane, but scarred and fluted down its absolutely vertical and impervious sides. This stupendous barrier was one of the most astonishing phenomena he had ever seen and he longed to climb up to the plateau, to roam at will round its natural defences and to enjoy the view. He had almost slipped through the gate that led to the single easy ascent when he was stopped by the guard, who insisted that he could not pass their post without permission from Meshed.

Before leaving the neighbourhood, however, he made a last bold attempt to enter Kelat-i-Nadiri. At 4.30 one black cold morning he began to ascend its steep stone precipice. He courageously edged his way up to within thirty feet of the top; but he was alone, and feared that the descent might prove awkward. He had to be content with climbing a neighbouring mountain from which he sketched the walls that had defeated him. Then, turning his face to the south, he rode on towards Meshed.

The most holy city in Persia owes its fame as a place of pilgrimage to Imam Reza, eighth of the twelve Imams, or Prophets, whose bones are buried in one of the most sacred shrines of the Mohammedan faith. Curzon did not choose to add his name to the role of those few intrepid European travellers who had penetrated in disguise to the very tomb itself. With so elaborate a programme of sightseeing before him, he prudently concluded that it would be foolhardy either to incur unnecessary personal risk or to bring his country into disrepute. 'If I must claim for myself any special distinction, it is the modest one of being the first English Member of Parliament who has entered the walls of Meshed.'

His description is scholarly and illuminating but not untouched by that critical scrutiny which the author brought to all foreign institutions. The Khiaban, or long straight street that is an unusual feature of an Oriental town, was, he noted, regarded by the inhabitants of Meshed as a veritable Champs-Elysées of urban splendour. For Curzon, however, its charm was marred by a canal – 'or as we should prefer to call it, a dirty ditch' – that ran down its centre and united the uses of drinking fountain, bathroom, laundry, depository for dead animals and sewer.

His sternest strictures were reserved for what he delicately called the provision of material solace available to pilgrims. In recognition of all they had endured, the ecclesiastical authorities permitted them to contract 'temporary marriages' during their sojourn in the city. 'In other words,' Curzon concluded, 'a gigantic system of prostitution, under the sanction of the Church, prevails in Meshed. There is probably not a more immoral city in Asia.'

Whatever its hygienic and moral shortcomings, Meshed was the last town to offer Curzon shelter until he reached Teheran, 500 miles to the west. There were two alternative methods of travel open to him. One was to form his own caravan by purchasing horses and baggage, animals and equipment for camping. Its advantage was freedom of movement; its disadvantages were expense, a slow rate of progress and the need to engage and supervise a whole retinue of servants. Curzon rejected such a plan in favour of riding *chapar*, or by Government post horse. Under this system the traveller, in effect a piece of animate freight, was carried swiftly and generally safely from stage to stage, spending each night in a post house that made few concessions to luxury. The cost of riding a horse was little more than a halfpenny a mile, together with a small tip to the post-boy. The gratuity, however, seems to have been optional and not once in 1,200 miles, Curzon noted, did a recipient ever deviate, even by accident, into an expression of gratitude

In this manner he covered about sixty miles a day. As the route from Meshed to Teheran was little frequented except by pilgrims, the horses to be found at each staging post were usually few and ill-conditioned. But he soon became skilled in selecting the least unreliable; he would choose the animal that could display most hair on its knees, as being reasonably sure-footed.

Curzon also learnt how to make himself at home in the draughty chambers set aside for foreign guests. He would stuff up gaping windows, nail curtains over ramshackle doors, spread a rug on the floor, light a fire and brew himself a cup of tea – 'the best beverage in the world'. In such a state of contentment, he boasted, he would not exchange his quarters for a sheeted bed in Windsor Castle: in the icy dawn of the next morning, packing his baggage by the light of a flickering candle, he felt less resolute.

Five hundred miles of desolate landscape brought Curzon to the gates of Teheran. He relished the contrast of those empty desert days with the bustle and clatter of his life at home, and delighted to weave romance even out of a passing cortège of camels: 'Suddenly, and without the slightest warning, there looms out of the darkness, like the apparition of a phantom ship, the form of the captain of the caravan. His spongy tread sounds softly on the smooth sand, and, like a great string of linked ghouls, the silent procession stalks by and is swallowed up in the night.'

Yet his moods were unpredictable. Like most newly arrived tourists in Teheran, he made an early expedition to see the Shah's jewels. He gazed on crowns and tiaras, swords and scabbards, cups and candlesticks, watches and snuff boxes. He saw a massive globe of the world alight with precious stones and mounted on a stand of solid gold; a mound of loose pearls he was allowed to let run through his fingers in cascades; jars crammed with uncut diamonds and emeralds, as higgledy-piggledy as bull's eyes or humbugs in a sweetshop. So glittering an Aladdin's cave might predictably have prompted him to display his most ornamental style, his most plethoric vocabulary. Instead he delivers a sombre sermon on the evils of hoarded riches and the neglected claims of material progress.

Nor did the rest of the contents of the Royal Palace evoke any happier reaction. It pained the son of Kedleston to see a more or less haphazard jumble of porcelain vases and gold-plated armchairs, Swiss musical boxes and meteorolites, antiquities without price and heads of game shot by His Imperial Majesty. 'They are eloquently typical,' Curzon wrote, 'of the life of mingled splendour and frippery, and of the taste, half cultured and half debased, of the Persian monarch and, it may be said, of the Persian aristocracy in general.'

As for the famous Peacock Throne, he denounced it, with a flourish of historical learning, as 'a fraudulent pretender to the honour of having supported the majesty of the Great Mogul.'

The ruling Shah, Nasr-ed-Din, or Defender of the Faith, had paid the second of his two State visits to Great Britain only a few weeks before Curzon's arrival in Teheran. To guide him through the labyrinth of European protocol he had included a Balliol man in his suite – Kasim Khan, the future Prime Minister of Persia better known as Nasr-ul-Mulk.* But neither in 1873 nor in 1889 had the Shah been a model guest. Staying with the Duke of Montrose in Scotland, he insisted on having two sheep killed each morning in the sight of his suite, rejected a William and Mary four-poster bed in favour of three mattresses piled on the floor, and blew his nose on the muslin curtains. His attentions to women, too, lacked finesse. During his first visit he took a fancy to Lady Margaret Beaumont, offering to buy her for his harem at a price of £500,000. During his second, he expressed his wonder that Lord Salisbury did not take a new wife; and when at Hatfield the Prime Minister presented to him the ageing Baroness Burdett-Coutts as the most celebrated philanthropist of her country, he gazed into her face and exclaimed '*Quelle horreur!*'

Arriving in Teheran a few weeks after the Shah's return to his capital, Curzon sought and was granted an audience. Although Nasr-ed-Din spoke a little French, he chose to conduct the interview in Persian through an interpreter. Curzon thought his short, jerky sentences more suited to a forensic cross-examination than to a conversation, but affable in tone. The single theme to which the Shah devoted their ten-minute talk was the Russian-built road from Askabad to the frontier and its continuation on to Persian soil. He could hardly have selected a subject on which his guest came better prepared.

Curzon subsequently devoted an entire chapter of his book on Persia to the character of the Shah. While conceding that Nasr-ed-Din applied himself industriously to the business of government, he emphasized the caprice that marred all plans for developing the resources of his country:

> One week it is gas; another it is electric light. Now it is a staff college; anon, a military hospital. Today it is a Russian uniform; yesterday it was a German man-of-war for the Persian Gulf. A new army warrant is issued this year; a new code of law is promised for the next. Nothing comes of any of these brilliant schemes, and the lumber-rooms of the palace are not more full of broken mechanism and discarded

* At Oxford, Curzon and his other contemporaries, with unsophisticated wit, dubbed him Curs'im.

bric-a-brac than are the pigeon-holes of the government bureaux of abortive reforms and dead fiascoes.

Curzon wrote scathingly about the ingrained pattern of corruption which ran through every department of Persian public life. 'From the Shah downwards,' he wrote, 'there is scarcely an official who is not open to gifts, scarcely a post which is not conferred in return for gifts, scarcely an income which has not been amassed by the receipt of gifts.'

Nor was he comforted by an examination of judicial procedure and the infliction of punishment; one he found to be arbitrary, the other ingeniously cruel. In Nasr-ed-Din's reign, he discovered, condemned criminals had been crucified, blown from guns, buried alive, flayed, mutilated, impaled, shod like horses, converted into human torches, torn asunder by being bound to the heads of two growing trees that were first bent together and then allowed to spring back to their natural position. As recently as 1884 robbers had been walled up alive in pillars of brick and mortar. The standard penalty was the bastinado, or beating of the soles of the feet. One victim, Curzon learnt, had endured no fewer than 6,000 blows.

By contrast, the Shah insisted upon kindness to animals, especially cats. His own pets accompanied him everywhere. One had its own baggage horse to carry a specially constructed cage with velvet-padded wires. Another had a pension of £400 a year settled on it in old age. A third one day fell asleep on the coat tails of a courtier who cut off a good foot of cloth rather than disturb the repose of the favourite.

An unsatisfied aesthetic appetite no less than a stringent timetable drove Curzon towards the South. Teheran was too recent a capital to boast those immense mosques and *madressehs*, or religious colleges, that dominate so many Oriental towns; and the trumpery confusion of the Royal palaces he dismissed with impatience. Isfahan, ancient seat of Shah Abbas the Great, beckoned him to worthier sights. Once more he submitted himself to the brisk tyranny of the *chapar*, or Government post.

For many modern travellers, neither the distant prospect of Venice from the sea nor the vision of the Parthenon turned to honey by the setting sun can quite match the first sight of Isfahan. There are domes and minarets of turquoise blue and daffodil yellow and Cornish cream; a square seven times the size of the Piazza di San Marco, fringed with some of the supreme glories of Mohammedan architecture; silent pools by which holy men squat in meditation; gardens alive with wagtails; bazaars where even the humblest utensils are adorned with painted roses.

It was not so in Curzon's day. He saw only the contrast between a past of grandeur and a present of sorrowfulness and decay. 'I know of no city in the world,' he lamented, 'that has ever struck me with greater pathos, or whose figure is wrapped in so melancholy a garb of woe.' He was wrong, however, in concluding that her former radiance was irrecoverable. Restored with the same care and fidelity that Curzon later brought to the ancient monuments of India, those of Isfahan have since emerged in all their glowing magnificence and remain as yet unsullied by the touch of mass tourism.

As for the inhabitants, Curzon continued, 'the Isfahanis enjoy an unenviable reputation alike for cowardice and morals. They are inordinately vain of their city and of themselves and in a country where lying is a fine art, are said to be incomparable artists.' And to illustrate their stinginess, he gleefully repeated the saying that a merchant of Isfahan will put his cheese into a bottle and rub his bread on the outside to give it a flavour.

Curzon hoped for better things at Shiraz, more than 300 miles to the south. It was, as he knew from its literature, 'the home of poets and rose-bowers and nightingales, the haunt of jollity and the Elysian fields of love, praised in a hundred odes as the fairest gem of Iran.' Once more he was disappointed. 'The panorama of the modern town contains nothing of distinction except three blue domes appearing above a crumbling wall and numerous enclosures thickly planted with cypresses which seem, in their sable stoles, to mourn like funeral mutes over a vanished past.' A closer inspection of its supposed attractions, including the tombs of the poets Sadi and Hafiz, confirmed his initial distaste.

About forty miles to the northeast of Shiraz, however, he found intellectual solace at Persepolis. In his *Persia and the Persian Question*, he later devoted eighty pages to a history and description of the tombs of the Achaemenian kings and the Sassanian rock carvings at Naksh-i-Rustam, to the ruined palaces of Xerxes, Artaxerxes and Darius. Indispensable to any serious student of those dynasties, they also illuminate the industry, erudition, reconstructive imagination and intense concentration which he brought to problems of archaeology.

It is therefore all the more surprising to read in his account of the bull-flanked portals of Xerxes an eloquent defence of vandalism:

> A structure so hopelessly ruined is not rendered the less impressive – on the contrary, to my thinking, it becomes the more interesting – by reason of the records graven upon it, in many cases with their own hands, by famous voyagers of the past, with whose names and studies the intelligent visitor to Persepolis is likely to be almost as familiar as he is with the titles of Xerxes.

He did not pause to consider what his reaction would have been on finding that a succession of Persian gentlemen had recorded their visits on the pillars of Stonehenge. He merely took out his knife and in a stone niche of the palace of Darius the Great added his own epigraph to the history of Persepolis. 'G. N. Curzon,' he scratched, '1889.'

The scholar and sculptor gave way to the man of action as Curzon embarked on 'the roughest and least propitious highway of traffic in the world'. The route from Shiraz to Bushire, on the Persian Gulf, first climbed a mountain pass to a height of 7,400 feet, then plunged down to the sea through a succession of sickeningly steep defiles. Since no *chapar* service could operate over such terrain, Curzon had to hire his own *yabu*, or pony, with a caravan of mules for the baggage. His first ordeal was the Pass of the Old Woman, which 'resembles an Alpine torrent-bed, minus only the torrent'. The second, deceptively named the Pass of the Maiden, was even steeper, and had been made into a hideously dangerous stairway by unskilled attempts to pave it with boulders. The third, that included a sheer drop of 1,200 feet in less than a mile, at least offered a sound surface conveniently indented by the hoofs of generations of mules. The fourth, the Kotal-i-Mallu, or Cursed Pass, had, Curzon concluded, been so named by ascending rather than descending wayfarers: for it was neither so precipitous nor so stony as its predecessors.

In spite of the jolts and jars that such conditions must have imposed on his weak spine, his determination and curiosity never deserted him. He made a detour to examine the ruins of Shapur and to cover page after page with meticulous description of its bas-reliefs. He recorded that the people of Borazjun boiled and ate locusts in the manner of shrimps, and that the Mamasenni, or nomads, kept honey bees in earthenware hives like drain pipes.

Five days after leaving Shiraz he stood on the shores of the Gulf. 'How glad I was,' he wrote, 'to take off the saddle and saddlebags and holsters, to say goodbye to my rickety *yabu*, and to feel that I had without any accident passed through Persia from sea to sea.' How swiftly, too, his spirits revived at the sight of the Union Jack streaming from the top of a gigantic mast that marked the British Residency. 'By far the loftiest object in Bushire,' Curzon wrote, and he may not have meant it only literally.

One of the most agreeable memories he brought back from Persia was the sight of English trade marks or figures on nine out of every ten bales of merchandise that passed on camel, donkey or mule. 'Manchester,' he proclaimed, 'is still the universal clothier of Isfahan.' Similarly at Bushire, the steamers lying at anchor were almost without exception British; the bazaars were crowded with British or Indian goods; the rupee was more readily accepted than the Persian kran.

To investigate the opportunities open to British commercial enterprise was one reason for Curzon's journey up the Karun, Persia's only navigable river, which flows into the Persian Gulf at a point more than 100 miles to the north-west of Bushire. His interest in its possibilities as an artery of trade had been reinforced by Sir Henry Drummond Wolff, the former member of Lord

Randolph Churchill's Fourth Party whom Lord Salisbury had subsequently rewarded with a succession of diplomatic posts in Turkey, Egypt and Persia.

Within a year of being appointed British Minister in Teheran at the end of 1887, Wolff had persuaded the Shah to open the Karun river to the mercantile marine of the world – a concession of infinitely more value to Great Britain than to any other nation. But as Curzon soon discovered, Persian local officials were determined to thwart the intention of the central government by imposing arbitrary and vexatious restrictions.

He experienced such ill-will for the first time on disembarking at Mohammerah, at the mouth of the Karun river, which he had reached from Bushire aboard a British steamer. The Persian official in charge of mercantile operations there sent a message demanding to see his passport – which had not once been asked for during his three months of previous travel through the country – and bidding him present himself at sunrise next morning. Curzon was not to be trifled with in this way. Ignoring the command, he went aboard the river steamer on which he had already booked his passage and at 6 a.m. began his voyage up the Karun.

At Ahwaz, some 120 miles up the river, the steamer could go no further because of dangerous rapids, and Curzon prepared to transfer to a smaller boat that plied the upper reaches. He had taken the precaution of bringing a letter of recommendation from the British Resident at Bushire to the Persian Governor-General of Arabistan, whose headquarters were at Shushter, another 100 miles upstream; it requested that the launch might be put at Curzon's disposal for the second stage of his journey. Accordingly, Curzon presented it to the Governor-General's deputy at Ahwaz, Mirza Akbar Ali, 'a model type of the genus Persian subordinate official, species first-rate obstructionist'. Having readily agreed that Curzon could embark for Shushter the next morning, the Mirza subsequently changed his mind and subjected him to hour after hour of frivolous objection and tortuous colloquy.

Curzon possessed a limitless fund of good humour that sooner or later would dissolve all the petty irritations and frustrations of foreign travel. They did not end with the insolence of the Mirza. Permitted at last to board the river launch, he abandoned her when only half-way to Shushter since her lack of speed threatened to upset his timetable. So he hired horses and set off cross-country. Soon after starting he heard a lion roar ahead of him. 'My guide, who was walking in front,' he wrote, 'informed me at the same moment that my horse was so much accustomed to go in advance that he would himself facilitate my progress by dropping to the rear; an act of friendly consideration on his part for which I shall ever remember the Arab.'

At Shushter, the most dilapidated and noisome town he had yet seen, he found further evidence that both officials and merchants were attempting to frustrate the concession of 1888 by means of a 'boycott'; so recently had the word been coined in Ireland that Curzon encased it in inverted commas. To his particular disgust, he learnt that the agent of the British steamship company had found it difficult even to obtain drinking water, as the pious Mohammedan inhabitants were unwilling to have dealings with 'an unclean thing'. He noticed, however, that nearly all the goods in the bazaars seemed to be of British or Indian origin; and he looked to the future with mild optimism.

The pride which kindled in Curzon's heart whenever he encountered the benevolent virility of British rule abroad continued to animate him as he sailed for Karachi and the long journey home.

'It is no exaggeration,' he wrote, 'to say that the lives and properties of hundreds of thousands of human beings are secured by this Protectorate of the Persian Gulf, and that were it either withdrawn or destroyed, both sea and shores would relapse into the anarchical chaos from which they have so laboriously been reclaimed. That the Persian Government has been enabled to reassert its authority upon the North littoral; that the pirates of the opposite coast have been taught that rapine is not a safe religion, and, where they once swept the sea with laden slave-dhows, now dive harmlessly for pearls; that the Arab tribes, instead of being subjected to the curse of pashas, retain the liberty they so dearly prize, is due to the British Government alone.'

The only comparable operation, he continued, had taken place in the Caspian: but there were differences. 'Where the Russians in the North have scared a few penniless buccaneers, the British in the South have effectively destroyed a pirate combination and fleet that recall the last century of the Roman Republic and the exploits of Pompey.' Even so, Russia had claimed the exclusive control of the Caspian as the reward for her exertions. His own country would demand no such price for the establishment of a Pax Britannica, however dearly it had cost her in men and money: the merchant navies of the world were free to compete without hindrance for the trade of the entire Persian Gulf.

So magnanimous a concession, however, depended upon one fundamental condition. 'I should,' he wrote, 'regard the concession of a port upon the Persian Gulf to Russia by any power as a deliberate insult to Great Britain, as a wanton rupture of the *status quo*, and as an intentional provocation to war; and I should impeach the British minister who was guilty of acquiescing in such a surrender, as a traitor to his country.'

That was the very essence of Curzon's interest in Persia. 'Turkestan, Afghanistan, Transcaspia, Persia – to many these names breathe only a sense of utter remoteness or a memory of strange vicissitudes and of moribund romance. To me, I confess, they are the pieces on a chessboard upon which is being played out a game for the dominion of the world.'

He conceded that Great Britain could not prevent Russia by force of arms from advancing on the northern provinces of Persia. But by establishing a mercantile and political ascendency in the south she had both stiffened the resolve of the Persian Government and blocked Russia's sea route to India. Such a policy embraced many virtues. It was practical: it was profitable: it was pacific. 'England,' Curzon proclaimed, 'does not covet one square foot of Persian soil. The eighth and tenth Commandments stand in no danger of being violated by us.'

Chapter Eighteen

UNDER-SECRETARY

A biography loses its charm when its subject either reaches the age of forty or becomes an Under-Secretary.

– C. R. W. Nevinson

Curzon had hardly arrived back in England at the end of February 1890, than his health gave way. For months he had driven himself mercilessly across the mountains and plains of Persia, so absorbed in his travels that he scarcely noticed discomfort or undernourishment, physical exhaustion or nervous strain. These prolonged privations now took their toll. He was in no state either to resume his parliamentary duties or to embark on the gigantic literary task of recording his Persian experiences. His doctors, moreover, suspected that he might be suffering from incipient tuberculosis. For once obedient to medical advice, he departed for the Mediterranean in search of sunshine and relaxation.

At Cannes he stayed with Prince Wagram, grandson of Marshal Berthier, and at lunch one day met H. M. Stanley, newly arrived from Africa. 'Short and solid,' Curzon recorded, 'almost podgy in appearance, a figure the reverse of elegant, dressed in clothes which were anything but smart. He was very shy when he came in and did not thaw till well into lunch, though he fortunately gave us the opportunity quite early in the day of turning the talk on to Africa and his adventures, by comparing the weather (it was raining cats and dogs) with the climate in the great equatorial forests where he wandered so long and where he said it was so dark and sombre that they could scarcely believe that the sun shone outside.'

Curzon enquired what question the explorer had first asked on emerging once more into civilization. First, Stanley replied, 'Does the Queen of England still live and reign?' Then, 'Is the Conservative Government still in?' – to which, he added, there came from every mouth the response, 'Thank God'. Whatever personal cordiality Curzon felt towards Gladstone, he warmed to Stanley's denunciation of him as 'the most dangerous and incompetent of statesmen', a man who had never visited Egypt, Turkey, India or the Colonies – or indeed been further afield than the Ionian islands – and was thus incompetent to rule the British Empire. There were two qualifications, Stanley concluded, that should be required of every Member of Parliament: that he should be under seventy and that he should have travelled in the British Empire. Curzon did not dissent.

From Cannes he went sailing with Lord Rosslyn, and then visited Rennell Rodd at the British Legation in Athens. There he embarked with other friends on a yachting cruise to Athos and Meteora. It struck a chord of family piety to follow in the wake of Robert Curzon, later fourteenth Baron Zouche and author of *Monasteries of the Levant.* Curzon could just recall the visits of his kinsman to Kedleston, 'a little old gentleman in a black swallow-tailed coat, habitually perched at the top of a ladder in a dim and dusty library'. And although he had at first been repelled by the title of Robert Curzon's classic work, he soon came to appreciate its wealth of lightly borne learning.

Not even on the Holy Mountain of Athos could Curzon rid himself of a familiar political spectre. At the Russian monastery of St Panteleeman, 'a great many of the monks whom I saw looked far better suited to shoulder a musket than to wear the cowl; and the entire establishment bore the appearance not of a retreat of pious-minded persons fleeing from the temptations of a wicked world, but of an enterprising colony bent upon aggravating its territories and providing itself with stores, depots, and all the necessary furniture of temporal aggrandisement'.

Curzon's religious scepticism, too, had not diminished with the years. At one monastery he noted that 'a French translation of the *Decameron* of Boccaccio and a modern guide-book to Paris seemed to indicate that the holy fathers found time to vary the austerity of conventual discipline with occasional dips into lighter literature'. At another he was shown an ancient ikon of the Virgin and Child. 'I fully expected to hear,' he wrote, 'that this painting was the product of St Luke, who is believed to have excelled with the brush, but the monks of Iberon would appear to have missed this excellent opportunity.' And he left smilingly for Meteora, where he enjoyed even the experience of being hauled up hundreds of feet of rock face, like a trussed quail in a net, to inspect other sacred treasures, including the vinegar and sponge offered to Christ upon the Cross.

With uncharacteristic meekness, Curzon decided not to retard his convalescence by embarking at once on his proposed book about Persia. But there was another matter connected with his travels which he could not afford to postpone. In the hope of turning to financial benefit the knowledge he had acquired during the past six months, he accepted an invitation to join the board of the Persian Bank Mining Rights Corporation, Ltd.

The company was incorporated on 16 April 1890, with a capital of £1,000,000. Its purpose was to acquire and work the mining rights granted

1 The chapel in Kedleston Church designed and dedicated by Curzon to the memory of his first wife, Mary. 'It was,' Sir Shane Leslie has written, 'as though a Gothic chantry had been made to enclose an Arabian Night.'

2 Curzon with some of his brothers and sisters at Kedleston (1869). 'I suppose no children well born and well placed,' he wrote in later years, 'ever cried so much or so justly.' But there were days of sunshine, too, when they escaped from the severe regime of their governess to play 'cricket with the flunkeys'. And George's watch and chain were almost certainly part of the rich harvest of presents he gathered each birthday.

3 Kedleston from the south. Matthew Brettingham's original plan was never completed, and the curved galleries and supporting wings of the north front were not repeated on the south side of the house. From the south, a later architect has written, Kedleston seems to float upon an ocean of green like a huge but finely proportioned silver ship towing two lesser vessels in her wake.

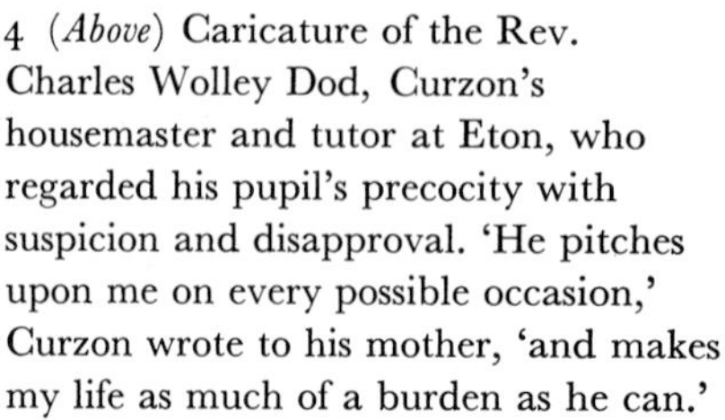

4 (*Above*) Caricature of the Rev. Charles Wolley Dod, Curzon's housemaster and tutor at Eton, who regarded his pupil's precocity with suspicion and disapproval. 'He pitches upon me on every possible occasion,' Curzon wrote to his mother, 'and makes my life as much of a burden as he can.'

5 (*Above right*) Resenting the chill austerity of Wolley Dod, Curzon sought sympathy and encouragement from another Eton master, the unconventional Oscar Browning. Although Browning was dismissed from Eton in 1875, Lord Scarsdale admired his character and allowed him to take his son abroad in the school holidays. This photograph was taken in Milan in 1878.

6 (*Right*) Edward and Alfred Lyttelton, who believed that cricket was next to godliness. In later life, as Head Master of Eton and a noted preacher, Edward confessed that he never walked up the nave of a church without bowling an imaginary ball. And W.G. Grace described Alfred's play as the champagne of cricket.

7 Curzon's Eton room. He kept an illicit cellar in the bottom drawer of his oak bureau. 'It was not that I cared for drinking,' he wrote, 'but I enjoyed the supreme cheek as an Eton boy of giving wine parties in my room. I used to make excellent champagne and claret cup.' Mr Gladstone knew nothing of these mild orgies, but when visiting Curzon in 1878 professed to be aghast at the luxury of an Eton boy's room compared with the plain living of his own day.

8 Mr Gladstone in his study (1896). The Grand Old Man found much refreshment from the cares of politics in a prolonged study of Homer. In 1878, at Curzon's invitation, he delivered a lecture to the Eton Literary Society on the epic poet. But meeting Curzon at dinner a few years later, he noted: 'What struck me painfully in him was the absence of any sort of reverence for anything like age or tradition.'

9 (*Right*) The Marquess of Salisbury, three times Prime Minister. In 1885 Curzon became one of his unpaid assistant private secretaries and wrote of him: 'His affability is almost embarrassing, for he poses as the recipient rather than as the donor of an obligation.' Later Curzon served him for three years at the Foreign Office and was rewarded by being appointed Viceroy of India.

10 George Leveson Gower is greeted by his friends on coming of age at Oxford, May 1879. Most of them acquired fame in later years.
Back row, left to right: Arthur Hardinge (British Ambassador in Madrid); Walter Lawrence (Curzon's private secretary in India); Harold Boulton (philanthropist and poet); Leonard Shoobridge (traveller and unsuccessful parliamentary candidate); William Radcliffe (holder of the world salmon record in Norway, having killed 1,352 fish in 51½ days).
Front row, left to right: George Curzon; Rennell Rodd (British Ambassador in Rome); George Leveson Gower (private secretary to Mr Gladstone and Commissioner of Woods and Forests); Richard Farrer (Fellow of All Souls and author of *A Tour in Greece*).

11 Dr Benjamin Jowett, Master of Balliol College, Oxford (1870–93). The devastating candour of his advice, however well-intentioned, was not always appreciated by his pupils. He told Curzon: 'It would be better if you were shorter in speaking, writing, conversation. I think it worth your while to consider how you can correct this defect – probably the only bar which stands in the way of your rise to eminence.'

12 (*Right*) Laura Tennant married Alfred Lyttelton in 1885 and died in childbirth within the year. 'My soul hankers after philosophy and poetry,' she told Curzon. In a lighter vein, she wrote: 'I have been reading about Bernal Osborne, and I think you are very like him, especially when he said his intentions to Miss Julia were *not* honourable.'

13 (*Below*) Charlotte Tennant, known as Charty, married Lord Ribblesdale in 1877. She was one of Sir Charles Tennant's five daughters, four of whom were not a little in love with Curzon. 'I hunger to look upon you and talk to you and hear you talk,' she wrote in 1886. 'Have I still got a little corner of your heart?'

14 Margot Tennant. 'I hear you are going to marry Margot Tennant?' a friend enquired of Arthur Balfour. 'No, that is not so,' he replied, 'I rather think of having a career of my own.' In 1894 she married another future Prime Minister, Henry Asquith. Queen Victoria, alarmed by stories of her disregard for convention, thought her 'most unfit for a Cabinet Minister's wife'.

15 Sibell, widow of Lord Grosvenor. 'I went to Eaton not long ago,' Alfred Lyttelton told Curzon, 'and made great friends with Lady Grosvenor, upon whose table I saw a photograph of you.' Curzon would like to have married this widow of sweet nature and unlimited means, but the prize fell to his friend George Wyndham.

16 George Wyndham. First a soldier, then a politician, Wyndham was at heart a man of letters whose elaborate style of oratory was never much to the taste of the House of Commons. Curzon described him as 'possessing the physical beauty of a statue and endowed with the chivalry of a knight errant, the fancy of a poet and the deep tenderness of a woman'.

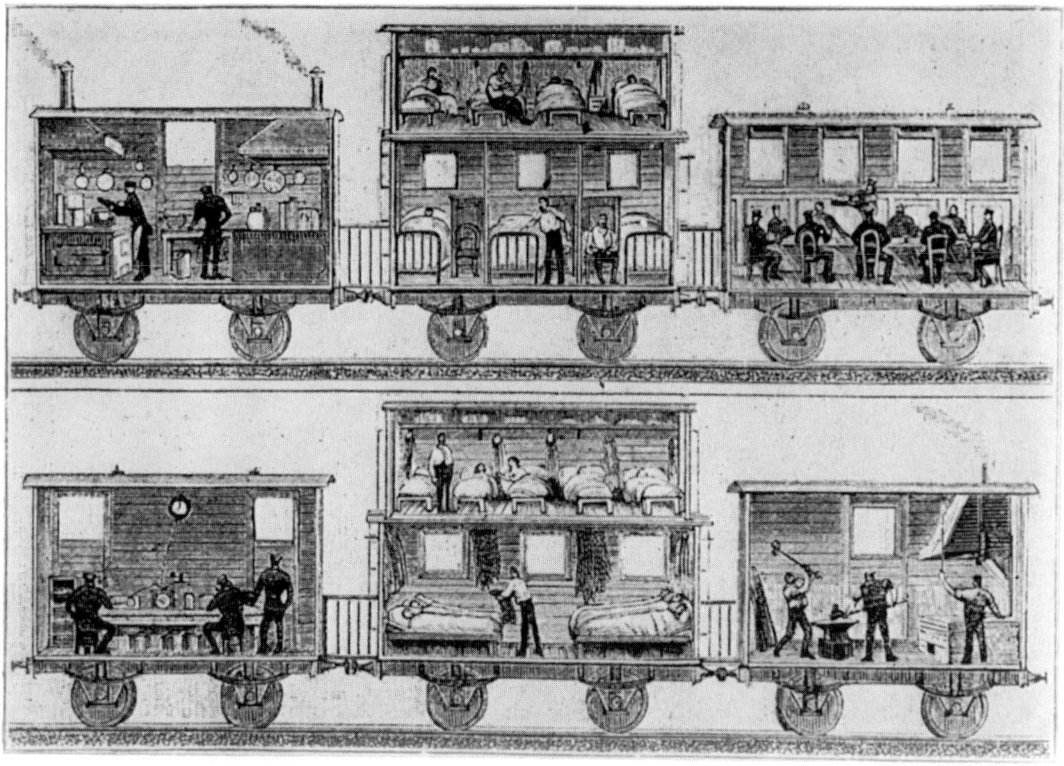

17 Section of the working train used to build the Transcaspian railway, that ran 900 miles from the eastern shore of the Caspian Sea to Samarkand. In 1888 Curzon became one of the first Englishmen to travel along the new route. Although fearing its political and military implications, he admired the skill of the engineers who had overcome an acute shortage of water and perpetually shifting sand dunes to lay the line at the rate of two miles a day.

18 (*Left*) Nasr-ed-Din, Shah of Persia, created a poor impression during his visits to Great Britain in 1873 and 1889. He had sheep killed in the sight of his suite each morning, blew his nose on the curtains and offered to buy Lady Margaret Beaumont for his harem at a price of £500,000. Curzon, who was received by him in Teheran, found him an industrious if cruel ruler, whose gleams of enlightenment were soon extinguished by endemic corruption.

19 Abdur Rahman Khan, Amir of Afghanistan. He loved cruelty as much for itself as for its effectiveness in governing a turbulent population. In twelve years, he confessed to Curzon when entertaining him in Kabul, he had slaughtered 120,000 rebellious subjects. The Amir was proud, too, of his accomplishments as a piano tuner, watchmaker and dentist.

20 Li Hung Chang, the Chinese statesman, visits Lord Salisbury at Hatfield in the summer of 1895. Also in the group are two lesser pillars of the Foreign Office: the Rt. Hon. George Curzon, Parliamentary Under-Secretary, and the Hon. Francis Bertie, an Assistant Under-Secretary.

21 Curzon brings his American bride, Mary Leiter, to Kedleston in May 1895, on returning from their wedding in Washington.
Mary found the formidable Lord Scarsdale, who stands behind her wearing a billycock hat, 'as tender and affectionate as my own father'.

22 Mary Curzon used to complain: 'People discuss my looks as though I were an oleograph.' Beauty was not her only contribution to a wonderfully successful marriage. She also brought encouragement and devotion; a subordination of her personality to that of her husband; and a huge fortune built on Chicago real estate.

23 Curzon as Viceroy of India. His friend Cecil Spring Rice used to say that one might as well talk of the P & O boats breeding Viceroys as of Eton breeding Governor-Generals: it was the only route for them to go by. Since his schooldays at Eton, Curzon had longed for the Viceroyalty of India and achieved his ambition before he was forty. It was for him less a political appointment than a divine mission.

24 (*Above*) St John Brodrick, 1st Earl of Midleton. One of Curzon's most intimate friends from Eton days. He became Secretary of State for India (1903), and within two years he and Curzon had embarked on a quarrel that never quite healed. Ostensibly it was over the conduct of Indian affairs, but at heart it lay in a clash of temperaments.

25 (*Above left*) Bishop J.E.C. Welldon. An impregnable fortress on the playing fields of Eton, he became Winston Churchill's Headmaster at Harrow. With more tact and ability to compromise, he might have become Archbishop of Canterbury. But differences with Curzon led to his premature resignation as Bishop of Calcutta.

26 (*Left*) Arthur James Balfour, 1st Earl of Balfour and Prime Minister (1902–5). In their youth, Curzon and his friends cherished Balfour's grace of body and of mind. But on two occasions he struck mortal blows at Curzon's ambitions with all the skill of an old political hand.

by Royal firman, or licence, to the newly established Imperial Bank of Persia. It thus held a monopoly of all iron, copper, lead, mercury, manganese, borax, asbestos and petroleum that belonged to the State and had not previously been ceded to other companies or individuals. The concession was to last sixty years – although all mining operations had to begin before 1899 – and the Shah was to receive sixteen per cent of the net profits. For the first time, Curzon wrote, the exceptionally rich mineral resources of the country, known to three centuries of travellers, were to be systematically and scientifically explored and utilized.

The search for oil occupied only a limited place in the programme of the Persian Bank Mining Rights Corporation. Throughout his long journeys Curzon noted the location of all the wells that lay along his route, mostly in the region of the Karun river. But they were of little commercial value: each yielded only thirty or forty gallons a day, used in lamps, for rubbing on camels, or as a cure for the itch.

Curzon's fellow directors were men of business ability and Oriental experience. They included Sir Lepel Griffin, a retired senior official of the Indian Civil Service; Mr Frederick Sassoon, the banker; and Baron George de Reuter, son of the financier who in 1872 startled the world by acquiring a concession to manage Persia's entire natural resources, industry and public works for a period of seventy years – a project so ambitious that it collapsed under its own weight. The lesser venture of 1890 also had at its disposal the advice of General Houtum Schindler. 'To the advantage of long residence in the country,' Curzon wrote, 'he adds the erudition of a scholar and the zeal of a pioneer.'

Such accumulated boardroom wisdom failed to impress the investing public, and the *Topical Times* proclaimed that the company should be called the Persian Bank Mining Rights and Wrongs Corporation, Ltd. 'This concern,' it said, 'is rotten to the core.' The company was certainly unfortunate. For three years, in the face of persistent local obstruction, its agents prospected for minerals and oil, but with practically no success. They carried out expensive borings for oil to a depth of more than 800 feet at Daliki, fifty miles northeast of Bushire. That, however, was not one of the places which, in the early years of the next century, was to resuscitate the entire economy of Persia with a seemingly limitless bounty. Having limped through a profitless decade, the Persian Bank Mining Rights Corporation went into voluntary liquidation in 1901.

The episode was hardly a financial disaster for Curzon, who had invested no more than £350 in the venture. Psychologically, however, it clouded his vision and led him to believe that others could not succeed where he and his colleagues had failed. As Viceroy of India he poured much scorn on the concession granted by the Persian Government in 1901 to William Knox D'Arcy – the Englishman who, after losing nearly every penny in his enterprise, was eventually rewarded when his engineers struck commercial quantities of oil in 1908 and so laid the foundations of modern Persian prosperity.

'I advise you,' Curzon wrote to Lord George Hamilton, the Secretary of State for India, on 31 July 1901, 'not to think that the industrial regeneration of Persia is going to make a new start in Mr D'Arcy's hands.' Two years later he repeated his pessimistic prophecy to Lord Lansdowne, the Foreign Secretary: 'Personally I do not believe in the likelihood of Persian oil deposits being worked at profit and should not fear sale of concessions to anybody else were it not that concessions in Russian hands would be worked in connection with Baku and might be utilised to spread a Russian influence in our sphere.'

'I hear you are working like a navvy,' Margot wrote to Curzon on Christmas Day, 1890. 'They all say your power of work is unrivalled Napoleonic. A. Balfour says he has never seen anyone like you.' After illness and recuperation, silent attendance at Westminster and the pleasures of the London season, a dutiful descent on his constituency and a visit to the Tennants in Scotland, he had at last begun to write the *magnum opus* of his life.

To ensure undisturbed quiet, he took lodgings in the London suburb of Norwood, where his only relaxations were to row in a boat each afternoon on the Crystal Palace lake and to read *The Count of Monte Cristo* while he dined. He had set himself a daunting task. It was no less than the compilation of the most comprehensive work on Persia to appear for half a century. Inhabitants, provinces, cities, communications, antiquities, institutions, government, policies, resources, trade, finance, present interests and future development – nothing Persian was foreign to his theme. He had read nearly all the works on the country written in European languages during the past 600 years; he had ridden for six months from one end of the country to the other; he had filled notebook after notebook with his observations; he had exchanged innumerable letters with scholars and administrators in every corner of the world. The map which was to accompany his book also cost him much anxious research and supervision, and was later acclaimed as a considerable addition to the knowledge of a region where no trigonometrical survey had yet been undertaken.

One particular handicap added to his toil. 'After Russia,' he wrote, 'where statistics exist but are systematically suppressed, I know of no country in which they are so difficult to procure as Persia, where they barely exist at all.' He found that facts and figures, in their very essence an insult to the Oriental imagination, could be established only after long and patient enquiry and the careful collation of the results of many independent investigations. 'I can truly say,' he wrote, 'that single lines in this book have sometimes cost me hours of work and pages of correspondence.' With exasperated hyperbole, he added: 'I am convinced that a true son of Iran would sooner lie than tell the truth; and that he feels twinges of desperate remorse when, upon occasions, he has thoughtlessly strayed into veracity.' Hence the implacable inquisition to which he had subjected more reliable witnesses. When staying with a British official of the Persian telegraph service on the track between Teheran and Isfahan, Curzon kept his host out of bed until the small hours, asking questions about the surrounding district. Early next morning he was ready with a full précis of their conversation, which he made the official criticize, correct and supplement before he took to the road again. Nor, at the end of a day's march, did he ever allow himself to relax without first marshalling in his mind the events of the past twenty-four hours and writing up his diary with a wealth of detail.

The labours of composition at Norwood were interrupted in January 1891, when a recurrence of ill-health sent him to St Moritz for a few weeks. But by March he had completed the first volume and by the autumn the end was in sight. The work ran to 1,300 closely printed pages containing more than half a million words. Even to transcribe *Persia and the Persian Question* would seem to be the task of years. For a busy Member of Parliament to have welded so huge a mass of material into logical sequence and luminous style is one of the most remarkable literary achievements of the nineteenth century.

In November 1891, when much of the book was at the printer and only a single chapter remained to be written, an unforeseen hazard threatened its early publication. Lord Salisbury invited the author to join his Government as Parliamentary Under-Secretary for India. By the standards of the day it was a notable promotion. In place of the fifty or so Ministers of State and Parliamentary Secretaries who today labour under the direction of nearly thirty Cabinet Ministers and other heads of departments, there were fewer than a dozen junior ministers in 1891. Curzon, moreover, was only thirty-two and had been a member of Parliament for barely five years.

His friends, however, thought his advancement belated. His brilliant maiden speech, his mature though infrequent interventions in debate, his strenuous travels and authoritative work on Central Asia – all combined to create an impression of confidence in his abilities. Salisbury, it is true, was generally reluctant to sacrifice older men in his administration to make room for rising talent: but St John Brodrick, by no means the intellectual peer of Curzon, had in 1886 been appointed Financial Secretary to the War Office at the age of twenty-nine.

One handicap that may have retarded Curzon's progress was a fatiguing verbosity. 'Above all things,' Dr Hornby once told him at Eton, 'take special pains about your peroration – you never know how soon you may require it.' That uncomfortably candid friend Dr Jowett gave him better advice. As late as 1889 he reinforced earlier warnings with this stern enjoinder: 'It would be better if you were shorter in speaking, writing, conversation. I think it worth your while to consider how you can correct this defect – probably the only bar which stands in the way of your rise to eminence.' Margot Asquith, admittedly in later years when their friendship had cooled, echoed the criticism. 'His words,' she wrote with brutal ingenuity, 'were a size too big for his thoughts.'

In October 1891, on the promotion of Sir James Fergusson to be Postmaster-General, it was widely forecast that Curzon would be appointed to fill the vacancy of Parliamentary Under-Secretary for Foreign Affairs. But Lord Salisbury's choice fell on James Lowther, another Conservative back-bencher. 'It is a bore,' Curzon wrote, 'to lose one of the few things for which I have combined taste and enthusiasm, as the chance may not recur. But I honestly think my friends were more disappointed than I. If I do not some day leave Lowther standing as still as a church steeple, I am not your obedient servant writing this letter.' His forecast was not entirely fulfilled. From 1905 to 1921, Lowther served with distinction as Speaker of the House of Commons.

Alfred Lyttelton was particularly incensed and wrote to commiserate with Curzon:

> Though J. Lowther is an old friend and a very good fellow, I have ever since been gathering increased wrath as a citizen of the Empire at your not being appointed. It is perfectly loathsome that the best men who have studied and become authorities on these subjects should be left out while important places be given to hacks, stump orators and regular voters. I am only consoled by the thought that by not being a front bencher in opposition you will cut these heavy bum-boats down to the water's edge in the future.
>
> Don't take any notice of this. I don't mean by it that old J. Lowther is one of those I have referred to – only I am furious at our best and most brilliant not being recognised.

Curzon was too absorbed completing the manuscript of *Persia and the Persian Question* to brood over this check to his political ambitions. He spent part of the autumn staying with Prince and Princess Wagram at Gros Bois, the spacious estate near Paris which successive French kings had given to their favourites and which Napoleon had ultimately bestowed on the Prince's grandfather, Marshal Berthier. Wilfrid Blunt, another frequent guest at Gros Bois, recorded how the Prince's father dedicated himself to its shooting, 'killing something every day in season and out of season, partridges on their nests if he could find no other, dogs and sometimes beaters'. The Prince, too, was much addicted to ancient ways, and would explain how the preserves had remained free of poachers since two or three had fallen to his own gun and been quietly buried where they fell.

In such feudal repose, Curzon received an unexpected letter from Lord Salisbury that dispelled the disappointment of the previous month and sent him hurrying back to England:

Gorst's migration to the Treasury has left vacant the Under Secretaryship for India. Are you disposed to undertake it? It concerns matters in which, without any official obligation, you have shown great interest in a very practical way; and it carries with it duties in the House of Commons, which sometimes involve important issues: issues on which whips feel very anxious.

The least attraction of the post, which Curzon did not hesitate to accept, was a salary of £1,500 a year. Almost from boyhood he had consciously equipped himself for the task of governing India, and the Under-Secretaryship now carried him appreciably forward to his ultimate goal. Among the letters of congratulation was one from Sir Mountstuart Grant Duff, who had held Curzon's new office in Mr Gladstone's administration twenty years before and later become Governor of Madras. 'I had rather have seen you at the Foreign Office,' he wrote, 'probably because I should have myself preferred going to it in 1868, if the choice had been offered to me; but I trust you are able to say as the Duke of Argyll did when he became Secretary for India, "I suppose I am the only man in the Government who has got *exactly* what he wanted".'

Curzon was touched, too, by a letter dictated from a sick bed by the Master of Balliol. 'I have never been more pleased at a political appointment than at yours,' Jowett wrote. 'There is the burning question of admitting the Natives to the Governor's Council, which has been pressed upon the Government by successive Governor-Generals, and which the best friends of India hope to have settled by a Conservative, and not by a Radical, Government.'

The author of *Persia and the Persian Question* soon discovered that less freedom of expression was permitted to a Minister of the Crown than to a private person. Within a few days of Curzon's appointment, Salisbury demanded to see the completed but unpublished text of the work and, if necessary, to excise any passage that might complicate Anglo-Persian relations. He perused the proof sheets, then delivered his verdict:

I think the part concerning the Shah cannot be published by a member of the Government. It is more severe than I expected when I spoke to you and I have no doubt it would give the deepest offence. I do not think the fact of your stating that it was in the printer's hands before you became a member of the Government would make any appreciable difference in his eyes. If this judgement does not commend itself to you, I would ask you to reflect what the consequences would be if some member of the Government – say James Lowther – were to publish a work dwelling at length on the parsimony of the Emperor William, on his 'petty economies and grudging gifts', on the 'meagreness of the acknowledgements received in this country by those who so sumptuously entertained him', stating that he had '£30,000,000 stowed in his vaults' while 'his country lay impoverished'; going on to point out that he had no claim to the honourable title of statesman, that he was 'entirely destitute of military knowledge and ability'; and that he enjoyed a military 'parade much as a child enjoys a Punch and Judy show'. Consider the supposed publication further stating that his reign had been 'disfigured by one or two acts of great barbarity of which the black and insufferable stain could never be washed out'; and then describing in detail the torture he had inflicted. Further imagine it to describe the manner in which the 'miserly sovereign' practised systematic extortion of various kinds upon his subjects; and then to finish with a personal delineation of the Empress of Germany, describing her as resembling a melon in her outline, and usually spending her time when at home in a ballet girl's dress with naked legs, and petticoats only half way to her knees.

Do you think it would be any answer to the Emperor of Germany that the member of the Government who had published this appreciation of himself and his surroundings was not a member of the Government when he marked it for the press?

Salisbury therefore required that the whole of the chapter on the Shah should be omitted or re-written, and in any case submitted for approval in its final form to Lord Cross, the Secretary of State for India. 'I write in the interests of the public service,' he concluded, 'without the slightest doubt or hesitation.' Further argument on Curzon's part was unavailing, and merely evoked a kindly but not less emphatic response from the Prime Minister:

I am afraid your feelings to me cannot be those of charity. You must be saying like Mr Puff 'The pruning hook! Zounds, Sir, the axe!'

But your plea in behalf of your utterances, that they are *true*, is quite inadmissible. That is precisely the circumstance that will make them intolerable to the Shah. ...

I do not think you are yet sufficiently officialised to be able to trust entirely to your own judgement as to particular phrases. It is not safe to handle the Shah with the truth or freedom which is permissible and salutary in the case of Mr Gladstone.

Curzon did, however, extract one concession from the Prime Minister. In place of Lord Cross, his censor was to be Sir Alfred Lyall, not only a former Foreign Secretary of the Government of India, but also a poet and essayist who could be expected to appreciate the feelings of a fellow man of letters. 'I am much obliged to you,' Salisbury wrote to Curzon, 'for accepting my suggestion in so kindly a spirit and allowing yourself to be Bowdlerised without resistance. I trust Sir Alfred Lyall's mutilations will not be barbarous.'

Lyall proved the most gentle of butchers, requiring the sacrifice of only a few sentences or phrases. Thus the reign of the Shah was no longer 'disfigured by one or two acts of great barbarity of which the black and insufferable stain could never be washed out'. Instead, it was 'disfigured by one or two acts of regrettable violence'. Nasr-ed-Din no longer displayed 'petty economies and grudging gifts', but merely 'mercantile instincts'. And his principal wife ceased to be melon-shaped but retained her short petticoats. When the lightly expurgated work was published a few months later, Curzon gracefully expressed his gratitude by quoting on the title-page these lines from Lyall's pen:

Shall I stretch my right hand to the Indus,
That England may fill it with gold?
Shall my left beckon aid from the Oxus?
The Russian blows hot and blows cold.
And the lord of the English writes 'Order
And Justice, and govern with Laws,
And the Russian he sneers and says, 'Patience,
And velvet to cover your claws';
But the kingdoms of Islam are crumbling,
And round me a voice ever rings
Of death, and the doom of my country –
Shall I be the last of its kings?

Even after censorship, Curzon's work can hardly have commended itself to the Shah and his subjects as a considered judgement on their country by a member of the British Government. To the passages of disparagement and disdain quoted in the last chapter must be added others of brutal offensiveness:

Persia is neither powerful, nor spontaneously progressive, nor patriotic. Her agriculture is bad, her resources unexplored, her trade ill-developed, her Government corrupt, her army a cypher.

They are ready enough to swagger about the glory and the beauty of their country, but there is not one in a hundred who would pull his sword from the scabbard to indicate its independence. In every manifestation of national spirit or activity they appear to have succumbed to a creeping paralysis which is slowly making its way upward from the extremities to the head.

Just as the Persian cottager would sooner absorb disease from a filthy pool at his threshold than walk 200 yards to a fresh spring, so does the State require to be prodded and goaded into any act of administrative energy or vigour.

They are consummate hypocrites, very corrupt, and lamentably deficient in stability or courage. .. With one gift only can they be credited on a truly heroic scale. .. I allude to their faculty for what a Puritan might call mendacious, but what I prefer to style imaginative, utterance.

Splendide mendax might be taken as the motto of Persian character. The finest domestic virtues co-exist with barbarity and supreme indifference to suffering. Elegance of deportment is compatible with a coarseness amounting to bestiality. The same individual is at different moments haughty and cringing. A creditable acquaintance with the standards of civilisation does not prevent gross fanaticism and superstition. Accomplished manners and a more than Parisian polish cover a truly superb faculty for lying and almost scientific imposture. The most scandalous corruption is combined with a scrupulous regard for specified precepts of the moral law. Religion is alternately stringent and lax, inspiring at one moment the bigot's rage, at the next the agnostic's indifference. Government is both patriarchal and Machiavellian – patriarchal in its simplicity of structure, Machiavellian in its finished ingenuity of wrong doing. Life is both magnificent and squalid; the people at once despicable and noble; the panorama at the same time an enchantment and a fraud.

In the very closing pages of the book, however, Curzon suddenly expresses a profound truth that helps to dispel his air of jaunty insularity:

Above all we must remember that the ways of Orientals are not our ways, nor their thoughts our thoughts. Often when we think them backward and stupid, they think us meddlesome and absurd. The loom of times moves slowly with them, and they care not for high pressure and the roaring of the wheels. Our system may be good for us; but it is neither equally nor altogether good for them. Satan found it better to reign in hell than serve in heaven; and the normal Asiatic would sooner be misgoverned by Asiatics than well governed by Europeans.

But the gleam of enlightenment was momentary, and found no place in the policies which Curzon later pursued as Viceroy of India. Only under European tutelage, he believed to the end of his days, could the Oriental preserve stability and seek salvation.

'Dear Mr Gladstone,' Curzon wrote from the India Office on 18 May 1892, 'I am venturing to send you from my publishers a copy of two portly volumes on Persia, which, after a hard but interesting three years of labour, I have at last finished and brought out.' Here was one reader, at least, who would appreciate *Persia and the Persian Question* for its ample proportions and elaborate style, its classical allusions and passages of Herodotus which the author had not thought necessary to translate from the Greek. But Gladstone would care less for its imperialist sentiments and warnings of Russian designs – themes which Lord Salisbury had deliberately left uncensored.

The self-confident tone of the work did not please all reviewers. 'Mr Curzon,' wrote one of them, 'seems to be under the impression that he has discovered Persia, and that having discovered it, he now in some mysterious way owns it.' Others complained of its prolixity: but without also sacrificing valuable information, the most severe verbal pruning could have removed no more than 200 of its 1,300 pages or one of its seven pounds in weight. All who knew the country had to admit that, thanks in part to the scrutiny and revision of every line by General Houtum Schindler, it was as scholarly as it was observant, as reliable on the provinces which Curzon had not been able to visit as on those which he had seen with his own sharp eyes.

He was proud to receive an accolade from Thomas Hardy: 'You have been much in my mind since we met. I had not then seen your monumental work on Persia – which I have done since. The amount of labour and enterprise it represents and the value to investigators of the facts acquired put some of us scribblers to shame.' He experienced another twinge of pleasure the following winter, during his second tour round the world. In the European club of the Chinese seaport of Chefoo, he picked up a copy of *Blackwood's Magazine* published since his departure from England and read: 'It is the best and most complete book on any Asiatic State in our language, not even excepting our Indian Empire.' From a journal that circulated widely among British expatriates the world over, that was praise indeed. Nearly eighty years later, those intending to visit Persia for a more than fleeting stay will still deny themselves much enlightenment and entertainment if they omit to consult Curzon's *magnum opus*.

The enduring value of the work has been reflected in its sales. Twenty years after it first appeared at two guineas for the pair of volumes, St John Brodrick wrote to the author: 'I have forgotten ever to ask you whether you have any idea of publishing a cheap edition of your *Persia*. It is getting so scarce that a bookseller offered me a copy for 10 guineas nearly a year ago.' It is today scarcer still, and a second-hand copy cannot usually be bought for less than £1000.

Curzon wrote his book in the interests of Indian defence and dedicated it 'to the officials, civil and military, in India, whose hands uphold the noblest fabric yet reared by the genius of a conquering nation'. He nevertheless hoped that it would also bring him a more than modest financial reward. That was not to be. By 1923 his total royalties on *Persia and the Persian Question* had amounted to no more than £405. 19*s*. 4*d*. 'A miserable return,' he scrawled across the account.

Curzon's first Ministerial appointment lasted barely nine months. He went to the India Office as Parliamentary Under-Secretary in November 1891, and resigned with the other members of the Salisbury Government after its defeat in the general election of July 1892. Although distracted by the completion, censorship, revision and publication of *Persia and the Persian Question*, he revelled in his introduction to political power and acquitted himself with distinction.

He could have found no more suitable training ground than the India

Office. So much of his life had already been devoted to studying the security and welfare of India, that he found himself instantly at ease with his new duties. The India Office, moreover, was a miniature Government in itself, grappling with a far wider range of administrative and executive problems than existed in any other single department of State.

The role of a Parliamentary Under-Secretary, as the title implied, was to represent his department in one or other of the Houses of Parliament. If the Secretary of State was a peer, the Under-Secretary sat in the Commons: if the Secretary of State sat in the Commons, the Under-Secretary was a peer, with a seat in the House of Lords. One important field of activity remained closed to a Parliamentary Under-Secretary. He had no responsibility for taking decisions. That task remained the prerogative of the Secretary of State, who would often lean for advice on the vast experience of his Permanent Under-Secretary and other senior officials, but would rarely consult his Parliamentary Under-Secretary.

A Parliamentary Under-Secretary, however, could not adequately defend a policy or answer supplementary questions unless he was familiar with the background of each topic. He was thus encouraged to read all the official papers and to master their contents. Free from the pressure of making decisions, he could slowly equip himself for the heavier responsibilities he would one day inherit as political head of a department and member of the Cabinet.

The Secretary of State when Curzon arrived at the India Office was Lord Cross. He had been called to the Bar, entered the House of Commons in 1857 as Conservative Member for Preston, personally defeated Gladstone in south-west Lancashire in 1868 and, without previous ministerial experience, been appointed Home Secretary by Disraeli in 1874. As the author of a Factory Act and a Licensing Act he had earned the popular jingle:

For he's a jolly good fellow,
Whatever the Rads may think;
For he has shortened the hours of work
And lengthened the hours of drink.

During the years of Conservative opposition between 1880 and 1885, he showed less vigour and, with W. H. Smith, earned the particular contempt of the rebellious Lord Randolph Churchill. The Queen, however, not only enjoyed his company but also, it was rumoured, appreciated his financial advice. Certainly he had a shrewd sense of money. From 1887 until his death in 1914, he drew an annual pension of £2,000 for every year he was out of office, amounting in all to £40,760. The intention of the Civil Offices (Pensions) Act of 1869, under which he received his solatium, was to enable former Ministers of the Crown and other public servants to maintain a comfortable standard of life should they lack other means: it was not to bestow a lifelong pension on all former Ministers, irrespective of their private means. Pained surprise, therefore, greeted the news in 1914 that the late Lord Cross's net personal estate had been sworn at £79,299.

Sir Arthur Godley, later created Lord Kilbracken, began his official career as one of Mr Gladstone's private secretaries and in 1883 was appointed Permanent Under-Secretary at the India Office, a post he held for an unprecedented period of twenty-six years. He thus occupied a position of exceptional influence in the Department, strengthened by the reluctance of Lord Cross to exert himself more than necessary. 'He was,' Godley wrote of him, 'when he came to us, a very pleasant, kindly old gentleman, perfectly capable of doing all that was required of him; and with the help of the official machine, which he left pretty much to itself, he got through his six years at the India Office well enough, and was throughout that time on excellent terms with all its inmates.' Curzon, who as an undergraduate once proposed the health of Cross at a dinner of the Oxford Canning Club, did not find it difficult to establish a placid and friendly relationship with his first Ministerial chief.

The new Parliamentary Under-Secretary was fortunate to acquire as his private secretary Mr Richmond Ritchie, one of the ablest officials of his generation and the eventual successor to Godley as Permanent Under-Secretary. His Eton career, academically as brilliant as Curzon's, did not absorb his entire energies; for while still a schoolboy he proposed marriage to his cousin, Anne Thackeray, daughter of the novelist. Rejected on the first occasion, he subsequently married her in 1877.

During his few months as a junior Minister, Curzon won the early esteem of Godley, who wrote of him: 'He was excellent: thoroughly interested in his official duties, most efficient as our representative in the House of Commons, and in every way agreeable and amusing to work with.'

An outside witness gave similar testimony. In the summer of 1891, a young officer called Francis Younghusband in the service of the Indian Government was arrested by a Cossack patrol while exploring the Pamir mountains and ordered to leave what his captors claimed to be Russian territory. Lord Salisbury reacted sharply to the incident, extracted an apology from St Petersburg and pressed successfully for the demarcation of the frontiers between Russia, China and Afghanistan in that remote part of Asia. A few weeks later, Younghusband arrived in London on leave and reported to the India Office. Lord Cross, he recorded, took only a perfunctory interest in the case, and could not think of much else to ask his visitor except if it was not very cold up there on the Roof of the World. The Parliamentary Under-Secretary, Younghusband continued, was very different. 'He engaged me in a long and *real* conversation. That is, he did not merely ask questions but gave forth his own views. He knew the whole subject well, and was keenly interested in it. No one else I had met – not even in India – was so well informed and so enthusiastic. And he was young and fresh and very alert and able. His name was George Curzon; and this was his first appointment.'

Soon after Parliament reassembled in February 1892, Curzon made his Ministerial debut in the Commons. An easy familiarity with the despatch-box manner and a close knowledge of the facts enabled him to demolish Mr Swift MacNeill, the Member for South Donegal and the most persistent of his antagonists, who charged the Government with a reluctance to employ Indians in the Public Service.

In March, Curzon was called upon to defend his fellow Soul, Lord Wenlock, the Governor of Madras, against accusations of incompetence in relieving famine. MacNeill declared that Wenlock held his appointment 'simply because he is a nephew of the Duke of Westminster ... he is a man of very moderate abilities indeed. He was given this office because he was in financial difficulties.' There was some substance in the allegations. Wenlock's experience of affairs was limited to three months as a Member of Parliament and the chairmanship of the East Riding of Yorkshire County Council; and on his death in 1912, his will was proved at £519,487 gross and £61,427 net, a disparity that points to the liquidation of huge debts. But he was an unpretentious and kindly man who, as Curzon was well able to demonstrate, had carried out his duties with vigour. The Under-Secretary's own performance drew a generous tribute from Sir Ughtred Kay-Shuttleworth, one of his predecessors at the India Office, who spoke of 'the readiness, grasp and ability he has displayed in the way he has dealt with an extremely important subject'.

Later the same month, Curzon moved the second reading of the India Councils Act (1861) Amendment Bill. Its purpose was to enlarge the existing Legislative Councils in India and to concede to them the rights of criticizing the Budget and of questioning the Government on policy and administration. Pressed from the Liberal benches for a bolder advance towards the elective principle – a proposal from which Mr Gladstone dissociated himself – Curzon replied, in a strain that was hardly to vary over the years: 'An elaborate system of representation for a people in this stage of development would appear to me to be, in the highest degree, premature and unwise.' On the committee stage of the Bill in April he put his case more cogently: 'We cannot have a Parliamentary system in India. ... The Government must be in a majority in India, and the majority must be the Government; it cannot resign, because there is no opposition to succeed it, as in this country.'

His friend 'Doll' Liddell, who was Chief Clerk in the Crown Office, walked across to the Commons to hear Curzon introduce the Bill and recorded his impressions: 'He stood at the table, looking like the great Sir Robert Peel, or some statesman of forty years' experience, instead of a young Under-Secretary in his first innings. However, he did what he had to do very well. His diction was rather Johnsonian, but clear, impressive and convincing. He ought to go far. He has such confidence that he gives his good abilities their utmost chance.'

Henry Lucy offered his readers a sharper etching of Curzon at the despatch box: 'His manner is marked by the imperturbability that comes of consciousness of personal superiority. He is able to greet with a smile of mingled geniality and pity attempts from other quarters to set him right on matters of fact or opinion.'

Nor could Curzon count on much deference from the Radical newspapers in his constituency. They were, he wrote, accusing him of 'brag, bluster, blatancy, bombast, buffoonery, foppishness, malignity and other political virtues'. At the general election of July 1892, however, Southport remained faithful to her sitting Member, returning him to Westminster by a majority of 604 over his Liberal opponent. Conservatism was also triumphant in East Worcestershire, where young Austen Chamberlain floored Oscar Browning. But as a party, the Unionists lost their majority in the House of Commons, so freeing Curzon from his lightly borne chains of office. Lord Salisbury, with his entire Government, resigned on 12 August. The following day his late Parliamentary Under-Secretary for India sailed for New York on yet another prolonged journey.

The purpose of Curzon's second world tour was still to satisfy a tourist's appetite for colour and contrast, for all that is ancient and beautiful and romantic. But he was also determined to make a deeper study of the Far East. Since the tour of 1887–8 he had held office for a few months in Lord Salisbury's Government as Parliamentary Under-Secretary for India: that, and his increasing influence as a much-travelled lecturer and author, spurred him to add to his armoury of knowledge by concentrating upon Japan and China, Korea and Cambodia.

Curzon had intended to cross the Atlantic with Wallace Cochrane-Baillie, who had recently succeeded his father as Lord Lamington. At the last moment Lamington had to remain in England. So Curzon turned to a more recent friend, Harry White, Secretary to the American Legation in London and husband of the captivating Daisy Stuyvesant Rutherford. Both were honorary Souls, immortalized in the rhyming roll-call of 1889.

America lends,
Nay she gives when she sends,

Such treasures as Harry and Daisy.
Tho' many may yearn,
None but Harry can turn
That sweet little head of hers crazy.

It suited their timetable best to travel to New York aboard a German ship, the *Fürst Bismarck*. Pleased to have a British Member of Parliament and an American diplomatist among the passengers, the owners offered them the best staterooms at absurdly low prices. Curzon was just the man to relish a bargain. 'Here I am,' he wrote jubilantly, 'enjoying for £16 15*s*. 0*d*. the comforts which are ordinarily appraised at £53 10*s*. 0*d*.' He was, however, obliged to pay a stiff penalty for the concession:

> As we gradually emerge and survey the company, a sepulchral gloom settles down on H. and myself. Of the hundreds of first class passengers crowding the great vessel, barely one has the appearance of a gentleman or lady. The majority are commercial Germans – with the unredeemed Teutonic type of face, figure, manner and dress. God! What a people! How coarse! How hideous! How utterly wanting in the least element of distinction!

The remainder were 'middle-class Americans, admittedly the least attractive species of the human genus. The guttural of the Germans and the twang of the Yankee combine in an aggravating dissonance which shudders up and down the long promenade deck.' It was no better in New York – 'architecture wholly unimpressive, and alternating between seven-stories braggadocio and the mild respectability of provincial suburbs: men busy, sallow, straw-hatted, perspiring: and the hum of business everywhere'. Washington was memorable for his having eluded the journalists who awaited his arrival and for his subsequent delight at seeing himself described in the newspaper as 'a portly man with a black mustache'.

After a swift tour of Canada he boarded the *Empress of Japan* for the voyage across the Pacific. This time his fellow passengers must have been less insufferable than usual, for he graciously agreed to address them one night on 'Election Humours'. Here is one example from his repertoire that has survived among his papers:

> Peter Rylands, the Liberal M.P. for Burnley up to 1886 or 1887, prided himself on being a great financial reformer and economist. He was always discovering and inveighing against the most atrocious financial abuses, by which the money of the nation was squandered and misused. On one occasion he was making a speech to his constituents, and explaining how he had moved in the House of Commons for an enquiry into one such abuse, how the motion had been accepted by Mr Gladstone, a Select Committee nominated to enquire into it, and himself appointed Chairman 'And' he went on to say, 'such was the interest that I took in this enquiry, that from the chair I asked no fewer than 763 questions myself!'
>
> Voice from the crowd: 'Why, what a hignorant old devil you must be!'

Curzon was disappointed by the response of his own audience. 'I am afraid,' he wrote in his journal, 'that half my jokes were not understood by the Americans and missionaries.'

He disembarked at Yokohama with a mound of baggage that had grown since his first visit five years before. It now included equipment to sustain him on long journeys into the interior of Asia: saddle and saddlebags, holsters, flask, sticking-plaster, camera, tinned salmon and a conversion table of the Centigrade, Fahrenheit and Réaumur scales of temperature. He had one immediate and unexpected stroke of luck. Approaching Tokyo, he confided to his host, Maurice de Bunsen, Secretary to the British Legation, that he would like to experience an earthquake. The same evening there was a sharp little shock to satisfy his curiosity.

Nature was less obliging to him when a few days later he attempted to climb Mount Fuji, only to be driven back from the summit by blinding rain. 'I was pretty well dead beat. Had not eaten since 12.30, i.e. for nearly 11 hours, and was cold, footsore and exhausted. ... We lit a fire. I drank a pint of Bunsen's champagne and tried to conjure warmth into my limbs. For a man who suffered from a permanent spinal weakness and who took no exercise in London except to walk home from the House of Commons after a late-night sitting, he displayed astonishing resilience and fortitude on his travels.

The tourist of 1887 became the pundit of 1892. From rummaging in the alleyways of Kobe, knowledgeably rejecting curios made from horses' hooves that masqueraded as tortoiseshell and dismissing the dancing girls as 'insipid', he had turned to examine that explosive element with which modern Japan was threatening to disrupt the Far East. The preface to his book on the subject warned the reader what to expect:

> There will be found nothing in these pages of the Japan of temples, tea-houses, and bric-a-brac – that infinitesimal segment of the national existence which the traveller is so prone to mistake for the whole, and by doing which he fills the educated Japanese with such unspeakable indignation. I have been more interested in the efforts of a nation, still in pupillage, to assume the manners of the full-grown man, in the constitutional struggles through which Japan is passing, in her relations with foreign Powers, and in the future that awaits her immense ambitions.

Curzon believed that these aspirations would drive her to become, on a smaller scale, the Great Britain of the Far East. For Japan was poised on the flank of Asia as Great Britain was poised on the flank of Europe, each exercising a powerful influence over the adjoining continent but not necessarily involved in its responsibilities. The prospect of her expansion did not alarm him. He deplored, however, the volatile and sometimes ridiculous outbursts of patriotic excitement to which the Japanese were addicted. 'In this respect,' he observed grandly, 'they may be termed the Frenchmen of the Far East.'

'The number of Englishmen who have travelled in the interior of Korea,' Curzon wrote, 'may be counted on the fingers of two hands.' In the autumn of 1892, armed with a contract to supply *The Times* with a series of articles about his journey, he set off from Tokyo. He was accompanied by Cecil Spring Rice, on leave of absence from his diplomatic duties. Curzon enjoyed renewing a friendship that went back to their years at Eton and Balliol. When the expedition was over he wrote in his journal: 'I have said goodbye to Springy, the best, cheeriest, most unselfish, most amusing of travelling companions, and am once more alone. For nearly two months we have been together at most hours of the day and night, and have not exchanged one jarring word.' In the preface to *Problems of the Far East* he also paid public tribute to his friend for revising the text and for advice.

Curzon might have been less generous in his appreciation had he been able to read Spring Rice's own account of the tour through Korea, published only after both of them were dead: 'He thinks the consular service appointed to help him on his journey, feed him and provide him material for his letters to *The Times*. He is deeply offended if the beds are not soft or the information not complete.' There were terrible scenes when a shortage of ponies seemed likely to delay his arrival in the capital: 'Curzon got very angry, explained that he was one of the most important people in England, and that it was a matter of most vital importance that he should see the King that week; and he threatened beatings and dismissals all round.'

Having arrived breathless at Seoul in time to be received at Court, Curzon wrote a richly comic description of his experience:

> Before proceeding to the royal audience, I enjoyed an interview with the President of the Korean Foreign Office, an old gentleman with a faultless black hat, a benign and sleepy expression, plump cheeks, and a long thin grey moustache and beard. I remember some of his questions and answers. Having been particularly warned not to admit to him that I was only thirty-three years old, an age to which no respect attaches in Korea, when he put to me the straight question (invariably the first in an Oriental dialogue), 'How old are you?' I unhesitatingly responded, 'Forty'. 'Dear me,' he said, 'you look very young for that. How do you account for it?' 'By the fact,' I replied, 'that I have been travelling for a month in the superb climate of His Majesty's dominions.' Hearing that I had been a Minister of the Crown in England, he inquired what had been my salary, and added, 'I supposed you found that by far the most agreeable feature of office. But no doubt the prerequisites were very much larger still.' Finally, conscious that in his own country it is not easy for anyone to become a member of the Government, unless he is related to the family of the King or Queen, he said to me, 'I presume you are a near relative of Her Majesty the Queen of England.' 'No,' I replied, 'I am not.' But, observing the look of disgust that passed over his countenance, I was fain to add, 'I am, however, as yet an unmarried man,' with which unscrupulous suggestion I completely regained the old gentleman's favour.

In more serious vein he analysed the problems of Korea. He described the country as a shuttlecock among nations, confronted by the cupidity of Russia, the latent force of China and the vainglorious interest of Japan. By herself, Curzon continued, she was quite incapable of resisting any one of those three: but in her intrinsic weakness lay her sole strength. For had she been powerful enough to render her own alliance an appreciable weight in the scale, she might have been tempted to adopt an attitude precipitating her final absorption. Curzon's commentary has a familiar ring to mid-twentieth-century ears.

China struck no cymbal of welcome in his honour. He found her people frugal and ungracious, her national character self-confident and stolid, her system of government still wrapped in the mantle of a superb but paralysing conceit. Not even her illimitable resources, he forecast, would save her from defeat at the hands of the relentlessly efficient Japanese should the two countries go to war.

On a lower plane of observation, he noted that Peking had certain disadvantages as a centre of tourism. The seasoned traveller, he wrote, 'may have seen the drab squalor of Bokhara and Damascus, have tasted the odours of Canton and Seoul, and heard the babel uproar of Baghdad and Isfahan; but he has never seen the dirt, piled in mountains of dust in the summer, spread in oozing quagmires of mud after the rains, like that of Peking; his nostrils have never been assailed by such myriad and assorted effluvia; and the drums of his ears have never cracked beneath such remorseless and dissonant concussion of sound'. The exactions of the Chinese monks – 'this nest of profligate scoundrels' – were by comparison almost bearable.

In July 1892, two weeks before setting out on his second journey round the world, Curzon had written to Lord Salisbury, then in his last days of office after his party's defeat in the general election. He asked the Prime Minister whether he might be entrusted with a mission on behalf of the British Government to decorate Prince Damrong of Siam, half-brother of the King and an enlightened student of European institutions. 'Of course,' Curzon admitted, 'such a commission would assist and dignify me: but I may honestly add that it is not the least on personal ground that I venture to suggest it. The Siamese question is becoming a very important one: and we must lose no opportunity of conciliating that Royal family and people.'

Curzon's request was less simple than he suspected. Salisbury replied that the Prince could not be honoured unless the King, too, received a decoration. The King, however, had already let it be known that he would not be content with the Star of India, often bestowed on protected Princes: as an independent Sovereign, he wanted nothing less than the Order of the Bath. But Queen Victoria would not consent to give an Oriental potentate so high a distinction, as its value would thereby be lowered in the eyes of European Royalty. 'I have found the problem quite insoluble and have long abandoned it', Salisbury wrote. Curzon was thus obliged to arrive in Bangkok as a private person.

There were compensations, however, for a political commentator. Hardly had Curzon reached Siam than France threatened her Government and despatched gunboats to blockade the capital. The crisis was not resolved until the summer. Curzon, meanwhile, with first-hand knowledge of a tense situation geographically remote from London, found a ready market for articles on the background to the dispute. He called for firm measures by Great Britain against France until she was persuaded to relinquish her claim to interfere in Siamese affairs. For just as it was essential that Afghanistan should stand as a buffer between Russia and the north-west frontier of India, so Siam must be maintained as a buffer between French Indo-China and the eastern frontier of India. To support France's claims to Siamese territory, he added, 'maps have to be specially constructed, history re-written and political jurisdiction invented, processes from which the French imagination is the last in the world to recoil'.

Curzon's Francophobia, defensible on strategic grounds, had emotional undertones. Travelling through French Indo-China in the weeks immediately preceding the Siamese crisis, he referred with distaste to 'snuffling little stubble-bearded Frenchmen of the most unattractive sort'. He continued: 'How tired I get of this type. No manhood about them. Every one of them like a hair cutter. All curl of the lip and smirk in address, but no real bonhomie or frankness, and a desperate jealousy and hatred of the English at bottom.' In two months, he recalled, he had not met a single Frenchman who could speak a word of English. And both intellectually and socially, he had found the French civil administrators inferior to their British counterparts: 'They worked a little in the morning, slept all the day from 11.30 to 3.30 and drove out and dined in the evening.' That was not Curzon's way of running an empire.

He reached London on 5 March 1893. He had been away, he noted, for 203 days and had spent £353 19*s.* 6*d.*, or £1 14*s.* 10*d.* a day. And with what he himself called his 'middle-class method', he compared the figures with those of his first journey round the world – '191 days costing £336 5*s.* 0*d.*, or £1 15*s.* 0*d.* a day.'

As a comparatively poor man, he was anxious to redeem the outlay by publishing a book about his travels. But the pressures of parliamentary business did not allow him to finish writing *Problems of the Far East* until the following year. Even then, he finished the task only by working long hours and by denying himself the convivial social life he so enjoyed. No critic could say of him, as was said of Robert Browning, that he had 'dinnered himself away'. A single volume proved inadequate for his bulky material and Corinthian style. He therefore devoted the first volume to a survey of Japan, Korea and China, intending to write a separate work on Indo-China and Siam. In the whirligig of his public and private life, however, the companion volume was never completed.

The knowledge he had acquired of French Indo-China was not entirely wasted. Some of it Curzon later embodied in a book of essays, some of it he used in a lecture to the Royal Geographical Society, when an unexpected incident lightened the solemnity of the occasion. The paper was followed by a series of slides thrown on to a screen, each of them introduced by a short commentary. 'I will now,' Curzon announced, 'show you a picture to prove that the native population of Annam, though possessing marked Mongolian features, are far from destitute of personal charm.' He snapped his fingers and there appeared, magnified to more than life size, the figure of a seated Annamite girl wearing no more than the merest shred of clothing. The operator of the lantern, in a spirit of forgetfulness or mischief, had selected a photograph of whose existence Curzon affected utter ignorance. From that moment, he wrote, 'the success of the lecture was assured in the same hour that the character of the lecturer was irreparably destroyed'. Among the audience was the Prince of Wales, later King Edward VII, who, after his fashion, never ceased to chaff Curzon for so daring but not unwelcome a challenge to the conventions of the age.

When *Problems of the Far East* appeared in the summer of 1894, fate conspired to help its sale. Japan had just gone to war with China over Korea, and there was a rush by the reading public to inform themselves about the dispute. The first edition alone brought Curzon a net reward of £423 8*s*. 0*d*., and three more editions were demanded. Spring Rice, his help generously acknowledged in the preface, wrote from his current diplomatic post in Washington to tell the author that the volume 'has been continually open in the U.S. State Department as well as quoted in the papers'.

Both money and reputation meant much to Curzon, and he confessed to having had 'a prolonged squabble about terms with my publisher' before the appearance of *Problems of the Far East*. But he would almost have been content to write that particular book without either reward or recognition. It was his gospel of imperialism, his glad recognition of what Great Britain had contributed – and would continue to contribute – to the East. He must sometimes have suspected that the Oriental races were not wholly worthy of European benevolence; certainly he liked to draw up careful balance sheets of their circumstances, behaviour and progress. In scenery, he wrote 'the dominant note of Asian individuality is contrast, in character a general indifference to truth and respect for successful wile, in deportment dignity, in society the rigid maintenance of the family union, in government the mute acquiescence of the governed, in administration and justice the open corruption of administrators and judges, and in every-day life a statuesque and inexhaustible patience which attaches no value to time and wages unappeasable warfare against hurry.'

That there were economic advantages to be drawn from the British connection with the East, Curzon did not deny. He wrote that of the 3,340 ships which passed through the Suez Canal in 1893, no fewer than 2,400 were British: next came the Germans with 270, the French with 190 and the Dutch with 180. 'We still are,' he added, 'and have it in our hands to remain, the first Power in the East. Just as De Tocqueville remarked that the conquest and government of India are really the achievements which have given England her place in the opinion of the world, so it is the prestige and the wealth arising from her Asiatic position that are the foundation stones of the British Empire.'

It would be wrong to assume that the commercial dividends paid by British investment in the East dominated his thoughts. The imperial mission of his country, he believed, was blessed by a Higher Power: and no one should grudge the dedicated schoolmaster his fee or the clergyman his offertory.

Chapter Nineteen
ROOF OF THE WORLD

> I would examine the *Caspian* Sea, and see where and how it exonerates itself, after it hath taken in *Volga*, *Iaxares*, *Oxus*, and those great rivers. ... I would find out with *Trajan* the Fountains of *Danubius*, of *Ganges*, and of *Oxus*.
>
> – Robert Burton's *Anatomy of Melancholy*

By the spring of 1893, when he returned from his second journey round the world, Curzon had completed rather more than half the ambitious literary plan devised nearly five years before. He had travelled along the Transcaspian railway and written *Russia in Central Asia.* He had ridden across Iran and written *Persia and the Persian Question.* He had toured Japan, China and Korea and written *Problems of the Far East.* He had collected a mass of material for an authoritative work on Indo-China which he hoped one day to complete.

There were two other regions which Curzon could not ignore in his study of British interests in the East. One was that mountainous tract on the north-west frontier of India known as the Pamirs, the other was the adjacent land of Afghanistan. Each was a focal point on which Russia continued to exert a pressure that at best created an atmosphere of suspicion and unease, at worst posed a direct threat to the security of India. It was not, therefore, surprising that members of Mr Gladstone's last Government declined to assist the inquisitive and observant George Curzon to roam those sensitive areas. Neither *Russia in Central Asia* nor *Persia and the Persian Question* had been accepted in St Petersburg as an entirely objective assessment of Russian foreign policy, and the author's descent on either the Pamirs or Afghanistan might well provoke Russia to sponsor similar expeditions. When, therefore, in the autumn of 1893 Curzon asked to be attached to a Government of India Mission which the Amir of Afghanistan grudgingly permitted to come to Kabul for talks on the demarcation of the frontier, the Secretary of State flatly turned down his request.

By nature, however, he was contemptuous of obstructive officialdom, and the fulfilment of the last phase of his travels through the East could not be postponed. His health, which had shown signs of strain in the winters of 1890 and 1891, was unlikely to grow more robust with the years. By 1893 he also realized that the electoral tide had begun to flow against the Liberals and that their defeat would not only recall him to office but also rob him, perhaps for ever, of his liberty to explore remote places. If he could not visit the Pamirs and Afghanistan under the auspices of the Government of India, he would do so as a private person.

Throughout 1893 and the early months of 1894, he was preoccupied with achieving what he called 'the last wild cry of freedom'. He planned to undertake in the autumn two successive but quite separate journeys across the north-west frontier, one to the Pamirs, the other to Afghanistan. But since each was to begin and end on Indian soil, neither was acceptable to the Viceroy and the Secretary of State, twin guardians of India's relations with her fretful neighbours.

It was to Curzon's disadvantage that both men were new to their jobs, a circumstance which reinforced their ingrained caution. The Viceroy was the ninth Earl of Elgin, son of a previous Viceroy and grandson of the peer who had ensured that the Greek marbles which bear his name should rest securely in the British Museum rather than be exposed to the vagaries of Balkan warfare. He had at first felt himself unfitted to accept Gladstone's invitation to become Viceroy, and never succeeded in overcoming a retiring disposition and a reserved manner. Lack of self-confidence, although allied to considerable administrative ability, made him more dependent on Whitehall than the traditional relationship between Viceroy and Secretary of State warranted. Curzon could expect no imaginative gesture from this shy, silent Scot.

Henry Fowler, later created Lord Wolverhampton, had once been a solicitor, and brought to politics all the prudence of his former profession. He was the first Wesleyan either to sit in Cabinet or to be made a peer. Mr Gladstone, however, had thought him socially inadequate to become First Lord of the Admiralty and on forming his last administration in 1892 had shunted him off to the respectable twilight of the Local Government Board. But two years later, when Rosebery succeeded Gladstone as Prime Minister, he was promoted to be Secretary of State for India. Fowler was a stubborn man, whose daughter once said of him, 'Father always lets us have his own way'. He was touchy, too. Owing to a mischance, it was a long time before Queen Victoria extended to him the traditional hospitality of dining and sleeping at Windsor. He would refer bitterly to the episode as 'the Windsor boycott'. Those were not qualities likely to endear him to Curzon's forceful and sometimes imperious entreaties.

United in their determination to thwart Curzon's peripatetic zeal, Elgin and Fowler communicated fussily with each other across 6,000 miles.

'Everybody is worrying, worrying, worrying about my journey,' Curzon wrote on 17 July, 'and trying to put spokes in my wheel. The Viceroy has sent an idiotic telegram from India. The fact is that none of these Government officials wants me to do a thing that they never have been able to do themselves, and all the forces of red tape are against me.'

That was not fair to Lord Elgin. 'Our position is very simple,' the Viceroy told Fowler, 'I cannot see what public advantage will be gained, and I see very considerable risk of public interest suffering. It is quite possible by the time he came out we should be compelled to prevent his crossing our frontier, and it is better, therefore, to stop him now, though I much regret having to disappoint him.'

Refusing to surrender to such querulous opposition, Curzon awaited the outcome of another and more impudent request. In the spring of 1894 he had made a personal appeal to the Amir of Afghanistan. Knowing that the Amir was intensely mistrustful of the Calcutta Government, Curzon calculated that he might be willing to converse with an Englishman who had been the Minister responsible for Indian affairs in the House of Commons, who was still a Member of Parliament, and who had invariably advocated the importance of intimate relations with Afghanistan. In a letter engrossed on vellum and sent by the hand of Sir Salter Pyne, the British chief engineer to the Government of Afghanistan and one of the Amir's most trusted advisers, he described his proposed journey to the Pamirs in the autumn and asked whether he might not also pay his respects to a ruler whom he had long admired and the independence of whose country he had loudly championed. In a spacious style which he knew would not come amiss in Kabul, he added:

> Throughout this time it has been my principal and incessant desire to be permitted to visit the dominions of Your Highness; so that I might both offer my salaams to the powerful and liberal minded Sovereign of whom I have so often written and spoken; and also that I might be able to stand up in the British House of Commons, when the affairs of India and Afghanistan were being discussed, to silence the mouths of the slanderers and to say to the British Government and the British people: 'I have myself been to Kabul as the guest of His Highness the Amir. I have conversed with this great Sovereign. I can speak for his sentiments. I desire to protect his interests.' Khorasan I have seen and visited; I have been in Bokhara and Samarkand. I have ridden to Chaman, and I have sojourned at Peshawar. But the dominions of Your Highness which are situated in the middle of all these territories like unto a rich stone in the middle of a ring, I have never been permitted to enter; and the person of Your Highness which is in your own dominions like unto the sparkle in the heart of the diamond, I have not been fortunate enough to see. Many books and writings I have studied and have talked to many men; but I would fain converse with Your Highness, who knows more about these questions than do all other men, and who will perhaps vouchsafe to throw upon my imperfect knowledge the full ray of truth.

Disappointingly, Curzon received no immediate reply from the Amir. But by early August the situation was shifting in his favour. The Russian Government withdrew its objections to his visiting Afghanistan, thereby removing the principal cause of Elgin's misgivings. Curzon was also astute enough to engage the support of Field-Marshal Lord Roberts, until recently Commander-in-Chief of the Indian Army, and even of the Prime Minister himself. Rosebery wrote to the Viceroy on 27 July: 'George Curzon is anxious to travel somewhere – I don't quite know where – as a veto has been placed on his original project. But I hope you will give him what assistance you can, consistently with the public service, in any legitimate voyage that he may undertake, as he is a very clever and very nice fellow.'

The traveller did not care to wait for official approval. Having sat up for four whole nights to complete the last chapter of *Problems of the Far East*, he left for India on 4 August, trusting that his powers of persuasion would change the Viceroy's mind once they came face to face. In spite of the Prime Minister's plea, Elgin was equally determined that his own will should prevail. 'On hearing Curzon had started,' he wrote to Fowler on 14 August, 'I consulted my advisers again, and we still do not see our way to permit his journey. I am sending a letter from the Foreign Department to meet him at Bombay.' And a little later: 'I thought it advisable to strengthen myself with a definite opinion of my Council, and we were unanimous in adhering to our prohibition.'

Curzon, however, knew how to blend charm with reason, cajolery with argument. Within a day or two of his arrival at Simla, where the Viceroy was spending the summer, he had cast his spell and found himself free to depart for the Pamirs. The price he had to pay for the withdrawal of Elgin's opposition was twofold. He agreed to a slight modification to his original itinerary, thus avoiding – 'for some mysterious reason', as he put it – the Victoria Lake and the Great Pamir. And he gave an assurance that he would try not to inflame political or diplomatic passions in the letters or articles he proposed writing for *The Times*.

There remained the problem of his proposed visit to Afghanistan, and this too was settled to his satisfaction. 'Sir Henry Brackenbury, then Military Member,' he wrote, 'and a man of great ability and much imagination, was my one friend; the Commander-in-Chief, Sir George White, was non-committal; the Viceroy, Lord Elgin, hesitated. At a meeting of the Executive Council, however, it was decided to let me cross the frontier (on my return from the Pamirs), provided that a direct invitation from the Amir arrived in the interim; but I was told that I must go as a private individual (which was exactly what I desired) and that the Government of India would assume no responsibility for my safety.'

'He dined with me on Thursday and seemed quite pleased,' the Viceroy reported to Fowler on 28 August, 'and left for Kashmir on Friday.' It was while camping there on the way to the Pamirs that Curzon received one of the most welcome telegrams of his life. It was the long awaited invitation from the Amir of Afghanistan.

The start of his trek to the Pamirs was deceptively gentle. 'In this Elysian valley,' Curzon wrote of the Vale of Kashmir, 'English flowers and fruit abound, English ladies move to and fro without escort, English children bloom.' But the euphoria did not last as he wended his way by pony up the recently constructed road to Gilgit, 200 miles to the north-west. It wound through an intricate maze of mountains and over a series of passes that even in the first week of September seemed to offer little more shelter than the peaks. He rode over the Burzil at 13,450 feet in a snowstorm, with the thermometer only one degree above freezing point; there he was shown a rock under which, not long before, five men had crouched to eat their supper and were found dead from exposure in the morning. And one of his servants assured him that he had been present when a coolie, the hindmost in a string, was forcibly seized and thrown into a neighbouring gully by a monstrous *jin* or demon, as tall as from the earth to the sky, and covered with hair over a foot long.

Having reached Gilgit untouched by such perils, Curzon pushed on along the Hunza valley to Baltit. Even to a traveller of his experience, the scenery was stupendous. Within a range of seventy miles there were eight crests with an elevation of over 24,000 feet, and the little state of Hunza alone, he was told, contained more summits of over 20,000 feet than there are of over 10,000 feet in the entire Alps. He recorded the spectacle in his most tasteful style: 'Nature would seem to have exerted her supreme energy, and in one chord to have comprised almost every note in her vast and majestic diapason of sound. For there she shows herself in the same moment both tender and savage, both radiant and appalling, the relentless spirit that hovers above the ice-towers and the gentle patroness of the field and orchard, and tutelary deity of the haunts of men.'

The apparition of Mount Rakapushi also touched his pen with magic: 'Everywhere visible as we ascend the valley, he keeps watch over the lower summits and over the smiling belts of green and the orchard plots below that owe their existence to his glacial bounty. But up above, where no raiment but the royal ermine clothes his shoulders, his true majesty is best revealed. There enormous and shining glaciers fill the hollows of his sides, the ice-fields stretch for mile on mile of breadth and height, and only upon the needle-point of his highest crest is the snow unable to settle. In that remote empyrean we visualise an age beyond the boundaries of human thought, a silence as from the dawn of time.'

Then the practical bent of his mind reasserted itself, and he rode on to

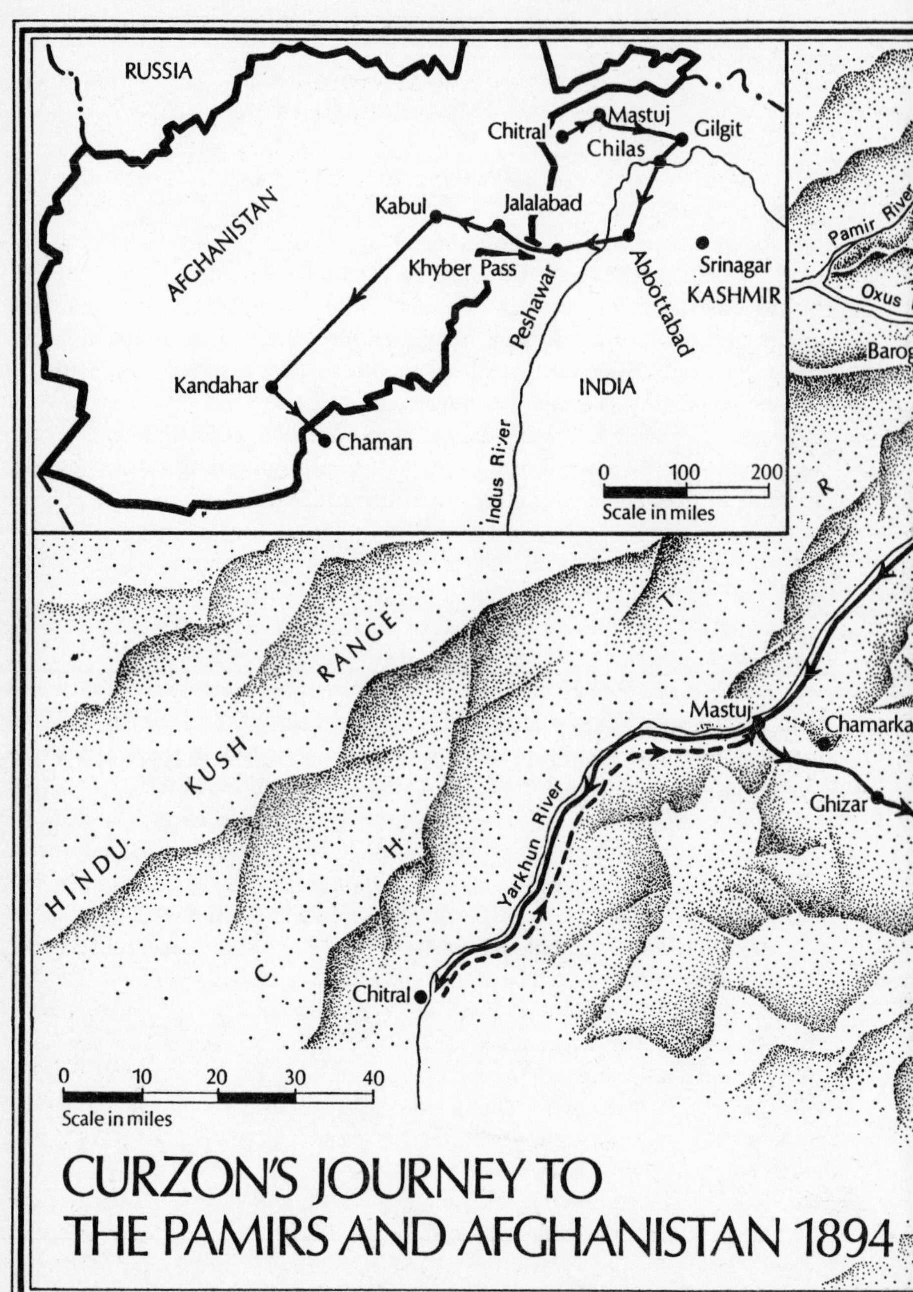

CURZON'S JOURNEY TO THE PAMIRS AND AFGHANISTAN 1894

GREAT PAMIR
To Lake Victoria
Lake Chakmak (13,100 ft)
Aksu R.
LITTLE
PAMIR
Wakh-jir Pass (16,100 ft.)
Kilik Pass (15,870 ft)
Bozai Gumbaz
Daliz Kotal
Sarhad
Pamir-i-wakhan
Source of the Oxus
L
Pass (12,460 ft)
HUNZA VALLEY
(Baltit, capital)
Hunza
Nagar
Pass
Gupis
Ghiza River
Raka Pushi (22,550 ft)
Gilgit
Indus River
Indus River
To Abbottabad
Chilas
From Srinagar

inspect the twin states of Hunza and Nagar that guard one of the principal gateways to India. Only three years before, the Government of India had launched a sharp and successful campaign to crush the pretensions of these two warlike peoples and to put an end to their harassing of the military forts established farther down the valley. Curzon noted approvingly how 'this nest of mountain-wasps, who stung and worried upon the frontier, and made Simla quake, had been converted into a useful and reliable outpost on the extreme ramparts of our Indian Empire'.

It was a sign of the prevailing cordiality between conquerors and conquered that British officers habitually joined the inhabitants in their native polo, a game played to the traditional accompaniment of drums and clarinets. Curzon proudly observed that even in the remoteness of the Hunza valley, the civilizing influence of Europe strove to exert itself. The occupying force had introduced a lighter ball of bamboo wood; had reduced the cheerful rabble of players to a manageable number; had abolished the rule by which a goal was not scored until one of the side striking the ball between the posts had dismounted and picked it up – 'with the result of a frightful and even dangerous scuffle'. But the orderly minds and commanding personalities of the sahibs had not yet succeeded in persuading the Hunza men to respect prohibitions against 'offside' and 'crossing'.

Curzon made a courtesy call on the Thum, or ruler, of Hunza in his five-storey castle at Baltit, the capital. To reach the reception chamber that opened on to the roof he had to climb a series of rude ladders and squeeze through a hatchway in the floor. 'This might be thought a primitive mode of entrance,' he reflected, 'but then the castle of Baltit is not precisely Windsor.'

Less than ten years later, when he was Viceroy, he invited his host and other border chieftains down to Calcutta as guests of the Government. And he liked to recall the happiness of one of them, who was not much accustomed to the use of a chair, seated on the marble floor of the pseudo-Kedleston, wearing an immense white turban, and stuffing a strawberry ice into his mouth with his fingers.

'In the course of a very few days,' Curzon wrote of the next stage of his journey towards the Pamirs, 'I underwent the bodily labours of a Parliamentary session and parted with the superfluous physical accretions of an entire London season.' The going was so rough that baggage animals could not keep their feet, and everything had to be carried on the backs of Hunza porters – 'strong, cheerful and willing', as he described them. Curzon himself rode a horse, but had to dismount several times a day to ford the swift, cold river or to pick his way across a glacier.

He was not alone in his ordeal. The Thum of Hunza, attended by his Wazir, or hereditary adviser, courteously accompanied him to the boundary of his territory. He also had the companionship and alert soldierly presence of Henry Lennard, an Eton contemporary who had taken part in the military operations of 1891 as a volunteer. On the sixth day of their march, a distance of eighty-one miles, they reached the top of the Kilik pass. Curzon completed a descriptive letter to *The Times*, which as usual was helping to bear the expenses of his journey, and allowed himself to dwell on the satisfaction of standing almost literally on the watershed of the Asiatic continent: 'India, with all its accumulated treasures, lay behind me, ring-fenced by the terrific barriers through and across which I had laboriously climbed. Central Asia, with its rival domination and its mysterious destinies, lay before me. I was on the southern eave of the Roof of the World.'

Much had been written about the Pamirs, but little that matched Curzon's meticulous standards of accuracy. A Pamir, he explained to the Royal Geographical Society on his return to England, is neither a down, nor a steppe, nor a plateau. It is a mountain valley of glacial formation which resembles a plain owing to the inability of the central stream to scour for itself a deeper channel. This in turn is the fault of the short summers which do not last long enough for the sun to melt the snow and so create a torrent.

He went on to describe some of the unattractive features of this scarcely known mountainous tract covering about 20,000 square miles. It possessed a mean elevation of between 12,000 and 14,000 feet, with peaks rising to 20,000 feet and higher; boasted an abundance of pasturage but total absence of timber or cultivation; was buried deep in snow during seven months of the year and often inaccessible for longer; scourged by icy blasts and destitute of any fuel except the dung of animals or the roots of desert scrub. There were few inhabitants, only the nomadic Kirghiz, with his sheep and goats, his yaks and ponies. And the numbers even of these hardy tribes were kept down by the difficulty of childbirth in so harsh a climate.

One form of life that does thrive in the Pamirs is the *Ovis poli*, or wild ram. Named after Marco Polo, who first described the species, it has always been much coveted by sportsmen for its magnificent horns, thick and long, with a wide span and sometimes a double convolution. Curzon spent four days stalking them to the very mountain peaks. He shot two head, one at a height of 17,000 feet where he could hardly breathe. Then he retired to his circular tent of felt spread over wickerwork, a snug speciality of Central Asia, and composed a learned dissertation comparing his bag with its distant kinsman, *Ovis karelini*.

That was not Curzon's only contribution to knowledge during his weeks in the Pamirs. Six years before, on his way to Bokhara by the Transcaspian railway, he had crossed the Oxus at Charjuri, 600 miles to the west. But there the river was in its sluggish middle course or, as his friend Matthew Arnold put it,

Oxus forgetting the bright speed he had
In his high mountain cradle of Pamere.

'With the poet,' he wrote, 'my imagination had flown eastwards and upwards to that aërial source, and had longed to pierce the secrets that were hidden behind the glaciers of the Pamirs and the snowy sentinels of the Hindu Kush.' Now his time had come. In the autumn of 1894, after months of research into all earlier authorities and reports, he became the first known traveller to gaze on the head waters of the Oxus as they emerged from their prison of ice.

It was from the top of the Wakh-jir pass that he caught sight of the river 2,000 feet below, a blue line winding away towards the Caspian between snow-crowned ridges. He dropped down the steep side of the valley, then rode up the shingle bed until his path was blocked by the precipitous snout of a glacier. At its foot the Oxus came tumbling out of two ice-caverns. One had a low overhanging roof from under which the water gushed to freedom: its neighbour was high enough for Curzon to peer into the interior and discern a long tunnel choked by huge slabs of ice. And all the while there was a ceaseless tumult of grinding and crunching.

Curzon spent the next few days making a survey of the Pamir lakes which lie to the north and the passes which connect them, then returned to the line of the river and from Bozai Gumbaz followed it along its westerly course. The ground was difficult and his ponies had to be unloaded and pushed or hauled up the rocky cliff tracks. Even so, they constantly slipped and fell, one of them disappearing down a steep ravine to instant death. At last mounting to the top of the Daliz Kotal, a pass of 13,500 feet, he saw far below him the splendid vista of the Oxus released from its mountain confines, spreading out in countless threads over a wide watery plain.

The realities of political power soon distracted him from the beauties of nature. At Sarhad, an outpost of Afghan rule occupied by 'a few seedy sepoys', he and Lennard were confronted by a *havildar*, or non-commissioned officer, and accused of being Russian spies. Anticipating just such an encounter, Curzon had previously written to the Amir of Afghanistan – whose guest he would be in the following month – telling him of his proposed return route from the Pamirs to India. The *havildar*, he was certain, had received instructions from Kabul to let the party pass, but had been unable to resist the temptation of humiliating foreigners before the inhabitants of a remote Afghan dependency. Curzon had experienced similar obstructiveness at the hands of Persian petty officials on the Karun river in 1890: and at Sarhad he settled the matter in the same way. He declined to be detained.

Later he complained to the Amir of the brusque officiousness to which he and Lennard had been exposed. But he had to admit that the *havildar*'s explanation of his conduct was so ingenious as to be almost convincing. 'He was still awaiting,' the *havildar* reported to Kabul, 'the arrival of the great English lord *sahib*, whose coming had been announced by His Majesty the Amir, and who would no doubt appear in uniform with an escort of a thousand men. In the meantime, two of the lord *sahib*'s servants had already passed through with an insignificant following. He himself would continue diligently to await the great lord.'

Brushing off the unwelcome attentions of the *havildar* at Sarhad, Curzon crossed the bed of the Oxus, by now three-quarters of a mile in width, and struck south over the Hindu Kush by the Baroghil pass. Having said good-bye to Lennard, whose route lay towards Gilgit, he continued down the gorge of the Yarkhun for seventy-two miles. It was a formidable ordeal. Twelve times in a single day he had to ford a broad and rushing mountain torrent whose force and volume almost lifted his pony off its legs. But the scenery was memorable, as though some vast Niagara, pouring from the skies, had suddenly been congealed in its descent and converted into pinnacles and towers of ice. On the third day he emerged into more open country and rode down grassy slopes towards Mastuj, where he was to meet his friend Francis Younghusband and march with him to Chitral. In the distance he saw a solitary horseman approaching him, and knew that this must be the native servant despatched by his host to guide him to camp. But it was no ordinary servant who now greeted him with a salaam. Curzon, parched and exhausted, uttered one word: 'Beer.' Without a moment's hesitation the bearer put his hand into the fold of his tunic and drew out a bottle of Bass. The traveller was once more within the comforting embrace of Pax Britannica.

Although only thirty-one, Captain Francis Younghusband had already acquired a reputation as one of the most intrepid and knowledgeable British officials on the Indian frontier. After Sandhurst he had joined a cavalry regiment and seen service at Meerut before undertaking a remarkable series of exploratory journeys through Manchuria and the Pamirs. His expulsion from Bozai Gumbaz by a Cossack patrol in the summer of 1891 had led to his first meeting with Curzon who, as Under-Secretary of State for India, received him warmly on his return to England on leave. Thereafter they corresponded freely on the subject of Russian expansion that was so close to both their hearts. Younghusband, having been appointed Political Officer in Hunza in 1892, was in the following year transferred to Chitral, where he rapidly won the confidence and affection of the Mehtar, or ruler. He later wrote a perceptive account of Curzon's visit to Chitral:

Curzon was then both a pleasure and a trial. He was perpetually discussing frontier policy, which was agreeable; but he was continually disagreeing with me, which was irritating. I did not discover till later that he was writing a series of letters to *The Times*, and that he was all the time forcing my views out of me. When he showed me the draft of the letter about Chitral which he had written, I found that it was entirely in accordance with my own views.

All the same, Curzon did have an argumentative turn of mind – I suppose it was the House of Commons debating habit – and it jarred on us up there on the frontier. We were most of us young men, and we were in responsible positions. We formed and expressed our opinions upon what was life or death for us personally in a quieter way than is usual in Parliament or at elections, where ability to talk and argue is the first consideration. And we resented Curzon's cocksureness. His manner grated on us on the frontier, as all through his life it grated on the British public. It might have been toned down if he could have been for a time with a regiment or served on the frontier; and he might then have attained the great position to which his ability, his tremendous power of work, his high sense of public duty, and his zeal for his country entitled him. But irritating though this manner was, it was yet compatible with remarkable tenderness of heart. In friendship he was warm and staunch. And for frontier officers he had a special affection. Soldiers in general he never understood or liked. But to frontier officers he always opened his heart, and all of us – and most certainly I – should be everlastingly grateful for the interest he took in our work and the way he supported us.

Like most of Curzon's friends, Younghusband soon came to know, to understand and even to forgive his paradoxical qualities of character. As a lifelong student of abstract speculation, he was both annoyed and pained by Curzon's arrogant disdain for philosophy. 'You won't get much out of them,' Curzon once told him, pointing to his library of philosophical works. But resentment soon melted in the sunshine of geniality. On Curzon's first morning in Mastuj he was offered jam at breakfast. 'I'll bet this is your last pot of jam,' he said. Younghusband admitted that as a matter of fact it was. 'There it is!' Curzon exclaimed, banging the table. 'Always on the frontier the guest finds the last of the best things produced for him!'

Friendship apart, what could not fail to unite them was a common conviction that Chitral – 'this small chink in the mountain palisade', as Curzon called it – must at all costs be closed to Russian infiltration. That he was the first Englishman not on official duty to visit the region underlines his absorbed interest in every facet of Indian defence.

It took two days to ride down from Mastuj to Chitral along the banks of the Yarkhun. In places the going was so rough that Curzon's sturdy pony began to spit blood and died in the night. Nor did he himself have an easy time of it. For the first time in his travels he used rope bridges to cross the river. Each bridge consisted of a thick cable of twisted birch or willow twigs on which to place the feet, with two lighter ropes of the same material to act as hand rails. Although stoutly made, the entire structure looked too frail to inspire confidence: and however tightly the passenger clung to the contraption, it was not agreeable either to sway a few inches above a raging torrent or to dangle hundreds of feet above a rocky gorge. Curzon shuffled his way across manfully, but one of the British officers who accompanied him, rather than trust himself to the cat-walk, insisted on swimming the swollen river on horseback. A few months later he was appointed to the Distinguished Service Order for conspicuous bravery in an operation against hostile tribesmen.

Four miles from Chitral, the Mehtar rode out to greet the party and to escort them into his tiny capital. He had the light curly hair, moustache and beard of an Englishman, and he wore a smart green velvet suit trimmed with gold braid. At first his manner was timid, almost cringing. 'But this shyness wore off completely as we became better acquainted,' Curzon noted, 'and although of weak character and debauched habits, he never in any situation looked anything but a gentleman.'

The Mehtar had arranged a princely entertainment for his guests. It began with a formal salute from two brass six-pounders presented by the Government of India and a *feu de joie* from several hundred Chitrali armed with matchlocks who lined the crest of the hills. Then there was polo. The custom of the place was for the beaten side to dance to the victors, and the Mehtar used to select as captain of the opposing team (which was invariably beaten) an old man who had once made an unsuccessful attempt on his life.

When lunching with his host, Curzon found the walls of the pavilion decorated with pictures from English illustrated papers, including a portrait of the recently married Margot Asquith. He and Younghusband gave a return feast, with a menu of tinned soup, army rations, pilau, chicken, stewed pears, beer, whisky and ginger wine. 'The whisky and the ginger wine were mixed together,' Curzon wrote, 'I am not sure that a little beer was not added, and I can recall the sight of one Chitrali nobleman pouring this amazing concoction down the throat of another, at the same time that he held him by the nose.' Then presents were exchanged, and Curzon received a *choga*, or loose woollen coat faced with silk, which for years he wore as a dressing-gown.

Curzon warmed to the Chitralis. They had neither the energy nor the warlike qualities that he so admired in the men of Hunza. But he liked their dignity and good-natured indolence, their dedication to hawking and horsemanship, their games and music, their stories and jokes. He was impressed, too, by the Mehtar's plea for a more emphatic definition of British responsibilities towards Chitral. The ruler asked that both the British officer attached to his court and the Indian Army escort should be stationed not at Mastuj, but at Chitral itself. Had this proposal been adopted earlier, Curzon came to believe, the subsequent history of the state might have run a happier course. Chitral had long been plagued by dynastic troubles, and little more than two months after Curzon's visit, the Mehtar was shot in the back while out hawking. The architect of the assassination was his half-brother, whom Curzon remembered as 'a sullen and repulsive figure, with long black locks and a look of gloom'.

The murder of the Mehtar on 1 January 1895, and the usurpation of his throne plunged Chitral into prolonged disturbance. The British force sent from Gilgit found itself bottled up in the very rooms where Curzon and the Mehtar had entertained each other, and it was not until April that a relief expedition arrived to restore order.

By then Curzon had visited Afghanistan and returned to England, where he flung himself into the controversy that raged on the future not only of Chitral but of the entire frontier policy. In letters to *The Times* despatched during his travels he had stressed in unequivocal terms the paramount need to retain, protect and strengthen a chain of outposts along the frontier of India. That the views of a former Parliamentary Secretary for India in a Conservative administration might be confused with those of the present Liberal Government, particularly when republished in foreign newspapers, alarmed both the Secretary of State and the Viceroy.

'I have been annoyed with Curzon's articles in *The Times*,' Fowler wrote to Elgin on 2 January, 'they do not reflect favourably on his discretion.' The Viceroy concurred: 'I am bound to say that we have some feeling here that he has gone beyond his engagements to us to use every caution and discretion in some of his expressions of opinion in *The Times*.' Sir Arthur Godley, the Permanent Secretary at the India Office, also had his say. 'Curzon must be thoroughly happy now,' he told Elgin. 'He has accomplished his great object, and has amassed material for a very considerable number of large fresh letters in *The Times*. But the time may come when he, being in "a responsible situation", may regret some of his utterances.'

Throughout the spring, Curzon publicly poured scorn on the considerable body of civil and military opinion that argued in favour of abandoning Chitral. It seemed unlikely, however, that his views would prevail. Both Rosebery and Fowler were persuaded that to hold Chitral and other such outposts would involve a ruinous outlay, an immense garrison, and the eternal and implacable hostility of the tribes. These were not sacrifices that commended themselves to a Liberal Government. But before their decision to withdraw could be made effective, the general election of July 1895 had returned the Conservatives to power.

Curzon, whom Lord Salisbury at once appointed to be his Parliamentary Under-Secretary, thus found himself in 'a responsible situation' sooner than Godley had expected. Nor did he have cause to 'regret some of his utterances'. Salisbury invited him to prepare a Cabinet minute on the vexed question of the Indian frontier, a task that he undertook with relish. The document included this passage:

> While not interfering (any more than we did before) with native institutions or customs, a British Political Officer should still be maintained at or near Chitral itself, with an escort adequate to secure his safety; and that British suzerainty should continue to be paramount along the entire Hindu Kush frontier. For a time more men may be required, and greater expense may be incurred than hitherto in the setting up of this new order. Later on the tension will be relaxed, and reduction will be possible. In any case, even increased outlay will be a cheap insurance against the future troubles and expenditure that present evacuation will some day involve.

Lord Salisbury and his colleagues found Curzon's argument convincing. A Political Officer was despatched to reside at Chitral: and when in 1897 an outbreak of tribal warfare set the whole frontier alight, Chitral remained tranquil under his influence. In the following year Curzon became Viceroy and completed the plans he had foreshadowed in 1895 by extending the telegraph line and forming corps of native levies or scouts. The British garrison was reduced to a single Indian battalion and Chitral lived happily ever after.

Having said good-bye to the ill-fated Mehtar in the autumn of 1894, the travellers retraced their steps up the Yarkhun valley to Mastuj. Here Curzon collected his mail, including a copy of *Problems of the Far East*, which had not been published until after his departure from England, and a stout bundle of newspaper reviews. 'Any author can sympathise with my emotions of pleasure,' he wrote, 'as, with the reins thrown on the neck of my horse, I rode up the steep and stony ascent that leads to the pass, reading the too-favourable notices of my book, and stuffing them into my holsters as I proceeded.'

They spent one night of their ten-day trek to Gilgit at the newly built fort of Gupis. The British officer in command was Captain Charles Townshend, soon to be besieged with his small garrison in Chitral, and subsequently to achieve fame as the defender of Kut in the Mesopotamian campaign of 1915–16. He combined an absorbing interest in military science with a nostalgic attachment to the joys of Paris. The mud walls of his quarters were relieved by daring coloured illustrations from Parisian magazines, and throughout what Curzon remembered as a very long evening he sang French ditties to the accompaniment of a banjo. His guest of honour was not tempted to linger, even by such unexpectedly cosmopolitan treats. He pushed on to Gilgit, followed the Indus river down to Chilas, crossed the Himalayas by the Babusar pass and stood once more on the soil of British India. He had no time to lose: in his pocket he carried his long-sought invitation to stay with the Amir of Afghanistan at Kabul.

Although news of its arrival had not reached him until the end of August, when he was camping in Kashmir on the first stage of his journey to the Pamirs, he had never doubted that he would achieve his purpose. Before leaving England that summer he had given meticulous care even to the clothes in which he should present himself at the Afghan capital. In 1893, when calling on the King of Korea, he had merely donned the drab blue civil uniform which he was entitled to wear as a former Under-Secretary at the India Office, and had been disappointed at the mediocre figure he cut. Later he recalled how an official of the Indian Political Department engaged on a Boundary Commission in Afghan Turkestan had been received with much deference after having a very broad gold stripe sewn on his trousers and girding a formidable sword at his waist. Curzon likewise decided that if he too were to produce a suitably startling effect in Kabul, he must dispense with the dress regulations laid down by the Lord Chamberlain at St James's Palace.

First he called at Nathan's, the theatrical costumiers in London, and for a modest sum hired a cluster of gorgeous stars of foreign orders, mostly from the smaller States of Eastern Europe. To these he added an enormous pair of gold epaulettes in a case the size of a hat-box. In Bombay he ordered a glittering pair of patent leather Wellington top boots. And while staying with General Sir William Lockhart at his headquarters at Abbottabad, en route for Afghanistan, he borrowed a gigantic curved sword with ivory hilt and engraved scabbard which had been presented to Lockhart in honour of a successful campaign. Someone produced a cocked hat, someone else a pair of handsome spurs, and his baggage was complete.

It was in more workmanlike clothes that Curzon left Peshawar for the ride of 180 miles to Kabul. He crossed the frontier by the Khyber Pass and was met by an escort of seventy men. The Amir had also given orders for relays of horses to await his guest along the route, thus enabling him to maintain an exceptionally high average of twenty-seven miles a day. A little way outside the walls of the capital, a tent had been pitched so that he could change into his ceremonial dress. But it was only after an hour's furtive work with needle and thread that he managed to sew the massive golden epaulettes on to his shoulders. Finally attired in all his splendour, and with an escort that had now grown to 200, he rode into the town and was conducted to the Durbar Hall of the Amir. There was a moment of embarrassment when the Amir asked Curzon for what services or exploits he had received such a galaxy of orders and decorations. 'To these inconvenient queries,' he wrote, 'I could only return the most general and deprecatory replies.' The Amir did not press the point. Apparently satisfied with the social standing of his guest – the only private person he had ever invited to Kabul – he installed him in the most sumptuous suite of his palace. 'The sheets of my bed are cerise coloured silk,' Curzon told Daisy White, 'the pillow is of flowered silk and the quilts of silk and brocade with gold and silver lace trimmings.'

To relieve Curzon of financial worries in a strange land, his host sent round 5,000 newly minted Kabuli rupees, worth about £230, on a tray. Pyne warned Curzon that to refuse the money would be taken as an insult; he should therefore accept it with gratitude, but spend it on presents for the Amir and tips for his servants. Curzon took his advice. A few coins, however, he thoughtfully saved for his old numismatist friend at All Souls, Charles Oman.

Abdur Rahman Khan, Amir of Afghanistan, had in early life experienced many of those twists of fortune to which oriental potentates are inured. He had fought and plotted to place first his father, then his uncle, on the throne: and when the death of one and the deposition of the other obliged him to flee the country, he had sought refuge at the courts of Meshed, Khiva and Bokhara. Ultimately he had lived for eleven years at Samarkand to be at hand when the day came for his recall. Early in 1880 he crossed the Oxus river into Afghanistan and, with British approval and support, fought a series of campaigns that by the summer left him impregnably installed in Kabul.

These vicissitudes were reflected in the savagery with which he crushed opposition and in the fear which he deliberately instilled in order to command an absolute obedience. But he loved such crude weapons of government as much for themselves as for their effectiveness. Curzon soon concluded that his host's passion for cruelty was one of his most inveterate instincts. He saw his first example of it as he rode towards Kabul: swinging from a tall pole was an iron cage containing the bones of a robber who had been caught and shut up alive in the contraption as a warning to others.

Curzon collected many other instances of ferocious rule which he satisfied himself were true. After one unsuccessful rebellion, the Amir had had many thousands of the guilty tribesmen blinded with quicklime. For crimes such as theft or rape, men were blown from guns or thrown down a well or beaten to death or flayed alive or tortured in the offending member. Thus a favourite penalty for petty larceny was amputation of the hand at the wrist, the raw stump then being plunged into boiling oil. An official who had outraged a woman was stripped naked and placed in a hole dug for the purpose on a high hill outside Kabul: it was mid-winter, and water was poured over him until he was turned into an icicle and frozen alive. The Amir remarked sardonically: 'He will never be hot again.'

When a woman of his harem was found to be pregnant, he had her tied up in a sack and brought into the Durbar Hall, where he ran her through with his own sword. Two men who talked of some forbidden subject had their upper and lower lips stitched together so that they should never offend again. Another man who openly accused the Amir of depravity had his tongue torn out by the roots. Even supposedly innocent acts which touched on his prerogative were punished. Thus a man who spoke to Curzon on his way to Kabul was thrown into prison, and another who offered him a pomegranate as he rode into Kandahar on his way back to India was severely beaten.

So ferocious a regime necessarily exposed the Amir to a perpetual risk of assassination. Once, when suffering from toothache, he saw that the surgeon had prepared chloroform to ease the pain of extraction, and asked how long he would have to remain insensible. 'Twenty minutes,' the surgeon said. 'Twenty minutes!' replied the Amir. 'I cannot afford to be out of the world for twenty seconds. Take it out without chloroform.'

The Amir, and the Amir alone, was the Government of Afghanistan. Nothing was too small, whether the cut of a uniform or the manufacture of a piece of furniture, to escape his attention. 'He was the brain and eyes and ears,' wrote Curzon, 'of all Afghanistan.' To maintain his omniscience, Abdur Rahman depended upon the detestable methods common to all despots. 'Life in Kabul,' Curzon told Elgin, 'is one gigantic funnel of espionage into which is collected the action and speech, almost the thought, of every man, while the Amir, like Dionysius of Syracuse, has his ear glued to the other end.'

During his previous travels, Curzon had usually found British communities overseas to be cheerful and harmonious. In Kabul, he discovered, the handful of British subjects employed by the Government of Afghanistan for their professional or technical skills were distressingly unsettled. Each regarded his neighbour with jealousy and suspicion; each indulged in what Curzon called 'a squalid maze of backbiting and lies'. For this 'kettle of unsavoury stew', he blamed the pretensions of the British wives. 'They are lifted into a position for which socially they are quite unfitted. The wives respectively of a tailor and a veterinary surgeon, in all probability of modest provincial origin, are admitted to the Harem and treated by the Queen as though they were representative English ladies and personal acquaintances of "her friend Victoria". They have assured the Queen that they are personal friends of H.M. Queen Victoria and have stayed at Windsor Castle.'

'I am standing on the brink of a small social volcano,' he noted, 'whose mutterings are audible at every turn.' He listened to all that his unhappy compatriots told him of each other's failings, but never forgot that the Amir was surely having him watched as closely as any Afghan official or satrap. He repeated no tittle-tattle, he made no mischief, he took no sides. But in the privacy of a secret memorandum to the Viceroy of India he recorded all that he had heard.

Only one European woman in Kabul won his entire admiration and respect. She was Miss Lillias Hamilton, who had originally come out to Afghanistan to teach music but had later been pressed into service as the Amir's medical adviser. It was a hazardous appointment, demanding qualifications far beyond the professional degrees she had obtained at Brussels and Edinburgh. The patient himself boasted a crafty knowledge both of diagnosis and of treatment which he was reluctant to abandon. He would relieve aches and pains by wrapping himself in the skin of a freshly slaughtered sheep, and preached an even more dramatic remedy for internal disorders. Confident they were caused by a worm, he claimed that he starved himself for a day, then sat in front of a large and delicious meal until the parasite was driven to crawl up his throat in search of food. As soon as it appeared, he would seize its head and draw it forth.

Miss Hamilton had other handicaps to overcome. If her treatment of the Amir's ailments were successful, she would be well rewarded: but if her patient should die, she would certainly be accused of having poisoned him and would be fortunate to escape with her life. The Queen of Afghanistan, she told Curzon, was deeply jealous of her: so too were the hakims, or court physicians. Hers was no enviable appointment. She nevertheless dealt competently with all Abdur Rahman's complaints, including stone in the kidney, flatulence and gout. The last of these was particularly troublesome, and frequent bulletins on the patient's progress would appear in the Indian newspapers. Whether by mistake or design, Curzon noticed, compositors used to read 'gout' as an abbreviation, and to print, not without truth, that the Amir was suffering from 'a bad attack of government'.

Curzon spent a fortnight in Kabul, and each afternoon would converse for several hours with his Persian-speaking host through an interpreter. The Amir loved to dwell on his self-professed skills of piano-tuning, watchmaking and practical dentistry; on his belief in the descent of himself and his people from the Lost Tribes of Israel; on the pernicious attachment of Europeans to monogamy – an inevitable result, he concluded, of an enervatingly damp climate; and on the prevalance of crime in Manchester and Birmingham compared to its disappearance from his own Utopia.

Each appreciated the company of the other. The Amir wrote of Curzon in his memoirs: 'He appeared to be a very genial, hard-working, well-informed, experienced and ambitious young man. He was witty and full of humour, and we often laughed at his amusing stories.'

Curzon, too, enjoyed matching his wits against a disputant who was no less a master of dialectic than himself. He paid the Amir the compliment of conceding that in argument or controversy it would be hard to find his equal on either front bench at Westminster. In other ways, however, the Amir was not a model parliamentarian. 'He is quite ignorant of the distinction between English parties or indeed the existence of party government,' Curzon wrote to Lord Salisbury. 'Happy Asiatic!'

It cannot have been easy to pursue great themes of statecraft amid the perpetual bustle and clamour of the Amir's court. There were doctors and surgeons, bodyguards and footmen, page-boys and grooms, musicians and priests, tailors and valets, astrologers and librarians, barbers and accountants, readers and story-tellers, doormen and sweepers, tea-makers and hubble-bubble keepers, coachmen and petitioners, catamites and drum-beaters, umbrella-carriers and flag-bearers, professional players of chess and backgammon.

In spite of the distracting atmosphere, Curzon managed to devote many hours of talk to the haunting topic of Russian aggression in Asia. Abdur Rahman had every reason to be concerned with the problem. He would describe his country as a poor goat, threatened from one side by a bear, from the other by a lion: and it was the bear he feared most. His gratitude towards Russia for the hospitality and small pension he had received during his years in Samarkand did not extend to any degree of trust in her pacific protestations. He told Curzon that while in exile he had secretly learned Russian and had enjoyed hearing his hosts discussing their plans for the occupation of Afghanistan in the presence of a seemingly simple-minded and unsophisticated visitor. Less dramatically, the Amir admitted in his memoirs that on many occasions he had openly discussed politics with the Governor-General of Russian Turkestan, and had convinced himself of Russia's determination to swallow up Persia, Turkey and Afghanistan. 'The Russian policy of aggression,' he wrote, 'is slow and steady, but firm and unchangeable.'

How was such a menace to be met? Initially, the Amir decided, by strengthening his armies, particularly along the north-west frontier of Afghanistan, the path down which Russia would one day attempt her descent on India. He told Curzon of an episode in the war of nerves which Russia was waging against him. A Russian officer wrote to say that he proposed to exercise a force of 500 men, both cavalry and infantry, on the north-west frontier, and he hoped that this would not alarm the Amir or be regarded as a hostile act. The Amir replied that he had no objection at all, the more so as he himself proposed to exercise a force of 5,000 Afghan troops opposite the same place.

As a long-term solution to the Russian threat, he proposed a stiffening of the alliance between Afghanistan and Great Britain. It was, he maintained, no less in the interests of India than in those of his own country: 'So long as Afghanistan does not join Russia, the invasion of India is impossible – and the joining of Afghanistan with Russia in such an invasion is still more impossible.' He had already offended Russia, his erstwhile host, by coming to an understanding with Great Britain. It ensured that the Amir would not communicate with the Government of Russia, or of any other foreign power, without the knowledge and advice of the British Government: and that the British Government would in return protect Afghanistan against any foreign aggressor.

The Amir, however, had become increasingly disillusioned by the development of his relationship with Great Britain. He felt slighted at being obliged to conduct all diplomatic business through the Government of India, and his request to establish a direct link with the British Government in London received a rebuff. He complained that Lord Lansdowne, Viceroy from 1888 to 1894, wrote to him in dictatorial tones that might sometimes be adopted towards a vassal but never to an equal. He resented the lack of response to his requests for arms, particularly for the fortification of his north-west frontier. As he said to Curzon again and again during their talks: 'England and Afghanistan are one house. One house should have one wall. Are your soldiers going to join mine in defence of that wall?'

On succeeding Lansdowne in 1894, Elgin was anxious to reach an amicable understanding with the Amir on all outstanding personal and political grievances. He therefore sent him, on behalf of the British Government, an invitation to visit England at an early date. The Amir, still smarting from the supposed discourtesies of Calcutta, declined to reply. In the course of his talks with Curzon, however, he admitted that he had long been anxious to make the journey to London provided two conditions could be fulfilled. One was that he could be assured of a welcome compatible with his own exalted conception of the dignity and prestige of the Afghan Sovereign: the other that he could safely absent himself from his country for several months without risk of revolution.

The Amir made some startling suggestions for the programme of his State visit. They included a public rebuke of Field-Marshal Lord Roberts, who in 1879 had marched with his army on Kabul to avenge the murder of the British Resident. Curzon kept a note of the Amir's conversation with him on this vexed topic:

'When I come to England and to London and am received by the Queen, shall I tell you what I will do?'

'Yes, Your Highness, I shall be glad to hear.'

'I understand that there is in London a great Hall that is known as Westminster Hall. Is not that so?'

'It is.'

'There are also in London two Mejilises [i.e. Houses of Parliament]. One is called the House of Lords and the other is called the House of Commons?'

'It is so.'

'When I came to London, I shall be received in Westminster Hall. The Queen will be seated on her throne at the end of the Hall, and the Royal Family will be around her; and on either side of the Hall will be placed the two Mejilises – the

House of Lords on the right, and the House of Commons on the left. Is not that the case?'

'It is not our usual plan; but will Your Highness proceed?'

'I shall enter the Hall, and the Lords will rise on the right, and the Commons will rise on the left to greet me, and I shall advance between them up the Hall to the dais, where will be seated the Queen upon her throne. And she will rise and will say to me, "What has your Majesty come from Kabul to say?" And how then shall I reply?'

'I am sure I do not know.'

'I shall reply: "I will say nothing" – and the Queen will then ask me why I refuse to say anything; and I shall answer: "Send for Roberts. I decline to speak until Roberts comes." And then they will send for Roberts, and there will be a pause until Roberts comes, and when Roberts has come and is standing before the Queen and the two Mejilises, then will I speak.'

'And what will Your Highness say?'

'I shall tell them how Roberts paid thousands of rupees to obtain false witness at Kabul and that he slew thousands of my innocent people, and I shall ask that Roberts be punished, and when Roberts has been punished, then will I speak.'

Curzon failed to convince him that things were not done in quite that way in London: that was how things were done in Kabul, and London meant no more to the Amir than a larger stage and a change of scene. On another occasion when they were discussing the proposed visit, the Amir removed his turban and began to scratch his head, which was shaved quite bald. 'In a moment,' wrote Curzon, 'he was transformed from the formidable despot to a commonplace and elderly man. I implored him when he came to London never to remove his turban or scratch his head; and, when I told him my reason, his vanity was at once piqued, and he promised faithfully to show himself at his best.'

Not until Curzon was about to depart did the Amir make up his mind about Lord Elgin's invitation. Then he announced that he would accept it, and composed a personal letter to Queen Victoria which he wrapped in violet silk and gave his guest to carry back to England. He also wrote with gratitude to the Prince of Wales and to the Duke of Connaught, the Queen's third son, whom he had met in 1884 when visiting India during Lord Dufferin's Viceroyalty. But only after much prompting from Curzon did he agree to send an official acceptance to Fowler, the Secretary of State in London.

Curzon, who could rightly claim some credit for having persuaded the Amir to resume a cordial relationship with the British Government, hastened to send the news to the Viceroy, together with a memorandum on his talks with Abdur Rahman. Unhappily, and characteristically, he could not resist alluding to events that were best forgotten. 'Though I confess I think that the Indian Government treated me very shabbily about my proposed journey this autumn,' he told Elgin, 'and though I know that they were not over anxious that I should come up here; yet I have myself, as I am sure you personally will believe, no interests other than theirs: and my object in coming to Kabul has assuredly been no gratification of private ambition, but the desire to render, in however humble a way, some public service.'

As Curzon was leaving Kabul for India, and so home to England, the Amir handed him a farewell present. It was a specially made gold star inlaid with diamonds and rubies and bearing a Persian inscription, an adornment that put his hired orders of chivalry to shame. Fortunately, he would never need to use those borrowed plumes again. 'Little more than four years later,' he wrote of the episode with satisfaction, 'I had as many genuine orders on my bosom (though not drawn from quite so wide a range) as it could conveniently hold; and I was corresponding with my friend the Amir as the authorised representative of my Sovereign.'

Hardly had Curzon returned to England at the end of January than he heard of the failure of his unofficial diplomatic mission. The Amir, although satisfied that a cordial welcome awaited him in London, decided that he could not leave his country without risking rebellion in his absence. Excusing himself, therefore, on the ground of ill-health, he withdrew his acceptance of the invitation. Curzon gleefully assured Lord Roberts that he would now be spared a public indictment before the Queen and the assembled estates of the realm: but the Field-Marshal was amused neither by the Amir's threats nor by his own reprieve.

In his place, Abdur Rahman sent his younger son Nasrullah to England, where he was received with kindness by the Queen. But the Amir was offended at the churlishness of the British Government in again refusing to sanction the establishment of a permanent diplomatic mission in London, and relations between Afghanistan and Great Britain continued to be clouded by mistrust.

On being appointed Viceroy in 1898, Curzon had every reason to hope that the friendship and trust shown him in Kabul four years before would enable him to charm Abdur Rahman into a more submissive state of mind. The Amir, after all, had confided to him even the closely guarded secret that he intended to nominate his eldest son Habibullah as his successor – by no means a predictable decision in the dynastic turbulence of Oriental courts. But the intimacy conceded to a private traveller was denied to the Viceroy of India. Abdur Rahman, Curzon complained, was 'a very difficult person to handle and a very formidable opponent to cross'. Nor did Habibullah, who duly succeeded to the throne on his father's death in 1901, prove more amenable. He continued to display an inveterate suspicion of British motives and a sense of betrayal at the reluctance of the British Government to supply Afghanistan with arms.

These disappointments lay in the future. In the spring of 1895 Curzon could congratulate himself on having completed his programme of travel and exploration, an achievement which in May brought him the Gold Medal of the Royal Geographical Society. Returning thanks for the honour, he offered some advice to other enterprising spirits who felt themselves drawn to remote and inaccessible places:

> In the first place, consult all the highest and most reliable authorities you can find. In the second place, read every book, good, bad or indifferent that has been written upon the country you propose to visit, so that you may know what to do and what not to do. In the third place, take no superfluous baggage – it only employs extra time and men. In the fourth place, realise that travel has not only its incidents and adventures, but also its humour. And in the fifth place, never expect any encouragement from the Government of your country.

Curzon's youthful disrespect for authority did not survive his own elevation to the Viceroyalty, and Lord Elgin himself could not have displayed a more obstructive immobility towards the adventurous globetrotter. A young journalist of the *Daily Telegraph* once sought permission to cross the frontier from India to Afghanistan, a feat which no unofficial Englishman since Curzon had performed. The Viceroy pointed out that Afghanistan was in a state of unrest, and that the journey could not, therefore, be sanctioned. The journalist persisted. 'But I have here a letter from Lord Burnham* asking you to do this very thing for me.' Curzon was not to be moved. 'I am extremely sorry,' he replied genially, 'but you have as much chance of entering the Kingdom of Heaven with a leaf of the Old Testament as you have of getting to Kabul with a letter from Lord Burnham.'

* Edward Levy-Lawson, first Baron Burnham, 1833–1916. Proprietor of the *Daily Telegraph.*

Chapter Twenty
MARRIAGE

Was there not something wonderful in this long trial, in the uncomplaining and faithful devotion of this darling girl? I think it was the foundation of the great happiness that she gave me, a happiness that no man has surpassed. Could there be a greater glory than to be the one and only love of such a woman?

– *From a manuscript note by Curzon on his marriage*

'I can't help thinking,' Charty Ribblesdale wrote to Curzon in 1886, just after Sibell Grosvenor had rejected Curzon's hand in favour of George Wyndham's, 'that there must be a woman in the world who would be able to help you more than she could. Perhaps nobody more darling to look at or more naturally angelic, but one wants more than this in the hard struggle of life, especially the life you have planned out for yourself which will always be at highest pressure. Though strength, I am told, is made perfect in weakness, hers is not that weakness whose very essence is strength.'

Curzon, however, was in no hurry to seek a substitute for Sibell. He bore his rebuff with a fortitude that soon turned to what looked suspiciously like relief. He was still handsome and high-spirited and the best of company: to these qualities he now added the irresistible attraction of a mildly broken heart. An adoring circle of Tennant sisters and others hastened to console him with an affectionate companionship that was much to his taste, and he acquired a reputation as a philanderer.

Miss D. D. Balfour, later to become Alfred Lyttelton's second wife, has described an episode in Curzon's career that was not apparently unique. In 1889 she was staying with Lord and Lady Elcho at Stanway for a large shooting party that included the Pembrokes, the de Greys, Doll Liddell (who was deeply in love with her) and Curzon. She wrote:

I wish I could reproduce George's swelling eighteenth-century manner and phraseology. 'I had heard of you,' he said, 'as a great addition to our circle, clever, brilliant, a good talker, and I had imagined to myself a woman of a certain age, without any other charms but those of intellect. What do I find? A young buxom creature, charming ...' He and I were alone at the breakfast table for a few moments. ... I got up to go, but before I had reached the door George got there in front of me, shut it and kissed me with fervour. I was rather bewildered but not displeased and got away – he had no physical attraction for me.

There were practical advantages, too, in exchanging the prospect of matrimony for the delights of dalliance. He not only saved himself from financial cares that neither his pocket nor his pride was equipped to bear, but also restored to himself the leisure necessary to complete his political education by travel and study. Not until 1890 did he again allow his heart to be touched by true love. Even then it took him two years to propose marriage, and a further three years to redeem his promise.

Mary Victoria Leiter was just twenty – eleven years younger than Curzon – when he met her for the first time during the London season, a few months after his return from Persia. She was the daughter of Mr and Mrs Levi Zeigler Leiter, of Washington and Chicago, who were in the habit of making a leisurely visit to Europe nearly every year. In spite of bearing one of the most honoured names in Jewry, Mr Leiter traced his descent to James van Leiter, a Dutch Calvinist who emigrated from Amsterdam to Baltimore in 1760. Levi, born in Maryland in 1834, sought his fortune in Chicago. With Marshall Field, a fellow clerk in the firm of dry goods merchants where he worked, he built up his own prosperous business from which he retired in 1881 to deal in real estate.

'It is huge and smoky and absorbed in the worship of Mammon in a grim and melancholy way,' Curzon wrote of Chicago during his first journey round the world in 1887. For the city's recovery from the disastrous fire of 1871, Leiter could claim considerable credit. He invested generously in the work of reconstruction, restored confidence among the insurance companies, helped to found an art gallery and a public library – and incidentally amassed a fortune of at least thirty million dollars.

It would have been more had he not been obliged to come to the aid of his son Joseph, who in 1897–8 tried to corner the market in wheat. Mary's brother was almost as astute as their father, but not even his fist could contain all the grain that commercial rivals poured on to the market to break his near monopoly. He had two strokes of bad luck. The war between the United States and Spain deterred European dealers from bidding for Chicago wheat in case their shipments were seized by the Spanish navy; and the harvest of 1898 was particularly abundant. The price of wheat plummeted, Joe was left with fifty million bushels on his hands and his father had to bail him out to the tune of ten million dollars.

Mrs Leiter was altogether less formidable, and established a name for herself in Washington society as much for her good nature as for her endearing malapropisms. 'At last I am back on terracotta,' she exclaimed on landing in New York after a stormy transatlantic crossing. And a fearless but uncertain command of French once led her, after Mary had scored a triumph at a fancy-dress ball, to hope that her daughter might be painted *en-sainte*. Perhaps, like her future son-in-law, she enjoyed living up to her public reputation. It was surely in a spirit of irony that, on hearing of a plan to erect a public lavatory near the family house on Dupont Circle in Washington, she wrote to President Cleveland suggesting that such an amenity ought more fittingly to be placed on P Street.

Curzon cannot have been unaware for long that the girl he met in a London ballroom in 1890 was a well-endowed heiress. But he was not a fortune hunter; nor was Mary Leiter's money her only passport to the houses of an English upper class whose predatory instincts were still nicely balanced by a costive social reserve. 'People discuss my looks as though I were an oleograph,' she once complained. That was not surprising: the oval of her face, Margot Asquith said, was almost as perfect as that of the Princess of Wales. She was tall and dark, with violet eyes and a slow smile of affecting radiance.

Intellectually, too, she could hold her own with the Souls. She had an alert mind and kept herself abreast of politics and international affairs. She was an enthusiastic pilgrim to the Wagner festival at Bayreuth. She read widely and displayed a gratifying taste for the works of George Nathaniel Curzon that survived even the author's warning of the role she might one day be required to play – 'amanuensis to a professional scribbler, drudge to a political pamphleteer'. Her farewell present before returning to Washington that first summer was a pocket edition of Horace's *Odes*. Curzon was enchanted. '*O fortes pejoramque passi, cras ingens iterabimus aequor*,' he replied. 'Brave hearts who have vanquished greater toils, tomorrow we put out again upon the mighty deep.' It was an appropriate but bowdlerized version of Horace. Curzon omitted the words, '*Nunc vino pellite curas*' – 'now banish care with wine'.

She spoke French better than her suitor, whose residence in the house of a Paris apothecary between Eton and Oxford did not succeed in eradicating an English accent. 'I want you to teach me French well,' he told Mary. 'If ever I am Foreign Minister I must be more supple and fluent than I am.' Alas, when eventually he did become Foreign Secretary, he had to serve under a Prime Minister who confessed that the only French he himself could understand was the Northumbrian variety spoken by Sir Edward Grey.

Between 1890 and 1895, Curzon saw Mary infrequently, but continued to write regularly to her from whichever mountain or desert or ocean he happened to be crossing. They were affectionate letters, but overlaid by a tone of badinage that concealed any intention he may have had of making her his wife. Thus from Saigon, during his second journey round the world: 'We are both getting old. I struck 34 three days ago, and you must be 23 or 24, I think. Are we more wise? I retain an unconquerable frivolity which, after being repressed during these six months of travel, will need some early outlet.'

Poor Mary, beset by other suitors, must have wondered whether there would ever be an end to Curzon's unconquerable frivolity. But her love for him stilled her doubts, and on 3 March 1893, they were reunited after a separation of nearly two years. Curzon was pausing for a single day in Paris on his way home from the East, and dined with the Leiter family at the Hotel Vendôme. Later that evening, alone with Mary in the private sitting room, he spoke the words for which she had waited so anxiously and so long. He asked her whether she would marry him – but not just yet, he added, in a year or two's time.

Curzon's conduct was not quite as heartless as it seems. He explained to Mary that in spite of knowing from the outset that they were destined for each other, he had not dared to propose marriage until he had accomplished his ambitious programme of Oriental travel and scholarship. Central Asia and India, Persia and Indo-China now lay behind him, and he asked Mary to be patient until he had visited the Pamir mountains and Afghanistan. In the meantime, their engagement was to remain secret, even from Lord Scarsdale and from Mr and Mrs Leiter.

'You were very sweet last night, Mary,' he wrote to her on the following day, 'and I do not think I deserved such consideration. While I ask you, and while you consent to wait, you must trust me, Mary, wholly, even as I trust you, and all will be right in the end. I will not breathe a word to a human soul. And since that is the line we take, it will be well that I should not write too frequently for fear of exciting suspicions. You need not fear that I shall not think of you, and rely upon your fidelity as upon a rock. You will let me hear how you are going on, Mary, won't you, and sometimes, if you are down in your luck, you will remember that my kiss of love has rested upon your lips. God bless you, my darling child.'

Their secret was well kept. A few weeks later Dr Jowett facetiously asked Curzon when he intended to exchange All Souls for one body.

With inspiring devotion, Mary remained faithful to her pledge for two more weary years. 'I like to think of you,' the fortunate Curzon wrote to her in the autumn of 1893. 'It is tranquillizing. I have often said that when engaged, if ever, I should frequently long to be out of the thing and should curse instead of hugging my chains. Not for one second have I had such a feeling. No, the fact that you have given yourself to me is a source of great pride and most serene happiness. I am spared all the anxiety of what is called a great courtship, and I have merely, when the hour strikes, to enter into possession of my own.'

If these sentiments ring a little callously, there is no evidence that Mary accepted them other than in a spirit of humble gratitude. Curzon nevertheless could display a more romantic style when he chose. 'Your loving letter received,' he wrote in 1894. 'Blessings for it. It contains one mistake only. You speak of *a* loving kiss. Why the singular number? Surely that would be criminal. I positively cannot let you off with one. There will be a number, a crowd, a bewildering sequence, an ardent succession, an ecstatic pell-mell.'

That summer he left for the Pamirs, the last formidable obstacle that stood between the betrothed pair and their marriage. Mary assured him that should he die on his travels, she would marry nobody else, but retire to a sisterhood. She nevertheless urged him to take no unnecessary risks, sensibly adding that it was better to dwell under a modest roof in England than perish on the roof of the world.

But even after his safe return to England in January 1895, little shadows continued to fall across the path of true love. Although he had just entered his thirty-seventh year, Curzon dreaded the ordeal of telling Lord Scarsdale that he wished to marry the daughter of an American dealer in real estate called Levi Z. Leiter. His anxiety, however, was misplaced. 'Blessed Mary,' he wrote to her on 5 February, 'I have been home and told my father. I had to make none of the apologies or explanations or defences that you imagined. He said: "So long as you love her and she loves you – that is all. You are not likely to make a mistake at your age, and she is old enough to know her own mind."' Mary's parents, too, raised no objection to the match, and Mr Leiter showed his approval by providing his daughter with a marriage settlement of 700,000 dollars. He also guaranteed an income of £6,000 a year to his prospective son-in-law of modest means.

At the end of February, just before the announcement of their engagement, Mary was disturbed to hear that Curzon had once more collapsed from spinal weakness, a reaction from which he nearly always suffered on returning from an exhausting foreign journey. With habitual resilience, however, he was soon on his feet once more.

Finally, there was the intervention of Cecil Spring Rice, who had often been entertained by the Leiter family during his first diplomatic post in Washington, and whose return there in 1893 allowed him more opportunity than Curzon for pressing his attentions on Mary. When she made it clear to him that her heart lay elsewhere, he betrayed disobliging confidences about her fiancé's cavalier ways with other women. Much troubled, Mary at once wrote to Curzon for an explanation. He had no difficulty in reassuring her of his own fidelity and in convincing her that Spring Rice's unkind gossip sprang from jealousy. Nor did he allow the episode to interrupt one of his oldest friendships. Curzon intended no irony when he wrote to Spring

Rice a few days after his engagement to Mary had been made public: 'I know that no one will rejoice with me more heartily over my good fortune than yourself.' He invited him to be an usher at the ceremony, apologizing that the duty of best man had already been claimed by Lord Lamington. And a few days after the wedding he left Spring Rice in no doubt of the welcome he would receive in the Curzon family circle: 'I am glad to know that you think I comported myself with credit in the international complications of last Monday and I need hardly say that when you come back to England you will be welcome at our home.'

So well had George and Mary kept their secret that the news of their betrothal on 2 March 1895 was received by other friends with amazement. 'It was clever of you and extremely characteristic to get engaged to Miss Leiter at Washington from the top of the Pamirs,' Lord Pembroke wrote to Curzon. 'You must tell me how it was done.' And Margot Asquith epitomized the delight of all Curzon's friends in a letter of exuberant congratulation:

Very Dear George,

I am as you know very genuine in my affections & you are among those I love best & count upon most. Your letter & news is a true joy to me. I have always cared for Mary; she has been sweetness itself to me & I think her a lovely sunny companion.

You are *so* right in what you are going to do. More than anyone *I* know, & have known, the difficulties of marrying – the courage & imagination that is wanted, & even in some ways nobility & steadfastness. I was not very well equipped for an undertaking that required these virtues but I can assure you I have been more than repaid & assisted by the love I have found & I think you – who have so much that is fine, loyal & warm in yr. character – will find yourself both better & happier for sharing your life and love with Mary Leiter. She is very beautiful & a great dear & I feel perfect confidence in your future.

Yes, you & I have as you say shared a great many things in life – great moments of joy & sorrow & death and perplexity. You must let no new tie lessen the old ones: & among all those who wish you happiness no one wishes it from a fuller heart than yr. dear & yr. friend.

Margie

Temporarily released by the Easter recess from attendance at Westminster, Curzon sailed for New York on 10 April and was married at St John's Church, Washington, twelve days later. Among the leaders of American society and politics, one alone seemed to be absent: the President of the United States was by custom debarred from attending private occasions. But Mrs Grover Cleveland was there, and sent the bride and bridegroom a silver loving cup from herself and her husband.

A complete list of wedding presents could – and ultimately did – fill a book. Mary alone received a thousand from her American friends and acquaintances, and Curzon did hardly less well in England. A dozen or so of his intimates subscribed towards a huge silver-gilt centre-piece. They included Arthur Balfour, George Wyndham, Alfred Lyttelton, St John Brodrick, George Leveson Gower, Wallace Lamington, Willie Grenfell, Godfrey Webb, Tommy Ribblesdale and Jim Cranborne. Oscar Browning sent an old English silver box, Welldon a pair of silver candlesticks, Rennell Rodd some gold and turquoise cuff-links. Cecil Spring Rice made reparation with a carved rosewood Chinese cabinet. W. H. Hutton, whom Curzon beat for the Arnold Prize, sent a silver sugar basin, Bob Raper a silver cream jug, and Sir William Anson, Warden of All Souls, two silver ale cups. From Augustus Hare came *The Story of Two Noble Lives* and a water-colour drawing; from Speaker Peel, a portrait of himself by Violet Granby; from Mr G. W. E. Russell, MP, *The Life of Mr Gladstone.* The name of only one old friend was missing from the list. Oscar Wilde had been arrested on 5 April, and in the following month was sentenced to two years' hard labour.

Few greetings can have given the bridegroom more pleasure than the letter he received from the Amir of Afghanistan, to whom he had sent a photograph of Mary:

> I pray God will keep you (my own wise friend) successful in all the desires of this life.
>
> I also congratulate you, my honest friend, that though you have only married one wife she is competent.
>
> From my knowledge of Phrenology she is very wise and a well-wisher of yours and better than 1,000 men.
>
> I hope it may be God's wish, my dear friend, that you will be happy and satisfied with her always. Thanks to the Almighty you have been fortunate enough to meet with such a wife, that in the whole of England there are but a few. Faithfulness, wisdom and honesty, all these I gather from her photo and according to Phrenology. May God bless you with a goodly offspring.
>
> If she should at any time thrash you I am certain you will have done something to deserve it. I am your sincere friend and well-wisher
>
> Abdur Rahman, Amir of Afghanistan.

Later that summer, Curzon was again reminded of his Oriental travels when bidden to Lord Salisbury's garden party in honour of Li Hung Chang, the Chinese statesman whom he had visited at Tientsin in 1892. While they were being photographed on the terrace at Hatfield, Li Hung Chang asked him how old he was. Curzon replied that he was thirty-six. 'Dear me,' Li Hung Chang said, 'exactly the same age as the German Emperor.' Curzon acknowledged the impeachment. The conversation continued:

Li Hung Chang: 'The German Emperor, however, has six sons. How many have you?'

Curzon: 'I have only recently been married, and I regret that so far I have none.'

Li Hung Chang: 'Then what have you been doing all this time?'

Curzon afterwards admitted that neither then nor subsequently could he find an appropriate answer.

A few weeks before his marriage, Curzon dined one night with Henry Lucy. The other guests included Arthur Balfour and Pearl Craigie, the novelist better known by her pseudonym of John Oliver Hobbes. She afterwards told her host: 'I thought Mr Balfour charming, but he does not convince me. Curzon may have less tact, but I swear he has more ability. What he knows he knows thoroughly; and his judgment in State affairs is astute to the last degree. When he is merrier and happier, and in a comfortable home, we shall see what we shall see! He has not had much of an opportunity yet.'

Through the generosity of his father-in-law, Curzon soon acquired the comfort – although not always the mirth and happiness – by which Mrs Craigie set such store. From bachelor lodgings in St Ermin's Mansions, Westminster, he moved temporarily with his wife into No. 5 Carlton House Terrace. Later that year they took a lease of No. 4 Carlton Gardens from Balfour, the new First Lord of the Treasury, whom Lord Salisbury allowed to live at No. 10 Downing Street. It was a tall, handsome house in the Nash terrace overlooking St James's Park, less than half a mile away from the Commons and even closer to the Foreign Office – the twin treadmills on which for the next three years he spent his working hours as a junior Minister in Lord Salisbury's third Government.

At once he took control of nearly all those domestic arrangements which a Victorian paterfamilias would usually leave to his wife. He was acutely sensitive to his surroundings. 'I have put the clock on a pink velvet bracket over the mantelpiece,' he told his mother during his first weeks at Eton. More than twenty years later it was he, not Mary, who decided exactly how the new house should be decorated and furnished, even to the precise shade of paint to be applied to the walls of the outer hall. He immersed himself, too, in the minutiae of household accounts: from childhood to the end of his days, he believed himself a martyr to the sloth, stupidity and greed of the shop-keeping class. 'Of course,' he wrote, 'that simple Swear *hasn't* sent my shirts as he said he would on Monday: they haven't arrived yet: and that silly idiotic little Mills sent my waistcoat but never altered it a bit so that it is just as bad as ever, and unwearable.' He was then thirteen.

At Carlton Gardens, he relieved Mary of the ordeal of engaging servants; only after they had survived his penetrating catechism was she permitted to inspect them herself. In spite of this preliminary ordeal, or perhaps because of it, few servants measured up to his own exacting standards. As an Oxford undergraduate he rebuked his scout, or college bedmaker, so severely for supposedly having cracked a teapot that the matter was carried before the Master of Balliol himself for judgement. And he angered Margot Tennant when staying with her at the Glen by wrongly accusing a footman of theft and refusing to apologize.

His Spartan upbringing never allowed him to depend overmuch on servants in an age that had not yet begun to regard them as a luxury. Not until 1886, when he was twenty-seven, did he feel that he could afford a valet. His subsequent experiences were disastrous. 'I seem to be the sort of leper whom no valet will serve,' he once wrote from his London house, 'so thought of going into hotel or lodgings.' Pain and overwork increasingly eroded what little patience he could command, and to the end of his life he would squander his limited reserves of strength on menial tasks best left to others. He filed his papers, packed his trunks, posted his letters, dusted his china, fastened pieces of cork on the backs of his chairs to prevent them from scraping the walls, took down and put back books from the highest shelves of his library.

'As the park keeper would not take the weed off the water,' he wrote from Kedleston after his father's death, 'nor keep the boat-house clean, nor keep the grass cut in front of it, I went into Derby myself and bought a scythe, a pair of clippers, a rake and a broom. Now he has no excuse.'

During his last years, he once told his second wife at a moment of political crisis: 'I look more like a butler out of a place than ever, and am sure that when we are turned out I can easily get a good situation.' Behind the irony lay much practical sense; no butler was ever such a master of the household as Curzon himself. Edgar D'Abernon described his friend's inspired gift in these words: 'Every item was thought out, every arrangement for comfort and convenience was elaborately drawn up and written down, not by proxy, but by the host himself; no detail was too paltry for his meticulous care, and neither wife nor secretary was allowed to mar or to dilute the majestic virility of the entertainment.' One guest at a dinner party in Calcutta noticed that the Viceroy himself had written out all the name-cards. Another, on a visit to the country, came on her host putting soap and towels in her room; later he showed her, inscribed in his own hand, the menu for every meal to be served in the housekeeper's room and in the servants' hall for the next fortnight.

At only one period of his life did Curzon's belief in the virtues of self-help prove indispensable: during his long journeys of exploration. Travelling through Persia, he cooked his own dinner every night and could dilate with authority on the merits of different provisions. Ever afterwards he found it difficult to adjust himself to the fanciful creations of professional cooks. Although not a greedy man, he was fastidious in his tastes – a relic, no doubt, of the unremitting tapioca dispensed by Miss Paraman. Yet he never seemed able to find a chef who did not attempt to drown him 'in elaborate and costly slushes with incomprehensible names'. The theme of discontent swelled with the years – 'At every meal since you left,' he told his second wife, 'I have swallowed (or refused to swallow) the horrid little mould of jelly or yellow blancmange with a bisected apricot or pear swimming at its base.' Again: 'The chef gets worse daily and I will give him notice before the end of the week. He has given me one ice three times in five days and a second, twice in two. Chicken five days running.' And yet again: 'The kitchen maid gives me everything that I detest and on this chill horrible day proposed mayonnaise of lobster and cold rabbit pie for lunch.'

The cuisine offended his lifelong sense of thrift, too. 'The household bills for June and July only which I have just been called upon to pay,' he complained, 'amounted without wages to £2,150! Of course we cannot go on at this rate. I think this chef is more expensive than the last. In one week he had £16 17*s.* 6*d.* of cream from London in addition to what comes from Kedleston. However I will not bore you with these repulsive details.' But he could not resist recording a mournful little tale of kitchen life at Kedleston: 'I have just tried to have some tea before starting and found only hot water and no tea leaves in the pot!'

Not even Edward VII was spared Curzon's gastronomic lament. 'Today is an important day in our calendar,' the Viceroy wrote to the King-Emperor on 2 September 1903, 'for after living on nothing but hard mutton, occasional beef, eternal turkey and indigestible pea-fowl for eight months, we suddenly plunge into the comparative luxury of tasteless hill-partridge and skinny pheasant.'

Working late through the night on his official papers, Curzon fell into the habit of supplementing the unpalatable fare dished up by his servants with a private hoard of chocolate or crystallized fruits. His secretaries always knew when he had been holding a solitary midnight feast: as they unpacked his red boxes the next morning, their desks would be sprinkled with flakes of sugar and fragments of silver paper.

Perhaps it was whispered from servants' hall to servants' hall that Curzon was a difficult employer, for those he engaged rarely stayed with him long. He was particularly tormented by the sins of his footmen. They got drunk or had bad breath or slept with the housemaids or used his private lavatory or gave notice on his wife's coroneted paper. 'How miserable,' he sighed, 'but how troublesome are these petty domestic details which make a burden of our lives.' And again: 'Our so called working classes are rotting at the core; and it is the upper classes and the older generation of working men who alone set the tone.' Even when they were industrious they broke things – a beautiful mirror and a Blue John vase once went in a single week at Kedleston – or turned his possessions upside down. 'During my brief absence,' he complained, 'that d—d fool Alice has routed out the whole of my room. Transposed all boxes and papers, shifted the books in the big bookshelf, so that I have got 1 to 2 hours work in putting it all back. The woman ought to be in Bedlam.'

Inevitably, they became sullen through fear or nervousness. Curzon addressed servants, a friend recalled, in language that would not have disgraced an oration by Cicero before the Roman Senate, and occasionally called them not by name but by the title of their station. 'Housemaid,' he would say, 'throw wide the casement', or 'Footman, add fuel to the flame'. Some servants, from a sense of loyalty, or perhaps pity, endured his irritable temper and scathing rebukes longer than others. There was once a butler who, having served Curzon for years, at last decided to leave and was asked whether he could recommend a successor. 'There are,' he replied, 'only two people who could take my place. One is Jesus Christ. I am the other.'

Curzon's marriage coincided with the first flourishing of the week-end habit. It was on a spring evening of 1895, readers of Sir Max Beerbohm's work will recall, that the Duchess of Hertfordshire asked Mr Maltby, the fashionable novelist, whether he was by any chance free on Saturday week. If so, he was to come to Keeb by the 3.30. It was only an hour and a quarter from Victoria, and there were always compartments reserved on a Saturday.

The custom of deserting London for a regular Saturday-to-Monday was recent and the word 'week-end' even more so, not appearing in *The Times* until 1892. As late as 1896 the Law Courts still sat on Saturday, regular Cabinet meetings were held at eleven o'clock in the morning, and even the gilded young clerks of the Foreign Office remained on duty. During the session 1893–4, Parliament met on four Saturdays. It was also a day for important diplomatic and political dinner parties.

The week-end received its strongest impetus from the restlessness of the Prince of Wales and his circle, leaders of the social if not the official world. By the middle of the 1890s it had become a recognized form of entertainment of the governing class, appreciated as much by the more sophisticated Souls as by the Marlborough House set. For years Curzon had enjoyed shooting parties at the houses of his friends without being able to return hospitality on the same magnificent scale. With his marriage and the vastly increased income it brought him, he was able for the first time in his life to have a country place of his own.

In the autumn of 1895, he and Mary took a lease of The Priory, Reigate, a spacious Georgian house little more than twenty miles from London, and at once embarked on a series of week-end parties. Max Beerbohm might well have had the visitors' book before him when he wrote of Keeb Hall: 'Statecraft and Diplomacy were well threaded there with mere Lineage and mere Beauty, with Royalty sometimes, with mere Wealth never, with privileged Genius now and then.' The first guests included Violet Granby, later

Duchess of Rutland; Mrs Craigie; Thomas Hardy; Bob Raper; and Henry Adams, the American historian. They were followed by St John and Hilda Brodrick, Jim and Alice Cranborne, Loulu Harcourt, Henry and Margot Asquith, Willie and Etty Grenfell, Edgar and Helen Vincent, Harry and Daisy White, Tommy and Charty Ribblesdale, Alfred and D.D.Lyttelton, Evan Charteris, Alfred Lyall and Richard Haldane.

No member of the Royal family adorned a week-end at The Priory, but George and Mary Curzon were invited that autumn to stay at Sandringham with the Prince and Princess of Wales, the other guests being Lord Rosebery, Arthur Balfour and Mr and Mrs Joseph Chamberlain. And in the following year they were commanded to dine and sleep at Windsor. The Queen wrote in her journal: 'Mrs Curzon, who is an American from Washington, is very handsome and ladylike. ... Had some long conversation also with Mr Curzon, who is clever and agreeable.'

During the summer of 1896 they took Inverlochy Castle, in Scotland, for the grouse-shooting. But for Curzon, holidays meant no more than a change of scene. By the time he set off with his guests for the butts soon after nine o'clock in the morning, he had already done several hours' work on papers sent up by the Foreign Office: and after dinner he would resume his labour. Not until within weeks of his death did he ever confess to a moment of idleness. 'I am doing no work for the first time in my life,' he wrote on 22 January 1925 from the South of France, 'having brought none to do!' Yet within a day or two he was immersed in compiling the index of his *British Government in India.*

In 1897 he again took a Scottish estate, Beldorney Castle, Aberdeenshire, and invited his father to come up for a week or two of his favourite shooting. One day Curzon drove over to call on Mr Gladstone, whom he had treated with reverent courtesy ever since the celebrated visit to the Eton Literary Society. He had for instance written to tell the G.O.M. of his forthcoming marriage in 1895. 'May I add,' he ended his letter, 'with what friendly admiration all your old Parliamentary friends and opponents alike regard the recovered vigour and health of what is indeed a magnificent old age.' Now, two years later, he saw him for the last time and wrote to tell his wife of the encounter. He found Gladstone 'immensely old and much bent. ... He talked, however, with perfectly clear and resonant voice; descanted upon the size of Aberdeenshire men's heads, upon the inability of Jew or Greek to compete in business with the canny Scotsman, upon the national characteristics of Bulgarians and Armenians, upon questions in the House of Commons, upon the merits of the station hotel at Perth, upon Scotch air, upon the health of Arabi Pasha, and upon the code of honour of John Bright. ... He wished me all success in fishing; but betrayed not the faintest interest in my public life or career.'

He died in the following year at the age of eighty-eight and was buried in Westminster Abbey. At his own request he was laid to rest clad in the scarlet robes of his Oxford doctorate; and among the mourners was the Rt Hon. George Curzon, quondam Fellow of All Souls.

'Matrimony,' Curzon told Cecil Spring Rice during the first year of his marriage, 'is a success so overwhelming that celibacy, once a delight, has now become a puzzle.' There was nevertheless a part of his life on which not even Mary was encouraged to trespass.

Margot Asquith once said that both Curzon's wives were more accomplices than critics, who sustained him by their love but did little for him by their advice. Consuelo Vanderbilt, who was married to the ninth Duke of Marlborough not long after the Curzon wedding, struck the same note. Mary, she observed, was able to subordinate her personality to that of her husband in a way generally considered to be beyond an American woman's power of self-abnegation. Nor was Mary herself in any doubt about the role she was expected to undertake. 'George will do with his career what he chooses,' she told her father, 'and *nothing on earth* can alter his iron will. I have long since realised George's iron will and never crossed it.'

Mary was obliged to make other adjustments in her life. Although she found Lord Scarsdale 'as tender and affectionate as my own father', there was no real cordiality between the two families, and her kinsmen experienced a discouraging lack of warmth during their visits to England. Among the Souls she herself would sometimes admit to a sense of detachment, although not of exclusion. 'I must say,' she once told her husband, 'no more critical set exists in the world than the friends, as they are merciless to anyone who can't keep up in the race for pleasure. In my cynical moments I know in my heart that the great fuss they make of me is because I am a novelty, unjaded, and the last edition of Georgian news.'

As the birth of her first child approached, she travelled up to London from The Priory in a horse-drawn carriage that Fred Streeter, then beginning his distinguished career as a gardener, had transformed almost literally into a bed of white roses. Irene, born on 20 January 1896, devoted much of her life to charitable and religious causes, and had a profound love of music. On the death of her father in 1925 she inherited the Barony of Ravensdale by special remainder and in 1958 became one of the first women to sit in the House of Lord as a Life Peeress. She died, unmarried, in 1966. In later years she would recall with gratitude the golden memories of her childhood and contrast them with the severity and punishment suffered by her father at the hands of Miss Paraman.

Mary bore her husband two other daughters but, to their sorrow, no son. One was Cynthia, born in 1898. She married Sir Oswald Mosley, the stormy petrel of British politics between the wars, and died in 1933. The other was Alexandra, who in 1925 married Major E. D. Metcalfe, equerry to the future King Edward VIII, now Duke of Windsor. As intrepid a traveller as her father, she has also occupied herself increasingly with charitable work, particularly on behalf of children.

It was of course Curzon himself and not his wife who engaged nurses and governesses for the children. After interviewing a candidate before the family left for India in 1898, he sent Mary a report that covered nine closely written sheets and displayed a singular power of observation:

> She is not the least like her photographs ... is ladylike, yet not quite a lady; neatly dressed, shows acres of gum and files of artificial teeth; has a rather curious way of rolling her lips when she speaks and an utterance very clear and precise and sometimes almost mincing in its accuracy. She is not in the least like a nurse, but exactly like an indigent lady placed in charge of children with a scientific and practical knowledge in which indigent persons are usually deficient. ...

The Viceroy-designate went on to discuss with his wife, in a wealth of detail, whether or not the nurse might be permitted to bring her bicycle with her.

Mary accepted such infringements of a mother's prerogative with calm and sometimes amused good humour. Much less was she tempted to resist her husband's political beliefs: but that did not prevent her from annexing them to her own creed with a fierce partisanship that surpassed conventional loyalty. Occasionally she fanned his innate ambitions too vigorously and aroused suspicions that were better left to slumber. When he was Parliamentary Under-Secretary at the Foreign Office she suggested to him that the Government was jealous of his ability and that Arthur Balfour 'placed stumbling blocks to prevent your prominence in the House'. During his years as Viceroy, too, she passed on the stray opinions of others that he was sacrificing a more fruitful career at home. 'Great as your work is in India,' she told him, 'there will be even bigger in England, where the party is slipping down the hill of indifference and incapacity.'

Save for these moments of restlessness, she brought him only joy and understanding. 'I am so proud when I see you run after, admired and adored,' he told her. 'What woman in London combines great beauty with exceptional intelligence, as well as a tact which is an inspiration?' In his eyes she was perfection itself. 'For me,' he told his friends, 'the American flag is all stars and no stripes.'

Chapter Twenty-one

FOREIGN OFFICE

> I have to thank you most earnestly for the unremitting labour and brilliant ability with which you have conducted the business of the Foreign Office in critical times – and have defended it with so much success in Parliament.
>
> – *Lord Salisbury to Curzon, 24 June 1898*

Accompanied by his bride and a thousand wedding presents, Curzon returned to England in May 1895, and impatiently awaited the end of the Liberal Government. It had already begun to disintegrate, little more than a year after Mr Gladstone's retirement in favour of Lord Rosebery. There was open dissension in the Cabinet, a falling majority in the Commons and a noticeable dwindling of confidence in the country. The Prime Minister, moreover, was suffering from the torture of prolonged insomnia and in no state of health to revive his party.

Characteristically, Rosebery allowed none of these misfortunes to deter him from giving many of his last hours in office to a minor but covetable little piece of patronage. The post of Secretary to Her Majesty's Office of Works had recently fallen vacant. It was a permanent, not a political appointment, and carried responsibility for the maintenance of public buildings, Royal parks and palaces, as well as a stipend of £1,500 a year. Two candidates, each an old friend of Curzon, solicited the Prime Minister for the vacancy. One was the penurious George Leveson Gower, who wanted to exchange his Liberal seat in the Commons for a paid occupation. The other was Reggy Brett, who did not suffer from the same acute financial worries, but who had lost his Liberal seat ten years before and often felt that he had missed his vocation by not going into the Civil Service.

Rosebery invited Leveson Gower to lunch at the Durdans, his house near Epsom, and told him that if he intended to marry in the near future, he could have the post: otherwise it would go to Brett. Leveson Gower was obliged to admit that he had no immediate matrimonial plans. On 4 June, therefore, the Prime Minister who by his own wish was to die to the strains of the Eton Boating Song appointed another pupil of William Cory to be Secretary to the Office of Works. And Leveson Gower, whose attachment to his schooldays was less fervent, had to wait thirteen years for the consolatory appointment of Commissioner of Woods and Forests.

Brett received his appointment just in time. On 21 June, the Liberal Government was defeated in the House of Commons. The architect of their doom was, somewhat surprisingly, St John Brodrick. As the Opposition expert on Army affairs, he had engineered a snap vote on the failure of the Secretary of State for War, Sir Henry Campbell-Bannerman, to maintain adequate stocks of ammunition. The Liberals, deserted by their own military following, found themselves in a minority of seven. Too demoralized to try to have the vote rescinded at the first available opportunity, the Cabinet determined to resign and Lord Salisbury became Prime Minister for the third time.

After ten years of uncommitted goodwill, the Liberal Unionists agreed to join his administration. Lord Hartington, who in 1891 had succeeded his father as Duke of Devonshire, refused the offer of the Foreign Office but accepted the less onerous post of Lord President of the Council; and Joseph Chamberlain became Secretary of State for the Colonies. Thus strengthened in forming his Government, Salisbury set about filling the lesser offices. On 27 June he wrote to Curzon:

> I have accepted the Foreign Office somewhat against my will. I had much rather that Devonshire had taken it. But he would not do so. And now having to undertake it at a time when much difficulty seems to impend, I am naturally trying to secure the best assistance that I can. Therefore I venture to turn to you. You are more familiar with Eastern questions than any man on our side, and your ability and position in the House of Commons will enable you to fight a good battle for us if our policy is attacked in the House. I hope, therefore, that you will not refuse to accept the Under Secretaryship of Foreign Affairs.

There was much to recommend instant compliance with Lord Salisbury's wishes. Curzon would now have sole responsibility for explaining and defending British foreign policy in the House of Commons; and, since Salisbury was again to assume the double burden of Prime Minister and Foreign Secretary, the new Under-Secretary could expect less supervision than most occupants of the office. He would, moreover, be working in close cooperation with a chief whose mind he had come to know and to admire during his apprenticeship as assistant private secretary ten years before.

Yet he had doubts. At the age of thirty-six he was now being asked to accept a place for which many had thought him outstandingly qualified in 1891. And in the meantime he had more than acquitted himself as Under-Secretary for India; published authoritative works on Persia and the Far East; discovered the source of the Oxus river; and parleyed on equal terms with the Amir of Afghanistan.

On 28 June he replied to Lord Salisbury's letter. Although he agreed to become Under-Secretary for Foreign Affairs, he felt entitled to draw the Prime Minister's attention to a personal difficulty:

> The Press and my friends had, rashly enough, formed even higher expectations of my probable employment. These expectations I had myself neither shared nor authorised. But their constant repetition will, I am afraid, lead many to assume that I must be disappointed, after the hard work of the past three years.

To assuage any embarrassment that might be felt, particularly in his constituency, he therefore asked Salisbury to nominate him for membership of the Privy Council, a distinction generally reserved for senior Ministers. The Prime Minister replied the same day, telling Curzon that he had already anticipated his request and adding that he was the youngest politician within living memory to receive the honour.

Within twenty-four hours Curzon was at Windsor to be sworn of the Privy Council in the presence of the Queen. The Duke of Devonshire's hands, he noticed, trembled so violently as he read out the list, that he almost dropped the sheet of paper. It is only fair to the memory of the Duke to record that, far from being intimidated by court etiquette, he had been known to display an unprecedented independence of character. Dining one night with his Sovereign, he was enjoying a saddle of four-year-old mutton, a speciality of the Windsor kitchens. But he had forgotten that as soon as the Queen had finished her own plate, it was the custom of the footmen to remove those of her guests. Pausing in the middle of his conversation, the Duke realized that his barely touched dinner had vanished. 'Here,' he said sharply, 'bring that back.'

The general election of July 1895 which confirmed the new Government in office with a majority of 152 seats once more returned Curzon as Member for Southport. This time he had a new Liberal opponent. Sir Herbert Naylor-Leyland's rise to eminence had been swifter than Curzon's but less orthodox. A Welsh land-owner who had served briefly in the 2nd Life Guards, he sat as Unionist MP for Colchester from 1892 until February 1895, when he unexpectedly resigned his seat and announced his sudden conversion to Liberalism. A few months later Lord Rosebery had him created a baronet, a remarkable measure of confidence in a man of thirty-one whose only claim to advancement was an abrupt change of political faith. Naylor-Leyland's precocious ennoblement, however, failed to dazzle the electors of Southport, who sent Curzon back to Westminster with an increased majority.

'Lunched with George Curzon at 5, Carlton House Terrace, which he has rented,' Wilfrid Blunt wrote in his diary on 15 August. 'He talked of things political, and of his own new position in the Government as Under-Secretary for Foreign Affairs. He prefers this to a minor place without power in the Cabinet.' Yet power was precisely what Curzon lacked at the Foreign Office. The task of the Under-Secretary was to expound in the House of Commons the policy determined by a Secretary of State, who from 1868 to 1905 was invariably a member of the House of Lords. In no way was it to be a deputy Secretary of State charged with relieving him of his responsibility for the conduct of foreign affairs.

Sir Henry Lucy, with his vast experience of parliamentary life, observed that when a strong and capable statesman such as Salisbury controlled the threads both of government and of foreign policy from his place in the House of Lords, he needed no more than the equivalent of a telephone in the House of Commons. It was a fate which some occupants of the office resented. St John Brodrick, for instance, who succeeded Curzon as Under-Secretary in 1898, wrote crossly to him a year later: 'Instead of the Parliamentary Under-Secretary being, as at the War Office, the pivot of the machine next to the Secretary of State, at the Foreign Office he is in most respects a *quantité négligeable*. I have rebelled, but quietly trusting to get some influence without a row.'

Curzon, too, came to resent his secondary role. He saw the most important of the telegrams and despatches, but was not asked to comment on, much less permitted to direct, the course of foreign policy. He could make fine orations in the House of Commons, but only within the limits laid down by the Secretary of State. He could impart his extensive knowledge of the East, but without any guarantee that his views would be acted upon or even considered. He was the representative and spokesman of the Cabinet, although hardly ever allowed to share or to influence its deliberations.

Curzon lacked the humility of his immediate predecessor at the Foreign Office, Sir Edward Grey, who commended the experience of a Parliamentary Under-Secretary for its intellectual discipline:

> He undergoes steady training in industry and despatch; he learns how to brace his mind to plough through the stiffest and least attractive material, to break up the most intractable clod; his memory is practised in storing things in an orderly way in his head so that each is out of the way when not wanted, and yet can be found at once when required. The habit of arriving at facile conclusions is checked; for he is brought in contact with limitations and difficulties, which are encountered inside a public office and were not apparent when he was outside; he finds the use of his own qualities, he is made aware of the inconvenience, perhaps the danger, of his defects.

What, Curzon might have enquired, did Grey suppose him to have been doing for the past decade except educate himself in precisely those ways? Had he not gathered and sifted and collated huge masses of material about Central Asia and Persia and the Far East, transmuting each into what was not only an historical chronicle and a geographical survey, but also a handbook of British foreign policy? Was he not on amicable, even intimate terms with the principal rulers of the East? Must the office of the Parliamentary Under-Secretary confine him so rigidly to the alphabet of statecraft?

But in his servitude he was at least spared the restrictions which in 1886 Queen Victoria had urged Lord Rosebery, the new Foreign Secretary, to impose upon his Parliamentary Under-Secretary, James Bryce. Doubtful whether the author of *The Holy Roman Empire* had a sufficient grasp of modern political realities, she made Rosebery promise that Bryce would write down every word of any statement he intended to make in the Commons and that he should be forbidden to depart from the approved text.

Neither the temperament of Lord Salisbury nor the cumbersome routine of the Foreign Office encouraged Curzon to depart from the traditionally subservient role of a Parliamentary Under-Secretary.

Salisbury had become Foreign Secretary for the first time in 1878, shortly before he accompanied Disraeli to the Congress of Berlin. With such a span of experience at his command he did not care for the officials of the Foreign Office to offer advice except on the rare occasions he requested it. He preferred to avoid discussion of any subject on which his opinion was undecided, finding that the intrusion of other men's thoughts was not only unhelpful but positively confusing. And once he had made up his mind, argument would at best make no impression on him, at worst rouse him to antagonism.

Sir Thomas Sanderson, the Permanent Under-Secretary, or senior official, recognized this. He differed from his successors in the office by regarding himself primarily as an administrator charged with carrying out the instructions of the Foreign Secretary. Salisbury came increasingly to rely on his immense knowledge, his retentive memory and a skill in drafting diplomatic documents based on the pellucid literary style of the Duke of Wellington's despatches; but neither Sanderson nor his master believed that it was the duty of an official to initiate policy.

Even so, the Permanent Under-Secretary occupied a far less subordinate position in the effective hierarchy of the Foreign Office than did the Parliamentary Under-Secretary. When Balfour acted as Foreign Secretary during Salisbury's illness in April 1898, it was Sanderson, not Curzon, whom the *locum tenens* summoned each morning to guide him through the intricacies of international affairs. 'I am now a sort of standing dish at Arthur Balfour's breakfast,' Sanderson wrote. 'When his attention is divided, as it was this morning, between me and a fresh herring there are alternatively moments of distraction while he is concentrating on the herring, and moments of danger when he is concentrating on foreign affairs.'

Known throughout the service as 'Lamps', from the large pair of spectacles that crowned his tall, thin, rather ungainly figure, Sanderson had joined the Foreign Office on leaving Eton in 1859. Although he served abroad only for brief periods, he had acquired much wisdom over the years, particularly as private secretary to successive Foreign Secretaries. His playful humour and genial sarcasm endeared him even to the junior clerks for whom in 1891 he wrote *Observations on the Use and Abuse of Red Tape.* It instructed them to learn 'the sizes of the various islands of the Samoan archipelago and whether the various inhabitants do or do not wear trousers'.

He insisted that all newly joined young men should pay particular attention to their handwriting. In his room he kept a framed minute by Lord Palmerston: 'The greater Portion of the Foreign Hands are excellent and admired by all but there are some few on the Establishment who might improve their Handwriting if they would take more Pains to form their Letters distinctly.' That Sanderson should continue to attach importance to calligraphy thirty years after Palmerston's death was no personal whim. The first lady typist was not introduced into the Foreign Office until 1889, and the bulk of documents continued to be written by hand for years to come. In March 1896, Curzon complained to Sanderson that copies of his answers to Parliamentary questions did not reach the Press gallery as quickly as journalists wished. 'Arrangements with typewriters begin today,' the Permanent Under-Secretary replied.

Until the early years of the century, the well-educated recruit to either the Foreign Office or the Diplomatic Service spent the first decade of his career immersed in the duties of an office boy. He would copy out despatches, cipher and decipher telegrams, put numbers on papers, and do up diplomatic bags with sealing wax and red tape. When Rennell Rodd sat for the Diplomatic competition, having taken a Second in Greats at Balliol, he came out top in two-thirds of his subjects but was disqualified for bad handwriting and spelling. In the following year he tried again and passed in at the head of the list.

In spite of her failing eyesight, the Queen herself helped to prolong this insistence on a legible hand by declining to read any telegram, despatch or draft – and she received all the most important of them – in typescript. She would scrutinize the handwriting of a Cabinet Minister or a Proconsul with the same attention that Sanderson brought to the script of his clerks. Goose quills of high quality were specially provided for the Foreign Secretary, and Lord Salisbury seems to have met her exacting standards. Curzon, who in early life wrote a clear, neat hand, allowed it to deteriorate under pressure of work, earning a mild rebuke from his Sovereign during his first year as Viceroy.

This Royal insistence on clerkly habits fell harshly on the Minister in Attendance who accompanied the Queen on her summer migration to

Balmoral. The prospect of a refreshing holiday in the Scottish Highlands proved chimerical. Forbidden to transact urgent business by word of mouth, he had to spend a part of each day in his bedroom, laboriously composing submissions on the official papers that arrived regularly from London. When he had finished, he would lock them in despatch boxes, ring for a footman, and have them carried to the Queen's private apartments. The replies would reach him a few hours later by the same cumbrous procedure.

A similar pattern governed the internal routine of the Foreign Office. Although attracted by the technical mysteries of the telephone, Salisbury mistrusted it as a serious instrument of communication. Nor did he care for personal interviews, which could as soon induce drowsiness or irritation as enlightenment. He preferred the written word. He himself was the least verbose of men when he put pen to paper. But others, including his Parliamentary Under-Secretary, invested the most meagre material with an epistolary flourish that did nothing to shorten the working day.

What laid the heaviest burden on Ministers and officials alike was the rising tide of paper that engulfed the Foreign Office throughout the nineteenth century. The number of telegrams and despatches rose from 9,059 in 1825 to 91,433 in 1895. Both Salisbury and Curzon had to read endless boxes of them, one to determine the course of foreign policy, the other to keep himself well enough informed to expound and defend it in the House of Commons. Salisbury also had to carry out the many additional duties of a Prime Minister; and Curzon to vote regularly throughout the evening at Westminster, as well as concern himself with the views of his Lancashire constituency. Each Minister had long been accustomed to work into the early hours of the morning. Salisbury once described his nocturnal regime in a charming letter to the Duchess of Rutland:

> At night, towards 1.30, when my business work is over, there always remains a certain residue of letters from my friends, and the question always arises for decision – shall I go to bed, or shall I write to my friends? And I am ashamed to say – degraded voluptuary that I am – that my fallen nature always decides in favour of going to bed.

A few months later he was laid low by a severe attack of influenza and his condition began to deteriorate. He pulled through, but hardly had the fever left him than he began dictating telegrams from his bed. 'I should much prefer,' his doctor said in despair, 'to be treating a half-starved patient living in the worst slum in London than to be responsible under such conditions.'

Successive occupants of the post of Parliamentary Under-Secretary found their lives no less encumbered. Grey had felt the strain acutely and complained that even in quiet times the interruptions of Parliamentary business made it barely possible for him to keep pace with the work of the Foreign Office. Curzon, who had trained himself from boyhood to toil away through half the night, conceded that the task was almost too much for him and collapsed at a critical moment in his fortunes. Brodrick, who succeeded him in 1898 on his appointment to India, suffered the additional disadvantage of slight deafness. He, too, could scarcely have endured for long had Lord Salisbury not arranged for his duties to be made lighter both at the Foreign Office and in the House of Commons. Few men ever laboured harder for a salary of £1,500 a year and the prestige of Ministerial office.

The permanent officials of the Foreign Office, although spared a politician's nightly attendance at Westminster, were nevertheless slaves of an exacting bureaucratic machine. Its fault lay less in the weight of paperwork it generated than in the uneven, not to say perverse manner in which it distributed its load. At the top of the hierarchy, men of judgement and experience found themselves oppressed, almost overwhelmed, by duties they were powerless to delegate. At the bottom, aspiring young men who had taken a good degree at the university, passed a stiff competitive examination and gone abroad to perfect two or three foreign languages, would find themselves deprived of all initiative.

These junior clerks worried not so much about how they could lead a lively social life on a salary of £100, for many of them had private means, as to how best to keep boredom at bay. They did not begin their mechanical grind of sorting and copying before mid-morning, and only occasionally were unable to dine out on time. They were discouraged, however, from leaving the office for luncheon, although two elegant gourmets used to have it sent in from a restaurant and ate it in the Ambassadors' waiting-room until discovered by a furious Sanderson.

So sybaritic a life was denied to the senior officials. As Permanent Under-Secretary, Sanderson found little leisure for his recreations: playing the flute, writing morality plays for children and following the progress of scientific thought. By the time he reached the Foreign Office at noon he had already done a hard morning's work at home, and would be fortunate not to have to take up his pen again after dinner. Inside the office, his control of the entire administration of British diplomacy was marked by a friendliness, patience and tact only occasionally clouded by irritability.

As well as bold handwriting, Sanderson insisted on certain sartorial standards. He demanded a tall hat and frock coat during the London season, even if the young wearer's only afternoon engagement was a game of stump cricket in the conveniently broad upper passages of the Foreign Office. It pained him to see anyone wearing a tweed suit on duty; and he was much put out when Eyre Crowe, the future Permanent Under-Secretary, whom he had requested not to wear a bowler, turned up next day in the ultimate informality of a straw hat. The lapse was doubtless put down to his having a German mother.

Eric Barrington, for twelve years Lord Salisbury's private secretary at the Foreign Office, exerted an influence that in some ways eclipsed even that of Sanderson. His appointment carried far more weight than its name implied. In addition to the usual duties of dealing with visitors and correspondence, the private secretary was responsible for the promotion and transfer of all but the most senior officials in the Foreign Office; and, except for the appointment of Ambassadors and Ministers to the more important missions, had a significant voice in all diplomatic promotions and postings.

Of the Assistant Under-Secretaries who ranked immediately below Sanderson, the most influential was Francis Bertie, known as 'The Bull'. He had a sharp mind, a caustic tongue and a courage that did not deter him from offering advice even when it was not sought. In fact it was he rather than Sanderson who wrote nearly all the long memoranda on foreign policy during the period. In his lighter moments he would divert his colleagues by demonstrating how high he could kick or how to cut a candle in two with a sword. From 1905 to 1918 he was British Ambassador in Paris, where he tyrannized the idle young men who worked in the chancery of his Embassy. But in Robert Vansittart he met his match. Bertie would plague him with telephone calls before breakfast until Vansittart told his servant to say not that he was out but that he had not yet come in. The persecution ceased.

Curzon also established an agreeable relationship with Schomberg McDonnell. He was not a member of the Foreign Office but for fourteen years acted as Lord Salisbury's private secretary in all matters other than foreign affairs. As Salisbury disliked working at No. 10 Downing Street, Pom McDonnell became a familiar and much-liked figure at the Foreign Office. He showed no trace of that haughty humour which sometimes afflicts the servants of great men. On the contrary, his manner was of a breeziness and volubility that unaccustomed callers often mistook for indiscretion: at the end of an interview, however, they found that their stock of information had not been appreciably augmented. He became a close friend of Curzon, whose years in India were enlivened by long letters of Paphian wit and shrewd political advice.

Curzon's own entourage consisted of a private secretary, Walter Langley, and a parliamentary private secretary, Ian Malcolm. One was a member of the Foreign Office who had successively served Fergusson, Lowther and Grey in the same post and proved himself an experienced guide to the routine of the Parliamentary Under-Secretary's department. The other was a fellow Conservative MP who out of friendship agreed to act as an unpaid parliamentary aide-de-camp. In the eyes of the fashionable world it was an advancement less remarkable than his marriage to a daughter of Lily Langtry, the outstandingly beautiful actress and intimate of the Prince of Wales.*

* Ian Malcolm was also the author of some sparkling verses about Curzon's later years as Secretary of State for Foreign Affairs. See Appendix, pages 390–1.

The little group of politicians and officials with whom Curzon worked most closely at the Foreign Office were almost all drawn from the same aristocratic or land-owning class that as late as the turn of the century continued to govern the country. Salisbury, of course, was descended from William Cecil, Lord Burghley, Queen Elizabeth's Lord Treasurer. Sanderson was the son of a Conservative MP and grandson of a Speaker of the House of Commons. Barrington was a son of the sixth Viscount Barrington. Bertie was a son of the sixth Earl of Abingdon. McDonnell was a son of the fifth Earl of Antrim. Malcolm was a son of the sixteenth laird of the family estates in Scotland. All had been educated at Eton. They toiled together by day and met in the same houses and clubs at night.

Thus within the Foreign Office there were currents of social affinity unknown to other Government departments. Between one official and another, and even between Ministers and officials, there were bonds of common interest that transcended a purely professional relationship. No 'Mr' or 'Sir —' was allowed between colleagues, and a middle-grade official would not be embarrassed at writing to the Permanent Under-Secretary as 'My dear Lamps'.

As Parliamentary Under-Secretary, Curzon ranked just below Sanderson, but his effective position was even inferior: no political sapling could grow in the shade of Lord Salisbury. Curzon addressed Sanderson as 'My dear Sanderson', and Sanderson addressed Curzon as 'My dear Curzon'. But with other officials, Malcolm later recalled, he maintained a stiffness of manner that was alien to the institution and a habit of calling them 'Sir —' or 'Mr —' long after most Parliamentary Under-Secretaries would have abandoned the formal prefix. When Malcolm questioned him about this lack of cordiality, Curzon replied that it was easier to preserve a constant formality than to drop it and later have to resume it if relations became strained. It was not an attitude of mind that augured well for the future.

When he became Foreign Secretary twenty-four years later, Curzon acquired a reputation among his officials as an inconsiderate chief. It was not only, as his private secretary Vansittart wrote, that 'he annexed their work as the Germans annexed Shakespeare'. He would treat even his Permanent Under-Secretary, Sir Eyre Crowe, with near contempt, constantly sending for him to return to the Foreign Office at night in spite of his victim's tragic, guttural complaint: 'I have to travel in the Unterground.'

Before taking his place on the front bench of the House of Commons each afternoon, Curzon would spend several hours at the Foreign Office. He read all important telegrams and despatches, discussed with senior officials the drafts of his speeches and answers to Parliamentary questions, and on matters of particular weight would seek the guidance of Lord Salisbury himself.

He was also given Ministerial charge of the Commercial Department, a tiny and socially unglamorous sphere of influence which he tried to enlarge at the expense of the Board of Trade. The Foreign Office, however, regarded itself as an instrument of diplomacy, not of commerce, and Curzon had to be content with redressing the grievances of British ship-owners, merchants and seekers of concessions.

Other minor questions, too trivial to engage the attention of the Prime Minister, were referred to him. Could the Mayor of Portsmouth accept a foreign decoration? Would the Foreign Office reserve a railway sleeping-berth from Berlin to Warsaw for the Bishop of Peterborough, who was to attend the Tsar's Coronation in St Petersburg? Could the Peruvian Consul at Brighton be given a seat to watch Queen Victoria's Diamond Jubilee procession, and the Colombian *Chargé d'Affaires* a ticket of admission to the Houses of Parliament? Does the Regius Professor of Physic at Cambridge need a letter from the Russian Embassy before visiting Moscow? Can the Foreign Office help a sportsman who wants to shoot in Albania, but has been refused permission by the Turkish Government owing to the disturbed state of that province?

One day there came a request from a writer who wished to examine the Foreign Office archives: he was told that they could not be shown beyond the year 1830. Another day there was a proposal from the Japanese Government that the Court of St James should go into mourning for the Empress Dowager of Japan. 'Better not make a precedent,' Salisbury advised Curzon. 'If there are several wives, are we to mourn for all?' A less agreeable communication was a complaint from M. de Staal, the Russian Ambassador, that Curzon, in answering a Parliamentary question on the Russo-Chinese Treaty, had used confidential information given to him by the Ambassador when both were dining one night with Lord Rothschild. Curzon denied that this was so, and attributed M. de Staal's lapse of memory to an excess of champagne. The Ambassador's imperfect intonation may have been a contributory cause of the misunderstanding. When the British Ambassador in St Petersburg once asked Salisbury for an account of a certain conversation in London with the Russian Ambassador, the Prime Minister replied: 'Staal's statements are like Virgil's mysterious verses: you only get the first four words of every sentence.'

Protests from the Society of Friends about slavery in Zanzibar fell to Curzon's lot. He agreed to receive a deputation, but on the understanding that a shorthand writer should take down his remarks so that he could check them before they appeared in the Press. The question then arose whether the Foreign Office or the Society of Friends should pay the scribe's fee, amounting to one guinea. A thick file accumulated on the subject, arousing even deeper passions than slavery itself. Eventually, and under protest, the bill was met by Her Majesty's Government. 'A flagrant imposition,' was Curzon's majestic reproof. In planning the British contribution to the international exhibition in Paris, he also found his temper tried by the Prince of Wales. 'H.R.H. is really too bad and unbusinesslike,' he complained to Salisbury.

Both the Prime Minister and his Parliamentary Under-Secretary found relief from graver matters in the hilarious episode of Sir Joseph Renals, the Lord Mayor of London who in the autumn of 1895 visited France. On the eve of his departure he called on Curzon at the Foreign Office to ask whether he should invite President Faure to visit London. Curzon reported to Salisbury: 'It would on the one hand seem to be rather curious if we should invite the President of the French Republic at the very moment when his Government is doing its best to injure us in every part of the world. On the other hand the French are so foolishly sentimental that such a compliment might predispose them to a more reasonable attitude.'

Sir Joseph was in euphoric mood during his visit to Paris. Lord Dufferin, the British Ambassador, told Wilfrid Blunt that among other gaucheries he had congratulated the President on his Royal bearing and invited him to stay as his guest at the Mansion House 'The irrepressible Lord Mayor came at his own request a second time to see me yesterday at the Foreign Office,' Curzon informed Salisbury at the end of September, 'in order to report upon the result of his self-imposed mission to France. He spoke in glowing terms of what seems to have been the very remarkable reception and entertainment devised in his honour. ...

> Thus by slow degrees [Curzon continued] the Lord Mayor arrived at his real point, which was to petition that some decoration (he was indifferent as to the number or nature of the letters) should be bestowed on himself. He was careful to explain that he had no personal desire for such a distinction, having already been made a Baronet by Lord Rosebery, and being superior to mundane ambitions. But he felt that such an honour to him would be regarded as a compliment by the entire French people, who indeed would feel somewhat aggrieved if it were not bestowed. .. No doubt the comparative twilight into which he is about to descend at the termination of his mayoralty would be greatly solaced and mitigated by an order.

'The Lord Mayor is superb,' Salisbury replied. 'His baronetcy is very much in excess of his deserts – and is due only to the fact of his being a City Liberal. His rash proceedings much disturbed the fountain of honour, and made it, for the time, quite an agitated stream.' Renals not only failed to receive his coveted decoration; a few weeks later he retired from office without the customary vote of thanks from the Court of Common Council of the City of London, whose sense of propriety he had offended by giving a banquet in honour of Mr Barney Barnato, the South African financier.

Such was the *hors-d'œuvre* of Curzon's day. The staple fare took him from the Foreign Office to the House of Commons where, on an average of two afternoons each week, he would answer questions on foreign affairs. It was a Parliamentary institution that had been steadily growing in importance throughout the century. As the State extended its legislative hold over new fields of activity such as health and housing, industry and communications, Government business necessarily encroached on the time previously claimed by private members to debate topics of their own choice. To compensate for these lost opportunities, the Commons made an increasing use of Parliamentary questions, by which Ministers were required to be in their places to answer for the conduct of their departments.

In 1850 about 200 questions were printed on the order paper: by the time Curzon went to the Foreign Office in 1895, the number in a single year had risen to 5,000. With the quickening of public interest in foreign affairs and colonial expansion, an increasing proportion of them was directed at the Foreign Office. There was a marked change in their tone, too. Members of Parliament used them not only to extract information, but to cross-examine, to pursue grievances and to score party points.

Most answers to Foreign Office questions in the Commons were drafted by officials and approved by Lord Salisbury, who would sometimes indicate the exact words to be used. Each written question, however, might be followed by one or more cunningly devised supplementary questions, of which Ministers received no warning. Salisbury insisted that diplomatic negotiations and other delicate aspects of foreign policy should be protected from public inquisition and instructed Curzon not to answer them. But on all other topics, the Parliamentary Under-Secretary had to be prepared to repel the Government's critics. During his first three weeks in office, he answered nearly forty separate questions. They ranged from the hanging of a British trader in the Congo to the tribulations of a Consul in China, from the forging of British patent-medicine stamps in France to the obstructiveness of the New York customs.

'I am a resolute champion of the old diplomacy and prefer curtness to indiscretion,' Curzon told Spring Rice. 'There is no other country in the world where foreign affairs are conducted by impromptu answers to premeditated questions.' He soon learnt to encase himself in what Sir Henry Lucy called the stiff buckram of the official manner. No Minister could more skilfully invest a deliberately evasive answer with weight and conviction or more thoroughly baffle an interrogator with polite irrelevance. 'When he has said nothing in half-a-dozen trim sentences,' Lucy wrote, 'and the importunate inquirer points out the omission, Mr Curzon's look of pained surprise is affecting, in some cases effective.' Under what flag, he was once asked, were military operations being carried on in the Sudan? Curzon declined to be trapped into a definition of the precise relationship between the Armies of Great Britain and Egypt. 'I do not know,' he replied innocently, 'I have not been there.'

When the Commons went into Committee of Supply on the Foreign Office estimates, he had particular need of a well-stocked mind, steady nerves and a nimble tongue. On these occasions the House exercises its right to roam at large over every aspect of a department's policy before voting the large sums of money demanded by the Government. That in no way daunted Curzon. In the course of a single evening he touched confidently on Siam and West Africa, on the Uganda railway and the Upper Nile, on China and Armenia and Zanzibar.

In the following year, Lucy noticed that Balfour, the Leader of the House, had left Curzon in sole charge of the Treasury bench during a similar debate on foreign affairs. 'Nor,' he added, 'was the confidence misplaced. Ready to conciliate where, as in the slavery question, promise of definite action was necessary, he showed himself ready to fight when, as in the matter of surrender to France in Siam, the foreign policy of the Government was attacked. His speech on the Siam business brought Sir Edward Grey into the field, and the audience, fit though few, watched with keen interest the encounter between the budding statesmen who by happy accident have succeeded one another in the Under-Secretaryship of the Foreign Office.'

Curzon scored another notable success later that year when he delivered an eighty-minute conspectus of foreign policy at Glasgow. Nobody could recall any other Minister not of Cabinet rank whose platform speech had been reported in full by the morning newspapers.

From time to time the measured tones of statesmanship gave way to an asperity that recalled Curzon's triumphs in the Oxford Union. During his first months at the Foreign Office he made a speech in the autumn recess that earned a personal rebuttal from no less Olympian a figure than the former Prime Minister, Lord Rosebery. Curzon claimed that he himself had never set foot in any overseas Consulate, Ministry, Embassy or Legation in which there was not rejoicing over a Conservative and lamentation over a Radical victory. That, replied Rosebery in the House of Lords soon after the reassembly of Parliament in February 1896, was not only untrue but also a grave and unjustified reflection on the impartiality of public servants. Curzon had also claimed that in the course of visiting a good many Courts and capitals of the world, he had never met one where there was not more respect felt for England under a Conservative than under a Liberal Government. Rosebery did not find that quite so easy to answer. He contented himself with the sort of jibe that came easily to Curzon's critics. 'Well, of course,' he said, 'a Liberal Minister has not the same opportunities of mingling in the Courts of the world as a person of Mr Curzon's position.'

Liberals in the Commons were no less annoyed by the disdain with which he castigated their opposition to the expedition up the Nile. 'Is there any resemblance,' he asked, 'between the lurid phantasmagoria which has been conjured up by the imagination of honourable Members opposite and the sober realities which I have attempted to put before the Committee?'

He even managed to wage a private little war with one of his senior colleagues in the Government. His survey of the Pamir mountains, undertaken just before the return of the Salisbury administration in 1895, was made public the following year in three successive issues of the *Geographical Journal*. The Royal Geographical Society then did the author the unusual honour of reprinting all three articles in a single volume. With it Curzon published a map of the Pamirs, partly based on information he had obtained from the War Office.

There must obviously have been some misunderstanding about the material, for early in 1897 the Viceroy, Lord Elgin, complained to the Secretary of State for India, Lord George Hamilton, of a breach of security. Hamilton accordingly raised the matter with Curzon, but received a sharp answer for his pains:

> I am sorry to think [he told the Secretary of State] that the Government of India think the publication of my map of the Pamirs a grave indiscretion. They did their best to prevent me from going to the Pamirs at all; and their hostility appears to extend to the consequences, as it did to the inception, of my journey. .. There is nothing in these maps that has not been communicated to me for use by the Intelligence Department of the War Office; and, if an error has been committed, it has been committed in good company and on high authority....

Hamilton sent on Curzon's reply to Elgin. 'I think that he did get full authority here,' he explained. 'The letter is written in Curzonese style, but that means nothing; George Curzon is George Curzon, and a very capable and accomplished man.' The Viceroy, too, decided to let the question drop. 'I am sorry that Curzon should still bear us a grudge for the conditions we thought it necessary to impose upon his journey to the Pamirs,' Elgin wrote sorrowfully to Hamilton. 'I thought from what he wrote to me afterwards that he had forgiven us. ... However, I am quite content to take your hint and attribute a good deal to style.'

Chapter Twenty-two

LORD SALISBURY

> Lord Salisbury is a delightful chief to serve under. He always sees the point in a good case, the flaw in a weak one. … I do not think however that he has any *a priori* fondness for strong measures.
>
> – *Curzon to Cecil Spring Rice, 28 November 1895*

Presiding over the Foreign Office in 1919, Lord Curzon had occasion to write to Mr Cecil Harmsworth, his Parliamentary Under-Secretary in the Commons:

> I am much obliged for the very clear and useful note which you have submitted.… But on looking through the papers I find copies of the letters and telegrams which you have written without any reference to me, to the Prime Minister and Lord Reading in Paris. I am sure you will pardon me, as an old Under-Secretary myself, if I point out that an Under-Secretary cannot write official or quasi official letters of this description, *on behalf of the Foreign Office*, without the knowledge and approval of the Secretary of State. The latter is the person responsible to the Cabinet, to Parliament and the nation, and I cannot conceive the situation in which if challenged to explain or defend the Foreign Office policy in the War Cabinet I had to confess that it had been carried on by my Under Secretary without my knowledge and behind my back.…
>
> I can quite understand how it has come about, and I suggest no blame. But I am sure that we ought to revert to the sound procedure which rests on an incontrovertible constitutional basis.

It says much for Curzon's high sense of duty and personal dedication to Lord Salisbury that during his own years as Parliamentary Under-Secretary at the Foreign Office he never exposed himself to such a reproach from his chief. By standards not exclusively his own, he brought a splendid array of talents to his subordinate office; yet at no time did he refuse to accept its customary limitations, however misguided he thought the policy of the Prime Minister and the Cabinet. He was the very epitome of loyalty.

He determined, however, that if he was to speak with authority in the

House of Commons, he should be no less well-informed than a Foreign Secretary in the House of Lords. He therefore asked Salisbury if he could see not only the telegrams and despatches circulated to him as a matter of course but also the more confidential communications between the Secretary of State and heads of British diplomatic missions overseas:

> I have to be the mouthpiece of the office here, and it would, I think, be an easier task if I knew always what was going on. It is not that the information could be used but that it might help one to know what not to say. I might also perhaps mention the records of your interviews with Ambassadors. I think I have only seen since last July the notes of what passed on two or three occasions with the French Ambassador about Siam and with the Turkish Ambassador about Armenia. ... I hope I am not making a very improper request. It is certainly not actuated by curiosity, and if you tell me that it is undesirable that I should see or know more I will be content. But I do feel the difficulty of having to speak here as if I knew all whereas I only know part; and I am sure you will exonerate me for mentioning it.

Salisbury readily allowed Curzon to see his private letters and telegrams, but explained that he no longer kept records of his conversations with foreign Ambassadors since discovering that Sir Charles Dilke had 'made an abominable use' of them on being appointed Parliamentary Under-Secretary at the Foreign Office in the Gladstone Government of 1880.

Dilke's alleged breach of the convention that Ministers do not search the departmental archives of their predecessors for political ammunition was not the only reason why Salisbury had discontinued his practice of making notes on conversations at the Foreign Office. He thought that it encouraged both Count von Hatzfeldt, the German Ambassador, and Baron de Courcel, the French Ambassador, to speak more freely with him than they might otherwise have done. 'They tell me, and I have no ground for disbelieving them,' he informed Curzon, 'that they on their side abstain to a great extent from formal reports.' Such informality enabled the Prime Minister to deliver an unpalatable decision without causing humiliation: on the occasion, for instance, that the French Government strenuously denied Great Britain's right to expel the Marchand expedition from the Upper Nile. In the friendliest possible manner, Salisbury told Courcel: '*Oui, oui, vous avez raison, mais il faut en aller.*'

The assiduous Parliamentary Under-Secretary had not exhausted his demands upon the overburdened man who held the offices of both Prime Minister and Foreign Secretary. In June 1896 he wrote to him:

> I do not quite know how it is, and no one in the office seems able to explain, but I have never once since I have been in the office heard of any intended deputation to you till after it has been and gone. I should very much like, for instance, to have

been present at the deputation about Indo-Chinese railways, a subject which I have long studied and in which I take a great interest. But the first I heard or saw of it was your speech in *The Times* next morning.

'I shall be only too glad to have your company,' Salisbury replied, 'on a remarkably dreary opportunity.'

While neglecting no source of official information, Curzon also added to his knowledge of foreign affairs by maintaining his own private intelligence service. Three close friends – Rennell Rodd, Cecil Spring Rice and Arthur Hardinge – were rising to responsible positions in the Diplomatic Service and corresponded more freely with him than with the officials in London who controlled their careers. During his travels, too, Curzon had met a wide range of men in Government Service whom he encouraged to write to him from time to time. They did so willingly, glad to have a friend at court. And if he thought their letters of sufficient interest, he would show them to the Prime Minister himself.

Lord Salisbury's family used to complain that he seldom remembered a piece of social gossip, and even more rarely was able to report it correctly: but if the item concerned a foreign statesman, he listened to it with interest and retained it with accuracy. His colleagues and subordinates were also inured to his vagueness. He was unable to recognize even those with whom he had sat in Cabinet an hour before, and would leave the most secret Foreign Office cipher books lying about on the hall table. Yet he somehow managed to absorb all that was needed by an omniscient Foreign Secretary. To a minute proposing that a certain Vice-Consul should be promoted to Consul, he appended the magisterial comment: 'Mr — beats his wife. S.'

Curzon added to the background knowledge of his chief. He sent on to him a letter from Charles Eliot, the British Minister in Sofia, about 'the backstairs intrigues of that squalid little court'; it contained an account of how the Bulgars urinated on the tomb of the recently assassinated nationalist leader, Stambouloff, while the gendarmes looked on. From Harry Cust in Pretoria came a description of his meeting with President Kruger: 'The old man dresses in a broad-cloth sleeping bag and swaddles a shocking bad topper in hat-bands of crepe. He dwells in a cloud of foul smoke and spits like a Maxim gun. We've had some quite bad rows but discovered that our birthdays are on the same day and wept and are going to exchange pipes.' Rennell Rodd wrote from Egypt about the shortcomings of the Khedive – 'a hopeless little wretch' – and later from Ethiopia during his mission to the Emperor Menelik. General Kitchener told him of his worries about cholera during the expedition against the Dervishes who threatened Egypt from the Sudan, and from Wady Halfa sent an imperious request for power to requisition boats. 'He must have been in a bad temper when he wrote', Curzon scribbled on the letter, and passed it to the Prime Minister.

Sometimes, it seems, Salisbury thought that Curzon's correspondents were making an unnecessary fuss about trivial matters. On reading a diatribe from Cecil Spring Rice in Berlin, he replied: 'I am afraid the German papers have the same effect upon Spring Rice's cuticle that *Punch* and *The Times* have upon that of the Emperor William. The world was much happier when the ruling classes in every country could read no language but their own.'

This marginal comment illuminates Salisbury's practical approach to statecraft. Having made up his mind on an issue, he would strive to achieve his purpose. But he believed that those charged with great responsibilities must deny themselves the luxury of emotional outbursts. 'He never laid claim,' his daughter wrote of him, 'to any peculiar right of moral condemnation or special loftiness of moral standpoint.' When Curzon once consulted him on the attitude of the Government to cruelties committed in the Congo, he replied: 'My impression is strongly against any interference on our part. We shall not reform our neighbour's ways by turning the philanthropic pack on him. They have no weapon but their tongues: and the only result they will achieve will be to make the tyranny better hidden, and therefore more cruel.'

Those who did not share his burden of responsibility for preserving peace would sometimes accuse him of an inglorious caution; and even those who appreciated his reluctance to resort to war except as an ultimate instrument of national honour or defence would urge him at least to express moral disapproval of other men's wickedness. He would answer each category of critic with disdain. 'Are you prepared to fight?' he demanded of one. 'Because if not you had better hold your tongue.' And to the other he declared: 'I have no belief in a policy of scold.'

Salisbury was not a pacifist. There were moments, he believed, at which the diplomacy of persuasion must be reinforced by a show of force. But a world of expanding populations in which the great powers jostled each other for elbow room and sought new markets for their industry in Africa and Asia required a calm restraint on the part of Great Britain. Curzon, whose education in international affairs had been acquired mostly in the East, preferred to settle international disputes by a more belligerent brand of diplomacy.

Thus differences both of temperament and of experience divided Salisbury and his Under-Secretary. Had either been a man of lesser stature, their partnership might have ended in personal reproach and bitterness: in fact it endured for three unclouded years. The Prime Minister, while remaining impervious to Curzon's pleas for a stiffening of attitude, was gently instructive and infinitely courteous towards his restless subordinate. And the Parliamentary Under-Secretary, while assuming an almost Royal prerogative to be consulted, to encourage and to warn, obediently expounded his chief's policy to the House of Commons with as much apparent enthusiasm as he would have brought to his own.

In private, however, he had misgivings and at one moment wrote to his friend Selborne, Parliamentary Under-Secretary at the Colonial Office, about French aggression in West Africa: 'I can't tell you how anxious and even how miserable I am. And next week I have got to be defending all this without the slightest idea what the Cabinet really think or by what steps they arrive at their mysterious conclusions.'

The printed reports of Parliamentary proceedings which record Curzon's utterances in the Commons between 1895 and 1898 betray no sign of his impotence. They reflect only his loyalty to the instructions which he sought from Salisbury whenever he had to speak on delicate or dangerous topics of foreign policy. The private exchange of correspondence between the two men, however, reveals an almost monotonous pattern of disagreement. The Parliamentary Under-Secretary could leave neither well nor ill alone, but was perpetually demanding strong words and even stronger actions. The Prime Minister, in his brief replies, would deprecate any hasty course that might inflame a situation and yet fail to achieve a solution.

Like the exploitation of the Congo by the King of the Belgians, the ill-treatment of Christians living in Armenia and elsewhere under Turkish rule aroused the conscience of all parties. Salisbury refused, however, to make promises of help that could not be fulfilled or to indulge in pinpricks against the Ottoman Empire that could bring scant relief to its victims.

One night Curzon received notice of a motion to be moved in the Commons on the following day, expressing sympathy with the sufferings of the Christian population in Asiatic Turkey and the hope that 'further endeavours' would be made to improve their lot. He suggested to Salisbury that the Government might safely accept the motion. 'Make it clear,' the Prime Minister replied, 'that in voting for the Motion we do not pledge ourselves to *armed* endeavours.' Next day, to loud cheers from the Conservative benches, Curzon declared that Her Majesty's Government was not prepared to plunge Europe into a Continental war for the sake of Armenia or to risk 'a perilous, if not a fatal philanthropy'.

Salisbury insisted that Curzon should strike the same note of detachment when Nizam Pasha, the Minister of Police in Constantinople was appointed Governor-General of the Turkish province of Beirut. There were protests at Westminster that a man so patently responsible for having failed to protect the Christians of Constantinople during the recent riots should now assume the rule of a substantial Christian population elsewhere. Curzon shared this sense of indignation and wrote to Salisbury about Nizam Pasha: 'I know him well – a treacherous old scamp and a corrupt Governor.' The Prime

Minister was in no mood to argue. He replied: 'I am afraid I cannot concur.' Two days later Curzon told the House of Commons: 'We have come to the conclusion that Nizam Pasha can scarcely be held responsible for many of the measures supposed to have been executed under his orders, and that there are not sufficient grounds for protesting against his appointment.'

The volatile foreign policy of France, that again and again in the last decade of the nineteenth century threatened British interests throughout the world, aroused Salisbury's misgivings no less than those of his Under-Secretary. When the French protested at some indiscreet observations made by a British Consul in Corsica, the Prime Minister told Curzon: 'If we were to measure out the same retribution to the French Embassy, they would long ago have forgotten the use of window glass.' But such private pleasantries found no place in his official instructions. Curzon once asked whether, in view of the persistent misrepresentation by French newspapers of British concern for Kiang Huang, he should make a Parliamentary statement about our rights in that Chinese province. Salisbury replied that it was a matter of little interest except to the journalists responsible for the attacks on Great Britain: 'I doubt if any one else will read or understand the question and answer. I fear the only result will be to make people think there must be something in the French contention, or you would not take so exceptional a course in order to refute it.' Again, when Curzon sought advice from Salisbury on how he should answer a Parliamentary question from Sir Edward Grey about a French breach of faith on Madagascar, he was told: 'I think that in a matter so grave we should at present be content with saying that the matter is being carefully considered.'

In June 1897, Curzon became exasperated at the supine attitude of his chief during the negotiation with France of a treaty governing British trade with the French Protectorate of Tunis. 'If I do not see you tomorrow before your talk with de Courcel,' he wrote to Salisbury, 'may I most respectfully implore you to secure for us our last draft or to break off negotiations? I should really be as unhappy if I had to defend anything less as I have hitherto been happy in the tasks that you have entrusted to me. I really do not think that we are grasping or contumacious. In any case, we are making a big surrender for somewhat problematical ends. But beyond a certain point it would seem to be unjustifiable that we should be asked to go.' And when Salisbury replied that a bargain consisted of give and take, Curzon replied with a touch of scorn that in French eyes a bargain was 'all take and very little give'.

Anglo-German relations were no less uneasy. The underlying cause was the conflict between Germany's colonial ambitions and those of Great Britain, a struggle aggravated by the mercurial and often mischievous temperament of the Emperor. In spite of the affection he bore his grandmother, Queen Victoria, Kaiser Wilhelm lost few opportunities of attempting to humiliate her Government. The most notorious example was the telegram of congratulation which he sent to President Kruger on the failure of the Jameson raid across the border of the Transvaal, a gesture that implied his disbelief in official British denials of responsibility for the illegal expedition.

Four days later, on 7 January 1896, Salisbury was giving a dinner party at Hatfield when a red despatch box was brought to the table. He asked the permission of Princess Christian, a daughter of Queen Victoria, to open it, and studied the short message it contained. Then he scribbled for a moment or two and had the box removed. The Princess asked him what it was. He replied that the German Emperor had landed 150 men at Delagoa Bay, in Portuguese East Africa, the only access of the Boers to the sea other than through British territory. 'What answer have you sent?' the Princess enquired. 'I haven't answered,' Salisbury said, 'I have sent ships.'

Curzon, too, was disturbed by the penetration of German influence in Africa. Commending the construction of the Uganda railway later that year, he warned the House of Commons that if Great Britain refused to recognize her obligations, Germany would step in and take her place. To a rebuke from Sir William Harcourt, the Leader of the Opposition, who accused him of making gratuitous and impolitic references to Germany, Curzon replied with heat: 'I have always been an ardent advocate of the *entente cordiale* with Germany.' Certainly he looked upon her as a less malevolent foe than France, and in April 1897 he gave proof of his goodwill.

He proposed to the Prime Minister that he should attempt to relieve the growing tension between Great Britain and Germany by seeking informal talks with the Emperor during a holiday in Berlin. He had, he added, taken the precaution of asking the Duke of Connaught, the Emperor's uncle, whether such a visit would be welcome, and had not been discouraged. The Parliamentary Under-Secretary at the Foreign Office was rarely entrusted with diplomatic duties: in the absence of the Foreign Secretary, it was not Curzon, but Sir Thomas Sanderson, the Permanent Under-Secretary, who received Ambassadors to the Court of St James. Salisbury nevertheless approved Curzon's unofficial mission to Berlin. 'I hope you will be able to discover why he has been seized with such an implacable suspicion of us and what he imagines we are scheming to do.'

Curzon's intention to talk the German Emperor into a less truculent state of mind was swiftly frustrated. The Kaiser curtly refused to see him, in itself, his would-be visitor assumed, a deliberate snub to the British Government. The disappointed Parliamentary Under-Secretary had to make do with Baron Marschall von Bieberstein, the German Foreign Minister, whose dignified and courteous manner could not conceal the bitter antagonism which his Government felt towards Great Britain. Curzon never afterwards cared much for Berlin. 'It was such an artificial show city,' he told his second wife more than twenty years later, 'with its statues and pillars and palaces and generally meretricious effect. The only good things were the collections.'

But even German questions sometimes had their lighter side. After the unification of the country under Bismarck, the Foreign Office continued to accredit diplomatic missions to some of the smaller States such as Darmstadt, Württemberg and Dresden, whose homely little Courts inspired affection rather than respect. 'The Queen would be grateful,' Sir Henry Ponsonby once wrote privately to her *Chargé d'Affaires* in Dresden, 'if you would request the *Chargé d'Affaires* in Dresden to take a less humorous view of Royal funerals.'

Yet there were those who saw no charm in such anomalies and determined to press Her Majesty's Government for the withdrawal or reduction of those minor diplomatic missions. Curzon warned Salisbury of impending trouble in the Commons, and received this reply from the Prime Minister: 'Decline to promise any alteration at present. I remember Palmerston's answer a long time ago always struck me as effective. He said that there were men in his party who never spoke and were thought of small importance in the House: but he found that on a division their votes were worth nearly as much as other people's.'

Curzon's humiliating experience in Berlin left him more than ever reluctant to defend Lord Salisbury's adherence to the Concert of Europe – the understanding that bound the great powers not to act independently of each other particularly in their relations with Turkey. In Curzon's judgement it would be farcical to extol an association whose harmony was so often and so wantonly broken by the discords of German ambition. 'It becomes a little difficult to go on singing the praises of the Concert of Europe,' he wrote to Salisbury, 'when its petty jealousies and rivalries become daily more apparent.'

Salisbury, who took a longer view of events than most statesmen, saw no reason why the aberrations of one member of the Concert should give a bad name to the whole. And in less than a couple of hundred words he provided Curzon with the theme of an important speech that the Member for Southport was about to deliver in his constituency:

> If you hinted without saying it that the extreme views of Germany have done much to mar its action, I do not see that you would be doing any harm. But we often think ill of the proceedings of Parliament; we do not in that see any reason for abandoning Parliamentary Government. The same with respect to the Concert of Europe. In spite of constant defects and errors, it is on the whole a beneficent institution. The things which our critics have to show and which they have not shown is that on any occasion things would have gone better if we had broken away from the

Concert. On several occasions our participation has done some good, though perhaps not much. On no one occasion has our participation hindered any good or done any harm. And this is the crucial question to be decided when it is disputed whether we ought to have withdrawn from the Concert as soon as we had ascertained that it was far from being likely to achieve all the good we desired.

The report of the speech which Curzon made at Southport four days later included these familiar themes:

You may say that the Concert of Europe is very slow in its operations. I grant you that it is very slow. Its operations have on more than one occasion been retarded by what appeared to us to be the exaggerated views that are entertained by some of its members. ... But though there are anomalies or weakness in an institution, you do not therefore necessarily condemn it. ... The House of Commons itself is not free from imperfections. There are many people who think it is tolerably full of them. But we should not for that reason applaud the action of any modern Cromwell who advanced to the table, removed the mace, expelled the members and ordered the door-keepers to shut the door. ... It is very easy for our critics to denounce the Concert of Europe. What they have to show, what they have not shown yet, is that matters would have proceeded any better or more smoothly if in the first place there had been no such Concert, or if in the second place Great Britain had broken away from it. I have shown you, I think, a number of occasions on which the Concert and the influence of this country in the Concert has done positive good. I know of no occasion on which our influence there has hindered any other Power from doing good; still less do I know of any occasion on which it has done harm. The Concert may not have done all the good we expected of it or desired; but if we had deserted it, we should have made ourselves ridiculous and should have retarded and not advanced the solution of the European problem.

However critical of his chief Curzon might sometimes allow himself to be in private, his public loyalty was absolute. It was a quality which Salisbury appreciated even more than the considerable intellectual pretensions of his Parliamentary Under-Secretary and one which could not fail to enhance Curzon's claim to high office in the months to come.

Curzon realized that his views on European and African problems deserved no particular respect from either the Prime Minister or from the permanent officials; he was, after all, merely an intelligent amateur in those fields. His record of Oriental travel and scholarship, however, led him to suppose that he would be consulted on relations with the Far East. It was not to be. Before becoming Disraeli's Foreign Secretary in 1878, Salisbury had spent four years as Secretary of State for India and had studied every nuance of the Eastern Question. In 1888 he had reacted with Curzonian firmness to a Russian advance on Herat, and again in 1891 during Younghusband's adventure in the Pamirs. He thus believed himself no less well equipped than his Parliamentary Under-Secretary to measure and contain the menace of Russian expansion. Again and again, Curzon's opinions were courteously brushed aside, and their author required to defend in public a policy which in private he despised.

He made an unfortunate start that cannot have increased confidence in his readily proffered counsel. Soon after beginning his duties at the Foreign Office, he heard that a new British Minister would shortly be required at Pekin and he addressed Salisbury on the subject. He pointed out, somewhat unnecessarily, that the next ten years would have a far-reaching effect upon the position of Great Britain in the Far East, and urged that the new envoy should be 'of first-rate abilities, of resolute character and with Eastern experience'. Salisbury agreed on the importance of the appointment, but asked whether Curzon could produce a diplomatist with those qualifications. He himself, he confessed, had looked in vain down the Foreign Office list to find a man of 'first-rate abilities, resolute character and Eastern experience' who was likely to accept the post. It would be possible, he concluded, to promote the senior man who knew anything of China, but doubted whether such an appointment would have 'a far-reaching effect on our position in the Far East'. Curzon never again forgot to do his homework before addressing his chief.

Five months later, the same episode caused Curzon further embarrassment when Salisbury's choice of a new Minister in Pekin fell on Sir Claude MacDonald, a professional soldier and colonial administrator. Much to Curzon's distress, a newspaper accused him of having expressed disapproval of the appointment. On a day that would otherwise have been gladdened by the birth of his first child, the unhappy Parliamentary Under-Secretary wrote to Salisbury: 'In case this grotesque fabrication should reach your ears, I hasten to say that I have never even mentioned the subject to a single soul outside the Foreign Office, and inside it only to Sanderson, Bertie, Eric and Pom. Nor of course in this case is the report anything but a concoction. Please do not trouble to answer; but if there is a suspicion calculated to wound, it is that of disloyalty.'

The incident left no blemish on Curzon's reputation. As the author of *Problems of the Far East* he had in any case established a reputation that entitled his views on Oriental affairs to some consideration. He had forecast the decline of China at Japan's expense, and so it had come to pass. He had also concluded that neither Russia nor Germany would hesitate to extend her sphere of influence in China as long as Great Britain looked impassively on. Salisbury was predictably unenthusiastic at any suggestion of British involvement. 'I should much deprecate any opposition to Russia,' he wrote to Curzon in November 1897, 'which is gratuitous or is motivated only by resentment or impatience. If any object is clearly to be gained by it I have no objection: but as a mere outlet to indignation or patriotic temper, it may do some harm and can do us no good.'

Before the end of the year, however, Germany had landed a party of marines at Kiao-Chau and Russia had despatched a naval squadron on a leisurely winter visit to Port Arthur. Each was a strategic point in the control of North China's maritime trade and a means of applying pressure to the seat of government at Pekin. Curzon hastened to send his appreciation of the problem to an unreceptive Lord Salisbury: 'Russia is always at the door of China by land; and if her occupation of Port Arthur is made permanent, will be so also by sea. Germany (if she makes a dockyard and a coaling station at Kiao-Chau) will be on the other side of the doorstep; and it will be more difficult for others to get in.' He went on to suggest that British interests must be protected by ordering the China squadron to Wei-hai-wei, the third of the important naval ports in the north, both as a warning to the interlopers and as a base for any future operations that might become necessary.

In March 1898 his prescience was confirmed when it became known that the Chinese Government had succumbed to pressure and leased both Port Arthur and the neighbouring commercial harbour of Talienwan (now known as Dairen) to Russia. For months he had been obliged to defend the passive policy of Salisbury while inwardly sympathizing with the more belligerent murmurings of public opinion. Now he was to come into his own. In the absence of the Prime Minister through illness, Balfour allowed him to address the Cabinet on the need to occupy Wei-hai-wei. After five sessions he carried his point, and the change of policy, approved by Salisbury from the South of France, was announced to the Commons on 5 April. It was an unprecedented triumph on the part of a mere Parliamentary Under-Secretary. At the time it restored much faith among Government supporters, and two years later, during the anti-European Boxer Rising in Pekin, the port proved invaluable as a base for the work of rescue and relief.

Throughout the summer of 1898, however, he continued to be harassed by the 'Pig-Tail Committee', a group of Tory dissidents in the Commons who demanded from the Government an even bolder reaction to the intervention of other European Powers in China. Curzon sighed to join their ranks, but contented himself with urging the Prime Minister to protest at the construction by a Russian railway syndicate of a line on the Yangtsze. Salisbury's reply was unhelpful: 'I do not see my way, if Russian Capitalists will throw their money about, to preventing the Chinese from picking it up. We must find some equally patriotic Capitalists on our side.'

Curzon had perforce to swallow his disappointment. But he later allowed his feelings to emerge in a letter to St John Brodrick, his successor at the Foreign Office. 'I know what an uphill job it is,' he wrote in 1900, 'with the Parliamentary Under-Secretary so to speak outside the show and with that strange, powerful, inscrutable, brilliant, obstructive dead-weight at the top.'

Curzon underwent three more Chinese tortures that year. The burden of office combined with the strain of defending a policy he privately deplored could hardly fail to fray his nerves. It was therefore in a mood of understandable irritation that he replied one day in the Commons to a question from an Irish Nationalist MP, John Dillon, a persistent tormentor and the man who a year earlier had three times in a day accused the Parliamentary Under-Secretary of lying. Why, Dillon demanded, had the Pekin correspondent of *The Times* been able to publish important facts several days before the Foreign Office knew of them? Curzon replied:

> It is the business of Her Majesty's representatives abroad to report to us facts of which they have official cognisance and to obtain confirmation of them before they telegraph. I hesitate to say what the functions of the modern journalist may be; but I imagine that they do not exclude the intelligent anticipation of facts even before they occur and in this somewhat unequal competition I think the House will see that the journalist, whose main duty is speed, is likely sometimes to get the advantage over the diplomatist whose main object is accuracy.

He had intended his jibe, he told Salisbury, to be no more than 'some mild chaff in which I indulged in a spirit of subdued compliment'. That was not how *The Times* took a reflection upon George Ernest Morrison, an accepted authority on Chinese affairs. When by error his death was prematurely announced in 1900, the obituary notice described the snub as 'the most genuine tribute ever wrung from unwilling lips to the highest qualities which a correspondent can bring to bear on his work'. Meanwhile, the newspaper turned on Curzon with savage dislike. That he had been an assiduous contributor of articles to *The Times* on his Oriental travels did not save him from a campaign of denigration. 'A Government cannot be said to be particularly fortunate,' ran one leading article, 'when it has to depend for the presentation of its policy to the House of Commons upon such speeches as that made by Mr Curzon.'

Lord Salisbury would have shrugged off the attack as one of those hazards inseparable from a political career. 'The only restraint I should like to impose on the liberty of the Press,' he used to remark, 'would be to make political abstractions penal.' But Curzon was wounded by such treatment, and a sense of grievance was never far from his thoughts whenever the newspapers chose to comment on him. Sometimes, it is true, he could be generous, as when he wrote from India:

> Many people sneer at newspapers and the lies and calumnies that they circulate. Quite true. But I can honestly say that out of the many scores of delinquencies and

abuses that I have detected and am every month detecting in this country, the clue to quite one-half has been given to me, often in some quite unintentional or unsuspecting fashion, by the Press.

More often, as the years rolled by and the Press continued to find little merit in his selfless labours, he would indulge in moments of self-pity. 'Oh! How those cursed papers have killed me for half a lifetime,' he wrote to his wife in 1923. 'I can never recover now.'

Another tribulation to which Curzon exposed himself that summer sprang from his exacting standards of literary composition. 'A man who cannot write a letter without some error in syntax, spelling or construction,' he observed, 'cannot be fit to control a great administration.' It was not only that he paid meticulous attention to his own literary work, whether it were two stout volumes on Persia or a brief note of gratitude for a dinner party: he could not bear to ignore the slipshod style of others.

Such sensitivity added cruelly to his labours. 'I have been spending the past few days in rewriting Mr Wheeler's Durbar Book for him, or rather for us,' he told a colleague in India. 'It is quite incredibly bad: not a spark of ability or a ray of imagination: only dull official details couched in language that would extract blushes even from a Gazette: and when he lets himself go, rodomontade that would earn reproach even from a Bengali Babu.' As a Cabinet Minister he would correct, and sometimes entirely redraft, the memoranda of civil servants. Official minutes hardly ever escaped annotation, even from the pen of a mere Under-Secretary.

In July 1898 Lord Salisbury decided that certain correspondence between Sir Claude MacDonald and the Yamen, or Chinese Foreign Office, should be published as a Parliamentary paper. During its preparation, Curzon laid hands on a printer's proof of the document and, presumably for the edification of Sanderson, or even of Salisbury himself, added his own marginal comment. By mischance the printer embodied Curzon's unamiable exegesis in the text, copies of which were sent to newspapers for publication the next morning. The mistake was not noticed in the Foreign Office until late at night, when frenzied appeals were despatched to editors asking them to omit the interpolations. Some of these requests arrived too late or were ignored, and Sir Claude MacDonald's letter appeared in this form:

Peking, February 9, 1898

Your Highnesses and your Excellencies have more than once intimated to me that the Chinese Government were aware of the great importance that has always been attached by Great Britain to the retention in Chinese possession of the Yang-tsze region, now entirely hers, as providing security for the free course and development of trade.

Strictly speaking, this is not grammar. 'China' has not been mentioned, only 'Chinese possession' and the 'Chinese Government', neither of which are of the feminine gender. 'Hers' can only refer, according to the ordinary rules of grammar, to Great Britain.

However, I suppose we must not be pedantic, but must leave Sir C. MacDonald and the Yamen to use bad grammar if they prefer.

I shall be glad to be in a position to communicate to her Majesty's Government a definite assurance that China will never alienate any territory in the provinces adjoining the Yang-tsze to any other Power, whether under lease, mortgage, or any other designation. Such an assurance is in full harmony with the observations made to me by your Highnesses and your Excellencies.

I avail, &c.,
(Signed) Claude M. MacDonald.

Connoisseurs of official discomfiture did not fail to point out a crowning touch of inspiration. Elsewhere in the Digest of correspondence the name MacDonald was spelt MadDonald.

However impetuous his tongue or his pen, Curzon had from the first days of his appointment dutifully observed the traditional bounds of his office; whatever his private thoughts, he had made no public pronouncement on foreign affairs that did not bear the approval of Lord Salisbury. He was therefore justifiably aggrieved one night in June 1898 when Joseph Chamberlain, the Colonial Secretary, clumsily intruded on his own preserve in the House of Commons. Curzon wrote in protest to the Prime Minister:

> We suffered agonies on the front bench as he proceeded to explain seriatim how we were not strong enough without an ally to stand up against Russia in the Far East, to preserve the independence of China, to exercise a controlling influence there, or even to maintain the 'open door'. ... Meanwhile in all our minds was the reflection '*Que diable allait il faire dans la galère?*' Why this lamentable dissension on the high principles of policy from one not primarily responsible for their execution?
>
> Of course I breathe not a word of this outside. But to you I may confess that that half hour was one to me of unmitigated gloom.

The ordeal of Lord Salisbury's Parliamentary Under-Secretary, however, was almost at an end. Exactly twelve days later he received a letter from the Prime Minister telling him that his name had been submitted to the Queen as the next Viceroy of India.

As Curzon's three years at the Foreign Office were drawing to a close, he told Lord Salisbury that he had learnt 'how premature first judgments are apt to be; what rewards there are for prudence and courtesy and consideration; and how wonderfully perseverance is justified to her children'.

Only in a personal sense did he believe those words to be true: the foreign policy he would have pursued in Salisbury's place was neither prudent nor courteous nor considerate. In 1900 he wrote to Selborne from India:

I never spend five minutes in inquiring if we are unpopular. The answer is written in red ink on the map of the globe. Neither would I ever adopt Lord Salisbury's plan of throwing bones to keep the various dogs quiet (Madagascar, Tunis, Heligoland, Samoa, Siam). They devour your bone and then turn round and snarl for more. No; I would count everywhere on the individual hostility of all the great Powers, but would endeavour so to arrange things that they were not *united* against me. And the first condition of success in such a policy is, in my opinion, the exact inverse of your present policy; for I would be as strong in small things as in big.

To be as strong in small things as in big was in Curzon's estimation a virtue, almost an essential, of statesmanship; others may judge it to be a fatal flaw. Admittedly, there were moments when snarling belligerency would have served British interests no worse than Salisbury's deliberate inaction. 'We have now managed in the last six months,' Wilfrid Blunt wrote on 9 January 1896, 'to quarrel violently with China, Turkey, Belgium, Ashanti, France, Venezuela, America and Germany.' That was a form of isolation to which not even the Prime Minister's most dedicated admirers would attach the familiar epithet 'splendid'.

It was, however, the nadir of Salisbury's diplomatic fortunes. Within a year, his preference for quiescence as an instrument of international understanding had healed the protracted boundary dispute between British Guiana and Venezuela, and in turn pacified a hostile United States Government. For Salisbury, such a settlement was the ultimate justification of his policy, what he called the 'substitution of judicial doctrine for the cold, cruel arbitrament of war'. Curzon, on his own admission, would have been unlikely to show a similar restraint – even towards the country from which he had so recently brought back both his bride and President Grover Cleveland's silver loving cup.

Salisbury himself confessed that it was not easy to decide the precise moment at which deliberate detachment and galvanic exertion should succeed one another. During disturbances on the Indian Frontier, he wrote to Curzon: 'If only we could take one line and stick to it. But our policy is Jingo and penitence in alternate doses. Unluckily the penitence usually coincides with a period of exhaustion on the part of our opponents: so that we miss our chance of settling the trouble once and for all.' Curzon, too, recognized the lack of consistency and told Brodrick: 'Of course the supreme lesson of the Foreign Office is that there is no pre-determined policy.'

During the imperialist scramble of the late nineteenth century, Salisbury nevertheless added 6,000,000 square miles and 100,000,000 subjects to Queen Victoria's realm without involving Great Britain in a war against any of the great powers. It was a feat that at the time earned him the gratitude of his country and the respect of the world. Cecil Rhodes thought it extraordinary that 'a man who never travels abroad further than Dieppe or the Riviera should have found out all the places in South Africa where an Englishman can breed, reserved them for Great Britain, and rejected all others'. Since then his reputation has been exposed to vicissitudes, a phenomenon he had observed elsewhere. 'In an Oriental Court,' he once told Curzon, 'call no man successful till he retires. Influence with these spoilt children wears out very rapidly.'

That Great Britain was in the end left dangerously rather than splendidly isolated is a debatable assertion which belongs more to a history of British foreign policy than an account of Curzon's relationship with Salisbury. What cannot be disputed is that Salisbury believed in certain methods of diplomacy which found no favour with his Parliamentary Under-Secretary: in the exercise of patience rather than of personal pique, in the value more of quiescence than of controversy.

For an immensely busy man he took pains to inculcate these virtues in Curzon. He could not always hope to convince him, nor is it likely that he sought a dialectical victory. But he would never refuse to explain the motives that governed his course of action or to satisfy a thirst for information. In this his generosity proved far beyond the bounds of what was due to a Ministerial mouthpiece in the Commons.

Curzon appreciated Salisbury's kindness and admired his intellectual dexterity. But he retained few of Salisbury's cherished precepts when in 1899 he assumed the direction of Indian foreign policy, even fewer when he came to preside over the Foreign Office in 1919. Perhaps, as William Cory used to say, the shadow of lost knowledge protects one from many illusions. For Curzon did achieve one spectacular triumph of diplomacy that not even a Salisbury would have scorned: the negotiation of the Treaty of Lausanne in 1923. In contrast to his transitory accomplishments elsewhere, it showed 'what rewards there are for prudence and courtesy and consideration; and how wonderfully perseverance is justified to her children'.

Chapter Twenty-three

PASSAGE TO INDIA

I think it was Carlyle who said of Oliver Cromwell: 'He coveted the place; perhaps the place was his.'

– *Winston Churchill in House of Commons, 28 March 1945*

In April 1897, while on his unofficial diplomatic mission to Berlin, Curzon was much disturbed to read a newspaper report about one of his colleagues in the House of Commons. It stated that the Marquess of Lorne, heir to the Duke of Argyll and husband of Princess Louise, Queen Victoria's fourth daughter, would soon receive a peerage with a view to a great appointment abroad. In Curzon's mind this could mean only one thing: Lorne was to succeed Elgin as Viceroy of India at the end of 1898. It was not a prospect that gave him the remotest pleasure.

He therefore sat down at once and wrote a long letter to Lord Salisbury, explaining what had prompted him to raise the question. 'You may perhaps have this, or still more likely, some other appointment in view,' he wrote, 'and in what I am about to say I may therefore be both premature and too late.' He continued:

I have long, however, thought that were the post in India to fall vacant while I was still a young man – I shall be 40 by the end of Elgin's term – and were it to be offered to me, I should like to accept it. It may be thought that this argues undue temerity on my part and that I am singularly deficient in the requisite qualifications.

Of this in many ways I am very conscious. But on the other hand it may perhaps be said for me that I have for at least 10 years made a careful and earnest study of Indian problems, have been to the country four times, and am acquainted with and have the confidence of most of its leading men.

If I have written books about its frontier problems – no doubt a risky venture – the views or forecasts I have been bold enough to express have I think on the whole turned out to be right: and I do not think, though my first book came out 8 years ago, I would cancel a single page in any one of them. I have been fortunate too in making the acquaintance of the rulers of the neighbouring states, Persia, Afghanistan, Siam, friendly relations with whom are a help to any Viceroy. At the India Office in 1891–92, thanks to the appointment with which you honoured me, I learned something of the official working of the great machine.

I seem rather to have been putting my wares, such as they are, in the shop window in this summary: but I have only done so to meet the obvious charge of presumption. It would perhaps be more pertinent to say that I believe a very great work can be done in India by an English Viceroy who is young and active and intensely absorbed in his work: who will at the same time try to do justice to the social part of his duties as the head of Anglo-Indian society (which Elgin certainly has not done) and will also establish the most friendly relations with the native chiefs and princes, and by keeping in touch with native feeling. For such a work a good deal of energy and application would be wanted and – what very few men take to India – a great love of the country and pride in the imperial aspect of its possession.

For myself all experience in administration might be very useful as giving me knowledge of men and things which I lack, and as neutralising the youth which is always thrown in my teeth.

It may well be that, apart from apparent disqualifications, you may have other ideas as to the kind of work to which I ought to be set: and the few of my friends who have sometimes suspected me of Indian hankerings have pressed upon me that I should be unwise to leave the House of Commons.

All these are considerations which do not now arise, and which it would be absurd to discuss in relation to a contingency which may never even occur.

I have only decided to make this confession to you as my chief in great trust and humility, not with a view to soliciting from you any opinion or reply, but simply that you may know, if at a later date you are considering the disposition of the high post to which I have referred, and should there be any question between a number of possible candidates, that I would be grateful if my name were at least considered among the latter.

Please do not look upon this as implying any indifference to my present work, which is a daily delight to me and which I can never sufficiently thank you for having assigned to me. I should be intensely reluctant to give it up. But after all I am discussing a contingency that will not arise for another year and a half. Even should it arise then.

Perhaps at a later date, should you not rule out my idea as vain and impracticable, you may be willing to let me discuss it with you. The fact of my having some day to go to the House of Lords has, of course, some influence on my own views, since I cannot in the nature of things look forward to a very prolonged House of Commons life.

But my strongest impulse is, I can honestly say, not a personal one at all: it is the desire, while one is still in the heyday of life, to do some strenuous work in a position of responsibility and in a cause for which previous study and training may have rendered one in some measure less unfit for the effort.

Salisbury's reply to this prolix apologia was friendly but evasive.

In view of the Peerage to which you are destined – or doomed – I am not surprised at the turn your thoughts have taken. If the idea which you mention should be realised, India will be very much the richer and Foreign Office the poorer by the transaction. No one could say of such an appointment that it had put upon the roll of Indian Viceroys a man not fully worthy of those who have gone before. If it falls to my lot to criticise such an appointment, I shall heartily applaud it. But whether it will be in my power to make it is another question, to which I cannot even suggest an answer. A year and a half is a long way off and where shall we all be then?

The months went by, and nothing more was heard of Lord Lorne's candidature. That in itself was satisfactory; but neither did any hint reach Curzon that his own cause was prospering. He waited until 19 April 1898, before once again laying his claims before the Prime Minister:

It is just a year ago since I was writing to you about India; and the contingency that you discussed in your reply, viz. of having to make the appointment yourself, seems likely to arise. Perhaps, unless you have already made other and wiser arrange ments, you may let me have a word or two with you about it when you return.

For 12 years I have worked and studied and thought – with a view should the chance ever arise – to fitting myself for the position. But I have also said to myself that I would not care to take it unless it were offered to me before I was 40: the reasons being that in my opinion the work is such as demands the energies of a young man in the prime of life, and that no older man can do it in the way in which I am convinced, from what I have seen in India, that it can and ought to be done: and in a less degree that I would like to get back to England while my father is still living, and before I am turned up into the House of Lords.

Then it seems to me that Viceroys as a rule can do nothing in their first year or two because they are new to the subjects and the work: and thus they are liable to be carried captive by the military men if the latter are strong in the Council, or by the financiers if they are to the front. My experience at the I.O. and elsewhere would to some extent relieve me of this source of weakness.

Trouble again must come when the Amir dies: it comes often enough with him while he lives. I think I possess to some extent his confidence and esteem. He constantly and regularly writes to me. I also know Habibulla, his successor. I think that while the father lives I could get on well with him; and that should he die while I was out there, there might be a little less chance of trouble with his successor.

I cannot think that personal ambition is at the bottom of any keenness I may exhibit in the matter. For many of my friends – talking to me on the slender suggestion of newspaper paragraphs – say to me that it would be folly to think of going away for five years, resigning a Parliamentary career and so on; and there is something to be said for this view, which I expect would be entirely shared by Arthur – to whom however I have never mentioned the matter. I can truly say that my anxiety in the case arises from an honest and not ignoble desire to render some service to a cause which I have passionately at heart.

On the other hand I frankly recognise the obstacles, the personal drawbacks and disqualifications and the strong reasons for a different appointment.

In that case I shall happily continue my work in my present post or in any other that you may desire.

Curzon must indeed have been agitated to send two such letters to Lord Salisbury. A clumsily applied veneer of humility that ill-cloaked the writer's honourable ambition and a scornful reference to Lord Elgin's shyness were unlikely to commend his interests to a Prime Minister of Salisbury's temperament. Nor could the excessive length of the pleas – the first of them ran to sixteen pages – fail to dilute the strength of Curzon's case in the eyes of a man already much encumbered by correspondence. Above all, Curzon had surely learned over the years how much his chief disliked being pestered for preferment.

In 1885, when Salisbury formed his first Government, the editor of *The Times*, Mr G. E. Buckle, was surprised by the cordiality with which the new Prime Minister received him. 'It is a pleasure to see you,' Salisbury exclaimed. 'You are the first person who has come to see me in the last few days who is not wanting something at my hands – place, or decoration, or peerage. *You* only want information.' He continued: 'Men whom I counted as my friends, and whom I should have considered far above personal self-seeking, have been here begging, some for one thing, some for another, till I am sick and disgusted. The experience has been a revelation to me of the baser side of human nature.'

To be set against Salisbury's distaste for dispensing patronage was the custom of the time: if a man wanted a job for himself or his friends, he did not hesitate to ask for it. Curzon's papers during his years as Parliamentary Under-Secretary at the Foreign Office include letters from, among others, Austen Chamberlain and the Speaker of the House of Commons, soliciting him for posts and places on behalf of their friends. And he in his turn wrote to Pom McDonnell, the Prime Minister's private secretary, with similar requests. Once it was to ask that Coningsby Disraeli, the nephew of his first political hero, should be appointed a Government Whip in the House of Commons. Another time it was to enquire whether FitzRoy Stewart, a son of the ninth Earl of Galloway, could fill a vacancy as Clerk of the Table in the House of Lords. Neither application was successful. 'Tell him it is in the Chancellor's gift, not mine,' Lord Salisbury minuted on the second of these importunate letters.

In writing so copiously to the Prime Minister about his own future in the spring of 1897 and again a year later, Curzon was thus taking a calculated risk. Against such a course of self-approbation lay Salisbury's preference for brevity of expression and modesty of demeanour. In its favour lay the increasing absent-mindedness of the Prime Minister and the indisputable armoury of qualifications for the Viceroyalty with which his Parliamentary Under-Secretary was able to jog his memory.

To Curzon's second letter, Salisbury replied that the appointment to India was much in his thoughts, but that he was not yet in a position to give a definite reply. As far back as January, however, the Prime Minister had written to the Queen, suggesting him as a possible candidate. 'He is a man,' Salisbury wrote, 'in many respects, of great ability, as well as of extraordinary industry and knowledge. ... His only fault is occasional rashness of speech in the House of Commons.' Early in June, the Queen gave her provisional approval, and about the middle of the month Salisbury spoke informally to Curzon. He told him that he was likely to be offered the Viceroyalty subject to a satisfactory state of health.

The condition was no mere formality at any time that summer, and certainly could not have been fulfilled when Curzon wrote to the Prime Minister from Reigate on 19 April. The letter is in pencil, a certain sign that he was lying on his back, stricken once more by spinal weakness and unable to manipulate pen and inkpot. Between 5 April and 9 May he took no part in the business of the House of Commons. 'I see it stated in the papers,' his old enemy Labouchere wrote on 27 April, 'that you are so bad that you will have to withdraw for some time from H. of C. then I see them contradicted. I sincerely hope that the contradiction is the right version, for you have made yourself such a splendid position in Parliament, that it would be too bad if your health were to break down for any time.'

Curzon cannot have suspected that this disability might impair his chances of becoming Viceroy. The Secretary of State for India, however, thought differently:

> As to his health [Lord George Hamilton told Elgin], I have my misgivings, so much so that when I knew he was to be appointed I pressed on the Prime Minister the necessity of a thorough medical certification and examination. ... The Indian climate suits him, and he is capable of greater exertion there than in England. He suffers from a slight curvature of the spine, and when greatly overworked he suffers pain and inconvenience, which I fancy affects his brain power, for he is obliged to lie on his back and do no work. The risk, I admit, is considerable, for a Viceroy being laid up in this way means a temporary stoppage of the Government of India; but he is a man of such high courage and resolution that he will do all that a human being can to morally subordinate and override his physical failings.

In obedience to Lord Salisbury's instructions, Curzon underwent a medical examination at the hands of Sir Thomas Smith, a surgeon who had served his apprenticeship under Sir James Paget. 'I hereby certify,' he wrote, 'that I have examined the Rt Hon. George Curzon and I can find no sign of disease about him and were I making a report to a life assurance office, I should recommend him for insurance at the ordinary rate for a 1st class life.' The same day Curzon sent the certificate on to the Prime Minister, accompanied by a personal letter: 'When you spoke to me the other day, I hardly found words with which to express my recognition of the compliment which your enquiries seemed indirectly to involve. Nor even now do I regard what you said as indicating more than a willingness to consider favourably my name in connection with the post of which we have spoken.'

He need not have written so anxiously. The appointment was as good as made. On 24 June, Salisbury replied:

I am very glad to see that Sir T. Smith gives so favourable an account of your case. Probably work in another climate with better hours will rather do you good than harm. I shall send in my submission shortly to the Queen, and unless she has just changed in her view, I shall have no difficulty in getting her approval. I enclose a transcript from a part of one of her letters which she charged me particularly to show you.

Queen Victoria's letter to her Prime Minister, written three days after she had entered her eightieth year, must surely rank among the most remarkable ever to come from the pen of that wise and perspicacious monarch. Its barely decipherable calligraphy, the result of failing eyesight, is itself a pathetic commentary on her devotion to duty:

The Queen read with much interest Lord Salisbury's letter respecting the future Vice Roy and his account of his conversation with Sir Wm. Lockhart with whom she feels sure he will have been pleased. His opinion of Mr G. Curzon is certainly of great weight and the latter's friendly feeling towards the Ameer and his knowledge of Affghanistan [*sic*] are very important.

But that is not all; the future Vice Roy must really shake himself more and more free from his red-tapist narrow-minded Council and Entourage. He must be *more independent, must hear for himself* what the *feelings* of the Natives really are, and do what he thinks right and not be guided by the *snobbish* and vulgar, over-bearing and offensive behaviour of our Civil and Political Agents, if we are to go on peaceably and happily in India, and to be liked and beloved by high and low – as well as respected as we ought to be – and not trying to trample on the people and continually reminding them and making them feel that they are a conquered people. They must of course *feel* that we are masters but it should be done kindly and not offensively which alas! is so often the case. Would Mr Curzon feel and do this? Would Mrs Curzon who is an American do to represent a Vice Queen?

Salisbury commended the Queen's words to Curzon. 'Putting aside the very un-official mode of expression, I entirely concur in the idea which is at the bottom of the extract. Paper and "damned nigger" are threatening our rule in India: and unfortunately as we grow more contemptuous, the Indian natives of all races are becoming more conscious of it, and more sensitive.' He went on to ask Curzon that his appointment to India should for the present be kept secret.

In a long and affectionate letter of thanks to the Prime Minister, Curzon, too, recognized the prescience of the Queen:

I shall not fail to bear in mind her wise injunctions. They might furnish a Rule of Conduct to any one about to occupy a position of authority over Asiatic races. In travelling I have seen something of these and have been thrown so much in their society that I hope I have lost – if indeed I ever had – the insular arrogance of the Englishman. One is more likely to find this among men who have lived long – often too long – in the East, and have become hardened and sometimes almost brutalised by contact, in posts of power, with people of a lower social and mental organisation. I recognise that the newcomer, unwarped by these associations, ought to set a different example and to keep in control the sort of spirit that made the French writer say of our rule in India: 'Ils sont justes mais ils ne sont pas bons.'

'That I should at my years,' he ended, 'receive from her hand this high post of trust which you are recommending her to confer upon me will lend a distinction to the honour that the winning of no other prize in life could give.'

'George Curzon is to be the next Viceroy,' Hamilton told Elgin on 5 August. 'I should have preferred Balfour of Burleigh, as he is a safe, reliable man, who has not committed himself in writing or speeches to any particular frontier views or policy, but the appointment is not mine but the Prime Minister's. Curzon is a charming fellow, and whose ability, industry, and courage make him in some respects admirably qualified. The spirit of adventure is somewhat developed in him, and an adventurous Viceroy has too many vistas of exploration open to him.'

Lord Balfour of Burleigh, Secretary of State for Scotland since 1895, had many of the sound but unspectacular qualities of Lord Elgin. He was competent, cautious, and uncomplicated. He possessed the administrative experience to grapple with the endemic problems of Indian famine and plague, and could bring a knowledge of the business world to the no less pressing financial difficulties of the sub-continent.

What tipped the scales against him was Curzon's deeper interest in the Indian frontier. In the previous year the entire north-west frontier had blazed into revolt, a conflagration extinguished only after costly operations involving the use of 60,000 troops. Although the Commander-in-Chief described Elgin as 'straight, clever and considerate', others charged the Viceroy with unpreparedness and indecision. Those were not failings of which Curzon had ever been accused. 'The soldiers almost always are on the side of confidence,' he had written to Salisbury about the Khyber Pass in August 1897. 'They think a fort sufficiently strong or a garrison sufficiently numerous. Only when the post has fallen and the garrison been cut up, is it realised that the one was untenable and the other inadequate.'

Hamilton, on whom fell the ultimate responsibility for Indian policy and its justification in Parliament, feared that Curzon's recorded opinions and belligerent attitude would be a handicap to his success as Viceroy. The Prime Minister, however, for all his dislike of military entanglements and excessive expenditure on defence, recognized the Indian frontier as an outpost of Empire that required a firm hand; and he later told Lady Curzon, with more enthusiasm than accuracy, that her husband's frontier policy would keep India for Great Britain fifty years longer than she would otherwise have kept it.

In recommending Curzon's name to the Queen, Salisbury made only one concession to Hamilton's qualms: he told the Viceroy-designate that his latest literary work, *On the Indian Frontier*, could not now be permitted to appear. The book was already in print, and the author had not only to return a handsome advance of £1,500 to the publisher but also to settle outstanding charges of £153 19*s*. By the time he returned from India seven years later, he considered the work to be out of date and it was never published. Curzon thought that Salisbury had behaved with 'a quite unnecessary punctilio'. He could nevertheless reflect that £153 19*s*. was not an excessive price to pay for the Viceroyalty.

The appointment was announced on 11 August. The following day Lord Scarsdale disengaged himself from shooting grouse to send a delighted letter to his son: 'I begin to realise what a splendid position you have deservedly won,' he wrote. 'Congrats pour in from every quarter and the country generally are as proud of you as I, your father, am, and more I cannot say.' Alfred Lyttelton's affectionate exhuberance epitomized the joy of Curzon's friends: 'And here is the top place of the Empire for you, my dear, I knew you would get to it, as I wrote once when first you got your foot on to the ladder, and some Dryasdust ventured to question. So here's to you, old boy, with every blessing for the future and every memory of the past.'

Greetings poured down on the new Viceroy from all sides of the House of Commons. Even Sir Henry Fowler, whose life he had once made a burden, wrote with warm goodwill: 'Although I may not always have agreed with some aspects of your policy, none wishes you success more heartily than I do.' Only *The Times* was coldly non-committal. 'We sincerely hope,' the leading article ran, 'for Mr Curzon's sake and that of the Empire, that Lord Salisbury's very interesting experiment will succeed.'

The author of those unenthusiastic words was nearer the truth than he probably suspected. For at the moment they appeared, Curzon lay helplessly on his back and in pain. Encouraged by the result of Sir Thomas Smith's medical examination in June, he had since driven himself too hard and paid the familiar penalty. Brodrick was disturbed to hear from Balfour that he and Salisbury were considering whether Curzon could still take up the appointment. At Brodrick's persuasion Balfour agreed to wait a few days, then called on Curzon to enquire after his health. He found the object of his solicitude, who had just bought a new and grander house to occupy on his return from India, transferring bottles of wine with his own hands from one cellar to another.

In spite of his astonishing resilience, Curzon was alarmed enough to seek further medical advice from Mr Howard Marsh, the future Professor of Surgery at Cambridge. For a fee of five guineas, he received this report:

There is nothing to suggest the least probability of the presence of organic disease. In fact it may be definitely said that none exists. Nor is there any ground for fear that any will, at any time, be developed.

There is strong reason to expect that the increase of curvature – which no doubt, so far as any has occurred, has been directly due to over work – will be corrected under the favourable conditions which can now be secured.

The best course will be to rest as much as possible in bed or on a couch till the pain of the present attack has subsided, and, for the next four weeks, to avoid muscular fatigue, and to have a good deal of horizontal, or reclining rest.

At Strathpeffer douching for the spine can be had. It should be douched once a day, with water as hot as can be borne without any discomfort. Rubbing after the douche could probably be useful. After a week, the douching with sea water can be carried on with a large bath sponge.

Dr J. feels that, as all the muscles and their nerves are perfectly healthy, and only much fatigued, electrical treatment does not promise any real advantage.

It is well worth trying the exercise shown today. In many cases it very materially improves the position of the hips.

There is strong ground for expecting that the rest which can now be secured will lead to much improvement: and that, in the future, the trouble will be much less than has recently been the case. But very much depends on the degree to which fatigue can be avoided, and reclining rest secured after work.

The stays, with the present amount of stiffening, should be used as long as they give relief.

He dutifully underwent a regime of douches and baths at Strathpeffer, the spa in the Scottish Highlands, and continued to encase his back in a steel and leather support. But he did nothing to remove the ultimate cause of his intermittent collapses: he did not know the meaning of rest.

On his way to Strathpeffer he was bidden to Balmoral by the Queen, who, he told Mary, 'talked incessantly'. She wrote in her journal on 4 September: 'Soon after luncheon saw Mr Curzon, and talked of all the difficulties lying before him, but he knows India well and is free from red-tapism, so that I hope he will do well.' He dined with her that evening, and was present when a dramatic telegram arrived from Kitchener announcing the victory over the Dervishes at Omdurman. A few days later she wrote to tell Lord Salisbury how satisfied she was with his choice of Viceroy.

Among the subjects which Curzon discussed with his Sovereign was his proposed title. In order that he should uphold the dignity of the Queen-Empress whom he was to represent in India, he had to submit to being made a peer. It was not a fate that he relished. Several times during his years in the House of Commons he had attempted to abrogate the custom that required a Member to abandon his seat on succeeding to a peerage. And now, it seemed, he was required to pay the penalty even before his father was dead.

Lord Salisbury offered a neat solution to the problem. He suggested that Curzon should be created an Irish peer. Such a dignity, while ensuring that he bore a lordly style indistinguishable from that of any other peer, would leave him free to seek election to the House of Commons on his return from India. By the Act of Union with Ireland in 1800, the Irish peers had received the right to elect twenty-eight of their number to sit for life in the House of Lords. But those who preferred to stand as candidates for the Commons were free to do so; and it was as an Irish peer that Lord Palmerston had sat in the Commons for nearly sixty years, for six of them as Prime Minister.

It was true that no Irish Peerage had been created since 1868 and that none was expected to be created: it was also true that Curzon was without Irish connections or property and that he had never set foot in Ireland for a single day. These considerations were set aside, and on 24 September 1898 *The Times* announced: 'The Queen has been pleased to confer the dignity of a peerage upon the Rt Hon. George N. Curzon, Viceroy designate of India, by the name, style, and title of Baron Curzon of Kedleston, in the Peerage of Ireland.' The fees he was required to pay amounted to £290: little enough ransom, he might have thought, to avoid premature and perpetual banishment to the House of Lords.

The newest Irish peer to be created – and indeed the last of them – would have liked to call himself simply Lord Curzon. At the end of the eighteenth century, however, Assheton Curzon, younger brother of the first Lord Scarsdale, had been created Baron Curzon, and a few years later, Viscount Curzon. This Viscounty had since been swallowed up in the greater dignity of the Earldom of Howe bestowed on Assheton's grandson in 1821: but it continued to be used as a courtesy title by the eldest son and heir of successive Earls.

In 1898 the heir to Earl Howe was George, Viscount Curzon, a near contemporary and friend of his distant cousin, George Nathaniel. Since 1885 he had sat in the Commons for High Wycombe, and had recently received minor political office as Treasurer of Her Majesty's Household. For the new Viceroy to call himself Lord Curzon would undoubtedly have led to untold confusion between the two public men; he was therefore obliged, at the very least, to add a distinguishing territorial designation to his name, and wrote to ask whether Earl Howe would mind if he called himself Lord Curzon of Kedleston. Howe was not altogether happy at the emergence of a second Lord Curzon, but gave his assent.

That was not the end of the matter. The Viceroy's official signature was Curzon of Kedleston. But as he immersed himself in the gigantic task of Indian administration, he fell into the habit of saving time by writing just Curzon. There was, after all, little chance that his signature would be confused with that of Viscount Curzon, MP, 6,000 miles away. And after 1900, when Viscount Curzon succeeded his father as fourth Earl Howe, there was no risk of uncertainty, for his courtesy title was assumed by a sixteen-year-old schoolboy. The new Lord Howe nevertheless felt that the rights of his family were being infringed; taking advantage of his place at Court as a Lord-in-Waiting to the new Sovereign, he appealed personally to the ultimate arbiter of such usages.

The King took the view that there was merit in Howe's case. Accordingly, his private secretary, Francis Knollys, spoke discreetly to the Prime Minister's private secretary, Schomberg McDonnell, who passed on a hint of Royal displeasure when next he wrote to his old friend the Viceroy. This was just such a controversy as Curzon relished; and in an immensely long letter that could have contained his full signature several hundred times, he defended himself with asperity. Piling precedent upon precedent, he pointed out that there was no law or custom that required a peer to sign his full title, and that in any case, as the representative of the senior branch of the family, he had an overriding claim to call himself simply Curzon.

'I would be as strong in small things as in big,' Curzon once told Selborne. He was speaking of British foreign policy, but his dictum applied no less to all that touched his personal pride. The dispute about his signature smouldered for years, bursting into flame for the last time in 1908, when Lord Howe noticed a letter in the *Morning Post* signed Curzon: it had not been written by his son. After another tart exchange with his kinsman, Curzon conceded that as the young Viscount was now married and beginning to make his way in public life – particularly as a pioneer of motoring – he himself would magnanimously revert to the practice of signing himself Curzon of Kedleston. In private correspondence he nevertheless continued to abbreviate his signature.

Throughout the autumn of 1898, Curzon pressed ahead with the domestic arrangements of his Indian appointment and subjected Lord Elgin, the outgoing Viceroy, to a characteristically exacting catechism:

> Do you leave me an A.D.C.? Is there not an admirable house steward? Do I take over carriages, plate, wine? Do the first two of these belong to Government, and are there sufficient? Must I bring a coachman and a chef? Is there a library at Government House at Calcutta or Simla, or must I bring out my own books? Have you any advice to give me as to uniforms or outfit? ...

Elgin's reply contained much sensible advice:

> It is a very big concern, for a census just taken in Simla showed our establishment to number 700 in all. ... As to libraries there is nothing in either house worthy of that name. ... The Privy Councillor's uniform is sufficient for all purposes. As a matter of fact the Viceroy wears uniform very seldom. ... A light grey frock coat is very useful for hot weather. As to outfit generally, I may, in the first place, pass on to

you the piece of advice I received from Dufferin – 'Take your fur coat'! Personally I have never used it, but I believe the underlying sentiment is sound i.e. do not provide only for tropical heat. A good deal of the Simla season is like ordinary summer weather at home, and both the beginning and end of it can be bracing, if not cold. On tour you may also find considerable differences of temperature. My own feeling is that one's tendency is to bring out too much. ... So much of your time is spent in the company of your study table that to be comfortably clad for working is making provision for a very large proportion of the whole day. ...

In his search for a private secretary, Curzon wrote to ask the advice of his old Balliol friend, Walter Lawrence, with whom he had spent a Christmas in Calcutta during his first tour round the world. The other Balliol contemporary at their reunion, Lord Herbrand Russell, had in 1893 succeeded his brother as eleventh Duke of Bedford and tempted Lawrence to retire from the Indian Civil Service in order to become his agent at Woburn. In reply to Curzon's enquiry for the name of a suitable private secretary, Lawrence suggested James Dunlop Smith, who had spent twenty years in India as a soldier and administrator; and he added that he wished he were available himself to accompany Curzon. The new Viceroy at once begged the Duke to release Lawrence, and so the matter was arranged.

No Viceroy has ever been more magnificently served than was Curzon by Lawrence. To an intense personal loyalty he added two other valuable qualifications. During his years in the Indian Civil Service he had acquired an entire familiarity with the machinery of government at every level; and having retired, he was able to manage all matters of promotion and preferment in an utterly disinterested spirit.

Winston Churchill, who at the age of twenty-three had just taken part in the charge of the 21st Lancers at Omdurman and, through his mother, received Curzon's congratulations, was tempted to offer himself as an aide-de-camp on the new Viceroy's staff. 'It is worth considering,' he told Lady Randolph, '£300 a year and no expenses of any sort.' But Curzon received fifty applications for the appointment and Churchill's claim, if pressed, was unsuccessful.

A succession of splendid feasts sped Curzon on his way. At the end of October more than 200 Old Etonians gathered at the Monico, in Piccadilly Circus, to celebrate the simultaneous appointment of Lord Curzon as Viceroy of India, of Lord Minto as Governor-General of Canada, and of the Rev. J.E.C. Welldon as Bishop of Calcutta.

Minto, nearly fifteen years older than Curzon, had seen much active service as a soldier and had several times ridden in the Grand National. He was a straightforward, decent, devout Scot who hated wearing a top hat and on his birthday chose to dine off oxtail soup and tapioca pudding. It would have surprised Curzon to learn that Minto had earlier that year speculated on his own claims to the Viceroyalty of India: and astounded him to know that Minto was to succeed him in Calcutta seven years later.

For Doon Welldon, however, he had long forecast early promotion to the episcopal bench. It was one of Curzon's most attractive characteristics to be as ambitious for his friends as for himself; and in 1896, when Parliamentary Under-Secretary at the Foreign Office, he had written to the Prime Minister:

> I am very reluctant to intrude in matters which do not directly concern me. But in the event of your being called upon to fill any vacancy on the Episcopal Bench, would you allow me to bespeak your friendly consideration of the name of Welldon, Head Master of Harrow? He is a man of high character, great abilities, considerable learning and no small powers of speech. I have known him intimately since we were at Eton, though he is some five years older than myself. His work at Harrow is practically completed and his real interests and ambitions are centred, I think, in the Church.

The seed fell on barren ground. But in 1898 Lord George Hamilton, as Secretary of State for India, was required to nominate a new Bishop of Calcutta. His thoughts turned to Harrow, of which he was both an old boy and a governor; and before the year was out Welldon had been consecrated.

Neither the menu nor the toast list on 28 October 1898 was cramped by modesty. The Old Etonians ate hors d'œuvre and two soups, turbot and red mullet, ham mousse and young pullets, saddle of mutton and roast grouse, soufflés and puddings, ices and desert. They drank sherry and moselle, two champagnes, claret and port, brandy and liqueurs.

The back of the menu card was no less satisfying. It bore two parallel lists of names: one of Governors-General and Viceroys of India who had held office during the Queen's reign, the other of Governors-General of Canada during the same span of sixty years. The names of Etonians were printed in light blue, those of less fortunate proconsuls in black. There was more blue than black.

St John Brodrick, who had succeeded Curzon as Parliamentary Under-Secretary at the Foreign Office, was deputed by the committee organizing the dinner to ask Lord Salisbury whether he would preside. The Prime Minister replied that much as he wished to honour the guests, he had never liked Eton and would feel out of place at such a glorification of the school. Lord Rosebery was thereupon invited, and agreed to take the chair. But as he knew nothing of Salisbury's refusal he was puzzled by the boisterous and gleeful cheers which greeted his solemn affirmation: 'In all my life I have met only one Old Etonian who did not like Eton, and he speedily went to the Devil.'

Curzon admired Rosebery's eloquence. 'It is gilded with happy phrases,' he once wrote, 'it sparkles with effervescence and laughter, and it becomes a part of the intellectual capital of the whole community.' That evening, however, his speech scarcely escaped the banal. With an irony so subtle that perhaps it did not exist at all, Rosebery claimed that a great deal more than the Battle of Waterloo had been won on the playing-fields of Eton. 'What, for example,' he demanded, 'would Canada have done without Eton, when out of the last six Governors-General all but one are Etonians? And although my friend Lord Aberdeen is an unhappy exception, I do not doubt but if he could have been, he would have been an Etonian.'

Gazing about him, Roseberry confessed that he almost needed a pair of sun spectacles to contemplate 'the various dazzling celebrities who owe their various successes to Eton'. Even allowing for the euphoria of the moment, Curzon cannot entirely have shared these filial sentiments. Although he would always look back upon his schooldays at Eton with affection and gratitude, he nevertheless thought of himself as a self-made man. There was much validity in his claim. No retrospect of Curzon's life is complete that omits his relentless industry, his conquest of pain, his will to succeed. Sometimes, it is true, he would exaggerate the severity of his struggle and invest his triumphs with a uniqueness that was unjustified. On being appointed a Knight of the Garter, he told the ninth Duke of Devonshire: 'You, Victor, of course, have got the Garter as the head of a Garter family. Dukes of Devonshire always get the Garter. It is no credit to you at all. But for me it is a personal honour.' And when the Duke protested that he had served his country in both Houses of Parliament, at home and overseas, Curzon waved aside his apologia. 'No, no, Victor,' he repeated, 'it means nothing to you. I have earned it myself.'

What, however, Curzon could not deny was the extent to which Etonians had thronged his path to fame and offered him help or encouragement. At the Monico that October evening of 1898, his Eton mentors were represented by Hornby and Browning, Warre Cornish and Luxmoore; his earliest friends of school and university by Welldon, Brodrick, Leveson Gower, Brett and the Lyttelton brothers; his later friends of Parliament, Crabbet and the Souls by Balfour, Wyndham, Vincent, Liddell and Charteris; the Foreign Office by Barrington, McDonnell and Bertie.

There was the Warden of All Souls, Sir William Anson; Curzon's travelling companion across the United States, Stuart Donaldson, and his fellow explorer of the Pamirs, Henry Lennard; the Indian official who censored his work on Persia, Sir Alfred Lyall; the soldier who interceded on his behalf with the Viceroy, Field-Marshal Lord Roberts; the President of Pop who had helped him to entertain Mr Gladstone in 1878, C.M.Smith.

Replying to the toast of his health, Curzon saluted Eton less fulsomely than Rosebery. He acknowledged his debt to the inspiring lecture of Sir James Fitz-James Stephen which had first fired his schoolboy mind with 'the fascination and, if I may say so, the sacredness of India'. Then he spoke some words which lifted the occasion from a mawkish festival of self-congratulation to a humble avowal of faith. 'The East,' he said, 'is a university in which the scholar never takes his degree. It is a temple in which the suppliant adores but never catches sight of the object of his devotion. It is a journey the goal of which is always in sight but is never attained. There we are always learners, always worshippers, always pilgrims. I rejoice to be allowed to take my place in the happy band of students and of wayfarers who have trodden that path for a hundred years.'

In the intervals of packing up his possessions and making inventories of furniture in his own hand, Curzon took his wife on a round of farewell visits to friends. Although conscious of the task that lay before him, he recaptured the buoyant spirits of his youth in an atmosphere that was never far from hilarity. After one such week-end at Panshanger, where Lord and Lady Cowper had assembled the Ribblesdales, the Brodricks, the Asquiths, the Grenfells and Arthur Balfour, the local train was late. So at the tiny station of Cole Green he wrote out an imperious telegram asking for the London express to be stopped for him at Hatfield. But he was not yet in India, and Ettie Grenfell later described how the old station master to whom he handed the message slowly read it out word by word: 'Lord Curzon of Kedleston, Viceroy Designate. ... Why, yer'll be there yerself before the wire.'

The final farewell took place on the evening of 9 December 1898, when most of the Souls he had entertained at the Bachelors' Club in 1889 and 1890 reassembled at the Hotel Cecil to say goodbye to George and Mary Curzon. It was considered rather daring to hold such a party at an hotel and not in a private house; to seat the company at small round tables; and to illuminate the courtyard with a powerful electric searchlight during the arrival and departure of the guests. The professional gossips also thought it necessary to note 'the presence of over a score of English ladies, leaders of English Society, in honour of the American lady who is about to occupy such an exalted position in the British Empire,' and to add that 'there were three more ladies of American birth to keep Lady Curzon's nationality in countenance – the Duchess of Marlborough, Lady Randolph Churchill and Mrs Henry White'.

After George and Mary Curzon, the hero of the evening was George Wyndham. Since his appointment as Balfour's private secretary in 1887 and his election as member of Parliament for Dover two years later, he had waited expectantly but in vain for Ministerial office. He was not appreciated in the Commons. 'His style,' Lucy wrote, 'was ornate, his phrases smelt of the lamp, and his delivery was marred by certain mannerisms not wholly free from suspicion of practice before the cheval glass.' Balfour gave him unpalatable advice. 'Dilute, my dear George, dilute,' he told him after an early speech. In 1895 he further bruised Wyndham's feelings by not only declining to recommend him to the Prime Minister for a place in the new

Government, but also by the brutal suggestion that he should abandon political ambitions for a literary career.

In the summer of 1898, however, all had changed. Curzon was appointed to India, Brodrick succeeded him at the Foreign Office, and Wyndham took Brodrick's place as Under-Secretary at the War Office. Salisbury was reputed to have said: 'I don't like poets.' That was a reproach which caused Wyndham no distress; and to celebrate the departure of the Curzons for India, he composed these rhymes in the deft style of Crabbet:

Eight years ago we sat at your table:
We were the guests and you were the host.
You were young, said the World, but we knew you were able
To justify more than your friends dared boast.
We knew you would win all wreaths in the end
And we knew you would still be the same dear friend:
And that's what we cared for most.

You wrote us some rhymes wherein friendship and laughter
Played in a blaze of affection and jest
Round the name of each one for whom no years thereafter
Could blunt the sharp edge of that festival's zest.
For we knew that your motto:–'Let Curzon hold
What Curzon held' – was no whit too bold
For its vaunt of your claim on each guest.

Nor was it. We're here; though eight years have rolled o'er us,
All fond of you, proud of you, sorry to part.
And we ought, one and all, to give in one chorus
The send-off you've earned from our love for your start.
But the Brave men and Fair ones, sealed of the tribe
Of Nathaniel, have told one incompetent scribe
To sing what each feels in his heart.

He obeys; and he bids you recall all you chanted
Of each man and each woman who sat at your board,
And, then, to believe that the tributes you granted
Too kindly are now, and more justly, restored
To you and the Lady whom none of us knew
Eight years ago; but whom now, thanks to you,
We have all of us known and adored.

So 'Go in and win!' what's five years but a lustre
To shine round a name that already shines bright?
Then come back, and we'll greet you and go such a 'buster'
As never was seen; no, not even to-night!

Come back in five years with your sheaves of new Fame:
You'll find your old Friends; and you'll find them the same
As now when you gladden their sight.

In bidding goodbye to his hosts, Curzon, too, played upon the theme of friendship: 'Surfeited as I have been with the public demonstrations of the past few weeks, squeezed dry as I am of the last platitudes about India, it is with positive relief that I find myself in the wholly frivolous and utterly irresponsible society that is collected round these tables. For here I see about me the friends, and sometimes the critics, of a tumultuous but absolutely unrepentant youth; the comrades of a more sober and orderly middle age; and, when I return five years hence, what I hope may be the props and the solace of dull and declining years.'

George Wyndham earned an apostrophe all to himself: 'Poet, statesman, warrior, Adonis: there has been no one like him since Sir Philip Sidney. May he enjoy a similar fame! May he escape a similar fate.' And Hugo Elcho was assured that when he came out to India as a Viceregal guest, arrangements would be made for him to shoot tigers from the backs of elephants or elephants from the backs of tigers – whichever he preferred.

'I said goodbye to Curzon today amid a great crowd of his friends,' Hamilton wrote to Elgin on 15 December. 'The conditions under which he enters his term of office are so exceptionally favourable that, knowing how the unexpected occurs in political life, I feel as if the auspices were almost too favourable.'

Nor was Curzon himself insensitive to the whims of fortune. 'Here I am being inordinately fêted,' he told the Viceroy whom he was about to succeed. 'There is something to me incongruous in the whole thing. It is all very generous and very encouraging. But surely the entertainment and congratulation ought to come after, not before, performance. One goes out amid the glare of magnesium. How shall I return?'

Epilogue
PARTING OF FRIENDS

> Try and suffer fools more gladly, they constitute the majority of mankind. In dealing with your colleagues and subordinates, try and use your rare powers of expression in making things pleasant and smooth to those whom you overrule or dominate. Cases have more than once come to my notice where persons have been deeply wounded and gone from you full of resentment in consequence of some incautious joke or verbal rebuke, which they thought was harshly administered.
>
> – *Lord George Hamilton to Curzon, 16 September 1903*

India was the watershed both of Curzon's public career and of his private happiness. From his schooldays until his fortieth year he had consciously educated himself for high administrative office, and in 1898 stood on the threshold of what few doubted would be a chapter of unparalleled brilliance in the history of British India. Yet he was not too busy for friendship during those formative, ambitious years. 'There is one commodity in which I have never been lacking,' he told the Souls on his departure from England, 'and that is the possession of whole-hearted and loyal friends.'

Seven years later he returned, bitter and betrayed. He had achieved much as Viceroy, although he would have been disagreeably startled to learn that mid-twentieth-century India remembers him only for his loving preservation and restoration of ancient buildings and monuments.* Even those triumphs, however, were turned to dust by the acutely painful circumstances in which his rule ended. At earlier moments of defeat and disappointment in his life, as when he missed a First in Greats or failed to win the hand

* Pandit Nehru, the first Prime Minister of India after Independence, told the Earl of Swinton, Secretary of State for Commonwealth Relations from 1952 to 1955: 'After every other Viceroy has been forgotten, Curzon will be remembered because he restored all that was beautiful in India.'

of Sibell Grosvenor – he had found strength and consolation in his friends. India, however, was the grave of his affection for both St John Brodrick and Arthur Balfour; and although he treated Doon Welldon with unusual tenderness when they disagreed about the value of missionary activity in the sub-continent, there were few other intimates of his boyhood, adolescence and early manhood who did not then or later feel the chill of his displeasure.

The seeds of asperity were in him before he became Viceroy. When his heart was touched, he displayed generosity and understanding; but he could also be callous and domineering. Cecil Spring Rice wrote of him in 1898: 'I am always in two minds about Curzon. He has a great deal of industry and courage and also of sterling qualities, but it isn't a fine nature.' And again, 'I can never leave his presence without a disagreeable feeling that he has made me appear like a fool.' Most companions of Curzon's youth, however, took a more magnanimous view of his failings, marvelling that the burdens he imposed on mind and body did not leave more obvious scars on his character.

From the moment he landed at Bombay, ill-health and overwork began to accentuate his emotional inconstancy, leading him to strain, sometimes to snap, the cherished personal ties of happier days. India was not the end of his public career; after a decade in the wilderness he was restored to high office. But he could not recapture the glad morning of his youth. He died almost friendless.

Ill-temper sprang from ill-health. Ironically it was St John Brodrick, the most savagely mauled victim of Curzon's later wrath, who alone dared warn the Viceroy against the dangers of needless fatigue. On 14 December 1898, a few hours before Curzon left England, Brodrick wrote him this letter from the Foreign Office:

My dear old boy,

If I had not seen you for that minute this evening, I intended to have written a few lines of farewell. I still do so for I have something to say.

You know how warmly I have welcomed your appointment. Except your wife, I doubt if anyone would have been more distressed if it had not come to you. Subject to one thing only I cannot doubt you will make your Vice-royalty memorable if not unique. You have knowledge, energy, talent and resolution in a degree I think never previously combined in the history of India.

But I, with many others, are sorely troubled – about your health. For years I have envied your marvellous nervous energy and recuperative power, and it is only because I seem to see that the one has been over-taxed and the other has ceased to come to the rescue that I now write – not on my own behalf alone.

You have lived a fuller life for the last 10 years than any man alive – and for the last 9 months you have hardly known a day's real health.

Since August things have multiplied upon you to cause a strain, when your friends felt that with the prospect ahead every day should have been reserved, and every action measured.

Do not think I am going to criticise what is past; you know I have never even referred to it, because I felt that no remonstrance could put on the drag, while it certainly would worry you.

But it is only fair to tell you that your meetings, your book, your new house, all competing for your time with necessary preparations, have caused much heart searching among your best wishers. I know both Lord Salisbury and Arthur Balfour have felt this very much; others who have seen you in your overstrain still more.

Please remember that all of us have but one aim. You cannot carry on as you have done these last 10 years. A man with heart complaint would not run 100 yards if he were late, and you, with overtired back and nerves, have *no right* to work when you are tired. ...

If you go on as at present you will come back like Dalhousie and Canning. For the appetite for work when one is overstrained (I know it well) becomes a disease.

You are to my mind bound by heavy 'recognizances' to spare yourself at the first symptom of fatigue. You owe it to those who have given you this great post; you owe it to us your friends who look forward to your subsequent career; you owe it above all to your wife, whose life is wrapped up in yours. You will not be angry with me for writing this. I have been asked over and over again lately to speak to you and have declined to worry you. But now – and for the only time – I speak as I feel. ...

Goodnight and goodbye. You will never want a friend, nor need of any assistance I could give, but no separation will ever make me feel that you and yours are altogether apart from one who has so long been

Your afft. Friend
St John Brodrick

In his reply Curzon promised to take Brodrick's well-meant advice to heart. But two and a half years later he was writing to Lord Ampthill, the newly arrived Governor of Madras:

You ask me how I get through my work. I think I can answer: (1) By never doing anything else. (2) By sitting up into the night. I invariably get $2\frac{1}{2}$ to 3 hours good work after dinner. (3) By rapidity in writing – the result of long practice. (4) By familiarity with most of the subjects, which are not entirely new to me, as I have been studying India for years. (5) By invariably devoting Sunday to some big subject, upon which I am working in independence of the ordinary routine. Thus I keep pace, more or less, with both. Again, I write the MS of letters in pencil, either in bed, or on a boat, or when dressing, or anywhere, whenever the thing comes into my mind: and these pencillings are then copied out and submitted to me for signature.

I am far from recommending my methods to any one else: for the concentration that they represent is the result of temperament far more than of training. I therefore take not the smallest credit for them, any more than I should for a good figure or a well-developed calf.

His appetite for work enabled him to penetrate into fields which other Viceroys had left untouched. 'Of course,' he said of outraged officials, 'I disturb and annoy these old fogies, looking into everything, writing about everything, picking out the flaws.' Not all of them resented it. Sir Evan Maconochie, after thirty-two years in the Indian Civil Service, called Curzon 'the greatest Indian Viceroy of our times – possibly of all times – fearless, creative, ardent, human'.

But the Viceroy added immensely and unnecessarily to his toil by undertaking absurdly trivial yet intricate duties. He would write up his personal accounts himself in enormous ledgers, a task not only tedious in itself but one which revealed the depressing conclusion that a salary of £16,680 still left him £8,500 out of pocket at the end of his fourth year in India. More precious hours were frittered away in detecting the peculations of a dishonest cook. 'We caught him redhanded,' he wrote in triumph to Pom McDonnell. 'He returned 596 chickens as having been consumed within a single month. We went to the tradesman who had the contract and found the figures were 290.'

Once he shocked even his devoted private secretary by correcting some proofs while presiding over a large dinner party. 'This reminded me painfully,' Lawrence wrote, 'of Archimedes at the fall of Syracuse.' The practice was never repeated, but Curzon continued to govern India with an attention to petty detail that again and again brought him to the edge of nervous and physical exhaustion. And to the racking pain in his back there was now added the torture of insomnia.

At first he was able to bear both the burden of paper-work and intermittent illness without injury to his personal or official relationships. 'I think you are too indifferent to other people's opinion to care much about what they say,' Pom McDonnell wrote to him in August 1899, 'but it may nevertheless interest you to know that we hear golden accounts both from civilians and soldiers of your work. I only hope you are not overdoing yourself.'

Before long, however, Curzon's letters began to display a malaise of spirit that could hardly fail to imperil his judgement. 'Grind, grind, grind,' he wrote to his wife, 'with never a word of encouragement; on, on, on, till the collar breaks and the poor beast stumbles and dies. I suppose it is all right and it doesn't matter. But sometimes when I think of myself spending my heart's blood here and no one caring one little damn, the spirit goes out of me and I feel like giving in. You don't know – or perhaps you do – what my isolation has been this summer. I am crying now so that I can scarcely see the page.'

The theme of self-pity continued to cloud his correspondence: 'Here I am, working away the whole day long and a considerable part of the night in the discharge of what I believe to be a serious and solemn duty. I am conducting the task in exile, in complete isolation from all friends and advisers, surrounded by forces and combinations against which it often requires great courage to struggle, habitually harassed, constantly weary and often in physical distress and pain.'

One reason for his growing depression was the inadequacy of the administrative machine he had inherited as an instrument of ambitious Viceregal designs. 'Nothing has been done hitherto under six months,' he told Mrs Craigie. 'When I suggest six weeks, the attitude is one of pained surprise; if six days, one of pathetic protest; if six hours, one of stupefied resignation.' Three years later he appeared to have inspired little improvement. 'The Government of India is a mighty and miraculous machine for doing nothing,' he wrote to the Secretary of State. 'It is worked by loyal and hard-worked men. I have not one word to say against their devotion to duty and their industry. But they are so absorbed with the daily grind that their eyes are never lifted from the ground. No ray of imagination strikes upon their minds. No spark of initiative springs from their breasts. If left to themselves, they will instinctively oppose and throttle every reform.'

Shortly afterwards Curzon recorded another stage in his disillusionment with the Indian Civil Service:

> The average young Englishman, who has been for ten years in the country, no longer has the affection for the people, or the love for India, that his fore-runner possessed in the days gone by. This is due to many causes; partly to the attitude and conduct of the Natives themselves; partly to the lamentable paucity in recent years of great men who could set a powerful example in the higher ranks of the service; much more to the absorbing attractions of home life and home associations, which, through the medium of improved steam and postal communications, and of the electric telegraph, are always drawing a man's heart away from India back to England, and teaching him to regard himself as an unfortunate exile in a land of regrets. This increase of interest in England means a corresponding diminution of interest and weakening of moral stamina here. It is being found out by the Natives themselves: they constantly complain in their newspapers that the Sahib is not what he used to be, and that the relations between the two races are not improving but going back. In the long run, unless we can arrest this inclination, it must be most injurious, and may one day be fatal, to our dominion in this country.

By 1903, the note of bitterness had become more marked. The greatest danger threatening British rule in India, he wrote, was 'the racial pride and the undisciplined passions of the inferior class of Englishmen in this country'. Another year, and the man who had once stood amazed at the benevolence of the British official overseas wrote this epitaph on his shattered ideals. 'It is to me,' he said, 'a melancholy and an inscrutable thing that the Indian Civil Service, the proudest and most honourable in the world, turns out from time to time, and as it seems to me with increasing frequency, some of the meanest and most malignant types of disappointed humanity whom it has been my fortune to meet.'

For the British Army in India he conceived a fierce dislike that was reciprocated. Shocked by the indifference of the military authorities to occasional incidents in which Indians were ill-treated by soldiers or killed by carelessly discharged rifles, he imposed stern corrective punishments on the regiments concerned. 'I will not be a party to any of the scandalous hushing-up of bad cases of which there is too much in this country,' he wrote to the King-Emperor's private secretary, 'or to the theory that a white man may kick or batter a black man to death with impunity because he is only a "d—d nigger". There is too much of that spirit abroad; and I have sacrificed ease and popularity in the effort to combat it.' Even in the midst of the glorious pageantry of the Coronation Durbar in 1903, he had to endure the humiliation of hearing one of the guilty regiments cheered with defiant exuberance by his own guests.

'One thing I will and do make a stand for here,' he told Alfred Lyttelton, 'and that is righteousness in administration. It is not that I have turned Pharisee, or that my spirits have gone sour. But the English people, and still more the English rulers, are here for an example. Every one of our actions should be open to inspection: every deed should be a duty. I set this before myself, and whatever is said I mean to go through with it. I will not connive at the scandals that go on: will not hush up ill-doing because it is found in high places. I decline to wink at all the little jobs and naughtinesses and frauds. Above all I see, oh so clearly, that we can only hold this country by our superior standards of honour and virtue and by getting the Natives to recognise them as such.'

The natives unfortunately showed scant appreciation of his struggles to protect their supposed interests: and for this Curzon was not without blame. 'I love India, its people, its history, its government,' the newly appointed Viceroy told his Etonian audience in 1898, 'I love the absorbing mysteries of its civilisation and its life.' Seven years later he was addressing the Convocation of Calcutta University in silkily offensive terms that betrayed the disenchantment of the intervening period and earned him lasting resentment:

> I hope I am making no false or arrogant claim when I say that the highest ideal of truth is to a large extent a Western conception. I do not thereby mean to claim that Europeans are universally or even generally truthful, still less do I mean that Asiatics deliberately or habitually deviate from the truth. The one proposition would be absurd, and the other insulting. But undoubtedly truth took a high place in the moral codes of the West before it had been similarly honoured in the East, where craftiness and diplomatic wile have always been held in much repute. We may prove it by the common innuendo that lurks in the words 'Oriental diplomacy', by which is meant something rather tortuous and hypersubtle.

In private correspondence he displayed even less confidence in the Indian character. When asked why more Indians were not employed in the highest ranks of the service, he replied: 'Because they are not competent, and because it is our constant experience that, when placed in authority, if an emergency occurs, they lose their heads or abdicate altogether.' He struck the same note of high-minded intransigence in a letter to Alfred Lyttelton: 'We cannot take the Natives up into the administration. They are crooked-minded and corrupt. We have got therefore to go on ruling them and we can only do it with success by being both kindly and virtuous. I daresay I am talking rather like a schoolmaster; but after all, the millions I have to manage are less than school children.'

Curzon once said that for him India was duty written in five letters instead of four. It was a proud and legitimate boast: but it was not enough. In alienating educated Indian opinion by an almost contemptuous want of tact, he denied himself both the gratitude and the respect of the governed. Lady Minto, wife of the man who succeeded him as Viceroy, struck a fair balance when she wrote of Curzon's departure: 'I believe a sigh of relief has gone up all over India; this has been a reign of terror and every official has been reduced to pulp, and Lord Curzon's marvellous ability and undefeated power of working beyond the endurance of any other man have dissected and laid bare the innermost workings of every department throughout India. But he has treated the 300,000,000 people as puppets.'

One old friend of Curzon who declined to treat Indians as puppets was Dr Welldon, the new Bishop of Calcutta. He believed that all Indians had souls, and that his mission was to enlist them under the banner of Christ, whatever other faiths happened to claim their allegiance. It was a conviction that cost him the trust of the Viceroy and ultimately his diocese.

'A very honest and able man with a long life before him,' Dr Jowett said of him in 1889, 'and if he is not too honest and open, not unlikely to be the Archbishop of Canterbury.' As the Master of Balliol discerned, Welldon possessed Christian virtues but little aptitude for ecclesiastical flexibility. Lord Salisbury, too, had presumably recognized this inadequacy when ignoring Curzon's plea that Welldon should be made a Bishop. Lord George Hamilton, however, had taken a broader view of the Anglican Church and appointed him to the See of Calcutta. The new Bishop, having shared with Curzon and Minto the profane benediction of his fellow old Etonians, reached India early in 1899.

The euphoria of the Café Monico did not long survive the climate and a fundamental disagreement between Viceroy and Metropolitan about the role of missionaries. Nearly twenty years had passed since Curzon, still an undergraduate, had presided in Derby over a meeting of the Society for the Propagation of the Gospel. He had then told his audience:

It is the history of the missionary enterprise, containing a martyr roll of great names of which all Englishmen are proud, that has done more than anything else to increase throughout the world that respect and admiration for the white race by which a triumph over fanaticism and over heathen tribes has been secured.

Subsequent travels through the East, however, had taught him that missionary activity could best touch the hearts of the unregenerate through education, charity and medical aid. As Viceroy, too, he insisted that whatever the intellectual shortcomings of the Indian peoples, their traditional creeds must on no account be disturbed by the proselytizing zeal of Christian missions. 'Imperialism,' he wrote, 'will only win its way in this country if it wears a secular and not an ecclesiastical garb.'

That was an attitude which Welldon found it impossible to condone. He feared that without Christian exhortation, all religious life in India might succumb to the alien influences of Western materialism. Such a belief encouraged him to take an insensitive view of Indian susceptibilities, and even before he left England, he had begun to alarm the Viceroy:

I am surprised [Curzon wrote to Hamilton in January 1899] at the extent to which the well-meaning but rather incautious utterances of Welldon in his various speeches and addresses at home appear to have prejudiced his reception here. ... He is alleged to have offended the natives by avowing that it was the Mission of the Church, and therefore his own, to convert them; the Army generally by saying that their morals are in need of reform; the Roman Catholics by some phrase which I have not heard quoted verbatim; and English Society at large by the impression that he is coming out to teach them all how to be good.

The Viceroy's surprise turned to pain and then to annoyance. 'I have a deep and affectionate regard for him in many ways,' he told the Secretary of State in February 1901, 'since he is one of my oldest friends, and I may almost say my oldest friend in India. ... I used to think of him as a future Archbishop of Canterbury. I do so no longer, for I doubt his capacity to fill a great position in which so many demands are made upon tactfulness, urbanity and the power to lead.'

By every mail, the Viceroy despatched to London a catalogue of the Bishop's failings. 'Welldon,' he wrote in June, 'thinks that the main duty of the English Church in India is towards the Indians. I think that it is towards the English.' And in July: 'He is thought to be bent upon forcing upon this country a policy of the Bible in education and proselytism in religion.'

Enormously corpulent, suffering from dysentery and malaria, disliked by his own clergy and unappreciated by his fellow countrymen, Welldon returned to England on prolonged leave in the summer of 1901. Winston Churchill, in his first year as a Member of Parliament, wrote to tell Curzon of his old Headmaster's arrival:

I am to attend a dinner to him next week. They ought to make him an English bishop. I am sure he is unhappy out in India. The East without wife, woman, sport, war, authority or pomp seems to me a very bad bargain – and in these days of lawlessness in the church, disciplinarians of the Welldonian type are a pressing necessity.

Churchill's suggestion of an English bishopric for Welldon had also occurred to Hamilton, who wrote to Curzon at the end of August:

> Poor Welldon! I am responsible for his appointment, and I should not like to ruin his career. .. I tried him for a Bishopric here, but Salisbury would not hear of him. He would do better as a Dean, where he would not come in contact with the clergy, and would have special opportunities of exercising his great powers of speech.

Even back in England and on the verge of resignation, Welldon could not resist another blunder:

> Finally [Curzon wrote to Hamilton], he goes home and makes a speech in which he intimates that the only test of loyalty in India is Christianity; that any Native who is not a Christian is a disloyal subject of the King, and that, if these dreadful pagans were left to themselves, they would rise against us and turn us all out tomorrow.

It stands much to Curzon's credit that in one of the most burdensome summers of his Viceroyalty he brought only tenderness and restraint to his correspondence with Welldon: not for him that withering style with which the Viceroy would pursue an obstructive official or chastise a deceitful soldier. Whatever the irritation and embarrassment which Welldon caused him, he never forgot the distant days of their early friendship; and he continued to address him as 'My dear old Doon.'

> India [Curzon wrote soothingly to him] is hardly the sphere for a great Churchman. It is scarcely the place for free and outspoken utterance on any point. The position of the Metropolitan as a servant of Government must inevitably place restrictions upon his freedom which a strong man is likely to resent. ... The spirit of a speech is not considered. The speaker is held bound by a hint of a sentence, I had almost said by a fraction of a word. ...
>
> In you I am about to lose my only friend in India and one of the chief and dearest friends of my life. Three years more are before me: and how solitary they will be without you, the experience of the present summer has enabled me to judge.

Welldon replied with resigned dignity. 'The Metropolitan of India is, as you say, the servant of Government. But he is also the servant of Christ. In that twofold service lies the difficulty of his position.' And he concluded with a tribute to the forbearance shown by Curzon throughout the years they had spent together in India:

> The sense of my own failure in India seems to be lost in the recollection of your own unvarying kindness to me while I have been there. No memory of India can be so vivid to me as that. That you must sometimes, and perhaps often, have felt my conduct to be unwise or inconsiderate I cannot doubt; but you have never said a word to give me pain; there has never been a shadow upon our affection. I do not

think there will ever be a day when you will not be in my thoughts and in my prayers.

As Hamilton had forecast, Welldon found solace in a Deanery, first at Manchester, then at Durham. And when he came to write his memoirs, he hardly mentioned his tribulations as Bishop of Calcutta. He did, however, erect a sorrowful tablet to the Viceroy: 'He preferred able men who went his way to stupid men who also went his way; but he preferred, I think, an inferior man who would follow him to a superior man who would resist him.'

A no less fundamental difference of belief clouded Curzon's intimacy with another of his closest friends, Arthur Hardinge, who in 1900 became British Minister in Teheran. They disagreed on the methods of diplomacy that could best secure a compliant demeanour on the part of the Persian Government. Hardinge favoured persuasion, Curzon coercion.

'How amusing is the appointment of Arthur Hardinge to Teheran!' Sir Arthur Godley wrote to Curzon from the India Office. 'And with Cecil Spring Rice as Secretary of Legation! What fun they will have. What with you, Hardinge, Spring Rice, and Brodrick at the Foreign Office, our Persian relations ought to be satisfactory, if John of Balliol and Dervorguilla his wife are good for anything.' Good Balliol man that he was, Curzon shared the pride of the Permanent Under-Secretary that responsibility for an important field of British foreign policy now rested in so many trusted hands. But his elation did not last.

Hardinge's intellectual brilliance, command of languages and courage had brought him a breastful of orders and decorations before he was forty. He had nevertheless retained the attractive qualities of his youth: by the standards of Victorian diplomacy he was absent-minded, unconventional and dangerously idealistic. His eccentricities of dress, for instance, although lacking the defiance of Eyre Crowe's straw hat, were held to reflect no credit on either the Foreign Office that was his first home or on the Diplomatic Service to which he later transferred. He displeased the Prince of Wales at a Levée by wearing a buttoned boot on one foot, an evening shoe on the other. And as Ambassador to Spain he would present himself for a Royal audience in a black morning coat put on as an afterthought over brown tweed trousers and waistcoat. He once visited a Government department in Madrid clutching a typist's parasol, and returned, quite accidentally, with the Minister of State's hat and umbrella.

He was similarly careless, not to say scornful, of administration. At Oxford his vagueness had cost him the Arnold Prize when he left the manuscript of his essay on Carthage in a London hansom cab. During his early days in the Foreign Office an important despatch known to have been in his care afterwards vanished and failed to come to light even after a thorough search. A week later a charwoman found it when dusting the broad ledge of a window that was invisible from the floor. While reading the document, Hardinge had jumped on to a chair to watch the ducks in St James's Park, and had then forgotten about it.

In later years, practical-minded subordinates used to bustle in his wake, bringing order out of administrative chaos. Their labours were not appreciated. Of one methodical young man, Hardinge was heard to remark that he had turned a gentleman's chancery into a counting-house. Curzon was pained by his indifference to the niceties of diplomatic procedure. 'He is a most casual person, sits down at the table, dashes off a rough draft, and has it despatched at once without consulting anybody.'

The Viceroy was nevertheless encouraged by Hardinge's appointment to Persia, a country in which for the past ten years he had taken a near-proprietorial interest. 'I feel rather happier now,' he told the new Minister in the course of a long complaint about the infirmities of British foreign policy, 'because you are at Teheran'.

In Hardinge, Curzon hoped, he had found a well-placed ally to prod the Cabinet into an awareness of Russian intentions in Persia. All the indications from London were that the Government regarded a Russian advance towards the Persian Gulf as inevitable, and hence not to be opposed. Neither during his travels of 1889–90 nor during his years as Parliamentary Under-Secretary had so supine a conclusion appealed to Curzon. He determined that an essential preliminary to meeting Russian aggression by force must be the stiffening of the Persians themselves.

As the months passed, however, he found that Hardinge was an unreliable representative of Viceregal thought in the Legation in Teheran. Curzon mistrusted and despised the Oriental mind. In 1901 he told Balfour: 'It is often said why not make some prominent Native a Member of the Executive Council? The answer is that in the whole continent there is not an Indian fit for the post.'

Hardinge's more accommodating approach was not to his taste. 'I do not think he has the least understanding of the Asiatic,' Curzon complained to Godley. 'He treats him as though he were a finished product of European diplomacy. He is nothing of the sort. His natural talent for duplicity and intrigue is much greater. On the other hand he requires sometimes to be spoken to with a brutal candour that would be regarded as "bad form" in the Chancelleries of Europe.'

Curzon pursued the same harsh theme in a letter to Lord Lansdowne, who in 1900 succeeded Salisbury as Foreign Secretary: 'Hardinge's whole attitude towards the Persian Government is that almost of a suppliant who must not offend them at any cost; who must always be making little compromises here and little concessions there, and who ought to be overwhelmed with gratitude at being allowed to lend money for no return to an impending bankrupt. Now I do not believe in wheedling the Persians or trying to twist them round one's finger. A good show of the boot now and then is very essential.'

The gist of Curzon's disparaging commentary on Hardinge's mission must surely have filtered back to Teheran, and cannot have been easy to bear. The Viceroy, after all, was not responsible for British relations with Persia, although his past experience of the country and his present duty of safeguarding India's frontiers entitled his opinion to respect. Hardinge took it well. His idealism – Curzon called it his hyper-subtlety – was itself an armour against the irritable reproaches of an old friend; and at no time did he allow differences of policy to poison a private relationship. In the winter of 1903 they made an official tour of the Persian Gulf together, an excursion marred only by a dispute between visitors and hosts about precedence. The Minister resisted Persian pretensions with Curzonian firmness, and later received the Viceroy's congratulations for the 'courage, imperturbability and force with which you have stated our side of the Bushire incident.'

Since Hardinge retired from the Diplomatic Service in 1920, only a few months after Curzon assumed the office of Foreign Secretary, no disagreement on policy was ever again able to disturb their friendship. Even by March 1904 Curzon's good nature had reasserted itself, and he ended a letter to Hardinge with the warm affection of Balliol days. 'Goodbye, my dear Arthur,' he wrote, 'I have been made Lord Warden of the Cinque Ports: and shall look forward to the day when your cheery laughter will resound along the battlements of Walmer Castle.'

Three years later, when Curzon stood against Rosebery for the Chancellorship of Oxford, Hardinge was Minister to Belgium. Exercising his franchise as a Master of Arts, he crossed from Ostend by the night boat, hastened down to Oxford to vote for Curzon, and returned the same evening.

Curzon's differences with Welldon and Hardinge cast a shadow over their intimacy; but their friendship survived. Neither dispute, after all, had a more than peripheral influence on the majestic tasks of Indian administration and defence that Curzon had set himself. That could not be said of his quarrels with Arthur Balfour and St John Brodrick.

An aristocratic structure of politics such as still survived at the turn of the century carries both benefits and perils. When government largely consists of a closely knit fraternity who have shared each other's thoughts and habits since boyhood, minor political problems can be solved in the lobby of the Commons or the smoking-room of a club, in a country house or across a dining-room table. But informal diplomacy, conducted rather in a code of common understanding than in the precise language of a state paper, is unfitted for the determination of high policy. If dedicated men collide on questions of principle, it is better that their contest should not be trammelled by past intimacy. For it is then that a sense of betrayal poisons official relationships; whereas the chance acquaintances of a more democratic society can debate their differences on an austerely intellectual plane.

Even so, Curzon's tenure of the Viceroyalty need not have ended in such anger and recrimination. His fatal blunder was to address the Prime Minister and the Secretary of State in the same terms of irritable and autocratic rectitude that he used towards his subordinates. And they resented it.

For the first two or three years of Curzon's Viceroyalty there was harmony between Calcutta and London. The Prime Minister had no wish to play more than a passive role in Indian affairs. 'Lord S.,' Brodrick told Curzon in 1901, 'though in health wonderful, is visibly failing and obstinate. He jokes in Cabinet, defers everything and is solely occupied with keeping us together till after the [South African] War – *après cela le déluge*.'*

Nor could Curzon have found a more experienced or less officious Secretary of State for India than Lord George Hamilton, who had held his office since 1895 and for four years been Parliamentary Under-Secretary for India while the Viceroy was still at school. Their early exchanges were agreeably conspiratorial. 'As you and I know,' Curzon wrote to him in 1901, 'though perhaps it is desirable that the world should not, India is really governed by confidential correspondence between the Secretary of State and the Viceroy.'

What he forgot, however, or chose to brush aside, was the constitutional right of the Secretary of State's Council to scrutinize his policies and proposals. Composed mainly of retired Indian civilians, members of Council seemed to delight in depreciating the labours of their successors and looked with jealous suspicion on any enterprising reform. Nor did they confine their examination to important matters. Curzon grumbled with justice at their having refused assent to the appointment of an efficient clerk of the works for Government House, Simla. Maynard Keynes, who began his career in the India Office, described Council meetings in King Edward's reign as 'government by dotardry,' observing that 'at least half those present showed manifest signs of senile decay, and the rest didn't speak'.

In May 1902, stung by the Council's criticism of his measures for police and educational reform, Curzon complained angrily to Hamilton of 'a desire on the part of your advisers in the India Office to thwart and hamper me in the work which I am endeavouring to undertake here. ... Unless I receive not only your support – for that I know has never wavered – but

* Although Lord Salisbury ceased to be Foreign Secretary in 1900, he continued to be Prime Minister until his retirement two years later, soon after the conclusion of peace with the Boers.

also the backing of your Council, I would prefer to resign my office.' With the letter he enclosed a memorandum listing twenty-two separate cases in which he had been 'nagged and impeded and misunderstood by the India Council'.

Hamilton was shocked by the outburst. 'I do not think,' he wrote, 'you could have drawn up the indictment you launch against the Council if you had not been so physically and mentally depressed as to be unable to take a fair, or I might even say a reasonable survey of your relations with the Council during the past two or three years.'

Curzon's reply was unrepentant: 'It is not against the exercise of superior authority that I have any complaint to make. It is against the assertion of an interference greater than has been exercised before and conducted in a spirit, not of confidence or helpfulness, but of distrust and suspicion.' And to Godley, the Permanent Under-Secretry, he scornfully observed: 'You send me out to India as an expert, and you treat my advice as though it were that of an impertinent schoolboy.'

The storm blew over. But almost immediately Curzon was engaged in yet another dispute between Calcutta and Whitehall. The point at issue was whether the cost of Indian representation at the Coronation of King Edward VII should be met out of Indian revenues, as the British Government insisted, or by the Treasury, as Curzon urged. The Viceroy maintained not only that the imposition was churlish, but that his acquiescence would establish a precedent and so burden the Indian Government with other charges that ought to be borne by Great Britain. He pressed his case in a vigorously phrased despatch which, Hamilton told him, had met with 'an absolutely universal chorus of disapprobation from the Cabinet'. And when asked to withdraw the document, he refused.

In the course of the conflict Curzon heard that Arthur Balfour had succeeded his uncle as Prime Minister, and hastened to congratulate him. 'I am as proud to have been your first Viceroy,' he wrote, 'as to have been Lord Salisbury's last.' He also hoped that Balfour would 'find time to assert that real control over the Cabinet and over the business of the entire Government which is reported to have steadily weakened in recent years, and to have been on the decline ever since the days of Sir Robert Peel'. He ended his letter: 'Good luck to you, old boy, in all that you undertake and do, and may God bless you in your noble task.'

To all except his intimates, Balfour was an enigma. 'He lives with his windows shut,' Laura Lyttelton said of him, 'and has a few false windows.' Curzon, however, was well aware that the new Prime Minister's lethargic distaste for action could be deceptive. 'Balfour has elevated political nonchalance to the dignity of a fine art,' he told Mrs Craigie, 'but it is largely superficial, and behind it all he is as patriotic and as capable of strenuous – though not detailed – work as any man.'

But if Curzon thought that Balfour's elevation to the Premiership had secured him a powerful advocate in London, he was soon disillusioned. Within a few days of taking office, the new Prime Minister added his voice to that of Hamilton in appealing for the withdrawal of the Viceroy's truculent despatch. The plea went unanswered; the Cabinet prudently decided not to force the issue; the despatch remained on the files; and Curzon was able to boast to his wife of 'a great victory over the India Office'. That is not how it seems in retrospect. Balfour had caught his first glimpse of Curzon's cloven hoof.

Three months later, in November 1902, the Viceroy again determined to challenge the Cabinet. He proposed to enhance the glory of the Delhi Durbar that celebrated the crowning of a new King-Emperor by announcing a reduction of taxation. After considerable discussion, Hamilton informed him that his suggestion was unacceptable: for if the Sovereign were to be identified with the bounty of a reduction of taxation, he might in the future incur the odium of an increase in taxation.

Curzon's response was unequivocal. He told the Secretary of State that he would resign if overruled by the Cabinet. He telegraphed to Sir Francis Knollys, against all constitutional practice, invoking the intervention of the King. And he appealed to the Prime Minister in terms that mingled cajolery with menace. 'You have never served your country in foreign parts,' he wrote. 'For your own sake, I hope you never may. English Governments have always had the reputation of breaking the hearts of their proconsuls, from Warren Hastings to Bartle Frere. Do you wish to repeat the performance? If the Government are fixed in their views, I feel disposed to say that it would be fairer upon me and fairer upon themselves that you should get someone else to carry them out. Do not make me the instrument of this great failure.' Lest he had not made his message clear, he added on the following day: 'The decision of the Government is not merely condemning the Durbar to a failure, but it is setting a similar and equally unmerited crown upon my own Indian career.'

This time the Cabinet refused to meet his demand, although allowing him to make a vaguer pronouncement about taxation that was not linked to the King's name. From Balfour he received a mild rebuke for having appealed to the Sovereign without the knowledge or assent of his colleagues, together with some healing words designed to soothe the Viceroy's troubled spirit:

> You seem to think that you are injured whenever you do not get exactly your own way! But which of us gets exactly his own way? Certainly not the Prime Minister. Certainly not any of his Cabinet colleagues. We all suffer the common lot of those who, having to work with others, are sometimes over-ruled by them. I doubt whether any of your predecessors have ever received so large a measure of confidence from either the Secretary of State or the Home Government. I am ready to add that probably none has ever deserved that confidence more: but do not let any of us

forget that there cannot be a greater mistake committed by a British statesman than to interpret any difference of opinion as a personal slight, or as indicating any want of confidence among colleagues.

Dear George, I do assure you that no one has marked with greater pride or greater pleasure your triumphant progress, and the admirable courage, energy and sagacity with which you have grappled with the immense difficulties of your task, than your old friend and colleague.

I have differed from you on this point or that point; I may have (who knows?) to differ from you on others. But nothing will for a moment diminish either the warmth of friendship or the enthusiasm of my admiration.

Curzon was not mollified. 'I start for Delhi tonight,' he told Hamilton, 'without the slightest ray of pleasurable anticipation, and with a feeling of indifference. ... This is due first and foremost to the great disappointment imposed upon me by you and the Cabinet, and which I shall never cease to think a first-class political blunder.'

He was not, during that Indian winter, an agreeable colleague. But worse was to come.

In September 1903, Balfour reconstructed his Cabinet. To replace Lord George Hamilton as Secretary of State for India he appointed St John Brodrick, who for the past three years had been at the War Office. It seemed an inspired choice. The two men who in their despatch boxes carried the destinies of 300 million Indians would now, Balfour assumed, work in an intimate partnership born of more than twenty years of friendship. The Prime Minister was mistaken. What in fact ensued was epitomized in some pencilled notes which Curzon wrote late in life and in a mood of bitterness:

St John Brodrick was a greater friend of mine at Balliol and in after life than at Eton. He was in some respects my closest friend in public until in an evil hour he became Secretary of State while I was Viceroy. In two years he succeeded in entirely destroying both my affection and my confidence. Burning to distinguish himself at the India Office as the real ruler of India, as distinct from the Viceroy, egged on by Councillors bitterly hostile to me, in a position to gratify a certain latent jealousy of my superior successes in public life – a feeling of which all our friends were cognisant – phenomenally deficient in tact, and tortuous and mean in his actual procedure – he rendered my period of service under him one of incessant irritation and pain, and finally drove me to resignation. Each one of the above propositions is demonstrated in the confidential papers with my summary of them, which I had printed before I left India. It was not till many years later that I forgave him and resumed friendly though never very intimate relations.

The roots of their quarrel were buried in youth. Two years separated them in age, and Curzon, the younger of the pair sometimes felt himself at a disadvantage. On 5 December 1880, the day after Brodrick's marriage to Hilda Charteris, he wrote from Balliol:

A year ago you and I sat and talked together in a position of almost (except for age) absolute equality. I am now far in the rear. You have got a start that many men would give more than one year of life to obtain. You are in Parliament. You have made a conspicuous success there. An article upon you appears in *The Times* – and (*finis coronat opus*) you have married some one of whom no higher praise can be spoken than by saying that she is worthy of you, while you are worthy of her.

As the years went by, Curzon continued to apostrophize Brodrick in the same strain. 'The one great delight of the whole thing,' he told him on being elected to Parliament in 1886, 'is the prospect of sitting with you.' And a few days before his own marriage in 1895: 'You have been a strong rock in my life: and to your counsel and sustenance I shall ever turn. May you be in my future life what you have *always* been in my past.'

In the race for political promotion, Brodrick continued for a time to hold his lead. He received his first appointment as a junior minister in 1886, when he was twenty-nine; Curzon had to wait until 1891, when he was thirty-one. Thereafter Curzon narrowed the lead, drew level and finally left Brodrick behind. In 1895, when Brodrick became Parliamentary Under-Secretary at the War Office – a sideways move from his previous post as Financial Secretary – Curzon became not only Parliamentary Under-Secretary at the Foreign office, but also a Privy Councillor. Brodrick, too, joined the Privy Council in 1897; but in the following year Curzon was appointed Viceroy of India, while Brodrick could do no better than succeed him at the Foreign Office.

By now, it seems, the affections of the two men for each other had begun to glow at different temperatures. Within the circle of the Souls, Curzon's liking for Brodrick was sometimes jocular, even condescending. Brodrick, however, continued to express himself in terms of hero worship or of earnest admonition that were not always reciprocated.

Just before Curzon left for India, Brodrick told him: 'You probably hardly know how much your departure means to me. ... It has been one of the brightest elements in my life to work with you and see you gaily flying the fences which I have laboriously climbed.' A few months later he wrote from Curzon's old room in the Foreign Office: 'Bless you, dear old boy. I would give worlds for a few hours of confidential talk. I pursue my education here without your guidance but I trust in your direction.'

Mary Curzon did not always take these sentiments at their face value, detecting in them a latent note of envy. But she conceded that 'at heart he is a true old dear and jealousy is his only occasional East wind'. And Curzon himself responded by assuring Brodrick: 'You have been the good genius of my life for twenty years.' He demonstrated his loyalty, too, when both Hamilton and Godley sent him reports of Brodrick's unpopularity at the War Office, largely attributable to deafness and tactlessness. 'Brodrick,' the Viceroy held, 'is a resolute man and has much strength of character as well as rectitude of purpose.' And a few months later he praised him for 'showing all the grit and courage with which I credited him'.

In the stormy autumn of 1902, however, there was a rift in the lute. Brodrick assumed the perilous role of candid friend and warned Curzon that if he elected to resign on the issue of the Durbar, the Cabinet would not press him to stay. The Viceroy was furious at this well-meaning intervention. 'Observe the amicable way,' he told Lady Curzon, 'in which he informs me that all the Cabinet, including himself (a humble participator) were quite prepared to throw me overboard ... what a light it throws upon human nature and upon friendship.' And to mark his disapproval, Curzon suspended his weekly letter to Brodrick for three whole months.

It was thus with qualified approval that in the following year he greeted Brodrick's appointment as Secretary of State for India. 'He is one of my oldest and closest personal friends,' Curzon told Godley, 'and our relations should therefore, I think, be one of the most confidential and satisfactory character. But I must honestly confess that I think there will have to be some change of clothes before he can be generally recognised as the whole-hearted champion of Indian interests.' Brodrick later saw this letter in the India Office and protested with wounded feelings. Curzon had not, however, misjudged the situation.

In the very first letter which Curzon wrote to Brodrick as Secretary of State, he repeated what he had earlier told Hamilton: 'The private correspondence between the Secretary of State and Viceroy is really the means by which the Government of India is carried on.' Four months later he was complaining of Brodrick's neglect of so valuable a channel of communication: 'I observe that you seldom mention the receipt of my letters, and that you rarely allude to the subjects that I have discussed in them. Your own letters in reply also differ a good deal from those which I was accustomed to receive from the late Secretary of State. ... My own work is so heavy here that I shall be quite ready to subscribe to any views that you may desire to express in the nature of the restriction of our correspondence.'

The Viceroy's rebuke was unkind but merited. Brodrick had none of Curzon's imaginative command of words and found neither pleasure nor relief in literary composition. The correspondence nevertheless continued for the time being, and occasionally would glow with its old cordiality. However pressing the burden of business, the humours of travel always found a ready place in Curzon's letters. He once described a worthy official as 'a gravestone with a moustache hung on in front in place of an inscription, and a wife like a custard pudding'. He told the King-Emperor of a triumphal arch bearing the legend, 'God Bless Our Horrable Lout', an ambiguous greeting which ought to have read 'Our Honourable Lat (or Lord)'. And in the very next letter he sent Brodrick after chastising him for his inadequacy with the pen, he resurrected another motto that had welcomed a Viceregal visit to Chittagong:

'He cometh as a bridegroom
Clad in the garment of love.'

'I did not dare institute any enquiries,' Curzon added, 'either as to the character of the raiment or the identity of the bride.'

Such gleams of humour became increasingly rare. 'My work has never been so hard as this winter,' he wrote a few days later, 'for days and even weeks together I have not got to bed before 2.30 or 3 a.m.' That in no way deterred him from undertaking a second term of office as Viceroy. 'In your own interests,' Balfour told him, 'I should personally advise you to come home before the tremendous strain of your labour produces, or has a chance of producing any ill effects. In the public interest I should hope that you will run the risk.'

Curzon did not hesitate; an appeal to him in the public interest was itself a command. But he foresaw that a second term of strenuous rule would earn him the hostility both of the Indians to whom he refused political concessions and of the European officials to whom he denied repose. 'I do not hesitate to predict that I shall suffer for it both in health and reputation,' he wrote to the Secretary of State.

With schoolboy resilience his spirits rose at the prospect of leave in England. Lord Ampthill, appointed Viceroy for the period of his absence from India, described their talks in a letter to Godley: 'My conversations with Lord Curzon, had the effect of rejuvenating and refreshing me in the most extraordinary manner, and although I was dead-beat when I arrived here, I have been able to start work feeling as fresh as if I had had a month's holiday. Lord Curzon's personality, ideas and marvellous powers are certainly most inspiring.' The Permanent Under-Secretary agreed. 'I am inclined to think, though it is a rash thing to say of a contemporary,' he replied, 'that Curzon has a touch of genius.'

Brodrick, in spite of his recent failings as a correspondent, was taken back into Viceregal favour. 'I am looking forward greatly to our merrymaking,' Curzon wrote to him from India, 'it will be a great day in our already well-stocked records of festivity.' But those gilded reunions of their youth eluded recapture.

After skirmishes on petty things such as Walter Lawrence's pension and the cost of Lady Curzon's passage to England, they were now to join battle on crucial questions – the policy to be adopted towards Afghanistan and Tibet, and the future of military administration in India. These were the issues that ultimately shattered thirty years of friendship.

Curzon was exposed to a succession of humiliations during his visit to London. In the previous year he had despatched his old friend Francis

Younghusband on an escorted mission to Tibet, charged with negotiating trade and frontier agreements. After many hardships the expedition entered Lhasa in August; a few weeks later, by the exercise of patient and ingenious diplomacy, Younghusband concluded a treaty with his unwilling hosts. The enterprise fulfilled all Curzon's hopes. 'If your mission had been anything but the most complete success,' he told his envoy, 'it would have been the ruin of me. Remember, throughout the rest of my life there is nothing I will not do for you.' The British Government, whose approval of the venture had from the start been hesitant and ambiguous, took a different view. Complaining that the terms imposed by Younghusband on the Tibetans were tantamount to annexation and far exceeded his instructions, they publicly repudiated him.

Colonel Peter Fleming, the historian of the episode, suggests that Brodrick, 'impelled by some strong but almost certainly subconscious impulse,' was striking at Curzon through Younghusband. It was under Younghusband's tutelage in Chitral ten years before that Curzon had strengthened his belief in a forward frontier policy; and in more recent months each shared a growing suspicion of Tibet as a source of Russian influence and mischief on the borders of India. The thoughts of Whitehall ran on more cautious lines, and it was only at the personal insistence of the King that Younghusband received a knighthood for his feat. The controversy left a shadow over his career. He served for a few years as Resident in Kashmir; then, aware that further advancement was closed to him, retired to study mystic philosophy and to promote the conquest of Everest.

There was an element of vindictiveness, too, in both the style and content of the Blue Book that deliberately suppressed Younghusband's side of the case. Curzon was on leave in England during Younghusband's shabby treatment at the hands of the British Government, but the censured envoy found a no less understanding protector in Lord Ampthill, the temporary Viceroy. By the time the Blue Book appeared, Curzon had resumed his office and felt impelled to join battle with Brodrick. 'I am unable to accept the contention that there was any obligation upon the Government to publish the distressing controversy which they did,' he wrote angrily to the Secretary of State, 'still less, as you know, can I accept the position that there was any ground for them to address the Government of India in the hectoring and pharisaical language which they employed, and which will have a permanent effect upon the prestige of our Government for years to come.'

There was as little comfort to be drawn from the Cabinet over Afghanistan as over Tibet. While Curzon was on leave in England, Ampthill sent a mission to Kabul, seeking to re-negotiate with the Amir Habibullah the agreements entered into by his late father, Abdur Rahman. Habibullah, however, declined even to discuss the draft treaty which the Indian Government presented for his signature. He merely produced a short document of his own that endorsed the promises of Abdur Rahman but was otherwise worthless in terms of Western diplomacy. As Ampthill's unofficial representative in London – and the man who was shortly to resume responsibility for relations between India and Afghanistan – Curzon attempted to stiffen the attitude of a Cabinet that had no relish for foreign entanglements. He did his best to persuade them that a failure to negotiate on the part of the Amir should be met by a refusal to continue either his subsidy or the import of arms from India. He repeated his appeals by telegraph soon after returning to Calcutta: but in vain. 'The Home Government are wobbling pitifully as they usually do,' he told Lady Curzon. He was not mistaken. The Secretary of State presently sent instructions that the envoy in Kabul was to sign Habibullah's unsatisfactory draft and withdraw. 'You may imagine also what are my sentiments about the Afghan surrender,' Curzon told Brodrick, 'but I have known all along that with a moribund Government, with fear of Russia on the brain, there would be no other ending.'

No man can ever have drawn less refreshment from his leave than did Curzon during those summer months of 1904. He felt increasingly misunderstood, frustrated and betrayed, and disturbed Brodrick by his nervous, irritable and excitable behaviour. Godley, too, was alarmed, and wrote to Ampthill:

> He seems almost to have lost sight of the merits of the various questions, in which he has differed from the Cabinet or from our Council (or they from him), and to be absorbed in a struggle for prerogative, control, independence. In any of these disputed matters, the thought that seems to rise in his mind is not 'I will prove to the Cabinet, or to the Council of India, that they are wrong about this and that I am right', but, 'I have given my opinion, I have even reiterated it in two or more despatches, I am the Viceroy of India, and, confound you, how do you dare to set your opinion against mine?' ... It is lucky for him that the Secretary of State is an intimate friend, who is most anxious to meet him at every point and to humour him as much as he can; for, constitutionally speaking, he has not a leg to stand upon, and an unfriendly person, in Mr Brodrick's position, might make things very unpleasant for him.

The view naturally taken in Whitehall was that even the most able and experienced proconsul must submit to Ministerial authority. John Morley, when Chief Secretary for Ireland, once attended a ball in Dublin given by Crewe, the Lord Lieutenant. 'Look at all those lovely dresses, jewels and decorations,' a guest urged him. 'Yes,' replied Morley, 'but the man with the black coat rules them all.'

Godley upheld the same doctrine in more conventional terms when he told Curzon: 'The responsibility for every one of your acts, great and small, lies with the Secretary of State, the Prime Minister and the Cabinet; and where the responsibility is absolute and unshared, there must be a corresponding right of control, absolute and unshared.' He developed the theme in a further letter to the Viceroy:

> I think we must all agree that the real government of India is in the House of Commons; that the Cabinet speaks with the authority of the House of Commons, and must decide everything with reference to the question – 'Can we defend this in the House?'; and that a Viceroy who cannot conscientiously acquiesce in and carry out the policy of the Cabinet has no choice but to resign.
>
> Let me assure you that I say this without implying in the smallest degree that the Cabinet is more likely to be right on any given question than the Viceroy is: on the contrary, my instinct always impels me to believe in the man on the spot. But the Cabinet has to take into account matters as to which the Government of India cannot be thoroughly informed: and, right or wrong, so long as the law and practice of the Constitution remain what they are, they are entitled, not only to the last word, but to the co-operation of the Viceroy.
>
> I do not know whether this will appear to you a hard saying: but I am quite sure that if you were to become Secretary of State for India, or Prime Minister, at the end of six months you would hold that doctrine quite as strongly as I do; and, what is more, you would enforce it.

The Permanent Under-Secretary then attempted to clothe his uncompromising interpretation of the Viceregal role in flattery:

> I am perfectly well aware that the difficulties of your position are actually enhanced by the energy, the ability, the ascendancy (to put it all into one word) with which you address yourself to public affairs. It is not only difficult, it is impossible, for such a man to bear in mind always the fact that there are at the other end of the wire men who have the whip-hand of him, and to practise the thousand little arts by which it is usually advisable to recognise that fact.
>
> But you must try to remember that our Acts of Parliament and our official traditions are based upon the average Viceroy, and not upon the exceptional one: and that the exceptional one, when he appears, has to reckon with a system of checks and balances which, in the long run, does more good than harm, though in his case it cannot fail to be a thorn in the flesh.

Curzon found no comfort in Godley's encomium. What he wanted was power. 'Should the day ever come,' he declared majestically to an audience of Indian Civil Servants, 'when the Viceroy of India is treated as the mere puppet or mouthpiece of the Home Government, who is required only to carry out whatever orders it may be thought desirable to transmit, I think that the justification for the post would have ceased to exist.'

The truth lay somewhere between the two extremes. So distant and so diverse were the problems of India that no Secretary of State in Council could expect his edicts to be binding in every instance. On the larger issues, however, no Home Government could tolerate a Viceregal degree of insularity that, as Balfour complained, raised India to the status of an independent and not always friendly autocracy.

It was a delicate relationship, depending ultimately on the temperaments of Viceroy and Secretary of State. Unhappily, neither was a man prepared to make concessions to the other. Curzon was conscious of an intellectual superiority and an Oriental omniscience which he barely troubled to disguise. Yet to the Viceroy's contemptuous astonishment, Brodrick refused to believe himself at a disadvantage in their trials of strength. 'You think me wholly lacking in Indian experience,' he told Curzon during their dispute on control of the Indian Army, 'whereas having spent nearly fifteen years dealing directly with soldiers, I feel to have a claim to a greater knowledge of their idiosyncrasies in administration than any civilian now in political life.'

Curzon convinced himself that Brodrick brooded on how best he could 'score off an old friend in private and humiliate the Viceroy in public'. Brodrick was no less certain that Curzon looked upon him as the Viceregal representative at the Court of St James, 'hoping that from our intimacy I should be able to carry for him points of policy of which he had utterly failed to convince my predecessor, George Hamilton, or the Cabinet'.

However tenaciously Brodrick asserted his authority as Secretary of State, he attempted to maintain a lifeline of cordiality. 'I cannot say how much I dislike the constant appearance of opposite views which seems to have recently arisen between us,' he wrote to Curzon in August. 'The result is that I have not had one conversation with you in the last eleven weeks except on business, and our official relations thus seem to overshadow private friendship.' And he signed himself, 'Ever your affectionate, St John Brodrick.'

Curzon would not be placated and appealed to Ampthill with his own apologia. 'I worked happily with the late Secretary of State for five years,' he wrote, 'though we did not always agree and he could not be described as strong. He was succeeded by one of my oldest friends. But I work under him with no pleasure whatever, for he seems to me to derive a peculiar satisfaction from disagreeing with me on the majority of the points to which, rightly or wrongly, I attach importance.'

Dejected by successive reverses at the hands of the Cabinet and embittered by the conduct of the man who had once been his dearest friend, Curzon prepared to resume the Viceroyalty. The scene at the railway station on his departure in November, Godley reported, was most painful. 'With most of those who were present he shook hands silently and mechanically: with two or three of those whom he knew best he broke down entirely, and shed tears. It is impossible to think that he is in a fit state to cope with the difficulties and, I fear, the disappointments which lie before him.'

Almost immediately on his return to Calcutta, Curzon was obliged to immerse himself in the most savage of all the disputes that clouded his

Viceroyalty. A profound principle was at stake: whether the Indian Army should remain under the control of the civil power, or pass entirely into the grasp of the Commander-in-Chief. The system which Curzon had inherited in 1898 vested control of the Indian Army in two separate authorities. The Commander-in-Chief, a senior general, was responsible for its fighting efficiency; the Government of India, acting through a less senior soldier known as the Military Member of the Viceroy's Council, was responsible for its administration. It was admittedly a somewhat cumbersome arrangement of duties that required the exchange of 10,000 letters a year between two departments sitting under the same roof. But the dual system embodied the constitutional supremacy of civil over military power as established in Great Britain. There was one difference, and that superficial. In both countries ultimate authority over the Army was vested in the Government. But whereas the Secretary of State for War was a civilian, the Military Member of the Viceroy's Council was a serving officer. The Military Member, however, had neither powers nor standing except within the framework of the Indian Government; he was essentially an expert on military problems fulfilling a civilian role.

Such was the machinery of military administration when Lord Kitchener, fresh from his South African triumphs, arrived as Commander-in-Chief at the end of 1902. Ironically as it later seemed, he had been appointed at the request of the Viceroy, who wished the most powerful soldier of his day to instil renewed vigour into the Indian Army. On 15 October, Curzon wrote to the King-Emperor.

> The Viceroy is looking forward greatly to the arrival of Lord Kitchener, who is an old friend of his, and whose unrivalled experience and wonderful ability should be of inestimable service in dealing with our Indian Military problems. The Viceroy will render to the new Commander-in-Chief every assistance in his power.

But within three days of taking up his command, and without previous knowledge of India, Kitchener demanded the abolition of the Military Member's department and the concentration of all military authority in his own hands. The conflict of views between Commander-in-Chief and Viceroy smouldered for eighteen months without personal rancour. Then Curzon, on leave in England, was disagreeably surprised to discover that Kitchener had been secretly pressing the Home Government to endorse his plan of military reform. 'He had intended to point Kitchener like a howitzer against the Amir,' Sir Shane Leslie has written, 'but Kitchener had turned into a blunderbuss and exploded in his hands.' On the Viceroy's return to India he asked the Commander-in-Chief to put his views of the existing system on official record. Kitchener responded by describing it as 'faulty, inefficient and incapable of the expansion necessary for a great war'.

Curzon's determination to maintain the dual system was from the outset doomed to failure, not by any weakness in his own case or strength in Kitchener's: but by the superior public prestige of his principal antagonist. The Cabinet knew that the resignation of a national hero like Kitchener could ensure their electoral defeat, whereas Curzon's premature departure from India would be less widely lamented. 'I often wonder if your advisers at the India Office desire secretly to drive me to resign,' the Viceroy wrote to Brodrick in March. 'And I have many times been pondering during the past few weeks whether you also contemplate this as a result of one and a half years of our co-operation. If so, I do not think that it will be very difficult to attain that end.' His veiled threat sounded no note of alarm in London.

The Government's acceptance of Kitchener's demands was patently anomalous. They were willing that he should add to his executive duties in India the entire administration of a great army. Yet they had just accepted the recommendation of Lord Esher's committee that such a system was unworkable in Great Britain. Their behaviour was disingenuous in other ways. Although claiming that Indian experience favoured the revolutionary change, they never dared to have the matter formally submitted to the India Council in London or fully debated by either House of Parliament. And in the end they accepted the recommendations of a single Member of the Viceroy's Council, Lord Kitchener, in preference to the united counsel of the Viceroy, the Military Member and every civilian Member.

Brodrick conveyed the decision of the Home Government to Curzon in a despatch dated 31 May 1905. It was a sweeping triumph for Kitchener, who acquired nearly all the additional powers he coveted, certainly all that could be exercised effectively by any one man. To present the illusion of an amicable compromise between Viceroy and Commander-in-Chief, the Government refrained from abolishing the Military Member. They stripped him, however, of all functions except the supervision of supply departments dealing with contracts, stores and remounts. 'A disembowelled Military Member has been left to prevent me from resigning,' Curzon wrote.

If the subsequent exchanges between Simla and Whitehall were ill-tempered, the fault lay as much with Brodrick as with the Viceroy. Instead of clothing a repugnant decision in language of gratitude and esteem, the Secretary of State seemed to have delighted in causing Curzon pain. The recipient described the tone of Brodrick's despatch as 'censorious, immoderate, spiteful and deplorably ill-advised'. Even the Commander-in-Chief called it 'nasty' and 'insulting'.

Freed from all restraint of economy, the wires hummed with amendments and intepretations: mailbags were heavy with recrimination. There were moments when the adversaries did not seem worthy of a great empire. Brodrick had earlier complained that Curzon never mentioned the work of the India Office in his numerous public speeches. Now it was Curzon's turn to protest that Brodrick had not paid tribute to the Viceroy when speaking on the Indian Budget at Westminster. Both failed to heed the dictum of Lord Dalhousie, 'that men who correspond over a space of 10,000 miles should watch their pens, for ink comes to burn like caustic when it crosses the sea'.

Ampthill was obliged to endure many confidences that summer. In June, Brodrick wrote to tell him of Curzon's latest transgression: 'This week he made the blunder of telegraphing to the Prime Minister behind or over the head of the Secretary of State. If instead of being one of his best friends wishing him to continue, I was his worst enemy and wished to bring him down, he could not have done anything which would give me greater support or cause more annoyance among my colleagues.'

That month Curzon broke off all personal correspondence with Brodrick, an unprecedented deterioration in relations between a Viceroy and a Secretary of State. 'My official existence,' he explained to Ampthill in July, 'has long ceased under Brodrick's treatment to be anything but a source of pain and distress, and I shall gladly and without repining bring it to a close. ... From England I have scarcely had one kind word, and from those who ought to have supported me, nothing but studied indifference or open humiliation.'

In August, Curzon resigned. 'The only mistake I can recall having made in this painful controversy,' he wrote to Ampthill a few days later, 'was in not resigning when the despatch first came. There I yielded to the urgent advice of my colleagues, and I thought – wrongly as it now seems – that duty required me to stay, while it might have looked like pique to go. No, I made one other mistake. I believed that H.M.G. were sincere in the modifications whereas it is now clear that they meant nothing and were merely bamboozling me. It may even be said that I made a third mistake, for I trusted K., whom I have now found to be without truth or honour.'

He was right to regret having lingered on as Viceroy: he was fretful, ill and exhausted, and knew in his heart of hearts that further controversy would be profitless. When he did resign, moreover, it was on a comparatively trivial issue. The constitutional responsibility for appointing Members of the Viceroy's Council lay not with the Viceroy but with the Secretary of State in London. Curzon nevertheless pressed on the Home Government the name of a certain general to be the first Military Member under the new system; and when the Cabinet turned down the suggestion, his patience ran out. In many eyes he thus appeared to have compromised in June on a critical issue of statecraft, yet resigned in August on a matter of personal pride.

That was not how he himself saw it. 'I have fought and fallen for the first principle of civil government,' he told St Loe Strachey, editor of the *Spectator*. Curzon found another ally in Winston Churchill, who had served in India as a cavalry officer and was now on the threshold of his first Ministerial office. In October, Churchill wrote to the leader of his party, Sir Henry Campbell-Bannerman, declaring that the new arrangement of duties in

India gave excessive and improper powers to the Commander-in-Chief who, he believed, was something very like a military dictator; and he offered to condemn the system from the Liberal benches of the House of Commons.

Curzon had to wait more than a decade, however, for his ultimate justification; until the Mesopotamian campaign of 1915–16 revealed the tragic inadequacy of Kitchener's Indian military system when put to the test of war. Addressing the House of Lords in July 1916, Lord Cromer spoke with the authority of a veteran proconsul:

> I claim that this change of system, this very important change which was introduced under Lord Kitchener's auspices should be judged by its results; and while it would certainly be a great exaggeration to say that the fiasco in Mesopotamia has been entirely due to that change, I cannot help thinking that it has very largely contributed to it. What has happened in Mesopotamia affords the most complete vindication of the attitude taken up by the noble earl opposite, the then Viceroy, in opposition to this drastic reform.

Kitchener was not there to dispute Cromer's judgement. He had been drowned at sea six weeks before.

The controversy over military administration in India has usually been interpreted in the public mind as a clash of wills between Curzon and Kitchener. It is true that Curzon found Kitchener a resolute, haughty and sometimes treacherous opponent, whose company he never again sought. But his enduring animosity was reserved for the Secretary of State who, he believed, had loaded the dice against him even before the start of their joyless game. Curzon might have harboured less bitterness had the instrument of his doom not been his oldest friend. As it was, he determined to cut Brodrick out of his life.

On the day Curzon telegraphed his resignation from Simla to London, he wrote to Lord Ampthill that he had been 'jockeyed out of office by a weak-minded Cabinet and a vindictive Secretary of State'. That was the pattern on which for the moment he distributed his animosity. The Prime Minister and all but one of his colleagues were branded with venial infirmity; for Brodrick alone was reserved the stigma of malevolence.

Balfour had from the beginning declined to quarrel with Curzon. Whenever the Viceroy hurled an epistolary thunderbolt at Downing Street he would judge it best either to send no answer or to reply with an affectionate understanding only lightly tinged by reproach. Immediately after Curzon's resignation he wrote:

> I have now no desire but to save from the political wreck all that is possible of private friendship and mutual esteem ... of one thing only shall I be mindful – that for nearly seven years, in sickness and in health, you have devoted with untiring

energy your splendid abilities to the service of India and of the Empire. And this is enough.

Curzon responded no less warmly to the Prime Minister's valediction:

There are many generous and affectionate sentiments in your letter of August 23 by which I have been much touched. I thank you for these, and I should indeed be sorry if anything that has passed were to impair a friendship which has also been one of my most treasured possessions.

But from the moment Curzon set foot on the platform of Charing Cross Station on 3 December 1905, goodwill vanished. According to the custom of the times, his friends had come to welcome him home. Among them, however, was not a single member of the Cabinet. No Balfour. No Brodrick. No Lyttelton. No Cranborne. No Selborne. No Wyndham. It is true that all these Ministers were preoccupied by business, for the Government resigned on the very next day. But their collective absence was to be interpreted in only one way. The returned proconsul could expect no indulgence from his Conservative colleagues, least of all from the man who three months earlier had spoken with honeyed words of 'private friendship and mutual esteem'.

At once the magnanimity of the outgoing Prime Minister was put to the test and found wanting. He declined to recommend Curzon for the earldom that would not only recognize the Viceroy's seven years of dedicated service but also enable him to take his place in the House of Lords.

On going out to India in 1898, Curzon had received an Irish peerage so that he could, if he wished, sit once more in the House of Commons on his return. It was always understood, however, that his path to the House of Lords would not be barred if at any time he changed his mind. While on leave in England in 1904 he received an offer from Balfour to submit his name for a peerage of the United Kingdom, and thus for a seat in the House of Lords. The Prime Minister feared that the Government might fall before the Viceroy's second term of office had run its course and that their Liberal successors would be unwilling to reward a political opponent. Curzon declined the offer. He had not yet decided in which House of Parliament he would pursue his political career on finally returning to England. In any case, he believed that as the office of Viceroy was a non-party post, his services would not be overlooked even by a Liberal Government. It was nevertheless agreed that the question should be put by Curzon to the Fountain of Honour himself.

Knollys replied on 21 September 1904. The King, his private secretary wrote from Balmoral, held the view that the Viceroy of India was outside party politics; and that should the Liberals be in power when Curzon finally returned to England, he would insist on their recommending him for the honour to which he was justly entitled.

The King's regard for his Viceroy was not limited to that pledge. In September 1905, three weeks after Curzon's resignation but before his return to London, the King urged Balfour to submit Curzon's name for an immediate earldom. The Royal advice was not well received in Downing Street, much less in the India Office. 'I respectfully suggest the "waiting, waiting game" is the one to play,' Balfour wrote slyly to Brodrick on 10 September. 'The pace is hot just now.' A month later he explained to Knollys why he had not yet acted upon the King's generous suggestion. The Prime Minister did not deny that Curzon's seven years in India deserved public recognition. But he was afraid that for the Government to reward him so soon after his controversial resignation could be variously interpreted as an admission of guilt, as a repudiation of Brodrick and Kitchener, even as an attempt to bribe a potentially dangerous critic into silence. He therefore proposed delaying further consideration of Curzon's peerage until January or February.

It was still, of course, open to Curzon to seek re-election to the Commons; and with the resignation of the Balfour Government on 4 December, a man of his acknowledged distinction would surely have had no difficulty in finding a suitable parliamentary seat in the impending general election. But on 6 December, when he was received in audience at Buckingham Palace, the King told him that he hoped a former Viceroy of India would not fight a contested election and so mar the dignity of his recently relinquished office. 'I asked the King,' Curzon later wrote, 'whether, if I were offered, without a contest, the representation either of the City of London or the University of Oxford (of which there was also a question) at forthcoming General Election, his objections would apply. H.M. replied that if I decided to re-enter the H. of C. he thought that either of these seats would be most appropriate.'

Curzon abided by the King's wishes and turned down invitations to stand for six constituencies. But to his disappointment, neither the City of London nor Oxford University proved available as an uncontested seat. Having for seven years ruled 300 million subjects of the Crown with outstanding ability, he found himself in February 1906 excluded from both Houses of the new Parliament.

On reflection he decided that he would abandon his efforts to re-enter the Commons, for neither his health nor his relations with former colleagues had yet recovered from the strain of India. And he let it be known that he would willingly accept a United Kingdom peerage on the recommendation of the new Liberal Prime Minister, Sir Henry Campbell-Bannerman. Recalling the King's pledge of September 1904, he anticipated no opposition to his wishes.

Campbell-Bannerman's initial reaction was favourable, and the only issue to be decided was the form of words in which the announcement should be made. The Prime Minister wished it to be known that Curzon's honour, although bestowed on the recommendation of the Liberal Government, would have been conferred by the Conservatives had they remained longer in power. Then silence fell. It was broken in March by a letter from Campbell-Bannerman to Knollys regretting that on two grounds he now felt unable to submit Curzon's name for a peerage. First, he claimed, because it was an honour which Balfour and his friends had 'frankly – I would almost say ostentatiously – withheld'. Secondly, because he and his Liberal colleagues had 'not always viewed with sympathy the methods and actions of Lord Curzon, although we all respect his devotion to the public service, and the industry and ability he has exhibited'.

Wounded and shocked by what he called 'the preposterous and disingenuous pleas' put forward in Campbell-Bannerman's letter, Curzon appealed personally to the King in a cogently reasoned letter of well over a thousand words. He argued that Balfour had only postponed and not withheld a public recognition which would certainly have been bestowed had the Conservatives remained in office until the new year; that he had received the almost unbroken support of the Liberals for his work in India; that at the King's request he had refrained from standing for any of the seats in the Commons that could have been his for the asking; that there was scarcely a Viceroy or Governor-General of the past hundred years who had been left unhonoured, even by political opponents; that the unprecedented slight put upon him would be much resented in India; and, above all, that in September 1904 the King himself had promised that a change of Government would not be allowed to deprive him of his traditional reward.

The King was embarrassed by the implied reproach. Through Knollys, he told Campbell-Bannerman that he considered the conferment of a peerage on Curzon to be 'a point of honour'. It was no use. The Prime Minister refused to budge. In June, the King sought further ministerial advice. He asked John Morley, the Liberal Secretary of State for India, whether there was any further action he could take to redeem his promise of 1904. Morley prepared a paper on the subject, the gist of which was that as Balfour had declined to recommend Curzon for a peerage either on the Viceroy's resignation or on his own four months later, Campbell-Bannerman did not conceive it his duty to do so; and that 'within the limits of well-established constitutional use', the King could press the matter no further.

When shown the document, Curzon was predictably indignant. 'This fastidious sense of constitutional propriety was held to be sufficient to override the twice repeated pledge of honour of the Sovereign,' he later wrote in a memorandum. 'To the few who are aware of the matter, the plea itself – in view of the general practice in the case of previous Viceroys – appeared to be disingenuous and grotesque: that it should be allowed to prevail shed an entirely new light upon the prerogatives of the Sovereign.'

Believing himself to be excluded from the House of Lords for the entire lifetime of the Liberal Government, Curzon turned his thoughts once more to the House of Commons. If the King, as a constitutional monarch, felt obliged to accept Campbell-Bannerman's decision as final, and thus to break his promise of 1904, Curzon felt no less absolved from his undertaking not to take part in a contested parliamentary election. He therefore wrote to Arthur Balfour asking for an interview at which he might enlist his help.

It was a painful occasion which can be reconstructed from the correspondence that afterwards passed between the former Viceroy and the former Prime Minister. Curzon set the tone by reproaching Balfour for not having recommended him for a peerage. It is true, he added, that he would have refused to accept any honour from the Ministry that had deserted him; but Campbell-Bannerman would not then have been able to claim that he was disqualified from conferring the peerage by Balfour's failure even to offer it.

Balfour replied that he had always intended to offer a peerage to Curzon in recognition of his Indian services, but that it would have been inappropriate at any time between the end of July 1905 and the submission of the final honours list in mid-December. In any case, he added, no man was bound to make an offer which he knew would be refused.

The disputants then turned to the immediate purpose of their meeting, Curzon's request for help in re-entering the House of Commons. Balfour was much nettled by the tone in which Curzon addressed him. 'Though I do not complain of the request,' Balfour told him in an enormously long letter more than a week later, 'I am sure you will not mind my saying that I do somewhat complain of the manner in which it was made. And I complain on two grounds. Your language seems to me to imply, in the first place, that you demanded the seat as the least reparation that could be made for some wrong that I had inflicted on you; and you hinted, not obscurely, that if a seat were not found by the ordinary organisation of the Party, it would none the less be found by some other means; but that, when thus found, its holder would feel himself free to take up a very different position to his Party and to his late colleagues than that which he would otherwise adopt. Now I do not admit the wrong, and I do not like the threat. Surely this is not the way which old friends like you and me should deal with one another.'

By now, however, Curzon no longer looked upon Balfour as a friend. 'I must disclaim having employed in our conversation the language of menace,' he replied coldly on the following day. 'I stated that of the two methods open to me of re-entering the House of Commons, the one with the approval and help of the leader of my party, the other by my independent efforts, I should greatly prefer the former, but that if it were not open to me, I must perforce

N

fall back upon the latter. I can see in this no threat but only a correct analysis of the situation.' And he concluded with a frigid 'I am, Yours sincerely, Curzon.' To Balfour, and to Balfour alone, he continued to attribute his exclusion from public life. He might, however, have spared both Balfour and himself the unpleasantness of that interview. For when invitations to stand for Conservative seats in the Commons did begin to reach him, he was obliged to turn them down on the orders of his doctor.

It was at this low point in Curzon's political fortunes that fate dealt him the most crushing blow of all: the death of his wife. Their years in India had witnessed the apotheosis of her devotion. On State occasions her majestic yet graceful bearing scorned the cruelty of a climate she soon came to dread; in her private hours she cherished her husband with a love that alone could ease the burden of a Viceroy's lonely life. When his plans prospered, she shared his triumph; when the skies grew dark, she gave him comfort and hope.

They found their occasional separations almost unendurable. 'My heart has stayed behind so completely,' she once wrote to her absent husband, 'that the void in my breast never stops aching.' And when ill-health obliged her to remain in England on his return to India in the autumn of 1904, he responded in the same leaden tones of melancholy. 'I have not dared to go into your room,' he wrote, 'for fear that I should burst out crying. And, indeed, I am utterly miserable and desolate. Nobody to turn to or talk to, memories on all sides of me and anxiety gnawing at my heart. ... It is a misery even to tear myself from writing to you and never in my life have I felt so forlorn and cast down.'

A few weeks later she courageously struggled out to join him for the last troubled months of his Viceroyalty. 'This will be like beginning life again after a hideous interlude,' he wrote, 'and all my efforts will be directed to make the new life happy and sweet – happier and sweeter if possible than the old. Every night and morning I thank God that you are coming out.'

But it was a false dawn. Two miscarriages and a desperate struggle for life at Walmer Castle in 1904 had undermined a constitution that was never robust. She died of heart failure at Carlton House Terrace on 18 July 1906.

That Mary had so brief a time to live was mercifully hidden from Curzon in the glad spring of 1905 which they shared at Simla. To celebrate what he took to be a permanent recovery, he wrote her these verses:

I would have torn the stars from the Heavens for your necklace,
I would have stripped the rose-leaves for your couch from all the trees,
I would have spoiled the East of its spices for your perfume,
The West of all its wonders to endower you with these.

I would have drained the ocean, to find its rarest pearldrops,
And melt them for your lightest thirst in ruby draughts of wine:
I would have dug for gold till the earth was void of treasure,
That, since you had no riches, you might freely take of mine.

I would have drilled the sunbeams to guard you through the daytime,
I would have caged the nightingales to lull you to your rest;
But love was all you asked for, in waking or in sleeping,
And love I give you, sweetheart, at my side and on my breast.

Kedleston is her tomb, this love song her epitaph.

Curzon recovered slowly from his grief. 'I am not fit for society,' he told a friend, 'and desire only to hide my head.' When at last he did begin to emerge from the shadows, his continued exclusion from politics denied him the employment in which he might have found diversion, if not solace. He bore his fate with an increasingly stoical acceptance. 'Such has been the fate of much greater and better men than myself,' he afterwards wrote, 'and when I thought of Warren Hastings in the solitude of Daylesford, I took heart anew. Indeed I began to feel a sort of gloomy pride in my undistinguished distinction, though sometimes I fumed at the penalty which it carried with it – of having no seat in either House of Parliament when Indian matters were under discussion.'

He allowed his hopes to rise again in the spring of 1907 when Rosebery, whom he had recently defeated in the election for a new Chancellor of Oxford University, magnanimously showed interest in his cause. But spinal weakness kept Curzon in bed, and he was unable to motor over to the Durdans for their proposed meeting. Even so, it is doubtful whether the former Prime Minister, already somewhat discredited in Liberal eyes, would have been able to sway the mind of his more radical successor.

There was yet another false dawn later in the year, when Morley had a change of heart and offered to intercede with Campbell-Bannerman. This time the Prime Minister's answer no longer depended on Balfour's laches of 1905; he now claimed unequivocally that his 'adherents in Parliament and in the country would not understand it, and would not like it'. The Labour leader, Philip Snowden, once described Campbell-Bannerman as in appearance the sort of man one would like to have for a grandfather or an uncle. But his heart was harder and the narrowness of his outlook, as Curzon complained with justice, 'not only humiliating to myself, but inconsistent with the finer traditions of our public life'. Curzon also suspected that he could no longer depend on the King's goodwill since the Prince of Wales later King George V, had returned from a tour of India as a strong partisan of Kitchener.

As Chancellor of Oxford, Curzon was summoned to Windsor Castle in November 1907 to confer an honorary degree on the German Emperor, and determined to thrash out the entire matter in a private audience with the King. But on the very morning of the ceremony he received a letter from Lord Lansdowne that offered a practical solution to his predicament. Would he allow himself to be nominated to fill a vacancy in the Irish Representative Peerage caused by the sudden death of Lord Kilmaine?

The proposal was not without irony. Curzon, who took no interest in Irish affairs, did not possess an acre of Irish land and never spent a single hour on Irish soil, had accepted an Irish peerage in 1898 for entirely non-Hibernian reasons; it was the only way in which he could assume the dignity of a Lord and yet remain free to return one day to the House of Commons. Now that ill-health debarred him from the Commons and Campbell-Bannerman's intransigence from the Lords, the same Irish peerage might serve to achieve precisely what he had wished to avoid in 1898 – a seat in the House of Lords. For by the Act of Union, the Peers of Ireland had received the right to elect twenty-eight of their number to sit for life in the Upper House at Westminster.

Lansdowne was supported in his well-intentioned plan by two of the most influential grandees in Ireland: the Duke of Abercorn, Lord George Hamilton's eldest brother, and Lord Londonderry. They hoped that Curzon's election would be unopposed, and were dismayed to discover that the bulk of Irish peers persisted in nominating men of predominantly Irish connection. What also weighed against Curzon's wish to occupy an Irish place in the House of Lords was that he would be likely before long to succeed his father, then aged seventy-six, and so inherit a seat in any case. Feeling that 'it would be preposterous to run you against an obscure Irishman,' Lansdowne and his fellow sponsors concluded that their candidate should not after all stand for election. Curzon, however, determined that he had spent long enough in the wilderness and insisted on being nominated. His courage was rewarded. In January 1908 he was returned at the head of the poll, albeit by only two votes over Lord Ashtown, who himself had only two votes to spare over the third candidate, Lord Farnham. His good fortune was in part the result of a noble gesture from St John Brodrick who, having nine months earlier inherited the Irish viscounty of Midleton among his father's other honours, quixotically voted in his favour. On 29 January 1908, Curzon took his seat for the first time in the House of Lords.

By a circuitous route, Curzon had now regained a place in the legislature. But he had still not received the honour customarily offered to all previous occupants of the office which he himself had held with distinction for seven years. That did not come until 1911, when King George v repaired the neglect by creating him an earl of the United Kingdom in the non-party Coronation Honours list. What little pleasure he could draw from such belated recognition was dimmed by prolonged and pedantic arguments about the special peerage remainders for which he asked. Having no male heir, he requested that the viscounty which is simultaneously bestowed with an earldom should at his death pass to his father, Baron Scarsdale, thence to his eldest brother; and that the new barony similarly bestowed on him should pass in turn to his daughters. After appealing to the King, he eventually had his way, although obliged to pay fees of no less than £2,080 2*s*. for the privilege.

'Thus ended the very unusual series of events,' wrote Curzon, 'by which the entry as a British peer to the House of Lords of a man who had twice been Viceroy of India and was already himself the heir to a British peerage, and later on an Irish Representative peer, was protracted over a period of seven years, and attended by circumstances which reflect credit on few of their authors and will probably (unless he be a politician) greatly surprise the historian. *Tantaene animis coelestibus irae!** May I, if ever I am placed in a like situation, give more generous measure than I have received.'

The belated earldom of 1911 did little to sweeten Curzon's character or to assuage the bitterness he harboured against his political enemies. He had lived too long with pain and exhaustion, grief and ill-usage, for the clouds instantly to roll away; and even the oldest of friends remaining to him had to tread carefully.

For Alfred Lyttelton alone was reserved the intimacy and trust of their schooldays. On leaving the House of Commons for India in 1898, Curzon had written to him: 'I cannot say how often, as I have been defending arguable policies or executing rhetorical capers, the sight of your dear old face aglow with sympathy as I turned round to the benches has cheered and helped me to go on.' And as Viceroy he sent letter after letter to 'My dear old Alf,' refusing to allow Lyttelton's implicit support in Cabinet for the policies of Brodrick to interrupt, much less shatter their confidences.

Curzon was profoundly moved by Lyttelton's fidelity in the bleak years that followed. 'Your words,' he wrote in 1908, 'affectionate and generous as ever, have warmed my heart, which is often very chill nowadays.' When Curzon stood against Lloyd George for the Lord Rectorship of Glasgow University, Lyttelton threw the weight of his attractive personality into the contest. 'How those undergrads must have loved you,' Curzon wrote, 'was anyone ever cut out to be such a hero to the young?' But he admitted – pessimistically as it turned out – that 'the little Welsh bruiser may leave me a mangled and eviscerated corpse'.

Alfred retained not only the endearing character but also the athletic

* Can heavenly spirits cherish resentment so dire. *Aeneid* I. ii.

brilliance of his youth. In June 1913 he was persuaded to take part in a game of cricket in his parliamentary constituency. He wrote next day: 'I was hauled out to play cricket! first time for ten years – poor wicket and professional bowling; saw it from first to last like a football and got 90.' But in the course of his innings he was struck by a ball; the injury aggravated an internal malady, and within a few days he was dead.

'He, perhaps, of all men of this generation,' Asquith told the House of Commons, 'came nearest to the mould and ideal of manhood which every English father would like to see his son aspire to, and if possible to attain.'

Curzon's more elaborate threnody, the finest thing he ever wrote, included words that touched the sublime:

> All will remember his endearing manner, that seemed almost to partake of the nature of a caress and was equally captivating to age and youth, to high and low, to women and to men. They will see again the sparkle of his merry eye and hear the shout of his joyous laughter. They will picture once more the virile grace of his figure, loosely knit, but eloquent of sinews and muscles well attuned, his expressive gestures and swinging gait. They will measure the quality of his mind, moderate and well-balanced in its inclinations, emphatic but not censorious in its judgments. They will think of his high and unselfish character and of his honourable and stainless life; and, as he passes into the land of silence and becomes a shadow among shadows, they will reflect with a lifelong pride that they knew and loved this glorious living thing while he shed a light as of sunbeams and uttered a note as of the skylark in a world of mystery, half gladness and half tears.

He was buried on the day of the Oxford and Cambridge cricket match; and at the hour of the funeral, the game was interrupted to allow players and spectators to stand in silence to his memory.

Lyttelton died before he could outlive Curzon's regard; another decade and even he might have felt the sting of that hasty tongue or received one of those plaintive yet menacing letters that flowed all too fluently from his pen. The ordeal was hard to bear by those who loved him, not because his conduct was of a sustained acerbity but because his darkest moods could alternate with bursts of warmth and sunshine that recalled happier days.

Allegiance varied with temperament. Cecil Spring Rice, who could be both mordant and morose, never deviated from the mild disparagement of his Balliol lampoon. 'His affection for his own glory makes it rather difficult for the Council to walk with him contentedly,' he had written of the Viceroy. 'I expect a man of the Elgin type is really what we want.' And a few years later he said of the recently elected Chancellor of his University: 'Curzon is making himself objectionable and ruling Oxford like an Indian province.'*

* Curzon not only departed from recent precedent by going into residence at the University, but also expected the dons to sign a gubernatorial visitors' book.

Rennell Rodd, a gentler character than Spring Rice – and one of the few friends of the Viceroy to greet him at Charing Cross Station on his melancholy return in 1905 – was another victim of Curzon's imperious manner. Shortly before he retired in 1920 as Ambassador to Italy, Leveson Gower asked him whether Curzon, the new Foreign Secretary, treated him with the easy familiarity of their youth. 'Sometimes, but not always,' Rodd replied. 'Ah,' Leveson Gower said, 'I suppose he digs you in the ribs and cracks jokes when you are alone but freezes up when foreigners are present?' Rodd answered that it was exactly the contrary: 'When foreigners are there, I get slaps on the back and am "*camarade de notre belle jeunesse*," and they are duly impressed by Curzon's cordiality to old friends; but when we are alone the atmosphere freezes.'

George Leveson Gower remained to the end of his life the ebullient Laxer of Balliol days. His good-humoured banter dispelled the dejection of a hard pressed Viceroy; and kinship with the great Whig families of England protected him from the slights which Curzon sometimes inflicted on those he supposed to be his social inferiors. From India, Curzon asked him to be a godfather to the son whose birth he eagerly awaited, although when Mary bore her husband a third daughter the invitation was not pressed.

But in later years Curzon treated him with scant courtesy. He once summoned Leveson Gower to the Foreign Office on a business matter, left him to cool his heels in a waiting-room for half an hour, then sent a curt message to say that the Foreign Secretary was too busy to see him. Nettled by such conduct, the Laxer bided his time; and long after Curzon's death he published the story, attached to a string of similarly disobliging anecdotes about his old friend. The splash of acid had bitten deeper than either suspected at the time.

Margot Asquith was another intimate who took her revenge in print after Curzon had carried a political dispute into private life and refused to ask her to a ball he gave during the Home Rule crisis of 1914. She also felt that Curzon had betrayed her husband by the haste with which he had transferred his loyalty to Lloyd George during the change of Government in 1916. Four years later, the girl who had once signed herself his 'most true and most loyal loving Margie' published an audacious autobiography that gave Curzon much pain. It exposed his 'poor sense of proportion and a childish love of fine people,' although it did mention his more agreeable qualities, too. 'The King,' Curzon told his wife, 'severely condemns Asquith for not reading and Crewe for reading and passing her scandalous chatter.'

Lord Crewe – the Lord Houghton of Crabbet days – provoked Curzon's discontent in other ways. It was not only that Crewe was a Liberal, Curzon a Conservative: from 1910 to 1915 Crewe was also Secretary of State for India, and so charged with reversing some of the most cherished measures of Curzon's Viceroyalty. There were occasional brushes, too, during the seven years that Crewe was Leader of the House of Lords. 'I found it exceedingly difficult to speak yesterday afternoon,' Curzon once wrote to him petulantly, 'because though I was answering a direct challenge from you to explain why I was against the Bill ... you scarcely paid me the compliment of affecting to listen but were talking to Morley the whole time. It was noticed by the whole of your Bench and must have been noticeable to the entire House.'

As Foreign Secretary, however, Curzon did not hesitate to cut daringly across political boundaries by begging Crewe to become British Ambassador in France in succession to Lord Hardinge. 'There, more than anywhere else,' he wrote, 'we want authority, influence, distinction, power.' Lord and Lady Crewe carried out their duties in Paris with urbane confidence. Yet only six months later Curzon was writing to his wife: 'As you say, there is no such thing as gratitude and the two Crewes are now firmly convinced that they got the place on their own merits.'

Even to the end, there were fitful gleams through the clouds. Curzon's condescension may have burnt into Spring Rice's mind like a corrosive. But when in 1912 Spring Rice was appointed Ambassador to the United States – a recognition of his talents as belated as Curzon's earldom – Curzon wrote him a letter of delighted congratulation. 'It is good,' he said, 'to see things come to the patient, the deserving, the competent, and above all the dear friend of a lifetime.'

Rennell Rodd may have been chilled by Curzon's official manner. But when he returned to London after eleven years as Ambassador in Rome and told the Foreign Secretary that he felt unnoticed and unappreciated, Curzon at once sent a letter that restored his spirits. 'The world has once more become full of sunshine and happiness for him,' Lady Rodd wrote gratefully to Curzon.

George Leveson Gower may have resented Curzon's rudeness to him at the Foreign Office; but well into his tenth decade he would chuckle over the pranks which they had played on each other seventy years before and luxuriate in recalling their shared pleasures of a world that cared for beauty in all its forms.

Margot Asquith may have been banished from Curzon's intimacy in 1920 after publishing her indiscreet autobiography. But five years later he invited her to dine so that they might end their quarrel – only to die on the day of their proposed reconciliation.

Crewe may have been exposed to Curzon's discontent in public and denigration in private. But when Curzon ceased to be Foreign Secretary in 1924, he bade farewell to the Ambassador in terms of unstinted generosity.

And although Winston Churchill never managed to establish an easy relationship with Curzon in Lloyd George's Cabinet, he recorded that of all the letters he received on his mother's death in 1921, Curzon's was the most noble and comforting.

Some of Curzon's old friends and acquaintances who in later years felt ill-used put themselves at a distance from him, and a thread of self-pity would run through his thoughts. In bed with phlebitis, he wrote from Carlton House Terrace to his wife: 'I sent for our book of visitors cards to see if any of my friends had called to enquire about me in the last ten days. Only two old Peels, unless that old Fox has forgotten to enter them. I think I must be entirely forgotten or have no friends left. ... Not a single one of the people whom I used to entertain year after year at Hackwood has written one line or even left a card. Well, such is the world. It does not wait even till you are dead to forget you, but if you are laid temporarily on the shelf it shuts and locks the door of the cupboard so as not to be reminded.'

Others who had to work with Curzon day by day consoled themselves for snubs and slights by mocking him behind his back. They included Lord Derby, whose patrician bonhomie was never sufficient armour against Curzon's patronizing rectitude. Once Curzon kept the entire Cabinet waiting without a message of explanation or apology. At last the green baize footstool with which he would relieve his phlebitic leg was borne in by an office-keeper. Derby exclaimed: 'Curzon himself has still not arrived, but we see premonitory symptoms.' And he rose and bowed to the footstool.

But there still remained one or two intimates who did not forget Curzon's genius for friendship before he went out to India. Even in moments of exasperation their thoughts touched on the battle against ill-health he had fought since boyhood; and they forgave all. 'His heart was sound enough, but his temper was hasty,' Esher wrote. 'What of that? A minor fault.'

Among those most anxious to wipe the slate clean was St John Brodrick. But India had dried up Curzon's affection for ever, and although in the small Edwardian world of society and politics the two men were obliged to see something of each other, even to correspond, the breach was never fully healed. The late Aga Khan did his best by inviting them to lunch with him at the Ritz Hotel. 'It was a failure,' he said. 'They confined their conversation to polite exchanges about the weather in Calcutta at different times of the year.' Alfred Lyttelton also tried his hand at arbitration and must have persuaded Curzon to accept a handshake of reconciliation, for Brodrick rewarded his diplomatic initiative with a silver inkstand. But Lord Newton, another man of goodwill, described himself as 'a kind of interpreter' between the two old adversaries during discussions on the reform of the House of Lords in 1911, even although they were generally in agreement.

It is to Brodrick's credit that he clutched at every possible opportunity over the years for holding out an olive branch, and warmly phrased letters were despatched on such occasions as Curzon's belated earldom in 1911, the death of Lord Scarsdale in 1916 and the negotiation of the Treaty of Lausanne in 1923. He even sent him little morsels of gossip, as when he wrote on 30 August 1914: 'Have you heard the statement that a force of Russians from Archangel has gone via Scotland to Southampton?' And although he had succeeded to his father's viscounty of Midleton in 1907, he would touch a heartstring of youth by signing himself 'St J.B.' Sometimes, however, presumably because he could not bring himself to write, 'My dear George,' much less 'My dear old boy,' he would plunge straight into the text of the letter without any superscription.

Curzon's enmity thawed a little in the comradeship of the Great War. In 1918, twenty years after Brodrick had last entered his house, the invitation was renewed. Curzon asked sixty eminent men to dine with him, and included Brodrick. That was not in itself an unusual form of hospitality; but the host made it so by leavening the masculinity of the evening with a mere dozen women. Those men whose wives had not been invited minded the insult more than they enjoyed the dinner. The Archbishop of Canterbury, for instance, came alone and to his unconcealed surprise found himself between Lloyd George and James Barrie. Brodrick, who had remarried in 1903 after the death of Hilda two years earlier, was another of those asked without his wife: he was much put out and wished he had never come. The bachelor Balfour, more fortunately placed next to Ettie Desborough, said it appeared strange to take the trouble of having a dinner for sixty people in difficult wartime days in order to offend thirty of them.

Curzon shared too many public and private interests with Balfour for his enmity to endure unabated. He never forgot how Balfour had abetted Brodrick in bringing his Viceroyalty to a humiliating end, subsequently denying him the peerage to which his services entitled him. But entry to the House of Lords in 1908 – albeit through a side door – and an earldom in the Coronation honours three years later encouraged him to resume an outward cordiality. From behind the mask he continued to gaze upon his old friend with a wariness little removed from mistrust.

In 1915, after ten years of Liberal government, both were recalled to power in Asquith's wartime coalition, Balfour as First Lord of the Admiralty, Curzon in the less onerous office of Lord Privy Seal – 'like a Rolls Royce car, with a highly competent driver, kept to take an occasional parcel to the station,' as Crewe described him. Eighteen months later, when Lloyd George superseded Asquith, Balfour became Foreign Secretary and Curzon a member of the War Cabinet. Even that did not mark the limit of their restored fortunes. At the beginning of 1919 Balfour accompanied Lloyd George to Paris for the Peace Conference and Curzon took his place as acting

Foreign Secretary,* while retaining his own office of Lord President of the Council.

The statesmen showed each other much courtly deference. 'The difficulty of running the Foreign Office in double harness,' Curzon told Balfour, 'has been not inconsiderable, although I need hardly add that it has been greatly alleviated by your consideration.' 'Thanks to your skill and wisdom,' Balfour replied, 'I do not think serious difficulties have arisen.' In private Curzon was less content with his lot. 'A.J.B. is in Paris pursuing one policy,' he told his wife, 'I am here pursuing another.' At the end of October, however, the two men exchanged posts. Balfour, now aged seventy-one, accepted the dignified repose of Lord President; and Curzon, formally appointed Secretary of State for Foreign Affairs, could look forward once more to the exercise of political power.

Humiliation and disappointment alone awaited him. Lloyd George, he soon discovered, was determined to be his own Foreign Secretary. 'He had,' Curzon wrote, 'no instinctive appreciation of diplomacy, no knowledge of his subject, no conception of his policy. He despised and disliked the instrument through which he was obliged ostensibly to work, viz. the F.O., never losing an opportunity in Cabinet or elsewhere of denouncing its officials and their work. He set up his own personal Secretariat to operate behind the back of the F.O., conducting intrigues, sending messages, holding interviews, of which we were never informed until it was too late, or only heard by accident or gathered from the intercepted telegrams of foreign governments.'

On a personal level too, Curzon was made to feel the smart of Lloyd George's contempt. 'I am getting very tired of working or trying to work with that man,' he told his wife. 'He wants his Foreign Secretary to be a valet, almost a drudge, and he has no regard for the conveniences or civilities of official life.' In 1921, it is true, the Prime Minister was responsible for his being created a marquess: but no recipient of an honour ever paid more dearly for it. Insulted in Cabinet, ignored in private and ridiculed behind his back, Curzon nevertheless refused to resign: if he could not have the substance of power, he would at least enjoy its shadow.

The greater part of his resentment he reserved not for Lloyd George but for Arthur Balfour:

> On the occasion of my visits to Paris he would expatiate with philosophic and almost cynical detachment upon the performances of the Big Four and the 'little man' in particular, as though they did not in the least concern him, the Foreign Minister of Great Britain. From that moment dated the practical supersession of the Foreign Office and the fatal domination of Lloyd George, which was later to have such deplorable results. It was always possible for him after his return to England to

* Curzon's appointment prompted Ian Malcolm to write the verses reproduced in the Appendix, page 390.

claim the right to deal with this or that question on the ground that he had been responsible for the policy pursued in Paris, and that the Versailles Treaty was his.

In a memorandum of 9,000 words begun in December 1922, Curzon composed an indictment of his old friend and colleague surpassed in bitterness only by the privately printed account of Brodrick's tenure of the India Office which he had written seventeen years before. Ranging over the whole of Balfour's Ministerial career, it dwelt on his 'careless precipitancy' when deputizing for Lord Salisbury at the Foreign Office in 1898; on his neglect of vital correspondence during Curzon's years as Viceroy; on his readiness to cede Cyprus to Greece during the war. 'I never felt since that he might not give up Gibraltar,' Curzon added scornfully.

Again and again, in passages of scathing contempt, Curzon returns to Balfour's supine subservience to Lloyd George at the Peace Conference in Paris. 'He played lawn tennis and attended concerts and presided with exquisite courtesy over the British Delegation and charmed everybody by his manners, and steadily day by day pulled the extinguisher more firmly down on the head of his own Department, until it almost ceased to have a separate existence. No one was more conscious of this humiliating self-suppression than Clemenceau, who used to speak of Balfour at this time as "cette vieille fille".'

I regard him [Curzon continued] as the worst and most dangerous of the British Foreign Ministers with whom I have been brought into contact in my public life. His charm of manner, his extraordinary intellectual distinction, his seeming indifference to petty matters, his power of dialectic, his long and honourable career of public service, blinded all but those who knew from the inside to the lamentable ignorance, indifference, and levity of his regime. He never studied his papers; he never knew the facts; at the Cabinet he had seldom read the morning's F.O. telegrams; he never got up a case; he never looked ahead. He trusted to his unequalled power of improvisation to take him through any trouble and enable him to leap lightly from one crisis to another....

In reality the characteristics that made him a failure and soon a danger as Foreign Minister were the same characteristics that made him a failure as Prime Minister. It was not lack of courage: he showed that in abundance during the Boer War; not lack of ability: he had that in a superlative degree; not onesidedness: he would always listen to any arguments. It was sheer intellectual indolence, a never-knowing his case, an instinctive love for compromise, and a trust in the mental agility which would enable him at the last moment to extricate himself from any complication however embarrassing....

The truth is that Balfour with his scintillating intellectual exterior had no depth of feeling, no profound convictions, and strange to say (in spite of his fascination of manner) no real affection. We all knew this, when the emergency came, he would drop or desert or sacrifice any one of us without a pang, as he did me in India, as he did George Wyndham* over Ireland. Were any one of us to die suddenly he would

* In 1905 Wyndham resigned as Chief Secretary for Ireland after criticism from his own party of the Home Rule tendencies of Sir Antony MacDonnell, his Under-Secretary.

dine out that night with undisturbed complacency, and in the intervals of conversation or bridge, would be heard to murmur 'Poor old George'.

Curzon completed his memorandum in January 1923, between sessions of the Lausanne Conference. 'For use by my biographer,' he wrote on the cover, then filed it away. As a denunciation of Balfour's conduct it is a formidable document; but through no fault of Curzon's, it is incomplete. Balfour still had one final, feline disservice in store for him.

In October 1922, a few weeks before Curzon left London for Lausanne, a majority of Conservative Members of Parliament decided to withdraw their support from the Coalition Government which Lloyd George had led since 1916. The Prime Minister at once resigned, a general election was fought on old-fashioned party lines and a wholly Conservative administration took office under Andrew Bonar Law, who had succeeded Balfour as leader of the party eleven years before. Many prominent Conservatives, however, including Balfour and Austen Chamberlain, remained loyal to Lloyd George; and they pressed Curzon to join them in declining to serve under Bonar Law.

He considered their proposal without enthusiasm. The ten bleak years which followed his resignation as Viceroy of India had given him a distaste for political exile; and the torments which Lloyd George inflicted on him at the Foreign Office had shrivelled his personal allegiance. Besides, Curzon believed in the continuity of British foreign policy; he also believed that a Conservative Government which did not include Balfour or Chamberlain would presently place him within reach of the Premiership. The balance of argument was irresistible. He remained Foreign Secretary.

Events outpaced his most sanguine hopes. On Saturday, 19 May 1923, Curzon went down to Montacute, his house in Somerset, for the long Whitsuntide week-end. On Monday morning he received a letter from Bonar Law. The Prime Minister had been stricken by cancer of the throat and given no more than six months to live. He was resigning immediately. The letter continued:

> I understand that it is not customary for the King to ask the Prime Minister to recommend his successor in circumstances like the present and I presume that he will not do so; but if, as I hope, he accepts my resignation at once, he will have to take immediate steps about my successor.

Since Balfour and Austen Chamberlain had put themselves out of the running at the fall of the Lloyd George Government seven months before, Curzon knew that the effective choice lay between himself and Stanley Baldwin. Measured by experience and intellectual ability, his own claims were overwhelming. He had been Viceroy of India for seven years and in the Cabinet for another eight; it was Curzon, moreover, who had presided over the Cabinet in Bonar Law's absence. Baldwin, by contrast, had been a Cabinet Minister for only two years and Chancellor of the Exchequer for a mere few months. But on grounds of temperament and character – although Curzon was perhaps unaware of it – the advantage lay the other way. One was thought to be high-handed, impulsive and unapproachable; the other respected for his honesty and calm good sense.

Curzon later described Bonar Law's letter as 'singularly curt and ungracious'. At the time, however, he seems to have interpreted it as a pointer to his chances – or why else, he thought, should Bonar Law have written it? It was therefore with something approaching complacency that Curzon waited at Montacute the whole of that Monday for a telegram summoning him to an audience at Buckingham Palace. As the house had no telephone,* he was necessarily isolated from the world of politics in London. Nor did he at once return to London by train, 'lest my action be misinterpreted,' he later wrote. That he wanted to be Prime Minister was indisputable; yet his placid inactivity on the crucial May day of 1923, his disinclination personally to press his cause in the higher ranks of the Conservative Party, is almost incomprehensible. Perhaps he did have doubts about the wisdom of keeping aloof. If so, they were laid to rest that evening when a policeman bicycled up to Montacute from the village post office bearing a telegram. It was from Lord Stamfordham, the King's private secretary. 'Would it be possible,' he asked, 'for me to see you in London tomorrow?' 'I will,' Curzon replied 'be at Carlton House Terrace at 1.20.'

When a Prime Minister resigns, it is customary for the Sovereign to determine his successor not by personal whim, but by consulting representative members of the appropriate political party. As soon, therefore, as it was known that Bonar Law had relinquished office, the friends and enemies of the two candidates embarked with animation upon their campaign. The retiring Prime Minister himself pleaded that he was too unwell to offer advice; but a document purporting to express his views was prepared by Mr J. C. C. (later Lord) Davidson, his parliamentary private secretary, and, unknown to Bonar Law, handed to Stamfordham for the King's perusal. It was unfavourable to Curzon's cause. Other Ministers, including W. C. Bridgeman, the Home Secretary, and Leo Amery, First Lord of the Admiralty, also declared against Curzon; but their opinions did not weigh heavily in the scale.

That could not be said of Lord Salisbury, Lord President of the Council

* This was less surprising in 1923 than it may appear today. Even as late as 1940 there was no private line between Chequers, the Prime Minister's official country house in Buckinghamshire, and No. 10 Downing Street. The only instrument in the house was connected to the local telephone exchange – and kept in the butler's pantry.

and as respected a sage in Conservative eyes as his father. Called from Devon at short notice, he made a dramatic dash to London by milk train in the early hours of Monday morning. And when received by Stamfordham, he pressed the claims of Curzon, his friend almost since boyhood.

There remained the only statesman other than Bonar Law who could speak with the authority of a Conservative Prime Minister. Balfour was staying at Sheringham, in Norfolk, when he received Stamfordham's summons. Although suffering from phlebitis, he shirked neither the journey nor the duty, and on the same Monday that Curzon sat waiting at Montacute, he sealed the issue.

In his talks with the King's private secretary, Balfour confined himself to a single theme: the problems that would face a Prime Minister who sat in the House of Lords. They were threefold. One difficulty was the unusually high proportion of Cabinet appointments already held by peers. Another was the resentment that would be felt by the House of Commons if this trend were extended to include the Prime Minister himself. A third was the hostility that would be encountered from the Labour Party; for although they held a majority of Opposition seats in the Commons, they were virtually unrepresented in the Lords and thus would be unable to question or challenge a Prime Minister who sat there. Together, Balfour declared, these three circumstances precluded the appointment of a peer as Prime Minister. 'I understood from Stamfordham,' he afterwards wrote, 'that these views were probably in very close conformity with those already held by His Majesty.'

At no time did Balfour urge that Curzon would be an unsuitable Prime Minister on personal grounds. On the contrary, Stamfordham recorded, 'Balfour said he was speaking regardless of the individuals in question, for whereas, on one side, his opinion of Lord Curzon is based upon an intimate, life-long friendship, and the recognition of his exceptional qualifications; on the other, his knowledge of Mr Baldwin is slight and, so far, his public career has been more or less uneventful and without any signs of special gifts or exceptional ability.'

It was with a clear conscience that on Tuesday Balfour resumed his holiday in Norfolk. He was greeted there by a party of friends, nearly all of whom had known Curzon since the days of the Souls: Hugo and Mary Wemyss, Ettie Desborough, Evan Charteris, Edgar D'Abernon. 'And will dear George be chosen?' one of them asked him. 'No,' he replied, 'dear George will not.'

Curzon, meanwhile, knew nothing of these portentous comings and goings. With Lord Stamfordham's telegram in his pocket he travelled up to London by train on the Tuesday morning in a mood of euphoria. The hours went pleasantly by as he discussed plans for the future with his wife: they would, he decided, continue to live and entertain at Carlton House Terrace, using No. 10 Downing Street only for official purposes. He also read the newspapers. 'I had found in the morning Press,' he later wrote, 'an almost unanimous opinion that, the choice lying between Baldwin and myself, there was no question as to the immense superiority of my claims and little doubt as to the intention of the King. The crowd of Press photographers at Paddington and my house – deceptive and even worthless as these phenomena are – at least indicated that popular belief.'

Lord Stamfordham was announced at 2.30, and Curzon asked his wife to remain in the room so that she might hear the fulfilment of their joint hopes from the lips of the King's private secretary himself. But the message he delivered was shatteringly different from what they had led themselves to expect. In faltering and embarrassed terms, Stamfordham explained that although the King recognized the predominant position held by Curzon both in the Government and in the political life of the country, he must regretfully lay aside personal considerations and select a Prime Minister who sat in the House of Commons.

'Lord Curzon,' Stamfordham recorded, 'listened quietly to all I endeavoured to say and then proceeded to reply with considerable feeling but with restraint and without bitterness. He said that the message which I had conveyed to him was the greatest blow and slur upon him and his public career, now at its summit, that he could have ever conceived. ... He most strongly protested against what he concluded was the principle implied by the King's decision – that no member of the House of Lords could be Prime Minister: and with that protest he should retire from public life, making it clear to the country his reason for doing so, but retiring with no animosity or feelings of opposition against his Party: but only with the deep wound which had been inflicted upon his pride, ambition and loyalty to his King, his country and his Party. ... While Lord Curzon naturally felt his supersession by a comparatively inexperienced and unknown man, he spoke in the warmest and most friendly terms of Mr Baldwin.'

Curzon readily forgave Stamfordham for having unwittingly raised false hopes; he appreciated that he had been summoned to London only to hear of the King's choice of Baldwin before it became public knowledge. There was another point, however, on which he later wrote with vexation:

> Stamfordham's visit to me had been delayed to an hour when all protest or appeal from me was futile. For at that very hour – 3.15 p.m. – Baldwin was already at the palace, receiving his mission at the hands of the King. In other words, the decision had been taken and acted upon without any chance being given to me, the Acting Premier and the Leader of the House of Parliament and the Senior Cabinet Minister, of even expressing an opinion.
>
> Such was the reward received for nearly forty years of public service in the highest offices. Such was the manner in which it was intimated to me that the cup of honourable ambition had been dashed from my lips, and that I could never aspire to fill the highest office in the service of the Crown.

But what if he had caught the first train to London on receiving Bonar Law's letter that fateful Monday morning? What if he had reminded colleagues of a Private Member's Bill that had failed to get a reading in the Commons only five weeks before, by which Ministers in either House were to be allowed to address the other House?* What if he had asked for their support in adopting such a measure as Government policy? What if Balfour's novel constitutional weapon had been blunted before it could be turned against him? What if his coronet, that first he dreaded and later coveted, had not ultimately become a crown of thorns?

Curzon was not a man to speculate on what might have been or to admit that he was the architect of his own doom. 'Of course it is a great disappointment,' he wrote to Crewe. 'But public life is made up of such: and the only thing is to go on and do one's best as I shall try to do.' He did not carry out his threat to retire from public life, but agreed to continue as Foreign Secretary. And a few days later he proposed the new Prime Minister as leader of the Conservative Party in a speech of graceful magnanimity.

He died less than two years later, some said of a broken heart.

* Leave to bring in the Bill was refused on 18 April 1923 by 244 votes to 100. The sponsor of the Bill was Capt. J. H. Thorpe, Conservative MP for the Rusholme Division of Manchester and father of Mr Jeremy Thorpe, the Liberal Leader from 1967.

APPENDIX

Crabbet Club poems by Curzon

CHARMA VIRUMQUE CANO (1891)

CHARMS and a man I sing, to wit – a most superior person,
Myself, who bears the fitting name of George Nathaniel Curzon.
From which 'tis clear that even when in swaddling bands I lay low,
There floated round my head a sort of apostolic halo.

Think not I mean thereby to say I am wholly 'without guile' –
That is a form of moral sloth that wears off in a while;
But take the Scriptural heroes from King David down to Daniel,
You'll find no better man than this particular Nathaniel.

In early days I'm sure I never did or said a thing
That the most captious critic at my memory could fling;
And if I never showed a sign of future elevation,
My Boswell can supply that need from his imagination.

At Eton other boys might quail before the brandished switches,
My virtue wore with modest pride the badge of intact breeches;
And he who knows not what a swell the Captain of the school is
For ever damned in my vocabulary as a fool is!

At Oxford I made speeches which might well provoke a fit
In persons jealous of the name and the fame of William Pitt;
And if the Schools Examiners deprived me of a First
It was because with envious spleen those blinking owls were curst.

'Tis true that when a seat I fain would win in Parliament
My native county did not smile upon that just intent;
But when they gave me notice in emphatic terms to 'off it'
I smiled and quoted from St Luke a phrase about a prophet.

With finer insight did a great Division in the North
To be their spokesman in the House of Chatter send me forth.
They took me in; and ever since, to pay the obligation,
I've taken them in with a truly honest exultation.

Superior Person

For me no mean ignoble stage – give me the wide whole world,
The seas of either hemisphere must see my sails unfurled.
I have furrowed many an ocean, I have trodden many a land,
From Chinquapin to far Cathay, from Fez to Samarkand.

I have walked in Salt Lake City in the steps of Brigham Young,
In fair Ægean isles have heard the songs that Sappho sung,
I have seen the houris of Tom Moore in the streets of Ispahan,
There has trembled on my lips the kiss of the maidens of Japan.

In tents of wandering Bedouin I have harkened more than once
To tales of prodigies performed by the great race of Blunts;
And if for me on Nilus' banks the Memnon would not sing,
It was because he's ceased to do so commonplace a thing.

Stanley in Darkest Africa may mix with dusky broods;
Give me mystery of the East, the Asian solitudes;
Ten thousand readers fall to sleep o'er Stanley's turgid pages;
Mine, though uncut, will light a fire for unbegotten ages!

To emulate a Stanley's fame tho' I'm in no great hurry,
I long have wished to find a Livingstone in Wilfrid Murray.
But now while in the distant States false rumour surges round him,
In England I have made my quest, at Crabbet I have found him.

I have a quite peculiar gift for unpoetic rhyme,
You've heard it and have greatly wondered at it all this time,
And when I say that now and then my conversation staggers,
You must not dully set me down among the empty braggers.

My looks are of that useful type – I say it with elation –
That qualify me well for almost any situation –
I've sometimes been mistaken for a parson, and at others
Have recognised in butlers and in waiters long-lost brothers.

Perchance with all these gifts you'll say, it's strange I am not wedded,
And preach a sermon on the woes of life when single-bedded,
But if Clarissa I adore, and rashly go and marry her,
To Chloe's subsequent embrace it may erect a barrier.

That I am most remarkable there cannot be a doubt,
Although no one remarks it when he once has found me out;
The only fear to which I own is lest some ass should blab it,
And I should nevermore be asked to lose the prize at Crabbet.

Appendix

SIN (1893)

IN an epoch so degenerate
That no one dares to venerate
The ruffian and the libertine, the criminal and rogue,
When all our old criteria
Have been shattered by Hysteria,
And the moral standard set by Stead is the new and patent vogue;

When biographers discover
That Nelson was no lover;
When Froude has whitewashed Henry as the model of a spouse;
When poor Parnell is driven
By Gladstone to Glasnevin
For innocently tampering with a married lady's vows;

When the too uxorious Verney's
Pursued by Crown Attorneys,
Because he did at Paris what the best Parisians do;
When Jabez is thought sordid
By the widows he defrauded;
When de Cobain's picking oakum just because the count was true;

When even our new Editor –
(Is there any here has read it, or
Disbursed a wasted penny on a fallen P.M.G. – ?)
Diverts the funds of Astor
To gibbet the Post Master
Because by gross venality he still is an M.P.

When merely to be vicious
Is voted a pernicious
And unpardonable infringement of the higher moral law;
When sentiment's so flabby
That genuine rogues like Labby
Are excluded from the Cabinet because they have a flaw;

In times so unromantic
And vulgarly pedantic
That history will style it a reproach to live therein,
We need some new Society
For the stamping out of piety
And the rehabilitation of uncompromising Sin!

Then let the names historic
Whose lustre meteoric
Has lit the sombre firmament of each successive age,
Let David be our hero,
Caligula and Nero,
The Cencis and the Borgias retread our modern stage!

For this sublime alliance
No lack is there of clients,
To play his own particular part each one of us is able;
Be this our sole prospectus –
'Let all the world inspect us' –
The laurelled veterans of vice are seated at this table!

Our *President* shall set us
And example that shall whet us
To practise all the naughty things he sings of in his odes;
Our lawyers, *Matthew*, *Mark*,
Will esteem it quite a lark
To defend us from the petty persecution of the codes.

The trinity of *Georges*
Shall institute fresh orgies
That will shame the classic record of the Emperor Tiberius;
And *Houghton*, when Home Rule
Has been passed, will be the tool
To prove the worst forebodings of the Ulstermen are serious.

Elcho shall lend his humour
To propagate the rumour
That wickedness adorned with wit is the cult to which we pander:
And *Gatty* shall defend us
And get damages tremendous
If any jealous critic vents his stupid spleen in slander.

The juvenile and tender,
Without regard to gender,
Shall be handed up to *Godfrey's* indiscriminate embrace.
And *Oscar* shall embellish
In a play that all will relish
The gradual and glorious declension of the race.

The Pall Mall under *Cust*
Shall ennoble forms of lust
That might have shocked the sensitive and squeamish soul of Stead.
And the fiends for this crusade
Shall be scrupulously paid
By *Loulou* from the Caucus that has Schnadhorst for its head.

By lectures to fair students
That will stimulate imprudence,
Shall *Morpeth* start the Mission which to *Leveson* is assigned
In deference to powers
That excel the rest of ours,
To wit the demolition of the whole womankind.

And so when some historian
Of the period Victorian
Shall crown the greatest exploit of this wonder-working age,
His eye shall light on Crabbet
And, if truth shall be his habit,
The name of everyone of us will shine upon that page.

To us will be the glory,
That shall never fade in story,
Of reviving the old axiom that all the world's akin,
That the true link of union
Which holds men in communion
Is frank and systematic and premeditated Sin!

Poems on Curzon by Sir Ian Malcolm

When Curzon was appointed acting 'Minister of Foreign Affairs', or Foreign Secretary, during Balfour's absence at the Paris Peace Conference of 1919, Malcolm drafted a series of imaginary minutes in verse that might have been addressed by Curzon to Sir Alfred Mond, the First Commissioner of Works:

I am acting M.F.A.;
Please remember what I say
Or you'll live to rue the day.
C. of K.

I must have a spacious room,
Not this loathsome living tomb
Filled with ghosts who've met their doom
How they loom

Bring me chairs and sofas new,
They should be of Royal Blue
Such as I'm accustomed to,
Entre nous

Buy me Persian carpets meet
For Imperial Downing Street,
Where on Wednesdays I greet
The Elite

Golden pen nibs I demand
Jewelled pencils at my hand;
Lacquer fire-screens; not japanned,
These are banned.

I regret I cannot pass
Inkstands made of brass and glass:
Get me one of Chrysophraz
From Shiraz.

And this paper! Well, I'm blest:
Neither monogram nor crest:
In my family interest
I protest

For remember, if you can,
That, although a warming-pan,
I am still a Christian
Nobleman.

The second set of verses which Malcolm wrote on Curzon was inspired by an incident at a meeting of the Middle East Committee of the Foreign Office. It was stated that some tribe worshipped a Peacock King, whose throne was temporarily vacant. Mr William Ormsby Gore, later Lord Harlech, thereupon suggested that Curzon would be a worthy occupant.

On a throne of Alabaster our Re-incarnated Master
Daily exercises his Vice-Regal craft:
Supervising now the Amir or apportioning a Pamir
Or composing some quite devastating draft.
From a cup of gold (not brass) he discovered in Kumassi
See him quaffing some exhilarating thing,
And amorously glancing at the houris that are dancing
For the pleasure of the Peacock King.

When he takes his morning bath he alludes to Amurath
As his predecessor, in all else but brains;
Or he serenades Jocasta or reflects on Zoroaster
With a fire to which Dutasta ne'er attains.
He never stops descanting in comparison enchanting
On the difference 'twixt Kedleston and Tring
Which explains why all the masses (as he calls the lower classes)
Madly venerate the Peacock King.

The people of Damascus did occasionally ask us
When this sublimated Monarch would retire:
They observed there was a chance of exporting him to France
Where some conference his presence would require:
But, before he could be asked, his ambition was unmasked
As he passed into the Inner Ring
And assumed the Foreign Office with the ardour of a novice
As the panache of the Peacock King.

ACKNOWLEDGEMENTS

Curzon Family Papers

My foremost debt of gratitude is to Viscount and Viscountess Scarsdale for their boundless help and friendship, encouragement and hospitality.

Lord Scarsdale, dedicated custodian of an ancient name and a splendid heritage, gave me complete access to his uncle's private and official papers at Kedleston before depositing them in the India Office Library in London. He also put at my disposal all other collections of Curzon family papers and photographs and answered innumerable questions, some of which required considerable research. Above all, he inspired me with a love for Kedleston that he himself inherited from his uncle and shares with his wife.

I am no less grateful to the Kedleston Trustees for permission to quote from Curzon's letters, memoranda and other literary works of which they own the copyright.

The late Baroness Ravensdale, Curzon's eldest daughter, lent me her father's scrapbooks and other documents. And Lady Alexandra Metcalfe, Curzon's youngest and only surviving daughter, kindly allowed me to quote from the correspondence of her parents.

Other members of the Curzon family who lent me documents and gave me advice were Mr and the Hon. Mrs T. Simpson Pedler, Sir Robert and the Hon. Lady Cary, Mr Roger Cary and Mr and Mrs Lawrence Tanner. I am much in their debt.

Other Manuscript Sources

I should like to thank all those who have given me permission to reproduce letters and other manuscript material of which they hold the copyright or who have allowed me access to papers in their possession or care:

Her Majesty the Queen, for extracts from the letters of Queen Victoria; and for extracts from letters written by Curzon to Queen Victoria and to King Edward VII.

Lord Ampthill, for a letter written by his father.

Lady Arthur, for letters written by her father, Sir Cecil Spring Rice, and for access to his papers.

The Earl of Balfour, for letters written by his uncle, the first Earl.

The Masters and Fellows of Balliol College, Oxford, for letters written by Benjamin Jowett, and for access to college archives.

The late Sir George Barnes, for access to letters written by Curzon to Sir Hugh Barnes.

Mr Charles Blacque, for a letter written by his grandfather, Lord Charles Beresford.

Mr Mark Bonham Carter, for letters written by Margot, Countess of Oxford and Asquith.

The Trustees of the British Museum for access to the papers of Arthur, first Earl of Balfour; St John Brodrick, first Earl of Midleton; Sir Henry Campbell-Bannerman; and Mr Gladstone.

Lord Brownlow, for a letter written by Harry Cust.

Miss Margaret Carleton, for access to the papers of Wilfrid Scawen Blunt.

Viscount Chandos, for letters written by his father, Alfred Lyttelton, and for access to his papers.

C. & T. Publications, Ltd, for a letter written by Sir Winston Churchill.

The Earl of Elgin, for letters written by his grandfather, the ninth Earl, and for access to his papers.

Viscount Esher, for letters written by his grandfather, the second Viscount.

The Head Master of Eton, for extracts from the minute book of the Eton College Literary Society.

Mrs Henry Farrer, for letters written by Richard Ridley Farrer.

The Trustees and Director of the Fitzwilliam Museum, Cambridge, for letters written by Wilfrid Scawen Blunt.

Sir William Gladstone, for letters written by his great-grandfather, William Ewart Gladstone.

Department of Palaeography, Durham University, for access to the papers of the fourth Earl Grey.

Mrs Vyvyan Holland, for letters written by her father-in-law, Oscar Wilde.

The Librarian of the India Office Library for Crown Copyright letters written by Lord Ampthill, Lord Curzon, the Earl of Elgin, Sir Henry Fowler, Sir Arthur Godley and Lord George Hamilton.

Colonel George Malcolm of Poltalloch, for verses written by his father, Sir Ian Malcolm.

The Earl of Midleton, for letters written by his father, the first Earl.

The Earl of Minto, for an extract from the journal of his mother, wife of the fourth Earl.

The *Observer* Trust, for access to the papers of St Loe Strachey.

Mr C. C. Oman, for access to the papers of his father, Sir Charles Oman.

The Earl of Pembroke, for letters written by the thirteenth Earl.

The Earl of Portsmouth, for letters written by his uncle, the seventh Earl.

The Keeper of Public Records, for the papers of Lord Curzon in the Public Record Office.

Lord Rennell of Rodd, for letters written by his father, the first Baron.

The Earl of Rosebery, for a letter written by his father, the fifth Earl.

Mary, Duchess of Roxburghe, for letters written by her father, the Marquess of Crewe.

The Marquess of Salisbury, for letters written by his grandfather, the third Marquess, and by his father, the fourth Marquess; and for access to the papers of his grandfather in the library of Christ Church, Oxford.

Viscount Simon, for a letter written by his father, the first Viscount.

Diana, Countess of Westmorland, and Mr Julian Fane, for letters written by Lady Ribblesdale.

Help and Advice

I must record a particular debt of gratitude and affection to the late Sir Harold Nicolson. Both as a dear friend and as the author of an illuminating work on Curzon as Foreign Secretary, he gave me over the years a wealth of guidance and encouragement.

Certain Fellows of All Souls College, Oxford, have given generously of their time and labour in helping me on specific points. They are the Warden, Mr John Sparrow; Dr E.F.Jacob; Dr A.L.Rowse; Mr Rohan Butler; Mr Robert Wade-Gery; the late Earl of Halifax; and the late Mr G.M.Young.

Other scholars to whom I owe unstinted thanks for patient, courteous and invaluable advice are Dr Edward Schofield, of the British Museum; Mr S.C.Sutton, Librarian of the India Office Library, and Dr Richard Bingle, of the same department; Dr David Dilks, historian of Curzon's Viceroyalty of India.

I am also much obliged to the following for personal reminiscences of Curzon, for tracing elusive facts and for wise suggestions: the late Aga Khan; the late Mr Leopold Amery; the late Baroness Asquith of Yarnbury; Mr Ian Ball; the Librarian and staff of Balliol College, Oxford; William Blackwood and Sons, Ltd; Mr Noel Blakiston, of the Public Record Office; the late Mr Gilbert Coleridge; the late Viscountess D'Abernon; Mary, Duchess of Devonshire; Lady Douglas-Home; Mr R.W.Ferrier, of British Petroleum; Capt. Richard Gatty; Mr John Gere, of the British Museum; Dr A.M.Gollin; Mr John Grigg; Sir Rupert Hart-Davis; the staff of the London Library; the late Sir George Leveson Gower; Sir Gilbert Laithwaite; Sir Fitzroy Maclean; Mr Angus Malcolm; Sir James Marshall-Cornwall; Dr J.F.A. Mason, Librarian of Christ Church, Oxford; M.René Massigli; Mr Richard Ollard; Mr Leo Russell; Mr Giles St Aubyn; the late Marchioness of Salisbury; the Marquess of Salisbury; the late Viscount Samuel; the Rev. Norman Sharp; Mrs George Steiner; the Earl of Swinton; Mr Jeremy Thorpe; Mrs Middleton Train; the late Mr Pembroke Wicks; Mr Frederick Worley; Sir Denis Wright; and the late Marquess of Zetland.

I should like to acknowledge the special skill of Mr Norman Knight, whose lively eye has saved me from several blunders and whose index is as much a work of art as of reference.

Finally, I must express gratitude to my publishers, particularly to Mr Anthony Godwin and Miss Rosemary Legge, for their patience and calm in dealing with an author who from time to time can be as exacting and as exasperating as Lord Curzon himself.

BIBLIOGRAPHY

I am grateful to the authors, publishers and copyright holders of the undermentioned books for permission, where necessary, to quote from them. Each individual mention is acknowledged in 'Source References'.

Books by George Nathaniel Curzon

Some Present Etonians, *Out of School at Eton: a Collection of Poetry and Prose Writings*,* Sampson Low, 1877.

'A Purified British Senate', *National Review*, March and April 1888.

Russia in Central Asia, Longmans, Green, 1889.

Persia and the Persian Question (2 vols), Longmans, Green, 1892.

Problems of the Far East, Longmans, Green, 1894.

The Pamirs and the Source of the Oxus, Royal Geographical Society, 1896.

Private Correspondence relating to Military Administration in India, 1902–1905, privately printed, nd [1905].

Indian Speeches (4 vols), Calcutta: Office of the Superintendent of Government Printing, India, 1900–6.

Frontiers (The Romanes Lecture, Oxford), OUP, 1907.

Modern Parliamentary Eloquence, Macmillan, 1914.

Subjects of the Day, Allen & Unwin, 1915.

Kedleston Church, privately printed, Chiswick Press, 1922.

Tales of Travel, Hodder & Stoughton, 1923.

British Government in India (2 vols), Cassell, 1925.

Leaves from a Viceroy's Note-Book, Macmillan, 1926.

Bodiam Castle, Cape, 1926.

Walmer Castle and its Lords Warden, Macmillan, 1927.

Tattershall Castle (with H. A. Tipping), Cape, 1929.

Other Works Consulted

Abbott, Evelyn, and Campbell, Lewis, *Life and Letters of Benjamin Jowett*, Murray, 1897.

Abdur Rahman, Amir of Afghanistan, *Memoirs*, Murray, 1900.

Ainger, A. C., *Eton Sixty Years Ago*, Murray, 1917.

Alington, C. A., *A Dean's Apology*, Faber, 1952.

* Curzon was both editor and a contributor

ALINGTON, C. A., *Things Ancient and Modern*, Longmans, 1936.
AMERY, L. S., *My Political Life*, vol. I, Hutchinson, 1953.
ARTHUR, SIR GEORGE, *Not Worth Reading*, Longmans, Green, 1938.
ASQUITH, LADY CYNTHIA, *Haply I May Remember*, Barrie, 1950.
ASQUITH, LADY CYNTHIA, *Remember and Be Glad*, Barrie, 1952.
ASQUITH, MARGOT, *Autobiography*, vol. I, Thornton Butterworth, 1920.
ASQUITH, MARGOT, *More Memories*, Cassell, 1933.
BAILEY, JOHN (ed.), *The Diary of Lady Frederick Cavendish*, Murray, 1927.
BAILLIE, ALBERT, *My First Eighty Years*, Murray, 1951.
BALFOUR, A. J., *Chapters of Autobiography*, Cassell, 1930.
BALSAN, CONSUELO VANDERBILT, *The Glitter and the Gold*, Heinemann, 1953.
BALSTON, THOMAS, *Dr Balston at Eton*, Macmillan, 1952.
BENSON, A. C., *Memories and Friends*, Murray, 1924.
BENSON, E. F., *Our Family Affairs, 1867–1896*, Cassell, 1920.
BENSON, E. F., *As We Were*, Longmans, Green, 1932.
BEERBOHM, MAX, *Seven Men*, Heinemann, 1920.
BIRKENHEAD, EARL OF, *Life, Law and Letters* (2 vols), Hodder & Stoughton, 1927.
BIRKENHEAD, EARL OF, *Contemporary Personalities*, Cassell, 1924.
BLAKE, ROBERT, *Disraeli*, Eyre & Spottiswoode, 1966.
BLUNT, WILFRID SCAWEN, *My Diaries, 1888–1914*, Secker, 1932.
BONHAM CARTER, MARK, Introduction to Margot Asquith's *Autobiography*, Eyre & Spottiswoode, new edition 1962.
BONHAM CARTER, LADY VIOLET, 'The Souls', *Listener*, 30 October 1947.
BOSWELL, JAMES, *Life of Johnson*, OUP, new edition 1938.
BOWRA, C. M., *Memories*, Weidenfeld & Nicolson, 1966.
BRETT, M. V. (ed.), *Journals and Letters of Reginald, Viscount Esher* (4 vols), Nicholson & Watson, 1934 and 1938.
BROWNING, OSCAR, *Memories of 60 Years*, Bodley Head, 1910.
BUCKLE, G. E., *Life of Benjamin Disraeli*, vol. v, Murray, 1920.
BUCKLE, G. E. (ed.), *Letters of Queen Victoria, 1886–1901* (3rd Series), vol. III, Murray, 1932.
BUTLER, A. S. G., *The Substance of Architecture*, Constable, 1926.
BUTLER, A. S. G., *Recording Ruin*, Constable, 1942.
CARTER, JOHN, *William Johnson Cory*, Rampart Lions Press, Cambridge, 1959.
CECIL, ALGERNON, *British Foreign Secretaries*, Bell, 1927.
CECIL, LADY GWENDOLEN, *Biographical Studies of the Life and Political Character of Robert, Third Marquis of Salisbury*, printed for private circulation, Hodder & Stoughton, 1948.
CECIL, LADY GWENDOLEN, *Life of Robert, Marquis of Salisbury* (4 vols), Hodder & Stoughton, 1921–32.

CHANDOS, VISCOUNT, *The Memoirs of Lord Chandos*, Bodley Head, 1962.

CHANDOS, VISCOUNT, *From Peace to War: a Study in Contrast, 1857–1918*, Bodley Head, 1968.

CHARTERIS, HON. EVAN, *Life and Letters of Sir Edmund Gosse*, Heinemann, 1931.

CHESTER, D. N. and BOWRING, NORA, *Questions in Parliament*, OUP, 1962.

CHILSTON, VISCOUNT, *W. H. Smith*, Routledge, 1965.

CHURCHILL, RANDOLPH S., *Lord Derby: 'King of Lancashire'*, Heinemann, 1959.

CHURCHILL, RANDOLPH S., *Winston S. Churchill*, vol. I 1874–1900, and companion vol. I, part 2, 1896–1900, Heinemann, 1966 and 1967.

CHURCHILL, WINSTON S., *Lord Randolph Churchill*, Odhams, new edition, 1951.

CHURCHILL, WINSTON S., *Great Contemporaries*, Thornton Butterworth, 1937.

COLE, G. D. H. and POSTGATE, RAYMOND, *The Common People*, Methuen, 1938.

COLERIDGE, GILBERT, *Eton in the 'Seventies*, Smith, Elder, 1912.

Complete Peerage (13 vols), St Catherine Press, 1910–59.

CORNISH, FRANCIS WARRE (ed.), *Extracts from the Letters and Journals of William Cory*, OUP, 1897.

CURZON OF KEDLESTON, MARCHIONESS, *Reminiscences*, Hutchinson, 1955.

D'ABERNON, VISCOUNT, *An Ambassador of Peace*, Hodder & Stoughton, 1929–30.

D'ABERNON, VISCOUNT, *Portraits and Appreciations*, Hodder & Stoughton, 1931.

DAVIS, H. W. CARLESS, *A History of Balliol College*, Blackwell, new edition 1963.

Dictionary of National Biography, supplementary volumes, 1901–50, OUP.

Dictionary of American Biography, vol. XI, OUP, 1933.

DUGDALE, BLANCHE E. C., *Arthur James Balfour, First Earl of Balfour* (2 vols), Hutchinson, 1936.

DUGDALE, E. T. S., *Maurice de Bunsen*, Murray, 1934.

ELLIOTT, SIR IVO (ed.), *Balliol College Register, 1833–1933*, OUP, 1934.

ESHER, REGINALD, VISCOUNT, *Cloud-Capp'd Towers*, Murray, 1927.

FABER, GEOFFREY, *Jowett*, Faber, 1957.

FARRER, R. R., *A Tour in Greece*, Blackwood, 1882.

FITZROY, SIR ALMERIC, *Memoirs*, Hutchinson, nd.

FLEMING, PETER, *Bayonets to Lhasa*, Hart-Davis, 1961.

FLETCHER, C. R. L., *Mr Gladstone's Visit to All Souls*, Smith, Elder, 1908.

GAMBIER PARRY, MAJOR E., *Annals of an Eton House*, Murray, 1907.

GATTY, CHARLES T., *George Wyndham: Recognita*, Murray, 1917.

GILBERT, MARTIN (ed.), *Servant of India: Sir James Dunlop Smith*, Longmans, 1966.

GLADSTONE, VISCOUNT, *After Thirty Years*, Macmillan, 1928.

GORELL, LORD, *One Man, Many Parts*, Odhams, 1956.

GOSSES, F., *The Management of British Foreign Policy before the First World War*, Leiden, 1948.

GOWER, LORD RONALD, *Old Diaries*, Murray, 1902.

GRANT DUFF, SIR MOUNTSTUART, *Notes from a Diary, 1896–1901* (2 vols), Murray, 1905.

GRAY, JOHN ALFRED, *At the Court of the Amir*, Richard Bentley, 1895.

GREY OF FALLODEN, VISCOUNT, *Twenty-Five Years*, Hodder & Stoughton, 1925.

GRUNDY, G. B., *Fifty-Five Years at Oxford*, Methuen, 1945.

GWYNN, STEPHEN (ed.), *Letters and Friendships of Sir Cecil Spring Rice* (2 vols), Constable, 1929.

HAMILTON, LORD GEORGE, *Parliamentary Reminiscences and Reflections, 1886–1906*, Murray, 1922.

(*Hansard*). *Parliamentary Debates: Official Report*, HM Stationery Office.

HARDINGE, SIR ARTHUR, *A Diplomatist in Europe*, Cape, 1927.

HARDINGE, SIR ARTHUR, *A Diplomatist in the East*, Cape, 1928.

HARDINGE OF PENSHURST, LORD, *Old Diplomacy*, Murray, 1947.

HARDINGE, W. M., 'Recollections of the Master of Balliol', *Temple Bar*, October 1894.

HARE, AUGUSTUS, *The Story of My Life*, vols IV, V and VI, George Allen, 1900.

HARROD, R. F., *Life of John Maynard Keynes*, Macmillan, 1951.

HASSALL, CHRISTOPHER, *Edward Marsh*, Longmans, 1959.

HENDERSON, SIR NEVILLE, *Water Under the Bridges*, Hodder & Stoughton, 1945.

HENSON, H. HENSLEY, *Retrospect of an Unimportant Life* (2 vols), OUP, 1943.

HENSON, H. HENSLEY, *Letters*, SPCK, 1950.

HISCOCK, W. G. (ed.), *Balliol Rhymes*, Holywell Press, Oxford, 1955.

HOGARTH, D. G., 'George Nathaniel Curzon, Marquess Curzon of Kedleston, 1895–1925', *Proceedings of the British Academy*, vol. XI, OUP, 1926.

HORNER, FRANCES, *Time Remembered*, Heinemann, 1933.

HOWARD, C. H. D., *Splendid Isolation*, Macmillan, 1967.

HOWARD, SIR ESMÈ, *Theatre of Life*, vol. I 1863–1905, Hodder & Stoughton, 1933.

INGE, W. R., *The Diary of a Dean: St. Paul's 1911–1934*, Hutchinson, 1950.

JACOB, H. E., *Six Thousand Years of Bread*, Doubleday, Doran, New York, 1944.

JAMES, HENRY, *Portraits of Places*, Macmillan, 1883.

JAMES, ROBERT RHODES, *Rosebery*, Weidenfeld & Nicolson, 1963.

JENKINS, ROY, *Asquith*, Collins, 1964.

KELLY, SIR DAVID, *The Ruling Few*, Hollis & Carter, 1952.

KENNEDY, A. L., *Salisbury*, Murray, 1953.

KILBRACKEN, LORD, *Reminiscences*, Macmillan, 1931.
KIPLING, RUDYARD, *Something of Myself*, Macmillan, 1937.
LAWRENCE, SIR WALTER, *The India We Served*, Cassell, 1928.
LEE, ELIZABETH, *Ouida: a Memoir*, Fisher Unwin, 1914.
LEE, SIR SIDNEY, *King Edward VII* (2 vols), Macmillan, vol. I 1925; vol. II 1927.
LESLIE, SIR SHANE, *Life and Letters of Mark Sykes*, Cassell, 1923.
LESLIE, SIR SHANE, *Studies in Sublime Failure*, Benn, 1932.
LEVER, SIR TRESHAM, *The Herberts of Wilton*, Murray, 1967.
LEVESON GOWER, SIR GEORGE, *Years of Content*, Murray, 1940.
LEVESON GOWER, SIR GEORGE, *Years of Endeavour*, Murray, 1942.
LEVESON GOWER, SIR GEORGE, *Mixed Grill*, Frederick Muller, 1947.
LIDDELL, A. G. C., *Notes from the Life of an Ordinary Mortal*, Murray, 1911.
LOCKHART, J. G., *Cosmo Gordon Lang*, Hodder & Stoughton, 1949.
LONGFORD, ELIZABETH, *Victoria R.I.*, Weidenfeld & Nicolson, 1964.
LUBBOCK, PERCY (ed.), *The Diary of Arthur Christopher Benson*, Hutchinson, nd.
LUCY, HENRY W., *A Diary of the Salisbury Parliament, 1886–1892*, Cassell, 1892.
LUCY, HENRY W., *A Diary of the Home Rule Parliament, 1892–1895*, Cassell, 1896.
LUCY, HENRY W., *A Diary of the Unionist Parliament, 1895–1900*, J. W Arrowsmith, 1901.
LUCY, HENRY W., *Sixty Years in the Wilderness*, Smith, Elder, 1912.
LUCY, HENRY W., *The Diary of a Journalist*, Murray, 1920.
LUXMOORE, H. E., *Letters*, CUP, 1929.
LYTTELTON, EDITH, *Alfred Lyttelton*, Longmans, 1917.
LYTTELTON, EDWARD, *Memories & Hopes*, Murray, 1925.
LYTTON, EARL OF, *Wilfrid Scawen Blunt*, Macdonald, 1961.
MACCARTHY, DESMOND, *Portraits I*, Putnam, 1931.
MACCARTHY, DESMOND, *Memories*, MacGibbon & Kee, 1953.
MACKAIL, J. W., *James Leigh Strachan-Davidson*, OUP, 1925.
MACKAIL J. W., and WYNDHAM, GUY, *Life and Letters of George Wyndham* (2 vols), Hutchinson, 1925.
MACMILLAN, HAROLD, *Winds of Change*, Macmillan, 1966.
MACONOCHIE, SIR EVAN, *Life in the Indian Civil Service*, Chapman & Hall, 1926.
MAGNUS, LAURIE, *Herbert Warren*, Murray, 1932.
MALCOLM, SIR IAN, *Vacant Thrones*, Macmillan, 1931.
MALCOLM, SIR IAN, *The Pursuits of Leisure*, Benn, 1929.
MALLET, VICTOR, *Life with Queen Victoria*, Murray, 1968.
MARSH, SIR EDWARD, *A Number of People*, Heinemann, 1939.
MARJORIBANKS, EDWARD, *Life of Sir Edward Marshall Hall*, Gollancz, 1930.

MASTERMAN, LUCY, *Mary Gladstone (Mrs Drew): her Diaries and Letters*, Methuen, 1930.

MERSEY, VISCOUNT, *A Picture of Life, 1872–1940*, Murray, 1941.

MIDLETON, EARL OF, *Records and Reactions, 1856–1939*, Murray, 1939.

MILL, HUGH ROBERT, *The Record of the Royal Geographical Society, 1830–1930*, Royal Geographical Society, 1930.

MILNER, VISCOUNTESS, *My Picture Gallery*, Murray, 1951.

MONTROSE, DUKE OF, *My Ditty Box*, Cape, 1952.

MOSLEY, LEONARD, *Curzon*, Longmans, 1960.

NEVILL, RALPH, *Life and Letters of Lady Dorothy Nevill*, Methuen, 1919.

NEWTON, LORD, *Retrospection*, Murray, 1941.

NICOLSON, HAROLD, *Curzon: the Last Phase, 1919–1925*, Constable, 1934.

NICOLSON, HAROLD, *King George the Fifth: His Life and Reign*, Constable, 1952.

O'MALLEY, OWEN, *The Phantom Caravan*, Murray, 1954.

OMAN, CHARLES, *Things I Have Seen*, Methuen, 1933.

OMAN, CHARLES, *Memories of Victorian Oxford*, Methuen, 1941.

OMAN, CHARLES, *The Text of the Second Betting Book of All Souls College, 1873–1919*, Oxford, 1938. Privately printed for members of the College only.

OXFORD AND ASQUITH, EARL OF, *Fifty Years in Parliament* (2 vols), Cassell, 1926.

OXFORD AND ASQUITH, EARL OF, *Memories and Reflections, 1852–1927* (2 vols), Cassell, 1928.

PARKER, ERIC, *Eton in the 'Eighties*, Smith, Elder, 1914.

PARTRIDGE, BURGO, *A History of Orgies*, Blond, 1958.

PEARSALL SMITH, LOGAN, *Cornishiana*, privately printed, Reading, 1935.

PEARSON, HESKETH, *Labby*, Hamish Hamilton, 1936.

PENSON, DAME LILLIAN, *Foreign Affairs under the Third Marquis of Salisbury*, University of London, Athlone Press, 1962.

PENTLAND, LADY, *Memories of Lord Pentland*, Methuen, 1928.

PHILLIPS, LISLE MARCH AND CHISHOLM, BERTRAM (eds), *Some Hawarden Letters, 1878–1913, written to Mrs Drew*, Nisbet, 1917.

PONSONBY, ARTHUR (Lord Ponsonby of Shulbrede), *Henry Ponsonby, Queen Victoria's Private Secretary: his Life from his Letters*, Macmillan, 1942.

PONSONBY, SIR FREDERICK, *Recollections of Three Reigns*, Eyre & Spottiswoode, 1951.

POPE-HENNESSY, JAMES, *Lord Crewe: the Likeness of a Liberal*, Constable, 1955.

PORTLAND, DUKE OF, *Men, Women & Things*, Faber, 1937.

RALEIGH, SIR WALTER, *Letters, 1879–1922*, edited by Lady Raleigh (2 vols), Methuen, 1926.

RAVENSDALE, BARONESS, *Little Innocents: Childhood Reminiscences*, edited by Alan Pryce-Jones, Cobden-Sanderson, 1932.

Reed, Sir Stanley, *The India I Knew*, Odhams, 1952.
Rendel, Sir George, *The Sword and the Olive*, Murray, 1957.
Ribblesdale, Lord, *Impressions and Memories*, Cassell, 1929.
Riddell, Lord, *Intimate Diary of the Peace Conference and After, 1918–1923*, Gollancz, 1933.
Riddell, Lord, *More Pages from My Diary, 1908–1914*, Country Life, 1934.
Robertson, C. Grant, *All Souls College*, F. E. Robinson, 1899.
Rodd, Rennell, *Songs of England*, David Stott, 1891.
Rodd, Rennell, *Rose Leaf and Apple Leaf*, Portland, Maine, 1906.
Rodd, Rennell, *Social and Diplomatic Memories* (3 vols), Arnold, 1922–5.
Ronaldshay, Earl of, *The Life of Lord Curzon* (3 vols), Benn, 1928.
Rosebery, Earl of, *Miscellanies: Literary and Historical* (2 vols), Hodder & Stoughton, 1921.
Rosebery, Earl of, 'Mr Gladstone's Last Cabinet', *History Today*, November 1951 and January 1952.
Salt, H. S., *Memories of Bygone Eton*, Hutchinson, nd.
Salter, Lord, *Slave of the Lamp*, Weidenfeld & Nicolson, 1967.
Scott, J. W. Robertson, *The Life and Death of a Newspaper*, Methuen, 1952.
Seaver, George, *Francis Younghusband*, Murray, 1952.
Simon, Viscount, *Retrospect*, Hutchinson, 1952.
Sitwell, Constance, *Bright Morning*, Cape, 1942.
Sitwell, Sir Osbert, *The Scarlet Tree*, Macmillan, 1946.
Smith, Mrs A. L., *Life of A. L. Smith*, Murray, 1928.
Smyth, Charles, *Cyril Forster Garbett, Archbishop of York*, Hodder & Stoughton, 1959.
Steiner, Zara, 'The Last Years of the Old Foreign Office, 1898–1905', *Historical Journal*, vi, i, 1963.
Steinhart, Harold (ed.), *The History of the Oxford Canning Club*, privately printed, Oxford, 1911.
Storrs, Sir Ronald, *Orientations*, Ivor Nicholson & Watson, 1937.
Tilley, Sir John and Gaselee, Stephen, *The Foreign Office*, Putnam, 1933.
Temple, Sir Richard, *Letters & Character Sketches from the House of Commons*, Murray, 1912.
The History of The Times, vol. iii, 1884–1912, *The Times*, 1947.
Tollemache, Lionel A., *Benjamin Jowett, Master of Balliol*, Arnold, 1895.
Tollemache, Lionel A., *Talks with Mr Gladstone*, Arnold, 1898.
Vansittart, Lord, *The Mist Procession*, Hutchinson, 1958.
Walpole, Horace, *Journals of Visits to Country Seats*, Walpole Society, vol. xvi, OUP, 1928.
Waterhouse, Norah, *Private and Official*, Cape, 1942.
Welldon, J. E. C., *Recollections and Reflections*, Cassell, 1915.
Wells, H. G., *Experiment in Autobiography*, Gollancz, 1934.

WEMYSS, COUNTESS OF, *A Family Record*, privately printed, 1932.
WINTERTON, EARL, *Orders of the Day*, Cassell, 1953.
WOODWARD, E. L., *Short Journey*, Faber, 1942.
WORTHAM, H. E., *Victorian Eton and Cambridge: being the Life and Times of Oscar Browning*, Arthur Barker, 1956.
YOUNG, ARTHUR, *The Farmer's Tour Through the East of England*, vol. 1, published London, Salisbury and Edinburgh, 1771.
YOUNG, KENNETH, *Balfour*, Bell, 1963.
YOUNGHUSBAND, SIR FRANCIS, *The Light of Experience*, Constable, 1927.
ZETLAND, MARQUESS OF, *Essayez*, Murray, 1957.

I am also grateful to the editors of *The Times*, the *Daily Telegraph* and other newspapers and periodicals from which I have quoted. Each individual mention is acknowledged in 'Source References'.

SOURCE REFERENCES

To avoid distracting the general reader, I have adopted a system of references that does not deface the text with innumerable figures or letters of the alphabet, yet allows each quotation or allusion in the book to be traced to its source. All references have been grouped together here, each being prefaced by the number of the page, the number of the line and a catch-phrase for easy recognition. The line number is that of the *last* line of the quotation or other statement in the main text.

Books and Periodicals

Each reference to a quotation or allusion consists of a catch-phrase to identify the topic, the surname of the author, the title of the book or article (sometimes abbreviated for convenience) and the volume number (where necessary) and page. The full name of the author, the title of the book, the publisher and the date of publication can be found listed alphabetically under the author's surname in 'Bibliography'.

If no author is specifically mentioned, the book is by Curzon, e.g. *Persia.* 1.107 refers to page 107 of volume 1 of Curzon's *Persia and the Persian Question*, and *RCA.* 80. to page 80 of Curzon's *Russia in Central Asia.*

The Earl of Ronaldshay's admirable and indispensable three volume authorized *Life of Lord Curzon* is referred to simply as Ronaldshay, followed by the volume and page number.

Letters

Each reference consists of a catch-phrase to identify the topic, the name of the writer of the letter, the name of the recipient and the date. I have given the place where the original letter is to be found only if this cannot be traced either from the notes printed here below or from the list of copyright holders printed above under 'Acknowledgements'.

Curzon is throughout referred to as C., his first wife as Mary and his second wife as Grace.

Where C. is the recipient, the letter is nearly always to be found in the Curzon Papers which have been deposited in the India Office Library in London. But family and personal letters during his years at Wixenford, Eton and Oxford, and sometimes beyond, remain in the archives at Kedleston, as do both sides of Curzon's correspondence with his second wife, Grace. Both sides of the correspondence between Curzon and his first wife are in the possession of their only surviving daughter, Lady Alexandra Metcalfe.

Most letters written by Curzon to the third Marquess of Salisbury are to be found in the Salisbury Papers in the library of Christ Church, Oxford. But there are also some letters between Curzon and Salisbury in the Public Record Office, in the section devoted to Curzon's official papers as Parliamentary Under-Secretary at the Foreign Office, 1895–8.

Curzon's letters to William Ewart Gladstone, to St John Brodrick and to Arthur James Balfour are in the British Museum. Those he wrote to Lord Elgin, Lord George Hamilton, Sir Arthur Godley and Lord Ampthill are in the India Office Library.

His letters to Oscar Browning and to Richard Farrer, returned to him after the death of the recipients, are at Kedleston. So are several letters which Lord Ronaldshay received from various correspondents when collecting material for his biography of Curzon.

Sometimes, but not often, copies of letters written by Curzon are to be found in his papers. During his Viceroyalty of India, however, all except the most private letters he wrote were copied, printed and bound up into volumes.

Other Manuscripts

Curzon left among his papers several autobiographical manuscripts of varying length, some of which he specifically marked for the use of his biographer. These are referred to as Notes, and where possible they have been dated.

His papers also include several longer memoranda on particular aspects of his career, mostly political. In these source references the titles he gave them are printed in ordinary type.

Personal reminiscences

Whether given by letter or in conversation, I have referred to them as, for example: Sir George Leveson Gower to author.

CHAPTER ONE: KEDLESTON

page 1	l. 18	Norman ancestry. Riddell. *Intimate Diary*. 120.
	l. 22	Unbroken tenure. *Persia and the Persian Question*. I.107.
page 2	l. 3	Country gentlemen. Riddell. *Intimate Diary*. 184.
	l. 29	Usurped name. Simon to C. 6 July 1915.
page 3	l. 26	Kedleston staircase. Butler. *Substance of Architecture*. 179.
page 4	l. 8	Tour of Kedleston. Walpole. *Journals of Visits to Country Seats*. XVI.64.

page 4	l. 16	Land Improvement. Young. *Farmer's Tour*. 192–3.
	l. 41	Dr Johnson. Boswell. *Johnson*. 122–3.
page 5	l. 7	Literary testament. Ronaldshay. III.73.
	l. 14	Unworthy ornaments. Mrs Hardress Waller. BBC talk. 12 April 1955.
	l. 15	Suburban fittings. C. to Grace. 8 Feb. 1921.
	l. 20	Hatfield alterations. The late Lady Salisbury to author.
	l. 25	Obtrusive tower. Newton. *Retrospection*. 164.
	l. 32	Flat dweller. Gorrell. *One Man, Many Parts*. 222.
	l. 38	Spacious places. Lockhart. *Lang*. 218.
page 6	l. 11	Asiatic pomp. *British Government in India*. I.64.
	l. 25	Utilitarianism. Hogarth. *Curzon*. 510.
	l. 36	Antiquarian activities. Hogarth and Ronaldshay *passim*.
	l. 40	Memorial Hall. *British Government in India*. I.177.
	l. 41	Sour observation. Lord Hardinge. *Old Diplomacy*. 244.
page 7	l. 6	Paris Embassy. C. to Grace. 3 Jan. 1923.
	l. 8	Hidden trophies. *Ibid*. 8 Sept. 1921.
	l. 16	Mahdo Singh. Lawrence. *The India We Served*. 215.
	l. 28	Charnel house. C. to Ampthill. 31 Oct. 1904.
	l. 37	Gothic chantry. Leslie. *Studies in Sublime Failure*. 222.
page 8	l. 22	Improving view. Raleigh. *Letters*. II.323.
page 9	l. 16	Cartoon. Leslie. *Mark Sykes*. 218.
	l. 36	Scholarly tasks. *Bodiam Castle*. 14–15.
page 10	l. 16	Kedleston contents. C. to Grace. 23 Sept. 1916.
	l. 22	No records. *Kedleston Church*. ix–x.
	l. 34	Windsor Castle. Vansittart. *The Mist Procession*. 273.
page 11	l. 1	Chatelaine. C. to Grace. 25 Sept. 1921.
	l. 6	Heartless. Grace to C. 15 Aug. 1920.
page 12	l. 13	Renovating Kedleston. Butler. *Recording Ruin*. 82–4.
	l. 16	New bath. *Ibid*. 85.
	l. 18	Garden estimate. C. to Grace. 3 Feb. 1924.
	l. 18	Flies. *Ibid*. 8 Oct. 1921.
	l. 20	Wrong flowers. *Ibid*. 5 Sept. 1921.
	l. 21	Christmas beef. *Ibid*. 23 Dec. 1923.
	l. 22	Lavatory. Butler. *Recording Ruin*. 85.
	l. 24	Mud and snow. C. to Grace. 29 Jan. 1925.
	l. 32	Departing guest. *Ibid*. 8 Oct. 1921.
	l. 39	Lying in bed. Butler. *Recording Ruin*. 92.
page 13	l. 6	Downing Street. Nicolson. *Curzon: the Last Phase*. 7.
	l. 20	Churchill epitome. W. S. Churchill. *Great Contemporaries*. 288.
	l. 26	Postcard in tomb. Marchioness Curzon. *Reminiscences*. 156.

CHAPTER TWO: CHILDHOOD

page 14	l. 7	Advowson. *Kedleston Church*. 104.
	l. 11	Bell Inn. *Ibid*. 24.
page 15	l. 2	Sunday apparel. *Ibid*. 23.

page 15 ll. 15ff. Peerage law. Kedleston archives and C. to Grace. 8 Sept. 1921.
l. 44 Broken match. Notes.
page 17 ll. 1ff. Scarsdale's character. Private information.
page 18 l. 11 Beggars Benison. Partridge. *History of Orgies.* 161–4.
l. 23 Sir Henry Wilmot. Private information.
l. 29 C.'s birth. Scarsdale. Diary. 11 Jan. 1859.
page 19 l. 4 Long hair. Scarsdale to C. 2 Dec. 1874.
l. 10 Roaming about. Riddell. *Intimate Diary.* 184.
l. 31 Paternal pride. Brodrick to C. 26 March 1916.
l. 35 Singapore letter. Scarsdale to Salisbury. 20 Dec. 1887. Christ Church.
l. 38 Perpetual tears. Notes.
page 20 l. 33 Childhood punishment. *Ibid.*
l. 43 Wicked fabrication. *Ibid.*
page 21 l. 3 Gold necklace. Alfred Curzon. Diary. 20 April 1875.
l. 22 Childhood treats. Notes.
l. 32 Cricket. Alfred Curzon. Diary. 19 Aug. 1875.
page 22 l. 4 Earliest speech. Notes.
l. 23 Cowley Powles. *Ibid.*
l. 31 Charles Kingsley. C. to Lady Scarsdale. 23 May 1869.
l. 33 F.D. Maurice. *Ibid.* July 1870.
l. 39 Frugal food. Notes.
page 23 l. 2 Bread and butter. C. to Lady Scarsdale. 12 May 1869.
l. 9 Request for hamper. *Ibid.* 5 Nov. 1871.
l. 17 Demand for music. C. to Alfred Curzon. 5 March 1870.
l. 23 Shakespeare reading. C. to Lady Scarsdale. 19 Nov. 1871.
l. 26 Mr Dunbar. *Ibid.* 5 May 1869.
Fn. R.S. Churchill. *Winston S. Churchill.* I.80.
page 24 l. 17 Dunbar's punishments. Notes.
l. 25 Fear of Eton. Cecil. *Salisbury.* I.16.
l. 36 School banker. Notes.
page 25 l. 9 Dunbar's kindness. C. to Lady Scarsdale. 29 April 1872.
l. 17 Unexpected friendship. Notes.
l. 22 Destroyed letters. Col. D. G. Proby to Lord Ronaldshay. 12 Nov. 1925. Kedleston.
l. 40 Visit to Palace. C. to Grace. 2 Dec. 1923.
page 26 l. 3 Lord Rosebery. Cornish. *Letters and Journals of William Cory.* 79.
l. 20 Scarsdale Will. *Complete Peerage.* IX.
l. 21 Mortgaged estate. Letter of Francis Curzon to *The Times.* 30 April 1934.
l. 25 Self-made man. Riddell. *Intimate Diary.* 412.
l. 29 Grumbling cabby. C. to Scarsdale. 12 June 1872.
l. 35 Dressing-gown. Marchioness Curzon. *Reminiscences.* 145.
l. 39 Book margins. Ronaldshay. III.28.
page 27 l. 5 Master of detail. C. to George Hamilton. 13 Jan. 1903.
l. 8 Lord Dufferin. *British Government in India.* II.247.
l. 22 Pembroke Wicks to author.

CHAPTER THREE: ETON

page 28 l. 5 Arrival at Eton. C. to Lady Scarsdale. 25 April 1872.
l. 6 Monstrous barrack. *Subjects of the Day*. 89.
l. 18 Wolley Dod. Ainger. *Eton Sixty Years Ago*. 53.
page 29 l. 20 Eton masters. Notes.
l. 38 Moral danger. Wolley Dod to Scarsdale. 10 Dec. 1872.
l. 41 Low in cash. C. to Lady Scarsdale. 21 Jan. 1873
page 30 l. 1 Civilized society. Wortham. *Oscar Browning*. 45.
l. 14 Climb Parnassus. C. to Browning. 17 March 1874.
l. 18 Not his pupil. Wortham. *Oscar Browning*. 101.
l. 28 Lamentable deficiency. Balston. *Dr Balston at Eton*. 58.
l. 34 Alpine climbing. Edward Lyttelton. *Memories and Hopes*. 133.
l. 36 Shelley and Harrow. Salt. *Memories of Bygone Eton*. 129.
page 31 l. 10 Browning's exercises. Wortham. *Oscar Browning*. 82ff.
page 32 l. 3 Browning exonerated. Scarsdale to Browning. 14 July 1874.
l. 11 Evil companions. C. to Browning. 20 July 1874.
l. 24 Income reduced. Wortham. *Oscar Browning*. 146.
page 33 l. 2 Stuffy confinement. Luxmoore. *Letters*. 159.
l. 6 Debt to Browning. Wortham. *Oscar Browning*. 300.
l. 9 Lent £100. *Ibid*. 298.
l. 15 Plea for KBE. Browning to C. 8 March 1919.
l. 25 Linoleum schools. Pearsall Smith. *Cornishiana*.
page 34 l. 9 Bet on Derby. Edward Lyttelton to C. June 1874.
page 35 l. 2 Private letter. *Ibid*. 27 July 1874.
l. 9 Boyish hero. Edith Lyttelton. *Alfred Lyttelton*. 414.
l. 20 Thirty years. Midleton. *Records and Reactions*. 25–6.
page 36 l. 42 Eton prizes. Notes.
page 37 l. 6 Life a burden. C. to Lady Scarsdale. 16 March 1875.
l. 9 Headache. Alfred Curzon. Diary. 24 March 1875.
l. 11 Bach's Passion. *Ibid*. 26 March 1875.
l. 12 British Museum. *Ibid*. 27 March 1875.
l. 16 Dr Jenner. *Ibid*. 31 March 1875.
l. 20 Spirit fled. *Ibid*. 4 April 1875.
l. 29 Dear face. C. to Alfred Curzon. 4 April 1875.
page 38 l. 12 Manuscript dated November 1875. Kedleston.
l. 18 Family surgeon. *Derby Mercury*. 7 April 1875.
l. 21 Sewer gas. R.R.Farrer to C. 27 Feb. 1882.
l. 22 Blood poisoning. C. to R.R.Farrer. 4 March 1882.
l. 27 Prince Consort. Longford. *Elizabeth R.I.* 297.
l. 30 Lord Chesterfield. Lee. *Edward VII*. I.321.
l. 33 War Office deaths. Kilbracken. *Reminiscences*. 4.
l. 36 Sir George Leveson Gower to author.
page 39 l. 4 Cribbing. Sitwell. *The Scarlet Tree*. 258.
l. 37 Eton escapades. Notes.
l. 40 Tall white hats. Coleridge. *Eton in the 'Seventies*. 119.

page 40	l. 13	System of action. Minute book of Eton College Literary Society. Eton.
	l. 22	Gladstone invited. C. to Gladstone. April 1878. Copy in C.'s Eton scrapbook
	l. 26	Pure atmosphere. Tollemache. *Gladstone.* 25.
	l. 29	Homeric theories. Magnus. *Herbert Warren.* 99–100.
	l. 33	Laughed to scorn. J.R.Harmer to C. 21 July 1878.
	l. 38	Feeble reply. Notes.
page 41	l. 3	Dr Hornby's wishes. Gladstone to C. 6 May 1878.
	l. 10	Anything for Eton. Notes and Eton scrapbook.
	l. 12	Sleepy assistant. *Ibid.*
	l. 19	Important communication. Coleridge. *Eton in the 'Seventies.* 238.
	l. 26	Old china. Tollemache. *Gladstone.* 29.
	l. 33	Pays respects. Notes.
	ll. 41ff.	Gladstone and Pop. Eton scrapbook and Coleridge. *Eton in the 'Seventies.*
page 42	l. 20	Derby winner. Rosebery. Speech at Eton. *The Times.* 15 July 1911.
	l. 28	Public life. Asquith. Speech in House of Lords. 23 March 1925.
	l. 35	Ironic lecture. Notes.
	l. 39	Silver cup. Eton scrapbook.
page 43	l. 2	Loss on magazine. Literary accounts. Kedleston.
	l. 5	Rejected articles. Notes.
	l. 12	Cheque for £5. Scarsdale to C. 4 June 1877.
	l. 29	Fourth of June. Eton scrapbook.
	l. 36	Flattery. Brett to C. 14 Feb. 1878.
	l. 39	Adroit priest. *Ibid.* 31 Aug. 1878.
	l. 40	Wily old serpent. *Ibid.* 19 Aug. 1878.
page 44	l. 5	Kissing hands. Brett. *Journals and Letters* II.149.
	l. 14	Flattery. C. to Brett. 4 March 1878. Quo. Brett. *Journals and Letters.* I.49–50.
	l. 29	Hornby's toast. Notes.
	l. 37	Real respect. Alington. *Things Ancient and Modern.* 192.

CHAPTER FOUR: BALLIOL

page 45	l. 2	Brief interval. Brodrick to C. 29 May 1878.
	l. 15	Examination report. *Ibid.* 2 Dec. 1877.
	l. 25	Fall at Kedleston. Lady Scarsdale to Cowley Powles. 19 Jan. 1871.
	l. 26	Fall from a pony. C. to Browning. 19 April 1874.
	l. 27	Broken collar bone. Alfred Curzon. Diary. 18 Oct. 1875.
page 46	l. 1	Easily knocked over. Francis Curzon to Lord Ronaldshay. 13 Nov. 1925. Kedleston.
	l. 7	Sir James Paget. C. to Alfred Curzon. Undated.
	l. 11	No late nights. Edward Lyttelton to C. 20 Nov. 1877.
	l. 24	Displaced hip. C. to Brett. 9 Oct. 1878. Quo. Brett. *Journals and Letters.* I.52.

page 46	l. 27	Second wind. Brodrick to C. 7 Oct. 1878.
	l. 31	Shattered health. Midleton. *Records and Reactions.* 189.
	l. 37	Going to bed. Alfred Lyttelton to C. 25 Dec. 1880.
page 47	l. 9	Agony of public appearances. Notes. 1910.
	l. 16	Elephant ride. C. to George Hamilton. 17 April 1901.
	l. 20	Royal penance. C. to Grace. 12 March 1920.
	l. 25	Sword seat. Marchioness Curzon. Reminiscences. 151.
	l. 36	Balliol men. *Balliol College Register.*
	l. 39	Balliol and India. Mackail. *Strachan-Davidson.* 81.
page 48	l. 4	Dr Jowett. *Balliol Rhymes.* 1.
	l. 8	Libel. *Ibid.* v.
	l. 10	Not omniscient. *Ibid.* v.
	l. 14	Beastly sherry. Inge. *Diary of a Dean.* 26.
	l. 18	Unmannerly dons. Abbott and Campbell. *Jowett.* II.154.
	l. 22	Advice scorned. Grundy. *Fifty-Five Years at Oxford.* 49.
	l. 28	Jane Austen. Lawrence. *The India We Served.* 5.
	l. 34	Influence towards good. Davis. *History of Balliol College.* 217.
page 49	l. 10	Most superior person. *Balliol Rhymes.* 19.
	l. 15	Self-assurance. Margot Asquith. *Autobiography.* 174.
	l. 23	Borrowed nightdress. Marchioness Curzon. *Reminiscences.* 30.
	l. 33	Aims and intentions. Alfred Lyttelton to C. Aug. 1878.
	l. 35	Would-be biographer. Zetland. *Essayez.* 172.
	l. 37	Awareness of superiority. Birkenhead. *Contemporary Personalities.* 87.
	l. 38	Suggested epitaph. D'Abernon. *An Ambassador of Peace.* I.52.
page 50	l. 3	Not enough heart. Brett to C. 23 Aug. 1878.
	l. 12	A great error. Alfred Lyttelton to C. 8 Sept. 1879.
	l. 17	Devastating sarcasm. Hon. Gilbert Coleridge to author.
	ll. 26ff.	Conservatism. Steinhart. *Oxford Canning Club.* 112ff.
page 51	l. 11	Stately eloquence. *Ibid.* 113.
	l. 20	Too much to say. Jowett to C. 31 Dec. 1884.
	l. 25	Unknown fledglings. C. to Brodrick. 12 Nov. 1882. BM 50073.
	l. 34	Distinguished scholar. Bowra. *Memories.* 243–4.
page 52	l. 13	Strachan-Davidson. *Balliol Rhymes.* 2.
	l. 22	Tobacco pouch. Mackail. *Strachan-Davidson.* 35–6.
	l. 28	Nettleship. *Balliol Rhymes.* 3.
	l. 35	Wonderfully beloved. Margot Asquith. *Autobiography.* 124.
	l. 37	Authorship attributed. *Balliol Rhymes.* 1 and 3.
page 53	l. 5	H. C. Beeching. *Balliol Rhymes.* 15.
	l. 27	Birthday greetings. Farrer to C. 11 Jan. 1880.
	l. 35	Charming friends. C. to Farrer. 14 Jan. 1880.
page 54	l. 2	Sheer labour. C. to Spring Rice. 11 July 1880.
	l. 13	Patient and gifted. Alfred Lyttelton to C. 12 March 1882.
	l. 18	Dignifying class two. C. to Farrer. 4 March 1882.
	l. 24	Written bosh. *Ibid.* 28 May 1882.
	l. 25	Logic a dodge. Tollemache. *Jowett.* 67.
	l. 39	Betting on a Second. C. to Farrer. 28 May 1882.

page 55	l. 5	Unconscious axe. Malcolm. *The Pursuits of Leisure.* 144.
	l. 22	Unfair failure. C. to Farrer. 23 July 1882.
	l. 32	Second Bible. Welldon. *Recollections and Reflections.* 9.
page 56	l. 4	Two distinctions. Scarsdale to C. 4 July 1882.
	l. 8	Personal ambition. Cowley Powles to C. 6 July 1882.
	l. 14	Affairs of luck. Edward Lyttelton to C. 4 July 1882.
	l. 20	Most famous Oxonian. Alfred Lyttelton to C. 4 July 1882.
	l. 23	Natural sphere. Jowett to C. 15 July 1882.
	l. 27	Respectable mediocrity. C. to Farrer. 23 July 1882.
	l. 31	Varied interests. Midleton. Speech at Eton. *The Times.* 7 Dec. 1927.

CHAPTER FIVE: BAND OF BROTHERS

page 57	l. 2	Hide my face. C. to Farrer. 23 July 1882.
page 58	l. 23	Breeding grounds. Luxmoore. *Letters.* 83.
	l. 41	Prejudice and craze. Grant Duff. *Notes from a Diary, 1896–1901.* I.271.
page 59	l. 9	Forty-eight hours. Midleton. *Records and Reactions.* 26.
	l. 15	Sumptuous tea. Alfred Lyttelton to C. Aug. 1878.
	l. 20	Obscure principles. Edward Lyttelton to C. 11 Nov. 1877.
	l. 22	Correspondence begins. Brett. *Journals and Letters.* I.2.
	l. 25	Break the ice. Brett to C. 14 Feb. 1878.
	l. 31	A fresh start. *Ibid.* 5 March 1878.
	l. 36	Looking backward. *Ibid.* 4 Aug. 1878.
page 60	l. 6	Cambridge topics. Edward Lyttelton to C. 20 Nov. 1877.
	l. 12	Etonianism preferred. Wallop to C. 13 March 1879.
	l. 19	Choice of newspaper. Spring Rice to C. March 1878.
	l. 27	Election to Pop. C. to Browning. 10 Sept. 1876.
	l. 31	Christian name. Brodrick to C. 29 Oct. 1876.
	l. 35	Confidence. *Ibid.* 2 Dec. 1877.
	l. 38	President of Union. *Ibid.*
	l. 43	Optional entertainment. Brodrick to C. 24 Sept. 1878.
page 61	l. 6	Acreage and income. *Complete Peerage.*
	l. 16	Mighty leg. *Subjects of the Day.* 89.
	l. 23	Lifelong friendship. Welldon to Ronaldshay. 14 Nov. 1925. Kedleston.
	l. 34	Cut and dried. Brett to C. 23 Aug. 1878.
	l. 40	Three months' leave. Spring Rice to C. 27 Nov. 1883.
page 62	l. 2	Chancellor of the Exchequer. Welldon to C. 3 Oct. 1878.
	l. 9	King-maker. Obituary appreciation, *The Times.* 20 July 1915.
	l. 27	Archbishopric not vacant. Raper to C. 25 March 1883.
	l. 35	Local governors. Edward Lyttelton to C. 30 March 1883.
	l. 38	Possible successor. Masterman. *Mary Gladstone.* 321.
page 63	l. 5	Welldon's promotion. Brodrick to C. 26 March 1885.
	l. 19	Middle-class idea. Alfred Lyttelton to C. 17 Aug. 1886.
	l. 22	Too much society. Lyttelton. *Alfred Lyttelton.* 79.

page 63	l. 33	Hams Hall. Farrer to C. 11 Jan. 1880.
page 64	l. 8	Party at Hatfield. C. to Farrer. 2 Dec. 1882.
	l. 14	Coming of age. *Ibid.* 14 Jan. 1882.
	l. 19	Unattainable region. *Ibid.* 17 Oct. 1880.
	l. 23	Empresses. Arthur. *Not Worth Reading.* 17.
	l. 30	Old friendships. C. to Farrer. 23 July 1882.
	l. 32	Homer. Gambier Parry. *Annals of an Eton House.* 331.
	l. 41	Unknown clergymen. Notes.
page 65	l. 5	To meet again. Hare. *Story of My Life.* v.284.
	l 8	Ideal boredom. C. to Spring Rice. 11 July 1880.
	l. 9	Met at Oxford. Hare. *Story of My Life.* v.296.
	l. 11	Augustuses. Leveson Gower. *Mixed Grill.* 126.
	l. 28	Ouida. Wallop to C. 14 Jan. 1877.
	l. 32	Gift of money. Lee. *Ouida.* 125
	l. 35	Inscription on fountain. *Ibid.* 230.
	l. 40	Shooting at eighty. Kedleston Game Book. 26 Sept. 1911.
page 66	l. 1	Walking with the guns. *Ibid.* 2 Sept. 1869.
	l. 2	16-bore gun. Alfred Curzon. Diary. 3 Sept. 1875.
	l. 7	Paternal grice. C. to Farrer. 17 Oct. 1880.
	l. 11	Fowls of the air. *Ibid.* 2 Dec. 1882.
	l. 13	Seven woodcock. Kedleston Game Book. 31 Dec. 1884.
	l. 22	Vulgar competition. Mackail and Wyndham. *George Wyndham.* I.318.
	l. 26	Lord de Grey. Portland. *Men, Women and Things.* 228–9.
	l. 29	Slaughter palls. *Problems of the Far East.* 114.
	l. 35	Shot well. C. to Francis Curzon. 17 Jan. 1901.
	l. 36	Record bag. *Ibid.* 17 Dec. 1903.
	l. 39	Three tigers. Ronaldshay. II.167.
page 67	l. 5	Dying sheep. Farrer to C. 3 Oct. 1880.
	l. 9	Brother's keeper. Leveson Gower. *Mixed Grill.* 22.
	l. 20	Beaters' strike. Crag Hall Game Book. 13 Sept. 1910.
	l. 25	Rook shooting. C. to Grace. Whit Sunday 1918.
	l. 29	Great effort. *Ibid.* 8 Sept. 1919.
	l. 36	W.G. Grace. C. to Browning. 23 Aug. 1874.
	l. 38	Illicit journey. Notes.
page 68	l. 6	Cricket at Lord's. *Ibid.*
	l. 9	Slog or shoot. C. to Alfred Lyttelton. 24 June 1901.
	l. 17	Family record. Edith Lyttelton. *Alfred Lyttelton.* 402–4.
	l. 19	50 not out. Parker. *Eton in the 'Eighties.* 169.
	l. 22	Imaginary ball. Chandos. *Memoirs.* 9.
	l. 25	Jolly Alfred. C. to Browning. 10 Sept. 1876.
	l. 30	Napkin fights. Edith Lyttelton. *Alfred Lyttelton.* 12.
	l. 31	Lightly flicking. *Ibid.* 15.
	l. 38	Disaster not averted. Bailey. *Lady Frederick Cavendish.* xix.
page 69	l. 3	Lear not funny. Margot Asquith. *Autobiography.* 38.
	l. 12	Canine assaults. Farrer. *A Tour in Greece.* 123.
	l. 26	Dog and tennis balls. Leveson Gower. *Mixed Grill.* 70.

page 69	l. 27	Fives balls. Edward Lyttelton. *Memories and Hopes*. 301.
	l. 28	Cart drivers. *Ibid.* 21.
	l. 34	Cat hunt. *Ibid.* 65.
	l. 41	Beaten horse. Rodd to C. Nov. 1881.
page 70	l. 12	Rudeness at a ball. Leveson Gower. *Mixed Grill*. 74–5.
	l. 23	An apology. Beresford to C. 14 Jan. 1885.
	l. 32	Wilde's kindness. Rodd. *Social and Diplomatic Memories*. 1.23.
page 71	l. 6	Effusive foreword. Rodd. *Rose Leaf and Apple Leaf. L'envoi* and 95–100.
	l. 9	Kindly meant. Rodd. *Social and Diplomatic Memories*. 1.23.
	l. 18	Dedication. Rodd. *Songs of England.*
	l. 20	Finer than Macaulay. Leveson Gower. *Years of Endeavour*. 126.
	l. 42	American lecture tour. Wilde to C. 15 Feb. 1882.
page 72	l. 4	Stranger gods. *Ibid.* July 1883.
	l. 12	Wilde at sea. Brodrick to C. 9 Aug. 1883.
	l. 23	Defence in Union. Wilde to C. Undated.
	l. 26	Inspector of Schools. *Ibid.* 20 July 1885.
	l. 38	Greek friend. Farrer to C. 11 Dec. 1882.
	l. 41	No personal experience. C. to Farrer. 29 Jan. 1883.
page 73	l. 3	Stare and itch. *Ibid.* 27 May 1883.
	l. 6	Travelling companion. C. to Spring Rice. 18 Nov. 1893.
	l. 14	Crumpled appearance. C. to Farrer. 2 Dec. 1882.
	l. 22	Berlin verse. Rodd to C. 25 July 1884.
	l. 31	Anti-feminist. Ronaldshay. 1.49.
	l. 38	Female globe-trotters. Mill. *Royal Geographical Society*. 110.
page 74	l. 6	Praise of women. Circular letter. November 1912.
	l. 8	Unfit to vote. C. to Mary. 9 July 1893.
	l. 12	Women at universities. Smyth. *Garbett*. 448.
	l. 18	Christmas visit. C. to Brodrick. 19 Dec. 1880. BM 50073.
	l. 28	Trying situation. Farrer to C. 22 Jan. 1881.
	l. 37	Immense sacrifice. Unsigned letter to C. 4 July [1882].
page 75	l. 2	Shut up together. Edith Lyttelton. *Alfred Lyttelton*. 77.
	l. 5	Against a family. Spring Rice to C. 27 Nov. 1883.
	l. 8	Waiting a bit. C. to Farrer. 23 July 1882.
	l. 30	Bull's discipline. Notes.
	l. 37	Very loose youth. Farrer to C. 31 March 1882.
page 76	l. 2	Drunken guest. Farrer to C. 19 Oct. 1881.
	l. 10	Low tastes. *Complete Peerage*. i.
	l. 13	Breach-of-promise. *Ibid.* ii.
	l. 16	Mendicity Society. *Ibid.* xii, Part 2.

CHAPTER SIX: CLASSICAL LANDSCAPES

page 77	l. 15	Talking of Eton. Edward Lyttelton to C. 24 Dec. 1877.
	l. 17	Obligatory silence. Alfred Lyttelton to C. 27 Feb. 1878.
page 78	l. 6	Youthful judge. *Tales of Travel*. 220–1.
	l. 13	Dress clothes. *Persia*. 1.55.

page 78	l. 20	General Boulanger. *Tales of Travel.* 24.
	l. 26	Stolen hat. *Ibid.* 230.
	l. 29	Theatrical orders. *Ibid.* 233.
	l. 36	Royal hockey. E. F. Benson. *Our Family Affairs.* 226.
page 79	l. 1	Grand Duke of Lucca. A. C. Benson. *Memories and Friends.* 135.
	l. 18	Ill-fated rulers. *Tales of Travel.* 7–8.
	l. 24	King Ludwig. *Ibid.* 8.
	l. 25	King George I. Rodd. *Social and Diplomatic Memories.* I. 107.
	l. 31	Homoeopathic chemist. Notes on Foreign Journeys.
page 80	l. 6	Travel with Browning. C. to Farrer. 17 Oct. 1880.
	l. 13	First long journey. *Ibid.* 26 Dec. 1882.
	l. 31	Roman impressions. Notebook.
	l. 33	Seasickness. C. to Farrer. 26 Dec. 1882.
	l. 36	Continues working. Edward Lyttelton. *Memories and Hopes.* 146.
page 81	l. 2	Horse and mules. Notebook.
	l. 5	Metallic French. *Viceroy's Note-Book.* 372.
	l. 17	Elgin Marbles. C. to Gladstone. 18 May 1890. BM 44510.
	l. 24	Lonely Caryatide. *Ibid.*
	l. 32	No opposition. Gladstone to C. 21 May 1890.
	l. 36	Leighton objects. C. to Gladstone. 23 May 1890. BM 44510.
	l. 37	Decisive coolness. Note on envelope containing correspondence.
page 82	l. 5	Schliemann. *Viceroy's Note-Book.* 370.
	l. 10	No fossils. Browning. *Memories of Sixty Years.* 198.
	l. 14	Advice on Troy. Schliemann to C. 11 April 1883.
	l. 23	Greek people. Notebook.
	l. 26	Lost rugs. C. to Farrer. 29 Jan. 1883.
	l. 38	Paying visits. Blunt. *My Diaries.* 58.
page 83	l. 5	Naples. Gower. *Old Diaries.* 231.
	l. 12	Venice. Margot Asquith. *Autobiography.* 37–8.
	l. 26	Victoria Station. Ribblesdale. *Impressions and Memories.* xxvii.
	l. 35	Well-earned laughter. *Persia.* I. 273.
	l. 43	Natal. C. Ribblesdale to C. 4 Aug. 1884.
page 84	l. 6	Tasmania. Wallop to C. 18 Feb. 1882.
	l. 24	Obtrusive inhabitants. Farrer. *A Tour in Greece.* 99 *passim.*
	l. 28	Talk and pilfer. *Ibid.* 128.
	l. 34	False quantities. *Ibid.* 48.
	l. 41	Hospitality spurned. *Ibid.* 70.
page 85	l. 23	Criticism of book. C. to Farrer. 2 Dec. 1882.
	l. 27	Spirit of indignation. Hardinge to C. 2 Feb. 1883.

CHAPTER SEVEN: UNTO CAESAR

page 86	l. 14	Voyage to Alexandria. Notebook.
	l. 26	Tel-el-Kebir. *Ibid.*
page 87	l. 9	Backside of an idol. C. to Farrer. 29 Jan. 1883.
	l. 18	Egyptian antiquities. *Ibid.* 9 Feb. 1883.

page 87 l. 41 Colossi of Thebes. Originally printed in *Edinburgh Review*, July 1886. Reprinted in *Tales of Travel*. 87–122.

page 88 l. 2 G.M. Young to author.

l. 21 Pyramids and Sphinx. C. to Farrer. 24 March 1883.

l. 24 Uncivilized. Notebook.

l. 42 Unprofitable Cairo. C. to Farrer. 24 March 1883.

page 89 l. 10 Historic shams. *Viceroy's Note-Book*. 359.

l. 12 Jerusalem plethora. C. to Farrer. 24 March 1883.

l. 21 Palestine. *Ibid.* 11 May 1883.

l. 34 Hostility to Zionism. C. to Balfour. 25 March 1919.

page 90 l. 9 On Dr Weizmann. *Ibid.* 9 Aug. 1919.

l. 23 Mount Carmel. Notebook.

l. 28 Sempiternal grottoes. C. to Farrer. 11 May 1883.

page 91 l. 41 Sustained irony. *Viceroy's Note-Book*. 361–4.

page 92 l. 1 Imaginary Holy House. C. to P.A. Barnett. 26 March 1883. Quo. Ronaldshay. I.88.

l. 6 Teach no lesson. Notebook.

l. 10 Christian creed. Ronaldshay. III.390. And Zetland. *Essayez*. 173–4.

l. 16 Corroding acid. Ronaldshay. III.390.

l. 22 Church-going habits. Edward Lyttelton to C. 1 March 1890.

page 93 l. 20 Need for religion. Brodrick to C. 7 April 1895.

l. 37 Thirty-Nine Articles. Abbott and Campbell. *Jowett*. I.239.

l. 43 Broad Church. Rodd. *Social and Diplomatic Memories*. I.11.

page 94 l. 2 Expansive spirit. Abbott and Campbell. *Jowett*. I.299.

l. 4 No religion good. Gwynn. *Spring Rice*. I.22.

l. 6 Praise of poverty. Tollemache. *Jowett*. 4.

l. 10 Free-thinking place. C. to Browning. 24 Nov. 1896.

l. 20 Theological cranks. Salisbury to C. 24 Nov. 1896.

l. 28 Social success. Rodd to C. [Aug. or Sept.] 1881.

l. 30 Spurgeon. Notes.

l. 36 Drummond lectures. Pentland. *Memories*. 23.

l. 42 Truth and falsehood. Faber. *Jowett*. 214.

page 95 l. 16 Kedleston incumbent. Waterhouse. *Private and Official*. 255.

l. 19 Belief in God. Margot Asquith. *Autobiography*. 136.

l. 27 Perfect humanity. Ronaldshay. III.393.

l. 31 Daily prayer. C. to Roberts. 26 Oct. 1914. Quo. Ronaldshay. III.394.

page 96 l. 11 British race. *Indian Speeches*. I.3.

l. 37 Be my judge. *Ibid.* IV.241–2.

page 97 l. 18 General Gordon. Notes.

CHAPTER EIGHT: FELLOWS

page 98 l. 6 Refuting examiners. Ronaldshay. I.54.

l. 21 Look of dullness. Kitchin to Raper. 11 May 1881. Kedleston.

page 99 l. 12 Lothian Prize essay. C. to Brodrick. 19 May 1883.

page 99	l. 28	How he triumphed. C. to Farrer. 27 May 1883.
	l. 32	Rodd's congratulations. Rodd to C. 17 May 1883.
	l. 34	Canning Club toast. Cranborne to C. 28 May 1883.
page 100	l. 13	Lost manuscript. Hardinge to C. 2 Feb. 1883.
	l. 34	Last-minute entry. Malcolm. *The Pursuits of Leisure.* 144.
	l. 41	Hawkins an absentee. Ronaldshay. 1.56.
page 101	l. 13	Church and State. Grant Robertson. *All Souls College.* 18.
	l. 20	Founder's kin. Oman. *Victorian Oxford.* 121.
	l. 26	Codrington library. Boswell. *Johnson.* 1.360.
	l. 28	A mind to prance. *Ibid.* 1.379.
	l. 30	Privilege eliminated. Grant Robertson. *All Souls College.* 197.
	l. 36	Stipend of £200. Simon. *Retrospect.* 37–8.
page 102	l. 6	100 to 1 chance. C. to Farrer. 23 July 1882.
	l. 10	No recommendation. Farrer to C. 1 Aug. 1882.
	l. 19	Report on examination. Raper to C. 7 Nov. 1882.
	l. 32	No regrets. C. to Farrer. 2 Dec. 1882.
	l. 41	Try next time. Farrer to C. 11 Dec. 1882.
page 103	l. 6	Grandiloquent pen. C. to Brodrick. 15 Aug. 1883.
	l. 8	Gibbon's style. Brodrick to C. 20 July 1879.
	l. 16	Note of pessimism. C. to Brodrick. 14 Oct. 1883.
	l. 19	Stomach deranged. Scarsdale. Diary. 3 Nov. 1883.
	l. 22	Asquith on All Souls. W.M.Hardinge. 'Recollections of the Master of Balliol'. *Temple Bar.* Oct. 1894.
page 104	l. 9	Eminent failures. Private information.
	l. 26	Cruelty at Winchester. Oman. *Victorian Oxford.* 36.
	l. 35	Roman coins. *Ibid.* 53.
	l. 39	Archaeological paper. *Ibid.* 95.
page 105	l. 5	Oman's omniscience. Amery. *My Political Life.* 1.64.
	l. 13	Collecting coins. Oman. *Victorian Oxford.* 126.
	l. 14	Romanes Lecture. C. to Oman. 23 Jan. 1906.
	l. 23	Repaying a debt. *Ibid.* 15 March 1907.
	l. 33	Congratulation on KBE. C. to Oman. 9 May 1920.
	l. 42	Medieval warfare. *Ibid.* 12 Sept. 1924.
page 106	l. 9	Hutton's encouragement. Henson. *Retrospect.* 1.4.
	l. 19	No public school. Henson. *Letters.* 240.
	l. 23	Welldon's bad taste. *Ibid. Retrospect.* 1.20.
	l. 30	Henson on research. Alington. *Dean's Apology.* 55.
page 107	l. 2	A great heart. Henson to C. 15 March 1922.
	l. 12	My old friend. Lockhart. *Lang.* 215.
	l. 18	Iron and magnet. Henson. *Letters.* 173.
	l. 24	Trouble ahead. Henson. *Retrospect.* 1.224.
	l. 27	Treason to All Souls. Alington. *Dean's Apology.* 42.
	l. 30	Worry from Durham. Lockhart. *Lang.* 294.
	l. 40	Able and excellent. Queen Victoria to C. 16 Feb. 1900.
page 108	l. 7	Swapping Mallard. Lockhart. *Lang.* 57–58.
	l. 10	Archbishop's curse. *Ibid.* 375.
	l. 19	French novels. Woodward. *Short Journey.* 148.

page 108 l. 28 Applauding Portsea. Lockhart. *Lang.* 114.
ll. 31ff. Light-hearted wagers. Oman, *Second Betting Book of All Souls College, 1873–1919. Passim.*
page 110 l. 4 No reverence. Arthur. *Not Worth Reading.* 17.
l. 10 Fletcher. *Mr. Gladstone's Visit to All Souls.* And Oman. *Things I Have Seen.*
l. 27 Fellows in Cabinet. C. to Grant Robertson. 25 June 1917.
l. 38 Codrington window. Woodward. *Short Journey.* 169.
page 111 l. 5 Also my college. Smith. *Life of A. L. Smith.* 272.
l. 10 No soup. Woodward. *Short Journey.* 166.

CHAPTER NINE: PRELUDE TO PARLIAMENT

page 112 l. 2 Parliament opening. C. to Scarsdale. 11 Feb. 1870.
page 113 l. 4 Disraeli. *Modern Parliamentary Eloquence.* 28–30.
l. 6 Brett. *Journals and Letters.* I.209.
l. 7 Rosebery. Blake. *Disraeli.* Preface xxi.
l. 8 Biography declined. C. to Mary. 3 March 1904.
l. 28 Gladstone. *Modern Parliamentary Eloquence.* 23–7.
l. 32 Not a Liberal. Edward Lyttelton to C. 22 April 1881.
page 114 l. 26 Burlesque exaggeration. *Modern Parliamentary Eloquence.* 37.
l. 32 Indulgence of atheism. W. S. Churchill. *Lord Randolph Churchill.* 200–1.
l. 40 Political invective. *Ibid.* 222.
page 115 l. 6 Book of Joel. Viscount Gladstone. *After Thirty Years.* 46–7.
l. 10 Marshall and Snelgrove. W. S. Churchill. *Lord Randolph Churchill.* 186.
l. 13 Pineries. *Ibid.* 268.
l. 19 Bits of paper. Lucy. *Salisbury Parliament.* 186.
l. 24 Randolph Churchill. C. to Farrer. 2 Dec. 1882.
l. 28 Smart fellow. *Ibid.* 17 Oct. 1880.
l. 34 Speech at Woodstock. Churchill to C. 3 March 1881.
page 116 l. 7 Mentioned in debate. Brodrick to C. 13 Nov. 1882.
l. 39 Chamberlain speech. 27 March 1884. Quo. Chilston. *Chief Whip.* 32.
page 117 l. 5 Single sofa. W. S. Churchill. *Lord Randolph Churchill.* 140.
l. 14 Great responsibilities. C. Ribblesdale to C. 24 July 1885.
l. 17 In their footsteps. Smith to C. 14 March 1883.
l. 37 Working for Gladstone. Leveson Gower. *Years of Content.* 159–60.
page 118 l. 7 Scientific instruments. Cecil. *Salisbury.* II.13.
l. 13 Explosion. *Ibid.* I.176.
l. 21 Electric light. *Ibid.* III.6.
l. 24 Telephone. *Ibid.* III.8.
l. 33 King's Cross. *Ibid.* III.213.
l. 36 Double doors. *Ibid.* II.16.
page 119 l. 1 Too busy. *Ibid.* II.235.
l. 10 Salisbury's affability. Diary. 4–9 Jan. 1886.

page 119	l. 30	Research for a speech. *Ibid.* 26–7 Jan. 1886.
	l. 40	Salisbury's oratory. *Modern Parliamentary Eloquence.* 35.
page 120	l. 2	Attorneys. Cecil. *Salisbury.* I.134
	l. 10	Bribery. Tollemache. *Jowett.* 79.
	l. 13	Election expenses. Hamilton. *Parliamentary Reminiscences.* 2–3.
	l. 20	Repton schoolmasters. *Derby Mercury.* 10 June 1885.
	l. 26	Clever young gentlemen. *Ibid.* 2 Dec. 1885.
	l. 37	Driven to suicide. Cranborne to C. 5 Nov. 1885.
page 121	l. 7	Canvassing. C. to Brodrick. 12 Nov. 1885.
	l. 11	Paper pellets. *Indian Speeches.* IV.29.
	l. 15	Miners' vote. Cranborne to C. 11 Dec. 1885.
	l. 25	Sorrow and sympathy. Salisbury to C. 3 Dec. 1885.
	l. 30	Railway men. Leveson Gower. *Years of Endeavour.* 72.
	l. 40	Intolerable position. Kennedy. *Salisbury.* 166.
page 122	l. 9	No fall till Easter. Diary. 4–9 Jan. 1886.
	l. 15	Keeping awake. Cecil. *Salisbury.* III.210.
	l. 20	German Poles. Diary. 4–9 Jan. 1886.
	l. 22	Next month's salary. Cecil. *Salisbury.* III.210.
	l. 29	Cranborne's influence. A. Hardinge. *A Diplomatist in Europe.* 78.
	l. 33	State will prosper. J.K. Stephen to C. 21 July 1885.
page 123	l. 12	Fall of government. Diary. 27 Jan. 1886.
	l. 28	Dines with Speaker. *Ibid.*
page 124	l. 9	Southport expenses. Ronaldshay. I.106–7.
	l. 19	Frederick Milner. Letter in *The Times.* 27 March 1931.
page 125	l. 15	Constituency advice. C. to Marshall Hall. 31 Oct. 1900. Quo. Marjoribanks. *Marshall Hall.* 137–8.

CHAPTER TEN: MAIDEN SPEECH

page 126	l. 16	Clergy in the cold. Bishop Ryle to C. 30 Dec. 1886.
	l. 19	Zoological garden. Cecil. *Salisbury.* III.142.
	l. 20	Bishops. *Ibid.* III.194.
page 127	l. 16	Protection from Mars. *Ibid.* III.218.
	l. 34	Conduct of legislation. W.S. Churchill. *Lord Randolph Churchill.* 565.
	l. 39	Increasing burden. Cecil. *Salisbury.* III.180.
page 128	l. 13	Conservatism. Article in *England.* Jan. 1887. Quo. Ronaldshay. I.113.
	l. 29	Randolph Churchill. Diary. 4–9 Jan. 1886.
	l. 33	Hosannas. C. to Arthur Godley. 31 Jan. 1901.
	l. 37	Queen uninformed. W.S. Churchill. *Lord Randolph Churchill.* 573.
	l. 38	Adventurer. *Modern Parliamentary Eloquence.* 38.
page 129	l. 1	Front-bench weakness. Cranborne to C. 31 Dec. 1886.
	l. 10	Churchill's speech. *Hansard.* 31 Jan. 1887.
	l. 26	Like an Angel. Chilston. *W.H. Smith.* 243.
	l. 37	Maiden speech. *Hansard.* 31 Jan. 1887.
page 130	l. 10	Nine days' wonder. Temple. *Letters and Character Sketches.* 202.

page 130 l. 16 Ineffable superiority. *Observer*. 13 Feb. 1887. Quo. Ronaldshay. I.115.
l. 27 No compliments. R. S. Churchill. *W.S.Churchill*. II.16–17.
l. 31 Overtrained. T. P. O'Connor. *Daily Telegraph*. 21 March 1925.
l. 41 Gladstone's oratory. *Modern Parliamentary Eloquence*. 24.
page 131 l. 5 Gladstone's routine. Lucy. *Salisbury Parliament*. 282.
l. 10 Coach stops. Gower. *Old Diaries*. 211.
l. 18 Home Secretary. *Modern Parliamentary Eloquence*. 33.
l. 20 Coined phrase. Lucy. *Salisbury Parliament*. 229.
l. 23 Troublesome colleague. Brett. *Journals and Letters*. II.414.
l. 27 Tearful valediction. Rosebery. 'Mr. Gladstone's Last Cabinet'. *History Today*. Jan. 1952.
l. 39 Sheer weariness. Notes. 23–5 Nov. 1895.
page 132 l. 8 Grow insupportable. Lucy. *Salisbury Parliament*. 167–8.
l. 11 Ink in receiver. Lord Asquith of Bishopstone. 'Giants of Those Days'. *Daily Telegraph*. 10 April 1953.
l. 15 Forensic. Mersey. *A Picture of Life*. 214.
l. 18 Corrected date. Jenkins. *Asquith*. 69.
l. 26 Roll of the drums. *Modern Parliamentary Eloquence*. 45.
l. 29 Never intimacy. Asquith to C. 15 Oct. 1891.
l. 34 Greek quotations. *Modern Parliamentary Eloquence*. 11.
l. 39 Home Rule speech. *Hansard* (Lords). 12 Feb. 1914.
page 133 l. 12 Middle Class. Chilston. *W.H.Smith*. 94.
l. 16 GCB declined. *Ibid*. 205.
l. 30 Likely to be PM. Esher. *Cloud-Capp'd Towers*. 22.
l. 32 Captain Balfour. Oxford and Asquith. *Fifty Years in Parliament*. I.33.
l. 36 The infernal. Masterman. *Mary Gladstone*. 66.
page 134 l. 1 Feeble speech. Diary. 27 Jan. 1886.
l. 6 Angry cats. Ribblesdale. *Impressions and Memories*. 198.
l. 16 Chief Secretary. Lucy. *Salisbury Parliament*. 29.
l. 22 Worshipping intellect. Diary. 4–9 Jan. 1886.
l. 29 Carlton Club. Balfour to C. 17 Jan. 1887.
l. 33 Hesitating. *Modern Parliamentary Eloquence*. 44.
page 135 l. 10 Gentleman-like. Buckle. *Disraeli*. V.362.
l. 12 Talkative. Mersey. *A Picture of Life*. 215.
l. 14 Slowly constructive. Brett. *Journals and Letters*. I.125.
l. 16 Treasure Island. Charteris. *Edmund Gosse*. 184.
l. 18 Late for dinner. Esher. *Cloud-Capp'd Towers*. 115.
l. 21 Run for something. Cecil. *Salisbury*. IV.220.
l. 27 Sustaining port. Lucy. *Salisbury Parliament*. 265.
l. 29 Jobbed man. Lucy. *Sixty Years in the Wilderness*. 375.
l. 32 Bad manners. Lucy. *Salisbury Parliament*. 418.
l. 38 Hate that man. C. to Brodrick. 5 Jan. 1882. BM 50073.
page 136 l. 3 Never for us. W. S. Churchill. *Great Contemporaries*. 69.
l. 21 Illimitable strength. *Modern Parliamentary Eloquence*. 50.
l. 30 George Brodrick. Midleton. *Records and Reactions*. 15.

page 136	l. 33	Rows of chairs. Lucy. *Home Rule Parliament.* 13.
	l. 38	Cranborne's apology. *Ibid.* 101.
page 137	l. 4	Irish peasantry. *Hansard.* 25 March 1887.
	l. 6	Chain-makers. *Hansard.* 17 June 1887.
	l. 14	Gladstone's magnanimity. Edith Lyttelton. *Alfred Lyttelton.* 213–14.
	l. 39	Smoking room. Malcolm. *Vacant Thrones.* 119.
page 138	l. 28	Unmitigated nuisance. C. to Ampthill. 22 Feb. 1902.
	l. 31	Queen of Spain. C. to Grace. 14 Nov. 1918.

CHAPTER ELEVEN: LORDS

page 139	l. 9	Weary strain. C. to Mary. 26 March 1893.
	l. 16	Home Rule Bill. C. to Spring Rice. 26 Aug. [1893].
	l. 22	Wisdom and ability. Steinhart. *Oxford Canning Club.* 139.
page 140	l. 20	Tory government. *Hansard.* 31 Jan. 1887.
	l. 28	Black beetles. *Truth.* 19 Nov. 1891. Quo. Ronaldshay. I.187.
	l. 35	Noble influence. *Hansard.* 21 March 1890.
	l. 40	Lord Taunton. Pearson. *Labby.* 68.
page 141	l. 7	Dogs and stick. *Hansard.* 21 March 1890.
	l. 18	Public service. *Ibid.* 9 March 1888.
	l. 29	Manageable dimensions. *Ibid.* 17 May 1889.
	l. 39	Democratic dash. Masterman. *Mary Gladstone.* 196.
page 142	l. 5	Carlton Club. *Hansard.* 21 March 1890.
	l. 8	Radical majority. *Ibid.* 9 March 1888.
	l. 12	Heirs to peerages. *National Review.* May 1888.
	l. 14	Two articles. 'A Purified British Senate'. *National Review.* March and April 1888.
	l. 39	Parliamentary Bill. *Hansard.* 16 March 1894. Col. 459.
page 143	l. 32	Affection for Commons. *Ibid.* 28 June 1894. Col. 420.
page 144	l. 1	Refusal to move. Midleton. *Records and Reactions.* 272.
	l. 10	Recent travels. C. to Brodrick. 6 May 1895.
	l. 21	Constitutional issue. *The Times.* 13 May 1895.
	l. 32	Choice of status. *Hansard.* 13 May 1895.
	l. 40	Precedents. *Ibid.* 14 May 1895.
page 145	l. 2	Prophecy. *Ibid.* 21 May 1895.
	l. 8	Peerikins. *Ibid.* 14 May 1895.

CHAPTER TWELVE: CLUBS

page 146	l. 9	Simple tastes. Edith Lyttelton. *Alfred Lyttelton.* 343.
	l. 12	Friendliest club. Notes.
	l. 17	Balfour dines. C. to Grace. 12 Sept. 1919.
	l. 21	Harry Chaplin. *Ibid.* 25 Sept. 1919.
page 147	l. 2	Unstoned grapes. FitzRoy. *Memoirs.* I.139.
	l. 4	Joins Athenaeum. Notes.
	l. 5	Salisbury seconds. C. to Salisbury. 9 March 1893. Christ Church.

page 147 l. 7 Stolen umbrellas. Brodrick to C. 28 July 1899.
l. 11 White's. Notes.
l. 13 Beefsteak Club. Kipling. *Something of Myself.* 145.
l. 22 Principal part. Notes.
l. 32 Sarah Bernhardt. *Ibid.*
l. 39 Grillion's. Grant Duff. *Notes from a Diary, 1896–1901.* 1.335.

page 148 l. 7 Tory candidate. Blunt. *My Diaries.* 522.
l. 10 Trespassers. Gwynn. *Spring Rice.* 1.346.
l. 12 Superior mechanic. Blunt. *My Diaries.* 315.
l. 16 See the stars. *Ibid.* 433.
l. 20 Blunt run in. Young. *Balfour.* 114.
l. 42 History of Crabbet. Blunt. *My Diaries. Passim.*

page 149 l. 24 Club rules. Lent by late Sir Harold Nicolson.
l. 26 Immortal wassail. C. to Blunt. 6 Oct. 1911.
l. 32 Motto. 'Crabbed age and youth cannot live together'. *The Passionate Pilgrim.* xii.
l. 34 Stark naked. Storrs. *Orientations.* 32.
l. 36 Flowing robes. Leveson Gower. *Years of Endeavour.* 84–6.

page 150 l. 6 Mixing the sexes. *Ibid.* 96.

page 151 l. 1 Dangerous jokes. MacCarthy. *Portraits.* 1.35.
l. 20 Respectable mediocrity. Howard. *Theatre of Life.* 1.74.
l. 22 Wilde embarrassed. MacCarthy. *Memories.* 204.
l. 28 Prime Minister. Blunt. *My Diaries.* 58.
l. 32 Twenty to dinner. *Ibid.* 112.
l. 41 Wyndham. Obituary appreciation. *The Times.* 10 June 1913.

page 152 l. 1 Handsomest man. Malcolm. *Vacant Thrones.* 127.
l. 11 Crabbet. Mackail and Wyndham. *George Wyndham.* 1.248.
l. 15 Asquith's income. Blunt. *My Diaries.* 639.
l. 22 Club's virtue. *Ibid.* 431.
l. 29 Webb. Margot Asquith. *Autobiography.* 182.
l. 36 Pregnant joke. C. Ribblesdale to C. 23 Oct. 1887.
l. 39 Valet's consolation. Horner. *Time Remembered.* 51.

page 153 l. 6 Cust. Obituary appreciation. *The Times.* 6 March 1917.
l. 14 French exam. Storrs. *Orientations.* 31–2.
l. 16 Fastidious critic. Margot Asquith. *Autobiography.* 200.
l. 17 Initial dislike. C. Ribblesdale to C. 23 Oct. 1887.
l. 18 Later warmth. Robertson Scott. *Life and Death of a Newspaper.* 371.
l. 26 Women. *Ibid.* 386.
l. 43 Presidential warning. Blunt to Cust. 25 Nov. 1892. Quo. Storrs. *Orientations.* 33.

page 154 l. 16 Pall Mall Gazette. Robertson Scott. *Life and Death of a Newspaper.* 377ff.
l. 17 Final word. Storrs. *Orientations.* 36.
l. 32 Gatty. Capt. Richard Gatty to author.

page 155 l. 6 Libel action. *The Times.* 17-21 June 1893.
l. 15 Damages reduced. *Ibid.* July 20.

page 155	l. 20	Lord Elcho. Chandos. *From Peace to War*. 58.
	l. 32	Pro-Derby. *Hansard*. 3 June 1890.
page 156	l. 2	Anti-Derby. *Ibid*. 31 May 1892.
	l. 6	On his hair. Cynthia Asquith. *Haply I May Remember*. 128.
	l. 33	President's homily. Blunt to C. 21 Nov. 1891.
page 157	l. 13	Another Caligula. Houghton to Blunt. 1892. Quo. Lytton. *W.S. Blunt*. 227.
	l. 23	Last of Viceroys. Blunt to C. 11 Aug. 1898.
	l. 28	Merited expulsion. C. to Blunt. 18 Aug. 1898. Fitzwilliam.
	l. 35	Forever young. *Ibid*. 6 Oct. 1911. Fitzwilliam.

CHAPTER THIRTEEN: HEARTS

page 158	l. 17	Sir Charles Tennant. Bonham Carter. *Introduction to Margot Asquith's Autobiography*. xvii–xx.
page 159	l. 13	Four sisters. Masterman. *Mary Gladstone*. 268.
	l. 24	Forgotten my existence. C. Ribblesdale to C. 5 Nov. 1882.
	l. 40	Two passions. *Ibid*. 3 Sept. 1883.
page 160	l. 9	Christian names. *Ibid*. 4 Aug. 1884.
	l. 20	Delicious letter. *Ibid*. 6 June 1885.
	l. 44	Clumsy indiscretion. *Ibid*.
page 161	l. 7	Jealous of Tommy. *Ibid*. 1 April 1886.
	l. 13	Not the food. *Ibid*. 1 April 1887.
	l. 35	Moving house. *Ibid*. 21 Aug. 1887.
page 162	l. 4	Confessions. Ribblesdale. *Impressions and Memories*. 189.
	l. 15	Tommy Ribblesdale. Verses composed for a dinner at the Bachelors' Club. 9 July 1890.
	l. 31	Husband's illness. C. Ribblesdale to C. 9 Jan. 1889.
	l. 43	Davos. *Ibid*. 19 Dec. 1886.
page 163	l. 4	Particular sister. *Ibid*. 9 Jan. 1889.
	l 10	Never grow old. *Ibid*.
	l. 20	Crossing sweeper. Horner. *Time Remembered*. 161.
	l. 23	Rejected lovers. Phillips. *Hawarden Letters*. 181.
	l. 28	Gerald Balfour. Laura Tennant to C. 20 March 1885.
	l. 36	Dilke's photograph. Margot Asquith. *Autobiography*. 147.
page 164	l. 3	You nice old boy. Laura Tennant to C. 27 June 1884.
	l. 16	Life at Glen. *Ibid*. 5 Aug. 1884.
	l. 22	Mediterranean Spring. *Ibid*. 20 March 1885.
	l. 30	Everlasting hills. *Ibid*. 28 Sept. 1884.
	l. 35	Bernal Osborne. *Ibid*. 20 Oct. 1884.
page 165	l. 12	No enemies. *Ibid*. 3 Dec. 1884.
	l. 20	Visit to Tennyson. Notes.
	l. 31	Exemplary life. Laura Tennant to C. 5 Aug. 1884.
	l. 38	To be married. *Ibid*. 30 Jan. 1885.
	l. 40	King Alf. *Ibid*. 20 March 1885.
page 166	l. 27	Eternal honeymoon. Alfred and Laura Lyttelton to C. 9 June 1885.

page 166	l. 32	Last letter. Laura Lyttelton to C. 5 Feb. 1886.
	l. 36	Death cannot enter. Margot Asquith. *Autobiography*. 47.
page 167	l. 3	Gladstone's condolence. *Ibid.* 51–2.
	l. 8	Ethereal emanations. Obituary appreciation of Alfred Lyttelton. *The Times*. 7 July 1913.
	l. 11	Blessed child. Note on letter of Laura Lyttelton to C. 5 Feb. 1886.
	l. 21	High on the list. Lucy Graham Smith to C. 5 Feb. 1887.
	l. 38	Gift of a cushion. *Ibid.* 12 Aug. 1892.
page 168	l. 2	Cheesemaking. *Ibid.* 30 Nov. 1886.
	l. 4	Facts and feelings. *Ibid.* 3 Aug. 1887.
	l. 8	Fatuous husband. Margot Tennant to C. 25 Dec. 1890.
	l. 9	Arthritis. *Ibid.* 17 June 1899.
	l. 10	Harry Cust. *Ibid.* 16 Dec. 1893.
	l. 11	Harrow. Lucy Graham Smith to C. 13 Feb. 1888.
	l. 26	A trio we meet. Verses composed for a dinner at the Bachelors' Club. 10 July 1889.
	l. 38	Hate the sea. Margot Tennant to C. 11 Nov. 1889.
page 169	l. 12	Opening a letter. *Ibid.* 4 Sept. 1884.
	l. 19	Laura's marriage. *Ibid.* 21 May 1885.
	l. 25	Rare combination. *Ibid.* 17 Oct. 1887.
	l. 35	Letter to Japan. *Ibid.* 25 Sept. 1887.
page 170	l. 6	Bon voyage. *Ibid.* 24 Sept. 1889.
	l. 9	Nasty things. *Ibid.* 22 July 1885.
	l. 19	Arch undertone. *Ibid.* 10 Oct. 1887.
	l. 20	Decorated face. *Ibid.* 28 April 1888.
	l. 25	Wilfrid Blunt. *Ibid.* 5 Sept. 1893.
	l. 31	Pretentious donkey. Margot Asquith. *More Memories*. 129.
	l. 35	Career of his own. *Ibid. Autobiography*. 169.
	l. 40	Home Secretary. Notebook of second journey round the world. 1892–3.
	l. 42	Delightful company. Margot Tennant to C. 28 Dec. 1892.
page 171	l. 7	Royal consent. Arthur Ponsonby. *Henry Ponsonby*. 281.
	l. 19	Lovely present. Margot Tennant to C. 22 April 1894.
	l. 42	Honeymoon letter. Margot Asquith to C. 10 May 1894.
page 172	l. 4	To the play. C. to Brodrick. Undated [late 1882].
	l. 14	Photograph. Alfred Lyttelton to C. 1 April 1883.
	l. 17	Angel in gauze. C. Ribblesdale to C. 3 Sept. 1883.
	l. 19	St Cecilia. Gower. *Old Diaries*. 8.
	l. 21	Unselfishness. Masterman. *Mary Gladstone*. 325.
	l. 22	Like vision. Margot Tennant to C. 6 Oct. 1888.
page 173	l. 4	Lower spirits. Laura Tennant to C. 25 Feb. 1885.
	l. 14	Born to be bright. Margot Tennant to C. 1 Sept. 1885.
	l. 20	Discovered nothing. C. Ribblesdale to C. 12 Sept. 1885.
	l. 25	Despair of the world. Mackail and Wyndham. *George Wyndham*. I. 188.
page 174	l. 16	Cherubin type. C. Ribblesdale to C. 19 Dec. 1886.
page 175	l. 23	£100 blackmail. Personal correspondence. Oct. 1920.

CHAPTER FOURTEEN: SOULS

page 176	l. 16	Coining the name. Balfour. *Chapters of Autobiography*. 232. And Lady Desborough, letter to *The Times*. 21 Jan. 1929.
	l. 22	Fresh coat of paint. Marchioness Curzon. *Reminiscences*. 139.
page 177	l. 11	Slightly ludicrous. Balfour. *Chapters of Autobiography*. 232.
	l. 12	The Gang. Margot Tennant to C. 11 Nov. 1889.
page 179	l. 2	Two instruments. Phillips. *Some Hawarden Letters*. 131.
	l. 7	Double staircase. *Ibid.*
	l. 12	Golf and politics. Balfour to C. 16 April 1896.
	l. 14	Noble minds. Lytton. *W.S. Blunt*. 226–7.
	l. 17	Kent courses. C. to Brodrick. 17 March 1904.
	l. 19	Hackwood golf. C. to Alfred Lyttelton. 19 Sept. 1907.
	l. 22	Ideal party. Masterman. *Mary Gladstone*. 120.
	l. 24	Very dear of him. C. Ribblesdale to C. 23 Oct. 1887.
	l. 34	Particular Soul. Midleton. *Records and Reactions*. 52.
	l. 38	Physical fulfilment. Young. *Balfour*. 134–8.
	l. 43	Inadvertently dined. Marsh. *A Number of People*. 203.
page 180	l. 7	Fancy Dress. Cynthia Asquith. *Haply I May Remember*. 20.
	l. 12	Few novels. Laura Tennant to C. 5 Aug. 1884.
	l. 21	Correspondence course. Lucy Graham Smith to C. 14 Dec. 1887.
	l. 26	Rousseau. C. Ribblesdale to C. 9 Dec. 1889.
	l. 30	Here to Australia. *Ibid.* 3 Sept. 1883.
	l. 34	Sad twaddle. *Ibid.* 9 Jan. 1889.
page 181	l. 8	Tennyson. Margot Asquith to C. 4 May 1891.
	l. 18	Churton Collins. Charteris. *Edmund Gosse*. 193–7.
	l. 26	Tennant family. Charteris to C. 25 Sept. 1888.
	l. 37	Talking menu. Laura Lyttelton to C. 3 Dec. 1884.
page 182	l. 1	Pale from boredom. Cynthia Asquith. *Remember and Be Glad*. 28.
	l. 5	Boring the Bore. Raleigh. *Letters*. II.366–7.
	l. 14	Soulful games. Cynthia Asquith. *Remember and Be Glad*. 12. And Lady Violet Bonham Carter. *Listener*. 30 Oct. 1947.
	l. 17	Quite chilling. Margot Tennant to C. 29 Aug. 1888.
	l. 20	Balfour is dead. Bonham Carter. *Introduction to Margot Asquith's Autobiography*. xxix.
	l. 27	Obituary eye. Salter. *Slave of the Lamp*. 29.
	l. 35	Tact defined. C. Ribblesdale to C. 3 April 1891.
	l. 43	Only faux-pas. *Ibid.*
page 183	l. 6	Balliol gaudy. Leveson Gower. *Years of Endeavour*. 243.
	l. 15	Elder sons. Lady Violet Bonham Carter to author.
	l. 39	Victim of tuberculosis. Lever. *The Herberts of Wilton*. 230.
page 184	l. 17	Medical advice. Pembroke to C. 19 May 1890.
	l. 23	Present of a rug. C. Ribblesdale to C. 14 Jan. 1891.
	l. 31	Pearls and jersey. Constance Sitwell. *Bright Morning*. 35.
	l. 36	Lurid proposals. Margot Tennant to C. 25 Sept. 1887.
	l. 43	Rather hard work. C. Ribblesdale to C. 23 Oct. 1887.

page 185 l. 1 Sailed alone. Constance Sitwell. *Bright Morning*. 35.
l. 2 Stumbled upwards. Sir Walter Raleigh. Quo. Margot Asquith. *Autobiography*. 187.
l. 9 Lobsters. Horner. *Time Remembered*. 160.
l. 21 Lovers' meetings. *Ibid.* 145.
l. 30 Ettie Grenfell. Margot Asquith. *Autobiography*. 188–9.
page 186 l. 5 Willie Grenfell. Portland. *Men, Women and Things*. 71.
l. 13 International financier. *Dictionary of National Biography*.
l. 19 Reigning beauty. Balsan. *The Glitter and the Gold*. 77.
l. 29 Lady Wenlock. Leveson Gower. *Mixed Grill*. 172.
l. 32 Another world. Liddell. *Ordinary Mortal*. 148–9.
l. 41 Ear trumpet. Marsh. *A Number of People*. 198.
page 187 l. 14 Sabbath cards. Wemyss. *A Family Record*. 196.
l. 23 Never a book. Bailey. *Lady Frederick Cavendish*. II.146.
l. 31 Royal persons. Margot Asquith. *More Memories*. 240–1.
l. 40 Henry Chaplin. *Dictionary of National Biography*.
page 188 l. 2 Unfiltered water. Lucy. *Home Rule Parliament*. 15.
l. 5 Effective orator. Riddell. *More Pages from My Diary*. 109.
l. 13 Shooting stars. Laura Tennant to C. 3 Dec. 1884.
l. 19 Balfour serenaded. Cynthia Asquith. *Remember and Be Glad*. 14.
l. 24 Copious irrelevance. Winterton. *Orders of the Day*. 69.
l. 26 Silver salver. Wells. *Experiment in Autobiography*. 766.
l. 37 Weak seat. Malcolm. *Vacant Thrones*. 120.
l. 40 Spirit of mischief. Rodd. *Social and Diplomatic Memories*. I.250.
page 189 l. 6 Disturbed dinner. Leveson Gower. *Mixed Grill*. 69.
l. 9 Glorious George. Rodd to C. 2 Oct. 1893.
l. 18 Six quails. Leveson Gower. *Mixed Grill*. 72.
l. 32 Lord Brougham. Notes. April 1890.
l. 41 Sir George Bowen. Rodd. *Social and Diplomatic Memories*. I.107–8.
page 190 l. 5 Leaps and bounds. Margot Asquith. *More Memories*. 166.
l. 7 Royal disapproval. Mallet. *Life with Queen Victoria*. 67.
l. 9 Fad and fancy. *Birmingham Gazette*. 3 Nov. 1892. Quo. Ronaldshay. I.166.
l. 12 Parasols. Phillips. *Some Hawarden Letters*. 136–7.
l. 19 Fast nor loose. Lady Violet Bonham Carter. *Listener*. 30 Oct. 1947.
l. 32 Democracy blighted. Midleton. *Records and Reactions*. 51.

CHAPTER FIFTEEN: EASTERN WINDOWS

Unless otherwise stated, all material in this chapter is drawn from the notebook which Curzon kept during his first tour round the world, from August 1887 to February 1888. It is now in the India Office Library.

page 191 l. 16 Parliamentary salary. *Hansard*. 29 March 1889.
l. 24 Kedleston economy. *Complete Peerage*. XI.
page 192 l. 11 Directors and fees. Mr D. J. Young, of the Clerical, Medical and General Life Assurance Society, to author.

page 192	l. 21	Eight-hour day. *Dictionary of National Biography.*
	l. 22	£250 a year. Mr M.R. Lindsay, of Hadfield's, to author.
	l. 28	Munitions. Midleton Papers. *Passim.* BM.
	l. 31	Veritable pauper. C. to Brodrick. 23 Jan. 1887.
	l. 36	Unable to travel. *Ibid.* 15 Sept. 1886.
page 193	l. 4	Vice-Chancellor. Lubbock. *Diary of A.C. Benson.* 245.
	l. 8	Portable bath. Alfred Lyttelton to C. 28 July 1887.
page 197	l. 2	Kioto wrestling. *Tales of Travel.* 183–5.
	l. 24	Sacred Empire. Derby. 28 July 1904. *Indian Speeches.* IV.30.
page 198	l. 25	Englishmen abroad. *Problems of the Far East.* 428–9.
	l. 30	Passion for games. *Ibid.* 427.
page 199	l. 33	Kedleston in India. *Indian Speeches.* I.XX.
page 200	l. 3	James Stephen. *Ibid.* I.V.
	l. 41	Prized recollections. *Tales of Travel.* 11–12.
page 201	l. 10	Taj Mahal. C. to Brodrick. 1 Jan. 1888. BM.
	l. 38	Frontier policy. C. to Hamilton. 12 March 1903.
	l. 42	Negotiating with Russia. Brodrick to C. 19 Aug. 1903.
page 202	l. 16	Aboriginal tribe. *Indian Speeches.* IV.36.
	l. 21	Respected and feared. C. to Scarsdale. 20 Dec. 1887.
	l. 32	Thunderous ocean. *Indian Speeches.* IV.8.
	l. 36	Pack of cards. *Ibid.* IV.44.

CHAPTER SIXTEEN: CENTRAL ASIA

page 203	l. 7	First question. Notebook. 1887–8.
	l. 10	Writer of articles. *Russia in Central Asia.* vii.
	l. 22	Nansen. Fleming. *Bayonets to Lhasa.* 23.
page 204	l. 7	Suppressed work. *Viceroy's Note-Book.* 158.
	l. 13	His boast. Malcolm. *Pursuits of Leisure.* 137.
	l. 16	Large slice. C. to Brodrick. 5 Sept. 1888.
	l. 18	Middle-class method. Margot Tennant to C. 29 Aug. 1888.
	l. 22	St Petersburg. *RCA.* 28.
	l. 28	Banks of the Wolga. Boswell. *Johnson.* II.538.
	l. 38	Separate authorities. *RCA.* 17.
page 205	l. 5	Early passengers. *Ibid.* 18.
	l. 16	Hotels. *Ibid.* 429.
	l. 21	Cost of food. *Ibid.* 62.
	l. 22	Cost of travel. *Ibid.*
	l. 27	Transcaspia. *Ibid.* ix.
	l. 43	Soldiers. *Ibid.* 48.
page 206	l. 4	Turned on its base. *Ibid.* 10.
	l. 12	No statistics. *Ibid.* 59.
	l. 24	At Russian mercy. *Ibid.* 97.
	l. 29	Merv. *Ibid.* 106.
	l. 34	Diplomatic protest. *Ibid.* 113.
page 208	l. 12	Skeleton of the past. *Ibid.* 140.
	l. 20	Oxus. Matthew Arnold. *Sohrab and Rustum.* Lines 875–9.

page 208	l. 29	Voice from the grave. Notes.
	l. 32	Soft cadences. *RCA*. 144.
	l. 38	Unknown lands. *Ibid.*
page 209	l. 30	Third-class carriages. *Ibid.* 155.
	l. 41	Indiarubber bath. *Ibid.* 170.
page 210	l. 14	Bokhara. *Ibid.* 172–5.
	l. 24	Bazaar. *Ibid.* 188.
	l. 33	Western civilization. *Ibid.* 193.
	l. 41	Convicted of fraud. *Ibid.* 194.
page 211	l. 3	Bribed jailer. Notebook. 1887–8.
	l. 18	Crime and punishment. *RCA*. 180–5.
	l. 21	Depraved tastes. *Ibid.* 200.
	l. 30	Dress-suit. *Ibid.* 201.
	l. 37	Most interesting city. *Ibid.* 203.
page 212	l. 4	Vague declarations. *Ibid.* 216.
	l. 9	Almost a paradise. *Ibid.* 213.
	l. 20	Righistan. *Ibid.* 220.
	l. 39	Ancient monuments. *Ibid.* 227–8.
page 213	l. 5	Tarantass. *Ibid.* 233.
	l. 26	Government House. *Ibid.* 244–5.
	l. 36	Degenerate scion. *Ibid.* 241.
page 214	l. 3	Tashkent library. *Ibid.* 248.
	l. 10	Self-purchase. C. to Arthur Godley. 13 May 1903.
	l. 12	Ambassador. Notes.
	l. 26	Russian character. *RCA*. 20–1.
	l. 38	Stupefied submission. *Ibid.* 276.
page 215	l. 16	Defence of India. *Ibid.* 306–8.
	l. 21	Hand-to-mouth. *Ibid.* 315.
	l. 30	Constantinople. *Ibid.* 321.
	l. 36	Imperial Crown. *Ibid.* 14.
page 216	l. 8	Eton debate. Minutes. 7 May 1877. Quo. Ronaldshay. I.144.
	l. 24	Eleven years old. C. to George Hamilton. 3 May 1899.
	l. 39	Harcourt's request. Quo. Ronaldshay. I.296.

CHAPTER SEVENTEEN: PERSIA

page 217	l. 14	Killing work. Balfour to C. 9 Sept. 1889.
	l. 17	Literary payment. Ronaldshay. I.49.
	l. 26	References. *Persia and the Persian Question.* I.viii.
page 218	l. 15	Clothes. *Ibid.* I.53–5.
	l. 19	Eton ice. C. to Lady Scarsdale. Feb. 1873.
	l. 26	Food. *Persia.* I.56.
	l. 38	Turkish customs. A. Hardinge. *Diplomatist in the East.* 29–30.
page 220	l. 2	Thousand Gehennas. C. to Margot Tennant. 28 Sept. 1889. Quo. Ronaldshay. I.149.
	l. 23	Transcaspia again. *Persia.* I.66–9.

page 221	l. 11	Saving face. *Ibid.* I.95.
	l. 31	Visit to Kuchan. *Ibid.* I.94–116.
page 222	l. 4	Kelat-i-Nadiri. *Ibid.* I.126–33.
	l. 15	Member of Parliament. *Ibid.* I.161.
	l. 30	Meshed. *Ibid.* I.165.
page 223	l. 3	Post horses. *Ibid.* I.30–2.
	l. 16	Keeping warm. *Ibid.* I.253.
	l. 24	Camels. *Ibid.* I.275.
	l. 35	Material progress. *Ibid.* I.317.
page 224	l. 2	Splendour and frippery. *Ibid.* I.328.
	l. 5	Peacock Throne. *Ibid.* I.318.
	l. 14	In Scotland. Montrose. *My Ditty Box.* 25.
	l. 17	Offer to buy. Hare. *Story of My Life.* IV.125.
	l. 21	Philanthropist. *Ibid.* VI.172.
	l. 30	Talk with Shah. *Persia.* I.396–408.
page 225	l. 2	Abortive reforms. *Ibid.* I.399.
	l. 7	Corruption. *Ibid.* I.438.
	l. 17	6,000 blows. *Ibid.* I.457.
	l. 23	Cats. *Ibid.* 399.
page 226	l. 2	Garb of woe. *Ibid.* II.61.
	l. 12	Stinginess. *Ibid.* II.43.
	l. 22	Shiraz. *Ibid.* II.93–4.
	l. 37	Persepolis. *Ibid.* II.156.
page 227	l. 29	Down to Bushire. *Ibid.* II.197–230.
	l. 33	Universal clothier. *Ibid.* II.41.
	l. 36	British goods. *Ibid.* II.236.
page 228	l. 17	Passport demanded. *Ibid.* II.341.
	l. 29	Tortuous colloquy. *Ibid.* II.355.
	l. 39	Friendly consideration. *Ibid.* II.362.
page 229	l. 4	Unclean thing. *Ibid.* II.368.
	l. 35	British policy. *Ibid.* II.464–5.
	l. 40	Chessboard. *Ibid.* I.3–4.
page 230	l. 7	Commandments. *Ibid.* II.619.

CHAPTER EIGHTEEN: UNDER-SECRETARY

page 232	l. 4	H.M. Stanley. Notes. April 1890.
	l. 13	Robert Curzon. *Viceroy's Note-Book.* 297–8.
	l. 30	Athos. *Ibid.* 299–320.
	l. 33	Meteora. *Ibid.* 330–3.
page 233	l. 6	Concession. *Persia.* II.513 and Curzon Papers.
	l. 9	Scientifically explored. *Ibid.* I.449.
	l. 15	Oil. *Ibid.* II.520.
	l. 25	Houtum Schindler. *Ibid.* I.xiii.
	l. 29	Rotten to the core. *Topical Times.* 26 April 1890.
	l. 33	Daliki. *Persia.* II.225.
	l. 39	£350 investment. Curzon Papers.

page 234 l. 6 Mr D'Arcy. C. to George Hamilton. 31 July 1901.
l. 12 Persian oil. C. to Lansdowne. 9 Dec. 1903.
l. 15 Like a navvy. Margot Tennant to C. 25 Dec. 1890.
l. 20 Row a boat. C. to Mary. 13 Oct. 1890.
l. 21 Monte Cristo. *Ibid.* 15 March 1899.
l. 38 Few statistics. *Persia.* II.469.
page 235 l. 1 Single lines. *Ibid.* I.xi.
l. 4 Strayed into veracity. *Ibid.* II.633.
l. 11 Gathering information. Hogarth. *Curzon.* 505.
page 236 l. 2 Peroration. *Modern Parliamentary Eloquence.* 70.
l. 6 The only bar. Jowett to C. 13 Sept. 1889.
l. 9 Big words. Margot Asquith. *More Memories.* 168.
l. 18 Lowther. C. to Mary. 10 Oct. 1891.
l. 32 Not recognized. Alfred Lyttelton to C. 17 Oct. 1891.
l. 41 Dogs and beaters. Blunt. *My Diaries.* 27.
page 237 l. 2 Poachers. *Ibid.* 77.
l. 10 Gorst's migration. Salisbury to C. 10 Nov. 1891.
l. 22 What he wanted. Grant Duff to C. 18 Nov. 1891.
l. 29 Burning question. Jowett to C. 23 Nov. 1891.
page 238 l. 20 Shah and Emperor. Salisbury to C. 27 Nov. 1891.
l. 33 Pruning hook. *Ibid.* 30 Nov. 1891.
l. 41 Not barbarous. *Ibid.* 5 Dec. 1891.
l. 43 Few sentences. Note on envelope containing correspondence.
page 239 l. 3 Regrettable violence. *Persia.* I.402.
l. 4 Mercantile instincts. *Ibid.* I.338.
l. 5 Short petticoats. *Ibid.* I.410.
l. 20 Lyall. *Verses in India.*
l. 28 Army a cypher. *Persia.* II.627.
l. 33 Creeping paralysis. *Ibid.* II.628.
l. 36 Administrative energy. *Ibid.*
l. 40 Hypocrites. *Ibid.* II.632.
page 240 l. 13 Enchantment and fraud. *Ibid.* I.15.
l. 22 Governed by Europeans. *Ibid.* II.630.
l. 30 Portly volumes. C. to Gladstone. 18 May 1892. BM. 44514.
l. 36 Left uncensored. Note on envelope containing correspondence.
l. 40 Owns it. *Sunday Sun.* 5 June 1892. Quo. Ronaldshay. I.156.
page 241 l. 3 Houtum Schindler. *Persia.* I.xii.
l. 10 Scribblers. Hardy to C. Undated. [Postmark June 1892.]
l. 15 Most complete. Notebook of second journey round the world, 1892–3.
l. 24 Bookseller's offer. Brodrick to C. 13 Nov. 1903.
l. 27 Indian defence. *Indian Speeches.* IV.156.
l. 33 Miserable return. Note on literary earnings.
page 242 l. 5 Wide range. Hamilton. *Parliamentary Reminiscences.* 68.
l. 19 Official papers. Cross to C. 16 Nov. 1891.
l. 32 Popular jingle. Quo. Blake. *Disraeli.* 550.
page 243 l. 4 Cross estate. Hansard. 28 April 1914.

page 243	l. 15	Excellent terms. Kilbracken. *Reminiscences.* 174.
	l. 16	Proposed health. Steinhart. *Oxford Canning Club.* 527.
	l. 25	Ritchie. *Dictionary of National Biography.*
	l. 29	Early esteem. Kilbracken. *Reminiscences.* 174.
page 244	l. 4	First appointment. Younghusband. *Light of Experience.* 63.
	l. 10	Public Service. *Hansard.* 12 Feb. 1892.
	l. 16	Financial difficulties. *Ibid.* 10 March 1892.
	l. 21	Huge debts. *Complete Peerage.* xii. Part 2.
	l. 27	Important subject. *Hansard.* 10 March 1892.
	l. 37	Premature. *Ibid.* 28 March 1892.
	l. 41	No opposition. *Ibid.* 25 April 1892.
page 245	l. 7	Like Peel. Liddell. *Ordinary Mortal.* 288.
	l. 12	Personal superiority. Lucy. *Home Rule Parliament.* 121.
	l. 16	Radical newspapers. Undated. Quo. Ronaldshay. i.190.
	ll. 27ff.	Unless otherwise stated, the source of the remainder of this chapter is Curzon's notebook of his second tour round the world, from August 1892 to March 1893.
page 246	l. 42	Election humour. Notes.
page 247	l. 13	Earthquake. Dugdale. *Maurice de Bunsen.* 104.
	l. 20	No exercise. C. to George Hamilton. 29 Oct. 1900.
	l. 34	Japanese ambitions. *Problems of the Far East.* ix.
	l. 39	Powerful influence. *Ibid.* 396.
	l. 43	Like Frenchmen. *Ibid.* 55.
page 248	l. 2	Two hands. *Ibid.* 8.
	l. 18	Deeply offended. Gwynn. *Spring Rice.* i.136–7.
	l. 22	Dismissals all round. *Ibid.* i.128.
	l. 43	Regaining favour. *Problems of the Far East.* 159–60.
page 249	l. 13	Paralysing conceit. *Ibid.* 237.
	l. 25	Profligate scoundrels. *Ibid.* 245.
	l. 35	Mission to Siam. C. to Salisbury. 26 July 1892. Christ Church.
page 250	l. 3	Insoluble problem. Salisbury to C. 28 July 1892.
	l. 18	History re-written. *Nineteenth Century.* July 1893.
page 251	l. 2	Robert Browning. Masterman. *Mary Gladstone.* 240.
	l. 23	Prince of Wales. *Tales of Travel.* 237.
	l. 27	Net reward. Note on literary earnings.
	l. 31	State Department. Spring Rice to C. 1 March 1895.
	l. 33	Prolonged squabble. C. to Spring Rice. 15 April 1894.
page 252	l. 4	No hurry. *Problems of the Far East.* 4.
	l. 14	Asiatic position. *Ibid.* 419–21.

CHAPTER NINETEEN: ROOF OF THE WORLD

page 253	l. 20	Sensitive areas. Elgin to Fowler. 17 July 1894.
page 254	l. 10	Cry of freedom. C. to Mary. 12 Nov. 1893.
	l. 26	Dependent on Whitehall. *Dictionary of National Biography.*
	l. 30	First Wesleyan. Oxford and Asquith. *Memories and Reflections.* i.167.
	l. 32	Socially inadequate. Brett. *Journals and Letters.* ii.303.

page 254	l. 40	Windsor boycott. Oxford and Asquith. *Memories and Reflections*. I.172.
page 255	l. 5	Red tape. C. to Mary. 17 July 1894.
	l. 11	Stop him now. Elgin to Fowler. 24 July 1894.
	l. 43	Letter to Amir. April 1894. Quo. Ronaldshay. I.206.
page 256	l. 4	Misgivings. Fowler to Elgin. 10 Aug. 1894.
	l. 5	Lord Roberts. Roberts to Elgin. 30 Aug. 1894.
	l. 11	Very nice fellow. Rosebery to Elgin. 27 July 1894.
	l. 13	Four whole nights. Midleton. Speech at Eton. 6 Dec. 1929.
	l. 20	Bombay. Elgin to Fowler. 14 Aug. 1894.
	l. 22	Unanimous prohibition. *Ibid.* 21 Aug. 1894.
	l. 29	Great Pamir. *The Pamirs and the Source of the Oxus*. 3.
	l. 31	Inflamed passions. Elgin to Fowler. 9 Jan. 1895.
	l. 41	No responsibility. *Tales of Travel*. 43.
	l. 43	Kashmir. Elgin to Fowler. 28 Aug. 1894.
page 257	l. 3	Amir's invitation. *Tales of Travel*. 43.
	l. 7	Children bloom. *Viceroy's Note-Book*. 152.
	l. 18	Burzil. *Ibid.* 165–6.
	l. 30	Haunts of men. *Ibid.* 176.
	l. 40	Rakapushi. *Ibid.* 177.
page 260	l. 8	Indian Empire. *Ibid.* 188.
	l. 20	Polo. *Pamirs*. 8.
	l. 25	Baltit. *Ibid.* 7.
	l. 31	Strawberry ice. *Viceroy's Note-Book*. 200.
	l. 35	Physical accretions. *Pamirs*. 9.
page 261	l. 11	Roof of the World. *Viceroy's Note-Book*. 205.
	l. 19	Create a torrent. *Pamirs*. 17.
	l. 29	Nomads. *Ibid.* 23.
	l. 38	Ovis poli. *Ibid.* 26–9.
page 262	l. 2	Matthew Arnold. *Sohrab and Rustum*. Lines 886–7.
	l. 5	Hindu Kush. *Pamirs*. 2.
	l. 18	Ceaseless tumult. *Ibid.* 31.
page 263	l. 9	Obstructed at Sarhad. *Ibid.* 59–61.
	l. 28	Pax Britannica. *Viceroy's Note-Book*. 347.
page 264	l. 22	Chitral. Younghusband. *Light of Experience*. 70.
	l. 27	Philosophy. Younghusband. 'Personal Recollections of Lord Curzon.' *Nineteenth-Century and After*. May 1925.
	l. 32	Pot of jam. Younghusband. *Light of Experience*. 69.
page 265	l. 7	River crossing. *Viceroy's Note-Book*. 116–8.
	ll. 8ff.	Chitral. *Ibid.* 121–35.
page 266	l. 20	Indiscreet. Fowler to Elgin. 2 Jan. 1895.
	l. 23	*The Times*. Elgin to Fowler. 9 Jan. 1895.
	l. 28	Responsible situation. Godley to Elgin. 10 Jan. 1895.
page 267	l. 10	Cabinet minute. *Viceroy's Note-Book*. 143.
	l. 27	Notices of book. *Ibid.* 138.
	l. 36	French ditties. *Ibid.* 139.
page 268	l. 25	Uniform. *Tales of Travel*. 231–5.
	l. 30	High average. *Pamirs*. 2.

page 268	l. 39	Inconvenient queries. *Tales of Travel.* 235.
page 269	l. 1	Lace trimmings. C. to Daisy White. 20 Nov. 1894. Quo. Ronaldshay. I.211.
	l. 6	Tips for servants. Memorandum on Afghanistan, completed 2 Dec. 1894. IO Mss. Eur. FIII.56.
	l. 8	Numismatist. Oman. *Victorian Oxford.* 126.
	l. 22	Amir's cruelty. *Tales of Travel.* 41–84 *passim.*
page 270	l. 13	No chloroform. *Ibid.* 80.
	l. 22	Funnel of espionage. Memorandum.
	l. 42	Social tensions. *Ibid.*
page 271	l. 12	Medical treatment. Gray. *At the Court of the Amir.* 477.
	l. 20	Amir's complaints. Memorandum.
	l. 24	Bad attack. *Tales of Travel.* 48.
	l. 32	Topics. *Ibid.* 41–84 *passim.*
	l. 36	Amusing stories. Abdur Rahman. *Memoirs.* II.141.
	l. 40	Westminster. *Tales of Travel.* 49.
page 272	l. 2	Happy Asiatic. C. to Salisbury. 22 Dec. 1894. Christ Church.
	l. 10	Courtiers. Abdur Rahman. *Memoirs.* II.87–9.
	l. 15	Bear and lion. *Ibid.* II.81.
	l. 21	Unsophisticated visitor. *Tales of Travel.* 46.
	l. 26	Russian aggression. Abdur Rahman. *Memoirs.* II.123.
	l. 36	Manoeuvres. *Tales of Travel.* 81.
	l. 42	Afghan-British alliance. Abdur Rahman. *Memoirs.* II.296.
page 273	l. 9	Rebuffed. *Ibid.* II.139.
	l. 13	No arms. *Ibid.* II.137.
	l. 15	One house. C. in House of Commons. *Hansard.* 15 Feb. 1898.
	l. 26	Invited to England. *Tales of Travel.* 61.
page 274	l. 18	Lord Roberts. *Ibid.* 63–4.
	l. 28	Removing his turban. *Ibid.* 50.
	l. 32	Queen Victoria. *Ibid.* 61.
	l. 37	Secretary of State. C. to Salisbury. 22 Dec. 1894.
page 275	l. 4	Public Service. C. to Elgin. 30 Nov. 1894.
	l. 8	Gold Star. *Tales of Travel.* 83.
	l. 13	Genuine orders. *Ibid.* 236.
	l. 17	Risk of rebellion. *Ibid.* 62.
	l. 19	Ill-health. Abdur Rahman. *Memoirs.* II.141.
	l. 22	Reprieve for Roberts. *Tales of Travel.* 65.
	l. 28	Continued mistrust. Abdur Rahman. *Memoirs.* II.143.
	l. 35	Name of successor. *Ibid.* II.8.
	l. 37	Formidable opponent. *Tales of Travel.* 83.
page 276	l. 13	Advice on travel. *Geographical Journal.* July 1895.
	l. 25	Lord Burnham. Malcolm. *Pursuits of Leisure.* 131.

CHAPTER TWENTY: MARRIAGE

page 277	l. 8	Strength and weakness. C. Ribblesdale to C. 19 Dec. 1886.
page 278	l. 6	No physical attraction. Chandos. *From Peace to War.* 38.

page 278 l. 14 Just twenty. The date of birth inscribed on her tomb at Kedleston is 27 May 1870. I have assumed this to be true in preference to the date 27 May 1871 inscribed on a leaf of the Leiter family Bible now in the possession of Mrs Middleton Train, of Washington.
l. 24 Levi Z. Leiter. *Dictionary of National Biography.*
l. 26 Chicago. Notebook of first journey round the world.
l. 31 Amassed a fortune. *New York Times.* 15 June 1904.
l. 41 Fifty million bushels. Jacob. *Six Thousand Years of Bread.*
page 279 l. 9 P Street. Mrs Middleton Train to author.
l. 15 Oleograph. Mary to C. Date not known.
l. 18 Affecting radiance. Margot Asquith. *More Memories.* 174.
l. 21 Bayreuth. Mary to C. 22 Aug. 1894.
l. 25 Political pamphleteer. C. to Mary. 12 Oct. 1894.
l. 31 Horace. *Odes.* VII.32.
l. 34 English accent. René Massigli to author.
l. 35 Foreign Minister. C. to Mary. 22 April 1894.
l. 39 Edward Grey. D'Abernon. *An Ambassador of Peace.* I.62.
page 280 l. 5 Early outlet. C. to Mary. 14 Jan. 1893.
l. 32 My darling child. *Ibid.* 4 March 1893.
l. 34 One body. C. to Spring Rice. 17 May 1893.
page 281 l. 2 Possession of my own. C. to Mary. 3 Sept. 1893.
l. 9 Ecstatic pell-mell. *Ibid.* July 1894.
l. 13 Sisterhood. Mary to C. 4 July 1894.
l. 15 Modest roof. *Ibid.* 30 July 1894.
l. 25 Lord Scarsdale. C. to Mary. 5 Feb. 1895.
l. 28 Guaranteed income. Mosley. *Curzon.* 57.
l. 33 Spinal weakness. *Ibid.* 58.
page 282 l. 3 Hearty rejoicing. C. to Spring Rice. 8 March 1895.
l. 4 Lord Lamington. *Ibid.* 3 April 1895.
l. 9 Welcome. *Ibid.* 26 April 1895.
l. 14 Clever of you. Pembroke to C. 3 March 1895.
l. 33 Congratulation. Margot Asquith to C. 3 March 1895.
page 283 l. 13 Wedding presents. Bound volume of names. Kedleston.
l. 32 Amir's letter. *Tales of Travel.* 68.
page 284 l. 3 Li Hung Chang. *Ibid.* 246.
l. 12 Merrier and happier. Mrs Craigie to C. 31 March 1895. Quo. Lucy. *Diary of a Journalist.* 42.
l. 27 Pink velvet bracket. C. to Lady Scarsdale. 12 May 1872.
l. 36 Unwearable waistcoat. *Ibid.* 4 May 1872.
page 285 l. 2 Cracked teapot. Balliol College archives.
l. 4 No apology. Margot Asquith. *More Memories.* 172.
l. 10 Hotel or lodgings. C. to Grace. 1 Nov. 1920.
l. 16 Menial tasks. Pembroke Wicks to author.
l. 20 No excuse. C. to Grace. 7 Sept. 1921.
l. 23 Good situation. *Ibid.* 29 Dec. 1923.
l. 30 Majestic virility. D'Abernon. *Portraits and Appreciations.* 29.
l. 31 Name cards. Late Aga Khan to author.

page 285	l. 35	Menus. Cynthia Asquith. *Remember and Be Glad.* 183.
	l. 39	Different provisions. *Persia.* I.56.
page 286	l. 1	Incomprehensible names. C. to Grace. 17 Oct. 1921.
	l. 5	Bisected apricot. *Ibid.* 14 Aug. 1919.
	l. 7	Too much chicken. *Ibid.* 15 May 1922.
	l. 9	Cold rabbit pie. *Ibid.* 1 Oct. 1922.
	l. 15	Repulsive details. *Ibid.* 28 Aug. 1921.
	l. 18	No tea in pot. *Ibid.* 21 Sept. 1921.
	l. 24	Skinny pheasant. C. to King Edward VII. 2 Sept. 1903.
	l. 30	Silver paper. Sir Harold Nicolson to author.
page 287	l. 2	In Bedlam, and other examples of unsatisfactory servants. C. to Grace. *Passim.*
	l. 6	Not by name. D'Abernon. *Portraits and Appreciations.* 28.
	l. 43	Statecraft and Diplomacy. Beerbohm. *Seven Men.* 59.
page 288	l. 6	The Priory. Visitors Book. Kedleston.
	l. 10	Sandringham. *Ibid.*
	l. 14	Windsor. Queen Victoria. *Letters.* 3rd series. III.108.
	l. 24	Compiling index. C. to Grace. 22 Jan. 1925.
	l. 32	Magnificent old age. C. to Gladstone. 14 March 1895.
	l. 42	Life or career. C. to Mary. 21 Sept. 1897.
page 289	l. 2	Oxford doctorate. Sir William Gladstone to author.
	l. 6	A puzzle. C. to Spring Rice. 28 Nov. 1895.
	l. 10	Accomplices. Margot Asquith. *More Memories.* 169.
	l. 14	Self-abnegation. Balsan. *The Glitter and the Gold.* 137.
	l. 17	George's iron will. Mary to L. Z. Leiter. 16 April 1903.
	l. 21	Lack of warmth. Mrs Middleton Train to author.
	l. 27	Georgian news. Mary to C. Date not known.
	l. 31	White roses. Fred Streeter. BBC Overseas Service. 12 April 1955.
	l. 38	Miss Paraman. Baroness Ravensdale. *Little Innocents.* 30.
page 290	l. 17	Nurse. C. to Mary. Date not known.
	l. 26	Stumbling blocks. Mary to C. 17 March 1896.
	l. 30	Incapacity. *Ibid.* 5 July 1901.
	l. 34	An inspiration. C. to Mary. Quo. Mosley. 116.
	l. 36	Stars and Stripes. Speech at Souls' dinner. 9 Dec. 1898.

CHAPTER TWENTY-ONE: FOREIGN OFFICE

page 291	l. 20	Missed vocation. Brett. *Journals and Letters.* I.185.
	l. 24	Matrimonial plans. Leveson Gower. *Mixed Grill.* 99.
page 292	l. 1	Eton Boating Song. R. R. James. *Rosebery.* 486.
	l. 10	Ammunition. Midleton. *Records and Reactions.* 90.
	l. 29	Under Secretaryship. Salisbury to C. 27 June 1895.
page 293	l. 7	Disappointment. C. to Salisbury. 28 June 1895.
	l. 13	Youngest politician. Salisbury to C. 28 June 1895.
	l. 17	Shaking hands. *Modern Parliamentary Eloquence.* 37.
	l. 25	Duke's dinner. Ribblesdale. *Impressions and Memories.* 120.
	l. 35	Change of faith. R. R. James. *Rosebery.* 379.

page 294	l. 2	Without power. Blunt. *My Diaries.* 173.
	l. 12	Telephone. Lucy. *Salisbury Parliament,* 393.
	l. 18	No influence. Brodrick to C. 13 Oct. 1899.
	l. 38	Danger of his defects. Grey. *Twenty-Five Years.* I.26.
page 295	l. 11	Approved text. Gosses. *British Foreign Policy.* 26.
	l. 23	Roused to antagonism. Cecil. *Biographical Studies.* 19.
	l. 30	Wellington's despatches. *Dictionary of National Biography.*
	l. 31	Initiating policy. Steiner. *Old Foreign Office.* 63.
	l. 41	Balfour's breakfast. Sanderson to Salisbury. 1 April 1898. Quo. Steiner. 64.
page 296	l. 9	Sanderson's character. Leveson Gower. *Years of Endeavour.* And Steiner. *Old Foreign Office.* 65.
	l. 11	Handwriting. Henderson. *Water Under the Bridges.* 22.
	l. 15	Palmerston minute. Tilley and Gaselee. *Foreign Office.* 59.
	l. 19	First typist. *Ibid.* 122.
	l. 22	Press gallery. C. to Sanderson and Sanderson to C. 27 March 1896. PRO. FO 800/147.
	l. 27	Red tape. Steiner. *Old Foreign Office.* 72.
	l. 31	Head of the list. Rodd. *Social and Diplomatic Memories.* I.30.
	l. 34	No typescript. Tilley and Gaselee. *Foreign Office.* 144.
	l. 37	Goose quills. *Ibid.*
	l. 41	Mild rebuke. Hamilton to C. 20 Oct. 1899.
page 297	l. 10	Mistrusted telephone. Baillie. *My First Eighty Years.* 99.
	l. 19	Telegram statistics. Foreign Office to author.
	l. 31	Going to bed. Salisbury to Duchess of Rutland. 30 June 1889. Quo. Cecil. *Salisbury.* IV.141.
	l. 36	Doctor in despair. *Ibid.* IV.264.
page 298	l. 5	Duties lightened. Steiner. *Old Foreign Office.* 63.
	l. 24	Furious Sanderson. Tilley and Gaselee. *Foreign Office.* 142.
	l. 28	Scientific thought. Steiner. *Old Foreign Office.* 142.
	l. 32	Occasional irritability. *Dictionary of National Biography.*
	l. 37	Tweed suit. Tilley and Gaselee. *Foreign Office.* 143.
	l. 40	Straw hat. O'Malley. *Phantom Caravan.* 47.
page 299	l. 8	Barrington. Steiner. *Old Foreign Office.* 61.
	l. 14	Bertie's memoranda. *Ibid.* 67.
	l. 16	Candle cutting. Tilley and Gaselee. *Foreign Office.* 131.
	l. 20	Bertie in Paris. Vansittart. *The Mist Procession.* 53.
	l. 30	Not indiscreet. Lucy. *Diary of a Journalist.* 204.
	l. 34	Parliamentary ADC. Malcolm. *The Pursuits of Leisure.* 127.
page 300	l. 18	My dear Lamps. Tilley and Gaselee. *Foreign Office.* 131.
	l. 22	Forms of address. C. to Sanderson. 27 March 1896. Sanderson to C. 21 Nov. 1896. PRO. FO 800/147.
	l. 29	Constant formality. Malcolm. *The Pursuits of Leisure.* 127.
	l. 33	Annexing Shakespeare. Vansittart. *The Mist Procession.* 44.
	l. 36	Tragic complaint. Kelly. *The Ruling Few.* 141.
page 301	l. 3	Board of Trade. C. to Salisbury. 23 Nov. 1897.
	l. 6	Commerce. PRO. FO 800/147 and 800/148 *passim.*

page 301 l. 18 Minor questions. *Ibid.*
l. 21 Not beyond 1830. *Ibid.* 24 May 1897.
l. 24 Mourning. Salisbury to C. 29 Jan. 1897.
l. 30 Excess of champagne. C. to Salisbury. 30 April 1896. PRO. FO 800/147.
l. 35 First four words. Notes. Beldorney Castle. Undated [1897].
page 302 l. 1 Majestic reproof. 18 Nov. 1896. PRO. FO. 800/147.
l. 3 Unbusinesslike HRH. C. to Salisbury. 17 Jan. 1898.
l. 13 Lord Mayor. *Ibid.* 5 Sept. 1895.
l. 17 Mansion House. Blunt. *My Diaries.* 177.
l. 31 Mitigated by an order. C. to Salisbury. 28 Sept. 1895.
l. 35 Agitated stream. Salisbury to C. 30 Sept. 1895.
l. 39 Barney Barnato. *The Times.* 2 Nov. 1907.
page 303 l. 12 FO Questions. Chester and Bowring. *Questions in Parliament.* 29.
l. 23 Delicate aspects. C. to Salisbury and Salisbury to C. 23 March 1896.
l. 29 Topics. *Hansard.* 22 Aug. to 3 Sept. 1895 *passim.*
l. 33 Impromptu answers. C. to Spring Rice. 19 July 1896.
l. 34 Stiff buckram. Lucy. *Unionist Parliament.* 71.
l. 39 Effective. *Ibid.* 133.
l. 43 Not been there. *Ibid.* 74. 12 June 1896.
page 304 l. 8 Single evening. *Hansard.* 21 Aug. 1895.
l. 18 In sole charge. Lucy. *Unionist Parliament.* 45. 27 March 1896.
l. 22 Platform speech. *The Times.* 15 Oct. 1896.
l. 39 Rosebery's jibe. *Hansard* (Lords). 11 Feb. 1896.
page 305 l. 3 Nile expedition. *Hansard.* 20 March 1896.
l. 8 Pamirs. Articles published in *Geographical Journal*, July, August and September 1896. Single volume, 1896.
l. 23 Controversial map. C. to Hamilton. 26 Jan. 1897. Copy in Elgin Papers.
l. 27 Accomplished man. Hamilton to Elgin. 29 Jan. 1897.
l. 32 Style. Elgin to Hamilton. 17 Feb. 1897.

CHAPTER TWENTY-TWO: LORD SALISBURY

page 306 l. 17 Constitutional basis. C. to Cecil Harmsworth. 23 Jan. 1919. Copy in Curzon Papers.
page 307 l. 15 Confidential records. C. to Salisbury. 24 March 1896.
l. 20 Abominable use. Salisbury to C. 25 March 1896.
l. 29 Formal reports. *Ibid.*
l. 34 Marchand expedition. André Mévil. *De la Paix de Francfort à la Conférence d'Algésiras.* 31. Quo. Algernon Cecil. *British Foreign Secretaries.* 307.
page 308 l. 3 Deputations. C. to Salisbury. 18 June 1896.
l. 5 Dreary opportunity. Salisbury to C. 18 June 1896.
l. 19 With accuracy. Cecil. *Biographical Studies.* 49.
l. 22 Cipher books. Frederick Ponsonby. *Recollections of Three Reigns.* 41.
l. 25 Wife-beater. Tilley and Gaselee. *Foreign Office.* 140.

page 308	l. 30	Stambouloff. Eliot to C. 27 Aug. 1895. PRO. FO 800/147.
	l. 35	Kruger. Cust to C. 4 Oct. 1896.
	l. 37	Khedive. Rodd to C. 28 Dec. [1895].
	l. 41	Dervishes. Kitchener to C. 5 July 1896 and 2 Feb. 1897.
page 309	l. 7	Berlin. Salisbury to C. 23 Dec. 1897.
	l. 13	Moral standpoint. Cecil. *Biographical Studies*. 9.
	l. 19	Congo cruelties. Salisbury to C. 25 June 1897.
	l. 27	No scold. Cecil. *Biographical Studies*. 61.
page 310	l. 8	Mysterious conclusions. C. to Selborne. 3 Feb. 1898.
	l. 30	Armed endeavours. C. to Salisbury and Salisbury to C. 2 March 1896.
	l. 33	Fatal philanthropy. *Hansard*. 3 March 1896. Col. 85.
page 311	l. 1	Cannot concur. C. to Salisbury and Salisbury to C. 13 March 1897.
	l. 5	No protest. *Hansard*. 15 March 1897. Col. 678.
	l. 12	Corsica Consul. Salisbury to C. 2 Feb. 1897.
	l. 21	Chinese rights. C. to Salisbury and Salisbury to C. Undated. [Summer–Autumn 1895 in C.'s hand].
	l. 25	Madagascar. *Ibid*. 23 March 1896.
	l. 38	Tunis. *Ibid*. 1 June and 2 June 1897.
page 312	l. 15	Delagon Bay. Violet Milner. *My Picture Gallery*. 87.
	l. 23	Entente Cordiale. C. to Harcourt. July 1896.
	l. 29	Proposed visit. C. to Salisbury. 6 April 1897.
	l. 33	Receiving Ambassadors. Steiner. *Old Foreign Office*. 65.
	l. 36	Unofficial mission. Salisbury to C. 9 April 1897.
	l. 43	Bitter antagonism. C. to Salisbury. 29 April 1897.
page 313	l. 3	Berlin. C. to Grace. 6 Oct. 1821.
	l. 11	Royal funerals. Arthur Ponsonby. *Henry Ponsonby*. 38.
	l. 20	Minor missions. Salisbury to C. 29 Aug. 1895.
	l. 29	Petty jealousies. C. to Salisbury. 3 Dec. 1897.
page 314	l. 5	Suggested speech. Salisbury to C. 6 Dec. 1897.
	l. 26	As delivered. Speech at Southport. 10 Dec. 1897. Quo. Ronaldshay. I.271.
page 315	l. 13	Minister in Pekin. C. to Salisbury. 28 Sept. 1895.
	l. 20	Snubbed. Salisbury to C. 30 Sept. 1895.
	l. 33	No disloyalty. C. to Salisbury. 20 Jan. 1896.
page 316	l. 2	Patriotic temper. Salisbury to C. 2 Nov. 1897.
	l. 16	Wei-hai-wei. C. to Salisbury. 29 Dec. 1897.
	l. 34	Pig-Tail Committee. *Ibid*. 11 April 1898.
	l. 39	Capitalists. Salisbury to C. 4 June 1898.
page 317	l. 2	Dead-weight. C. to Brodrick. 19 July 1900.
	l. 9	Accused of lying. C. to Mary. 30 March 1897.
	l. 18	Intelligent anticipation. *Hansard*. 29 March 1898. Col. 1245.
	l. 20	Mild chaff. C. to Salisbury. 11 April 1898.
	l. 25	Genuine tribute. *History of The Times*. III.355.
	l. 31	Unfortunate Government. *The Times*. 4 Aug. 1898.
	l. 35	Political abstractions. Cecil. *Salisbury*. III.115.
page 318	l. 3	The Press. C. to Hamilton. 16 Oct. 1901.

page 318	l. 7	Cursed papers. C. to Grace. 18 Nov. 1923.
	l. 11	Writing a letter. C. to Hamilton. 7 June 1899.
	l. 20	Bengali Babu. C. to Sir Hugh Barnes. 6 Sept. 1903.
	l. 22	Redrafting. L. S. Amery to author.
page 319	l. 15	Sir C. MacDonald. *Daily News*. 30 July 1898.
	l. 30	Chamberlain's intrusion. C. to Salisbury. 12 June 1898.
	l. 34	Viceroy of India. Salisbury to C. 24 June 1898.
	l. 38	Perseverence justified. C. to Salisbury. 20 June 1898.
page 320	l. 10	Small things. C. to Selborne. 9 April 1900.
	l. 17	Quarrels. Blunt. *My Diaries*. 212.
	l. 26	Arbitrament of war. Kennedy. *Salisbury*. 263.
	l. 36	Sticking to a line. Salisbury to C. 2 Sept. 1897.
	l. 38	Not pre-determined. C. to Brodrick. 3 May 1899.
page 321	l. 5	Rhodes. Malcolm. *Vacant Thrones*. 5.
	l. 8	Spoilt children. Salisbury to C. 14 Oct. 1897.
	l. 26	Lost knowledge. Carter. *Cory*. 1.

CHAPTER TWENTY-THREE: PASSAGE TO INDIA

page 323	l. 41	Request for Viceroyalty. C. to Salisbury. 18 April 1897.
page 324	l. 5	Evasive reply. Salisbury to C. 26 April 1897.
	l. 42	Second application. C. to Salisbury. 19 April 1898.
page 325	l. 17	Base human nature. Cecil. *Salisbury*. III.142–3.
	l. 23	Posts and places. PRO. FO 800/148 *passim*.
	l. 27	Coningsby Disraeli. C. to McDonnell. 29 June 1895. Christ Church.
	l. 29	FitzRoy Stewart. *Ibid*. 14 April 1896.
page 326	l. 2	Rashness of speech. Salisbury to Queen Victoria. *Letters*. Third Series. III.225.
	l. 5	State of health. C. to Salisbury. 20 June 1898.
	l. 16	An old enemy. Labouchere to C. 27 April [1898].
	l. 29	Physical failings. Hamilton to Elgin. 28 Sept. 1898.
	l. 36	Medical certificate. 20 June 1898. Christ Church.
	l. 41	Favourable consideration. C. to Salisbury. 20 June 1898.
page 327	l. 6	Queen's approval. Salisbury to C. 24 June 1898.
	l. 27	Advice to Viceroy. Queen Victoria to Salisbury. 27 May 1898.
	l. 34	To be kept secret. Salisbury to C. 24 June 1898.
page 328	l. 6	No other prize. C. to Salisbury. 25 June 1898.
	l. 14	Vistas of exploration. Hamilton to Elgin. 5 Aug. 1898.
	l. 26	Indecision. *Dictionary of National Biography*.
	l. 31	Forts and garrisons. C. to Salisbury. 26 Aug. 1897.
	l. 34	Belligerent attitude. Hamilton to Elgin. 7 Sept. 1898.
	l. 40	Frontier policy. Mary to C. May 1901.
page 329	l. 10	Book suppressed. *Viceroy's Note-Book*. 158.
	l. 15	Paternal pride. Scarsdale to C. 12 Aug. 1898.
	l. 20	Top place. Alfred Lyttelton to C. 11 Aug. 1898.
	l. 25	Hearty wishes. Fowler to C. 11 Aug. 1898.
	l. 27	Interesting experiment. *The Times*. 11 Aug. 1898.

page 329 l. 38 Bottles of wine. Midleton. *Records and Reactions*. 191.
page 330 l. 23 Medical advice. August 1898. Kedleston.
l. 29 Talked incessantly. C. to Mary. 4 Sept. 1898.
l. 34 Omdurman. Queen Victoria. *Letters*. Third Series. III.274.
l. 35 Satisfied. *Ibid*. III.280.
page 331 l. 1 Salisbury's solution. Memorandum No. 1 written by Curzon on the promise and refusal to him of a British peerage 1905–6, dated 1 July 1906.
l. 17 Fee of £290. Draft letter, C. to Asquith. 18 Oct. 1911.
l. 37 Howe's permission. Viscount Curzon to C. 4 Sept. 1898.
page 332 l. 15 Claim to name. C. to Knollys. 10 June 1901.
l. 26 Abbreviated signature. Memorandum on the title 'Curzon of Kedleston'. Undated.
l. 34 Exacting catechism. C. to Elgin. 12 Aug. 1898.
page 333 l. 8 Practical advice. Elgin to C. 31 Aug. 1898.
l. 19 Private Secretary. Lawrence. *The India We Served*. 220.
l. 25 Disinterested. Hamilton to Elgin. 11 Nov. 1898.
l. 30 £300 a year. R.S. Churchill. *Winston S. Churchill*. Companion Volume I. Part 2. 982.
l. 31 Fifty applications. *Ibid*. 975.
l. 32 Unsuccessful claim. Churchill to C. 22 Aug. 1905.
l. 40 Top hat. Gilbert. *Servant of India*. 46.
l. 41 Tapioca pudding. *Ibid*. 91.
l. 43 His own claims. Ronaldshay. I.293.
page 334 l. 13 Pushing Welldon. C. to Salisbury. 15 Oct. 1896.
l. 38 To the Devil. Midleton. *Records and Reactions*. 9. And Rosebery. *Miscellanies*. II.284.
l. 41 Happy phrases. *Modern Parliamentary Eloquence*. 41–2.
page 335 l. 6 Lord Aberdeen. Rosebery. *Miscellanies*. II.284.
l. 9 Dazzling celebrities. *Ibid*. II.281.
l. 23 Earning the Garter. Macmillan. *Winds of Change*. 135.
page 336 l. 6 The East. *Indian Speeches*. I.vii.
l. 8 Inventories of furniture. Ronaldshay. III.86.
l. 18 Imperious telegram. Portland. *Men, Women and Things*. 75.
l. 25 Searchlight. *Court Journal*. 17 Dec. 1898.
l. 31 American wives. *Table Talk*. 17 Dec. 1898.
l. 38 Ornate style. Lucy. *Diary of a Journalist*. I.305.
l. 40 Dilute. Cynthia Asquith. *Haply I May Remember*. 55.
page 337 l. 2 Bruised feelings. Lucy. *Diary of a Journalist*. I.305.
page 338 l. 18 Farewell speech. 9 Dec. 1898. Copy of a manuscript written out by C. for Lady Ribblesdale.
l. 20 Too favourable. Hamilton to Elgin. 15 Dec. 1898.
l. 26 How shall I return. C. to Elgin. 17 Nov. 1898.

EPILOGUE: PARTING OF FRIENDS

pvge 339 l. 8 Loyal friends. Speech at Souls' dinner. 9 Dec. 1898.

page 339	Fn.	Lord Swinton to author.
page 340	l. 13	Like a fool. Gwynn. *Spring Rice*. I.257–9.
page 341	l. 27	Overwork. Brodrick to C. 14 Dec. 1898.
	l. 29	Advice accepted. C. to Brodrick. 19 Dec. 1898.
	l. 43	Daily routine. C. to Ampthill. 10 April 1901.
page 342	l. 2	Old fogies. C. to Hamilton. 29 Aug. 1900.
	l. 5	Greatest Viceroy. Maconochie. *Indian Civil Service*. 122.
	l. 8	Enormous ledgers. Lord Hardinge. *My Indian Years*. 5.
	l. 9	Salary. C. to Hamilton. 1 Oct. 1902.
	l. 10	Out of pocket. *Ibid*. 13 April 1903.
	l. 15	Chickens. C. to McDonnell. 25 July 1900. Quo. Ronaldshay. I.106.
	l. 18	Proof-reading. Lawrence. *The India We Served*. 237.
	l. 22	Insomnia. C. to Hamilton. 13 June 1900.
	l. 29	Golden accounts. McDonnell to C. 29 Aug. 1899.
	l. 38	See the page. C. to Mary. 23 July 1901.
page 343	l. 2	Distress and pain. C. to Hamilton. 28 May 1902.
	l. 7	Stupefied resignation. C. to Mrs Craigie. 17 April 1899. Quo. Ronaldshay. II.27.
	l. 15	Throttling reform. C. to Hamilton. 9 April 1902.
	l. 32	Declining interest. *Ibid*. 21 May 1902.
	l. 35	Inferior class. C. to Brodrick. 2 Oct. 1903.
	l. 42	Malignant types. *Ibid*. 5 April 1904.
page 344	l. 9	Shooting cases. C. to Knollys. 14 Dec. 1902.
	l. 12	Guilty regiment. C. to Hamilton. 8 Jan. 1903.
	l. 23	Superior standards. C. to Alfred Lyttelton. 29 Aug. 1900.
	l. 28	Love of India. *Indian Speeches*. I.iv.
	l. 39	Calcutta University. *Ibid*. IV.75.
page 345	l. 2	Lose their heads. C. to Hamilton. 23 April 1900.
	l. 8	School children. C. to Alfred Lyttelton. 29 Aug. 1900.
	l. 10	Five letters. *Indian Speeches*. IV.52.
	l. 19	Puppets. Lady Minto. Diary. 20 Nov. 1905. Indian Institute, Oxford.
	l. 27	Honest and able. Margot Asquith. *Autobiography*. 122.
page 346	l. 2	Missionary enterprise. *Derby Mercury*. 6 Oct. 1880.
	l. 5	Medical aid. *Persia*. I.509.
	l. 9	Imperialism. C. to Hamilton. 7 Aug. 1901.
	l. 12	Western materialism. Welldon. *Recollections and Reflections*. 229.
	l. 22	Viceroy alarmed. C. to Hamilton. 12 Jan. 1899.
	l. 29	Power to lead. *Ibid*. 21 Feb. 1901.
	l. 33	English Church. *Ibid*. 11 June 1901.
	l. 34	Proselytism. *Ibid*. 31 July 1901.
page 347	l. 2	Lawlessness. Churchill to C. 3 June 1901.
	l. 8	Powers of speech. Hamilton to C. 29 Aug. 1901.
	l. 15	Another blunder. C. to Hamilton. 7 Aug. 1901.
	l. 31	My dear old Doon. C. to Welldon. 21 Aug. 1901.
page 348	l. 2	In my prayers. Welldon to C. 12 Sept. 1901.

page 348	l. 8	Superior man. Welldon. *Recollections and Reflections*. 226.
	l. 19	Balliol men. Godley to C. 17 Aug. 1900.
	l. 32	Odd shoes. Leveson Gower. *Mixed Grill*. 95.
	l. 36	Hat and umbrella. Rendel. *The Sword and the Olive*. 42–3.
page 349	l. 5	Duck. Leveson Gower. *Mixed Grill*. 96.
	l. 9	Counting-house. Rendel. *The Sword and the Olive*. 43.
	l. 12	No consultation. C. to Brodrick. 28 Jan. 1904.
	l. 17	Happier now. C. to Hardinge. 13 June 1901.
	l. 31	No fit Indian. C. to Balfour. 31 March 1901.
	l. 38	Bad form. C. to Godley. 17 June 1903.
page 350	l. 4	Show of the boot. C. to Lansdowne. 3 April 1903.
	l. 10	Hyper-subtlety. C. to Hamilton. 19 March 1903.
	l. 17	Bushire incident. C. to Hardinge. 8 April 1904.
	l. 25	Walmer Castle. *Ibid*. 24 March 1904.
page 351	l. 15	Salisbury failing. Brodrick to C. 22 Nov. 1901.
	l. 22	Confidential correspondence. C. to Hamilton. 18 June 1901.
	l. 27	Jealous suspicion. Hamilton to C. 16 Jan. 1902.
	l. 30	Clerk of works. *Ibid*. 9 Jan. 1901.
	l. 34	Dotardry. Harrod. *Keynes*. 123.
page 352	l. 4	Nagged and impeded. C. to Hamilton. 28 May 1902.
	l. 9	Mentally depressed. Hamilton to C. 19 June 1902.
	l. 13	Suspicion. C. to Hamilton. 9 July 1902.
	l. 16	Impertinent schoolboy. C. to Godley. 18 June 1902.
	l. 26	Disapprobation. Hamilton to C. 7 Aug. 1902.
	l. 36	Noble task. C. to Balfour. 16 July 1902.
	l. 38	False windows. Chandos. *From Peace to War*. 29.
	l. 43	Strenuous work. C. to Mrs. Craigie. 12 March 1900. Quo. Ronaldshay. II.122.
page 353	l. 7	Great victory. C. to Mary. 27 Aug. 1902.
	l. 18	Threatened resignation. C. to Hamilton. 13 Nov. 1902.
	l. 20	The King. C. to Knollys. 15 Nov. 1902 and 17 Nov. 1902.
	l. 28	Instrument of failure. C. to Balfour. 20 Nov. 1902.
	l. 31	Failure. *Ibid*. 21 Nov. 1902.
page 354	l. 10	Admiration. Balfour to C. 12 Dec. 1902.
	l. 15	Political blunder. C. to Hamilton. 28 Dec. 1902.
	l. 38	Brodrick. Notes.
page 355	l. 6	Far in the rear. C. to Brodrick. 5 Dec. 1880.
	l. 9	Elected to Parliament. *Ibid*. 8 July 1886.
	l. 12	Strong to rock. *Ibid*. 10 April 1895.
	l. 32	Laboriously climbed. Brodrick to C. 14 Dec. 1898.
	l. 35	Confidential talk. *Ibid*. 7 July 1899.
	l. 40	Good genius. Midleton. *Records and Reactions*. 187.
	l. 42	Unpopularity. Hamilton to C. 13 Feb. 1903.
page 356	l. 1	Rectitude. C. to Godley. 3 Jan. 1901.
	l. 2	Grit and courage. C. to Hamilton. 1 April 1901.
	l. 6	Not pressed. Brodrick to C. 20 Nov. 1902.
	l. 10	Human nature. C. to Mary. Dec. 1902.

page 356	l. 11	Correspondence suspended. Midleton. *Records and Reactions.* 193.
	l. 18	Whole-hearted champion. C. to Godley. 23 Sept. 1903.
	l. 19	Wounded feelings. Brodrick to C. 15 Oct. 1903.
	l. 24	Private correspondence. C. to Brodrick. 2 Oct. 1903.
	l. 31	Restriction. *Ibid.* 11 Feb. 1904.
	l. 39	Custard pudding. Quo. Ronaldshay. ii.170.
	l. 41	Lout and Lord. C. to King Edward vii. 11 June 1903.
page 357	l. 4	Identity of bride. C. to Brodrick. 23 Feb. 1904.
	l. 7	Bed at 3 a.m. C. to Sir Hugh Barnes. 27 Feb. 1904.
	l. 12	Run the risk. Balfour to C. 18 June 1903.
	l. 18	I shall suffer. C. to Hamilton. 17 June 1903.
	l. 26	Inspiring. Ampthill to Godley. 5 May 1904.
	l. 28	Touch of genius. Godley to Ampthill. 19 May 1904.
	l. 32	Records of festivity. C. to Brodrick. 18 May 1904.
	l. 35	Petty skirmishes. *Ibid.* 1 Dec. 1903.
page 358	l. 8	Successful mission. Seaver. *Younghusband.* 255.
	l. 15	Striking at Curzon. Fleming. *Bayonets to Lhasa.* 288.
	l. 21	Younghusband's knighthood. *Ibid.* 282.
	l. 38	Effect upon prestige. C. to Brodrick. 30 March 1905.
page 359	l. 11	Wobbling Government. C. to Mary. 9 Feb. 1905.
	l. 16	No other ending. C. to Brodrick. 2 March 1905.
	l. 33	Constitutional position. Godley to Ampthill. 17 June 1904.
	l. 39	Morley. Riddell. *More Pages from My Diary.* 5.
page 360	l. 1	Right of Control. Godley to C. 1 Jan. 1904.
	l. 18	House of Commons. *Ibid.* 8 Jan. 1904.
	l. 31	Thorn in the flesh. *Ibid.* 3 March 1904.
	l. 37	Mere puppet. *Indian Speeches.* iv.229.
	l. 43	Independent autocracy. Midleton. *Records and Reactions.* 198.
page 361	l. 11	Claim to knowledge. Brodrick to C. 18 May 1905.
	l. 13	Humiliated Viceroy. C. to Sir Hugh Barnes. 14 Sept. 1905.
	l. 17	Court of St. James. Midleton. *Records and Reactions.* 200.
	l. 24	Ever affectionate. Brodrick to C. 5 Aug. 1904.
	l. 31	Peculiar satisfaction. C. to Ampthill. 31 Oct. 1904.
	l. 39	Shed tears. Godley to Ampthill. 25 Nov. 1904.
page 362	l. 10	Same roof. Midleton. *Records and Reactions.* 203.
	l. 28	Kitchener welcomed. C. to King Edward vii. 15 Oct. 1902.
	l. 32	Demand for abolition of Military Member's department and subsequent events leading to Curzon's resignation in August 1905. *Private Correspondence relating to Military Administration in India, 1902–1905.* This volume, privately printed in India in 1905, consists of a closely reasoned narrative of 68 pages, supplemented by a further 54 pages of appendices.
	l. 38	Exploded blunderbuss. Leslie. *Studies in Sublime Failure.* 215.
	l. 41	Faulty and inefficient. Ronaldshay. ii.374.
page 363	l. 10	Driven to resign. C. to Brodrick. 2 March 1905.
	l. 30	Disembowelled. C. to Clinton Dawkins. 21 June 1905. Quo. Ronaldshay. ii.383.

page 363	l. 37	Insulting. *Private Correspondence*. 40.
	l. 42	India Office ignored. Brodrick to Ampthill. 30 Dec. 1904.
page 364	l. 1	No Viceregal tribute. C. to Balfour. 19 July 1905.
	l. 3	Burn like caustic. Dalhousie to President of Board of Control. 28 June 1854.
	l. 10	Annoyance. Brodrick to Ampthill. 30 June 1905.
	l. 18	Open humiliation. C. to Ampthill. 23 July 1905.
	l. 27	Truth or honour. *Ibid.* 12 Aug. 1905.
	l. 39	First principle. C. to St Loe Strachey. 28 Sept. 1905. *Observer* Trust Papers.
page 365	l. 3	Military dictator. Churchill to Campbell-Bannerman. 28 Oct. 1905.
	l. 15	Cromer's verdict. *Hansard* (Lords). 20 July 1916. Col. 854.
	l. 29	Vindictive. C. to Ampthill. 12 Aug. 1905.
	l. 36	Affectionate understanding. Balfour to C. 18 June 1903.
page 366	l. 2	Political wreck. *Ibid.* 23 Aug. 1905.
	l. 7	Treasured possessions. C. to Balfour.
	ll. 8ff.	Absence of goodwill. Memorandum No. 1, written by Curzon on the promise and refusal to him of a British peerage, 1905–6. Dated 1 July 1906. It was followed by Memorandum No. 2, on the second promise and refusal to him of a British peerage, 1907 (dated 18 Feb. 1909); and finally by Memorandum No. 3, on the concluding phases of the peerage question, Jan. 1908 to Feb. 1912 (dated 5 Aug. 1912).
page 367	l. 7	Waiting game. Balfour to Brodrick. 10 Sept. 1905.
	l. 15	Delay proposed. Balfour to Knollys. 7 Oct. 1905.
	ll. 28ff.	Audience with King. Peerage Memorandum No. 1. 1906.
page 369	l. 37	Old friends. Balfour to C. 2 July 1906. Letters accompanying Peerage Memorandum No. 1. 1906.
page 370	l. 3	Frigid conclusion. C. to Balfour. *Ibid.* 3 July 1906.
	l. 7	Doctor's orders. Peerage Memorandum No. 2. 1909.
	l. 18	Aching breast. Mary to C. 6 March 1899.
	l. 25	Cast down. C. to Mary. 13 Dec. 1904.
	l. 30	Coming out. *Ibid.* 16 Feb. 1905.
page 371	l. 8	Love song. The manuscript bears a note in Curzon's hand: 'I wrote these verses in India in 1905 and gave them to my darling.'
	l. 11	Hide my head. C. to Earl Grey. 29 Nov. [1906]. Durham University, Department of Palaeography.
	l. 20	Warren Hastings. Peerage Memorandum No. 2. 1909.
	l. 32	Would not like it. Morley to C. 15 Oct. 1907.
	l. 37	Tradition of public life. Peerage Memorandum No. 2. 1909.
	l. 40	Partisan of Kitchener. *Ibid.*
page 372	l. 7	Representative Peerage. Lansdowne to C. 14 Nov. 1907.
	l. 27	Obscure Irishman. *Ibid.* 1 Dec. 1907.
	l. 36	Quixotic vote. Midleton. *Records and Reactions*. 210.
page 373	l. 8	Fees of £2,080. Peerage Memorandum No. 3. 1912.
	l. 16	Unusual series of events. *Ibid.*

page 373	l. 27	Aglow with sympathy. C. to Alfred Lyttelton. 19 Aug. 1898.
	l. 32	Very chill. *Ibid.* 5 Jan. 1908.
	l. 38	Eviscerated corpse. *Ibid.* 21 Oct. 1908.
page 374	l. 4	Got 90. *Eton College Chronicle.* 10 July 1913.
	l. 9	Asquith's tribute. *Hansard.* 8 July 1913.
	l. 23	Curzon's threnody. *The Times.* 7 July 1913.
	l. 37	His own glory. Gwynn. *Spring Rice.* II.320.
	l. 39	Indian province. *Ibid.* II.119.
page 375	l. 12	Atmosphere freezes. Leveson Gower. *Mixed Grill.* 75.
	l. 19	Godfather. *Ibid. Years of Endeavour.* 236.
	l. 26	Disobliging anecdotes. *Ibid. Mixed Grill.* 76.
	l. 37	Love of fine people. Margot Asquith. *Autobiography.* 175.
	l. 38	The King. C. to Grace. 9 Nov. 1920.
page 376	l. 6	Talking to Morley. Pope-Hennessy. *Crewe.* 155.
	l. 10	Appointment to Paris. C. to Crewe. 30 Oct. 1922.
	l. 14	Own merits. C. to Grace. 9 May 1923.
	l. 21	Friend of a lifetime. Gwynn. *Spring Rice.* II.174.
	l. 27	Sunshine and happiness. Lady Rodd to C. 23 Oct. 1919.
	l. 32	Tenth decade. Sir George Leveson Gower to author.
	l. 36	Proposed reconciliation. Margot Asquith. *More Memories.* 205.
	l. 39	Unstinted generosity. C. to Crewe. 23 Jan. 1924.
page 377	l. 2	Comforting letter. W.S. Churchill to Lady Curzon. 24 March 1925.
	l. 13	Self-pity. C. to Grace. 22 May 1922.
	l. 21	Premonitory symptoms. Late Lord Samuel to author.
	l. 26	Minor fault. Brett. *Journals and Letters.* IV.298.
	l. 34	Calcutta weather. Late Aga Khan to author.
	l. 36	Silver inkstand. Chandos. *From Peace to War.* 64.
	l. 39	Interpreter. Newton. *Retrospection.* 161.
page 378	l. 5	Russians. Brodrick to C. 30 Aug. 1914.
	l. 24	Offended guests. R.S. Churchill. *Lord Derby.* 272–3.
	l. 39	Rolls Royce. Crewe to C. 7 Jan. 1916.
page 379	l. 6	Consideration. C. to Balfour. 24 June 1919.
	l. 7	Skill and wisdom. Balfour to C. 1 July 1919.
	l. 9	Two policies. C. to Grace. 19 Aug. 1919.
	l. 24	This and subsequent passages describing Curzon's relations with Lloyd George and with Balfour are based on a manuscript document to which Curzon gave the title: 'Confidential Memorandum written by me at Lausanne Dec. 1922–Jan. 1923 concerning the fall of the Lloyd George Government and other cognate matters for use by my biographer'.
	l. 29	Almost a drudge. C. to Grace. 22 April 1921.
page 380	l. 2	On Balfour. This passage is drawn from a manuscript document to which Curzon gave the title: 'Memorandum on some aspects of my tenure of the Foreign Office'. It is dated November 1924.
	ll. 3ff.	Confidential Memorandum, 1922–1923.
page 381	l. 35	Resignation. Bonar Law to C. 20 May 1923.

page 382	l. 10	Curt and ungracious. This and subsequent passages are drawn from a manuscript document to which Curzon gave the title: 'Narrative of the events of May 1923 when I failed to become Prime Minister'.
	l. 25	Exchange of telegrams. Nicolson. *King George the Fifth*. 377.
page 383	l. 23	Close conformity. Young. *Balfour*. 431.
	l. 31	No exceptional ability. Nicolson. *King George the Fifth*. 376.
	l. 37	George not chosen. W.S. Churchill. *Great Contemporaries*. 287.
page 384	l. 6	Popular belief. Narrative of the events of May 1923.
	l. 29	Most friendly terms. Nicolson. *King George the Fifth*. 377–8.
	l. 43	Service of the Crown. Narrative of the events of May 1923.
page 385	l. 13	Do one's best. Pope-Hennessy. *Crewe*. 168.

INDEX

Compiled by G. Norman Knight, MA, *Vice-President of the Society of Indexers*

The entry under **Curzon, George Nathaniel,** has been confined to those sub-headings which cannot be readily found under other entries. Apart from that heading his name has throughout the index been abbreviated to C. Similarly, Oscar Browning is sometimes abbreviated to O.B. The abbreviation 'q.' denotes 'quoted'.

Page reference numbers in bold type indicate that a substantial part of the page(s) in the text is devoted to the item. Reference numbers in italics denote maps.